THE BUSINESS OF ARMAMENTS

How did Britain's most prominent armaments firms, Armstrongs and Vickers, build their businesses and sell armaments in Britain and overseas from 1855 to 1955? Joanna Spear presents a comparative analysis of these firms and considers the relationships they built with the British Government and foreign states. She reveals how the firms developed and utilized independent domestic strategies and foreign policies against the back-drop of imperial expansion and the two world wars. Using extensive new research, this study examines the challenges the two firms faced in making domestic and international sales including the British Government's commitment to laissez faire policies, prejudices within the British elite against those in trade, and departmental resistance to dealing with private firms. It shows the suite of strategies and tactics that the firms developed to overcome these obstacles to selling arms at home and abroad and how they built enduring relationships with states in Latin America, Asia and the Middle East.

JOANNA SPEAR is Research Professor of International Affairs at George Washington University. She works on armaments, arms sales and arms control issues and is the author of *Carter and Arms Sales* (1995).

THE BUSINESS OF ARMAMENTS

Armstrongs, Vickers and the International Arms Trade, 1855–1955

JOANNA SPEAR

George Washington University

Shaftesbury Road, Cambridge CB2 8EA, United Kingdom

One Liberty Plaza, 20th Floor, New York, NY 10006, USA

477 Williamstown Road, Port Melbourne, VIC 3207, Australia

314–321, 3rd Floor, Plot 3, Splendor Forum, Jasola District Centre,
New Delhi – 110025, India

103 Penang Road, #05–06/07, Visioncrest Commercial, Singapore 238467

Cambridge University Press is part of Cambridge University Press & Assessment,
a department of the University of Cambridge.

We share the University's mission to contribute to society through the pursuit of
education, learning and research at the highest international levels of excellence.

www.cambridge.org
Information on this title: www.cambridge.org/9781009297523

DOI: 10.1017/9781009297516

First published 2023

A catalogue record for this publication is available from the British Library.

ISBN 978-1-009-29752-3 Hardback

In memory of my academic sisters:

Dr. Karen Ballentine (1961–2010)

Dr. Chandra Lekha Sriram (1971–2018)

And

Dr. Janne Emilie Nolan (1951–2019)

Sorely missed by all who knew them

CONTENTS

FIGURES AND TABLES

Figures

Tables

ACKNOWLEDGMENTS

I am indebted to the various archives and libraries that assisted me in writing this book. Special thanks are due to the Syndics of Cambridge University Library for access to the records of the Vickers firm, the Tyne and Wear Archives at the Discovery Museum for access to the Armstrong papers, and the British National Archive, for access to British Government documents. I also benefited from access to records held by the British Library, the Cumbria Archive and Local Studies Centre in Barrow-in-Furness, the Kendal Archive Centre, the Wiltshire and Swindon History Centre, the Sir Winston Churchill Archive and the British Newspaper Archive. The Gelman Library at George Washington University was unfailingly helpful (especially during the pandemic). The British Library was a vital place to access rare sources and a conducive place to work, as was the Westminster Research Library. I thank the librarians and archivists at all these institutions for the help that they continually give to me and to others.

I am grateful to my institutional home, the Elliott School of International Affairs at the George Washington University. I am lucky to have great colleagues there and I have benefited from many talented assistants, who helped me with my directing jobs, creating a little space for research. Special thanks are due to Samia Ausaf, Rory McGuire, Zlatko Kaurin, Alexander da Silva, Hibbah Kaileh, Miho Moon and Caleb Darger, who were all vital to keeping me (relatively) sane. For the past eight years I have enjoyed working full time with the Foreign Area Officer Community. I am grateful to Chatham House in London for welcoming me as a Visiting Scholar in the early stages of this project, to the Institute for Defence and Security Analyses in New Delhi for a two-month fellowship, and to the Royal United Services Institute (RUSI) for hosting me as a Senior Visiting Scholar in 2013. I also truly appreciate my colleagues who attend the "Just Write!" sessions I run at the Elliott School and my writing buddy, Dr. Aisling Swaine. I also benefited from writing time at the homes of Jane Sharp and Susan Bryant Kimball. Thank you everyone.

Inevitably a historical work like this stands on the shoulders of giants, but any wobbles in facts or analysis are my responsibility. I am grateful to the following individuals for their help and advice as this project evolved: Hugh Agnew, Matthew Bell, Michael E. Brown, Michael Clarke, Neil Cooper, Alex Downes, Andrew Gamble, Charles Glaser, Jonathan Grant, Keith Hayward, Ben Hopkins, Matthew Levinger, John Louth, Edward McCord, Zoe Nielsen, Graham Pitts, Jen Spindel, Daniel Stahl, Arturo Sotomayor, Trevor Taylor, Karin von Hippel, Paul Williams and Claire Yorke. I have always benefited from interesting conversations with Professor Sir Laurence Freedman, previously my boss in the Department of War Studies, King's College London. I particularly remember the discussion where we agreed that a proper review of secondary sources was a vital element of good historical research. That has haunted me!

I benefited from opportunities to discuss the ideas for this book at the Foreign Policy Program at The Brookings Institution, the Institute for Security and Conflict Studies at the Elliott School, the RUSI weekly seminar and Women in International Security UK.

I am indebted to the two anonymous reviewers who provided important (albeit contrasting) feedback on the first draft of this manuscript. I appreciate the forbearance of Michael Watson at Cambridge University Press as I juggled pandemic work demands and revising the manuscript, and the help of the whole team in getting the manuscript into publication. I also am grateful for Dr. Victoria George's work in preparing the index and to David Sturtevant for the fabulous artwork.

I so appreciate my lovely family and friends in Britain, India, Singapore, Ireland and the United States: inspirations and distractions in nearly equal measure. They have long been asking when this book would be finished. Well, it is now, so can we all go out and party?

ABBREVIATIONS

BL	British Library Manuscripts
BNA	British Newspaper Archive
BoE	Bank of England
CHAR	Chartwell Papers, Churchill Archives Center, Cambridge University
CID	Committee of Imperial Defence (Cabinet)
DNC	Director of Naval Construction
ESC	English Steel Corporation
GUAS	Glasgow University Archives
HMG	His/Her Majesty's Government
HMS	His/Her Majesty's Ship
MAP	Ministry of Aircraft Production
NSS	National Shipbuilders Security Ltd.
SCC	Shipbuilding Consultative Committee
SLSL	Sheffield Local Studies Library
TNA	The National Archive
TWA	Tyne and Wear Archive
VA	Vickers Archive, Cambridge University Library
WSBC	Warship Building Committee

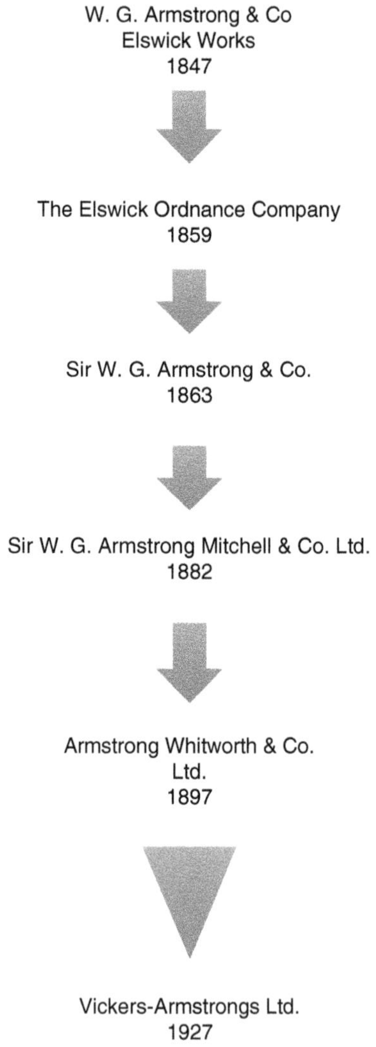

W. G. Armstrong & Co
Elswick Works
1847

The Elswick Ordnance Company
1859

Sir W. G. Armstrong & Co.
1863

Sir W. G. Armstrong Mitchell & Co. Ltd.
1882

Armstrong Whitworth & Co.
Ltd.
1897

Vickers-Armstrongs Ltd.
1927

Figure 1   The evolution of Armstrongs

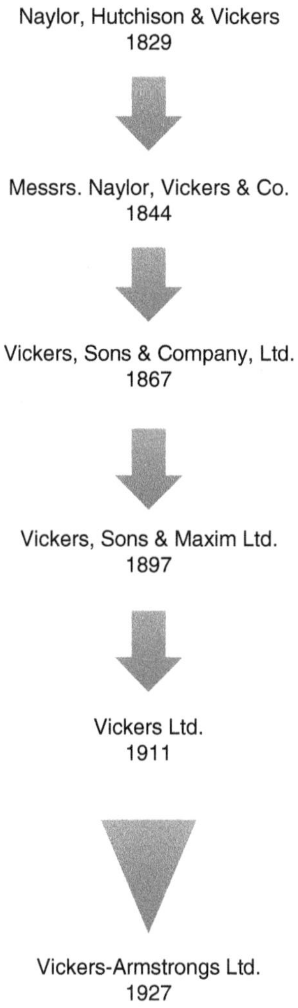

Naylor, Hutchison & Vickers
1829

Messrs. Naylor, Vickers & Co.
1844

Vickers, Sons & Company, Ltd.
1867

Vickers, Sons & Maxim Ltd.
1897

Vickers Ltd.
1911

Vickers-Armstrongs Ltd.
1927

Figure 2   The evolution of Vickers

Introduction

British Armament Firms' Independence and Power

This book looks at a relatively familiar issue – British armaments production and sales between 1855 and 1955 – from the perspectives of two prominent British firms. Armstrongs and Vickers invented, manufactured and marketed armaments, and built relationships with the British Government and with other states. The book argues that Armstrongs and Vickers developed and utilized independent domestic strategies and foreign policies. These were initially necessitated by the British Government's indifference to their existence, attempts to exploit them and resistance to helping them sell abroad. Even as their relationships with the British Government grew, the firms maintained their own interests, strategies and foreign policies. They were independent actors.

Throughout the century considered here, the British Government consistently worked in its own interests. The firms' most prominent customer disregarded contracts and canceled orders, disputed royalties, brought in new firms to invigorate competition, worked to reduce firms' profits and assumed no responsibility for keeping them in business. The firms strategized in response. Relationships with the British Government were therefore a wary dance for Armstrongs, Vickers and other armament firms.

Selection of Firms

The first firm is commonly known as "Armstrongs," after its founder, William Armstrong of Newcastle upon Tyne. He was a Victorian inventor interested in problem-solving and engineering, with a good understanding of business and finance. From the early 1860s, when "Armstrong Guns" were first produced at the Elswick Ordnance Works in Newcastle, until around 1900, Armstrongs was the most prominent British armament firm and enjoyed buoyant overseas sales. After 1900 there was more competition in the domestic and international armaments markets and the firm became less successful. In the interwar period Armstrongs struggled to adapt to the depressed market and its efforts to diversify into civilian markets were disastrous, leading to their amalgamation as a junior partner with our second firm.

This firm, colloquially called "Vickers," was a family business in Yorkshire engaged in milling before moving into steel production. An entrepreneurial firm, they moved into armor manufacture in 1888. Vickers was particularly adept at bringing in talented managers and salespeople. The firm grew significantly around the turn of the century via inspired mergers, acquisitions and licensing deals. In the Edwardian period Vickers grew as Armstrongs struggled. In 1927 Vickers cherrypicked the best of Armstrongs, amalgamating into Vickers-Armstrongs Ltd., thereby becoming the premier British armament firm.

Although Armstrongs and Vickers faced the same markets, their responses to them were somewhat different. The firms emphasized different strategies, reflecting their varying strengths, and developed distinct organizational cultures. Both firms faced significant peaks and troughs in orders over the century covered in this book, so there are many opportunities to see their domestic strategies and foreign policies in operation and to assess their success. The centrality of these two firms to British armaments production, their distinct strategies, their subtly different relationships with the British state and their approaches to exports make them important subjects for analysis.

Both firms left extensive archives. The Armstrongs papers are available at the Tyne and Wear Archive housed in the Discovery Museum, Newcastle upon Tyne. The Vickers Archive is housed in the Department of Manuscripts and University Archives, Cambridge University Library, Cambridge. These archives are invaluable for understanding how Armstrongs and Vickers assessed their situations, developed their strategies and responded to the many crises they faced. Documents held by regional archives and local newspapers also reveal insights into the firms. British National Archive documents show how Armstrongs and Vickers' most prominent customer, the British Government, perceived them and what British Embassy staff observed of the firms' behaviors abroad. Together these sources provide an excellent basis for examining the domestic strategies and foreign policies of Armstrongs and Vickers, and for assessing the degrees of independence and power they held in their relationships with the British Government. These relationships evolved over time, the increasing reach of the state gradually bringing them closer together. However, the catalysts for major changes in the relationship were the two world wars, as is now briefly illustrated.

The Arc of the State–Firm Relationship

When Armstrongs and Vickers were founded, there were well-established Royal Arsenals and Dockyards serving the state, so the firms were – necessarily – completely independent. The British Government initially used the firms instrumentally, employing Armstrongs to create and manufacture a new gun (then casting them aside) and Vickers to create domestic competition in armor production (before casting them aside too). This set the pattern. Early on the government stole armament firms' patents and refused to pay royalties.

Indeed, the War Office consistently regarded private firms as unwelcome competition to the Royal Arsenals and first sought to exclude them from the British market, before moving to treating them as producers of last resort.

Initially the British Government was committed to *laissez-faire* (the principle that government should not control business) and provided neither subsidies nor export help. Armament firms therefore had distant relationships with the British Government. This contrasted with the situations in Germany and France, where armament firms received domestic subsidies and help to sell abroad. The British firms often complained about the disparity. For example, in 1888 the Armstrongs agent in Turkey protested that "any German subject who has business with or claim upon the Turkish government gets the most powerful support from his ambassador here. We get absolutely *None*."[1] However, because the firms were independent, they did not need to align with British strategic interests, giving them great freedom. The lack of British secrecy laws until 1889, and the weakness of those enacted, gave Armstrongs and Vickers a relatively free hand in foreign markets.

The armament firms sometimes undertook exports that the British Government opposed but was powerless to prevent. The 1870 Foreign Enlistment Act was the first legislation enabling the British Government to restrict private firms' exports, and then only to states at war. In peacetime the firms had the freedom to pursue their own foreign policies. This sometimes resulted in the Admiralty buying products destined for export as this was the only way to prevent the recipients from acquiring more sophisticated warships than Britain. The government incrementally instituted export controls. While initially indifferent to the impact of armament firms' exports – unless they affected British neutrality or reserves for war – after 1886 the British Government realized the economic advantages of sales and began to edge into providing sporadic and limited help in marketing armaments abroad.

Laissez-faire ruled the British Government's approach to armament firms for many decades. Consonant with that, Armstrongs and Vickers pursued their own domestic strategies and foreign policies. However, the government's approach changed completely during the Great War because the armament firms were vital to the war effort. Now the government strongly regulated production. As Armstrongs' Chairman John Meade Falkner sorrowfully told shareholders in 1915, "instead of private enterprise we have become a Government arsenal under Government control."[2] The firms now built exclusively for the British Government, thereby sacrificing many foreign policy goals and long-term relationships. While government domination of production and trade ended in 1918, regulation never retreated to prewar levels. *Laissez-faire* in the

---

[1] Leak to Elswick, October 20, 1888. TWA, 31/4187. Emphasis in original.
[2] Cited in Bastable, *Arms*, p. 172.

armaments sector was partly extinguished and firms' relationships with the state grew, but it was often an uneasy connection.

Armstrongs and Vickers had expanded their capacities enormously for the war effort but in 1918 British orders were immediately canceled and armament firms were cast adrift into a depressed market. Subsequently, the British Government's commitment to naval arms control severely limited both domestic production and exports. After trying to diversify into civilian fields, many armament firms went out of business during the interwar years. Our two firms became Vickers-Armstrongs. While the Admiralty and Air Ministry drip-fed domestic ship and aircraft contracts to keep the surviving firms afloat, the War Office did not. By the 1930s, influenced by rising unemployment and the Great Depression, the British Government began to give more assistance to firms to market their wares abroad. Nevertheless, in 1935, under pressure from negative public opinion, there was a Royal Commission investigation into the profits and behavior of armament firms. With German revanchism casting a long shadow, the British Government and Vickers-Armstrongs worked in parallel – but, crucially, not in collaboration – to oppose the demand for the nationalization of all weapons production. They were successful.

As war loomed once again and rearmament began, Vickers-Armstrongs asked to be allowed to maintain some level of exports to countries such as Portugal and Turkey because it would be hard to restart such relationships after a complete hiatus. The government agreed. The relationship between armament firms and the British state further deepened during World War Two. The firms again freely loaned senior personnel to the government for the war effort. The state gave armament firms subsidies to increase capacity and develop new weapons systems; it gave them responsibility over many "Shadow Factories" and closely supervised all armament production and export. Once again, regulation receded postwar, but not to prewar levels.

In the early 1950s Britain adopted industrial strategies for key sectors such as military production. This clipped the wings of British armament firms, a process further accelerated by the nationalization of Vickers-Armstrongs' English Steel Corporation, something they had strongly resisted. Nationalization changed the firm–state relationship quite dramatically. Vickers-Armstrongs had lost an innovation hub and was now reliant on the products of the British Steel Corporation. The government nevertheless still prioritized national strategic interests over industrial concerns. Luckily, the export interests of Vickers-Armstrongs now often coincided with the state's interests in retaining a share of international markets and sustaining strategic influence in key areas of the globe in the face of strong international competition and the burgeoning Cold War. Now the British Government actively supported arms exports to markets such as Latin America and the Middle East. Hence, by 1955, where this book closes, the arc of the relationship between armament firms and the state had evolved from independence to interdependence.

A Military–Industrial Complex?

This book's focus on the power and independence of Armstrongs and Vickers casts light on debates over relations between armament firms and states. Considering armament firms as independent actors is a rather different framing from many works in history and political science. These disciplines have traditionally assumed a dependent relationship between all types of firms and sovereign states, with the latter by far the dominant actors, making firms unnecessary for analysis.[3] In 1961 a different paradigm of the armament firm–state relationship emerged, something that President Dwight D. Eisenhower termed a "Military Industrial Complex."[4] This important concept reflected the Cold War reality that the United States now needed to consistently innovate and manufacture armaments, rather than just turning to production when war loomed. This shift created a cadre of permanent armament firms constantly interacting with the military services and the legislative committees charged with appropriating defense funds and building strong relationships; this sometimes created "Iron Triangles" which the executive branch struggled to control.[5] While this concept was initially used to explain the contemporary situation, there has developed an interesting body of scholarship tracing the roots of the United States' military–industrial complex back to the nineteenth century.[6] Importantly, as Maurice Pearton astutely noted, the military–industrial complex is a peculiarly American phenomenon, and therefore "The term fails to explain with any degree of precision what takes place elsewhere, where values and practices differ."[7] Moreover, the relationship between armament firms and the state "depends upon the political culture in which they are experienced. They work out differently in different societies."[8]

The British parliamentary system, with executive branch dominance, strong and disciplined political parties and a legislature with a minimal role in defense budgeting, does not easily lend itself to the classical military–industrial complex paradigm. However, that does not in itself mean that there was no military–industrial complex in Britain during the period 1855–1955. What did contemporary critics say? There were two phases when British armament firms were under sustained fire, first around 1906–08 and, more acutely, in the 1930s. In each case, though, the criticism was not that there was a military–industrial complex, but rather that armament firms were *independent* "merchants of death" fomenting wars to reap profits, acting in their own interests, colluding with international firms and disregarding the interests of their home states.

[3] A notable exception was the British East India Company. Dalrymple, *Anarchy*.
[4] Eisenhower, "Farewell Address."
[5] Adams, *Iron Triangle*.
[6] Hackemer, *U.S. Navy*; Cooling, *Grey Steel*; Baack and Ray, "Political Economy."
[7] Pearton, *Diplomacy*, p. 8.
[8] Pearton, *Diplomacy*, p. 7.

The critics charged that armament firms were more responsive to their share-holders than to the needs of the state. As Christopher Miller has noted, the idea of a military–industrial complex and the concerns in the 1930s about the merchants of death "do not sit well with each other. One asserts that the state and industry had an uncomfortably close relationship, while the other argues that arms manufacturers caused wars by playing nations against one another."[9] In the 1930s the critics' preferred solution was the nationalization of armament firms. Clearly the state was not perceived as part of the problem – indeed, it was the solution – whereas the independence of armament firms was the issue. During both phases of public criticism, the British Government was largely silent, refusing to engage with critics in the House of Commons, until its hand was forced by various peace ballots. At the subsequent 1935–36 Royal Commission on the Private Manufacture of and Trading in Arms (Bankes Commission), important government figures arose to defend the armament firms. They were regarded as critical if the country was to survive any future conflict with Germany.

Katherine Epstein's book *Torpedo* does claim to have identified a military–industrial complex in Britain. This is particularly relevant as in 1906 both Armstrongs and Vickers took shares in Whiteheads, the firm at the center of her British case study. Epstein follows the development of torpedoes in the United States and Britain from their origins in the 1860s to their deployment in the Great War. She argues that torpedo technology led to a "new procure-ment paradigm" because "Industrial naval technology was so sophisticated and expensive that traditional methods of building weapons in public-owned factories or purchasing them as finished products from private contractors did not suffice. Instead, governments had to invest in private-sector technology during the experimental phase."[10] She sees this as indicating the emergence of military–industrial complexes in both countries.[11] However, the evidence sug-gests that this interpretation fits the United States better than Great Britain.

Regarding Epstein's claim of a new procurement model with state investment in research and development, this is not how the government behaved in the cases of Armstrongs and Vickers, two of Britain's most important suppliers. In fact, the omnipotent Treasury ensured that *laissez-faire* always prevailed. There was complete unwillingness to subsidize research and development until the point at which an armament firm had already developed an innovative product; the government would then "reward" the firm with a contract for a limited num-ber of experimental models. Indeed, this is what happened with the Whitehead torpedo and later with Whitehead's experimental gyroscopes – four of these

---

[9] Miller, *Planning*, p. 6.
[10] Epstein, *Torpedo*, p. 2.
[11] The assertion is in the introduction and in the last paragraph of the book. Epstein, *Tor-pedo*, p. 229.

were tested and then a large order placed.[12] Rather than the British procurement model showing the existence of a military–industrial complex, it showed the government having a limited relationship with firms, one that shifted the risks onto them, only rewarding successes with contracts. In turn, armament firms sought to price their products to include profits that would compensate them for their up-front investments in research and development.

To this author, Epstein's detailed account of the long negotiations between the Whitehead Company and the Admiralty shows something other than a military–industrial complex. The relationship was defined by extremely defensive behavior on both sides and constant disputes over prices, royalties and even patents. Two examples from 1896 illustrate the difficult relationship. Six years after Whiteheads had established a factory at Weymouth with Admiralty encouragement, the Admiralty brought in Greenwood and Batley to make torpedoes too, ending Whitehead's monopoly and ability to set prices.[13] The same year, a Whitehead tender for a contract to produce 220 torpedoes to a Royal Gun Factory design raised the proposed price per torpedo on the grounds that it had tendered the previous time without being informed of the accuracies required. The firm also complained about earlier delays in getting drawings and specifications from the Admiralty and "having to incorporate 'glaring errors in design' in the RGF [Royal Gun Factory]-pattern torpedoes."[14] Although Admiralty officials had themselves been critical of the Royal Gun Factory designs, they now banded together to criticize the firm. In these interactions over torpedoes spanning three decades, the state and the firm were jockeying for position, disputing over money and rights, and not behaving as though there was a strong confluence of interests between them. Epstein's claim that there was a British military–industrial complex prior to 1918 are not proven.

Jon Sumida recounts the conflictual relationship between Arthur Hungerford Pollen, inventor of a fire-control system, and the Royal Navy. In his dealings with the Admiralty between 1900 and 1914, Pollen encountered conservatism, bureaucratic inertia, administrative rigidity, financial restrictions and difficult personalities. These combined to inhibit the evaluation and acceptance of his important new technology, which was ultimately rejected in 1910. It was only after the failures of Royal Naval gunnery in battles such as Jutland that the service was finally prodded to adopt Pollen's fire-control system in the mid-1920s.[15]

More broadly, the fact that the Admiralty kept lists of approved suppliers does not indicate *per se* a military–industrial complex.[16] The *content* of those relationships must be considered. As is shown in subsequent chapters,

---

[12] Epstein, *Torpedo*, p. 220.
[13] Epstein, *Torpedo*, pp. 4, 8 and 42.
[14] Epstein, *Torpedo*, p. 42.
[15] Sumida, *Defence*.
[16] LeClair mentions a "nascent military industrial complex" in the 1870s, but then talks himself out of it. LeClair, *Supervising*, pp. 257–58.

Armstrongs, Vickers and the state were locked in difficult and conflictual (albeit polite) relationships. The interests of the state and firms differed, especially over money and risk, and they constantly struggled for advantage.

There is another strand of literature that abuts on discussions of a British military–industrial complex. It debates the question of British military strength between the wars, pitting "declinists" such as Corelli Barnett against academics such as David Edgerton and Edward Packard, who argue that the British state (and by extension British armament firms) was not left fundamentally weak by the interwar years but was what Edgerton terms a "Warfare State."[17] Edgerton shows how, during the interwar period, the British state, particularly the military, became dominant in research and development, after a long period where the armament firms were major initiators.[18] The major theme of Edgerton's impressive oeuvre is correcting the standard view of Britain as a declining, anti-militarist state between the wars, and defeating the historical tropes that have resulted from that (in his view, incorrect) solely "welfarist" interpretation of British history.[19] Edgerton's task is much broader than the one taken on in this book – no less than revising the historiography of twentieth-century Britain – but his views of the period 1920–70 must be considered as he explicitly makes arguments about, and uses the language of, a British military–industrial complex.

The condition of British armament manufacturers, including Vickers-Armstrongs, is important to this debate over British strength and preparedness prior to World War Two.[20] Edgerton assumes that British armament firms (broadly defined) were fully at the disposal of the British state and that there was therefore a military–industrial complex. However, as this book shows, Vickers-Armstrongs always maintained some interests distinct from those of the British Government, and even at this point of interdependence in the 1930s, still clashed with the state.

For his analysis of the strength of the armaments industry, Edgerton relies on a mix of official histories (though critical of their coverage and analysis[21]), an authorized history, J. D. Scott's *Vickers: A History*, and other works covering Armstrongs and Vickers and an array of British firms.[22] Edgerton notes dismissively that these "Specialist inquiries into each armed service and the arms industry have habitually presented detailed accounts and explanations to match

---

[17] Barnett, *The Audit of War*; Edgerton, *Warfare*.
[18] Edgerton, *Warfare*, pp. 167–68.
[19] Edgerton, *Warfare*, pp. 21–33 and 33–48, respectively.
[20] Edgerton, *Warfare*, pp. 36–41.
[21] *History of the Second World War: United Kingdom Civil Series*. Edgerton is particularly critical of two volumes: Postan, *British*; and Hornby, *Factories*. Edgerton, *Warfare*, pp. 17, 43 and 63.
[22] He cites among others: Grant, *Steel*; Scott, *Vickers*; Davenport Hines, *Dudley* and unpublished PhD thesis; Peebles, *Warshipbuilding*; and Warren, *Armstrongs*.

the gloomy conclusions of the general accounts."[23] Many of these accounts are based upon company archives such as those of Armstrongs and Vickers, with the result that they present the "gloomy conclusions" of the firms themselves during the interwar period, when there was a precipitous decline in work.[24]

In the interwar years many armament firms significantly reduced their production capacities, either independently or through organizations such as the National Shipbuilders Security Ltd. Many firms went out of business and there were major amalgamations and subsequent rationalizations of production. Consequently, overall British armaments production capacity was reduced and remained largely unmodernized. The problems were most pronounced in artillery and land systems since the War Office penchant for favoring the Royal Arsenals left the remaining producers – including Vickers-Armstrongs – in poor shape. The Admiralty and Air Ministry had kept their remaining producers on contractual life support, so they were in a somewhat better position.

Packard's work is important because he broadly follows Edgerton's line, but his research utilizes the archives of Vickers and Vickers-Armstrongs. It is an elegant piece of scholarship. Packard argues – contra the declinists – that Vickers-Armstrongs had great strength during the interwar period, but that the British Government thought otherwise, and those assumptions guided state policies.[25] However, this analysis prompts a vital question: If there was a British military–industrial complex, would the state so misunderstand the strength of the premier British armament firm?

The major works on Armstrongs and Vickers do not allude to a military-industrial complex.[26] However, many of these studies focus only on business history. Work by Clive Trebilcock seeks to rehabilitate the image of British armament firms from the "merchants of death" formulation, particularly concerning the use of domestic and international and armament trusts (rings).[27] His important book on Vickers is framed by examining structural relations between the firm and the state, specifically the consequences of oligopoly and monopsony.[28] However, this focus on economic explanations minimizes the role of politics and relationships in the story of the British Government and Vickers. His works nevertheless show that the British Government was constantly seeking to rein in the armament firms by introducing new suppliers to keep competition keen and innovations flowing, using the Royal Arsenals and Dockyards as benchmarks for pricing, and using contracting to restrain expenditure and profits. In turn, the firms were seeking to maximize profits from government work, minimize state intervention in their activities and

[23] Edgerton, *Warfare*, p. 16.
[24] Edgerton, *Warfare*, p. 334.
[25] Packard, *Whitehall*.
[26] Bastable, *Arms*; Scott, *Vickers*; Warren, *Armstrongs*.
[27] Trebilcock, "Radicalism."
[28] Trebilcock, *Vickers Brothers*.

pursue independent strategies abroad. There is less evidence of confluence than there is of the two sides seeking to outsmart the other. For a military–industrial complex to occur there would need to be a record of a significant, consistent confluence of interests between the British state and the firms. As this book will demonstrate, initially there was no such overlap of interests, and it grew only episodically over the century considered here.

By 1955, when this study ends, the relationship between armament firms and the state was interdependent and close because of the state's dominance of industrial planning and regulation, provision of subsidies for research and development, and support for exports. However, collaboration did not equal harmony. Armament firms and the state still retained distinct and incompatible interests: over domestic procurement and spending restraint; over profit levels; over levels of subsidies; over research and development expenditures; over exports; and over regulation. They were two actors in a relationship that were constantly sparring over a range of issues, albeit now with the deck stacked in the state's favor. This was not a seamless military–industrial complex.

Assessing the Independence and Power of Armstrongs and Vickers

If Armstrongs and Vickers were creating independent relationships and running their own foreign policies, there should be evidence of this in their archives. Further, if they were truly independent, there should be areas where the foreign policies the two firms pursued were significantly different to those of the British Government, and this should be reflected in official records. Two propositions are derived from this:

- If armament firms were independent actors, there will be evidence of them selling to whomever they wanted; and
- If British armament firms had independent foreign policies, there will be examples of them doing things that the British Government did not approve of, especially in terms of exports. There should also be evidence of divergent opinions between them and the British Government, reflecting their different goals and interests.

To test these propositions, the book uses extensive case studies to explore the firms' foreign relations with Latin America, Asia and Turkey.

The armaments trade is oligopolistic. That is, there were always a limited number of armaments producers, domestically and internationally. This was because of the very high costs of becoming, the escalating costs of remaining and the financial risks associated with being an armaments manufacturer. Those costs limited the number of suppliers, particularly at the technologically innovative end of the market. This had implications for power relationships. The oligopolistic structure of the market meant that the British Government did not have many alternative suppliers and would have faced extremely steep reentry costs if it decided to bring sophisticated armament production inhouse. This gave armament firms some power in their relationship with the state. However, while oligopoly handed some power to firms, monopsony handed some back to the government. As the major recipient of the armament firms' products, the British Government had significant power in those relationships. The armament firms depended on government business, so were obliged to accommodate the wishes of the state in terms of pricing, profits, exports, and so on, while also developing strategies and tactics designed to curb the British Government's power as a monopsonist.

The domestic independence of the firms prompts a bigger question: Did this independence reflect or give them any *power* in their relationships with the British Government? Also, as the relationship between armament firms and the British Government changed over the century covered in this book, how did the power of the firms in relation to the government evolve over time? To answer these questions, it is helpful to briefly unpack ideas from political science about what power is and how it can be used. As Britain is a democracy, it is appropriate to begin from the classic pluralist stance which sees power as dispersed and not just lying with the state.[29] It is important to see where, beyond the government, power lies and how it is wielded. This investigation has been helpfully done through various iterations of democratic theory by considering different dimensions, or "faces," of power. These dimensions reflect a hierarchy, with each face representing a more "powerful" version; the more powerful an actor, the less power it needs to expend to achieve a desired outcome. Moreover, in creating their own taxonomy of power, Michael Barnett and Raymond Duvall make the important point that these conceptions of power are not competing but are connected (indeed, this author would say cumulative).[30] Considering these "faces" of power provides a framework for analyzing the degree of power that the armament firms were able to wield – or not – in their relationships with the British Government.

The "first face of power" is the most straightforward. Power is used by one actor to influence the behavior of another. This is relational power. It exists in the relationship of one actor to another actor, and the ratio of power varies depending on the actors involved. Our concern is the British Government's relationships with the armament firms, and vice versa. Most obvious was the power of the British Government to structure the regulatory environment in which armament firms operated, for example, directly through restrictions on exports, rules on secrecy, ceilings on profits and so on. The state also shaped the economy in which armament firms operated through policies on infrastructure, regulation, education, production and so on. This is often called "authority"; it signals the legitimacy of the government to exercise that power.

[29] Derived from the classic work by Dahl, *Who Governs*.
[30] Barnett and Duval, "Power."

The British Government was initially slow to use that direct authority but over time exercised more of it over the armament firms through regulation. Ironically, though, in parallel the government became more invested in the armament firms' success, reflected in the growth in contracts awarded to Armstrongs and Vickers and increasing government support for research and armaments exports. Growing interdependence saw the firms retain some power and leverage in their relationship with the state even as they lost some independence.

In the British democratic pluralist system, actors such as armament firms potentially have some power, essentially derived from their positions in the economy. Their economic heft and the employment they provide can create political support for armament firms, which might enable them to: influence the government's selection of one weapon over another; gain permission to export an armament; win a subsidy; or prevent something bad from happening to them – such as contracts going to a rival, a tax being imposed on their profits or nationalization being pursued. Where an armament firm sought to make something happen – or to prevent something from happening – and was successful, they would have shown they had relational power and exercised the "first face" of power in relation to the government. Indeed, even a negotiation between an armament firm and the government over an issue such as subsidies, weapons choices, exports or industry structure is a signal that a firm (or firms in concert) had some power in that relationship. Two propositions can be derived from this:

- If Armstrongs and Vickers had relational power in relation to the British Government, there will be evidence of interactions in the records of the firms and the state, for example, showing the firms successfully negotiating over relevant issues.
- Armstrongs and Vickers will have been shown to have strong relational power if they have influenced the British Government to act in their favor. The firms should win victories or concessions on issues such as subsidies, costs, profits, competition, penalty clauses in procurement contracts, export controls, patent rules, taxation levels and so on.

The "second face of power" is defined as an actor being able to set the agenda. It is a more effective form of wielding power because not as many resources need to be expended to achieve the desired ends. While agenda-setting power might be expected to lie with the government, if a firm has more than relational power, it should be able to set the agenda on issues it cares about. Agenda-setting can be both positive – for example, support for building more warships – or negative (a "nondecision") – for example, preventing substantive discussions of the profits or behavior of armament firms.[31] This can be formulated as:

---

[31] For a discussion of power as the ability to structure the environment or "mobilize bias" to put issues on or keep issues off the agenda, see Bacharach and Baratz, "Two Faces."

- In Armstrongs and Vickers' relationships with the British Government, the second face of power will be in evidence if the two firms were able to put favorable issues such as more military spending or generous profit levels on the agenda and to keep negative issues – such as investigations into their behavior or limits on their profits – off the agenda.

Finally, the "third face of power" is what Steven Lukes calls "ideological power," that is, effectively structuring the political environment so that alternatives are completely excluded and actors do not realize that other possibilities exist. This ideological power is described as the ultimate form of power as the holders do not need to expend any of it to achieve their ends because they have so successfully structured the realm of possibilities.[32] This can be formulated into the following proposition:

- In the relationship between Armstrongs, Vickers and the British Government, the firms will show ideological power if there is evidence of the British Government unquestioningly adopting the interests of the firms in terms of issues such as military spending, armaments sales at home and abroad, profit levels and subsidies.

Considering this three-level framework, this book uses process-tracing techniques to examine the behaviors of Armstrongs and Vickers in relation to the British Government and key foreign governments. The book proceeds as follows. Part One covers selling weapons at home. Chapter 1 lays out the challenges the two firms faced in making sales, specifically, the British Government's commitment to *laissez-faire* policies, prejudices within the British elite against those in trade, and departmental resistance to dealing with private firms. It then establishes the suite of strategies and tactics that the firms developed to overcome these obstacles to selling arms at home and abroad. Chapters 2–5 provide a chronology of the firms' experiences of dealing with the British Government and the many peaks and troughs in that central relationship. Chapter 2 covers the Victorian era, when Armstrongs rose to prominence. Chapter 3 discusses the Edwardian era, which saw Vickers successfully challenging Armstrongs' dominance. Chapter 4 examines the difficult interwar period when both firms struggled to survive, but Armstrongs failed. Chapter 5 charts Vickers-Armstrongs responses to the challenges of rearmament, World War Two and postwar nationalization.

Part Two considers selling weapons abroad. Armstrongs and Vickers built surprisingly enduring relationships with recipient states over the century considered here. Chapters 6–8 are case studies of armament exports to Latin America, Asia and Turkey, respectively. These relationships endured despite royal successions, abrupt changes of leadership, coups and – importantly – changes in the strategic interests of the British state. To create and maintain

---

[32] Lukes, *Power*.

those relationships, Armstrongs and Vickers developed a suite of independent foreign policy strategies and tactics, while always leading with their technologically sophisticated armament products. In each case, Armstrongs was the pioneer in the foreign market, but by the beginning of the twentieth century Vickers was a strong competitor and they often colluded against foreign firms. Chapter 9 returns to the conceptual framework laid out here to assess the domestic strategies and foreign policies of the two firms and reflect upon the power and independence that Armstrongs and Vickers exhibited in their relationships with the British state.

PART I

Selling at Home

1

Armstrongs and Vickers Become Armament Firms

The Challenges They Faced and the
Strategies They Developed

The Industrial Revolution began in Europe and emanated outwards. A key feature of the era was the rapid pace and continuous cycle of military technological change. As David Stevenson recounted, in the century and a half prior to the 1840s naval and land armaments had scarcely changed, but from then on industrialization had a transformative effect on destructive capabilities.[1] The technological and industrial capacities needed to manufacture modern weapons demanded major changes in the way that the British state procured weaponry, with the government turning to private firms to create armaments that had proved beyond their technological – and financial – capabilities and for wartime production surges.[2]

Innovations came especially fast in the naval sphere, with important and costly technological advances in gunnery, speed and torpedoes. Constantly improving seaborne artillery meant that ships needed ever heavier armor, leading to a dependence on private suppliers.[3] As Lord George Hamilton noted, "After 1860 each subsequent decade outdid its predecessor in the improvements and development of power – so much so that fighting ships were almost obsolete before they had completed their first commission."[4] The Admiralty still led in ship design, but even here private firms created designs to catch the eye of the First Sea Lord and to sell abroad.[5]

Determined British entrepreneurs such as William Armstrong, Joseph Whitworth, William Beardmore, Charles Cammell, John Brown, Thomas Vickers and Albert Vickers – and the competition between them – propelled armament developments from 1855 onwards.[6] An incentive for many entrepreneurs (except Armstrong) to begin armaments production was the intense

---

[1] Stevenson, *Armaments*, p. 15.
[2] After France launched the first ironclad, *La Gloire*, in 1859, the shipbuilding market expanded quickly. Slaven, *British*, pp. 44–45.
[3] Grant, *Steel*, pp. 20–21.
[4] Hamilton "Introduction," in Manning, *William White*, p. v.
[5] Lyon, "Admiralty," pp. 37–64.
[6] Bastable, *Arms*; Harkavy, *Arms Trade*, p. 32; Hume and Moss, *Beardmore*; Scott, *Vickers*; Trebilcock, *Vickers Brothers*.

competition in the civilian iron and steel markets.[7] Our two firms, colloquially known as "Armstrongs" and "Vickers," became vital sources of technological innovation and capital investment in armaments production. They are now discussed in turn.

The Armstrongs Origin Story

William Armstrong's shift into armaments manufacture has been recounted several times.[8] He was "the son of a Cumberland yeoman and born in Newcastle in 1810."[9] Although Armstrong initially trained for the law, his heart was in engineering and in 1847 with friends he formed W. G. Armstrong & Co., with a site at Elswick, to manufacture his innovative hydraulic engines and cranes.[10] The first ever hydraulic crane was installed at the Albert Dock in Liverpool in May 1848, earning the firm £1,000. That year, while the crane business was growing, the firm sought to diversify into locomotive production, but this was a failure.[11] At the 1851 Great Exhibition, Armstrong demonstrated his hydraulic cranes and hydraulic engines (though it was the German firm Krupp's six-pound cannon that won the gold medal).[12] By the 1850s Armstrongs products were transforming docksides.

In 1854, during the Crimean War, the War Office asked Armstrong to design a submarine mine capable of blowing up the Russian ships that had been sunk and were blocking Sevastopol harbor.[13] This he did, and although the War Office did not deploy the mines, "what was important about the incident was that Armstrong had been taught to think about military matters, and had been provided with acquaintances in the War Office."[14] By November Armstrong was turning his mind to guns.

As his longtime associate Stuart Rendel later recounted, William Armstrong's real shift into armaments came out of a combination of problem solving and patriotism. Armstrong and James Rendel, Stuart's father, were animated by newspaper accounts of the problems that British soldiers experienced in moving and firing guns at the 1854 Battle of Inkerman. James Rendel set Armstrong the task of designing a better gun, which Armstrong did quickly and with good effect. "[B]y the following month he had designed a gun on entirely new

---

[7] Grant, *Rulers*, pp. 4–5.
[8] Rendel, *Personal Papers*; McKenzie, *W.G. Armstrong*; Warren, *Armstrongs*; Bastable, *Arms*; Heald, *William Armstrong*.
[9] Cochrane, *Romance*, p. 166.
[10] Fairbairn, *Elswick* records that the works commenced in 1847, "this date being shewn on weather vane on old blacksmiths shop," VA, Doc. 593.
[11] Warren, *Armstrongs*, p. 256.
[12] Picard, "Great"; Payne, *Private Spies*, p. 129.
[13] Cochrane, *Romance*, p. 167.
[14] Scott, *Vickers*, p. 25.

principles and had also himself interviewed the Duke of Newcastle, then War Minister, who gave him an order to make up to six guns to his design."[15] In all, twenty-three inventors were given money to develop their ideas.[16] William Armstrong received £7,219 toward his work on large, wrought-iron, rifled breechloaders and was aided by the brilliant inventors James Nasmyth and Isambard Kingdom Brunel.[17] His 3-pound model was submitted to the War Office in July 1855, followed by a 5-pound model in 1856; and "within two years he had an 18-pounder."[18] At Elswick Armstrong spent £12,000 on building a gun shop.

The Armstrong Gun, utilizing a build-up method of construction, was trialed by a commission against models designed by others, including Joseph Whitworth (igniting a bitter rivalry). As the Secretary of War informed Parliament in 1859, "The Report of the Commission was that, after giving the fullest attention to the subject, they considered Sir William Armstrong's invention superior to all others." He explained:

> The great advantages of this gun were its extreme lightness, the extent of its range, and its accuracy. An Armstrong gun throwing a projectile of 18 lb. weighed one-third as much as the guns now in use discharging shot of that weight. The range of a 32 lb. gun, fired with a charge of 5 lb. of powder, was a little more than five miles and a quarter. ... The precision of the gun was still more extraordinary than its range. The accuracy of the Armstrong gun at 3,000 yards was as seven to one compared with that of the common gun at 1,000 yards; while at 1,000 yards it would hit an object every time which was struck by the common guns only once in fifty-seven times; therefore, at equal distances, the Armstrong gun was fifty-seven times as accurate as our common artillery. Its destructive effect, also, exceeded anything which had hitherto been witnessed.[19]

Unfortunately, the Crimean War was over before the War Office accepted the Armstrong Gun in 1859. With reports of the gun's success, the Royal Navy requested "in the strongest manner" that the War Office supply them with a "large number" of 70- and 110-pounders.[20] In 1859 Armstrongs' 7-inch, 110-pound, rifled breechloaders were fitted to the Isaac Watts designed HMS *Warrior* without having undergone naval trials. Ultimately the cast iron guns

---

[15] Fairbairn, *Elswick*, p. 50; William Armstrong, "Report on the Construction of Wrought Iron Field Guns," July 14, 1855. TNA, WO 33/11.
[16] Whitworth was given nearly £13,000 to develop rifling machinery for small arms. Bastable, *Arms*, pp. 28–29.
[17] Armstrong received "by far the largest amount." Bastable, "Breechloaders," p. 218.
[18] Bastable, "Breechloaders," p. 221.
[19] House of Commons Debates, Army Estimates – Supply. March 4, 1859, *Hansard* Vol. 152, c. 1319.
[20] Bastable, "Breechloaders," p. 225. Citing "Report from the Select Committee on Ordnance," *Parliamentary Papers* 11 (1863), p. 5.

could not withstand the shock created by the propellant, exactly as Armstrong had warned.[21]

In accepting the Armstrong Gun, the War Office implicitly acknowledged that it was beyond anything the Royal Arsenal at Woolwich could produce. According to the firm's historian, patriotism dominated Armstrong's motives: He "had not patented his new inventions and furthermore he had declined the £20,000 reward which was offered him, so the Government took out patents in his name for the guns and their complete outfit, and by an Act of Parliament, withheld publication of the patents."[22] Marshall Bastable also sees Armstrong's actions as an astute political move because "[i]n return he demanded a guarantee that the capital investment in the new company would not be lost if the government decided to build all the guns at Woolwich or contract them out to others."[23] In 1859 Armstrong was given a ten-year contract (backdated to April 1, 1856 so as to cover the expenses that he incurred in developing his gun) as Engineer for Rifled Ordnance to the War Office, a knighthood and an annual salary of £2,000, plus payment for the "draughtsmen employed by him" and his travel expenses. His contract specified he was to "give his best attention to the maturing and perfecting of his system of rifled ordnance." It gave him "authority to direct the methods to be adopted and the conditions to be observed in the construction of such articles" at Woolwich Arsenal.[24] As Bastable notes, in addition to training Army engineers to make his guns, Armstrong would use his position to "develop his build-up method for larger guns at government expense."[25]

With Sir William in government service, his former associates in Newcastle formed a new department at Elswick, named The Elswick Ordnance Company, financed with public capital.[26]

> The Partners ... were Mr. Cruddas, Mr. Lambert and Mr. George Rendel, while the capital guaranteed by the Government was £50,000, afterwards increased to £85,000. The new Company engaged to work solely for the British Government, and their charges were to be checked by Government auditors ... The beginning of this Company can be dated as January, 1859, the date of a formal agreement between the three above-mentioned partners and General Peel, Secretary of State for War.[27]

---

[21] Bastable, "Breechloaders," p. 225; Armstrong testimony at the Select Committee on Ordnance, 1863.

[22] Fairbairn, *Elswick*, p. 58.

[23] Bastable, "Breechloaders," p. 223.

[24] "Definitions of Sir William George Armstrong's Duties as 'Engineer for Rifled Ordnance' and forms of his appointment," signed by Sir William Armstrong, February 23, 1859. Wiltshire and Swindon History Center, 2057/F8/V/A/32, paragraphs 1 and 4.

[25] Bastable, "Breechloaders," p. 224.

[26] "History of Sir W. G. Armstrong's Introduction of his Gun, with Reports of Experiments &c.," pp. 3–5. TNA, WO 33/9.

[27] Fairbairn, *Elswick*, p. 60.

The Elswick Ordnance Company received a grant to extend the factory and plant, and the government held a monopoly over the Armstrong Guns it produced.[28] Sir William played no active role in the firm, though this was not precluded by his contract.[29] At Elswick "[t]he utmost secrecy was preserved, and the intrusion of foreign observers was rigorously prevented."[30] Stuart Rendel marveled: "Considering ... the bitter contentiousness over the private manufacture of rifled ordnance, it is noteworthy that a single private firm should have enjoyed so great and profitable a monopoly without cavil."[31]

In London Sir William was elected to the Athenaeum Club, where his friend James Rendel was already a member. This started a tradition of the firm's management becoming members of that gentlemen's club.[32] Despite this handy connection to the elite, things were hard for Sir William: "[H]e was assailed by inventors over whom he had obtained preference."[33] There was continuing conflict with the indefatigable Whitworth, who complained that "to place him in office at the War Department was to prejudice the fair consideration of all new ideas not emanating from himself" and still refused to accept that Whitworth guns were inferior.[34] Moreover, despite the appearance of advantage, Sir William's experience of government service was frustrating because Woolwich Arsenal was outmoded and – like the War Office – was stacked with conservative figures hostile to innovation. There was also parliamentary concern that Armstrong was now the inspector of the guns made by his former partners at Elswick.[35] Regardless, in three years Sir William had rebuilt Woolwich to independently manufacture Armstrong Guns, leading the government to terminate Elswick's contract. Sir William returned to Newcastle and the new combined company of Sir W. G. Armstrong was formed. With the Armstrongs firm thus established, this chapter now turns to the birth of the firm that became its major rival, Vickers.

The Vickers Origin Story

There are fewer published accounts of the origins of Vickers, partly because it is more a story of managerial competence, hard work and the search for profits

---

28   House of Commons, "Minutes of Evidence Taken Before the Select Committee on Ordnance," July 2, 1862. *Report of Committees Vol. VI* (1862), question 35, p. 2; Pearton, *Diplomacy*, p. 80.
29   It stated: "8th Sir William George Armstrong shall remain at liberty to carry on his present business, or any other in which he may think proper to engage." "Definitions of Sir William George Armstrong's Duties," paragraph 8.
30   "Andrew Noble," p. 266.
31   Rendel, *Personal Papers*, pp. 271–72.
32   Wheeler, *The Athenaeum*, p. 27.
33   Fairbairn, *Elswick*, p. 63.
34   Rendel, *Personal Papers*, p. 274; Bastable, *Arms*, pp. 75–78; Tennent, *Story*, pp. 333–44.
35   Parliamentary Question from Sir Frederick Smith, August 3, 1860, *Hansard*, Vol. 160, c. 654; Motion for a Select Committee from Mr. Henry Baillie, House of Commons, June 13, 1867, *Hansard*, Vol. 187, c. 1789.

than a glamorous tale of patriotic endeavor and burgeoning elite connections.[36] According to Douglas Vickers' 1920 *History of Vickers*, there had been a firm with the Vickers name since around 1750.[37] The steel dynasty began with the marriage of miller Edward Vickers (1804–1897) to Anne Naylor (1804–1881) in August 1828. Anne was the daughter of George Naylor, who, along with his son William, was a partner in a local steel melting firm. William Naylor also independently had a rolling mill.[38] In 1828 George Naylor and his new son-in-law, Edward Vickers, founded Messrs. Naylor, Vickers and Company, to produce steel for objects such as cutlery, tools and files, operating two works, the River Don works at Wadsley and the Sheffield Millsands works.[39] Naylor Vickers had an agency in the United States selling steel products, where German émigré Ernst Benzon went to work and flourished.[40] After George Naylor senior retired in 1829, Naylor, Hutchinson & Vickers was formed by his son George Portus Naylor, Edward Vickers and John Hutchinson. The firm operated the Millsands and River Don works, a file manufacturer in Orchard Street and a forge at Wadsley Bridge, and had representation in New York.[41]

Edward Vickers saw the potential of the railways for the nation, as new business for Naylor, Hutchinson & Vickers, and for improving the firm's supply chain. During the 1830s he was involved in committees for the Sheffield and Manchester Railway, the Sheffield and Rotherham Railway, the North Midland Railway and the Doncaster, North Midland and Goole Railway.[42] By the 1840s Edward was an established figure in Sheffield and was continuously active in local politics. Over time his political affiliations moved to the right, in parallel with those of most members of the Sheffield merchant and manufacturing class.[43] He unsuccessfully stood for Alderman in 1843.[44] Edward was the elected mayor of Sheffield in 1847–8 and the 1851 census recorded the merchant and steel manufacturer as being an Alderman and Borough Magistrate.[45] Successive members of the family and managers of Vickers were members of the Sheffield Club, established in 1843, which "acted as a centre for information on political and financial developments

---

[36] The classic published accounts are Scott, *Vickers* and Trebilcock, *Vickers Brothers*. Scott's *Vickers* is an excellent account, but he provides few citations to the specific documents in the Vickers Archives he drew from, making it hard to trace his primary sources or to check his interpretations.

[37] Vickers, *History of Vickers*, 5th draft, March 18, 1920. VA, Doc. 762, p. 1.

[38] Tweedale, *Giants*, pp. 65–72.

[39] White, *Formation*, p. 68; "1930 Industrial Britain: Vickers-Armstrongs Limited."

[40] Vickers, *History of Vickers*, Older Draft, p. 1, Folio 4. This draft puts the date as the 1860s, but Naylor & Vickers was active in Sheffield in 1852. Tweedale, *Steel City*, p. 51, Table 1.4.

[41] "Naylor," Citing "1933 History and Directory of Sheffield, Rotherham," in "Naylor, Hutchinson, Vickers and Co.," *London Gazette*, August 12, 1834.

[42] "Edward Vickers," *Grace's Guide*.

[43] White, *Formation*, pp. 206 and 220–21.

[44] White, *Formation*, p. 148.

[45] "Edward Vickers," *Grace's Guide*.

in the rest of the country and the world," taking many newspapers and business journals.[46] This was not a gentleman's club, but a functional business organization. In 1854 Edward Vickers was involved in the creation of a "Sheffield Exchange and News Room," where the businessmen of the city could meet and receive their telegrams. On March 2, 1857 he became president of the new Sheffield Chamber of Commerce: "[I]ts aims were to further the interests of Sheffield trade, and to provide a conduit for effective lobbying of Government."[47] In the same year Edward supported a local Tory candidate and signed a petition in favor of the pro-trade government of the Whig Lord Palmerston and, as president of the Chamber of Commerce, personally presented it to the prime minister.[48]

Two of Edward Vickers' sons, Thomas Edward (1833–1915) and Albert (1838–1919), finished their technical schooling in the 1840s with spells in Germany.[49] Thomas studied in Neuwied-on-the-Rhine and Albert in Hamein-on-the-Weser.[50] In 1854 these talented young men joined the family firm. Thomas was an excellent metallurgist and engineer, who by the age of twenty-eight had patents to his name.[51] Albert was an effective manager and salesman for the firm. The firm was flourishing and in the mid-1850s Vickers brought German "melters" to Sheffield to introduce pioneering crucible processes for making complex steel castings, and by 1860 the firm was successfully producing steel bells, steel castings and steel railway tires.[52] Thomas managed the Sheffield plants from about 1855, and Albert "spent a considerable portion of his life in the United States, representing the Firm."[53] It would be a further two decades before Vickers entered the armaments market.

With our two firms now established, this chapter turns to the three main challenges that private firms faced in selling armaments to the British Government and around the world.

Challenge One: *Laissez-faire* and Free Trade Policies

When Armstrongs and Vickers emerged, the British Government was strongly committed to *laissez-faire*, the principle that governments should not control business, and to free trade. Consequently, the government would not help

---

[46] White, *Formation*, pp. 36–37.
[47] White, *Formation*, pp. 204, 200.
[48] White, *Formation*, pp. 199, 204 and 209.
[49] Tweedale, *Steel City*, p. 150.
[50] "Colonel Thomas Edward Vickers"; "Albert Vickers."
[51] Scott, *Vickers*, p. 14.
[52] Tweedale, *Steel City*, p. 47; "1930s Industrial Britain: Vickers-Armstrongs Limited."
[53] Vickers, *History of Vickers*, 5th Draft, p. 6. This seems an exaggeration of his time in the United States, though he did marry an American. Wilson, *Middle-Class*, p. 41. Albert did not live in Sheffield, though. Census records show he lived in turn in London, Aldermin-ster, London and Eastbourne. "Albert Vickers," *Grace's Guide*.

struggling businesses, provide any subsidies or help firms market overseas. Firms were independent actors and sank or swam by their own efforts. The bastion of *laissez-faire* thinking within the government was the extremely powerful Treasury, though the Foreign Office and Diplomatic Service also strongly upheld the doctrine. The Treasury exercised an iron grip on spending and had no qualms about disciplining a department that might want to stray from the approved line.

The commitment to *laissez-faire* and free trade also empowered the government to give short shrift to the rights of firms. Firms were regarded as something to be used in the interests of the state. For example, in the early part of this era patents seem to have been ignored as often as they were acknowledged. This favored Armstrongs when it was accused of stealing the inventions of Theophilus Blakely. The government's commitment to Armstrongs was absolute and it would not hear the patent complaint or allow competition, leading Blakely to leave Britain in 1863.[54]

In the 1880s the government's commitment to *laissez-faire* was challenged by the Long Depression and resulting mass unemployment. Lord Salisbury appointed a Royal Commission to investigate the causes and consequences of the depression, at which Thomas Vickers appeared as a witness.[55] However, the Commission's eventual report did not stray from *laissez-faire*.[56] The government also investigated Britain's overseas trade, resulting in the "Bryce Memorandum" of July 17, 1886, designed to boost exports.[57] James Bryce suggested "stimulating the interest of our present diplomatic and consular officers in commercial affairs and … giving them both a stronger motive and better facilities for activity in this department of their duties."[58] However, even after this political recognition that exports helped the state, the strong commitment to *laissez-faire* and free trade remained a "formidable" inhibitor to change within the Foreign Office and Diplomatic Service.[59] As a result, armament firms needed to conduct their own foreign policies.

Challenge Two: Class Prejudices

All firms faced a barrier to working with the government: class prejudice. As David McLean reported, in the 1880s there was a "social gulf which still divided the world of business and of British officialdom."[60] The resulting snobbery included distain for anyone who had to accumulate wealth through active

---

54 Bastable, *Arms*, p. 36.
55 Thomas Vickers, *Report of the Royal Commission*, p. 109, Q. 3438.
56 Howe, *Free Trade*.
57 "Memorandum by Mr. James Bryce," p. 5.
58 *Report of the Royal Commission*; Bryce Memorandum, "Correspondence."
59 Platt, *Finance*, pp. 102–40.
60 McLean, "Commerce," p. 475.

work, that is, the middle and lower classes. Indeed, the term "trade" was used pejoratively. While social class was a barrier to trade generally, it was doubly so for "dirty" industries such as steel, armaments and warship production. Exacerbating this perception was the fact that many of the armament firms were begun by northern entrepreneurs in Newcastle, Glasgow, Sheffield, Manchester and Liverpool, meaning that most had northern accents, another point counting against them for the southern elite that dominated government and the civil service.[61]

Nevertheless, different attitudes toward Armstrongs and Vickers can be detected in British Government documents and secondary materials spanning this period, with Armstrongs generally more favored. Armstrong had clear patriotic motives for becoming engaged in armaments production, and this was appreciated.[62] His record of government service and his role as a prolific inventor all recommended him to the state. His support for local charities, his innovations at the home he built at Cragside, Northumberland, his connections to Liberal politics and his role in public life all increased his favor with Queen Victoria and the Prince of Wales. Reflecting this burgeoning relationship with the elite was his elevation to a baronetcy in 1887. As J. D. Scott reports, Lord Armstrong "had the gift, so important in British public life, of not seeming to try too hard, and this contributed to the position which the Armstrong firm enjoyed of being something more than a commercial organization, something more like a national institution."[63] The subsequent elevation of Armstrongs' Stuart Rendel to a peerage, the rotation of warship designers between the firm and the Admiralty (see Chapters 2 and 3) and the increasing prominence of the firm meant Armstrongs earned a degree of acceptance from government officials, enhanced by Sir William's courtly manner in all his dealings with the state.

By contrast, Vickers, while earning admiration for its industrial prowess and business savvy, was viewed differently. The firm built its reputation as an innovative steel and armament firm, not as an adjunct to the elite. The Vickers family did not build fancy houses or integrate into the British national elite.[64] Although Vickers supported some local charities this was not done to the same extent or with the panache of Sir William or fellow steelmaker Mark Firth of Sheffield, so did not lead to royal attention or invitations to Court.

---

[61] The southern English aristocracy's failure to compete with northern industrialists led those "gentlemanly capitalists" to focus on advancing imperialism. Cain and Hopkins, *British Imperialism.*

[62] Bastable, *Arms,* p. 109.

[63] Scott, *Vickers,* p. 89.

[64] Some fellow Sheffielders did pursue these routes: George Wostenholm built Kenwood House, Sir John Brown became a friend of Palmerston and Mark Firth hosted the Prince and Princess of Wales at Oakbrook in 1875 when they opened Firth Park to the public. Tweedale, *Steel City,* pp. 155–56 and 73; Wilson *Middle-Class,* p. 66.

The Vickers family played roles in local society as members of the Sheffield Club, the Chamber of Commerce, the Cutlers' Company and the Sheffield Exchange and News Room, all of which furthered their business interests and reflected their status as part of the local urban elite (or upper middle class). According to the *Daily Telegraph*, Albert "did not allow his energies to be frittered or his spirits to be disturbed by other pursuits: there were only two things in the world that interested him – his business and his shooting."[65] Albert Vickers' excellent moorlands may have helped cement relations with important foreign customers, and shooting and hunting were also increasingly fashionable among British industrialists.[66] Thomas Vickers was a local Justice of the Peace and a founder of the Hallamshire Rifles, in which by 1861 he and Albert were both Captains; the firm also provided Ensigns Natrop and Mitchell.[67] Tom was made a Colonel in 1884 after twenty-five years of service.[68] He was made a prestigious Sheffield Master Cutler in 1872. He and Albert were described by Scott as "very handsome men, and they had style. They were natural aristocrats, and looked it."[69] This may have been the perception in Yorkshire, but it did not carry to London.

After the turn of the century more of Vickers' management had been in government employment, but they tended to have been in technical, rather than political, positions. Locally Douglas Vickers was made a Master Cutler 1908 and was a Conservative Member of Parliament for Sheffield Hallam in 1918–22, though he "was one of the most silent" MPs.[70] Overall, the family did not interact with the southern elite in the way that Armstrongs' directors did. Moreover, the businessmen of Vickers were at least as interested in keeping strong connections with financiers and bankers as they were in building relations with the British Government.[71] While the directors of the firm were patriotic, they were also strategic in that patriotism and government officials understood that. This perception of Vickers lingered late into the 1920s and the firm had to consistently strategize to overcome these prejudices.

Challenge Three: Departmental Resistance

The final challenge that armament firms faced in dealing with the British Government was the resistance of some departments. Bastable has perceptively

---

[65] Tweedale, *Steel City*, p. 143. Citing *Daily Telegraph*, July 16, 1919.
[66] Letter Book 12, May 16, 1904, January 4, 1910. VA, Doc. 1004; Albert hosted Grand Duke Michael of Russia at a shooting party in 1910. Trebilcock, *Vickers Brothers*, pp. 34, 128; White, *Formation*, p. 68.
[67] White, *Formation*, p. 85, Table 3.8.
[68] Hamilton, *Misses Vickers*, p. 27.
[69] Scott, *Vickers*, pp. 76–77.
[70] Tweedale, *Steel City*, p. 144.
[71] Trebilcock, *Vickers Brothers*, p. 129.

noted that armament firms experienced different relationships with the state depending on which ministries they were interacting with.[72] Initially the key departments for the armament firms were the Admiralty and the War Office (both in the thrall of the Treasury), and the Foreign Office and Diplomatic Service.

Interestingly, the initial relationship established between armament firms and a military service set up an enduring path dependency for future relationships, and there was considerable variation in paths between the services. From the first the relationship between Armstrongs and Vickers and the Admiralty was broadly positive – though not necessarily intimate – because armament firms were the only sources for resilient armor, heavy guns and mountings, and an increasingly important source for ships' hulls and design personnel. As former First Naval Lord Sir Richard Hamilton made clear in 1896: "It is highly important … for the country that happy relations should be preserved with contractors. Upon this depends the ability to increase upon emergency our constructive means."[73]

The Admiralty's needs drove generally positive relationships, particularly with Armstrongs, who supplied it with a succession of directors of naval construction. Around the turn of the century "relations between Vickers and the Admiralty remained formal and cool. Vickers might have hoped for a more sympathetic attitude from the Board, but their representations of matters directly affecting them were often rejected; as were those of Armstrongs."[74]

The Admiralty made a move early in the era designed to give itself more control over armament firms: It split all armor and ship contracts, even if the firm manufactured both, making delays "less easy to conceal than if they were hidden in the departments of one large firm."[75] This was frustrating to the major firms, who wanted to profit from whole deals. The distance the Admiralty sought from even key suppliers was justified, though, because the private firms had their own agendas; for example, Armstrongs and Vickers had a secret price fixing agreement between 1906 and 1913.[76] Additionally, sometimes firms sought to manipulate the Admiralty: "Not all tenders were genuine, since firms would occasionally tender at absurdly high prices solely for the purpose of gaining insight into the latest Admiralty designs in order to make use of them in their work for foreign navies."[77] This was effectively espionage, the hallmark of an armament firm thinking as a completely independent actor. In turn, the Admiralty sometimes undertook its own espionage, calling for firms to submit designs, ostensibly for production, but in reality to ascertain what innovations

[72] Bastable, *Arms*, p. 14.
[73] Hamilton, *Naval*, p. 179.
[74] Scott, *Vickers*, p. 51.
[75] Lyon, "Admiralty," p. 41.
[76] "Armstrong Whitworth & Co. Ltd: Arrangement with Vickers on Armament Orders 1906–13," VA, Doc. 551, Folios 135–37.
[77] Pollard, "*Laissez-Faire*," p. 107.

they had developed.[78] These design tenders also gave the Admiralty insights into what talent the firms had, and these people were then invited to sit on government committees, as happened to George Rendel of Armstrongs.

Overall, working with the Admiralty was a reasonably constructive experience for armament firms. By contrast, as Armstrongs found, producing Army artillery was a tortuous affair. The War Office fundamentally wanted to use products from the Royal Arsenals and disliked having to deal with private firms. Moreover, the procurement system was staffed by "fiscally and technically conservative officers and officials."[79] A major feature of the system from 1855 was the Ordnance Select Committee, which was tasked with both developing weapons indigenously and evaluating armament firms' gun designs, so "Woolwich was now in direct competition with the trade and yet had access to their secrets."[80] They were perfectly willing to harvest the best technologies from the private firms but unwilling to acknowledge ownership of these ideas or pay royalties. "The accusations made in the 1850s that the War Office stole designs from private inventors, were confirmed in the 1860s. After rejecting the designs of private inventors, the War Office and Admiralty coolly used them to build their own mix-and-match versions."[81] In response to these outrages, the armament firms eventually turned to politics and to the courts to gain redress. Moreover, "as Whitworth discovered in 1863–64, even a definitely superior product might not be accepted by procurement officials".[82] The relationship clearly posed dilemmas for firms: In putting forward design proposals to the War Office they risked them being stolen for the Arsenals, but the firms did not want to ignore potential sales opportunities. As Richard Davenport-Hines puts it: "Relations between these privileged manufacturers and their client were a strained mixture of wary collaboration and mutual exploitation."[83]

The relationships the Admiralty and War Office's air branches established with the emerging private aircraft producers shows path dependency from their existing relationships with armament firms. The Army controlled production, with the Royal Aircraft Factory at Farnborough playing a dominant role in Army aircraft design and manufacture. Armstrongs and Vickers only produced for the Army using designs from the factory.[84] For the Army, the

---

[78] Between 1859 and 1880 the Admiralty called for ship designs on five occasions. From all these competitions, the Admiralty approved only one design, and then reluctantly, the Lairds-built *Captain* designed by Cowper Coles, which unfortunately sank on her maiden voyage, taking her inventor with it.

[79] McNeill, *Pursuit*, p. 278.

[80] Bastable, *Arms*, p. 28.

[81] Bastable, *Arms*, p. 37.

[82] McNeill, *Pursuit*, p. 278.

[83] Davenport-Hines, "British," p. 147.

[84] Hayward, *British*, p. 10.

private sector's role was just to provide talent they could harvest. By contrast, the Admiralty's more positive view of private industry endured. Keith Hayward records: "The Admiralty ... tended to look both to private industry and to the Royal Aircraft Factory for aircraft for the Royal Naval Air Service."[85]

The challenges that Armstrongs and Vickers experienced with the services were only magnified in their dealings with the Foreign Office and the Diplomatic Service, which were institutionally disinclined to help firms trade internationally thanks to a difficult combination of ideology, snobbery and organizational culture. Their strong commitment to *laissez-faire* and free trade was a significant barrier to their providing any trade assistance. The most diplomats would do was to try and ensure equal treatment for British firms in foreign competitions and to speak out against the imposition of tariffs on imports. Of course, *laissez-faire* was also a convenient excuse for diplomats disinclined to act for firms.

The Foreign Office and Diplomatic Service were bastions of snobbery. Martin Horn highlighted the Foreign Office's "dominant aristocratic ethos," which denigrated finance and trade.[86] The Foreign Office recruited mainly from the upper classes. The 1914 Royal Commission on the Civil Service found that the Foreign Office was the second most expensive in the world – and the most snobbish. As late as 1919 half of the clerks on the Foreign Office list had been to Eton, though Sir John Tilley commented defensively that "the critics have been too ready to assume that the Service suffered in consequence."[87]

Zara Steiner reported: "The Diplomatic Service, an entirely separate service, was even worse, more exclusive than the Foreign Office in social background and education. Diplomats spent almost all of their professional lives abroad, moved only in restricted social circles and took little or no interest in commercial affairs."[88] Until 1919, men without a minimum private income of £400 a year were barred from joining the Service. Candidates were also expected to know at least two languages, which generally meant having spent several years studying abroad, limiting the pool to the rich and well-connected. Diplomats were also expected to personally pay for any losses incurred on Diplomatic Allowances due to currency fluctuations. This was only changed, with some difficulty, during the Great War.[89]

Francis Hirst, editor of the *Economist*, gave a "violently critical account" of the Diplomatic Service in testimony before the 1914 Royal Commission, claiming that the "only commercial agents received at the Embassies abroad were the agents – normally aristocrats, ex-officers, or officials – of the great armament companies" and that other branches of trade were not afforded such Embassy

---

[85] Hayward, *British*, p. 9.
[86] Horn, *Britain*, p. 15.
[87] Tilley and Gaselee, *Foreign Office*, p. 88.
[88] Steiner, "The FCO," p. 20.
[89] Tilley and Gaselee, *Foreign Office*, pp. 68 and 87.

hospitality.[90] There is evidence that Armstrongs and Vickers' representatives were received at some – but far from all – British Embassies abroad.

The Foreign Office and the Diplomatic Service organizational cultures emphasized the practice of "high" politics, shunning commercial diplomacy. Substantive evidence of this had been gathered by Bryce and influenced his 1886 memorandum to Embassies.[91] The Foreign Office delegated trade issues down to the Consular and Commercial Attaché Services and there was no sympathy between them; retired Consul-General Sir Roger Casement bemoaned that "nobody in the Foreign Office has ever been a consul, or knows anything about the duties of a consul."[92] The Consular Service provided retrospective compilations of trade statistics, which, Bryce had noted, were not produced sufficiently regularly and were likely out of date before they were published.[93] The Service also avoided dealing with individuals or firms.[94] Rather, the armament firms relied mainly on their own intelligence gathering and local networks in their search for sales and consistently complained that the governments of other countries – such as Italy, Germany and the United States – gave their armament firms much more help. It was not until the early twentieth century that "the Foreign Office was willing … to put traders in touch with possible markets by means of introductions through consular officials."[95]

Intervention on behalf of individual firms therefore fell to the – extremely reluctant – Diplomatic Service. In 1907 Foreign Secretary Sir Edward Grey asked all British missions overseas to delegate one person to assist British businesses. This had little impact.[96] David McLean has suggested that the Foreign Office operated on two levels during the nineteenth century, the "official" and the "unofficial," arguing that while it was hard to move the Foreign Office officially, diplomats did more unofficially to aid British trade in China.[97] There is some evidence of Armstrongs and Vickers getting some unofficial help, but usually the firms were completely autonomous. Prior to 1914 any government help abroad was unsystematic; it depended on the willingness of individual diplomats to informally act for firms and on the ability of the firms' representatives to find those amenable diplomats. According to Davenport-Hines, "The relations of a company like Vickers with the Foreign Office were always those of a government supplier dealing with a department of its main

---

[90] Platt, *Finance*, p. XVIII; Royal Commission on the Civil Service, *Parliamentary Papers*, Cmnd. 7749.
[91] "Correspondence," Part I.
[92] Royal Commission on the Civil Service.
[93] Platt, *Finance*, p. 140.
[94] Platt, "Role," pp. 494–97.
[95] Platt, "Role," p. 504.
[96] Boyce, "Economics," p. 11.
[97] McLean, "Commerce," pp. 464–76.

customer. There was deference, and the Foreign Office always dictated the pace and direction of events."[98]

After the turn of the century the "the ripples of government circled ever wider."[99] Now in addition to maintaining relations with the military services and the Foreign Office and Diplomatic Service, the armament firms had to build relationships with a wider range of departments, including those in charge of factory inspections and taxation. This expansion of government involvement was somewhat eased for manufacturers by the growing presence of a new generation of civil servants, one drawn from a broader swath of British society and less susceptible to the class prejudices of their predecessors.

Armament Firms' Strategies and Tactics

To deal with these perennial challenges and other issues that arose, Armstrongs and Vickers developed a suite of strategies and tactics.

Strategy One: Building and Maintaining Relationships in Britain

Cultivating relationships with the British state was vital for both firms. A benign – but ideally favorable – relationship with the British Government was necessary not only for facilitating domestic purchases and for official legitimation of their products, but also, once regulation of armaments exports began, for permission to sell abroad. Two types of relationships in Britain were important for armament firms. First, the relationships with elites, such as senior politicians, members of the aristocracy and the royal family; and second, the relationships with civil servants and the military, including the members of the services who oversaw trials and competitions, dealt with procurement and increasingly visited factories. These latter relationships were significant as civil servants held a lot of power in procurement decisions and their behavior toward armament firms early in the era reflected official distain for firms' profits, patent rights and survival. Armstrongs excelled at elite relations. Vickers would have liked to pursue an elite strategy, but impermeable upper-class resistance and institutional snobbery initially made that impossible. Instead, they built relations with key civil servants and military officials. From their unique experiences the two firms developed the following appropriate tactics:

Tactic 1: Relationship Enhancement through Interchanges of High-Level Personnel
Armstrongs focused on developing relations with the elite, enhancing those relationships through a tactic of interchanging high-level personnel, particularly with the Admiralty. Chapters 2 and 3 show Armstrongs' implementation of that strategy and Vickers' attempts to emulate it.

[98] Davenport-Hines, "British," p. 168.
[99] MacDonagh, "Nineteenth-Century," p. 17.

Tactic 2: Relationship Building through Selective Intelligence Sharing
Vickers did not have the elite connections of Armstrongs and found it harder
to create them. Instead, Vickers tried to be useful as a substitute for being
acceptable and sought to earn government respect by providing intelligence.
Chapters 2–5 show this tactic in action.

Strategy Two: Building and Maintaining Relationships with Elites in Other States

Building relationships with elites in other countries was considered vital for
securing foreign sales. Armstrongs and Vickers constantly conducted international diplomacy, aiming to build consistent relationships with foreign
governments.[100] They had to be attuned to shifting politics in buyer countries.
Following local politics was particularly important in the coup-prone countries of South America (see Chapter 6), in China (Chapter 7) and in Turkey
(Chapter 8), all places where politics could change fast. In international markets Armstrongs and Vickers needed extra tools to build these relationships,
especially given international competition. Two tactics were normal practice
and considered vital by Armstrongs and Vickers:

Tactic 1: Using Agents for International Diplomacy
The firms relied on agents to cultivate relationships with well-placed figures
within foreign military and political establishments to gain consideration of their
products. Successful "traveling ambassadors" for the firms were effective com-
municators; they were usually cosmopolitan by nature and credible to foreign
governments thanks to either prior military service, technical expertise or connections. The firms also used lawyers who understood local laws – and the actual
practices – in the countries where they were selling armaments.[101]

Tactic 2: Commissions and Bribery
Providing bribes and commissions in markets where they were a normal part of
business was routine for Armstrongs and Vickers.[102] All types of firms paid bribes
and commissions. These business methods looked unsavory from the vantage
point of well-regulated democratic systems, and certainly damaged the reputation
of Vickers-Armstrongs during the 1930s. However, the British Government never
cut ties with the firms over bribery and in the case of Venezuela in 1950 endorsed
Vickers-Armstrongs' payment of bribes to the military junta (see Chapter 6).

---

[100] Krupp of Germany had a similar strategy for exports, involving agencies, representatives, bribes and presents, "though their success was mostly limited. Like its British rivals,
Krupp could thus neither create demand nor decisively influence governmental decisions
about armament contracts." Epkenhans, "Military-Industrial," p. 17.
[101] Miller, *Britain*, p. 142.
[102] Scott, *Vickers*, p. 81.

Strategy Three: Excluding Competitors

Armstrongs was a first mover in armaments production, but by the mid-1880s Vickers was beginning to compete. Ideally, Armstrongs wanted to keep Vickers out of the domestic market and limit the firm's impact on the international market. However, that proved impossible. By the early twentieth century the two firms had pragmatically set aside many areas of competition and now worked together to try to exclude other firms from the domestic market. This strategy was in Armstrongs and Vickers' interests but was directly opposed to those of the British Government, which wanted to keep the oligopoly loose, as competition kept prices down and encouraged innovation.

Strategy Four: Cooperating and Colluding with Other Firms

While Armstrongs and Vickers initially competed fiercely with each other and with other domestic and foreign firms, at times there was cooperation, and even collusion. While many of these secret alliances were domestic, some were international. Domestically, these alliances were usually to keep prices comparable (for example, for armor plate) and were regarded as a defensive strategy against British Government attempts to play firms off against each other in procurement competitions. In lean times, the arrangements sometimes included creating "rings" or "trusts" for setting high prices and splitting the profits with unsuccessful bidders to keep them in business, meaning that the appearance of competition was a chimera. Sometimes the British Government tolerated these behaviors. Revelations about these collusive strategies badly rebounded on armament firms in the 1930s, but for decades these behaviors served them well.

Strategy Five: Diversifying

When business was lagging, armament firms undertook various strategies of diversification, including:

Diversification into Exports:
A major diversification strategy was into foreign markets. Basil Collier noted that armament firms sought to sell abroad to compensate for a lack of orders at home.[103] This problem certainly brought Armstrongs into the international market (see Chapter 2). Diversification into exports could help smooth out the peaks and troughs of domestic procurement cycles. However, according to Clive Trebilcock, when orders for Vickers were scarce at home they were also scarce abroad.[104] This was certainly true for all firms during the 1908–11 recession and again during the interwar period.

---

[103] Collier, *Arms*, p. 4.
[104] Trebilcock, *Vickers Brothers*, pp. 76–77.

Once export relationships were established, international connections were retained for their intrinsic value and profits; they became essential to the firms' strategies. Between 1868 and 1927, 42 percent of Armstrongs' warship tonnage was exported. Sidney Pollard noted that in the 1880s the profits from ship exports were larger than those from domestic sales, increasing the incentives to export.[105] From Vickers' entry into the warship market in 1896 to the 1927 amalgamation, Barrow was more tied to the Admiralty and exported only 18.4 percent of its warship production.[106] Krupp of Germany found that "In contrast to the domestic market, where aggressiveness and high prices could seriously affect the relations with the army or the navy, the foreign market did not know any such restrictions."[107] The effort put into foreign relations by Armstrongs and Vickers is evidence that the economic rewards of international exports were consistently important to them. But what if protectionism locked them out of a foreign market? Firms then turned to different diversification strategies.

Diversification through International Subsidiaries and Partnerships:
Diversifications into subsidiaries and partnerships were strategic decisions for Armstrongs and Vickers, involving forming long-term relationships within – or even with – a particular state, and rested on their assessments of future procurement decisions and likely profits. These were initially completely independent decisions. Even after 1889, if nothing breached the new Official Secrets Act, the British Government had no say in them. These diversifications carried significant risk, requiring that a firm transfer technology, plant and knowhow to a recipient country.[108] A partnership might involve sharing these with another firm, possibly an erstwhile rival. Forming a local subsidiary or partnership was therefore usually a defensive strategy to maintain market access.

Technological and Sectoral Diversifications:
These could be into adjacent armament fields (near diversifications) – for example, the move from guns into gun mountings. They could be along their supply chain – for example, buying a coal mine or a railway used by a yard (backwards integration) – or into producing the warships, tanks or aircraft to carry the guns they manufactured (forwards integration). Diversification could also be into completely new technologies or sectors (sectoral diversifications) – for example, Armstrongs and Vickers' moves into railway equipment and motor car production, and their interwar forays into various civilian markets (far diversifications).

[105] Pollard, "*Laissez-Faire*," p. 107. Citing evidence to the 1887 Government Committee on Contracts.
[106] Brook, *Warships*, p. 19, Table 1/5.
[107] Epkenhans, "Military-Industrial," p. 20.
[108] Krupp refused to establish subsidiaries, refusing to enable "other countries to manufacture good artillery material themselves." Epkenhans, "Military-Industrial," p. 19. Citing Memo, "Erfahrungen im Kriegsmaterial-Geschäft mit dem Auslande," p. 73.

Strategy Six: Financing

In terms of finance for private firms to develop and produce armaments, the British Government provided no upfront capital (the development of the Armstrong Gun being a notable exception). Firms were expected to fund research and development themselves. Financing for innovations in armaments therefore came from the fruits of private firms' own labor, either from the profits made on contracts or from raising private capital. Those latter investments initially came from the families and friends of entrepreneurs. Later, wealthy backers, including prominent politicians, military leaders and industrialists, bought preferential shares in armament firms. If the armaments they developed were successful, a firm might then receive a British Government contract.

A notable feature in international markets was that the states that wanted armaments were often short of money. This made working in the international market very different – and much riskier – than making domestic sales. Therefore, financing strategies were often a make-or-break element for securing and completing an export. This was Vickers' forte and providing recipients access to finance was a very successful strategy for the firm.

Strategy Seven: Innovating

Existential to all private armament firms' survival was the need to create products that attracted new orders. While both Armstrongs and Vickers began as innovative and nimble firms, after 1900 Armstrongs gradually lost its innovative edge and became weighed down by internal disputes. By contrast, various technologically risky moves by Vickers paid off handsomely in armament orders. This developed into a unique Vickers organizational culture; they consistently innovated in times of poor orders – at considerable risk – developing new products and building new machinery so that they were ready to secure new business when the opportunity came.

Summary

For a century, Armstrongs and Vickers and the amalgamated Vickers-Armstrongs consistently pursued all these strategies: building and maintaining relationships with the British elite and civil servants; developing international relationships; competing or collaborating with other firms; diversifying when necessary; financing sales; and innovating.

Importantly, though, the ways in which the two firms were perceived by the state had an impact on the emphasis each firm placed on individual strategies and tactics. Armstrongs put more emphasis on elite relationships, naval sales abroad and exchanges of personnel with the Admiralty, whereas Vickers put more emphasis on investing in research and development, generating financing and providing intelligence to the government. Ultimately it was Vickers that survived and Armstrongs that went under in the brutal downturn of the interwar period, the better businessmen winning out over a firm with more elite connections. The next four chapters chart the fortunes of our two firms in dealing with their most important customer, the British Government.

2

Selling Armaments in Britain 1860–1900

Armstrongs Rises and Vickers Evolves

This chapter charts the early years of Armstrongs and Vickers, when they were developing what became their major domestic strategies and their distinct organizational cultures were becoming clearer. For much of this period Armstrongs was the premier armament firm in Britain, but by the late 1890s Vickers had become a very strong competitor.

These four decades saw major technological progress in armaments and ratcheting competition between guns and armor. Innovations in one produced counter-innovations in the other, driving progress. Sir William Armstrong believed that the gun would triumph, but the firm could not rest on its laurels and constantly innovated. New technologies were also appearing – for example, the torpedo – and warship builders had to innovate in response. The fast pace of technological change created significant risks for suppliers. If firms built factories and plant to manufacture a new armament, they faced uncertainty whether the "new facility would continue to be used or would instead have to be discarded after the completion of a single contract because some new device or design had come along in the meanwhile and rendered it obsolete."[1] This was a risk that the British Government was happy for private armament firms to shoulder.

The 1860s

At the start of the decade Sir William was still working in London. He and Lady Armstrong remained prominent members of Newcastle society, regularly entertaining at their Jesmond Dene home, described as "the abode of art, literature and luxury."[2] Sir William encountered many members of the British elite, though he wrote to his wife in March 1861: "I must say that my taste for court does not increase."[3] Nevertheless, this type of elite interaction would later prove important for the company. Sir William was also ruffling feathers at Woolwich

---

[1] McNeill, *Pursuit*, p. 289.
[2] Cochrane, *Romance*, p. 167. In the early 1860s they added a banqueting hall to entertain Elswick workers and their families. Heald, *William Armstrong*, p. 141.
[3] Heald, *William Armstrong*, pp. 125 and 111.

Arsenal, where he was modernizing the works to produce the Armstrong Gun. Stuart Rendel recounted: "The civilian management he had substituted for military management at Woolwich gave serious umbrage to the Artillery Corps."[4] This made Armstrong's time working for the government fraught.

In parallel with his modernizing work, Sir William was handed a political hot potato. The War Office charged him with creating large guns for a series of coastal forts deemed necessary to protect Britain from bombardment by the new French ironclad *La Glorie*. The forts were already under construction at a cost of £12 million, despite continued debate over their military value. Sir William was under immense pressure. As Lord Palmerston reported to Queen Victoria, if Armstrong could make a gun capable of sinking *La Glorie* at 1,200 yards despite the ironclad's 4.5 inches of armor "then there can be no doubt as to the usefulness of the forts."[5] Otherwise, the government had wasted a colossal amount of money on them. Armstrong's response was a 300-pound gun, trialed in April 1862.[6] The guns penetrated the target at the right distance, proving three things: first, the capability of the guns to meet the challenge of French ironclads; second, Armstrong's engineering prowess (though this exacerbated his competition with Joseph Whitworth, who proclaimed his gun was more successful); and third, the value of the government forts. This should have won Sir William favor at the War Office, but it did not. "The whole situation was thoroughly distasteful to Armstrong, but he carried out his duties for three years, until Woolwich was fully equipped with plant and skilled men for the manufacture of guns."[7]

Consequently, in October 1862 the government "announced the cessation of its orders to the Elswick Ordnance Company."[8] As they were contractually bound to serve only the British Government, this effectively meant the end of the firm. Sir William immediately resigned his government position and returned to Newcastle, where a new company was formed, combining the engineering and ordnance works into Sir W. G. Armstrong, colloquially known as "Armstrongs." While contractually allowed to buy the portion of the plant paid for by the government, the firm was not permitted to. The firm therefore offered to sell the factory's machinery to the state for the "most reasonable figure" of £137,000, "compared with the actual capital expenditures on it of £168,000," but this was flatly refused. Consequently, "the question of compensation was referred to arbitrators, who had no difficulty in reaching agreement, but the Government repudiated their award. After taking two legal opinions, the Government finally agreed to pay the amount of the award, £85,000."[9]

4 Rendel, *Personal Papers*, p. 273.
5 Bastable, "Breechloaders," p. 231.
6 Bastable, "Breechloaders," pp. 235–44.
7 Fairbairn, *Elswick*, VA, Doc. 593, p. 63.
8 Fairbairn, *Elswick*, p. 64.
9 Fairbairn, *Elswick*, pp. 64–65; Bastable, *Arms*, p. 100.

The new firm therefore began nearly from scratch. Nevertheless, at the 1862 London International Exhibition, Armstrongs were displaying their "Breech-loading and muzzle-loading ordnance, with projectiles."[10]

Over the previous four years, the Elswick Ordnance Company had handsomely profited from producing field guns for the government: "In 1858–9, the company sold guns worth under £8000 to the government; in 1859–60 it sold over £30000 of guns; in 1860–61 and 1861–2, revenues were £400000."[11] Now there was a precipitous drop. Between 1863 and 1878, combined War Office gun orders reached only £24,804.[12] This was a wild change of fortune. Elswick's official historian, A. R. Fairbairn, recorded: "It was ... the first experience of a peculiar difficulty which was to recur throughout the Works history; to be regarded as a Government arsenal as long as the need remained, but to be thrown on their own resources as soon as the emergency has passed."[13]

Among the engineering talents recruited to Armstrongs by Sir William were George Rendel, Hamilton Rendel and Andrew Noble. George Rendel had worked for Elswick from the beginning as an innovator in hydraulics. He was an exceptional engineer and at Armstrongs moved into designing innovative ships, as well as heading the ordnance department. Hamilton Rendel (brother of George and Stuart) joined Armstrongs after graduating from Cambridge. He was described by Stuart as the "soundest and most scientific engineer connected with the firm," and designed and installed the original hydraulic mechanism for Tower Bridge in London.[14] He worked in the Armstrongs engineering department, eventually heading it. Captain Andrew Noble was a ballistics expert and Secretary to the 1858 Ordnance Committee on Rifled Cannon, where he met Sir William.[15] Noble was promoted to Assistant Inspector of Artillery in 1859, but against the advice of Army friends, resigned his position and joined Elswick in 1860, though he remained on the government's Committee on Explosives until its dissolution in 1880, and continued his experimental work.[16] As he gained seniority at Armstrongs he increasingly became part of the elite; for example, he was elected to the Athenaeum in 1873.[17] Noble worked at a frenetic pace, continuing his experimental work on propellants while also interacting with

---

10 *International Exhibition 1862: Official Catalogue*, p. 40.
11 Bastable, *Arms*, p. 99.
12 Bastable, *Arms*, p. 106, ff. 125.
13 Fairbairn, *Elswick*, p. 65.
14 Rendel, *Personal Papers*, p. 282; Scott, *Vickers*, p. 31.
15 Armstrong to Noble, February 22, 1860. TWA, DF/NOB/1/1; Series TWA, DF/NOB/1/1-71; "A Great Victorian: Sir Andrew Noble," p. 22. TWA, D/VA/74/3/3; Bastable, "Breechloaders," p. 235.
16 "Obituary: Sir Andrew Noble"; "Andrew Noble," p. 266. In 1873 John Fisher cited Noble's experimental work on gunpowder. Fisher to Captain Henry Boys, 31 October 1873. In Marder, *Fear God*, Vol. 1, pp. 86–87.
17 Wheeler, *Athenaeum*, p. 27.

British and foreign dignitaries.[18] Another crucial addition to the new firm was the lawyer Stuart Rendel, who had worked in London on behalf of the Elswick Ordnance Company. Subsequently, he became Managing Director of Armstrongs London office. "Apart from Lord Armstrong himself, Rendel was the most important link to the British social and political elite."[19] Stuart Rendel, like his father, was a member of the Athenaeum.

Sir William continued to innovate, and the Armstrong Gun was followed by ever larger rifled, muzzle-loaded guns and increasingly large and heavy gun mountings. Noble's new and improved propellants and developments in steel enabled the firm to develop large breech-loading guns. The firm also diversified into artillery to be carried on ships and into heavy guns for coastal defense.

Sir William was still having to defend his invention against attacks from the indefatigable Whitworth. The House of Commons was an arena for the dispute.[20] Seven official committees had concluded in Armstrongs' favor, but Whitworth's supporters in the House (and in the letters' column of the *Times*) still agitated.[21] Such was the hue and cry that a new Committee of Inquiry was established to carry out extensive tests on the two guns. It was staffed by service personnel, plus a civilian representative of each firm. An important member of the committee was General Lintorn Simmonds, "a scientific engineer officer, a convinced advocate of Mr. Whitworth, and a decided opponent of Lord Armstrong."[22] Whitworth's first representative, marine engineer Mr. Penn, resigned because Whitworth expected him to be an advocate for – not judge of – the Whitworth Gun. His replacement was Mr. MacDonald, a well-known manager of the *Times*. Professor Pole, Armstrongs' first representative, resigned "on finding that his health and nerves were unequal to the strain of the experimental ground."[23] His replacement, Stuart Rendel, also found the trials extremely politicized and stressful – and loud (more than 50,000 rounds were fired). The trials were extensively covered in the national and international press. After a month of competition, the *Times* noted that it was hard to declare "the ultimate success of either."[24]

Armstrongs faced an immediate crisis: Without British Government orders, how could it survive? Sir William later explained, "the firm had no alternative but to commence a new career, based on foreign support, and it was by that

---

[18] His diary for March 9, 1898, illustrated his strong work ethic. Heald, *William Armstrong*, p. 329. Citing: Noble, *A Long Life*.

[19] Bastable, *Arms*, p. 231.

[20] Parliamentary question from the Earl of Hardwick, February 9, 1864, *Hansard*, Vol. CLXXIII. cc., 311–14 and 318–20; Duke of Somerset's responses, cc., 314–18.

[21] For example, Halsted's 1864 letter: *The Armstrong Gun: A Rejoinder to the Letter of Sir William Armstrong*. Armstrong to Noble, February 16, 1865, TWA, DF/NOB/1/4; Armstrong to Noble, April 4, 1865, TWA, DF/NOB/1/16; Rendel, *Personal Papers*, p. 274.

[22] Rendel, *Personal Papers*, p. 275.

[23] Rendel, *Personal Papers*, p. 18.

[24] "Armstrong & Whitworth Trials," p. 3.

support – and not by government patronage –" that Armstrongs flourished.[25] This pivot came despite the strong reservations of Sir William. He noted that although he had foregone the £20,000 reward for creating his gun, he had received "a knighthood, C.B., and a well-paid office under the War Office; and that … he could not possibly so soon as he had left office, start on the supply of his guns to foreign powers."[26] Stuart Rendel was the instigator of the move into exports, and knew the best arguments to sway Sir William. Rendel told Armstrong that: "[H]is first patriotic duty was to maintain the prestige of the system he had induced the Government to adopt … [and] that the manufacture of arms for foreign powers was far from an unpatriotic act" because British capacity was increased by sales, "whereas foreign countries were disadvantaged to the extent to which they were dependent on us for their munitions of war."[27] According to Rendel, despite these arguments,

> Lord Armstrong still looked upon the matter with much indifference. He made, however, this concession to me: "If these are your opinions you are perfectly at liberty to try to give them effect and if you can obtain any orders for Elswick by all means do so and to make it worth your wile [sic] we will give you five percent commission upon the orders you bring us."[28]

Work on the Gun Committee had given Stuart Rendel in-depth knowledge of Armstrong Guns, making him an ideal salesman.

In 1863 the firm received its first order, "for guns for some English merchant ships seeking protection from pirates."[29] Their first foreign order came from the Union States fighting the American Civil War, secured through Sir William's personal contacts.[30] This Union contract was closely followed by orders from their opponents, the Southern States.[31] These were secured by Stuart Rendel.[32] In each case, the buyers initiated the sales, reflecting the firm's technological credibility. For Marshall Bastable, "The name Armstrong was the company's most effective marketing weapon. Other guns were available, but the publicity gained by the Armstrong gun in England between 1854 and 1863 was beyond purchase …. All in all, the marketeering entrepreneurship of Armstrong was built into his technology."[33]

[25] Scott, *Vickers*, p. 31.
[26] Rendel, *Personal Papers*, p. 277; "Resume of Lord Armstrong's contributions to arms manufacture for the government," no date, TWA, DF/A/3/23.
[27] Rendel, *Personal Papers*, p. 277.
[28] Rendel, *Personal Papers*, p. 277.
[29] McKenzie, *W.G. Armstrong*, p. 75.
[30] Rendel, *Personal Papers*, p. 277.
[31] Stuart Rendel to George Rendel, 1 February 1864, TWA DF/NOB/5/1-54; D/NOB/5/36/1-2 shows that business was done and paid for in December 1866; Rendel, *Personal Papers*, pp. 277–78.
[32] Rendel, *Personal Papers*, pp. 277–78.
[33] Bastable, *Arms*, p. 110.

Stuart Rendel saw three years of gun trials to a successful conclusion. In 1864 the Ordnance Select Committee again found in favor of the Armstrong Gun.[34] Writing the final report took months of negotiation between Simmonds and Rendel, who admitted later that "how we came to produce a report fairly capable of construction as generally favourable to Armstrong I can scarcely understand. But so it was."[35] Also in 1864, the *Times* reported on the success of Armstrongs' new 600-pound steel shell against John Browns' 11-inch armor plate.[36]

While in private business in Newcastle, Sir William maintained good relations in London. Decades later he recalled his first meeting with William Gladstone, then Chancellor of the Exchequer. He was introduced by the former Secretary of War, Sidney Herbert, who declared Armstrong "the worst enemy a Chancellor of the Exchequer could have" because of the costly guns he was producing.[37] They became close friends, which is ironic as in government Gladstone consistently sought to hold back defense spending to avoid public debt.[38]

According to Richard Davenport-Hines, early in the era interactions between armament firms and the state were mediated through civilian agents; with a shift to direct relations in the 1880s.[39] However, from the first Armstrongs used core personnel to interact with the government, including during the fifteen-year famine in government orders. Internationally, Armstrongs' directors generally handled European sales, meeting diplomats passing through London and traveling to the continent, but further afield the firm employed agents to secure sales. Risk was a constant part of exporting armaments. Armstrongs allowed local agents to finance transactions themselves, shifting the responsibility onto the agents. Armstrongs' first Japanese agents, Thomas Glover & Company, generated orders in the 1860s by lending the Satsuma feudal domain the money for the guns. John Pitman, an Armstrongs agent in China, financed a deal with a Canton (administrative division) personally with the help of Butterfield and Swire, a large trading house in Asia. Glover subsequently went bankrupt, proving both the inherent risks in the armaments trade and Sir William's sagacity.[40]

Stuart Rendel developed a network to gather intelligence. Many large firms had intelligence departments to compensate for the shortcomings of the British Consular Service.[41] Armstrongs used their international agents to gather information on local conditions, including from local newspapers.[42]

---

[34] Rendel to Noble, April 14, 1864, TWA, DF/NOB/5/8.
[35] Rendel, *Personal Papers*, p. 275.
[36] Bastable, *Arms*, p. 113.
[37] Dolman, "Notable Men," p. 574.
[38] French, *British*, pp. 11–12.
[39] Davenport-Hines, "British Marketing," p. 147.
[40] Bastable, *Arms*, p. 118.
[41] Platt, "Consular," p. 499.
[42] For example, Intelligence Department to Stuart Rendel, 1869. Enclosing a clipping from *The Evening Journal*, May 22, 1869. TWA, 31/1938.

More spectacularly, Rendel formed a relationship with C. M. Boys of the Intelligence Department of the Electric and International Telegraph Company. Boys would provide Rendel with intelligence on what the telegrams handled by the company were reporting on key issues, while Rendel provided him with professional introductions.[43]

Armstrongs' directors sought entrées to the key decision makers in the countries they were targeting and entertained these officials lavishly in their home capitals and in Britain. This meant a stream of visitors to Stuart Rendel's home in London, to the Elswick works, and to Sir William's and Andrew Noble's Jesmond Deane homes. Rendel's domestic and international networks soon brought in further orders, the approach evolving to become the firm's foremost strategy: creating relationships with international elites. He secured orders from Italy for guns via contacts with Captain Augustus Albini, the Italian naval attaché in London (Albini became an Armstrongs agent as well as an Italian rear-admiral and count); guns for Egypt via contacts provided by a college friend, George Goschen MP, with Colonel Efflatoun Pasha, himself a personal friend of the Khedive (later Efflatoun became a friend of Sir William and Noble and an agent for Armstrongs); guns for new Turkish ironclads being built in Britain; and guns and warships for Chile via introductions by Rendel's London neighbor, George Gibbs of Anthony Gibbs and Sons of Valparaiso.[44] Rendel also built lasting relationships with key foreign officials, such as Sir Robert Hart of the Imperial Chinese Customs Service (see Chapter 7). Some of Stuart Rendel's efforts failed, though. He could not overcome the dominance of Krupp in Russia, despite assistance from his father-in-law, who had business there. He unsuccessfully sought orders in Austria and in Spain, and he sought further orders in Turkey but without results. In Prussia, a contract he had won to arm the ironclad *Koenig Wilhelm* "fell through under Krupp influence."[45] For twelve years, Stuart Rendel facilitated exports for Armstrongs.

With foreign orders now ensuring the firm's survival, Armstrongs began to acquire promising patents. In November 1866 they struck an exclusive agreement with a retired British Army officer, Major William Palliser, for patents "relating to compound cast and wrought iron guns and also under those relating to the manufacture of chilled shot and shell."[46] Palliser had invented a system of converting outdated smooth-bore, cast iron, muzzle-loading guns into rifled muzzleloaders. His simple process could save the War Office money and spare them from buying new guns, including the new breechloaders which Armstrongs wanted to sell them.

[43] Rendel–Boys correspondence, TWA, 31/1749–75.
[44] Rendel, *Personal Papers*, pp. 278–80; Collier, *Arms*, pp. 50–51; Bastable, *Arms*, p. 113.
[45] Rendel, *Personal Papers*, p. 280; 278–80.
[46] "Memorandum of Agreement between Major Palliser and Sir W. G. Armstrong," November 22, 1866. TWA, 31/868.

Palliser was having an experience familiar to Sir William, needing to defend the utility of his inventions, which were being debated in the House of Commons and disparaged in the *Times*.[47] Concurrently, the Ordnance Select Committee repeatedly asked to see Palliser's drawings of the converted guns; he demurred, but noted it was "rather a ticklish thing to refuse them."[48] He explained to Stuart Rendel:

> You are quite right in supposing that I could have no distrust of the O.S.C. [Ordnance Select Committee] but I know the drawings will be forwarded to the Royal Gun Factories where they will be scrutinized by Mr. Fraser. Every possible fault will be found with them and at the same time every thing useful to him will be pirated without the least acknowledgement, and my plans will form a basis for him to make slight modification on and bring out as the "Fraser" system of conversion.[49]

While this may seem paranoid, the Royal Arsenal often behaved like this toward firms and inventors. A War Office Director of Contracts admitted in 1887: "Everybody knows that independent inventors have a dread of approaching our departments because they think ... that their inventions are in danger of being copied without recognition."[50] The War Office bought the rights to use Palliser's conversion techniques.[51] Palliser's chilled shot was also approved by the British Government on October 21, 1867.[52] This also saved the state money as it enabled existing projectiles to penetrate armor more efficiently.

Armstrongs first sectoral diversification was into naval production. In 1867 the firm struck a deal with Dr. Charles Mitchell, who had a naval yard at Low Walker, to build the gunboats they were designing as platforms for Armstrong Guns. Armstrongs also moved into engine design and production. Subsequently, the firm benefited from Mitchell's linguistic talents and foreign connections; since 1862, Mitchells had been building ships for the Russian navy based at St. Petersburg.[53] In 1868 the George Rendel-designed HMS *Staunch* gunboat was launched at Low Walker. It was described as "a Floating Gun Carriage of fair speed and handiness."[54] The firm sold only a few of these innovative gunboats to the Admiralty, but this legitimation led to good export sales, including to Australia and China, with Armstrongs reaping the rewards of this bold act of diversification.

By the late 1860s Armstrongs customers included Turkey, Austria, Spain, Egypt, Denmark, Holland, Chile and Peru, as well as, notably, Italy in 1866

---

[47] Palliser to S. Rendel, July 30, 1867. TWA, 31/888.
[48] Palliser to S. Rendel, September 26, 1867. TWA, 31/889.
[49] Palliser to S. Rendel, September 27, 1867. TWA, 31/890.
[50] Morley Committee, 1887, Q. 3914.
[51] "History of the Palliser System of Converting Cast-Iron Smooth-Bored Guns into Rifled Muzzle-Loading Guns," TNA, WO 33/21A/1870/425A.
[52] Palliser received a Companion of the Order of Bath in 1868 and was knighted in 1872. He became an MP in 1880.
[53] Heald, *William Armstrong*, p. 179.
[54] Scott, *Vickers*, p. 35.

when war with Austria looked likely.[55] These overseas orders brought the firm more independence, and potentially leverage over the British Government, but also allowed the state to feel no responsibility for the firm, with Armstrongs' success apparently vindicating government *laissez-faire* policies. Despite official indifference to the firm, Sir William's ties with the British elite were maintained and increased, reinforced by his work as an inventor and his many acts of philanthropy.

Turning to Vickers, in the 1860s Naylor, Vickers & Company was a growing Sheffield steel firm headed by Edward Vickers and his brother-in-law George Portus Naylor. Through the energetic Ernst Benzon's London agency, Naylor Benzon & Company, the firm was selling to America, "where they carried on very prosperously as American merchants among other things, shipping large quantities of rails to America to meet the demands of new railway construction there."[56] As the sole American agent for Vickers, Benzon's firm earned 5 percent on all sales.[57] At Naylor Vickers, "The growth of the business ... and the change toward a heavier type of product led to the decision to build new works on a larger scale, and ... works were laid out and begun, which formed the nucleus of the ... River Don Works."[58] The firm decided to make only crucible steel. This was a gamble as cheaper alternatives were appearing.[59] The resulting works at Brightside was highly praised by an American iron and steel expert as "the best specimen of mechanical engineering at present in existence."[60] This shows that Vickers already had an organizational culture marked by what J. D. Scott terms "technical boldness."[61] While this courageous approach was not the standard behavior of British armament firms, it was true to the culture of Sheffield steel firms.[62]

Nevertheless, Naylor Vickers' bold expansion at the River Don Works nearly left them bankrupt: The firm was heavily in debt by 1866; it had a mortgage of £60,000 and had spent £204,000 on the River Don Works.[63] While this might have been ridden out, "Unfortunately for the partners this construction coincided with the financial crisis that led to the Overend & Gurney [bank] failure of May 1866, and their supplies of money being cut off they turned to Naylor Benzon & Company for assistance."[64] Effectively, Benzon saved the firm, but demanded that Vickers become a limited liability company. As Thomas Vickers subsequently acknowledged to a Royal Commission in 1886: "It has been an

---

[55] Scott, *Vickers*, p. 33.
[56] Vickers, *Vickers A History*, 5th Draft, VA, Doc 762, p. 1.
[57] Scott, *Vickers*, p. 12.
[58] Vickers, *Vickers A History*, p. 1.
[59] Scott, *Vickers*, p. 17.
[60] Warren, *Armstrongs*, p. 47; Scott, *Vickers*, p. 17. Citing: Carr and Taplin, *British Steel Industry*.
[61] Scott, *Vickers*, pp. 16–17.
[62] Tweedale, *Steel City*, especially pp. 60–98.
[63] Scott, *Vickers*, p. 16.
[64] Vickers, *Vickers A History*, pp. 1–2.

advantage to my company to be a limited liability company because I have had as much power as a director in this company I had previously had as a partner, and the resources of the company were greater than those of the partnership."[65]

Vickers, Sons & Company was established on April 17, 1867, taking over the debts and the assets of the old firm.[66] The firm's capital of £155,000 was divided equally between Benzon, on the one hand, and Edward Vickers, his four sons and employee William Whitehead, on the other. Benzon was chairman, and his superior (and conservative) financial approach guided the firm out of debt. Whereas in 1867 profits were only £1,270, by 1868 they were £39,120, despite the works being only half-full at the beginning of the year.[67] Vickers continued to innovate and in 1868 undertook a sectoral diversification into manufacturing marine shafting, their first contact with shipbuilding. It now also produced steel and steel forgings for guns. One of Vickers' customers was Armstrongs.

Reflecting the firm's improving fortunes, the Vickers family were living increasingly well. Whereas in the 1840s Edward's family had been living just a mile from Sheffield's city center at Weston Bank, by 1862 they had purchased Taplow House.[68] In 1863 Edward purchased Tapton Grove, with eight acres of land and a small lake, demolishing the Georgian house and building a modern house, Tapton Hall.[69] Edward, now fifty, retired from the business and handed the reins to Thomas and Albert.[70] In 1869 with Vickers, Sons & Co. flourishing, Thomas, now thirty-six, bought a substantial family house at Bolsover Hill, close to the new works in the Lower Don Valley.[71] His family lived there, tended by seven servants.[72] These Sheffield homes were respectable residences, but could not compete with Sir William's Jesmond Deane home and park. Nor were they intended to. According to Nyra Wilson, "Vickers of Tapton Hall built for their own satisfaction: in true Sheffield style they acted to please themselves and were largely indifferent to the opinion of others."[73] This independence likely protected them from the snobbery they encountered as they increasingly interacted with national elites and tastemakers.

1870s

During this decade improvements in propellants (some due to Noble and Abel's experimental work on slow-burning powder) and in steel enabled Armstrongs

---

[65] Vickers T. Minutes, p. 109. Question 3438.
[66] Naylor had died without heirs.
[67] Scott, *Vickers*, pp. 16–17.
[68] Wilson, *Middle-Class*, p. 34.
[69] Wilson, *Middle-Class*, pp. 59, 65.
[70] Wilson, *Middle-Class*, p. 65.
[71] Wilson, *Middle-Class*, p. 34.
[72] 1871 Census. Cited in "Thomas Edward Vickers"; "Bolsover Hill."
[73] Wilson, *Middle-Class*, p. 62.

to make increasingly powerful rifled, breech-loading guns for the international market. However, hopes of new British Government orders were dashed with the Royal Artillery's 1870 decision, taken for a mix of economic and technical reasons, to renounce breechloaders and rely on muzzle-loading artillery. Armstrongs was also building cruisers, ever-heavier guns and, from around 1877 Quick Fire guns for the international market. In 1870 Armstrongs made a near-diversification, expanding its armaments catalogue by buying a license to manufacture an early semi-automatic gun, the Gatling.

In 1870 Joseph Whitworth was still seeking to overturn the primacy of Armstrong Guns. He was demanding a costly new competitive trial of his 35-ton gun, made using a new material, compressed steel, against the Armstrong Gun – now called the "Woolwich Service Gun." In the House of Commons there were complaints about trial costs. In the words of the First Lord of the Admiralty:

> Sir Joseph Whitworth had valued his gun at £6,000, and the Woolwich gun, that was to compete with it, would cost at least £3,000 or £4,000, while the manufacture of the projectiles to be used by them would also involve a very considerable expenditure; and the question, so far from being set at rest, would be set rolling, and would entail a cost of many thousands of pounds.[74]

Some in the Navy were against reopening the Armstrong–Whitworth gun debate because of cost and because "they were perfectly happy with the 'Naval Service Gun.'"[75] On the other side, the Secretary of State for War and the Director of Naval Ordnance had been sufficiently impressed on a visit to Whitworth's Manchester works to recommend a new trial.[76] The controversy continued, leading Stuart Rendel in 1875 to pen *The Question of the Guns*, defending the Armstrongs system.[77]

Scott recounts an incident in 1870 illustrating the chilly professional relationship between Armstrongs and the British Government. Sir William asked to meet with Hugh Childers, the First Lord of the Admiralty, "'under the belief that Mr Childers will be desirous of making himself acquainted with issues upon artillery questions.'" This overture was "courteously snubbed. Mr Childers informed him that he would be happy to see him, 'but the pressure of public business at the present time must prevent me from giving attention to any question, except such as it may be necessary to discuss in reference to the

---

[74] Cited in Statement of Sir John Hay. House of Commons Debate, March 3, 1870. *Hansard*, Third Series, Vol. 199, cc. 1150–54.

[75] Statement of Mr. Hanbury-Tracy, citing Admiral Cowper Key. House of Commons Debate, March 3, 1870, *Hansard*, Third Series, Vol. 199, cc. 1154–55.

[76] Statement of Mr. Childers. House of Commons Debate, March 3, 1870. *Hansard*, Third Series, Vol. 199, cc. 1158.

[77] Warren, *Armstrongs*, p. 257.

current business of this department.'" Sir William saved face by claiming not to have received this reply, but he never again sought to meet Childers.[78]

On October 28, 1870, George Rendel wrote to his brother Stuart: "I enclose a copy of a letter received from Mr. Albert Vickers, a younger member of Vickers Sons and Company Limited, a large Sheffield firm that supplies us with a good deal of steel for gun barrels. I think it would be well for you to call and see Mr. Vickers if convenient."[79] There were also the seeds of a potential collaboration, with Noble writing to Stuart Rendel: "George asked me to let you know that he has no objection to tell Vickers that should we get the order referred to, we should let them have the barrels."[80] Nothing seems to have come of this potential overseas order, though.

Stuart Rendel took "part in discussions which led to the adoption of designs of the first four great Italian ironclads of the *Duilio* class, and received an Italian decoration for that service."[81] The two lead ships, *Duilio* and *Dandolo*, were to carry Armstrongs guns. The initial intent in 1873 was for them to be armed with 38-ton rifled muzzleloaders, but by the time they were completed in 1880 they carried a main battery of four Armstrongs 17.7-inch guns, weighing 100 tons, then the largest guns afloat.[82] These ironclads got the attention of the Royal Navy as the ships were both faster and carried larger guns than its own ironclads. "So impressed were the British that they produced a near-copy in the *Inflexible*."[83]

Armstrongs realized that enabling ships to travel further up the Tyne River would facilitate new business. Working with the River Tyne Commissioners, they dismantled the old low stone bridge, and then engineered and paid for an innovative swing bridge, which opened to road traffic in June 1876. The *Europa*, collecting a 100-ton Elswick gun for Italy, was the first ship to pass through, on July 17, 1876.[84] Additionally, in 1878 Armstrongs built a cartridge factory at Erith, outside London. This diversification proved very successful. Less so was the firm's Gatling gun. The machine gun underwent official trials at Shoeburyness against other guns, and lost out to the Gardiner model, which had a simpler mechanism.[85] The Gardiner itself was eclipsed during the 1880s by the revolutionary Maxim gun, in which the Vickers family had a hand.

For Armstrongs the famine in War Office artillery contracts lasted for sixteen years. The Russian war scare of 1878 saw the British Government scramble

[78] Scott, *Vickers*, p. 51. No citations provided.
[79] Warren, *Armstrongs*, p. 47. Citing: George Rendel to Stuart Rendel, October 28, 1870. TWA.
[80] Warren, *Armstrongs*, p. 48. Citing: Andrew Noble to Stuart Rendel, July 27, 1871. TWA.
[81] Rendel, *Personal Papers*, p. 280.
[82] Gardiner, *Conway's*, p. 340.
[83] Beeler, *British*, p. 197.
[84] "Elswick Works, Part. 1."
[85] Scott, *Vickers*, p. 36.

to purchase four 110-ton guns that Armstrongs was building for Italy.[86] This presaged a change of course, as the British Government realized the extent to which Woolwich Arsenal had fallen behind the private firms.

Vickers was on the periphery of the armament sector for much of this decade. It continued to provide Armstrongs and other armorers with gun steel. The firm was expanding steel production through developing and adapting new technologies – thanks to Thomas Vickers' technical skills – and diversifying into new areas of business. They added new buildings to their works in 1872 and installed Siemens regenerative gas furnaces, innovating in how the furnaces were fed steel and doubling the size of the pots in the melting holes, thus saving a lot of money.[87] At the beginning of the 1870s Vickers mainly manufactured railway tires, axels, castings, steel bars and "steel castings made to pattern," being one of only two firms in the world able to do the latter.[88] With its increased capacity Vickers made ever bigger castings. In 1872 the firm cast its first marine screw propeller. The firm was now prosperous. Pre-1867 debts were wiped out and during the 1870s bonus shares were regularly issued to shareholders. Vickers expanded again in 1874 with the acquisition of thirteen acres of land, where they built a rolling mill to capitalize on their growing melting capacity. The firm continued to expand toward what Thomas Vickers termed "the very heavy trade," which would help as American import taxes on railway steel ensured that market dwindled.[89]

1880s

Armstrongs had moved into designing and producing cruisers, including George Rendel's "protected" cruisers, and by the mid-1880s had progressed to building battleships. The firm also made rifled breechloaders with a "robust interrupted screw-breech mechanism."[90] Around 1885 Armstrongs developed Quick Fire guns for pre-dreadnought battleships (including the 120mm Quick Fire gun for navies working in the metric system). The guns rate of fire was five to six rounds per minute. HMS *Sharpshooter* was the first British ship to carry the equivalent 4.7-inch guns.[91] Quick Fire naval guns became an important export for Armstrongs.

Stuart Rendel became the Member of Parliament for Montgomeryshire in 1880, though as a major shareholder he remained an active member of the Armstrongs Board. Armstrongs expanded in November 1882, amalgamating with Mitchells of Low Walker, becoming Sir W. G. Armstrong Mitchell & Co. Ltd.[92] This gave the firm a thriving civilian business. While as a limited liability company,

[86] "Andrew Noble," p. 266.
[87] Scott, *Vickers*, p. 19.
[88] Scott, *Vickers*, p. 17. Citing: *Engineering*, 1867.
[89] Scott, *Vickers*, p. 18.
[90] "Elswick Works, Part 1."
[91] Gardiner and Lambert, *Steam*, p. 161.
[92] McKenzie, *W.G. Armstrong*, pp. 98–99.

the firm had more freedom of action and was exposed to less risk, Stuart Rendel thought the effect was "to defeat altogether the family character of the old firm" and to create a "mischievous separation between capital and management."[93]

The new Armstrongs Board included William Siemens and Josiah Vavasseur, each owning multiple useful patents.[94] Siemens was a friend of Sir William. A prolific inventor, his developments included the regenerative furnace used by Vickers, and he had the skills to assist with Armstrongs' planned backward integration into steel. Unfortunately, he died ten months after joining the Board.[95] Vavasseur ran J. Vavasseur & Co., known as the London Ordnance Works. He was an inventor who worked on the construction of build-up steel guns and gun mountings. In 1877 Vavasseur had developed a naval hydraulic gun mounting that was accepted by the Royal Navy due to "the ease and certainty with which it worked"; it was adopted by every navy afloat.[96] By 1883 his firm was overwhelmed with business, and he welcomed an amalgamation.[97] It was a happy combination. Vavasseur, who had strong networks around the capital, ran the London Office and Armstrongs benefited from his existing patents, continued inventions, and his firm's overflowing order books. Another addition was Colonel Charles Younghusband. A member of the Ordnance Committee between 1863 and 1867, he had worked with Noble, including on high muzzle velocity guns, and concluded his government career as superintendent of the Royal Gun Factories.[98] Younghusband became a director in 1883. In 1889 Andrew Noble recruited George Hadcock from Woolwich to become his personal assistant on experimental work. Hadcock took on increased responsibilities at Armstrongs over the coming decades.[99]

Not all moves were to join Armstrongs. George Rendel had come to the Navy's attention through his work on two committees on ship design and "Two First Lords in successive Governments invited him to quit Elswick and join the Admiralty. Domestic pressure for departure from Newcastle, long urgent, now increased, and a third offer to join the Admiralty was accepted. He became an extra Civil Lord of the Admiralty and quitted the firm."[100] The "domestic pressure" was his desire to escape from Noble's increasingly autocratic management of Elswick. Sir William regarded George and Stuart Rendel's departures "as though we had both rather deserted Elswick and himself."[101] The fissures emerging at Armstrongs were to widen over the coming years.

[93] Rendel, *Personal Papers*, pp. 283–84.
[94] Fairbairn, *Elswick*, p. 89; Brook, *Warships*, p. 11.
[95] "Sir William Siemens"; Warren, *Armstrongs*, p. 29.
[96] "Obituary Josiah Vavasseur," *1908 Institution*.
[97] "Obituary Josiah Vavasseur," *The Engineer*.
[98] Younghusband to Noble, 10 January 1874. TWA DF/NOB/6/7.
[99] d'Eyncourt, "Obituary," p. 141.
[100] Rendel, *Personal Papers*, p. 281.
[101] Rendel, *Personal Papers*, p. 282.

Early in this decade Armstrongs made a major decision to invest in a shipyard and new steelworks at Elswick. This was in response to Krupp's attempts to enter the British market. The investment enabled Armstrongs to keep a monopoly on Admiralty artillery orders for longer.[102] The move was facilitated by appointing Colonel Henry Dyer, who, Sir William thought "will supply excellently the kind of experience we want for our steel works."[103] Dyer was a Director at Whitworths in Manchester (he had previously served at the Government Small Arms Factory at Enfield).[104] Sir William calculated that "by getting him away from the Manchester company we enormously lessen the chance of that company readily becoming a rival to Elswick in gun-making."[105] The new steelworks included two 21-ton Siemens furnaces; Dyer was in sole charge.[106] This was a classic backward integration, and ended Armstrongs' dependence on steelmakers such as Vickers.

The shipyard expansion was possible because of the new swing bridge across the Tyne River. The bridge and the new works drew a continuous stream of politicians and technical experts to Armstrongs, where they inspected new equipment, observed gun and ship trials, and attended ship launches. As Bastable recounted: "The involvement of Elswick managers in party politics enabled the firm to develop and maintain access to the British government whatever party was in power. Thus, when Sir Stafford Northcote visited Newcastle in 1884, it was Cruddas, not the Liberal (Unionist) Armstrong, who ushered that influential Tory to his social functions."[107]

Armstrongs' first international diversification was a defensive move, strongly encouraged by their ambassador-agent Admiral Albini, to fend off exclusion from the Italian market. The fear of losing market access plus the opportunity to gain a government-subsidized factory was a winning combination. The Pozzuoli factory near Naples was set up in 1884 and managed by Albini and George Rendel.[108] An Armstrongs' document adds flavor to the decision. After George left the Admiralty, he moved to Italy for his health. "The climate did his health good; so much so that in about 1886 he proposed to Sir William Armstrong that an Italian branch of Sir W. G. Armstrong & Company be founded there and supervised by himself."[109] The Pozzuoli diversification was successful; however, in 1889 Armstrongs decided against establishing a shipyard there.

Armstrongs used Sir William's newly designed Cragside mansion to entertain important guests. Cragside reflected "every convenience of wealth

---

[102] McNeill, *Pursuit*, p. 271.
[103] Warren, *Armstrongs*, p. 29. Citing: Armstrong to Stuart Rendel, October 10, 1882. TWA.
[104] "Colonel Dyer."
[105] Warren, *Armstrongs*, p. 29. Citing: Armstrong to Stuart Rendel, October 10, 1882. TWA.
[106] Scott, *Vickers*, p. 34.
[107] Bastable, *Arms*, p. 231. George Cruddas had joined Armstrong in his hydraulic crane venture and remained on the Board.
[108] Bastable, *Arms*, pp. 133–34.
[109] "Vickers and Armstrongs in Italy," VA, Vickers Doc. 552.

and taste."[110] The first house lit by hydroelectricity, Cragside was a marvel of technology and grandeur, attracting global interest. He entertained Lord Grey there on several occasions.[111] Sir William had formed strong relationships with Queen Victoria and particularly the Prince of Wales, who was fascinated by technological developments and armaments advances.[112] The Prince and Princess of Wales and their children visited Cragside in August 1884.[113] The occasion was Sir William and Lady Armstrong's gift of sixty-two acres of parkland in Jesmond Dene valley, their Jesmond Dene home and the Banqueting Hall to the people of Newcastle.[114] This came with an endowment of four houses in the Dene whose rent would cover the costs of maintaining the Dene and the Banqueting Hall. However, as this revenue proved inadequate, until 1899 Sir William also paid for maintenance, "which has been considerably in excess of the rents of the houses."[115]

Armstrongs continued to market its wares. In 1884, when the Royal Arsenals still held a monopoly on gun production, Sir William was approached by the *Pall Mall Gazette* with the opportunity to air his views on the issue. The editor wheedled, "An article from so great an authority as yourself might exercise a great influence."[116] At the request of Sir Fredrick Bramwell, Sir William contributed £1,000 to guarantee the 1885 International Inventions Exhibition.[117] This was a strategic investment as Queen Victoria was Exhibition Patron, and the Prince of Wales was President of the Council. Additionally, Bramwell served on the Ordnance Committee and would be a valuable ally.[118] Armstrongs exhibited "various rifled-guns and machine guns. Included amongst the former is a short rifled howitzer, and a screw gun which takes to pieces for convenience of transport."[119] In 1887 Newcastle hosted an international exhibition to mark Queen Victoria's Jubilee. Armstrongs'

[110]   Cochrane, *Romance*, p. 167.
[111]   Grey to Armstrong, 30 August 1884. TWA, DF/A/1/18/2.
[112]   Francis Knollys [Private Secretary to the Prince of Wales] to Armstrong, 10 July 1884. TWA, DF/A/1/20/1.
[113]   Sutherland to Armstrong, 11 July 1884, TWA, DF/A/1/34/1; Francis Knollys to Armstrong, 18 July 1884, TWA, DF/A/1/20/1; Francis Knollys to Armstrong, 27 August 1884, TWA, DF/A/1/20/2; Charlotte Knollys [Private Secretary to Princess Alexandra] to Armstrong, 20 September 1884, TWA, DF/A/1/20/4. Lord Grey had also been invited but could not attend due to infirmity. Grey to Armstrong, 6 August 1884, TWA, DF/A/1/18/1; Cochrane, "Obituary: Lord Armstrong," p. 327.
[114]   Dolman, "Notable," p. 578. Subsequently, Sir William gave more parkland and in 1886 gifted the Corporation all the contents of the Banqueting Hall. "Report of the Parks Committee," 1899, p. 434.
[115]   "Report of the Parks Committee," p. 435.
[116]   Milner to Armstrong, 17 December 1884. TWA, DF/A/3/13.
[117]   Bramwell to Armstrong, July 15, 1884; Bramwell to Armstrong, July 24, 1884. TWA DF/A/1/7.
[118]   "Obituary: Sir Frederick."
[119]   *International Inventions Exhibition*, p. 23; Hobhouse, *Crystal Palace*, p. 214.

exhibits included a 110-pound naval gun and models of two fast protected cruisers for Japan.[120]

Armstrongs had much to offer the government in terms of products and expertise. Consequently, there was an increasing exchange of experts between the firm and the government. Armstrongs' strongest links were with the Admiralty, where exchanges began with Admiralty architect William Henry White.[121] Early in the decade, White designed an armored cruiser for Argentina, which Armstrongs built. Then in 1883 he joined the firm as Chief Naval Designer in charge of the new Warship Yard at Elswick and was responsible for the design of the early Elswick cruisers.[122] He earned £1,400 more annually than he had at the Admiralty. White's ability to call upon relationships with former colleagues was clearly helpful for Armstrongs, reflecting the success of the firm's elite strategy.[123] White's expertise cultivated international sales for Armstrongs. For example, his memorandum for Austria resulted in a contract for the torpedo cruiser *Panther*, followed by an order for the *Leopard*.[124] He endured a frustrating trip to Madrid in search of orders for a battleship and some third-class cruisers, waiting for weeks for an audience with the king, but losing out to a French firm. Nevertheless, White had meetings with the Minister of Marine and Admiral Polo.[125] He eventually secured the smaller contract.[126] After the former Chief Constructor Sir Edward Reed was "dropped" by the Greek Commission in 1884, White advised that Armstrongs not seek further entrées through him.[127]

There were many competitions held between increasingly powerful guns and ever-stronger armor, all extensively covered in the national and international press. As Hugh Lyon noted, firms would invite Admiralty officials to attend such trials, often wining and dining them.[128] For example, three officials attended the 1884 Armstrongs trials of the innovative *Esmeralda* (designed for Chile but later sold to Japan). After the trials, White authored a piece on *Esmeralda* for the *Times*.[129] Sir Edward Reed responded in the letters' column, disparaging the protected cruisers designed by White (previously his subordinate at the Admiralty) and singling out the *Esmeralda* for attack; he followed this over the next year with criticisms of the *Admiral* class.[130] White's riposte,

[120] Conte-Helm, *Japan*, pp. 61–62.
[121] "Obituary, Sir William Henry White," p. 324.
[122] Parkinson, *Late*, p. 158.
[123] For example, he asked his former colleague Nathaniel Barnaby for "an opinion on the proposed use of cast steel struts." Manning, *William White*, p. 124. Citing: White to Barnaby, October 24, 1883.
[124] Manning, *William White*, pp. 130–33, 136.
[125] Manning, *William White*, pp. 145–52.
[126] Brook, *Warships*, p. 65.
[127] Manning, *William White*, p. 127. Citing: White to Noble, February 13, 1884.
[128] Lyon, "Admiralty," p. 41.
[129] Manning, *William White*, p. 112; the *Times*, August 6, 1884.
[130] Manning, *William White*, p. 164. Citing: Reed to the *Times*, October 20, 1884.

published by the *Times* on April 4, 1885, settled the dispute decisively, demolishing Reed's arguments, and displaying such expertise as to ensure that White became favorite to be the next Chief Constructor.

In 1885 the new First Sea Lord, Lord Hamilton, sought to bring White back as Chief Constructor, contacting Sir William, "who by return of post most patriotically gave up White, provided that the Admiralty would allow him to take another officer from the Corps of Naval Constructors."[131] White's replacement was Philip Watts, a rising Admiralty architect, who remained at Elswick until 1901. Sir William's other condition was that White should sometimes consult with Armstrongs, with the Admiralty stipulating that this must be unremunerated. White's government post was upgraded to Director of Naval Construction (DNC) in October 1885. His Armstrongs connection was unsuccessfully used by critics trying to create trouble for him.[132] Indeed, DNC White dealt with armament firms impartially by always ensuring competitive tendering.[133] Lord Hamilton noted, though, "The system of select firms for contracts is not without danger …. The door to favouritism has been laid open, and it rests largely with high-minded officers that all works well."[134] Toward the end of the decade, as he was taking on more of the management of the firm, Noble brought in John Meade Falkner to be Company Secretary.[135] Falkner had begun as the private tutor to Noble's children and his suitability for the role (he was a renaissance man and novelist) has been debated.[136]

Cordial relationships with the Admiralty began to pay off for Armstrongs mid-decade. In 1886 John Fisher, the new Director of Naval Ordnance, a good friend of Vavasseur and an admirer of Noble's ordnance work, was permitted to buy "economically" from private firms. He immediately placed an order for Armstrongs' Quick Fire guns for use against torpedo boats.[137]

Sir William was granted the Freedom of the City of Newcastle in 1887 for his contributions to the city. During Queen Victoria's Golden Jubilee, Sir William became Baron Armstrong of Cragside, reflecting his national standing. As ever, there were also multiple foreign visits to the armament factories, yards and testing grounds of the firm. International visitors to Cragside included many important guests from Japan.[138] Li Hung Chang (Li Hongzhang) of Imperial China, the King of Siam, the Shah of Persia and the Crown Prince of Afghanistan were all entertained at Cragside and toured Elswick.[139]

---

[131] Cited in Manning, *William White*, p. 178.
[132] Manning, *William White*, pp. 180, 204–206, 209–12.
[133] Manning, *William White*, pp. 414–15.
[134] Hamilton, *Naval*, p. 155.
[135] Warren, *Armstrongs*, p. 67.
[136] Warren, *John Meade Falkner*, pp. 125–26; Scott, *Vickers*, p. 89.
[137] Heald, *William Armstrong*, p. 195.
[138] Conte-Helm, *Japan*, pp. 62–63, 103–104 and 132–35.
[139] Wilson, *Victorians*, p. 384.

In a diplomatic innovation, Armstrongs began to use their ship launches to strengthen ties with their international customers. Whereas in 1880 the Japanese gunboat *Tsukushi* had been launched at the Walker Shipyard without fanfare, in 1885 the *Naniwa* was launched by Lady Armstrong and the *Takachiho* by the wife of the Japanese Ambassador, Madame Kawasi.[140] Attention to ship launches increased and the firm began printing commemorative cards. On April 9, 1887, HMS *Victoria* was launched from Elswick by Mary Anne Forwood, wife of the Secretary to the Admiralty.[141] Armstrongs astutely lent a model of the *Victoria* for display at the South Kensington Museum.[142]

Meanwhile at Vickers, as Scott records,

> The outcome of the prosperity of the Seventies was seen in 1881, when the fixed assets of the company were written up by £200,000, and £50,000 were transferred from the profit and loss accounts to reserves and this quarter of a million was, once again, issued to the shareholders in bonus shares, thus increasing the capital of the company to £750,000.[143]

In 1884 the Vickers family began an important business relationship with an American inventor called Hiram Maxim. He was working in Europe on electrical business when he was allegedly inspired to develop a machine gun by a conversation in Vienna with an American counterpart. As George Chinn recounts, that friend, "[d]isgusted with the delay and red tape encountered in this field … stated to Maxim, 'Hang your chemistry and electricity! If you want to make a pile of money, invent something that will enable these Europeans to cut each other's throats with greater facility.'"[144] In a workshop in Hatton Gardens, Maxim experimented until he had a prototype machine gun, which – after a short spell of disbelief among observers at what Maxim had achieved – attracted the attention of HRH the Duke of Cambridge, Lord Wolseley and War Office officials.[145] Maxim produced a revolutionary gun that harnessed the power of a bullet's recoil to eject the spent cartridge and draw in a new one. He created a belt system to continuously feed in the cartridges, making the gun automatic. It could shoot at various speeds and was relatively simple, rugged and portable.

Armstrongs was producing the Gatling under license, so Maxim contacted Vickers.[146] In 1884 Albert became chairman of the newly established Maxim Gun Company Ltd. and Edward took 100 shares and Thomas seventy-five. The company's new facility in Crayford manufactured a gun to exhibit at the 1885

---

[140] "Ships built for the Japanese Navy," TWA, D/VA/21/2 (1899). Previously the womenfolk of yard workers launched the boats.

[141] The ship and its ordnance caused many problems for Armstrongs. Hough, *Admirals*, pp. 47–52.

[142] South Kensington Museum, *Catalogue*, p. 12.

[143] Scott, *Vickers*, p. 18.

[144] Chinn, *Machine Gun*, p. 128.

[145] Chinn, *Machine Gun*, p. 132.

[146] Scott, *Vickers*, p. 38.

International Inventions Exhibition. The Maxim Gun won a gold medal and stunned observers because "its rate of firing – 770 shots a minute – is at least three times as rapid as that of any other machine gun."[147] In 1885 Maxim demonstrated the machine gun to the British Army and in 1887 the Royal Navy trialed it, buying three.[148] The new firm used Hiram Maxim as "its principal agent, salesman and publicity agent."[149]

In 1887 Maxim traveled to Switzerland for a trial of the machine gun against the Gatling, the Gardner and the Nordenfelt, with the Gardener strongly favored to win orders. "On this occasion he was accompanied by Mr. Albert Vickers, who was now deeply interested in the business …. Vickers did the firing and showed great skill as a machine gun marksman, as he outshot the Gardener in spite of its improved ammunition."[150] Other trials followed. Albert Vickers was present at a competition in Vienna and alternated with Maxim to fire the gun "practically the entire day," impressing Archduke William, Field Marshall of the Austrian Army.[151] The British Government were the first to adopt the Maxim Gun, taking out a license in 1889 (though orders were not large), followed by Austria, Germany, Italy, Switzerland and Russia. "In January 1887 Albert Vickers resigned as chairman in favour of General Sir Andrew Clarke, RE, but the general was merely a figurehead, and Albert remained on the Board."[152] Soon after, Maxims amalgamated with Nordenfelt, forming the Maxim Nordenfelt Gun and Ammunition Co. The combined firm inherited Nordenfeld's agent, Basil Zaharoff, a formidable salesman who had competed with Maxim in 1886–88 and was not above a little industrial sabotage.[153] The combined firm produced a variety of rapid-fire naval guns, and two automatic weapons: the 37 mm "Pom-Pom" and a rifle caliber gun, the Maxim-Nordenfelt.[154]

Though Vickers thrived in the early 1880s, storm clouds were forming. All of Sheffield's traditional steel businesses were going into a slump, exacerbated by Washington's imposition of tariffs on tool steel imports.[155] Vickers needed to act, and some new sectors were beckoning. "Already the process of product diversification was bringing them to the end of shipbuilding and ordnance. In the mid-1880s they were making some of the biggest marine shafts in the world, as well as steel castings for ordnance manufacturers."[156] In 1884 Vickers had the

---

[147] Cochrane, *Romance*, p. 178.
[148] Simpkin, "Hiram"; Chivers, *The Gun*, p. 84.
[149] Payne, *Private Spies*, p. 136.
[150] Chinn, *Machine Gun*, p. 137.
[151] Chinn, *Machine Gun*, p. 137.
[152] Scott, *Vickers*, p. 38.
[153] For example, a sabotaged Maxim gun failed during a competitive test in Vienna. Payne, *Private Spies*, pp. 138–39.
[154] Chinn, *Machine Gun*, p. 143.
[155] Tweedale, *Steel City*, p. 147–48.
[156] Warren, *Armstrongs*, p. 48.

perspicacity to enlarge their Sheffield works so that they could undertake ordnance work, making a forward integration to utilize their steel. They installed a large forging press and a crane able to lift 150 tons, enabling them to make ingots for large guns. But they planned to expand further.[157]

In 1881 Thomas Vickers and his family were still living at Bolsover Hill, now attended to by nine servants.[158] In 1884 the Vickers brothers commissioned the up-and-coming American artist John Singer Sargent to paint family portraits. Sargent was selected by Thomas' wife, who had studied art in Paris.[159] Before coming to Sheffield, Sargent had been criticized for the picture "Portrait of Madam X," exhibited in Paris, which was seen as over-sexualized. Though Sargent feared losing the commission, Thomas did not withdraw his request, having his own portrait painted and one of his three eldest daughters.[160] Sargent spent three weeks in Sheffield completing the latter painting, describing the city as a "dingy hole."[161] *The Misses Vickers* was met with distain in London. *Pall Mall Gazette* readers voted it the worst picture of 1886 at the Royal Academy.[162] Undeterred, Thomas then commissioned Sargent to paint his wife and sons, and other family members.[163] Other paintings included portraits of Albert's wife Edith and of Albert and Edith's children Dorothy and Billy, as well as "A Dinner Table at Night (Mr. and Mrs. Albert Vickers)." The Vickers family continued to follow their own path, disregarding elite opinion.

In 1887 Vickers undertook its first international diversification, establishing the Placencia de las Armas Company Limited in Spain. This wholly owned Vickers subsidiary was set up by agreement with the Spanish government to manufacture guns and ordnance. Unfortunately for Vickers, Placencia was not profitable in the short or medium term, although their agent, Zaharoff, always talked about the firm's "Spanish business," "which for twenty or thirty years has always been brilliant."[164] That was truer for him than for Vickers.

---

[157] LeClair, *Supervising*, p. 292. Citing: "Sheffield Trade for 1885," the *Times*, January 5, 1886, p. 13.

[158] 1881 Census. Cited in "Thomas Edward Vickers."

[159] Wilson, *Middle-Class*, p. 41; 228.

[160] Fairbrother, *John Singer Sargent*, p. 189; Portrait of Colonel Thomas Edward Vickers, by John Singer Sargent. At: www.johnsingersargent.org/Portrait-Of-Colonel-Thomas-Edward-Vickers.html.

[161] Hamilton, *Misses Vickers*, p. 43.

[162] At: www.jssgallery.org/Paintings/The_Misses_Vickers/The_Misses_Vickers.htm. Now highly regarded for its "modern" approach, it resides at Sheffield City Art Gallery.

[163] Portrait of Mrs. Thomas Edward Vickers (Frances Mary Vickers) by John Singer Sargent. At: www.johnsingersargent.org/Portrait-Of-Frances-Mary-Vickers.html. Portrait of Douglas Vickers. At: www.johnsingersargent.org/Douglas-Vickers.html. Fairbrother, *John Singer Sargent*, p. 190.

[164] Zaharoff to McLean, April 15, 1929. "Aviation: Spanish Correspondence 1929–1936," VA, Doc. 571.

Armstrongs experienced a problem in 1887. They were building *Dogali* for the Greek Government, which could not pay and canceled the order when the ship was well underway. Armstrongs' solution was classic; they sold the ship to Italy – it became the *Salamis*. The following year Armstrongs completed three ships for Italy, the fastest cruiser in the world, *Piemonte*, equipped entirely with Quick Fire guns, and the twin-screw gunboats *Polluce* and *Castore*, which were assembled at Pozzouli.

In spring 1887 Vickers decided to move into large scale armaments production, increasing their capital by a share issue and focusing on armor plate and large guns. The Sheffield firms John Brown, Charles Cammell and Thomas Firth were planning the same move.[165] Vickers had tested their first gun by September 1888 and tested their first armor plate a few months later.[166] The firm's timing was exquisite, and orders soon followed. The trigger was the naval scare which began in late 1887 and led to the passing of the Naval Defence Act of 1888. The Act aimed to restore British naval superiority over other powers by spending £16 million on warships (including £10 million for the private yards) and £5.5 million on armament (£4.5 million going to private firms). As Clive Trebilcock noted, "as warships grew increasingly in size, the proportion of total naval tonnage which could be obtained from the Royal Dockyards grew inexorably smaller; consequently, the Admiralty was forced to waive its distrust of private yards – it had drawn upon their design capabilities only five times between 1859 and 1882 – and to resort increasingly to the independent builders."[167] This was an important opportunity for Armstrongs and Vickers.

The Admiralty also needed better armor plate. In January 1888 there had been unsuccessful trials of the "compound" armor plate produced by Browns and Cammells. Traditionally the Admiralty "did not provide direct financial encouragement to firms entering the armour industry; instead it gave advice and contracts."[168] This was true for Vickers, who had discussed a move into armor production with DNC White.[169] Now half a dozen firms – including Vickers – were invited to submit trial plates to the Admiralty. Vickers' first attempt at armor plate triumphed, leading to substantial Admiralty orders. Adding Vickers as an armor plate maker loosened the oligopoly in favor of the government.

After armor came guns. At this point only Armstrongs and Whitworths were producing large naval guns, but Vickers, Cammells and Firths were invited by the Admiralty to start production. Vickers were offered guaranteed orders of £200,000. Of the three, only Vickers "braved the problems of

165   "Sheffield, 2nd October 1889," p. 327.
166   Warren, *Armstrongs*, p. 48.
167   Trebilcock, *Vickers Brothers*, pp. 52–53.
168   Lyon, "Admiralty," p. 51.
169   Warren, *Armstrongs*, p. 49.

large-scale ordnance technology" and moved wholeheartedly into armaments.[170] The result of this bold strategy was an 1888 Admiralty order for large guns.[171] Vickers also won orders from Italy, including one for forty guns worth over £14 million; "in the following year their contracts with the ministries for the navy and war, and with an Italian firm named Tempini were worth £67 million."[172] These large orders vindicated their organizational culture. Vickers also integrated backward into collieries, giving them dedicated coal supplies for their steel mills.

As so often with armament orders, an opportunity was also a crisis, and so the Naval Defence Act proved for both the Royal Arsenals and private firms. The timelines for completing warships were much shorter than usual. Compounding this, these vast orders created a bottleneck in gun production, as the massive guns ordinarily took twelve months to complete and now the Navy needed 540 pieces of ordnance for the seventy new ships (including ten battleships). This chokepoint also affected Army artillery. In 1889 Armstrongs were planning to increase their floating capital by a million pounds, a move necessitated "through the enormous increase in the company's business, which in the year ending June 30th, involved an expenditure upon articles manufactured of £1,958,974, as against £863,103 expended under the same head in 1882."[173] Armstrongs was very behind in heavy gun production and "were so badly placed that they were found to be postponing contracts for the British Government in order to make good outstanding commitments to foreign clients; if they were celebrated for quality, they were becoming notorious for delay."[174]

1890s

Vickers had supplied the armour for six second-class cruisers and in 1890 was "busy making all-steel plate for the first-class cruisers in the Admiralty program …. The company is also engaged upon thirty large guns for the Government."[175] Still innovating, "Messrs. Vickers were the first to have a forging press in operation in Sheffield" and were planning to install a second, of 6,000 tons, "by far the heaviest in the Sheffield district."[176] They were the first European firm to license the Harvey method of producing hardened steel and pioneered rolling Harveyized armor plate in 1892.[177] Where Vickers led, others followed. International armor firms formed a pool to acquire the patent for the

[170] Trebilcock, *Vickers Brothers*, p. 55.
[171] Collier, *Arms*, p. 67; Scott, *Vickers*, p. 20.
[172] Segreto, "More Trouble," p. 317.
[173] "Messrs. Armstrong, Mitchell & Co.," *Industries and Iron*, p. 327.
[174] Trebilcock, *Vickers Brothers*, p. 54.
[175] "The Sheffield District," p. 161.
[176] "The Sheffield District," p. 161.
[177] Tweedale, *Steel City*, p. 102; Collier, *Arms*, p. 60.

Harvey system. In 1894 this arrangement became a price-fixing syndicate where foreign orders were divided up by drawing lots.

Despite the competition from Vickers and other armament firms, Armstrongs still relied upon their elite connections and marketing at major exhibitions. In 1891 Lord Chamberlain visited Cragside for a weekend.[178] Queen Victoria was Patron and the Prince of Wales President of the 1891 Royal Naval Exhibition, which they attended alongside a host of dignitaries.[179] The *Engineer* carried a long account of what the public could see.[180] The Navy staged the exhibition to push for a greater share of the Parliamentary estimates, particularly as rearmament was being considered. The Exhibition had two galleries of naval ordnance, torpedoes and other equipment. Armstrongs products occupied a whole gallery.[181] It included "fine models" of the firm's warships and the "battery deck and turrets of a modern man-of-war for which … Messrs. Armstrong, Mitchell and Co., must have incurred considerable cost in the undertaking."[182] The exhibition catalogue included a supplement dedicated to the work of Captain Noble.[183] Reflecting the firm's elite strategy, Sir William sent copies of a new supplement to his book to politicians and other influential figures in 1899.[184]

Armstrongs also had extensive showrooms at Elswick: "[T]here is always kept a stock of ordnance of different kinds and sizes. It is from the specimens kept in these large galleries that the representatives of the war offices of the world give their orders. They are sold ready-made when guns are required at short notice in any quarter of the globe."[185] Beyond the showrooms, a magazine reported that:

> Elswick is a domain rather jealously guarded …. They are constantly on the alert at Elswick for the designing engineer and the enterprising foreigner, the American being more particularly an object of suspicion. Hence, the rigid exclusion of the stranger. As it is, there are several "shops" where important models and designs are kept, which only a few members of the staff at "Armstrongs" are ever allowed to enter.[186]

Armstrongs and Vickers needed a London presence to secure domestic sales. Both firms had established offices in Westminster, Armstrongs on Great George Street and Vickers on Victoria Street before moving to The Broadway.[187]

---

[178] Dolman, "Notable," p. 581.
[179] Photograph of Queen Victoria and dignitaries outside the P&O Gallery: *Historic England*, Heritage Explorer.
[180] "The Naval Exhibition," pp. 530–33.
[181] *Royal Naval Exhibition*, p. XV.
[182] Pall Mall Gazette, *Royal Naval Exhibition*, pp. 53 and 60.
[183] Ibid. p. 61.
[184] Salisbury to Armstrong, March 4, 1899. TWA, DF/A/1/31/1.
[185] Dolman, "Notable," p. 582.
[186] Dolman, "Notable," pp. 581–82.
[187] Rendel to Pallister, June 13, 1867. TWA, 31/877.

As states increasingly set up legations in the capital, these premises also facilitated relationships with overseas buyers.

By the early 1890s Vickers had invested around a million pounds in armaments production, but business had slumped. In 1893 shareholders were informed that since "the amount of business done by this company was considerably reduced, there has consequently been a large falling off in the profits earned."[188] This was Vickers' first experience of a trough in government orders. In response, they followed their strategy of investing during downswings and extended their plant in 1894. Initially this did not bear fruit, with Vickers' Directors explaining to shareholders that they "'[R]egret to say they have been disappointed in not getting the orders for large guns which they were led to expect when they laid down their extensive gun plant.'"[189] Vickers did get naval gun contracts, but no War Office orders. Recovery followed, though. Whereas in 1890 the dividend to shareholders had been 7.5 percent, by 1895 it was a healthy 10 percent and it rose thereafter, hitting 20 percent in 1899.[190]

Armstrongs also experienced an order trough and employed their default strategy. As Admiral Jacky Fisher recounted to the First Sea Lord in 1894:

> Lord Rendel spent over an hour with me on Friday last saying exactly, but at greater length, all that is contained in [his] letter to you. What he wanted was to get the order for 7 ships for Elswick instead of only 5, and he frankly told me Noble had sent him for that purpose. I asked him in reply whether five-sevenths of an order of over half a million was not a good share for Elswick? ... and did he deliberately propose that a firm of the European eminence of Whitworth, who had succeeded admirably in producing efficient mountings for two existing battleships, were not to have any orders at all! Of course, he had nothing to say, but went off on what he called "general principles." I told him that the question had been decided as to the mountings for the 7 battleships and that there was no likelihood of any alteration in the decision, which had been arrived at after most careful consideration.[191]

A year later Fisher reminded Earl Spencer of Armstrongs' elite lobbying, recalling "our memorable interview in your room with Lord Armstrong and Sir Andrew Noble, when they vehemently accused the Admiralty of giving an undue proportion of orders to the ordnance factories to the great detriment of the private traders of this country."[192] Despite this vigorous lobbying, Armstrongs' classic strategy failed. The firm then considered, but rejected, an invitation to build an armor factory at the Barrow naval yard. This left the door open for Vickers to buy the site.

[188] Scott, *Vickers*, p. 43.
[189] Warren, *Armstrongs*, p. 49.
[190] Tweedale, *Steel City*, p. 128 and profits table 3.1, pp. 124–25; Scott, *Vickers*, p. 43.
[191] Fisher to Earl Spencer, October 22, 1894, in Marder, *Fear God*, Vol. I, p. 123.
[192] Fisher to Earl Spencer, May 23, 1895, in Marder, *Fear God*, Vol. I, pp. 125–26.

As Vickers grew and gained prestige, they attracted senior recruits brought in for their technical abilities, not their elite connections. In 1896 Trevor Dawson joined from Woolwich Arsenal, where he had been an Experimental Officer. "[T]he promotion of so young and untried a man might not unnaturally have been deemed something of an experiment," showing another aspect of Vickers' boldness.[193] Dawson was extremely successful in business, kept good relations with the government and was perceived by the service departments as "amenable and handy."[194] James Dunn, who had been a Senior Constructor under DNC White, joined Vickers as a director in 1897.[195] Albert Vickers created good links with British finance and made diverse investments on behalf of the firm, further widening his network. These connections were cemented and internationalized by the recruitment of two men to the firm, Sir Vincent Caillard and Frank Barker. Caillard was an associate of Sir Ernest Cassel and through his work in Turkey had wide connections in the financial world. Barker hailed from a Constantinople banking family. He had strong knowledge of business in Eastern Europe and had developed a special interest in Russia.[196] As Trebilcock reports, "these facilities and friendships were not irrelevant to the capital-intensive traffic in armaments; indeed, they gave Vickers a distinctive advantage over all other British producers and over many continental ones."[197]

The year 1897 was a momentous one, with Vickers making two key purchases. It bought Maxim Nordenfeldt for $1.3 million, becoming Vickers, Sons & Maxim Ltd.[198] The acquisition brought in three important figures. The first was the energetic inventor, Hiram Maxim, who "remained an active participator until his seventy-first birthday."[199] The second was the firm's youthful director, Sigmund Loewe, a protegee of Lord Rothschild with connections to financier Sir Ernest Cassel.[200] Loewe had returned Maxim Nordenfelt to profitability between 1895 and 1896.[201] Loewe brought to Vickers a connection with submarine pioneer Isaac Rice and the Electric Boat Company, and informally acted as financial controller until his untimely death in 1903.[202] Third, Vickers inherited the – already legendary – salesman Basil Zaharoff, though Vickers records show he was selling

193 "The Late Sir Trevor."
194 Davenport-Hines, "British," p. 158.
195 "Barrow," p. 105.
196 Scott, *Vickers*, pp. 78–79.
197 Trebilcock, *Vickers Brothers*, p. 129.
198 Tweedale, *Steel City*, p. 126.
199 Chinn, *Machine Gun*, p. 144.
200 Notes of an interview with Sigmund Loewe's daughter, Mrs. Orbach, January 19, 1959. "Arms Enquiry Sundry Papers: Sir Basil Zaharoff." VA Doc. 788.
201 Scott, *Vickers*, p. 43. An 1896 Maxim-Nordenfelt catalogue was printed with English and Chinese text in parallel. "Loewe Papers," VA, MS 1933, A/5.
202 Scott, *Vickers*, pp. 44–45, 77.

armor plate for them before 1895.[203] Zaharoff was a brilliant ambassador-agent with a network of informers: "It was a useful intelligence service in miniature well-tailored to the needs of competing with a rival firm. It brought in industrial as well as political intelligence."[204] Zaharoff brought Vickers strong international networks that helped to compensate for Armstrongs' advantages in elite connections, and he consistently utilized commissions and bribes. Scott mildly concluded: "[T]here is evidence that on two or three occasions in Serbia in 1898, in Russia later, and probably in Turkey, Zaharoff paid secret commissions, or bribes, of sums running from £100 to possibly several thousand pounds." For Scott, these payments were designed to "forestall German and other rivals" and did not justify the legends of the trade.[205] However, £100 in 1898 was equivalent to £14,447 in August 2022, so even small bribes were of significant value in the poorer countries, where, of course, sterling already went a long way.

Second, Vickers made a historic forward integration, acquiring the Naval Construction & Armaments Company Limited of Barrow for £425,000.[206] They could now manufacture warships and "for this special work ... Messrs. Vickers are undoubtedly well prepared" because they already produced armor and guns they could put on Barrow battleships.[207] As Warren explained: "Until then, lacking shipbuilding facilities, they had to supply others, firms whose demand varied and which could play off one armour maker or gun supplier against another. There was always the export trade, but that was uncertain, scope for taking business in armour at least being limited by agreements between major producers."[208] When Vickers later issued shares to increase the firm's capital by £1,250,000, the shares were immediately oversubscribed.

Still innovating, in the late 1890s Vickers took a license from Krupp for nickel-chromium steel plate.[209] As Luciano Segreto noted, "Big investments in scientific research in the 1890s put Vickers at the forefront of the international market which Krupp (artillery), Schneider (warships) and Holtzer (artillery shells) had previously dominated."[210] Vickers was now a direct challenger to Armstrongs. Even more gallingly, ex-Armstrongs employee DNC White "gave their new rivals an endorsement when he came to the Barrow launching of the cruiser, HMS *Amphitrite*, in July 1898."[211]

---

[203] Lawrence to Secretary of the Royal Commission, and enclosure on "Sir Basil Zaharoff," March 11, 1936. Bankes Commission: Reports and Submissions. Vickers Ltd.: evidence; note by Secretary. TNA, T 181/56; Scott, *Vickers*, p. 79.

[204] Payne, *Private Spies*, p. 136.

[205] Scott, *Vickers*, p. 81.

[206] Scott, *Vickers*, p. 44.

[207] "Barrow," p. 105.

[208] Warren, *Armstrongs*, p. 49.

[209] Collier, *Arms*, p. 60.

[210] Segreto, "More Trouble," p. 317.

[211] Warren, *Armstrongs*, p. 49.

As Scott records, "Armstrongs – some members of the Armstrong's board at least – were watching this bold expansion and most ruthless moderniza-tion of the Vickers plant with anxiety and apprehension."[212] The elevation of Noble's acolyte John Meade Falkner from Company Secretary to the Board did not calm Stuart Rendel's fears. Armstrongs was not standing still, though. In 1897 it amalgamated with its Manchester rival, Sir Joseph Whitworth & Co., with Colonel Henry Dyer, who had previously worked at Whitworths "largely instrumental in bringing about the amalgamation."[213] At Whitworths' Openshaw site Armstrongs added a new armor plate works, and new shops were built at Elswick. In 1899 Armstrongs purchased land at Scotswood, out-side Newcastle, for a factory for fuses, shot and shells.

Vickers was soon complaining that they had extended their armor produc-tion plant at the urging of the Admiralty, but "the subsequent Admiralty orders were insufficient to keep it fully employed; and for this reason they had been compelled to take a large contract with a foreign Government." However, the Admiralty calculated that Vickers was fully employed with the British con-tract and "the contract with a foreign Government was taken with the object of securing a higher profit, and for no other reason."[214] Vickers was prioritizing its own interests – to the chagrin of the Admiralty.

Meanwhile, the firms were engaged in complex negotiations with the gov-ernment over their patents and royalties. At least three negotiations, cover-ing several of the two firms' products, were proceeding in parallel in 1894 and continued into the next century. These negotiations provide insights into Armstrongs and Vickers' wary relations with the British Government. First, a negotiation was finally concluding over the Admiralty's infringement of Armstrongs' patents for "Hydro-pneumatic Carriages, Recoil Carriages for Quick Fire Guns, Powder Cases and Shrapnel Shells."[215] In 1894, Cruddas applied for £9,649 to be paid "by the Admiralty on account of the infringement of certain Patents held by this Company."[216] However, the Accountant General of the Navy proposed deferring the settlement because it had been calculated on the basis of an estimate. The War Office responded tartly: "To keep Messrs. Armstrong waiting longer for payment of the sums due would, in Mr Campbell Bannerman's opinion, be unjust."[217] Armstrongs got their money at the end of June.

Second, Armstrongs was negotiating with the Admiralty and War Office over future royalties on their gun mounting patents. While the Admiralty

[212] Scott, *Vickers*, p. 49.
[213] "Sudden Death."
[214] Manning, *William White*, p. 410.
[215] "Sums due to Sir W. G. Armstrong & Co. in connection with their patents for certain war-like stores," June 30, 1894. TNA, ADM 1/7833.
[216] Cruddas to Admiralty, June 11, 1894. TNA, ADM 1/7833.
[217] War Office to Accountant General of the Navy, June 30, 1984. TNA, ADM 1/7833.

agreement had officially come into force on April 1, 1894, the royalty negotiation continued. Rejecting an Armstrongs proposal, the Admiralty counter
offered:

> [T]he following scheme which has been decided upon after full consider-
> ation of the matter, is considered to be fair and equitable in its application
> to all parties concerned, viz:-
>
> (1) For any orders for mountings, of which Elswick patents may then
>   still be in force, not given to Elswick during any financial year, and
>   accounting to one-third (or less) of the total value of the orders to
>   Elswick, there shall be paid a nominal royalty of £1 per mounting (on
>   orders to Woolwich), and 10 percent. on the contract price (on orders
>   to contractors other than Elswick): and
> (2) For any such further orders (not given to Elswick) in excess of one-
>   third of the total value of the orders to Elswick, there shall be paid 5
>   percent. on actual cost (on orders to Woolwich), and 12½ percent. on
>   contract prices (on orders to contractors other than Elswick):
> (3) For any such orders not given to Elswick, when Elswick receives no
>   orders during any financial year, there shall be paid 5 percent. on
>   actual cost (on orders to Woolwich) and 12½ percent. on contract
>   prices (on orders to contractors other than Elswick).[218]

Noble refused this, responding that "the proposals which their Lordships now
forward differ very materially from those submitted by us, and we trust the
question may be further considered." Armstrongs were particularly concerned
about clauses (2) and (3) because the effect was:

> that we are to receive the same royalty whether (for example) about one-
> tenth of the mountings are ordered from us or none at all. This is obviously
> an oversight, and we suggest the following:-
>
> 1. For any orders for any class of mountings (on which we have patents)
>   not given to Elswick during any financial year, and amounting to one-
>   third (or less) of the number of mountings actually given to Elswick
>   there shall be paid a nominal royalty of £1 per mounting on orders to
>   Woolwich, and 10 percent. on the contract price on orders to contrac-
>   tors other than Elswick.
> 2. Should the number of mountings referred to in (1) ordered from
>   Elswick be greater than one-third, and less than two-thirds of the total
>   number ordered during any financial year, there shall be paid 5 per-
>   cent. on the total actual cost in respect of orders to Woolwich, and
>   12½ percent. of contract price in respect of orders to contractors other
>   than Elswick.
> 3. Should all the mountings referred to in (1) be ordered away from
>   Elswick, or should the number ordered from Elswick be less than

---

[218] Admiralty to Elswick, August 9, 1894. TNA, ADM 1/7833.

one-third, there shall be paid 7½ percent. on the total actual cost in respect to orders given to Woolwich, and 15 percent. on contract price in respect of orders given to contractors other than Elswick.[219]

Noble concluded:

> We are exceedingly anxious to meet the views of the Admiralty in every possible way, but at the same time it is absolutely necessary that designs which have cost us very large sums in experiments &c. should not be placed, without expenditure, at the disposal of rivals, who are thus put in a position successfully to compete with us, especially when, as at present, we are maintaining a large unemployed plant to meet demands should they occur.[220]

Armstrongs wanted to exclude other firms from the market. Noble proposed a conference to solve the issue.[221]

In November 1894 the Admiralty responded:

> My Lords … while unable to assent to the proposals which you have made … are willing to modify the scheme proposed in Admiralty letter of 9th August 1894, as follows, in order to meet your views as far as possible, vis:-
>
> (a) If your Firm receives 75% or more of the value of the total orders for these transferable gun mountings, the Admiralty will pay a Royalty on the balance of the orders of – £1 per mounting for those mountings ordered from Woolwich. 10% of the Contract price of orders given to other contractors.
> (b) When you receive 25% or more (but less than 75%) of the total value of the orders, the Royalty payable to be – 5% of the value of Woolwich orders. 12½% of contract price of orders to other Contractors.
> (c) When you receive less than 25% of the total value of orders, or no orders at all, then the Royalty to be paid will be – 7½% of value of Woolwich orders. 15% of Contract price of orders given to other Contractors.[222]

This scheme was accepted by Armstrongs, but this triggered further government discussion of royalties on mountings ordered before April 1, 1894.[223]

By 1896 the Admiralty were struggling to calculate the royalties due to Armstrongs on guns made by Woolwich, because the actual cost was often known only long after an order was completed. Armstrongs provided the solution, proposing that the average price paid to them for any gun mounting of

[219] Noble to Admiralty, August 23, 1894. TNA, ADM 1/7833.
[220] Noble to Admiralty, August 23, 1894. TNA, ADM 1/7833.
[221] Noble to Admiralty, August 23, 1894. And follow up: Falkner to Admiralty, August 31, 1894. TNA, ADM 1/7833.
[222] Macgregor, Admiralty to Sir W. G. Armstrong & Co., November 27, 1894. "Royalties on Transferable Gun Mountings," TNA, ADM 1/7833.
[223] Noble to Admiralty, November 29, 1894. TNA, ADM 1/7833.

their patented design should be used as the basis for calculating the Woolwich royalty. The Admiralty forwarded the proposal to the Treasury, noting that "this method ... will be a beneficial arrangement for the Crown, as the general rule is that the mountings made at Woolwich are dearer than those supplied by Elswick."[224] The Treasury accepted Armstrongs' solution, adding that if the arrangement did not actually benefit the Crown, it should be revised.[225] Armstrongs was informed of this acceptance in August.[226]

The Admiralty–Armstrongs agreement was open-ended, a flaw that became obvious in 1898 when a new gun mounting manufacturer had emerged and new royalty terms had to be negotiated, initiating a long intra-government debate. A memorandum recorded:

> When the existing royalty agreement with Elswick was framed no other important English gun mounting firms were contracting to the Admiralty, and the agreement was considered equitable by both parties for the use of the Elswick firm's patents.
>
> Another firm has now obtained large orders for mountings to their own designs and it will be necessary to make some agreement with them for the use of their patents to provide for the manufacture of their mountings by Woolwich or other contractors as found necessary or desirable. The objections to the existing arrangement appear to be:
>
> 1. That no specific patents are referred to, the period of operation of the agreement is indefinite and it will apparently continue in force as long as Elswick patents on gun mountings for the navy exist, unless specifically terminated.
> 2. The amount of the royalty payable on the mounting remains the same although the original patents may have expired and only minor ones are still in force.
> 3. By adding small patented fittings the royalty on which should be trifling, the full royalty based on a proportion of the value of the mounting may be claimed.[227]

Vickers was the new supplier. Their design for a 12-inch gun was approved and ten were ordered by the Admiralty. The Vickers 6-inch Quick Fire gun design was also approved, with a potential order of ninety-five if the trials were successful.[228]

Vickers also wanted land orders, making the War Office a bold offer: "Provided we are allowed a sufficient amount of time we are prepared to manufacture guns and mountings up to any amount."[229] They had installed

---

[224] MacGregor, Admiralty to Treasury, July 16, 1896. TNA, ADM 1/7833.

[225] Mowatt, Treasury to Admiralty, July 25, 1896. TNA, ADM 1/7833.

[226] Admiralty to Armstrongs, August 22, 1896. TNA, ADM 1/7833.

[227] "Agreements as regards Royalties with makers of guns Armstrongs," reviewed September 5, 1898. TNA, ADM 1/7833.

[228] Director of Naval Ordnance, "Patents for and Royalties on Guns and their Equipment, excluding Mountings," December 8, 1897. TNA, ADM 1/7833.

[229] Scott, *Vickers*, p. 49.

substantial specialist machinery, because "[l]arge naval mountings required the attention of 500 machines per unit, including 30-foot circular saws for the roller bearings and multiple cutters working in harness so as to achieve the parallel recoil paths for the big guns."[230] They were successful. The War Office adopted the Vickers breech mechanism for 6-inch guns and there was the potential for orders of this mechanism for use in 4.7-inch guns.[231]

The Admiralty and War Office agreed that the 1894 Armstrongs agreement was not the model for one with Vickers.[232] The Admiralty drafted a candid letter to the War Office: "[M]y Lords think that with regard to the Vickers Q.F. [Quick Fire] gun patents it is probable better terms may be obtained if the question is discussed before the patentees know whether their patents will be accepted or not."[233] The version sent was more diplomatic: "[I]t has been found by experience very inconvenient and the cause of much delay to defer making terms with Patentees until after their Patents have been adopted in the service," and asked permission to negotiate with Vickers on three distinct patents, "assuming without prejudice to fuller enquiry that these patents are valid."[234]

The Admiralty informed Vickers in March that they would pay royalties for gun mountings produced by the Ordnance Factories or other contractors. If Vickers was willing to accept those terms, they requested the firm "forward as soon as possible a list of the patents held by you which are used in the designs of gun mountings which have already been submitted by your firm," and that this be followed by:

> a statement of the royalty you would require for the use of each of these patents. The designs referred to are:-
>
> 12 inch Hydraulic Mountings for "Vengeance", "Irresistible" and "Venerable."
> 9.2 inch Hydraulic Mountings for "Higue", "Sutlej", "Euryalus" and "Bacchante."
> 6 inch Q.F.P. Mark IV.
> Maxim Tripods.
> Sighting Gear for Gun Mountings
> And any others which have already been submitted.[235]

---

[230] Trebilcock, *Vickers Brothers*, p. 8. Citing: Richardson, *Vickers*.
[231] Kenyon, War Office, "Royalty on Quick Firing Guns and Land Service Mountings," November 7, 1899. Copy in TNA, ADM 1/7833.
[232] "Agreements as regards Royalties with makers of guns Armstrongs," reviewed September 5, 1898. TNA, ADM 1/7833.
[233] Draft, Admiralty to War Office, December 23, 1897. TNA, ADM 1/7833.
[234] Admiralty to War Office, December 31, 1897. The War Office consulted the Ordnance Council on potential terms with Vickers. Knox, War Office to Admiralty, February 11, 1898. TNA, ADM 1/7833.
[235] MacGregor, Admiralty to Vickers, and enclosure undated. "Proposed Letters to Messrs. Vickers in Regard to Their Patents on All Naval Gun Mountings," February/March 1899. TNA, ADM 1/7833.

The proposal specified that any new design of gun mounting submitted should provide full patent information, that Vickers should indemnify the Admiralty against "all liability in the event of any patent held by the firm on which a royalty is paid being held to be an infringement of any Patent not held by the firm," and that the Admiralty be informed when any patents expired.

In January 1899 Vickers confirmed that "our new Maxim Tripod Mounting to design Nos. 1615 G and 1616 G is covered by Provisional Patent No. 364/99."[236] However, in July the Admiralty were still waiting for an answer to their proposal on royalties on other gun mountings.[237] Dawson sent a long-winded reply, apologizing for the slow response, "owing to the very important nature of the subject matter contained therein," and enclosing their patents list. Dawson also laid out at length Vickers' views, many of which concerned excluding other firms from the market:

> We have paid very large sums of money in order to endeavour to establish ourselves in the ordnance business, and in addition to this, we have laid out our Works in Sheffield, Barrow, and Erith for ordnance production, with a view to meeting Admiralty requirements, at a very heavy cost to ourselves, amounting to upwards of a million sterling, which is a very large commitment for the purpose of securing a special type of business. If therefore our designs and experience are handed over to other Makers, they will at once become our competitors, not only for work connected with the British Admiralty and War Office, but also in Foreign markets.
>
> We will however state in the first place that we are prepared to endeavour to meet any wishes the Admiralty may express to us, after having taken into consideration our position, and we are prepared to grant licenses, where we do not assist in creating new competition against ourselves. Up to the present, the only important firm in competition with us in Foreign markets, is Messrs. Sir W. G. Armstrong Whitworth & Co. Ltd. ... [W]e may say that, notwithstanding our commercial rivalry, and in order to meet the Admiralty requirements, we are prepared to allow them to manufacture naval mountings for Great Britain and the Colonies, and all Countries under the Crown, at a Royalty of 5% of their selling price on the mountings; provided we are given a fair and equitable portion of orders which are placed ....
>
> Should, however, their Lordships send our drawings to other large Firms, it would have the effect of enabling them to compete with us in our foreign trade at our expense, in money and experience.[238]

Dawson embellished the case for excluding other firms by noting the money Vickers had invested in machine tools and gauges, none of it yet bringing any reward to the firm. Dawson concluded that Vickers were prepared to allow their patents and designs to be used by the Ordnance Factories

---

[236] Dawson to Admiralty, January 7, 1899. TNA, ADM 1/7833.
[237] MacGregor, Admiralty to Vickers, 4 July 1899. TNA, ADM 1/7833.
[238] Vickers to Admiralty, July 20, 1899. TNA, ADM 1/7833.

at a nominal royalty of £1 per each mounting, excepting where we have had to pay large sums of money for the purchase of the patents, and are committed to a large amount, when we will lay the matter before their Lordships, and agree to a royalty to be mutually decided upon, taking the circumstances of the case into consideration; on the understanding that such negotiations are kept absolutely confidential to the Admiralty, and that we are given a fair amount of the order to enable us to keep our Works satisfactorily employed.[239]

Dawson's letter was acknowledged – "the matter is receiving careful consideration" – but it met with resistance in the Admiralty.[240]

An Admiralty memorandum recorded dissent on two important points: "(1).- That a clear hand must be left with the Admiralty as to placing orders with other firms besides Elswick, with whom, it appears at present very unlikely that we shall place orders to Vickers' designs. (2).- They imply in their terms proposed for Elswick a royalty on their entire mounting instead of on the patents actually in force." It noted that the Admiralty policy of having alternative manufacturers (in case, for example, of strikes)

cannot be abandoned; every effort is and will be made to treat the firm whose design is adopted with consideration and to give them a fair share of orders but this is a point on which the final decision must rest with the Admiralty …. If these principles be approved they should also be applied to Elswick so as to put the two Firms on an equal footing and that firm have as a matter of fact behaved very reasonably as regards the new type of 12pr. [twelve pounder] mounting under consideration.[241]

Officials clearly did not appreciate Vickers' negotiating behavior.

By 1899 there is evidence that Armstrongs and Vickers were collaborating to exclude others from Admiralty gun mounting orders. Dawson stated:

We would point out that in regard to the Firm of Messrs. Sir W. G. Armstrong Whitworth & Co. Ltd. as they are now doing a very large business, we have no reason to suppose that the advantages they would gain from being in possession of our designs would be greater than if we were in possession of their designs and therefore taking this fact into consideration, we should have no objection whatever to letting them have full details in connection with our mounting designs. Should, however, their Lordships send our drawings to other large Firms, it would have the effect of enabling them to compete with us in our foreign trade at our expense, in money and experience.[242]

[239] Vickers to Admiralty, July 20, 1899. TNA, ADM 1/7833.
[240] Admiralty to Vickers, November 29, 1899. TNA, ADM 1/7833.
[241] "Vickers Sons Maxim: Patents held by the firm as to terms for use of patents by other manufacturers," July 20, 1899. TNA, ADM 1/7833.
[242] Vickers to Admiralty, July 20, 1899. TNA, ADM 1/7833.

This collaboration foreshadows their subsequent efforts to exclude the Coventry Ordnance Works from the British gun market (see Chapter 3).

The negotiation with Vickers triggered further discussion with Armstrongs in 1899 on the status of the 1894 agreement on Elswick Naval Gun Mountings. The Admiralty wrote to Armstrongs in January 1899 asking them to state what patents held by the firm covering any portion of the mountings were in force on April 1, 1894, when each patent would expire, and if any further patents covering the mountings or any part of mountings had been taken out since then and when those patents would expire.[243] Armstrongs was slow to respond, despite a chasing letter in early March and a telegram two weeks later.[244] The firm explained that they found definitively answering some of the questions on patents difficult as "it is much more likely that a rival manufacturer would try to evade our patents than to blindly copy them," and therefore "we are frequently compelled to take out patents to cover ground a little outside certain designs so that an imitator may be prevented not only from exactly copying our design, but also from evading the claims in the patent on which the actual design mainly depends." They enclosed a list of 100 Armstrongs patents connected to guns and mountings, and their dates of application.[245] The Admiralty requested copies of each specification from the Patent Office, plus information on whether they were still in force, "and, if not, which of them have expired or been abandoned."[246] The Patent Office swiftly provided ninety-six specifications, noting that three more were in process and one had been abandoned.[247]

In November the Admiralty wrote to Armstrongs: "My Lords are of opinion that the time has arrived when the subject should be reviewed." This was with an eye to cost cutting. "My Lords are further of opinion that any sliding scale, as in the agreement of 1894, is objectionable, though they are quite prepared to assent to differentiating between mountings made in Ordnance Factories and those made by private firms, other than yours, if the terms of differentiation submitted by you appear to My Lords to be reasonable."[248] The Admiralty wanted new designs for naval gun mountings (other than hydraulic) to be under new terms.[249] The proposals paralleled terms offered to Vickers:

1. When submitting a design for gun mountings &c. the firm to forward a list of the patents they hold (with copies of the specifications) which cover the design or any portion of the same, on which they ask for a

243 MacGregor, Admiralty to Armstrongs, January 3, 1899. TNA, ADM 1/7833.
244 Admiralty to Armstrongs, March 4, 1899; Telegram, Admiralty to Armstrongs, March 14, 1899. TNA, ADM 1/7833.
245 Armstrongs to the Admiralty, March 11, 1899. TNA, ADM 1/7833.
246 MacGregor, Admiralty to Comptroller General, Patent Office, May 8, 1899. TNA, ADM 1/7833.
247 Patent Office to Admiralty, May 16, 1899. TNA, ADM 1/7833.
248 Copy of Admiralty to Elswick, November 11, 1899. TNA, ADM 1/7833.
249 Admiralty to Armstrongs, November 24, 1899. TNA, ADM 1/7833.

royalty, and to name the royalty they would require for the use of each individual patent, for each Mounting manufactured –

(a)   In a Government Establishment

(b)   By a private firm or firms (other than the holder of the patents) manufacturing for the Government.

2.   The Firm to indemnify the Admiralty against all liability in the event of a patent held by the firm on which a royalty is paid, being held to be an infringement of any patent not held by the firm.

3.   The firm to inform the Admiralty immediately after the expiration or abandonment of any of the patents covered by this agreement, so that after the date of such expiration or abandonment no further royalty for use shall be paid.[250]

Armstrongs acknowledged this letter in late November 1899.[251] In April 1900 Noble responded, acknowledging the changes that the Admiralty wanted, but still asking for royalties on whole systems and denying other firms access to their patents. Armstrongs had toughened their stance on competition. Using similar language to Vickers, Noble elucidated:

> In previous discussions upon this subject we have pointed out to their Lordships the enormous cost of our experimental work, and we have frequently stated that our sole wish is to prevent designs which may have cost us thousands of pounds passing, without any trouble or expense, into the hands of rival Contractors, and we trust their Lordships will forgive our citing one or two cases in support of our contention.
>
> The whole of the Hydraulic Mountings of the present day are, with certain modifications, based on our designs. These designs cost us very large sums and much experimental work to perfect them.
>
> The Admiralty agreed to our stipulation that our drawings should not be copied for manufacturing purposes, but it is within our knowledge that a rival manufacturer was permitted to make drawings of all details from the mountings and machinery themselves.
>
> We may cite also the case of the High Angle Mounting. The design was considered so novel that we were informed it could only be adopted after a successful trial of which the expenses were to be borne by us.
>
> The trial was entirely successful, cost us nearly £12,000 and the manufacture was subsequently placed in the hands of another Firm who had incurred no expense at all ....[252]

Noble did not mention that Armstrongs' work on High Angled Mountings was in response to an inquiry from a foreign government, and that the firm had

[250] Enclosure B, "Proposed Arrangement for Future Designs," in Admiralty to Armstrongs, November 24, 1899. TNA, ADM 1/7833.

[251] Armstrongs to Admiralty, November 30, 1899; Armstrongs to Admiralty, January 23, 1900; Admiralty to Armstrongs, January 31, 1900. TNA, ADM 1/7833.

[252] Noble, Armstrongs to Admiralty, April 12, 1900. TNA, ADM 1/7833.

subsequently sold them for use on "a considerable number of vessels, chiefly in foreign navies,"[253] so the firm likely recouped that investment.

Noble's letter sent the Admiralty into a spin. Armstrongs had not accepted their proposal, had made several allegations and had introduced an entirely new issue: overhead royalties. After internal debates, an extensive memorandum dealt with each issue and reported "the mountings referred to as being manufactured by another firm contained other novelties besides the possibility of high angle fire which latter is an extension, under suitable precautions, of the ordinary limit of elevation." Armstrongs' fears of losing technology to a competitor were dismissed as "too remote a contingency to take into consideration." Ultimately, "the increased sources of supply and the advantages to be derived from competition resulting from the employment of additional firms are beneficial to the service .... [I]t is further considered to be undesirable to give any information as to the reasons which induced the Admiralty to accept designs from another firm."[254] The Admiralty was formulating a reply to Armstrongs when a War Office letter suspended the process.[255] The War Office had consulted a patent expert and Honorary Fellow of the Chartered Institute of Patent Agents, James Swinburne.[256] He had denied the validity of Armstrongs' continued claims for royalties on gun mountings for the War Office.[257] As the War Office noted, "It seems that if these questions had been put to the patent expert before, we – and still more, the Admiralty – might have saved large sums."[258] The War Office now wanted to inform Armstrongs that it would pay royalties only for orders made before November 22, 1899, when the patents expired, but wanted to be in step with the Admiralty on this.

An Admiralty file noted:

> The War Office is advised that the last of the firms principal patents expired on 22.11.99 and that no more royalties should therefore be paid on any mountings *ordered* after that date ... this completely alters the aspect of the case so far as the Land Service is concerned. But as pointed out by DGO [Director General of Ordnance] in his minute of 17.5.00 the Admiralty and the War Office made their own terms separately and the opinion of the Solicitor ... seems to be against the prospect of our attaining any legal relief from the Agreement of 1894 until the last patent however small which Elswick held on 1 April 1894 expires.

253 "Elswick Naval Mountings," p. 88; "Naval Summary," p. 143.
254 "Elswick: Gun Mountings Royalties for Patents in Connection With, Statement of Case," April 12, 1900. TNA, ADM 1/7833.
255 Draft Admiralty to Armstrongs, May 30, 1900. "Royalty on Transferable Gun Mountings: Draft reply to E.O.C. letter of 12th April," TNA, ADM 1/7833.
256 Freeth, "Swinburne," p. 260. By 1902 Swinburne was President of the Institution of Electrical Engineers and held "highly original" views on patents and patent laws. *The Electrical Review*, p. 522.
257 Swinburne to War Office, "Armstrong Michell's Claims for Royalties," March 12, 1900. Copy in TNA, ADM 1/7833. Chapter 3 shows that Swinburne would thwart Armstrongs again.
258 Kenyon, War Office DGO, note, April 5, 1900. TNA, ADM 1/7833.

It was proposed to "refer to solicitor for opinion whether the expiring of the 'Ground Patents' releases us."[259] Another note stated: "Mr. Swinburne's report fully confirms the opinion expressed … that royalties should only be paid on the value of the parts covered by valid claims and not on the whole cost of a mounting."[260] While the Admiralty decided to wait for "the results of the proposed War Office communications to Elswick before taking any independent actions," there was speculation about whether the 1894 agreement was valid if the "ground patents" had expired, "although minor patents, dealing with small details might still be in existence. Whether the arrangement would be so construed judicially is open to doubt. But to relations between Elswick & the Admiralty & War Dept may be such as to make the possibility of legal proceedings very remote."[261]

In August 1900 the Admiralty consulted Mr. Swinburne directly, noting that their case was different from the War Office's relating to Land Service mountings because "in several instances the patent specifications of the latter describe in detail the actual arrangement for the parts of such mountings." They asked "whether the claims for royalty on account of the Naval mountings of Elswick patented design are in reality valid or not."[262] In early December, Swinburne sent a series of technical questions about the gun mountings the Admiralty utilized, to which the Admiralty responded.[263] The issue of gun mountings patents continued and is discussed in Chapter 3.

A third track of discussions were begun in 1894 over Admiralty use of Armstrongs drawings for aiming rifles/tubes for Quick Fire guns. A minute notes that: "The Company state that, although these aiming rifles are not patented, the finished design cost them some trouble and money, and they hope that if the system is adopted in Her Majesty's Service they may count upon a considerable order. They remark that the prices they ask are exceedingly moderate."[264] The Admiralty asked the firm for confirmation that once the drawings for aiming rifles had been supplied at a rate of 1*l*. 1*s*. (one pound, one shilling) each, they could be used by the government "as may be considered desirable, in order to enable the articles to be made in the Ordnance Factories or elsewhere, without further reference to the Company."[265] The Firm's response was recorded as:

[259] Note on file, "Royalties on Transferable Gun Mtgs," June 4, 1900. TNA, ADM 1/7833. Emphasis in original.
[260] Note on file, "Royalties on Transferable Gun Mtgs," June 16, 1900. TNA, ADM 1/7833.
[261] Note on file, "Royalties on Transferable Gun Mtgs," June 30, 1900. TNA, ADM 1/7833.
[262] Admiralty to Swinburne, August 25, 1900. TNA, ADM 1/7833. It seems that the Admiralty had not worked with him before.
[263] Swinburne to Admiralty, December 7, 1900; Admiralty to Swinburne, December 24, 1900. TNA, ADM 1/7833.
[264] Armstrongs to the Admiralty, April 5, 1894. "Aiming Rifles for Quick-Firing Guns, designed by Sir W. G. Armstrong & Co., and adopted for use in the Royal Navy: Question of remuneration to Sir W. G. Armstrong & Co., for the use of designs, &c.," p. 4. TNA, ADM 1/7833.
[265] Admiralty to Armstrongs, May 30, 1894. "Aiming Rifles," p. 4. TNA, ADM 1/7833.

they did not intend that the drawings referred to, and for which they quoted at a rate of 1*l*. 1*s*. each, should be shown to rival manufacturers. They remark that, in the course of an interview between Lord Armstrong and Sir A. Noble and the First Lord of the Admiralty a few days previously, the question of the use, by rivals, of designs got out by them was gone into at some length, and their position in this respect was fully explained. They trust that this explanation may be taken into consideration in the present instance.[266]

The Admiralty replied, referring to their proposal:

This procedure had been decided upon for the purpose of avoiding in future the difficulties which had so often arisen as to the settlement of claims for the use of drawings or designs in the Ordnance Factories or by private manufacturers other than the original patentees, and the Admiralty understood that the proposal was concurred in by the Company.

The acceptance of the aiming tubes in question, without previous arrangement as to the terms for the use of the drawings in anyway which might hereafter appear desirable, might lead to a recurrence of what happened with regard to powder cases, recoil carriages for Q.F. guns &c.

The Admiralty, therefore, desire the Company to reconsider the matter, not with special reference to present orders, but to possible future requirements, and remark that, apart from the Company's concurrence in this procedure and the arrangement of terms for use of drawings, &c., they may be reluctantly compelled to abandon the idea of adopting the Company's pattern in this instance.[267]

Armstrongs hastily responded that they had "misunderstood the memorandum of 30th May, and had no intention whatever of avoiding an arrangement with the Admiralty on the subject of future manufacture of their aiming tubes." They enclosed a War Office letter to the firm that proposed differentiated payments, depending on where the aiming tubes (for 6-pr. or 3-pr. Hotchkiss guns) were ordered from and in what numbers, with the most money paid to them – 5*s*., double the cost to the Ordnance Factories – when tubes were "ordered elsewhere than from the Ordnance Factories or themselves." The firm included a sliding scale of payments depending upon the percentages of work undertaken by the Ordnance Factories and themselves. The letter concluded that if the Admiralty accepted those conditions the "Company will furnish working drawings to be used as the Admiralty think best, at the nominal change of 1*l*. 1*s*. per drawing, and they will supply model aiming tubes at the ordinary price quoted in their letter of 5th April."[268] This was accepted by the Admiralty on July 28, 1894.[269] The War Office subsequently noted that as the aiming tube designs were

[266] Armstrongs to Admiralty, June 1, 1894. "Aiming Rifles," p. 4. TNA, ADM 1/7833.
[267] Admiralty to Armstrongs, June 20, 1894. "Aiming Rifles," p. 5. TNA, ADM 1/7833.
[268] Armstrongs to Admiralty, June 25, 1894. "Aiming Rifles," p. 5. TNA, ADM 1/7833.
[269] Admiralty to Armstrongs, June 28, 1894. "Aiming Rifles," p. 5. TNA, ADM 1/7833.

not patented, "a payment of so much per article, would not be, strictly speaking, a royalty, but rather a reward or honorarium to the inventors."[270] The War Office consequently wanted the Admiralty to pay Armstrongs directly, which they agreed to do.[271]

In January 1896 the Admiralty reported to the Treasury that Armstrongs' new pattern aiming rifle for Quick Fire guns from 3-pr. upwards had been introduced to the Navy. As the Admiralty "do not consider it desirable to have to depend on one firm alone for the supply of these aiming rifles," they had "been endeavouring to make equitable arrangements with those contractors for the use of their drawings and patterns, for calling for tenders from other manufacturers, including the Ordnance Factories."[272] The Admiralty proposed that Armstrongs should receive differentiated payments, with any aiming rifles produced at a rival firm earning Armstrongs more.[273] The Admiralty explained to a skeptical Treasury:

> That the proposal that a royalty should be paid for every aiming rifle made by an outside contractor, other than the inventor, appeared to them to be a fair and equitable one. It could hardly be expected that the inventors of a successful plan, while willing to forego their claim to remuneration for the use of the articles manufactured in a Government factory, would agree to make a similar concession in the case of rival manufacturers who would be making profits out of the results of their labour and ingenuity.

Further, "The Elswick Company are not desirous of concluding any arrangement by which competing firms should be put in possession of their drawings and so be in a position to manufacture in competition with Elswick, not only for us, but for foreign governments as well." And "the Company consider that they are entitled to be paid for the use of their drawings on all such articles made by other private firms."[274] The Admiralty had clearly accepted Armstrongs' arguments.

Things became more complicated when the Morris Tube, Ammunition, &c., Company claimed that Elswick pattern aiming rifles were covered by their patents. They had written to Armstrongs in May 1894 to say that a patent of Captain Lloyd and Mr. Haddock (sic), No. 8102 of 1893, appeared to their company "to be a mere putting together of various patented inventions belonging to them, and so covered by or included in the Company's prior patents, and the opinion of Mr. Moulton, Q.C., had confirmed this view."[275] Morris explained to the Admiralty in May 1896 that their claims applied particularly to "aiming

---

[270] War Office to Admiralty, October 26, 1894. TNA, ADM 1/7833.

[271] Admiralty to War Office, October 1, 1895. TNA, ADM 1/7833.

[272] Admiralty to Treasury, January 8, 1896. "Aiming Rifles," p. 7. TNA, ADM 1/7833.

[273] Admiralty to War Office, April 18, 1896. "Aiming Rifles," TNA, ADM 1/7833.

[274] Admiralty to Treasury, April 4, 1896. "Aiming Rifles," p. 8. TNA, ADM 1/7833.

[275] Morris to Captain Lloyd, Elswick, May 7, 1894. Provided to the Admiralty by the Morris Company. TNA, ADM 1/7833.

rifles for Q.F. guns, 12-pr. to 6-in." As a memorandum recorded, Morris now claimed to be entitled to a large measure of favourable consideration from the British Government.[276]

While the Admiralty had approved Armstrongs' aiming rifle designs in July 1895, Elswick had received no orders, even though manufacturing was being carried out in the Ordnance Factories. Armstrongs had initially said that the aiming rifle was not patented, but the Admiralty noted in January 1896 that for the larger guns, "it was thought that the Elswick firm would claim that they were covered by patent No. 8102 of 1893, taken out by Captain Lloyd and Mr. Haddock (sic), the validity of which was questioned by … Morris."[277] That proved to be so, and Armstrongs declared that "Elswick, Q.F. 6-in. to 12-pr. were covered by their patents Nos. 8102 of 1893 and 11325 of 1894."[278]

The Morris Company asked to inspect the Armstrongs' design. This was refused by the Secretary of State in June 1896, but the government undertook a detailed review of the Morris and Elswick patterns and consulted an expert, Dr. Hopkinson, who considered the two firms' patents and drawings.[279] Hopkinson concluded that while the Armstrong patents considered were novel, two – and possibly three – of the Armstrongs drawings infringed a Morris patent.[280] As the Inspector General of Ordnance noted in July 1897: "Although the patent has not long to run, the circumstances mentioned seems to be deserving of consideration, both in regard to possible claims from the Morris Company, and to the question of how much of the Elswick designs is really original, and such as Sir W. G. Armstrong & Co. have valid claim for compensation in regard to."[281]

This led the Ordnance Council to decide that a conference should be arranged "without prejudice, with representatives of the Company," to invite "a confidential interchange of experts' opinions, so that the question as to infringement of patent may be, if possible cleared up before further steps are taken."[282] This took place at the War Office in January 1897, with Armstrongs represented by Mr. John Noble and Mr. Carpmael. Dr. Hopkinson's conclusions about the Elswick infringement of the Morris patent were discussed. The Armstrongs' representatives argued that the Morris claim, if interpreted broadly, was invalid, "being anticipated by Nordenfelt's patent No. 5337 of 1881," which they produced; and if it was interpreted narrowly, the Morris

---

[276] "Aiming Rifles," p. 10. TNA, ADM 1/7833.
[277] Admiralty to Treasury, January 8, 1896. TNA, ADM 1/7833.
[278] Armstrongs to Admiralty, May 14, 1896. TNA, ADM 1/7833.
[279] "Aiming Rifles," comparisons at pp. 11–15, Dr. Hopkinson's consideration at pp. 16–17. TNA, ADM 1/7833.
[280] "Aiming Rifles," pp. 16–17. TNA, ADM 1/7833.
[281] "Memorandum by Inspector-General of Ordnance," July 20, 1896. "Aiming Rifles," p. 17. TNA, ADM 1/7833.
[282] "Proceedings of the Ordnance Council held at the War Office on 27th November 1896." TNA, ADM 1/7833.

claim was invalid because the means Elswick used were different to those in the Morris patent.[283] This contention was then sent to Dr. Hopkinson for his consideration. He noted that he had not known of the Nordenfelt patent when he made his last judgment and concluded of the Morris patent: "On the whole I am of opinion the patent is bad having regard to Nordenfelt's patent No. 5337 of 1881."[284]

In May 1897 the Ordnance Council resolved that the Admiralty's terms to Elswick set out in letters of January 8, 1896 and April 18, 1896 "should be approved," and that "in computing the proportions of orders, and arranging for payments, the term 'aiming rifle' shall be understood to mean the apparatus complete with all necessary fittings and components; and that no payment should be made on account of any spare parts or fittings ordered with the aiming rifles, or separately."[285] This was a victory for Armstrongs, as the Admiralty had threatened to pay royalties only for novel components rather than the whole system.

Turning to business, by 1898 Vickers were reaping the benefits of their expansions, with Thomas Vickers reporting to shareholders that "all the works [were] well supplied with orders" from abroad.[286] Just before the outbreak of the Boer War in 1899, Vickers was planning to deliver guns to the Transvaal Government. According to Albert Vickers, "I went personally to try to see Mr Chamberlain, to tell him that the guns were going out by the next steamer … I did see Lord Ampthill, who told me that they had no power to stop the guns, but that they would be obliged if I delayed them one steamer, which I did."[287] The Vickers-Maxim "Pom-Pom" gun was soon used *against* British forces, a bitter irony because the gun had been developed at the request of the British Army but then disparaged by their artillery experts. "The War in South Africa disproved their evaluation."[288]

In 1899 Armstrongs approached the War Office to ask, given the rising tensions in South Africa, if they should increase their output of shrapnel shell. The War Office said no. However, two months later the Army asked Armstrongs for a fortyfold increase in production of shrapnel shell. In parallel, Vickers, who had never made a field gun for the British military, was given huge orders during the first weeks of the war.[289]

---

[283] "Question of remuneration to Sir W. G. Armstrong & Co., for the use of designs, &c." pp. 3–4. "Aiming Rifles," TNA, ADM 1/7833.

[284] "Question of remuneration to Sir W. G. Armstrong & Co., for the use of designs, &c." pp. 4–5. "Aiming Rifles," TNA, ADM 1/7833.

[285] "Proceedings of the Ordnance Council held at the War Office on 14th May 1897." TNA, ADM 1/7833.

[286] Scott, *Vickers*, p. 81.

[287] Letter Book 31, VA, Doc. 1005, folio 130.

[288] Chinn, *Machine Gun*, pp. 143–44.

[289] Trebilcock, "War," p. 149.

The outbreak of the Boer War was clearly both an opportunity and a crisis for our firms as Britain was ill-prepared for an industrial-scale war. While the government has been blamed for relying on a *laissez-faire* production system and for failing to anticipate the demands imposed by the conflict, the firms bear some responsibility too. As Trebilcock recounted, "in answer to the government's inquiries concerning the emergency armament programme, Trevor Dawson replied that his firm could complete the entire artillery provision of the defence scheme within four years and the entire ammunition allocation within a single year, while Noble, hardly less optimistic, pledged Armstrongs to deliver the whole programme within two years."[290] Soon after the conflict began, both firms realized how naïve their declarations had been.

In a coda to the era, on December 27, 1900, Baron William Armstrong died aged 90. A new phase was beginning at Armstrongs.

Summary

During four decades of growth and expansion, Armstrongs and Vickers developed a suite of strategies designed to see them through good times and bad. First, both firms sought to cultivate relations with British elites and senior government officials. This was far easier for Armstrongs than for Vickers, thanks to the success of Sir William's gun, his subsequent War Office service and his burgeoning relationship with the Royal Family. During the sixteen years when there were no Army orders, Armstrongs' relationship with the War Office languished, but the relationship with the Admiralty strengthened, partly from necessity but also because Armstrongs developed a tactic for improving relations with the naval brass: exchanges of personnel. William White's time with Armstrongs was short, but Armstrong made a good bargain in allowing White to return to the Admiralty while getting Philip Watts in exchange. Armstrongs would repeat this tactic. The firms also began intelligence sharing. At the close of the era, with the outbreak of the Boxer Rebellion in late 1899, Armstrongs gave the British Government information on all the guns they had supplied to China since 1894.[291]

As Vickers became an armament firm it seemed somewhat indifferent to cultivating elites, though this was possibly a defensive response by the Sheffield steelmakers to the snobbery they had encountered or expected to encounter. Again, it was the Admiralty that first forged a relationship with the firm. From the start of the Boer War, a relationship began with the War Office.

In terms of developing relationships with international elites, Armstrongs naturally led for much of this period. They had been crafting foreign policies toward various states and regions, and had assembled a stable of

---

[290] Trebilcock, *Vickers Brothers*, p. 67. Citing *Secret Committee on Reserves*, 1900, TNA, WO A617.
[291] Bastable, *Arms*, p. 216.

ambassador-agents who assisted in cultivating relationships with international leaders. Toward the close of the century, as Vickers entered the international arena, it built upon the relationships of the firms they acquired, especially those of Maxims and Barrow. Inheriting the services of Basil Zaharoff opened many doors internationally for the firm. Moreover, the British obsession with class was not held internationally, so for Vickers the environment was more welcoming. As Vickers came of age, they naturally adopted standard marketing behaviors, but abroad put more emphasis on bribery (see Chapters 6–8).

In terms of interfirm collaboration and collusion, there is more evidence of Vickers' involvement in collusion, in part because as a steel and armor producer it was involved in international pools to obtain patents. These morphed into arrangements to set prices and ensure profits to all members of the pool, not behavior the British Government approved of. More importantly, both firms sought to exclude others from the British market and by the 1890s they were working together to keep the oligopoly tight. This brought them into polite disputes with the government.

Both Armstrongs and Vickers made important diversifications into armaments production, Armstrongs moving from hydraulics and engineering, and Vickers from steel production. Each then made sectoral diversifications into new areas of armaments production. They made successful backward integrations (to obtain steel or coal) and forwards integrations (into ships to carry their guns, and into armor to utilize their steel).

In terms of their organizational cultures, whereas Armstrongs was cautious with money and relied on elite strategies, Vickers prioritized building relations with the financial and banking systems (where class mattered less) and preferred their tried and tested method of innovating during downswings in the market, though they were now complaining that the government had denied them the armament orders to ensure that these investments paid off immediately.

3

Selling Armaments in Britain 1901–1918

Vickers Rises and Armstrongs Responds

The years 1901–18 saw Armstrongs and Vickers face multiple challenges: a surge in orders for the Boer War, prickly relationships with the British Government, a precipitous decline in orders after the war ended, a recession crimping Admiralty procurement plans, and a new surge in orders as another war looked inevitable – capped off by four years of struggle to produce sufficient armaments for the Great War. Initially the two firms were competing fiercely but over time they began to collude on domestic prices and increasingly cooperated in international markets.

Additionally, Armstrongs was experiencing personnel issues. Soon after he became Chairman, Andrew Noble fell gravely ill. The Board considered a government replacement, to tackle what the firm perceived as Admiralty "'hostility in high places.'"[1] Admiral John Fisher (an inveterate gossip) informed journalist Arnold White:

> Quite unknown to me, when Sir Andrew Noble ... was nearly dying lately, the Directors very kindly unanimously proposed to invite me to take his place with his perquisites (that is, Dictator with £10,000 a year!). Although Sir A. Noble has made a wonderful recovery, and the matter is in abeyance at present, it may still come off later on, I think ... *Please don't mention a word of this to anyone*, as Noble, who is a lifelong friend, is very sensitive naturally, and I have heard nothing direct except through the indiscretion of two of the Directors.[2]

With Noble recovered and now a baronet, his sons John and Saxton, son-in-law Alfred Cochrane and former personal secretary John Meade Falkner were all elevated within the firm. Eustace Tennyson d'Eyncourt also rejoined Elswick as their naval architect. Henry Gladstone (Stuart Rendel's son-in-law) joined the Board in 1903, bringing needed business experience.[3] Nevertheless, as Scott tartly reported, Sir William "had both an innate and a trained understanding

---

[1] Scott, *Vickers*, p. 51.
[2] Fisher to White, January 28, 1901. In Marder, *Fear God*, Vol. I, p. 185. Emphasis in original.
[3] *London Gazette*, p. 4738.

81

of financial matters, but he had always sought, and set a high value on professional advice. In all these respects Sir Andrew Noble differed from him."[4]

Noble's high-handed management also led to debilitating fissures in the Board that distracted the firm, affected decision making and inhibited innovation. Stuart Rendel often clashed with Noble over business strategies and the financing of the firm, and was dismayed at Armstrongs increasingly losing out to Vickers. While both firms were advantaged by increased British Government orders, Vickers ultimately capitalized on them more effectively.

In stark contrast to Armstrongs, the organizational culture that evolved at Vickers empowered younger innovators and managers.[5] Thomas Vickers was an effective Chairman, though shareholders "soon came to realise that curiosity was a folly which could not be indulged in pleasantly while this man of iron occupied the chair. In time the enquiring shareholder became as extinct as the dodo, and the annual meeting of Messrs. Vickers was ... compressed within four or five minutes."[6] In 1906 Vincent Caillard became Finance Director, and in 1909 Albert Vickers became Chairman and Trevor Dawson and Douglas Vickers were made Managing Directors.[7] Dawson became Vice Chairman in 1912, helping to see Vickers through the difficult war years.[8] The Vickers Board was packed with talent: "from the family, from banking, from the army and the navy, they brought a mixture of hereditary experience, profound technical knowledge, 'user experience', prudence and alertness .... They were by any standard a formidably able Board of Directors [and] were supported by outstanding technical and production men."[9] The business skill of the firm was its paramount advantage. As Clive Trebilcock noted, "At Vickers, all the board, from the Chairman to the financiers, technologists and designers, would sell if they needed to; at Armstrongs, though there were no specialists, there were no commercial generalists either."[10]

Boer War Production

Vickers 1897 acquisitions had included establishments that proved vital to Boer War production. They owned Maxim's Crayford machine gun works, "the North Kent Iron Works for making shells, ... the former Nordenfelt Works – Erith – for making machine guns, the Birmingham Works for manufacturing cartridge cases, [and] the Dartford factory for ammunition."[11] The Erith plant

4   Scott, *Vickers*, p. 90.
5   Scott, *Vickers*, p. 90.
6   Tweedale, *Steel City*, p. 143. Citing: *Sheffield Daily Telegraph*, October 20, 1915.
7   *The Statist*, p. 672.
8   "Obituary: Commander Dawson."
9   Scott, *Vickers*, p. 79.
10 Trebilcock, *Vickers Brothers*, p. 141.
11 Scott, *Vickers*, p. 48.

was substantially extended. Crayford produced the Maxim Automatic water-cooled .303-inch machine gun for the Army from 1899. The War Office also eventually adopted the converted Maxim machine gun, the "Pom-Pom," a 37 mm one-pounder able to fire sixty rounds per minute up to 1.68 miles.[12] This procurement came after a direct intervention by *de facto* second in command Kitchener, responding to pleas from the field. Fifty were sent to South Africa.

These adoptions by the War Office and the "storm" of British orders meant that Vickers was under immense pressure to create more machinery and produce machine guns, artillery, shells and ammunition at vastly higher levels than ever before.[13] By contrast, at Armstrongs, "The beginning of the Boer War at the end of 1899 made little difference to the Works, except that there was an increased demand for ammunition, and more call on the production of the Shell Department at both Elswick and Scotswood."[14] However, soon both firms were significantly behind in production. In 1900 government inspectors found that Armstrongs' Elswick plant was poorly organized, cramped, inadequately supported by its own supply chain and inefficient. Vickers was judged to be in better shape but nevertheless had production bottlenecks.[15] The two firms reported to the 1903 Royal Commission into the War in South Africa (Elgin Commission) that Armstrongs had spent almost £3 million on capacity between 1896 and 1903 and that Vickers had invested around £2 million between 1898 and 1903.[16]

The Director General of Ordnance admitted to the Elgin Commission that the War Office had assumed that industry "would supply what we wanted from week to week," confessing: "I thought that you could get anything you wanted out of the trade of this country at short notice. I found it was impossible."[17] This illustrates the gulf between the War Office and armament firms. Dawson and Noble (who had overestimated their firms' production abilities in responding to the government in 1900) now appeared before the Elgin Commission, emphasizing that private firms were wary of specifically fitting out factories for government work because orders were simply cut once an emergency passed. They reported, "if they had been in receipt of substantial War Office orders before 1899 it would have enabled them to keep sufficient trained men and machines" to quickly ramp up production to meet Boer War needs.[18] Dawson went much further, advocating that the government reverse policy and give all

---

12 "Pom Poms."
13 Trebilcock, *Vickers Brothers*, pp. 65–66.
14 Fairbairn, *Elswick*, p. 99. Around 1900, 8,200 women were working at Elswick, predominantly in the Finishing Shops, though some operated precision machinery. "Elswick Works, Newcastle, Part 2 (1882–1928)."
15 Trebilcock, "War," p. 146. Citing: "War Office Report on the Current Contracts of Messrs. Armstrong Whitworth and Vickers Maxim, 1900," TNA, WO 32/300 7101/2474.
16 *Minutes of Evidence*, Cd. 1790. Q. 20899 Noble, Q. 20945 Dawson.
17 *Minutes of Evidence*, Cd. 1790. Q. 1732 Maj. Gen. Sir H. Brackenbury.
18 French, *British*, pp. 44–45. Citing *Minutes of Evidence*, Cd. 1790. Q. 20915 Dawson, and Q. 20862 and Q. 20899 Noble.

armaments orders to the private firms, while keeping the Arsenals as a reserve in case of war.[19] Unsurprisingly, this was ignored.

In 1900 Vickers bought an important twenty-five-year licensing agreement from the American firm Electric Boat Co. Ltd to manufacture submarines for the British Empire and European markets.[20] Vickers then signed a deal with the Admiralty agreeing not to sell in Europe – or even discuss the boats – in return for a monopoly over British submarine orders.[21] Submarines were a successful sectoral diversification for Vickers. They innovated from the original John Philip Holland submarine design, patenting many improvements, and producing A, B, C, D and E classes of ever larger, ever faster boats.[22]

When William White's retirement as DNC was announced in 1901, the *Marine Engineer* lamented: "It would be a pity if the Admiralty have to select his successor outside the Corps, for such a course directly implies that the constructors in the Royal Corps are not sufficiently expert marine architects."[23] However, that is what happened. Armstrongs' Philip Watts became DNC in 1902, showing that their elite strategy still worked.

In 1902 Armstrongs purchased the Thames Ammunition Works at Dartford. They also considered overseas diffusions, purchasing a controlling interest in Ansaldo of Italy, though ultimately deciding against a move into North America. By contrast, in 1901 Vickers attempted a bold expansion into the American naval market. Loewe had been scouting out transatlantic opportunities for some time, assessing potential partners and meeting President McKinley.[24] Dawson, James McKechnie a marine architect at Barrow and Albert Vickers toured potential firms.[25] They needed an American face for a Vickers-dominated enterprise because the United States Government would only buy American hardware.[26] Now, working with the Cramp shipyard Vickers sought to merge with Bethlehem Steel. Albert's knowledge of the American steel market and Bethlehem's participation in the Harvey Steel pool underpinned this move. As Thomas Heinrich notes, "by the standards of the military-industrial complex … Cramp-Vickers-Bethlehem would be a virtual behemoth building hulls, engines, armor, and guns for Britain and the United

---

[19] *Minutes of Evidence*, Cd. 1790, Q 20918, Dawson.
[20] Davenport-Hines, "Vickers as," p. 57.
[21] "Contract for the construction of His Majesty's Vessels Submarine Boats Nos. 1–5 [Holland Type] 1902." VA, Doc. 736, p. 1. Vickers skirted this agreement, providing boat specifications to M. Schauenburg in Berlin and suggesting he should work through Electric Boat in America. "Letter book The Electric Boat Company January 10, 1901, to October 1, 1907." VA, Doc. 1003, Folios 245, 259 and 292.
[22] Collier, *Arms*, pp. 73–74; Scott, *Vickers*, p. 67.
[23] "Naval Matters," p. 355.
[24] "Loewe Memorandum on American Visit," 1898. VA, Microfilm 307, Folio 30.
[25] VA Microfilm 307, Folios 1–194.
[26] Trebilcock, *Vickers Brothers*, pp. 137, 139.

States …. No other naval concern, including Armstrong and Brown, built capital ships for two world powers."[27] The deal stumbled on the concerns of one set of American financiers, which opened the door to a press campaign against British ownership of a U.S. shipbuilder.[28] Vickers were unable to complete the deal, but showed their entrepreneurialism, a contrast with Armstrongs' hesitancy.

Vickers also conducted interfirm diplomacy, in 1901 developing a long-term relationship with Deutsche Waffen und Munitionsfabriken (DWM), the Berlin firm of Sigmund Loewe's brother Ludwig. The initial agreement franchised DWM's production of the Maxim Gun, with DWM selling "in Germany and to any other Government (except the British Empire, France and Her Colonies and the USA) guns and various other parts, improvements etc."[29] The profit split strongly favored Vickers.[30] In 1907 the Colt Patent Firearms Company joined what became a cartel dividing the machine gun market between the three firms.

After the turn of the century Armstrongs' connections with the British elite gradually weakened without Sir William's strong relationships. Armstrongs regarded sharing intelligence as a patriotic duty, but it now had the side benefit of shoring up elite relationships. Marshall Bastable notes that after the outbreak of the 1904 Russo-Japanese War, the firm provided the Admiralty with details of the performance of Armstrong-supplied guns used against the Russian fleet at Port Arthur.[31]

In contrast, Vickers' elite relationships grew. Lord Kitchener visited their River Don works in 1902 and "spent considerable time in examining a new quick-firing gun just finished, capable of firing twenty-seven 14lb shots per minute."[32] In August 1903 Princess Louise launched HMS *Dominion* at Barrow, and Vickers issued a commemorative medallion.[33] Trevor Dawson served on several government technical committees, burnishing Vickers' reputation. Vickers' intelligence sharing was patriotic but also for relationship building. The example of this *par excellence* was Dawson. Davenport-Hines notes that Dawson's activities included recruiting a secret agent for the government during the Boer War, and in 1904 providing the War Office with information on Russia's policy in Tibet.[34]

[27] Heinrich, *Ships*, p. 66.
[28] *Philadelphia North American*, "British Gold Seeks the Control of Shipbuilding and Armor Plate Industries by Buying American Plant." VA, Microfilm R 307, Folio 614.
[29] "Agreements with Deutsche Waffen und Munitionsfabriken," Evidence Prepared for the Bankes Commission, p. 1. VA, Doc. 57, Folder 14.
[30] Trebilcock, *Vickers Brothers*, p. 98.
[31] Bastable, *Arms*, p. 216.
[32] "Lord Kitchener," p. 453.
[33] Loewe Papers VA, Doc. 1933, F/2.
[34] Davenport-Hines, "British Marketing," p. 158.

A Collapse in Orders

By 1902 Armstrongs, and particularly Vickers, were experiencing an evaporation of demand. Vickers begged the War Office for orders to keep their plant open. Dawson had reminded the Director of Naval Ordnance: "We have paid very large sums of money in order … to establish ourselves in the ordnance business, and, in addition to this, we have laid out our works at Sheffield, Barrow and Erith for ordnance production … at a very great cost to ourselves, amounting to upwards of a million sterling."[35] The government was unmoved by these appeals. Armstrongs and Vickers therefore began to collude to exclude other firms from the British armament market, resisting the government's intention to expand its range of suppliers.[36]

Warship building was hit. In 1902 the First Lord of the Admiralty, Lord Selborne, was a guest in Sheffield, and the Lord Mayor pointedly asked when orders for armor plate would be placed for the recently approved battleships. Lord Selborne ignored the question, but when he visited Vickers and other steelmakers, "the silent testimony of unused forges, idle plant, motionless machinery, and workshops empty of workers must have appealed to his Lordship … eloquently."[37] The Selborne program had planned for firms to construct seven battleships and first-class cruisers per year until 1906–07, but by 1908–09 this had been whittled down to one battleship and one battle cruiser annually.[38] Armstrongs and Vickers' response was to collude with other firms on armor plate prices.[39] As Falkner noted in 1901, without "the convention" controlling supply and keeping prices at around £115 (£15,711 in August 2022) per ton, the competitive selling price would have been around £40 (£5,465 in August 2022) a ton.[40] The Admiralty was somewhat sympathetic and endorsed the firms' "arrangement" for armor plate orders, which shared profits to keep them all in business.[41] Others were less understanding. The *Times* reported in 1906 that Britain was paying roughly 40 percent more per ton for armor plate than the United States, adding about $100,000 to the cost of a *King Edward VII*-type vessel.[42]

With the collapse of orders, Vickers' profits had slipped to 10 percent by 1903 and Armstrongs experienced a similar reversal.[43] However, the way the firms

[35] Dawson to Admiralty, July 20, 1899. "Director of Naval Ordnance, Correspondence and Papers," TNA, ADM 1/7833.
[36] Trebilcock, *Vickers Brothers*, p. 91.
[37] Letter to the Editor, April 21, 1902, *British Trade Journal*, May 1, 1902, p. 185.
[38] Sumida, *Defence*, p. 186.
[39] On keeping different company's prices close, see: VA, Doc. 1006A, Folio 422.
[40] Bastable, *Arms*, p. 214. Citing: Falkner to Vickers, July 16, 1901. TWA, 31/7033.
[41] Barker to Falkner, Letter Book No. 33 VA, Doc. 1006A, Folio 163–64; VA, Doc 1006, Folios 251–52 and 255 confirm that the ring for bidding on contracts had stood for "many years."
[42] Cited in: "Armor Plate," p. 1225.
[43] Trebilcock, "'Special Relationship,'" p. 366, ff.1. Citing: *Arms and Explosives*, Monthly Trade Report, 1903–05; Tweedale, *Steel City*, p. 128 and profits table 3.1, pp. 124–25.

reacted was completely different. Vickers' continued their organizational culture of investing during downturns. The firm invested £2.25 million in plant
and machinery between 1898 and 1903, including aping the newly amalgamated
Cammell Laird in establishing a metallographic laboratory and bringing in the
metallurgist J. H. S. Dickenson in 1903.[44] These developments were funded by
multiple share issues between 1899 and 1903, which "raised the issued capital
from £2,500,000 to over £5,000,000."[45]

Vickers also acquired half the ordinary share capital of Beardmores, the
Scottish warship and armor plate makers. Armstrongs decided against investing, fearing Vickers was trying to get it to share Beardmores' substantial debts.
There are disagreements over Vickers' motives for this investment. Trebilcock
emphasizes the firm's interests in preserving market share by preventing
Beardmores' planned move into ordnance.[46] However, as Beardmores was
also heavily indebted to Vickers, Scott considers that Albert Vickers may have
wanted to secure that investment.[47] The Admiralty is said to have encouraged
Vickers to invest because they feared Beardmores would fail (as others had),
disrupting the supply of warships.[48] Regardless, "Beardmores were not only
removed as … a direct competitive threat but converted into a valuable defensive screen for the larger firm: in 1904 the Clydeside works executed a useful
diversionary manoeuvre by submitting its 'own' designs for the important
artillery rearmament contracts."[49]

Both firms undertook some diversifications. Armstrongs moved into manufacturing cars and trucks, buying Wilson Pilcher in 1904 (without the knowledge of the full Board!).[50] Initially they shipped parts in from Paris for assembly
at Elswick. Later Scotswood became involved in car design and manufacture,
facilitating the invention, by Major Walter Wilson, of the petrol-engine,
armored gun tractor.[51] Armstrongs also contemplated a backward integration
into steel through an association with Hadfields of Sheffield, but after considering the move for three years it was rejected by the Board in 1907.

Vickers also diversified into car production, acquiring Wolseley in 1902
and creating the Wolseley Tool and Motor Car Company. This was a forward
integration to use their forgings and steels.[52] They installed motor car pioneer
Herbert Austin as General Manager.[53] While a far diversification into civilian

[44] Tweedale, *Steel City*, p. 109.
[45] Scott, *Vickers*, p. 81.
[46] Trebilcock, *Vickers Brothers*, pp. 91–93.
[47] Scott, *Vickers*, p. 49.
[48] Hume and Moss, *Beardmore*, p. 52.
[49] Trebilcock, *Vickers Brothers*, p. 92.
[50] Warren, *Armstrongs*, p. 146; Irving, "New Industries," pp. 154–56; 164.
[51] "Elswick Works, Newcastle, Part 2 (1882–1928)."
[52] Tweedale, *Steel City*, p. 105.
[53] Warren, *Armstrongs*, p. 146.

production, it seems that the "Board had half an eye on the military possibilities: 'Such self-propelled machines' they believed 'must be of great use in future
military operations.'"[54] This was the origin of Vickers' involvement with military transport, leading eventually into innovative work on tanks.

Royalty Negotiations

Negotiations over government royalties on Elswick-patented gun mountings
dragged on and became a vehicle for Armstrongs to try to exclude competitors
from this market. In 1900 the Admiralty had sent a list of 100 Armstrongs gun
mounting patents to James Swinburne. He submitted a twenty-six-page document demolishing most of Armstrongs' patent claims. His summary was brutal:

> Of all the hundred patents there is only one which covers anything in the
> mountings, and is apparently valid …. This is only a detail of one mount-
> ing, and not a matter on which a royalty on the whole mounting or any
> sort of general monopoly in mountings should be based. The other patents
> are mostly irrelevant, but those which are relevant are generally invalid,
> and often even these cover only unimportant details in the mountings in
> question. In my opinion the broad claims for royalties are not valid.[55]

The War Office waited impatiently for the Admiralty to decide their next
steps.[56] The Admiralty were debating three things. First, how to terminate
the 1894 Agreement. Second, the question of up to what date royalties should
be paid: Should this be the date of termination or the date the ground patent
expired? Third, whether to reclaim from Armstrongs royalties paid on patents
termed invalid by Swinburne. Admiralty Solicitor R. B. D. Ackland provided
the legal opinion. The first issue was easily solved; a letter would be sent notifying the firm that the Admiralty was terminating the 1894 Agreement. On
the issue of royalties, Ackland declared, "so long as the Agreement exists the
Admiralty are bound under the Agreement of 1894 to continue to pay Royalties
with reference to Patents which Mr. Swinburne has advised are invalid." And
he thought the Admiralty could not recover royalties already paid.[57] Ackland
subsequently elucidated:

> Speaking generally money paid under a mistake of *fact* can be recovered
> back. It would be incumbent on the Admiralty to prove that as a matter of
> fact the articles manufactured by them were not covered by the patents.

[54] Scott, *Vickers*, p. 83.
[55] Swinburne to Admiralty, "Armstrong Mitchell's Claims for Royalties," January 16, 1901.
  TNA, ADM 1/7833.
[56] "Royalties on Elswick Patents: Applications from War Office," April 7, 1901. TNA, ADM
  1/7833.
[57] Ackland, "Sir W. G. Armstrong & Co's claim to Royalties on Gun Mountings for which
  they hold Patents: Opinion," May 23, 1901. TNA, ADM 1/7833.

This no doubt would be contested and the Admiralty would be obliged to remove the suspicion which would be sure to exist in the mind of the tribunal that the Admiralty, with all the skilled technical opinion at their disposal would not have paid unless they actually made use of the patents.[58]

This was a powerful point against seeking to recover royalties.

The Admiralty noted the War Office intention to act in tandem in writing to Armstrongs to terminate the agreement. On the issue of reclaiming money from Armstrongs, "It may be noted that the War Office do not propose to reclaim any payments already made."[59] This was because the War Office recognized that "as ... we tacitly admitted the validity of the Armstrongs patents it is now too late to dispute it."[60] The Admiralty also noted, "It may well be argued by Elswick that the agreement is the basis for payment and until it is cancelled payment is due. In case of the Firm arguing this point it would appear that to contest it would involve exactly the same difficulties as the Solicitor anticipates in recovering payments already made."[61] A year later the Admiralty was still debating these issues, with draft letters prepared in January and April 1902, the latter draft was shared with the War Office, who agreed to it in May.[62]

It was not until June 1902 that the government was ready to make a new patent arrangement with Armstrongs for transferrable gun mountings.[63] The Admiralty wrote to Armstrongs on July 10, 1902, terminating the 1894 arrangement and notifying them that a final payment would be made for the period April 1, 1899, to October 22, 1899, "in view of the fact that the ground patents for the Mountings in question expired on 22 October 1899." The Admiralty advocated that the firm accept the new terms, declaring: "Your suggestion that the Admiralty should pay an overhead Royalty upon the total value of an order, whether the design be wholly or partially patented or not, would appear to be entirely separate from the question existing between a sliding scale Royalty and the fixed Royalty." The Admiralty closed with some moral pressure: "[T]he new terms are put forward with the intention of conceding so far as the Public Interest allows every possible consideration to a firm whose

[58] Ackland, "Armstrong's Patents: Further Opinion," June 3, 1901. TNA, ADM 1/7833. Emphasis in original.
[59] Notes of August 8, 1901, "Royalties on Gun Mountings Payable to Messrs. Sir W. G. Armstrong & Co. Adjudication on the validity of the patents for mountings upon which royalty is payable." TNA, ADM 1/7833.
[60] Brackenbury, War Office DGO [Director General of Ordnance], note May 17, 1900. TNA, ADM 1/7833.
[61] Note by Director of Naval Ordnance, August 23, 1901, "Royalties on Gun Mountings." TNA, ADM 1/7833.
[62] Two drafts: Admiralty to War Office, April 15, 1902; Fleetwood Wilson, War Office to Admiralty, May 13, 1902. In "Royalties on Transferable Gun Mountings," TNA, ADM 1/7833.
[63] War Office, "New Arrangement for Payment of Royalties," June 18, 1902. TNA, ADM 1/7833.

designs may be adopted."[64] The letter laid out the terms the Admiralty wanted for royalties on future Elswick designs and, reflecting government learning, were designed to preempt patent disputes:

1. When submitting a design for gun mountings &c. the firm to forward a list of the patents they hold (with copies of the specifications) which cover the design or any portion of the same, on which they ask for a royalty, and to name the royalty they would require for the use of each individual patent, for each Mounting manufactured –
   (c) In a Government Establishment
   (d) By a private firm or firms (other than the holder of the patents) manufacturing for the Government.
2. The Firm to distinctly understand, however, that all enquiries and replies will in no way prejudice the rights of the Crown as regard the terms on which the inventions will be [taken] should they be adopted for His Majesty's service, and also that the use of patents held by the Firm would not be postponed [by] settlement of terms.
3. The Firm to indemnify the Admiralty against all liability in the event of any patent held by the firm on which a royalty is paid, being held to be an infringement of any patent not held by the firm.
4. The firm to inform the Admiralty immediately after the expiration or abandonment of any of the patents covered by this agreement, so that after the date of such expiration or abandonment no further royalty for use shall be paid.[65]

The War Office sent an identical letter to Elswick. Six months later they had received no response, and the Admiralty informed Armstrongs that "an answer is urgently needed."[66]

In their reply Armstrongs resisted the Admiralty's plan: "We respectfully submit that it would be most unfair to this Firm to antedate the period of the notice, and we consider we should be paid on all mountings the orders for which were given out prior to the date of the letter under reply."[67] Noble continued:

As regards the future, we are quite prepared to place every design we have at the disposal of the Admiralty for manufacture, either in the Government Establishment or by Messrs. Vickers Sons and Maxim free of any royalty, but we submit that so long as these three Establishments, who

---

[64] Admiralty to Armstrongs, "New Arrangement for Payment of Royalties," July 10, 1902. TNA, ADM 1/7833.

[65] Idem. Apart from 2. this is identical to the terms proposed by the Admiralty in Enclosure B, Admiralty to Elswick, November 11, 1899 (elsewhere dated as November 24, 1899). In "Elswick Royalties, Aiming Rifles," TNA, ADM 1/7833.

[66] War Office to Admiralty, December 17, 1902, and Admiralty to Armstrongs, December 31, 1902. TNA, ADM 1/7833.

[67] Armstrongs to Admiralty, January 12, 1903. "Payment of Royalties on Transferable Gun Mountings," TNA, ADM 1/7833.

both like ourselves spend very large sums on experiments, are in a position to meet all the requirements of the Admiralty, we should not be asked
to allow our designs to be spread broadcast among rival manufacturers.[68]

This was a concerted effort from Armstrongs and Vickers to exclude other firms
from the gun mountings business.[69] As Trebilcock records, "a free exchange of
their designs for British work, each abdicating its royalty rights ... was the first
step in a process of wide-ranging conciliation" for Armstrongs and Vickers.[70]

The proposal from Armstrongs would keep the oligopoly tight, giving the
government few opportunities to bring in new innovators or control prices
through competition. Within the government there was nevertheless some
relief that the "new arrangement" with Armstrongs and Vickers would significantly simplify the royalties question – because none would need to be paid.[71] A
War Office memorandum complacently noted:

> As regards the future, if it is considered that Elswick, Woolwich and Vick-
> ers between them will be able to easily meet all requirements, and will fur-
> nish sufficient competition to keep prices down to reasonable figures, the
> Firm's proposal to charge no royalty if orders are confined to these three
> might perhaps be accepted. If later on it were found necessary to go out-
> side those three sources, some arrangement would have to be made with
> the Firm for use of any of their patents involved, and could best be done, it
> is considered, by direct negotiation in each case when it occurs.[72]

Fleetwood Wilson of the War Office noted in September 1904 that "It seems
important to keep a firm hand as to bringing in outside firms if at any time such a
course is necessary in the public interest. But at present the balance of advantage
lies in completing orders as approved to the two firms & to Ordnance Factories."[73]

The Admiralty accepted the advice of the Treasury Solicitor that they must
pay royalties for the period between April 1, 1899, and July 10, 1902, even though
the ground patent had expired in October 1899 and the remaining patents were
considered "invalid" by Swinburne.[74] The Admiralty then informed the War
Office that it planned to pay royalties for those three years.[75] The War Office

[68] Armstrongs to Admiralty, January 12, 1903. "Payment of Royalties on Transferable Gun
Mountings," TNA, ADM 1/7833.
[69] "Vickers and the British Admiralty," in "Vickers Limited and Vickers-Armstrongs Limited, Particulars of Licences," p. 1, VA, Doc. 58, Folder 24.
[70] Trebilcock, *Vickers Brothers*, p. 95.
[71] Memorandum, "Elswick: Royalties on Transferable Mountings, Termination of 1894
Agreement, Remarks on," January 12, 1903. TNA, ADM 1/7833.
[72] War Office Memorandum, April 20, 1903. "Payment of Royalties on Transferable Gun
Mountings," TNA, ADM 1/7833.
[73] War Office, Fleetwood Wilson Memorandum, September 18, 1904. "Payment of Royalties
on Transferable Gun Mountings," TNA, ADM 1/7833.
[74] Admiralty discussion, April 20, 1903. "Payment of Royalties on Transferable Gun Mountings"; Admiralty to War Office, February 6, 1905. TNA, ADM 1/7833.
[75] Admiralty to War Office, February 6, 1905. TNA, ADM 1/7833.

grudgingly agreed to do the same.[76] Consequently, in April 1905 the Admiralty paid Armstrongs a final sum of £19,536-13-11 for mountings made by Woolwich between April 1899 and July 1902.[77] Noble accepted the payment.[78] It had taken Armstrongs six years to get these final royalties.[79] Nevertheless, the issue of bringing in new firms still lingered.

Relations with the Government

While Vickers' connections with government elites were growing, there were sometimes problems in the relationship. For example, in December 1904 Trevor Dawson inadvertently made an enemy of Secretary of State for War, H. O. Arnold-Forster. Dawson had complained directly to Prime Minister Balfour that Vickers' completion of the new Field Gun contract had been delayed by the War Office's failure to deliver drawings. Balfour used that information during a Cabinet meeting, to the chagrin of Arnold-Forster. While in November 1904 Arnold-Forster had written to his subordinate Sir James Wolfe Murray criticizing his failure to properly supervise the progress of the Field Gun, to Balfour Arnold-Foster laid the blame outside of his department.[80]

Dawson was swiftly called to a meeting with Arnold-Forster, who complained that Dawson had not brought these concerns directly to him. Dawson, however, "continued to impress upon the Secretary of State that in his interview with the Prime Minister, he made no complaint against the War Office for this delay. He, however, did his best to evade the question put to him by the S. of S." and "eventually admitted that it would have been better had he reported the non-delivery of the drawings and the probable delay in the execution of the orders, to Mr. Arnold-Forster."[81] Arnold-Forster then wrote to privately to Balfour:

> Yesterday I saw Dawson of Vickers'. You will remember, at any rate I do, how you quoted him the other day and brought him up as a witness to the delays and the improvidence of the War Office. I was rather sorry you did this because I know Dawson pretty well, and I should have preferred to have an opportunity of examining the charge before it was repeated in the presence of all my colleagues. I feel confident both you and they would have taken a somewhat different view of the matter if Dawson had told you all the facts.[82]

[76] War Office to Admiralty, March 1, 1905. TNA, ADM 1/7833.
[77] Admiralty to Armstrongs, March 15, 1905. TNA, ADM 1/7833.
[78] Noble, Armstrongs to Admiralty, March 17, 1905. TNA, ADM 1/7833.
[79] In 1905 Armstrongs was at the High Court fighting demands for royalties from William Edward Corrigall. They succeeded. Cutler, "Corrigall v. Armstrong," p. 268.
[80] Arnold-Forster Confidential letter to Sir J. Wolfe Murray, November 25, 1904. BL, Arnold-Forster Papers Vol. LV (XV), Folios 227–33.
[81] Interview between Lieutenant Dawson (of Vickers, Sons, & Maxim) and Mr. Arnold-Forster, December 21, 1904. BL, Arnold-Forster Papers Vol. LV (XV), Folios 164–65.
[82] Arnold-Forster private letter to Balfour, "New Field Gun: Delay in Supplying Drawings to Messrs. Vickers." December 21, 1904. BL, Arnold-Forster Papers Vol. LV (XV), Folio 143.

He then proceeded to lay out those "facts," including claiming that the lack of detailed drawings made no difference. However, Arnold-Forster was subsequently proved wrong by his own staff, who reported that Vickers had needed Armstrongs' detailed drawings and received them later than other contractors, so orders were delayed. However, this fact was never made public.[83]

Dawson's chastisement was not the end of the issue, though. In 1905, when production of the New Field Gun and Carriages fell behind, a government report showed that although all the contractors were behind, Vickers' performance was worse than Armstrongs' and the Ordnance Factories' but was on a par with Cammell Lairds'.[84] Arnold-Forster wrote to his staff, "The delay at first sight appears to be solely due to the default of the manufacturers." He suggested that stiff fines should be levied.[85] The next Master General of the Ordnance minute focused solely on Vickers' slow production, ignoring Cammell Lairds' problems. While agreeing that under the gun contract a fine could be in order, the Master General of the Ordnance mildly recommended that Vickers be warned that without satisfactory reasons for the delay a fine would be levied.[86] Arnold-Forster's minute in response suggests that he had not forgiven Dawson:

> I agree with the action proposed at 'A' [a fine] but I take a strong view on this case. This firm has constantly professed its readiness and ability to perform any kind of work we choose to entrust to them. They have urged us to add to their orders, and we have done so. They have constantly endeavoured to impress us with the magnitude of their operations and the success of their methods. Relying upon these representations, we have entrusted a large share of a very important order to the Company, & the first result is that they break down sooner & more completely than any other manufacturer …. If there had been a war, the position would have been most serious. Explanations should be asked for, but a mere statement that "the firm has experienced difficulties in obtaining material from their sub-contractors", or that they have been "unsuccessful in obtaining sound castings", should not be accepted as adequate excuses.[87]

Clearly, the relationship between Arnold-Forster and Vickers had broken down. Nevertheless, that year the King and Queen visited Vickers during a visit

---

[83] Master General of the Ordnance's Minute to the Secretary of State, December 24, 1904. BL Arnold-Forster Papers Vol. LV (XV), Folio 21.

[84] Report from Master General of the Ordnance, August 1905. BL, Arnold-Forster Papers Vol. LV (XV), Folio 197.

[85] "New Field Gun Delay in Deliveries. Default of Contractors." Arnold-Forster Minute to Master General of the Ordnance, October 7, 1905. BL, Arnold-Forster Papers Vol. LV (XV), Folios 167–68.

[86] H. Williams Master General of the Ordnance (c) to Arnold Forster, Vickers' Delay in Delivery of Guns and Carriages, October 11, 1905. BL, Arnold-Forster Papers Vol. LV (XV), Folio 170.

[87] Minute by Arnold-Forster, October 24, 1905. BL, Arnold-Forster Papers Vol. LV (XV), Folio 170.

to Sheffield, and a large Admiralty party attended a cruiser launch.[88] Arnold-Forster left office when the Balfour government was dissolved in December, but Vickers' relationship with the War Office remained strained.

This became obvious when the War Office and Admiralty encouraged the newly formed Coventry Ordnance Works (created by Cammell Laird, Fairfield and Browns) to bid on contracts for guns, gun mountings and armor.[89] The War Office practice of including patented aspects of weapons into their own designs and sharing the results with rival firms continued too, with two of the Royal Ordnance's quick-firing artillery pieces using Armstrongs barrels, Vickers recoil systems and Royal Ordnance sighting and elevating gears.[90] "When Vickers and Armstrongs pleaded that they and Woolwich should monopolize production in order to recover development costs, the War Office insisted on the rival Coventry Ordnance Works taking a share of orders."[91]

At Armstrongs, according to Admiral Fisher's correspondence with Private Secretary to the King, Viscount Knollys, (and therefore with the King), in 1905 Noble made a "frightfully secret" attempt to recruit him: "I may explain SECRETLY that an immense combination of the greatest shipbuilding, armour-plate, and gun-making firms in the country are willing to unite under my presidency (and practical dictatorship!) and I fancy I would have about £20,000 a year, as I see my way to double their dividends." The monarch was opposed. Fisher therefore remained as First Sea Lord, being compensated "with the Order of Merit in June on the King's initiative."[92] Fisher remained a friend to Armstrongs though, in April 1906 writing to Noble:

> SECRET
>
> I must discourage you about 20 12-inch guns at present. I suppose that never has such thought been given to fighting considerations as in designs of *Dreadnought* and *Invincible* class. Well, we are going further next year, in a quite new design, and the tendency will be to reduce the ten 12-inch guns of the *Dreadnought* to the 8-inch of the *Invincible*, as getting the most fighting work for the money ... with the 8 inch guns differently arranged than in *Invincible*, you will get 100 percent of them on the broadside, and a battleship action will be a broadside action, for inevitably and surely the faster fleet will assume this formation in the crowning moment of victory.

---

[88] Vickers Ltd. Visit of HM King and Queen, 1905. SLSL, 338.45SF. Albert Vickers to J. D. Siddeley, September 19, 1905. VA, Doc. 1004.

[89] Lyon, "Relationship," p. 43; Davenport-Hines, "British Marketing," pp. 150–51.

[90] Wilson and Lewendon, *The Gun*, p. 65. Cited in Stevenson, *Armaments*, p. 26.

[91] Stevenson, *Armaments*, p. 26; "Correspondence with the War Office re Horse and Field Artillery Requirements," VA, Doc. 800.

[92] Fisher to Knollys, March 3, 1905. In Marder, *Fear God*, Vol. II, p. 53. Bastable dismisses Fisher's account as a "fantasy" and "part of his machinations at the Admiralty." Bastable, *Arms*, p. 238.

Ever yours,
J.F.
BURN THIS
But if you have some wonderful plan for getting 20 12-inch guns on broad-
side, then all right![93]

Clearly, this information would save Armstrongs effort and enable them to be
ready to compete for 8-inch gun contracts.

In 1906 Dawson was invited to a late-night meeting at the Admiralty and asked
whether Vickers and their associates might be "disposed" to buy Whiteheads
to ensure it remained in British hands. Dawson thought this likely, and Vickers
and Armstrongs each acquired a quarter of Whiteheads shares for £200,272
(£27,065,899 in August 2022), securing control of the torpedo works in Fiume
(Austria) and Weymouth.[94] This was a sectoral diversification for both firms,
though Armstrongs already had some experimental work on superheaters underway. Unfortunately, in a classic change of fortunes, "having purchased more than
600 torpedoes in FY [fiscal year] 1905–1906, and more than 550 in FY 1906–1907,
the Admiralty ordered just 113 in FY 1907–1908."[95] This hurt Whiteheads – and by
extension Armstrongs and Vickers – badly. Epstein considers that Armstrongs'
June 1908 threat to claim a patent infringement by an Admiralty employee was
likely a ploy to garner more torpedo orders.[96] Patent expert Swinburne concluded
that Armstrongs' claim that Hardcastle's torpedo superheater infringed their patent failed for "want of subject matter" thwarting them once again.[97]

Dawson continued to provide intelligence to the government. In 1907 he provided Prime Minister Henry Campbell-Bannerman with a letter from Albert
Vickers in Zurich which recounted: "To our surprise on coming out of the dining room last night we met Mr. Schauenberg. He says that Germany is secretly
preparing for war, that they have ordered the materials (uniforms &c.) for the
equivalent of 20,000 reserve officers. Some of our own people might like to
know this." According an explanatory note: "Mr. Schauenberg was employed by
the Govt. through the agency of Lt. Dawson in the Boer War on very secret work
and is absolutely trustworthy."[98] Schauenberg is likely Dawson's secret agent.

[93] Fisher to Noble, April 14, 1906. In Marder, *Fear God*, Vol. II, pp. 74–75. On the admonition
      to "BURN THIS," Arnold White informed the second Lord Fisher: "His 'burn and destroy'
      meant 'publish as widely as possible, but don't give me away.'" Marder, *Fear God*, Vol. I,
      p. 355.
[94] Dawson recounted this story at the February 1931 Whiteheads annual dinner. VA, Doc. 58,
      Folder 85.
[95] Epstein, *Torpedo*, p. 115.
[96] Epstein, *Torpedo*, p. 116.
[97] Epstein, *Torpedo*, p. 121, ff. 47. Nevertheless, Armstrongs sued in 1922, when they were in
      desperate straits.
[98] Albert Vickers in Zurich to Dawson, January 4, 1907. BL, Campbell-Bannerman Papers
      Vol. XXVI, Folio 112 and calling card of Lieut. Dawson, Folio 111.

Another example of Dawson's intelligence sharing subsequently came to light. Admiral Sir Reginald Bacon recalled that in 1909, when he was Director of Naval Ordnance, he heard from Dawson

> that Krupp was a member of the Nickel Syndicate in Europe and all the members of the Nickel Syndicate were supposed to place their orders to Nickel through the Syndicate. Instead of that they heard, and found out, that Krupp had placed a very large order for nickel outside. The only infer-ence to be drawn from that, as nickel was almost entirely used either for gun or armament manufacture, was that Krupp was laying up secretly a large supply of Nickel .... Naturally I passed on the information to the First Lord of the Admiralty and the information proved correct.[99]

Admiral Fisher passed the information to the King.[100] Vickers' strategy of intelligence sharing was appreciated, and Dawson was knighted in December 1909.[101]

Despite these strong relationships there was another precipitous decline in government armament orders between 1907 and 1910. Albert Vickers declared to shareholders that "The Company's finance has been seriously inconve-nienced by the lean years which commenced with the cessation of demand at the conclusion of the Transvaal War."[102] The lower domestic orders were reflected in the reduced dividends paid by Vickers, Armstrongs and other firms.[103] Indeed, between 1908 and 1910 Armstrongs made no provisions for depreciation (reducing values to reflect wear and tear on machinery) in order to maintain a 10 percent dividend and mask the effects of the recession.[104] Falkner noted privately in 1908, "Our order list is very small; and today we got our tender for 108 4 mountings refused ... I suppose Coventry [Ordnance Works] will have taken most."[105]

Early Airpower Work

Vickers now undertook a sectoral diversification into airpower. In 1908, prompted by the Admiralty (who were ahead of the Committee of Imperial Defence), Vickers began work on airships under the direction of Director of Naval

[99] "Allegations Re War Scares and Armament Firms' Endeavours to Defeat Reductions in Armaments," VA, Doc. 58, Folder 73, p. 31.
[100] Fisher to Sir Arthur Davidson, March 27, 1909. In: Marder, *Fear God*, Vol. II, p. 236.
[101] *London Gazette* 28321, December 24, 1909, p. 9763. At: www.thegazette.co.uk/London/issue/28321/page/9763.
[102] Trebilcock, *Vickers Brothers*, p. 78. Citing: *Arms and Explosives*, April 1909.
[103] Trebilcock, "Special Relationship," p. 366, ff.1. Citing: *Arms and Explosives*, Monthly Trade Report, 1903–05.
[104] Irving, "New Industries," pp. 152 and 170.
[105] Falkner to Saxton Noble, November 17, 1908. TWA, DF/NOB/3/2/1.

Ordnance Captain Reginald Bacon.[106] More daringly, as he was an evangelist for heavier-than-air designs, Hiram Maxim continued some independent work on airplanes, which Albert Vickers paid for as "the company itself are not prepared to spend more money on it."[107] The Admiralty sent Vickers specifications for the lighter-than-air Rigid Naval Airship No. 1.[108] Vickers had already bought the patent rights to Duralumin and roughly estimated costs at £30,000 (£3,969,016 in August 2022) for all the materials, with the firm paying for the housing for airship construction. Albert noted, "No allowance is made in the above process for experiments, &c."[109] Bacon reviewed the estimates and reported: "I am of opinion they will not manufacture the hull for this sum owing to the entirely new nature of the work and the very careful workmanship required. It is largely the advertisement and confidence in future orders which causes them to tender moderately and supply [the] £20,000 shed for nothing."[110] The Admiralty accepted the estimate and provided further specifications to Vickers, noting: "You are to be responsible for the general structural efficiency of the ship and the attainment of the guaranteed power of the engines, but My Lords do not hold you in any way responsible for the general performance of the vessel, her manoeuvring or the speed she may practically obtain."[111] If Vickers were thinking that any deficits would be made up by future orders, they were to be disappointed.

The Admiralty carefully drew up the contract: "[T]here should be proper safeguards for the immediate and possibly ultimate interests of the Admiralty, in the event of contingencies arising in the course of carrying out the contract, and of the placing of future contracts. The experience of similar arrangements in connection with the construction of submarines, to which the DNO referred, should be had in mind."[112] Also, as Vickers were working alongside Admiralty officers, both sides needed guidelines over patents. The Admiralty drew up a two-year agreement which noted: "8. Developments in aeronautics are expected to be very rapid. Patents will sometimes have to be taken out quickly to prevent their being forestalled. To avoid any delay the Inspecting Captain of Airships will represent the Admiralty and can be approached at any time with regard to joint patents."[113]

---

[106] Admiralty to Vickers Sons & Maxim, August 14, 1908; Vickers to Admiralty, April 22, 1909. "Naval Airship No. 1: Tender & Contract Papers etc. Vickers Ltd. 1909–1914," TNA, AIR 1 2306/215/15.

[107] Telegram, Albert Vickers to Maxim, December 1, 1909. Letter Book 31, VA 1005, folio 53; Andrews and Morgan, *Vickers Aircraft*, pp. 1–4.

[108] "SECRET: Vickers Sons & Maxim Ltd. Specification for H.M. Airship No. 1 L," TNA AIR 1/2464.

[109] Albert Vickers to Captain Bacon, Admiralty, September 8, 1908. TNA, AIR 1/2306/215/15.

[110] Bacon memorandum. September 9, 1908. TNA, AIR 1/2306/215/15.

[111] Admiralty to Vickers, March 9, 1909. TNA, AIR 1/2306/215/15.

[112] Note on file, September 9, 1908. "Contract for Construction of Airship," TNA, AIR 1/2306/215/15.

[113] Admiralty to Vickers Sons & Maxim, March 10, 1910, "Air-Ship patents. Suggested heads for an Agreement with Messrs. Vickers Sons and Maxim," TNA, AIR 1/2306/215/15.

Development, design and production of Rigid Naval Airship No. 1 was a painful process and involved many setbacks. Vickers had to master completely new areas of materials science, aerodynamics, technology and sophisticated theoretical mathematics. The airship, known as *Mayfly*, was a problematic build and ultimately unsuccessful, fatally breaking her back when caught by a gust of wind exiting the shed at Barrow (assistant H. B. Pratt had calculated this outcome, but was ignored).[114] The Admiralty ordered no more and in 1912 Vickers were seeking to recover some of their costs for the *Mayfly*. Inevitably, some of their costings were disputed.[115] Vickers then offered the Admiralty two different proposals for airships, but neither was accepted. Government support for airships had, at that point, evaporated due to lack of success.[116]

Even while Vickers labored on airships, they sought to interest the government in aircraft. In February 1909 Hiram Maxim wrote to Winston Churchill, then President of the Board of Trade: "it is almost certain that my fellow directors in the Vickers Maxim Company will back me up in making flying machines for the Government." Maxim offered access to large buildings at Crayford and enthused about his collaboration with an expert on gas and gasoline motors.[117] However, in 1910 Vickers entered the aircraft industry as a private venture because the government was not prepared to support them. The company had a choice of in-house development or licensed production. Prompted by Captain Murray Sueter, they chose the latter, buying a Robert Esnault-Peltier design.[118] However, this was a misdirection, as ultimately the Admiralty declined to buy the resulting R.E.P. aircraft from Vickers.[119]

There was another bump in the relationship in 1910, when the Royal Navy commandeered guns being built by Vickers for Ansaldo of Italy. The Italian firm's response was to begin a court case, not against the Navy but against Vickers. As the court costs mounted, Vickers' lawyer Mr. Dawes advised Albert Vickers that they should settle because, in addition to the court costs, "in any case we shall have to pay some damages." This happened, with Vickers losing £20,000 (£2,618,448 in August 2022), plus their costs.[120] Vickers obviously could not afford to bear grudges and maintained relations with the Admiralty.

At Armstrongs, by 1910 the comparatively low bridges of the Tyne River were inhibiting both civilian business at Low Walker and naval business at Elswick.

---

[114] Scott, *Vickers*, pp. 71–73.
[115] Note of Captain Murray F. Sueter on file, January 24, 1912, "Naval Airships: As to Disposal of &c, Firm state £7678.13.10. is due to them," TNA, AIR 1/2306/215/15.
[116] Dawson pitched the "Zodiac" design. Vickers to Admiralty, January 22, 1912. TNA, AIR 1/2306/215/15; Scott, *Vickers*, p. 73.
[117] Maxim to Churchill, February 2, 1909. CHAR, 11/19, Folio 14.
[118] Zaharoff initially acted for the French inventor, M. Esnault-Pelterie. Zaharoff to Barker, November 16, 1910. "Pelterie Monoplanes," VA, Doc. 284.
[119] Scott, *Vickers*, p. 74.
[120] Diamond to Albert Vickers, February 7, 1910, and Dawes to Vickers, February 10, 1910. Letter Book No. 31. VA, Doc. 1005, Folios 271 and 279.

With the Admiralty signaling that contracts would soon be forthcoming, the Board decided to create a new shipyard downstream from Newcastle, the High Walker Yard. Capitalizing on scientific developments, they also created a new Electrical Department, which worked on dynamos, motors, motor car sparking cells and electric firing mechanisms.[121] Noble's protegees were progressing in society. In 1908 John Meade Falkner was elected to the Athenaeum; later Noble's son-in-law, Alfred Cochrane, was elected to the club.[122] Nevertheless, simmering internal disputes continued to distract the firm. While Andrew Noble was a prodigious worker and Stuart Rendel praised the "energy and devotion which have so wonderfully marked your life-long labours," Noble's lack of financial acumen and autocratic style were problematic.[123] Rendel had made numerous complaints about bad investment decisions and money wasted at Armstrongs.[124] Now there were complaints about financial irregularities, including the five executive directors taking large salaries and commissions without the knowledge of the ordinary directors.[125] While Rendel could not prevent the "coup" that further elevated John Noble and Alfred Cochrane and made John Meade Falkner Managing Director in 1911, he was able to strike a deal to bring new men onto the Board "on the understanding that no more would be said about the large renumerations secretly appropriated in past years."[126] New Board members Sir Percy Girouard, a protégé of Lord Kitchener, former Secretary of the Committee of Imperial Defence Sir Charles Ottley, and former Treasury official Sir George Murray were appointed in 1912. "To a considerable degree, the infusion of new blood secured, above all by Stuart Rendel's persistence, worked."[127] All three brought excellent connections to the British elite, reviving the firm's traditional strategy, though none had international financial networks.[128]

Collaboration on Prices

Given the depressed market, Armstrongs and Vickers had a confidential arrangement between 1906 and 1913 to avoid international price competition; they competed on designs and innovations but kept their prices comparable to box in recipients.[129] Profits were shared with whichever firm lost the competition.

[121] "Elswick Works, Part 2."
[122] Wheeler, *Athenaeum*, p. 27.
[123] Quoted in Warren, *Armstrongs*, p. 181.
[124] Warren, *Armstrongs*, pp. 97–99, 109, 128.
[125] "Copy of Report of Salaries Committee May 11, 1910," TWA, Private Minute Book C40, p. 2.
[126] Collier, *Arms*, p. 148.
[127] Warren, *Armstrongs*, p. 182.
[128] Bastable, *Arms*, p. 236.
[129] "Armstrong Whitworth & Co. Ltd: Arrangement with Vickers on Armament Orders 1906–13," VA, Doc. 551, Folios 135–37.

The scope of the scheme embraced some nine important markets; it provided for a simple comparison of prices in Italy, and agreement to "work together" in Argentina and Portugal, an exchange of commissions in Greece and Chile, a division of armour and ordnance orders for Turkey, an equal division of all work in Japan and Spain, and a division of profits for Brazilian work.[130]

In 1907 Falkner sought to avoid a debilitating competition (threatening duplication and price cutting) between Ansaldo-Armstrong and Vickers-Terni. He:

reached the brink of success, despite acrimony between Orlando and Perrone. "Mais comment faire un rapprochement entre ces messieurs qui se traitent en voleur et assasin?" [But how do you make a connection between these gentlemen who treat each other as thieves and murderers?], Falkner asked his colleague Lord Rendel, quoting a Schneider director who hastened to add "et ils le sont" [and they are].[131]

Ultimately, it proved impossible to bring the companies together; Italy was one of the few markets where Vickers and Armstrong still genuinely competed, though they still compared prices. In 1909 Vickers was negotiating with Ansaldo over gun prices. Albert Vickers reported to John Noble that "Perrone demands reduction so utterly ridiculous we have apparently broken off negotiations." Albert explained to Zaharoff: "Mario asked for fifty percent reduction on artillery and absolutely declined [to] accept less." He added: "[T]his means not only no profit but an actual enormous loss for us and we have informed Mario we cannot possibly agree to it."[132] Vickers may have been hoping John Noble could influence them.[133]

The Armstrong–Vickers collusion had to remain secret, even internally. In January 1910 Caillard was reminding one of their auditors, W. B. Peat, about profits on ships sold to Brazil:

I would add that our people in Barrow are not supposed to be aware of the details of our private arrangement with Armstrongs, and I think, therefore, that you had better ask your people not to raise any question with them on this subject, as they simply work according to fixed prices arranged upon between Armstrongs and ourselves for all the material which Barrow has to supply to Armstrongs.[134]

The firms collaborated on prices to Japan for a warship contract, though submitting independent designs. Albert Vickers wrote to their Naval Architect

---

[130] Trebilcock, *Vickers Brothers*, pp. 95–96. Citing: Albert Vickers to Barker, February 25, 1913. VA Microfilm 214.

[131] Segreto, "More Trouble," p. 319.

[132] Albert Vickers telegram to John Noble, December 6, 1909, and Albert Vickers telegram to Zaharoff, December 6, 1909. Letter Book No. 31. VA, Doc. 1005, Folio 66.

[133] Segreto, "More Trouble," p. 318.

[134] Caillard to Peat, January 25, 1910. Letter Book No. 31. VA, Doc. 1005, Folio 253.

George Owens: "For your information I enclose Armstrongs prices and ours, as tendered for the Japanese ship. I am informed that they will probably select the big ship, 28 knots."[135] Vickers won the contract for the *Kongō*.[136] Vickers' agents, Mitsui Bussan Kaisha, secured the order by bribing a senior naval official. Admiral Fujii received large sums of money in return for declaring Vickers' warship bid superior to all others.[137] Checks from Mitsui to Vice Admiral Matsumoto Kaza were initially marked in the firm's ledger and transfer book as "secret service expenses"; this was later altered to "provisional payments" to (unsuccessfully) make those transfers look innocuous.[138]

In 1910 there was collusion between Vickers, Armstrongs and DWM to keep gun tenders to Serbia comparable.[139] A new global market-sharing agreement was signed by Vickers and DWM in March 1911. Trebilcock admiringly recounts, "Vickers emerged from this transaction as they had entered it: successfully marketing a superior weapons pattern, dictating terms to powerful competitors, winning useful accommodations while themselves retaining a commercial advantage."[140] Also in 1911 Albert Vickers complained when Fiat offered their Fiat-Rivelli gun to the British War Office at £88 per barrel:

> [I]t makes it very difficult for us to compete with them. Knowing that Mr. Orlando [Vickers-Terni] was connected with the Fiat Company ... I told him that his friends were simply spoiling the whole machine gun business by quoting such prices, and he happened on the same day to meet the Vice-President of the Fiat Company and told him so. This gentleman agreed that they were evidently making a mistake and that he would look into the question.[141]

Clearly, keeping prices comparable was a rational – and acceptable – strategy.

---

[135] Albert Vickers to Owens, August 1, 1910. Letter Book No. 32. VA, Doc. 1006, Folio 130.

[136] Lawrence to Secretary, including Appendix A: "Extracts from the Times," Appendix B: Parts I and II, Extracts from "The Japan Chronicle," Appendix C "Extracts from Parliamentary Debates," February 19, 1936. "Vickers Ltd.: evidence: note by Secretary." TNA, T 181/56.

[137] Engelbrecht and Hanighen, *Merchants*, p. 78.

[138] Lawrence to Secretary of the Bankes Commission, with enclosures, Appendix B Parts I and II, Extracts from "The Japan Chronicle," pp. 1–2. February 19, 1936. TNA, T 181/56. When investigations were underway in 1914, the issue was raised in Parliament. MPs questioned whether Vickers should remain eligible for Admiralty work. On each occasion the government rebuffed the question. Lawrence to Secretary, Appendix C "Extracts from Parliamentary Debates," "Armaments Trial (Tokio), 22 July 1914," p. 1. TNA, T 181/56; Parliamentary answer of Sir Edward Grey to Mr. King, July 23, 1914. *Hansard*, Vol. 65, cc. 626–27.

[139] Dawson to Deutsche Waffen und Munitionsfabriken, February 11, 1910. VA, Doc. 1005, Folio 282; Dawson to Armstrongs, February 11, 1910. VA Doc. 1005, Folios 284–85.

[140] Trebilcock, *Vickers Brothers*, p. 99.

[141] Letter to Albert Vickers, February 6, 1911. Letter Book No. 33. VA, Doc. 1006A, Folios 240–41.

In 1910 Zaharoff thought that Vickers faced "terrible odds" in the international market.[142] Nevertheless, Vickers scored some spectacular victories over strong competition. In 1908 Vickers had won Spanish orders worth £6 million at the expense of Germany (thanks to Zaharoff), and in 1911 Russian warship orders of £7 million were stolen from France (thanks to Barker). At Krupp's expense, Vickers secured Turkish contracts worth £2 million in 1911 – despite British Government opposition to the deal (see Chapter 8). In each case Vickers overcame their rivals' traditional diplomatic ties, all without assistance from the British Government.

International Diversifications

As exports were still depressed, Armstrongs and Vickers used a strategy of market expansion through diversifying into international subsidiaries and partnerships. The firms' willingness to make such moves reflects the increased competition in the international armaments market. Vickers had the Vickers-Terni Società Italiana di Artiglierie e Armamenti company at La Spezia, founded with Italian firms in 1905, with Vickers providing all artillery designs and technical aid.[143] By 1910 it was producing land and naval artillery and helped to break Armstrongs' Italian naval gun monopoly.[144] In Russia, Vickers established Chantiers Nicolaiev in 1912. Barker worked from Russia on the deal, while Caillard sought French finance for the dockyard. Trebilcock recounts, "By the end of the year he had drawn in not only the important French *banque d'affaires*, the *Société Générale*, but also some of the most important figures in Russian high finance, including Vyshnegradskii from the International Bank and Outine of the Discount Bank."[145] Vickers had a 10 percent stake and provided technical assistance to the dockyard. The Tsaritsyn Gun Foundry, begun in 1913, involved Vickers designing and building three battleships in Russia. Finally, there was Canadian Vickers, founded in 1911 to build warships and aircraft to capitalize on the Naval Service Bill of 1910, which mandated the creation of a Canadian navy. Vickers held 94 percent of the shares in Canadian Vickers. As Graham Taylor has noted, this was a far larger proportion than Vickers normally invested.[146]

In 1912 Armstrongs also undertook a Canadian diffusion, setting up the steel firm Armstrong, Whitworth of Canada, Ltd. Headquartered in Montreal,

[142] Zaharoff to Albert Vickers, July 28, 1910. VA, Microfilm 307.
[143] Segreto, "More Trouble," p. 318.
[144] Stevenson, *Armaments*, p. 33.
[145] Trebilcock, *Vickers Brothers*, p. 130.
[146] Taylor, "Negotiating," p. 141. Additionally, Dawson, Caillard and Albert Vickers were on the London Advisory Board for Canada Steamship Lines Ltd. This was expected to yield liner contracts. "Canada," p. 2.

the firm was headed by Sir Percy Girouard, who worked from London – an inefficient arrangement. The firm produced a variety of steel ingots and other products.[147] Armstrongs had been similarly enticed by the promise of Canadian naval building and the increased need for steel.

Many diffusions were joint ventures between them. For example, the Nihon Seiko Sho (Japan Steel Works) ordnance works in Muroran, a 1907 Japanese Government initiative, involved Armstrongs, Vickers and Japanese firms.[148] In Italy there was Società Anonima Italiana Whitehead, where Vickers and Armstrongs took 50 percent each. Further Torpedo ventures were Société Française de Torpilles Whitehead, a French joint venture in which Armstrongs had a 75 percent stake and Vickers 25 percent; the Austro-Hungarian Whitehead Torpedo Fiume, a 1906 joint venture in which again Armstrongs had a 75 percent stake and Vickers 25 percent; and from 1914 the Whitehead Company in Russia, a joint venture in which Armstrongs and Vickers held 25 percent each. In Turkey the Ottoman Dock Company was a prewar joint venture (see Chapter 8). In Spain La Sociedad Española de Construccion Naval, founded in 1909, was a subsidiary of the British group composed of Vickers, Armstrongs and John Browns.[149]

Unfortunately for Armstrongs, in most of these joint agreements Vickers got the better of them, as Stuart Rendel consistently complained. Armstrongs records are clear-eyed on this: "Vickers bested us in Italy ... the worst defeat we have yet had at Vickers' hands"; the Turkish arrangement "gives the greatest part of the work to Vickers"; and in Japan, "Vickers get the whole of the work and we take a secret *solatium* [consolation] only," with the Brazil agreement "the only case where we have the better of Vickers."[150] The Vickers victories were due to superior diplomacy. By February 1913, Vickers was thinking globally. Albert telegraphed to Barker: "'Taking a broad view of the whole situation, we are inclined to think it is desirable to agree to combine general agreement with Armstrongs for equal share of business in all parts of the World.'"[151] This never happened, however, as rearmament took precedence.

Armstrongs and Vickers made all these international diffusions independent of the British Government. As Segreto observed, "Vickers' foreign investment decisions, while they took account of international diplomacy, nevertheless rested on company strategies." Davenport-Hines made similar points about Vickers' direct investments in Italy and Japan.[152] Moreover, the firms could not

---

[147] *Directory of Iron and Steel*, pp. 38–39.
[148] Scott, *Vickers*, p. 85.
[149] Scott, *Vickers*, p. 84.
[150] Trebilcock, *Vickers Brothers*, p. 96. Citing: "Memorandum on Arrangements between Vickers and Armstrong, Whitworth in respect of Foreign Orders," undated. VA, Armstrong, Whitworth file.
[151] Trebilcock, *Vickers Brothers*, pp. 95–96. Citing: Albert Vickers to Barker, February 25, 1913. VA Microfilm 214.
[152] Segreto, "More Trouble," p. 316; Davenport-Hines, "Vickers and Schneider," p. 124.

expect any government support if they got into an international business dispute. This lack of protection presented real risks for them.

Crisis/Opportunity: Rearmament for War

The naval arms race preceding the Great War inevitably pushed armament firms and the Admiralty together.[153] By 1910–11, of the £13 million to be spent on naval construction, over £9 million was to be spent on contracts with private yards with the rest for the Royal Dockyards.[154] Armstrongs and Vickers had prepared for new warship orders. Vickers had also expanded capacity for submarine construction in 1911, but they thought the orders they received in 1913 did not do justice to those investments.[155] As manufacturing capacity was increasingly devoted to domestic production, the two firms' emphasis on foreign relations decreased and strategic interactions with the home state became more intense and more important.

There were now constant negotiations between the firms and the government over costs. As Dawson reported to Zaharoff in October 1912:

> I think I have left everything at the Admiralty in good shape. I have seen
> Sir Francis Hopwood today and Mr. Black and the Third Sea Lord and I
> have told them that it is impossible for us to reduce our price for the new
> Armour Plates as the costs we put in to the Admiralty were not for the new
> Plate but for the Krupp Plate and there were two or three more operations
> necessary in our new Plate which made it more expensive, besides which
> the costs of raw materials have gone up considerably and as we have had
> to spend a quarter of a million sterling to increase the plant to do the work,
> it would be very hard on us to ask us to reduce, when we have such a big
> debit on Capital Account. I rubbed this in very strongly both to Sir Francis
> Hopwood and Mr. Black.[156]

Although there was concern among radicals about the power that armament cartels wielded prior to the Great War, Trebilcock sees that as overplayed, noting: "However energetically the armourers might employ 'ring' tactics to drive up prices, they still depended on the government's *acceptance* of their price – there was no alternative source of demand within the home market once the service ministries had declined to do business."[157] That said, the Admiralty was unaware of firms' profit margins. As F. W. Black, the Director of Contracts, minuted in February 1914, "The evidence in our possession, so far as it goes, indicates that the firms are not making excessive profits, and most of the statements regarding the unduly high prices paid by the British Admiralty are based

[153] Bastable, *Arms*, p. 167.
[154] Scott, *Vickers*, p. 56.
[155] Scott, *Vickers*, pp. 67–68.
[156] Dawson to Zaharoff, October 22, 2012. VA, Doc. 788.
[157] Trebilcock, "Radicalism," p. 185. Emphasis in original.

on insufficient or inaccurate information."[158] Vickers were devious about their profits, though, as recorded in a 1913 letter from Caillard to Zaharoff discussing dividends to shareholders and the bonuses due to the firm's directors: "I particularly agree with you that the Dividend should not be increased. The only point about Bonuses is that in order to distribute them we must show very large profits, which Dawson, for some political reasons, does not think advisable. Income bonds (with no capital rights) would get over this difficulty."[159]

Armstrongs and Vickers had received few artillery orders since the Boer War, indicating that the War Office had not considered preparing for demand escalation in wartime. Triblock notes, "the perilous gap between peace-time and war-time levels of demand" seen in the Boer War "was very effectively *widened*" by the dearth of orders to private firms.[160] Shockingly, "In the financial year 1913–14 only four complete guns and two outfits of ammunition were produced by the trade for the War Office."[161] As Trebilcock astutely concluded, while the state was committed to industrial mobilization, it had not provided any mechanisms for actually achieving it.[162]

Armstrongs and Vickers were therefore severely disadvantaged when ordnance orders suddenly poured in: in the five weeks after war was declared, total War Office contracts for standard field guns and howitzers nearly equaled purchases over the previous ten years.[163] Whereas both firms had extensive plants and shipyards for meeting naval needs, they lacked suitable plant when called upon to suddenly meet urgent artillery needs.[164] Machine tools and gauges had to be created and installed, and workers trained before production could begin. As David French noted, at appearances before the 1907 Departmental Hadden Committee, representatives of Armstrongs and Vickers had declared that the private firms would be able to quickly meet government needs in a national emergency. Unfortunately, "the committee took them at their word."[165] Notably though, these declarations predated the deep trough in government artillery orders from 1907 to 1913.[166]

---

[158] Buxton and Johnson, *Battleship*, p. 219. Citing: "Armour Plate for Battleships 1910–1915," TNA, ADM 116/3456.

[159] Caillard to Zaharoff, September 25, 1913. VA, Doc. 788.

[160] Trebilcock, "War," p. 153. Emphasis in original.

[161] French, *British*, p. 47. Citing: "Statement Showing Orders for Guns, Ammunition etc. Placed with manufacturers from 1913 to 1915," August 30, 1916. TNA, MUN 5/6/170/15.

[162] Trebilcock, "War," p. 154.

[163] *History of the Ministry of Munitions*, Vol. I, Part I, pp. 72–74.

[164] Dewar, *Great*, p. 75.

[165] French, *British*, p. 46. Citing: *Factories: Royal Ordnance (Code 49(A)): Government and Workshops Committee*, Q. 2182–84 and Q. 2201, Noble and Q. 2325 Dawson. TNA, WO 32/4734.

[166] Between 1908 and 1913 only twenty-one private firms had received orders from the government, of which only four produced large guns and only nine produced shells. *Bankes Commission*, "Sir Maurice Hankey: evidence," TNA T 181/50. Also cited in French, *British*, p. 44.

In a tragic repetition of the Boer War experience, government armament orders came late and in vast numbers. There was a dawning recognition that Britain was unprepared for the demands of modern industrial war, demonstrated by the "shell crisis" – the lack of sufficient artillery ammunition for the British Army – of 1915.[167] Armament firms and the Royal Ordnance Factories struggled to meet demand. The reasons for the shell crisis included the British Government's assumptions that: the war would not require the creation of a large army; that shrapnel shells were adequate and high explosive shells unnecessary; and that "business as usual" could be maintained as the war would not last long.[168] Shells were used at an unprecedented rate. The static nature of the conflict and the consequent use of artillery against trench fortifications meant that munition use was far, far beyond what had been predicted. The government initially had no idea of what private firms could produce and how quickly they could do it, so just asked for what they wanted: "[A]s the campaign developed the projected maximum scale of effort was itself rapidly enlarged, so that the maxima of one month became the minima of the next, while the unforeseen increase in the rate of consumption, especially in the case of gun ammunition, tended to widen the breach between output and immediate requirements."[169]

The government's response to early production problems was fivefold.[170] First, a government committee looked at how to increase output and concluded that "it would be best to extend sub-contracting at first among non-munitions firms," leaving the most exacting work of armaments assembly to the established armament firms.[171] Second, in October 1914 the new Cabinet Committee on Munitions Supply held a meeting with both the Royal Ordnance Factories and the six key private armament firms (in itself unprecedented). As a first step the Committee promised that if the firms increased output, "the capital required for extension would be found, and that they would be fully compensated for any consequential loss."[172] Vickers agreed to double its production of 9.2-inch howitzers from sixteen to thirty-two, and to nearly double its production of 18-pound guns from the 360 currently on order to 640. Armstrongs was also to increase its production of 18-pound guns from 450 to 700, with both firms to deliver the 18-pounders by August 1915 [173] Vickers increased production of 6-inch howitzers by making the gun and mechanism themselves, while farming out the manufacturing of the carriages and gun sights to a range of small engineering concerns around Manchester.[174] The Committee applied

[167] "Shell Shortage," p. 8; "The Great Need," p. 2; "The Shell Shortage," p. 3.
[168] French, *British*, pp. 39–50.
[169] *History of the Ministry of Munitions*, Vol. I, p. 14.
[170] In contrast, Barnett identified two responses. Barnett, "Audit of the Great War," p. 110.
[171] Dewar, *Great*, p. 27.
[172] *History of the Ministry of Munitions*, Vol. I, pp. 89–90.
[173] Hume and Moss, *Beardmore*, Table 5.1, p. 106; Scott, *Vickers*, p. 99.
[174] Simmonds, *Britain*, p. 72.

significant pressure to the firms, with Sir Vincent Caillard calling its methods "inquisitional."[175] These orders were soon significantly increased again as the government realized the scale of need for artillery given the emerging stalemate on the Western Front. In a speech to the House of Commons on April 20, 1915, Minister of Munitions David Lloyd George explained that in the two weeks of fighting around Neuve Chappelle in March 1915 the ammunition used was about equal to the total amount expended in the Boer War.[176]

Third, the crisis led to the hasty formation of the powerful Ministry of Munitions in early 1915.[177] The old free enterprise production system was replaced by a state-led system.[178] Fourth, "and even more revolutionary in terms of traditional Victorian *laissez faire* no fewer than 218 national factories were built on green-field sites to manufacture products" for the war effort.[179] These "National Factories" were often managed for the government by the private armament firms. For example, in terms of shell factories, Beardmores ran three National Factories in Glasgow, Armstrongs ran a National Factory near Gateshead and Vickers ran one in Lancaster.[180] National Factories were vital in terms of ammunition production and were important for rifles and small arms.[181] Also, firms in the woodworking, light engineering and (particularly effectively) bus manufacturing sectors became successfully engaged in aircraft production.[182] Additionally, Vickers and Armstrongs' Whitehead Torpedo Company was taken over by the government in 1914 because of its strategic importance and was returned to the private sector in 1918.

Fifth, a final important change was the passing of the Munitions of War Act on July 2, 1915. This was the culmination of discussions within the government over the management of armament firms. Initially the government contemplated nationalizing all the major firms and placing them under military discipline. However, Sir William Plender suggested an alternative scheme that involved leaving the firms independent but limiting excess profits, with the side benefit that this met a core trade union demand. This Treasury Agreement became the basis for wartime management of the private firms.[183] A British newspaper reported: "There is a general recognition that he [Lloyd George] could not ask labour to make sacrifices in the national emergency without making similar demands on employers."[184]

---

175 Trebilcock, "War," p. 157.
176 Dewar, *Great*, pp. 11 and 26–27.
177 Miller, *Planning*, pp. 15–16.
178 Trebilcock, "War," p. 155.
179 Barnett, "Audit of the Great War," p. 110.
180 Simmonds, *Britain*, p. 74.
181 Hornby, *Factories*, p. 12.
182 Barnes, *Shorts Aircraft*, p. 13.
183 Hume and Moss, *Beardmore*, pp. 111–12. Citing *History of the Ministry of Munitions*, Vol. I, pp. 71–87.
184 "War Profits," p. 3.

In March 1915 President of the Board of Trade Walter Runciman had begun negotiations with representatives of Armstrongs and Vickers. According to French, "The companies knew they were in a strong position and drove a hard bargain, making the government pay dearly for their help."[185] The government wanted to limit the shareholder dividends paid during and immediately after the war. The discussion evolved into negotiations over the level of profits that armament firms would be allowed to make. Runciman wanted a 15 percent limit, whereas Armstrongs and Vickers wanted 20 percent and would not compromise. The eventual agreement limited the two to no more than 20 percent above the profits made in the last two years of peace – ironically, a ceiling neither came near to breaching.[186] This agreement formed the basis for the Munitions of War Act, which was paralleled by the Finance (No. 2) Act of 1915, which taxed firms' non-armaments profits that exceeded by more than £100 the profits on their Income Tax Assessments of 1914–15.

War Office inspectors became regular visitors to all Vickers' establishments, constantly assessing the firm's capacity and strategy for shell production.[187] The 1915 Act gave the government much more control over armament firms, enabling factory inspectors from the Ministry of Munitions to take on issues such as wage levels, working hours and even mealtimes. In these "controlled establishments," the government was able to impose labor agreements and prevent workers leaving. Startlingly, "special Munitions Courts were set up to hear cases involving infractions of the rules by either management or labor."[188] As Ralph Adams comments, "With this legislation munitions workers came under a degree of state control no British workers had experienced in modern times."[189] This was true for Armstrongs and Vickers too. As Falkner reported to shareholders in 1915, "instead of private enterprise we have become a Government arsenal under Government control."[190] While "the management of the companies was left undisturbed … in practice their actions were severely circumscribed."[191] Armstrongs and Vickers had temporarily lost their independence.

Even as the government assisted Armstrongs and Vickers with increasing production, help was often given in the form of loans rather than subsidies. For example, in 1915, as it sought to fill vast orders from the government, Vickers needed to rapidly recruit more skilled workers for Barrow, but lacked the requisite accommodation. To facilitate the expansion the government lent the company £75,000 to purchase land and build houses for workers and their families.

---

185   French, *British*, p. 162.
186   Scott, *Vickers*, pp. 129–30 and 133; Adams, "Delivering," p. 241.
187   See: Lloyd-Jones and Lewis, *Arming*, p. 112.
188   Adams, "Delivering," p. 242.
189   Adams, "Delivering," p. 241.
190   Cited in Bastable, *Arms*, p. 172.
191   Hume and Moss, *Beardmore*, p. 112; Turner, *Businessmen*, pp. 39–40.

The loan was to be repaid over forty years at an interest rate of 4.5 percent per annum.[192] The standard interest rate in Britain in 1915 was 5 percent, so the firm did not receive a big concession from the government, though the repayment time seems generous.[193] The government still favored granting contracts rather than providing money for research and development, which meant that the firms did a lot of financial juggling.[194] Despite this assistance, Barrow experienced serious problems in recruiting skilled labor as it was a relatively remote location.[195]

For Vickers and Armstrongs the scale of government demand was unparalleled; in 1914 Vickers had produced fewer than twenty 18-pound guns for the War Office, but it suddenly had orders for 2,400 for delivery by June 1915, and only managed to fulfill about half the order.[196] Prime Minister Asquith, at the center of the shell crisis storm, averred:

> The great munition manufacturers were summoned, and orders were place with them which they thought they could undertake, and they undertook to execute them. If they had carried out that undertaking it would have placed the country in a tremendous position and we should have had a surplus. The placing of the orders was done by the committee, and the manufacturers did their best to execute them, but difficulties arose in the relations between capital and labour which confounded all the calculations of the manufacturers.[197]

Trebilcock gives a very different explanation: "[C]aught without adequate stocks, a desperate government again pushed the responsibility for the future military situation on to private industrialists who could not carry it – and protested that they could not."[198]

In October 1915 the Cabinet decided to raise existing contracts for 18-pounder guns from the current order of 892 guns to 3,000 to equip sixty-two New Army divisions, rather than the eighteen divisions originally planned for. However, the Cabinet had not considered the practicalities of this escalation, assuming that the private firms could rise to the challenge. As French recounts:

> The next day the Cabinet Committee actually put these new orders to representatives of the ordnance factories and the trade. It wanted Vickers and Armstrongs to promise to deliver 1,000 18-pounder guns each by 1 June

---

[192] "From the War Department for purchase of land to erect houses at Barrow, 1915." VA, Doc. 909.
[193] Rogers, "Interest Rates."
[194] Scott, *Vickers*, p. 309.
[195] Schofield, *Industry*.
[196] Scott, *Vickers*, pp. 97–98 and 99. However, that figure is contradicted by *History of the Ministry of Munitions* figures, Vol. 1, Pt. 1, p. 23.
[197] "The Shell Shortage: Mr. Asquith," p. 4.
[198] Trebilcock, "War," p. 158.

instead of the 360 and 450 they had already been contracted for. Both firms flatly refused to agree, and it was only with considerable reluctance that they agreed to *try* to deliver 640 and 850 guns respectively.[199]

While the shell shortage was largely a result of the government's assumptions and choices, armament firms, including Armstrongs and Vickers, were roundly criticized for failing to quickly meet the exponential growth in demand.[200] As the same industrial expansion was also occurring in France and Russia, there was competition for resources and rising prices. Vickers was quickly behind on machine gun orders for the new Ministry.[201] Firms had to build new sheds and factories and install more "huge hydraulic machines and furnaces, boring and turning gear, fuse-makers, chemical apparatus, and tools varying from 100-tons to those delicate enough to shave a watch spring."[202] Vickers' production of high explosive shells was delayed by five months as they waited for machine tools.[203] Worse: there was a shortage of the tungsten powder needed to produce high-speed steel for machine tools because Germany monopolized the processing of tungsten ore. In response, a consortium of about thirty leading Sheffield tool making firms, plus Armstrongs, created High Speed Steel Alloys Ltd. in late 1914 and built a factory in Widnes to process tungsten powder. By 1916 supplies were adequate, thanks to the factory and two mines in Burma.[204]

Asquith did not lay the blame for the shell crisis at the door of Armstrongs, Vickers and other armament firms, but others were more skeptical. In 1915 a newspaper explained:

> The British contractors ascribe their inability to deliver the goods on time to labour troubles (this cause has been exaggerated), to difficulties in obtaining materials owing to the congestion at the ports, where military requirements were supreme, to obstacles to transit arising from the same cause. While there is validity in these pleas and excuses, the root-trouble was the failure at the outset to organise in systematic fashion the immense engineering resources of the United Kingdom.[205]

There were other calls for the government to take over private armament firms.

Particularly in the early years of the war – when production was inadequate to meet demand – War Office Inspectors were continually assessing Vickers' capacity for shell production.[206] Once machines were installed, as they were in constant use, with two or three shifts daily, they wore out more quickly. In addition to

---

[199]   French, *British*, p. 135. Emphasis in original.
[200]   "The Facts," p. 5; "Shell Shortage: Remarkable," p. 5.
[201]   *History of the Ministry of Munitions*, Vol I., p. 120.
[202]   "The Truth," p. 3.
[203]   French, *British*, p. 154.
[204]   Tweedale, *Steel City*, pp. 195–96.
[205]   "The Facts," p. 5.
[206]   Lloyd-Jones and Lewis, *Arming*, p. 112.

substantially expanding their own plants, Vickers subcontracted work on artillery fuses to seven bicycle makers, including the Raleigh Cycle Company, in their attempt to keep up with spiraling demand.[207] In 1914–15 Vickers needed to rapidly recruit more workers for Barrow, but lacked the requisite accommodation. In August 1914, it was announced that many workers from other shipyards were traveling to Barrow and that the "firm are appealing to the people of Barrow to afford all the accommodation they can, on patriotic grounds."[208]

The attempts by the armament firms to ramp up production were hampered by the voluntary nature of military service at the start of the war. Many men from the armament firms had heeded the call to enlist and were reluctant to return to munitions work when the government sought to reverse course. The government called for War Munition Volunteers and many from other areas of industry stepped forward, as did many women.[209] For the armament firms, "their task was more difficult because they were lending men to instruct the inexperienced workers in the new firms working on munitions for the nation."[210] After a rocky start, munition production increased markedly.[211] In December 1915 the *Sheffield Independent* was declaring the shell shortage over and hailing the "Private Firm's Splendid Service," particularly the contributions of the local firms who had put themselves at the disposal of the Ministry of Munitions.[212] As Douglas Vickers recorded, "During the recent war the whole of the Company's Works were devoted to the needs of the nation, and were kept going night and day for a period of five years."[213]

In 1915, Noble died and Falkner inherited the Armstrongs' Chairmanship. Principal shareholder Stuart Rendel noted, "with all his admirable gifts, Falkner is no expert."[214] Basil Collier considers that Falkner "was at least an adequate chairman during the years when Armstrongs, like Vickers, were virtually under government control."[215] George Hadcock was now elected to the Board of Armstrongs, and subsequently became the Managing Director of the Elswick Works (and, following firm tradition, a member of the Athenaeum).

In lighter-than-air craft, Vickers had spent £50,000 on the equipment and housing for the Rigid Naval Airship, but no contracts were forthcoming.[216]

[207] Lloyd-Jones and Lewis, *Arming*, p. 112.
[208] "New Warships," p. 5.
[209] "Rush," p. 3.
[210] Dewar, *Great*, p. 28.
[211] "Chart Showing Shells, Cartridge Cases, Fuses and Primers Manufactured by Armstrong Whitworth," 1914–1918, TWA, D.VA/49/5; "Chart Showing Guns, Mountings, Including Repairs and Tanks Manufactured by Sir W.G. Armstrong Whitworth and Company Limited," TWA, D.VA/49/3; "Tables of Proportionate Increases in Munition Output and Capacity from August 1914 to May 1916," TNA, MUN 5/177/1200/12.
[212] "Labour's Splendid Achievement," p. 7.
[213] Vickers, *History of Vickers*, 5th draft, p. 1.
[214] Warren, *Armstrongs*, p. 187.
[215] Collier, *Arms*, p. 149.
[216] Scott, *Vickers*, pp. 67–68, 73.

By 1914 Admiralty interest had waned (again) and Vickers was being told to "dispose of the airship etc. as favourably as possible."[217] War restored Admiralty interest. However, in 1915, when Vickers was on the brink of successful airship production, the Admiralty changed course again and declared that the airship works at Cavendish Dock was to be turned into a Royal Naval Air Service flying station. This decision was itself soon reversed because of the toll being extracted by German Zeppelins. When airship orders were finally placed, they also went to Armstrongs and Beardmores.[218] "The level of the Admiralty's financial support to Beardmores was a source of irritation to Vickers who had spent about £130 000 on providing their own facilities at Barrow and were obliged to accept fixed-price contracts."[219] Worse, as the only firm that had worked on airships, Vickers was expected to teach their rivals how to manufacture them. Even after Armstrongs and Beardmores had been recruited to help build airships, the Admiralty still vacillated. Scott concluded: "[F]rom 1908 to 1918 the Board of Admiralty never had a policy for airships; what they had were merely a series of reactions to German successes …. Vickers' loyalty … was so great that it was generally assumed that the Admiralty must have good reasons for its actions."[220]

In 1916 the firm British Cellulose and Chemical Manufacturing Co. (later British Celanese Ltd.) was created with the support of the Ministry of Munitions to produce cellulose acetate "dope" used as a varnish for warplanes and airships. The firm was given a monopoly over production in addition to starting capital.[221] Subsequently, Board member Trevor Dawson and Chairman of British Cellulose Walter Grant Morden were accused in the *London Chronicle* and elsewhere of speculating on British Celanese shares, of seeking various government concessions for the firm, of improper relations with government departments and of using undue influence over Chancellor of the Exchequer Reginald McKenna. Apparently, the original investors saw their 6*d*. (penny) shares increase in value by 5,700 percent.[222] This was investigated as war profiteering by the 1918 Sumner Inquiry. While the inquiry was underway, Morden, now an MP, asked about decisions over the firm in Parliament! The final report found little wrongdoing but noted annual payments to the Managing Directors and £5,000 to Morden for living and entertainment expenses, "it being expressly agreed that no detailed account of these expenses needed to be presented." The report found no improper use of the monies, but "only mention[ed] the fact

217 "Naval Airship No. 1 Particulars of Amounts Realized by Sale and Appropriation," August 17, 1914. "Naval Airship No. 1 Tender & Contract Papers etc. Vickers Ltd. 1908–1914." TNA, AIR 1/2306/215/15.
218 "HMR 25, the first Armstrong Whitworth rigid airship, in flight," 1918. TWA, D.VA/20/1.
219 Hume and Moss, *Beardmore*, p. 129.
220 Scott, *Vickers*, p. 125.
221 Cerretano, "Treasury," pp. 92–93.
222 "Investigate British War Company," p. 7.

lest it might appear to have been overlooked."[223] None of the allegations against Dawson had stuck, but the result of the publicity was that he did not receive a peerage in 1917 as planned. Scott fails to mention any of this in his exhaustive study of Vickers.

Despite government indifference, Vickers had independently pushed ahead with aircraft, setting up an aviation department at Brooklands, where G. H. Challenger developed their FB.1 biplane.[224] A prototype FB.1, armed with a Vickers machine gun, was shown at the Olympia Aero Show in 1913.[225] By 1914 Vickers had produced only twenty-six aircraft, at great cost.[226] Nevertheless, this changed dramatically with the outbreak of the Great War. The FB.1 and its successors became the backbone of the Royal Flying Corps in the early years of the war. Vickers subsequently became the first private firm to have a wind tunnel, and by 1918 was considering amphibian aircraft for civilian passenger travel.[227] Armstrongs was slower to become involved in airpower, creating an "Arial Department" at Dukes Moor, Gosforth in 1913 to manufacture biplanes for the War Office to a design by the Royal Aircraft Factory. From there, they went on to design and produce their own aircraft, but "the first of these did not appear before 1915."[228]

Once the government turned to airplanes, Vickers found it hard to meet British Government aircraft requirements and hatched a plan in 1915 for Vickers-Terni to build an aircraft factory to meet some of those needs. However, there were disagreements within the Italian Government over details of the deal (costing Vickers an order for 100 airplanes that could have been made at Vickers-Terni) and ultimately it failed. Interestingly, Vickers' famed market nous did not predict the vast orders for aircraft from the Italian Government when it declared war and Vickers-Terni missed out on that pro-curement feast.[229]

By October 1915, "pressure from the Western Front ... forced the Royal Aircraft Factory to 'open up design to the trade' and the system of military requirements, specifications and invitations to tender was instituted."[230] This adoption of the Admiralty approach to procurement encouraged some of the major armament firms "to create design departments of real strength" and a "partnership between government and industry was formed which was to survive the war and another greater aerial war after it."[231] Total national

---

[223] "British Cellulose Inquiry," p. 194. Citing Sumner report.
[224] Collier, *Arms*, p. 78.
[225] Scott, *Vickers*, p. 75.
[226] Scott, *Vickers*, pp. 74–75.
[227] Scott, *Vickers*, p. 177.
[228] Collier, *Arms*, p. 78.
[229] Segreto, "More Trouble," p. 322.
[230] Hayward, *British*, p. 10.
[231] Scott, *Vickers*, pp. 120–21.

production, which had stood at ten planes per month at the start of the war, had expanded to 1,229 airframes per month by 1917.[232] Private firms produced the majority of the aircraft; of the more than 55,000 aircraft produced, only 482 aircraft and 2,000 aircraft engines came from the Royal Aircraft Factory.[233] "Armstrongs supplied over a thousand aeroplanes, starting with 6 in 1914 and ending with 423 in 1918; and they experimented with new types, such as a single-seater high-power fighting scout, at the time of the Armistice."[234] They also made three airships.

Vickers undertook serial production of the Royal Aircraft Factory's B.E.2 multirole biplane, of which approximately 3,500 were built over five years, built 125 FB.5 (Gunbus) armed scout biplanes – a derivative of the Farman MF.11 – in 1915, and by the close of the war had designed and built 200 of the innovative Vimy bomber.[235] As Hugh Driver concluded of Vickers' aircraft:

> The war, then, ultimately brought out the best in Vickers and its aircraft. Initially the firm had struggled to find its niche. Despite the fact that the company started trading with all the financial and industrial advantages of a large, expansive manufacturing concern … it at first failed to match the success of smaller competitors such as Sopwiths, Avro and Shorts. This was because its products had generally lacked the innovative quality of its main rivals. Yet, increasingly, financial backing for expensive development programmes was becoming the key to design innovation.[236]

After an awkward pause while the Italian Government decided which side to back in the war, Vickers-Terni was able to produce the Farman MF.11 Shorthorn aircraft under license from the French, as Vickers was doing. Vickers-Terni also accelerated artillery production, as did Armstrongs' Pozzuoli factory. Canadian Vickers made some contributions to the war effort. The naval spending – which had prompted Vickers to set up there – did not appear until the outbreak of war in 1914; consequently, Canadian Vickers faced the same problem as its parent in gearing up quickly for wartime production. For Canadian Vickers, a key problem was raising sufficient capital to extend factories and plant. The planned solution was a new issue of debentures in 1914. However, the issue only came two years later, and "the parent firm, which had already provided over £1 million pounds in capital and loans to Canadian Vickers, was obliged to guarantee a substantial portion of the total."[237] As a consequence of these delays, Canadian Vickers was only reaching peak production toward the end of the Great War, and still carried a large debt burden. Armstrongs and

[232] Ritchie, *Industry*, p. 7; Scott, *Vickers*, p. 118.
[233] Hornby, *Factories*, p. 426. Citing: *History of the Ministry*, Vol. XII, Pt. I, p. 173.
[234] Dewar, *Great*, p. 79.
[235] "Vickers Company Chronological Aircraft List"; Marshall, "Tools of War."
[236] Driver, *Military Aviation*, p. 129.
[237] Taylor, "Technology Transfers," p. 142.

Vickers' joint investments in Turkey seemed lost as she sided with Germany in the conflict.

In the naval sector, over the four years of the war Armstrongs built twelve armored ships, eleven cruisers, eight sloops, eleven submarines and ninety-seven torpedo tubes for the Royal Navy.[238] According to Armstrong's historian: "In the end, the Firm was responsible for one third of the national output of guns and mountings, besides aircraft, tanks, warships, and shells."[239] Vickers "drove forward in a hot frenzy of production. It delivered to the armies and navies 100,000 machine guns, 2528 naval and field guns, thousands of tons of armor plate, built four battleships, three armored cruisers, fifty-three submarines, three subsidiary vessels, and sixty-two smaller boats."[240] It also made aircraft. Vickers and Armstrongs' wartime production made decisive contributions to the British war effort.

During the conflict Vickers took over two firms which provided them with important sub-components. First, Vickers bought a 70 percent stake in T. Cooke & Sons, manufacturers of a fire-control system, rangefinders and anti-aircraft predictors. The second acquisition was James Booth & Company Limited, which manufactured the Duralumin that Vickers used in its airships for the Admiralty, and which had potential for aircraft production.[241]

In addition to taking on exponential amounts of work, the firms also lent personnel to the government. For example, Vickers' Commander Charles Craven joined the government when war broke out, serving in the submarine service, "but was released in 1916 at the request of Vickers Ltd. to rejoin their staff at Barrow, in order to supervise the construction of submarines and airships."[242] By 1917 he was the naval assistant to the Managing Director of the Barrow works, and soon after the end of the war was appointed as a Special Director. Armstrongs' Sir Percy Girouard took a government post in 1915, returning to Elswick in 1917.[243] George Hadcock "went to France several times personally to inspect the new guns and mountings in use at the Front; and after the War was a member of a commission sent to Germany on behalf of the Government to inspect the dismantling of the arms factories there. For his war services he was created a K.B.E."[244] Many from industry served in the wartime administration. It was, however, a practice neither businessmen nor civil servants wanted to perpetuate in peacetime.[245]

[238] Dewar, *Great*, p. 75.
[239] Fairbairn, *Elswick*, VA 593, p. 114.
[240] Flynn, *Men of Wealth*, Section VIII.
[241] Scott, *Vickers*, p. 132.
[242] Williams, *Who's Who*, p. 8.
[243] Warren, *Armstrongs*, p. 189.
[244] d'Eyncourt, "Obituary: Sir George Hadcock," p. 143.
[245] Platt, *Finance*, p. XXXII.

Sharing Wartime Intelligence

In 1914, as war grew likely (and after Britain had seized two dreadnoughts that Armstrongs was building for Turkey, as recounted in Chapter 8), Sir Charles Ottley passed intelligence to the Foreign Office, visiting Eyre Crowe on August 6 to share what he had learned from Captain Harry Vere, who was supervising the reconstruction of the Turkish docks. Ottley followed up with a written report that not only provided intelligence, but also recommended a policy to the government:

> Enver Bay and a considerable section of the Turkish public are in favour of joining the Austro-German alliance, and are using the fact that we have seized the two Turkish Dreadnoughts as an appeal to popular animosity against England. If – as is rumoured – Italy now joins England, our Turkish friends tell us that this will be represented as a plain indication that there is an anti-Mussulman [Muslim] crusade on foot. Should this idea gain headway in Constantinople the effect might be to turn the scale and bring Turkey into belligerency against us. Merely to inform the Turkish Government by diplomatic channels of the friendliness of our intentions is therefore (say our friends) not enough …. What is wanted [is] to get into the Turkish *press* a statement that England is friendly to Turkey.[246]

Ottley's intelligence sharing was in the Armstrongs patriotic tradition.

Vickers was active too. First Lord Winston Churchill reported to the Admiralty's Intelligence Division in September 1914 that Trevor Dawson had visited him and provided a paper on the progress of German shipbuilding. "He says the two Schicahu ships at Dantzig are valuable vessels three quarters finished. The Russian advance is now only 60 miles from Dantzig, and Dawson suggests that we should point out to the Russians the great importance of smashing up these ships, if possible, where they lie on the slips, by bombs from aircraft or bombardment."[247] Dawson was also going beyond providing intelligence and recommending actions that Churchill agreed with. While in the United States in May 1915, Dawson twice telegraphed information to Churchill, first concerning the German distribution of rifles to German citizens in American cities for use if the U.S.A. declared war.[248] The second telegram covered issues that included apparent German plans to plant bombs aboard British liners. Dawson also noted, "In case I do not get through wish to report German Syndicate calling for design of about 5000 ton submarine cargo boat from Electric [Boat] Company to carry copper and other essential

---

[246] Miller, *Straits*, p. 229. Citing: Ottley to Crowe, August 6, 1914. TNA, FO 371/2137/38809. Emphasis in original.

[247] Minute Churchill to Captain Reginald Hall on Warship Construction in Germany, September 8, 1914. CHAR 13/29/140.

[248] Telegram from Sir Trevor Dawson in New York to Winston Churchill, 6 May 1915, CHAR 13/70/44.

stores ... Company will act as Admiralty wish ... taking contract and delaying completion or refusing."[249] Given Vickers' alliance with Electric Boat, they
could make that happen.

During the war Sir Vincent Caillard and Basil Zaharoff took intelligence sharing
to a whole new level, moving from provision to action. Declassified records show
that Zaharoff was engaged in several schemes on behalf of the British Government
in the Balkans, with Caillard acting as the intermediary in London. This brought
them both into contact with the British elite.[250] In an *aide-mémoire* reviewing his
activities during the war, Zaharoff's first statement is, "I did not ask for this mission."[251] What is unclear is whether the British government approached Vickers
or if Caillard had offered Zaharoff's services to the Crown – the more probable
scenario as Caillard had previously worked for the government.

The schemes sought to leverage Zaharoff's excellent contacts in Greece and
Turkey to shorten the duration of the war, first by bringing the Greeks to the
Allied side and later by trying to persuade the Turks to become neutral. Zaharoff
was given money to bribe various Greek political figures. In January 1916 he
briefed Prime Minister Asquith and Chancellor of the Exchequer McKenna on
the success of his mission. After this he suggested several avenues for further turning Greek public opinion against the Germans, including by establishing a pro-
British newspaper in Greece.[252] When the British Government declined to fund
the scheme, Zaharoff and his contacts put up the money themselves, publishing
pro-British propaganda, with some success. In the summer of 1916, when Greece
descended into a political crisis, Zaharoff maneuvered in support of his pro-
British friend Venizelos, who became Prime Minister and swiftly brought Greece
into the war on the Allied side. Subsequently Caillard and Zaharoff, working for
Prime Minister Lloyd George, were involved in trying to bribe Turkish officials
to sign a separate peace treaty with the Allied Powers. At the same time, Foreign
Secretary Arthur Balfour (ignorant of their activities) was trying to achieve the
same outcome. Zaharoff worked on this project on and off until the end of the war.

For Joseph Maiolo and Tony Insall, who first accessed these declassified papers,
the major lesson to be learned from them is that Caillard and Zaharoff (despite
the freewheeling image of those later branded "merchants of death") could not
decisively influence the behavior of the British Government. This is certainly
true. They also note in passing "[e]vidence of Caillard lobbying Asquith and
Lloyd George on behalf of heavy industry."[253] Vickers' strategy of relationship

---

[249] Telegram from Sir Trevor Dawson in New York to Winston Churchill, 10 May 1915,
CHAR 13/70/47.

[250] For example, on September 1, 1918, the King invited Caillard to Buckingham Palace.
Papers of Sir Vincent Caillard, TNA, FO 1093/47, Folio 365.

[251] Papers of Sir Vincent Caillard, TNA, FO 1093/47 File 1, Item 1, Folio 1.

[252] Zaharoff to Caillard "urging action in Greece," November 23, 1915. Papers of Sir Vincent
Caillard TNA, FO 1093/47 File 1, Item 7.

[253] Maiolo and Insall, "Sir Basil," p. 822.

building through being useful to the British state was an additional motive for action. Caillard used these interactions to discuss armament industry issues. In a 1916 letter to Zaharoff, Caillard recounted a conversation with Asquith:

> I might just add here that I also spoke to the Chairman strongly about the (in my opinion) disastrous financial policy of the government, which is having the effect of crushing all spirit of enterprise in the productive industry of the country. He told me he had a very searching enquiry going on about this subject now, that he took careful note of what I told him, and would pass it on personally himself to the Treasurer, and that as I was going to see him on other subjects, I might mention that also to him.[254]

Caillard subsequently met with McKenna and discussed postwar industrial planning, but reported back to Asquith that he did not share McKenna's optimism and wait-and-see approach.[255] Additionally Caillard also used the wartime relationship to lobby the Prime Minister on the idea for a Federation of British Industries.[256]

The strength of Vickers' elite connections now was illustrated by Dawson's presence at the American Club Lunch and Pilgrims' Club dinner celebrating America's entry into the war in 1917. No one from Armstrongs was in attendance.[257] The acceptance of Vickers into the establishment was further evident in 1918 when *Tatler* magazine featured a portrait of Dawson's new daughter-in-law.[258] James McKechnie, Managing Director at Barrow during the war, was knighted in January 1918. At a Barrow event in his honor, McKechnie "said he considered the honour the King had conferred upon him should be shared by the 36,000 men and women employed at the Barrow works, who, during the last three years, had stood the strain well and rendered faithful services."[259] Douglas Vickers took over the role of Chairman from his Uncle Albert in September 1918, shortly before the war ended.[260]

State–Firm Frictions over Costs and Profits

Despite the heavy government control of armament production during the war there was popular concern about the profits being made by firms,

---

[254] "Letter to Z about C's lunch with P.M., financing Venizelos and Turkish idea," Papers of Sir Vincent Caillard TNA, FO 1093/50 File V, Folio 142.
[255] "Letter to Asquith about Turkish idea and bringing Sir E. Grey into the picture re activities in Greece," July 9, 1916. TNA, FO 1093/50 File V, Folio 144.
[256] "Letter to Asquith about Credit for Z," August 6, 1916. Promising to send a memo on the Federation of British Industries. Papers of Sir Vincent Caillard, TNA, FO 1093/51 File VI, Folio 159.
[257] *Pamphlets*; "Companionship in Arms," p. 31.
[258] "Some Recent Portraits," p. 133.
[259] "Honouring Sir James."
[260] Scott, *Vickers*, p. 392.

notwithstanding the excess profit clause in the 1915 Act. During the war years Vickers moved money into secret reserve funds and established a disproportionately large reserve against debtors, thereby deflating the firms' public wartime profits by £1,190,000.[261] Armstrongs made similar moves, with generous contingency funds and charges for "special depreciation," shielding profit levels. The two firms were clearly able to manipulate their profit levels. It seems that Armstrongs did not pay Excess Profit Duty or the Munitions Levy during the war, and this became an issue in state–firm negotiations beyond the end of the war.[262]

There were difficult wartime negotiations between the specialist armament firms and the government over prices, especially once non-specialist firms became engaged in production. The armament firms understood that the window for recouping the costs of buying dedicated machinery was likely to be limited, so fought hard to recover the money, ruffling feathers in the government. In 1916 Christopher Addison, the Deputy Minister of Munitions, wrote: "Trevor Dawson metaphorically shrouded himself in the Union Jack and almost wept as I expostulated that these great patriotic firms were charging too much."[263]

The armament firms collaborated and actively skirmished with the government over costs during the war, as the case of armor plate firms shows. In 1916 the five producers – Armstrongs, Vickers, Beardmores, Cammell Lairds and Browns – coordinated on prices for gun shields and other equipment rather too obviously. As the Navy Auditor General reported, the five had been invited to tender and all "quoted an identical, and, in the opinion of the Admiralty, excessive price." Four were contracted to urgently deliver the shields "with a request for revision of the price. In reply, each of the firms offered a similar small reduction," which was accepted because of the urgency. However, the deliveries were between two and six months late, and "the high prices obtained do not appear to have been further reduced in consequence."[264]

These firms were meeting regularly and were coordinating prices for armor plate. A February 1917 meeting involved the five firms' representatives and their auditors, with the aim of ensuring that the "figures are all prepared on the same lines, and that, if disclosures are necessary, they will be made around the table when the next Armour Plate Makers' meeting takes place."[265] That was the meeting in March 1917 "to discuss the question of armour prices."[266]

---

[261] Arnold, "Service," p. 302.

[262] Arnold, "Service," p. 303.

[263] Davenport-Hines, "British," p. 155. Citing: Christopher Addison, diary February 8, 1916, Bodleian Library, Oxford.

[264] Report of the Comptroller and Auditor General, *Navy Appropriation*, p. 16.

[265] Caillard to Forster (Messrs. Peat & Co.), February 21, 1917. VA Microfilm R 246, Folio 34; Benthall to Browns, Cammell Laird and Beardmores, March 16, 1917. VA Microfilm R 246, Folio 30.

[266] Benthall to Vickers, London, March 13, 1917. VA Microfilm R 246, Folio 26.

In late October 1917 the five firms met to discuss Falkner's desire to ask for a price increase and the Admiralty's parallel request for details of their armor plate costings, including labor and materials costs. Falkner was apparently concerned that the low wartime prices would cast a bad light on prewar prices.[267] While Vickers had considered and dismissed asking for a price increase, Caillard nevertheless brought the firms together to discuss this. Vickers Director J. L. Benthall was very concerned about meeting the Admiralty request. He had pointed out to Albert Vickers and Dawson that

> it would be the greatest mistake imaginable to start discussing prices for armour with the Admiralty as you will not only not get any increase in price, but you will find that they will want to cut down prices already given and we have been strongly advised by our friends at the Admiralty not to raise the question with them at all.[268]

The upshot of the meeting was an agreement that the five were to get their accountants and auditors to discover the actual costs of armour in 1917 on actual and estimated output and "to form an estimate as to what the cost would have been on the basis of present-day prices of material and labour, both based on this year's output."[269]

It seems an Advisory Committee on armor plate matters was being considered, making Falkner "very nervous about attempts to form anything in the shape of an Association or Committee. The existence of such a body must inevitably lead to demands for information from the Taxing authorities and this information will no doubt in due course reach the Admiralty." Falkner added a handwritten warning: "[W]e want to waltz very warily, and that any systemization … into combinations is at present to be depreciated."[270] Given the postwar investigations into the behavior of armament firms, this was a prescient concern.

In 1918 the Armor Plate Makers were again planning to meet and in preparation Mr. Forster, for Vickers' accountants Peat & Co., was preparing the costings, noting, "As I have not heard yet of any settlement having been made with Somerset House in respect to Depreciation, I have charged the Depreciation in the Costs on the basis of the latest scheme suggested …. This results in a considerable increase in the costs of the Plates."[271] Vickers then suggested a meeting of the five firms with Sir Henry Livesey, Director of Contracts, along the lines of the 1917 meeting.[272] The firms collaborated

---

[267] Caillard to Albert Vickers, October 20, 1917. VA Microfilm R 246, Folios 7–8.

[268] Benthall to Vickers, London, October 23, 1917. VA Microfilm R 246, Folio 3.

[269] Caillard to Vickers, Sheffield, November 5, 1917. VA Microfilm R 246, Folio 15.

[270] Falkner to Caillard, December 4, 1917. VA Microfilm R 246, Folio 25.

[271] Forster to Caillard, February 11, 1918. VA Microfilm R 246, Folios 36–37.

[272] Benthall to Browns, Cammell Laird and Beardmores, April 4, 1918. VA Microfilm R 246, Folios 37–38. Benthall to Vickers London, April 10, 1918. VA Microfilm R 246, Folio 38. (37–38 is used twice.)

on the layout of their armor plate costs and then each firms' figures were submitted to Sir Henry. The submission letter noted: "[W]e also show on the list the cost of armor per ton at the present day prices of material and wages. From these we think it clearly demonstrated that the present schedule is quite inadequate." At the conference, the firms wanted to request "that the schedule prices be raised to such figures as will cover all rises in material and wages and give us a profit of above 25 percent in view of the small amount of orders that are now given out by the Admiralty when compared with the enormous plants that we have to keep up in anticipation of urgent requirements."[273] Interestingly, whereas the armor plate costs per ton at present prices of Beardmore (£130.0.0), Brown (£141.0.0), Cammell Laird (£157.3.7) and Vickers (£135.15.11) were close, Armstrongs' costs were an outlier (£199.2.6) and possibly anticipate their postwar problems. Even after the submission discussions continued.

An indication of the scale of the issue comes from Caillard's correspondence with Sheffield about adding depreciation costs. The Directors had suggested "£25 per ton ... in view of the small output of the past year and of the small output which we think we can reasonably look forward to," considering the figure "quite justifiable."[274] However, Forster was concerned that with such a figure, total costings could not be guaranteed to the Admiralty. Benthall concluded: "I think it better to leave our costs with the depreciation at 18.1 percent, or £13.15.3 per ton which is the only figure that Mr. Forster is prepared to sign for."[275] Caillard subsequently negotiated with Forster the addition of a contingency because costs were likely to go up "to cover for this, 5% for the past figures, and 7½% for present-day figures."[276] Vickers clearly wanted to give the Admiralty the highest possible figures.

By July 1918 Vickers were coordinating another meeting of the armor plate makers, necessitated by "further information received in conversation ... [Armstrongs] have had with Sir Harry Livesey. It is very necessary that a meeting ... should be called as early as possible."[277] The information regarded "settlement of armour plate prices." Vickers asked the other firms to bring with them their latest figures – as well as their auditors – "so that some common analysis of these costs could, if possible, be made at this meeting."[278] After the meeting the firms wrote a joint letter to Sir Harry suggesting:

[273] Armour Plate Firms to Livesey, including figures, April 10, 1918. VA Microfilm R 246, Folios 53–54.
[274] Caillard to Benthall, April 22, 1918. VA Microfilm R 246, Folio 49. (The papers are out of order.)
[275] Benthall to Caillard, April 25, 1918. VA Microfilm R 246, Folio 47.
[276] Caillard to Benthall, April 26, 1918. VA Microfilm R 246, Folio 45.
[277] Caillard to Benthall, July 9, 1918. VA Microfilm R 246, Folio 63–64.
[278] Vickers to Armstrongs, Beardmores, Browns and Cammells, July 9, 1918. VA Microfilm R 246, Folio 61.

the following schedule for the 1917 Armour:-

For the 10,800-tons ordered, the price should be ... £149 per ton.

For the 1918 Armour, allowing for the rise in material and extra wages, we suggest the following schedule:-

If 5,000-tons ordered ... ... £186 per ton

If 10,000-tons ordered ... ... £181 per ton

If 15,000-tons ordered ... ... £ 178.10.0 per ton

If 20,000-tons, and upwards ... £ 176 per ton

As it seems advisable that the present Armour Plate schedule of prices issued in 1913 should be still retained for all classes of Armour, we would suggest that in the case of the 1917 Armour, the prices as now fixed by that schedule should each be raised by 62%.

For the 1918 Armour, we would suggest the present schedule be raised:-

If 5,000-tons ordered, by 101%

If 10,000-tons ordered, by 97%

If 15,000-tons ordered, by 94%

If 20,000-tons, and upwards by 91%.[279]

The firms declared that the figures were the average of those sent to Livesey in June "plus a small profit, which varies according to the amount of tonnage given out by the Admiralty each year."[280]

The response of the Admiralty was to initiate an investigation into the firms' costs and to send a team under Arthur Whinney, Adviser on Costs of Production, to visit each firm. Whinney had noted to the Accountant General of the Navy that "the Schedule of Prices which has up to recently been in operation was drawn up in August 1913 based upon Costs extracted in 1911 and previous years, and it is desired that the present enquiry should commence from the year 1912."[281] This caused a panic among the firms: "Sir William Ellis and Mr. Tongue seem to think that those costs ought to be considered dead, as they are afraid the Admiralty's idea is to take our profits over all the good years of 1913-14-15 and [decrease] our prices accordingly, which they do not want."[282]

The Admiralty plan was a dual threat, legitimating both retroactive audits and the government demand to investigate their books. The issue was taken up by the Federation of British Industries (set up in 1916 as an organization to represent industries and where several Vickers Directors were prominent players), which advised "if you are approached by any Government Department to enter into any new contract embodying a clause which provides for the investigation of costs, you should request that the matter be deferred" until the Federation of British Industries had concluded their

---

[279] Benthall Vickers to Livesey, July 18, 1918, V A Microfilm R 246, Folio 70.

[280] Ibid., Folio 71.

[281] Copy of Whinney to Accountant General Admiralty, October 1, 1918. V A Microfilm R 246, Folio 93.

[282] Benthall to Caillard, October 2, 1918. V A Microfilm R 246, Folios 91–92.

negotiations with the government on this.[283] Caillard sought to fend off a retroactive audit. He informed Benthall that if the Admiralty's investigation of costs in 1918 was a continuation of an existing investigation, then information should be provided, but if it was a new investigation, "then until the Federation have agreed the future method of investigation of costs with Lord Colwyn's Committee, no information should be given."[284] A few days later Benthall was explaining that Mr. Allen of Browns had understood that the resolution of a recent Federation of British Industries meeting was to be wholly cooperative with the Admiralty investigative team under Mr. Whinney, the Adviser on Costs of Production. It was the opposite.[285] Benthall followed up with Browns to "find out exactly what they had done and they have noted as you told us to do, i.e. put Mr. Whinney's people off when they came down ... by telling them that they could only have the particulars for the 10-months of 1917 and these they would need to get through their, and our Auditors."[286] The Admiralty team visited both Vickers and Browns on the same day and seem satisfied with the information from 1917. However, by December no decision on the prices for 1918 had been taken, and the Admiralty was asking for information and a revision of the armor plate price. The firms' responded: "To give details of the work done in the various armour plate shops would be quite impossible with the depleted staffs that we have at present, and therefore we regret we are unable to answer your letter more specifically."[287]

At the close of 1918 the five firms were:

> now going into important Reconstruction questions of considerable magnitude, and it is therefore essential they should have some general information as to the probable future requirements of the Navy, so that each can form an opinion of what proportion of their enormous Armour Plate Plants can be used for other purposes, if any, and what must be kept to meet the Navy's demands.[288]

While Vickers was in a robust financial position at the start of the war, as the conflict went on, and given the vast amount of work it was undertaking, the firm had to take large loans from the government to work on contracts for the government that were only paid for after the armaments were delivered. Sometimes the government was slow to pay. Albert Vickers pointed out this "absurdity" to Caillard in March 1918, later grumbling:

[283] Tennyson, Federation of British Industries, to Caillard, October 21, 1918. V A Microfilm R 246, Folio 111.

[284] Caillard to Benthall, November 18, 1918. V A Microfilm R 246, Folio 78.

[285] As set out in Caillard to Benthall, October 5, 1918. V A Microfilm R 246, Folio 90.

[286] Benthall to Caillard, November 21, 1918. V A Microfilm R 246, Folios 80–81.

[287] Benthall to Admiralty, December 12, 1918. V A Microfilm R 246, Folio 99.

[288] Benthall to Admiralty, December 12, 1918. V A Microfilm R 246, Folio 88.

Table 3.1 *Armstrongs and Vickers' profits after taxation, 1901–1919*[289]

Year	Armstrongs Profit £	Vickers Profit £	Vickers
1901	564,864	646,332	
1902	652,698	541,434	
1903	631,359	556,121	
1904	618,414	686,895	
1905	652,639	787,778	
1906	652,639	879,905	
1907	722,409	786,525	
1908	491,350	416,848	
1909	500,325	288,044	
1910	611,345	510,668	
1911	681,138	641,686	
1912	761,765	872,033	
1913	877,684	911,996	
1914	925,522	1,019,035	
1915		1,000,000++	
1916			
1917	} 4,053,605	}	6,612,439
1918		} 4,494,000*	
1919			

* The profits for 1916–19 were combined because Vickers' accounting system had "succumbed to the pressure of over-work and disorganization." Scott, *Vickers*, p. 132.

No member of any government ever thinks of what they ought to do in the interests of the contractor, they only think out how to pay as little money as possible, and if (as I should like to see) a sudden peace came about they would probably stop paying out anything they could help and leave us in a very dangerous position.[290]

This assessment was to prove prescient.

Table 3.1 shows the profits of Armstrongs and Vickers. For the first decade of the century, Vickers' profits averaged 13.3 percent.[291] However, this also masked some extreme swings. While Vickers' profits had slumped around the turn of

289 Brook, *Warships*, p. 21 Table 21; Scott, *Vickers*, pp. 132–33 and 389–90.
290 Scott, *Vickers*, pp. 130–31.
291 McNeill, *Pursuit*, p. 288; Scott recorded that this was tax free. Scott, *Vickers*, p. 82.

the century, by 1905 the company's results had rebounded "largely due to the increase of business done with foreign countries." There was another decline in profits from 1907–11 (not masked as Armstrongs' had been), but then results picked up. "The improvement was an all-round one, but the foreign business of the company and the business of the subsidiary companies in particular had flourished."[292] A. J. Arnold records that from 1910–14 Vickers' average returns on total capital were 10 percent; Armstrongs' were eight percent.[293] As Sir Noel Birch subsequently noted: "[B]efore 1914 [armament firms] made a great deal of money ... [but] for their ultimate welfare the money was perhaps too easily made."[294] The combination of the Treasury Agreement, the Munitions of War Act and the Finance (No. 2) Act of 1915 kept the profits at Armstrongs and Vickers in check. While profits increased, they were in proportion to the extra production the two firms had undertaken.

Summary

The Great War had brought profound changes to Armstrongs and Vickers, including in their relationships with the state. As they had remained independent, the government took no responsibility for their futures, and they also faced growing public disapproval. At the end of the war in November 1918, C. P. Scott in the *Manchester Guardian* expressed the hope of millions:

> The vast machine of military munitioning may continue to work for a little, as it were by force of habit, but with fast-diminishing energy and with no serious purpose before it except that of bringing itself, as soon as possible and with as little injury as possible to the millions of men and women it has absorbed, to a complete standstill.[295]

These expectations were to be a major challenge for the postwar period. Another was outlined by Sir Herbert Lawrence: "As regards the period of the War, except for supplies to the Allied Forces, foreign business so far as the Vickers Company was concerned, of course, was non-existent."[296] The firm would therefore face the dual challenges of reduced domestic markets and the need to reestablish diplomatic relationships with foreign countries.

[292] Scott, *Vickers*, p. 82.
[293] Arnold, "Service," p. 300.
[294] Quoted in Davenport-Hines, "British," p. 154.
[295] Scott, "The Great Day," *Manchester Guardian*, November 12, 1918. In: *C. P. Scott*, p. 173.
[296] Sir Herbert Lawrence to the Commission, March 11, 1936. Evidence Prepared for the Bankes Committee, Volume III. VA, Doc. 59, Folder 134, p. 3.

4

Selling Armaments in Britain 1919–1935

Interwar Struggles and Vickers-Armstrongs Is Born

In 1919, as Albert Vickers had predicted, armament firms found themselves in a "dangerous position."[1] There was an immediate collapse of demand, followed in the 1920s by various international arms control negotiations (in which the British Government played a major role), with severe implications for the survival of armament firms. Armstrongs and Vickers responded by diversifying into other businesses, but with limited success.

The contraction of the armaments market led the two firms to merge. Vickers-Armstrongs was born into difficult times on October 31, 1927. The Great Depression further eroded military spending and dashed hopes of expanding exports. In the early to mid-1930s three things happened simultaneously: the international situation deteriorated; arms control proceeded but did not solve international insecurity; and there was growing public ire about the past behavior of armament firms. The interwar period was therefore an extended existential crisis for Armstrongs and Vickers.

In terms of technologies, this period also saw the maturation of aircraft and tanks, and the increasing sophistication of warships, submarines, artillery and military electronics. Armstrongs and Vickers played important roles in advancing many of these technologies. However, there was reluctance within the government to accept how far technological progress had changed the conduct of war, causing problems for armament firms throughout this period and for the British state as it planned for rearmament in the mid-1930s.

Crisis: The End of the War

At the end of the Great War, the British Government immediately terminated all orders with armament firms. The Admiralty canceled orders for 480 warships and 414 sloops and small vessels, as well as merchant construction and repair work.[2] According to Eustace Tennyson d'Eyncourt: "Great numbers of ships then under construction were stopped, and the work already done on them

---

[1] Scott, *Vickers*, p. 131.
[2] Slaven, "War," in Davenport-Hines, *Business*, p. 67.

broken up and scrapped ... any ships with which we were reluctantly allowed to proceed took a long time in building, some of them progressing so slowly that it was six or seven years before they were completed."[3] This was a severe blow to warship builders. Worse, the government held plentiful reserves across all services. For example, "the Air Ministry held three years' supply of aircraft and engines for the RAF [Royal Air Force] and there was little prospect of new orders of appreciable scale."[4] These developments threw armament firms into financial difficulties. Armstrongs "was faced with a catastrophe involving the casting out of employment of many thousands of workmen, some of whom had been with them all their working lives."[5] Vickers had expanded the most during wartime and faced a massive adjustment in people, products and profits.

Additionally, as previously agreed with the government, the armament firms now took over all the buildings, plant and machinery that had been installed in their works for wartime production.[6] Firms were therefore saddled with significant redundant capacity.[7] Whereas the National Factories (see Chapter 3) swiftly reverted to their civilian functions of making buses, railway carriages and bicycles, armament firms were stymied because many of their products – and the equipment to build them – could not be "civilianized."

Vickers declared it found wartime accounting "so complicated that an exact apportionment among the various years was ... [too] so difficult," and they produced only brief amalgamated accounts covering the period up to December 1919.[8] However, the Vickers Archive shows that such accounts existed but were hidden from the public; the same was true at Armstrongs.[9] Moreover, "it is apparent that the profit figures for the Barrow yards shown in their head-office books were deflated during the war years by special depreciation charges and write-offs and by the creation of local secret reserves."[10] Both firms had systematically deflated their returns in 1914–19. "In the case of Vickers the distortion during the war years appeared to have reduced the returns to equity interests by only 1% but at Armstrongs it implied returns to equity of over 15%, as compared with the 10.4% published."[11]

In 1919 Armstrongs, Vickers, Cammell Lairds, Browns and Beardmores tried to get compensation for their obsolete plant through negotiations with the Admiralty on the long-running question of the costs of armor plate. As noted

[3] d'Eyncourt, *Shipbuilder's*, p. 129.
[4] Hayward, *British*, p. 11.
[5] d'Eyncourt, *Shipbuilder's*, p. 149.
[6] *History*, Vol. III. Part 3, Chapter 4.
[7] "Sheffield's Case," *Sheffield Daily Telegraph*, December 31, 1925. Cited in Tweedale, *Steel City*, p. 240.
[8] Arnold, "Service," p. 300. Citing: Vickers *Annual Report 1919*, VA Doc. 1480.
[9] Arnold, "Service," p. 301. Citing: *Annual Reports 1910–24*. TWA 130/1329–86.
[10] Arnold, "Service," p. 306.
[11] Arnold, "Service," p. 310.

in Chapter 3, in July 1918 the firms had proposed significant price increases on armor plate that included "a small profit."[12] In early 1919 the Admiralty still had not accepted their figures, despite discussing them with the five firms. Director of Contracts Sir Frederick Black now asked to meet with the firms' accountants, who were to provide costings for 1912 (the base year), costings for ten months of 1917 and "any information they possess which bears upon the capital expended on plant and machinery in each case for the manufacture of armour plates and how much of that capital has been written off and how much is included in the costs of manufacture of Armor at each of the works for interest or depreciation on existing plans and buildings."[13]

Caillard asked Forster to represent Vickers, hoping that the issue "might be settled at a round-table conference in his office, without having to have the Admiralty Auditors coming down here to the works and going into our books … as the Admiralty seem to wish." He reported that Sir Frederick "is most anxious to meet us in every way he possibly can and not to cause unnecessary trouble."[14] Directors and accountants for the five firms met with Sir Frederick and Sir Arthur Whinney, Adviser on Costs to the Admiralty. Sir Arthur asked forensic questions about the firms' accounting procedures and discovered that they had taken different approaches to depreciation.[15]

At the same time, Cammells was telling Vickers: "We think the time has arrived when the question of depreciation and obsolescence of Buildings, Plant, and Machinery employed in the manufacture of Armour Plate should be closely considered, and a substantial writing-down out of Excess Profits Duty secured from the Inland Revenue Authorities."[16] Caillard thought that "the point of view held by Cammell's [sic] is quite right and equitable," and that the five firms should collaborate on a plan.[17] The firms achieved a good measure of success. Subsequently, "Armstrongs merged a receipt from the government with their depreciation fund in 1921 and was able to recognise a large surplus in 1923,"[18] and Vickers received "rebates or refunds equal to almost the entire £4M of Excess Profits Duty and Munitions Levy paid during the war."[19]

Nevertheless, Douglas Vickers complained that "when the company had made profits, excess profits [tax] and one thing and another took away practically everything but what was left in the shape of bricks and mortar."[20]

[12] Benthall Vickers to Livesey, July 18, 1918, VA Microfilm R 246, Folio 71.
[13] Black to Vickers, January 7, 1919, reproduced in Vickers to Armstrongs, Beardmores, Browns and Cammells, January 9, 1919. Folio 115; Black to Vickers January 10, 1919, Folio 114.
[14] Benthall to Forster, January 9, 1919. VA Microfilm R 246, Folio 112.
[15] Forster to Caillard, January 16, 1919. VA Microfilm R 246, Folios 117–20.
[16] Allan, Cammell Laird to Vickers, January 14, 1919. VA Microfilm R 246, Folio 126.
[17] Caillard to Benthall (Sheffield), January 16, 1919. VA Microfilm R 246, Folio 116.
[18] Arnold, "Service," p. 313.
[19] Arnold, "Service," p. 302.
[20] Packard, Whitehall, p. 115. Citing: The Times, April 16, 1925.

Now Vickers – and Armstrongs especially – hid problems by moving money from the reserves and making no provision for depreciation.

Vickers planned to work itself out of its financial problems. In 1919 an observer reported: "The directorate is drawn from whatever genius can any-where be found." Visiting the Vickers' London Head Office was "more like a visit to a great Government department than to a private firm ... all are bound by one rule; they are full-time directors. You find them at their desks as early and assiduously as their clerks or their secretaries."[21] This organizational work ethic could not compensate for canceled orders, however.

The British Government's expectation that peace would last created further dilemmas for armament firms. In November 1918 the interim report of the McKinnon Wood Committee, considering the decentralization of Woolwich Arsenal's work, concluded:

> Assuming, therefore, that a Government factory is kept in existence, and that the supply of armaments is greatly reduced in quantity, it more or less follows that the present outlay of the larger private firms for armament production will be considerably reduced, *and such manufacture will not improbably disappear as a specialty. It is also probable that the country will insist on the production of all armaments being confined to Government factories* .... [S]pecializing in the future on the part of a limited number of firms will probably not be necessary for the safety of the country.[22]

This was an important signal about the future of domestic procurement. For the firms, worse followed. In August 1919, Winston Churchill, the Secretary of State for War and Air, advocated adopting a Ten-Year Rule, because war was unlikely within a decade. This became the government's working assumption. The Ten-Year Rule was later institutionalized by the Committee of Imperial Defence, at (now Chancellor) Churchill's urging, making it a rolling ten-year period.[23] The messages were clear: Increased domestic procurement was unlikely; Armstrongs and Vickers needed to diversify and find new markets.

Usually in this situation Armstrongs and Vickers would cut prices, but this failed as there was no demand to stimulate.[24] Their other standard strategy – turning to exports – failed due to the international surfeit of weapons and deficit of money, compounded by Britain's return to the Gold Standard, which made exports more expensive. Douglas Vickers reported to the 1921 annual meeting that "As far as armaments are concerned there has been a little relief through the orders obtained from the Japanese Government about twelve months ago, but except for that this year has been no better for ordnance work than the

---

[21] O'Connor, *Daily Telegraph*. Cited in Tweedale, *Steel City*, p. 137.

[22] Hornby, *Factories*, p. 15; Postan, *British*, p. 393. Citing: *Report of the Enquiry into the Royal Ordnance Factories, Woolwich*, p. 8. Emphasis added.

[23] Postan, *British*, p.1.

[24] Miller, *Planning*, pp. 40–41.

previous one."[25] Vickers was nevertheless "under persuasion from Whitehall" to maintain armament production capacity, though no orders were in sight.[26]

Strategies for Survival

Vickers and Armstrongs responded by licensing armaments for production abroad. This was not enough to keep them afloat, though, so other strategies were pursued. Vickers employed strategies of diversification, divestment, consolidation and development. Armstrongs relied upon diversification strategies.

In the emerging field of aircraft production there were near diversifications into civilian production and backward integrations into producing aeroengines. Armstrongs was an early mover. In 1919 it amalgamated Armstrong Siddeley Motors Ltd., Armstrong-Whitworth (Aircraft) Ltd., A.V. Roe & Co. and the Gloster Aircraft Co. into the Armstrong-Whitworth Development Company.[27] Vickers continued to develop aircraft and record-breaking vividly showcased their expertise. For example, footage of Alcock and Brown's 1919 transatlantic fight in a Vickers Vimy aircraft was shown in movie theaters across the Empire.[28]

While aircraft firms could produce for civilian or military markets, both were depressed.[29] In 1918 industry output had been 30,000 aircraft, but in 1924 the industry produced only 503.[30] The government now recognized that the sector needed to be maintained, and the Navy model of relationships with firms was adopted. New initiatives provided design work to select firms – known as "the family" – keeping them in business. To Keith Hayward the interwar aircraft industry was "a state pensioner."[31] In 1930 Vickers' Board Member Sir Mark Webster Jenkinson remarked privately that "these various aircraft Companies cannot live indefinitely on subsidies from the Air Ministry."[32]

Vickers and Armstrongs diversified into civilian products. Vickers had set up a Peace Products Committee in 1917 and planned to exploit the expected booms in railways, ships and electricity.[33] Armstrongs had established their "After the War Conditions" subcommittee in 1916. For near diversifications, the subcommittee had considered reentering the civil engineering field but decided instead on marine engine building. Armstrongs also moved into merchant shipping

[25] "Company Meetings," *The Scotsman*, p. 3.
[26] Scott, *Vickers*, p. 144.
[27] "Article concerning Aircraft Department by Captain Fairbairn Crawford, 29 January 1957," TWA, D/VA/6/9–10.
[28] *British Pathé News*, "Alcock."
[29] "General Sykes," p. 11.
[30] Hornby, *Factories*, p. 18.
[31] Hayward, *British*, p. 7.
[32] Webster Jenkinson to Zaharoff, July 7, 1930. VA, Doc. 786.
[33] Scott, *Vickers*, p. 137.

and electro-engineering, and resumed motorcar production. For the third time in its history, Armstrongs decided to diversify into locomotives, with the Scotswood plant designed to be the "largest self-contained locomotive building establishment in the world," producing 300–400 engines per annum.[34]

There was a problem with diversification into nearby areas: The armament firms often had similar survival strategies. For example, in railway equipment Vickers and Armstrongs found themselves competing with Beardmores, with the Royal Arsenals, which were also attempting ("woefully") to build locomotives, and with existing civilian producers.[35] Vickers' sally into locomotive production ended in 1920 when their contract tender was significantly higher than the civilian firms' bids.[36]

Armstrongs was chasing Moscow railway orders in the spring of 1920.[37] By May, the firm had a preliminary five-year agreement to repair around 300 locomotives annually, conditional upon the concluding of a general trade agreement by the two governments. Armstrongs desperately wanted the contract, which was expected to keep 3,000 employed on the Tyne and bring in around £8,000,000 (£397,424,498 in August 2022).[38] The agreement was signed in March 1921.[39] Armstrongs was surprisingly unsophisticated about production; it planned to work on nine different locomotive models and was unwilling to speed up production.[40] Anthony Heywood notes, "The British government and Armstrong Whitworth … leave the impression that they felt … rightfully entitled to a large Soviet railway order, for which complacency they paid accordingly."[41] That said, the Moscow Representative of the British Government was skeptical that the contract would be executed.[42] He likely realized that domestic Soviet politics was making the deal difficult to defend.[43] There ensued "two fraught sessions" with the Soviet trade delegation in London, and the result was "Armstrongs giving way almost completely on 3 October and settling for just 200 new boilers" at only £797,500 (£39,618,255 in August 2022).[44] Ultimately, the contract – which the Soviets saw as a political gesture – was abandoned in

[34] Warren, *Armstrongs*, pp. 205–06.
[35] Heywood, "Armstrong," p. 66. Citing: Conclusions of a Conference of Ministers, May 28, 1920. TNA, CAB 23/21, p. 200; Hume and Moss, *Beardmore*, pp. 184–85; "Beardmore Locomotives," pp. 6–7.
[36] Scott, *Vickers*, p. 137.
[37] Heywood, "Armstrong," p. 60.
[38] White, *Commercial Relations*, p. 270, ff. 67. Citing: Ottley to Gregory, December 31, 1920. TNA, FO 371/6885.
[39] White, *Commercial Relations*, pp. 129–32.
[40] Heywood, "Armstrong," p. 68.
[41] Heywood, *Lenin's Russia*, p. 231.
[42] White, *Commercial Relations*, p. 292, ff. 17. Citing: Hodgson, Moscow No. 34 (R), March 26, 1921. TNA, FO 371/6929.
[43] Heywood, "Armstrong," pp. 76–84.
[44] Heywood, *Lenin's Russia*, p. 177; Heywood, "Armstrong," p. 83.

late 1921. Armstrongs were no more successful at this attempt to move into locomotives than they had been in the past.

Armstrongs had practically ceased motorcar production at their Scotswood plant at the start of the war. When the firm resumed production, it was in the Midlands. In early 1919 they bought the Siddeley-Deasy Company of Coventry, whom they had previously done business with. The firm became Armstrong Siddeley, and by 1923 had produced what the *Times* declared "a praiseworthy attempt to produce a British family car."[45]

Armstrongs invested further in merchant shipbuilding.[46] While this was moderately successful, it could not halt the slide of the firm.[47] Warship builders had hoped that passenger liners would be a lifesaver, but demand for Atlantic travel was depressed and they were competing with dedicated constructors.[48] Vickers had some successes, having contacts to draw on.[49] Sir Basil Zaharoff secured contracts for two liners to be built at Barrow for the Peninsula and Orient Steam Navigation Co., sealing the deal with the P&O Chairman after Lord Inchcape had won 100 francs at the Monte Carlo casino.[50] Armstrongs and Vickers found civilian ship sales insufficient even with assistance from the Overseas Trade (Credits and Insurance) Act of 1920 and the 1921 Trade Facilities Act.[51]

The Washington Naval Conference of 1920–21 was another problem (discussed later in the chapter). Douglas Vickers informed shareholders, "The Company obtained a fair share of the orders placed a few months ago for the four battle cruisers, although all the hulls were placed elsewhere. These orders raised a hope of better times, both for us and our workmen, but owning to the discussions at the Washington Conference, instructions were received recently to suspend work on them altogether."[52] This was a bitter blow.

As Scott recounts, at Vickers, business "was already very bad in 1920."[53] Hope came with a contract for three P&O passenger ships, obtained by Craven through "stalking Lord Inchcape with grim determination."[54] In 1922 two "Treaty ships" were commissioned. The *Nelson* was to be built by Armstrongs and the *Rodney* at Cammell Laird in Birkenhead. These firms had submitted

45 Warren, *Armstrongs*, p. 158. Citing: "Cars of Today."
46 Collier, *Arms*, p. 13; Scott, *Vickers*, pp. 137–38.
47 Lillicrap, "d'Eyncourt," p. 353.
48 Parkinson, "Shipbuilding," p. 82; Miller, *Planning*, pp. 30–31.
49 Albert Vickers to Albert Booth, Cunard, October 24, 1910. Letter Book 31, VA, Doc. 1005, Folios 237–39.
50 "When Lord Inchcape Won," p. 6.
51 R.M.S.P Meat Transports Ltd. were lent £2,300,000 for seven years for the construction of three ships at Vickers' yard. Cerretano, "Treasury," p. 87, Table 2; Contributed, "Export Credits Guarantee Department," pp. 50–51; Aldcroft, "Early History," pp. 69–71.
52 "Company Meetings: Vickers," p. 3.
53 Scott, *Vickers*, p. 143.
54 Scott, *Vickers*, p. 185.

the lowest tenders; Armstrongs' bid at £1,479,000 for hull and machinery was far below Vickers' bid of £1,858,000.[55]

In 1919 Vickers made a near diversification into electro-engineering, inspired by Board member Dudley Docker, acquiring Metropolitan at a (high) cost of £13 million, then buying British Westinghouse and renaming them the Metropolitan-Vickers Electrical Company.[56] While Vickers had some background in the field (in 1915 manufacturing generators for a Philadelphia power station), more heft was required to take on the German electro-engineering giants, and subsequently an agreement was struck with Brown Boveri, which included restrictions on where Vickers could sell equipment. Vickers had to take out an expensive bank loan to complete the deal, though Sir Francis Barker considered it a "very promising acquisition."[57]

In parallel, Armstrongs bought the electrical engineering firm Crompton & Co. In 1920 they acquired an interest in the Pearson and Knowles Coal and Iron company of Lancashire – a logical backward integration. However, most of Armstrongs' diversifications were speculative leaps. They bought the Glasgow designer and ceramic decoration maker Messrs. A. and J. Maw. In 1921 they acquired the Bury paper machinery works of Charles Walmesley, and a year later undertook a fateful diversification into paper mills and hydroelectric power in Newfoundland, Canada.[58] This was disastrous. The companies could not compete with existing high-volume industries and lacked the knowledge and skills to develop and market new civilian products.[59] The Newfoundland Power and Paper Co. Ltd. was "a bottomless pit for funds" and from the mid-1920s was controlled by Armstrongs' bank, the Bank of England (BoE).[60]

Vickers diversified into a dizzying variety of civilian products. By 1919 the firm was advertising sewing and washing machines. At the 1920 Ideal Home Exhibition they showed a "Vickers Ideal Cottage" filled with their products, which ranged from flooring to furniture to children's toys.[61] In 1920 Douglas Vickers noted: "It may be said that practically the whole of the Company's Works have now been diverted to Peace Products, with the exception of a small portion of some of the Works, which are still employed on armaments."[62]

---

[55] Johnston and Buxton, *Battleship*, p. 36.
[56] Scott, *Vickers*, p. 142. My grandfather, Percy Spear, worked at Metro-Vicks in Trafford Park during WWII.
[57] Segreto, "More Trouble," p. 328. Citing: Board of Director's Minutes, "Brown Boveri," meetings September 26 and December 11, 1919. VA.
[58] Warren, *Armstrongs*, pp. 214–21.
[59] Lillicrap, "d'Eyncourt, p. 353.
[60] Tolliday, *Business*, p. 192; Cerretano, "Treasury," p. 89.
[61] *Vickers News*, Vol. 1, No. 2 (October 15, 1919), p. 18; *Vickers News*, Vol. 1, No. 10 (February 15, 1920); "Vickers Darenta Toys: A Transition from War to Peace," *Vickers News*, Vol. 2, No. 22 (August 15, 1920), pp. 153–57. VA, Doc. 1910.
[62] Vickers, *History*, VA Doc. 762, p. 2.

At the 1920 Great War Exhibition all the major firms showed both their war-time and peacetime products.[63] A late 1920s Vickers brochure showcased new products, including brewery tanks and bicycles.[64] However, civilian markets were very competitive. Vickers also diversified their investments, buying into Bryant & May, the British Lighting and Ignition Company Ltd., the Bromley and West Kent Newspaper Company Ltd., the British Refrigerating Company Ltd. and many more firms.[65]

A Vickers employee recalled that the "worst year for Barrow was 1923," when the yard was so empty that birds were nesting in the cranes.[66] Vickers did not pay dividends on ordinary shares in 1920 or between 1923 and 1926.[67] In winter 1921–22, Sir Mark Webster Jenkinson, a Chartered Accountant from Sheffield (and future Board member) who had previously worked at the Ministry of Munitions, was tasked by the Vickers Board with reporting on the state of the company.[68] His conclusions were sobering: "Experience has shown that combinations or trusts can only be successful if confined to one trade or class of trade."[69] He recommended splitting the firm into independent units, with existing shareholders granted shares in each, and hinted at writing down share value. Though not acted on, these recommendations were harbingers of things to come.

Crisis: The Threat from International Arms Control

With British firms struggling, arms control negotiations were a new threat. First came moves to negotiate multilateral agreements to prevent armaments reaching European colonial territories.[70] The British Government strongly supported the League of Nations' attempt to develop a comprehensive legal framework to regulate arms transfers to Africa, Turkey and the Middle East. The result was the 1919 Convention for the Control of the Trade in Arms and Ammunition, and Protocol (known as the St. Germain Convention).[71] This worked in harmony with the Covenant of the League of Nations, signed by member states, and the proposition that arms exports were only allowed where they were explicitly licensed by a government.[72] The aim was to make exports

---

[63] "The Great War Exhibition," pp. 2–4.
[64] *The Activities of Vickers Limited*, brochure circa 1928–29. "Guides to the Company and its products," TWA, D/VA/2/9.
[65] "Register of Investments 1903–1930," VA, Doc. 1919.
[66] "Barrow recollections of Mr. V. H. Crozier," VA, Doc 596, Folio 123.
[67] Davenport-Hines, *Business*, p. 266.
[68] He had also published a book on accountancy. Webster-Jenkinson, *Bookkeeping*.
[69] Scott, *Vickers*, p. 157.
[70] Harkavy, *Arms Trade*, p. 214; Committee of Imperial Defence, "Report of the Sub-Committee on Arms Traffic," January 1917, p. 1. TNA Cabinet (CAB) 16/44.
[71] "Official Documents: Convention," pp. 297–313; Anderson, "International," p. 760.
[72] Goldblat, *Arms Control*, p. 22.

the exception, not the rule. While the major armament producing states signed the Convention, they did not ratify it.[73] Neil Cooper notes the strength of support for imperial armaments restraint: "[E]ven though the convention never came into force the European powers informally agreed to carry out its provisions in Africa and the Middle East."[74]

While these measures potentially hit Vickers' machine gun business (Maxim-Nordenfeld had been marketing them to the King of Abyssinia and "Indian princes"[75]), the main result was to prevent British firms from trading with states that had not signed the St. Germain Convention. Daniel Stahl shows that the Convention had direct implications for Armstrongs and Vickers, and they vigorously lobbied the government on the issue.[76] They were particularly concerned about exports to Spain. Even though it had not ratified the Convention, the British Government rigorously implemented it, denying export licenses for armaments to non-signatory powers. Both firms lobbied for permission to complete some export agreements. In May 1920 Vickers' agent Brigadier-General Rudkin and Sheffield MP Major Ralph Glynn met Under-Secretary of State Cecil Harmsworth to discuss the issue.[77] Harmsworth reported:

> Meanwhile according to Gen. Rudkin, both France and the United States are sending munitions into Spain (Gen. Rudkin understands that the French Government winks at this infraction of the Convention on the plea that the French Parliament has not yet ratified the Convention.) So strictly, on the other hand, are we interpreting the Convention that guns ordered of Messrs. Vickers in 1910 for a Spanish battleship are not allowed to be delivered.[78]

The Board of Trade contacted the Foreign Office about the issue:

> Attention is again invited to the particular application made in January of this year by Messrs. Armstrong Whitworth & Co. Ltd., for the export of two twelve-inch guns, together with their mountings, intended for the battleship "Jaime 1", of an approximate value of 370,000 pounds sterling. In this case it is understood that the arms were ordered for the Spanish Government before the outbreak of war, and Messrs. Armstrong Whitworth are now placed in the unfortunate position, through no fault of their

---

[73] Stone, "Imperialism," p.19.

[74] Cooper, Evidence to Committees on Arms Exports.

[75] Loewe Papers, A/4, VA, Doc. 1933.

[76] Stahl, "Decolonization," p. 7.

[77] Rudkin, a former ADC to King George V, was Vickers' global representative for military artillery between 1920 and 1923. Davenport-Hines, *Markets*, p. 177.

[78] "Spanish Arms Commission in England," Memorandum of Cecil Harmsworth, May 4, 1920. TNA, FO 371/4421. I am grateful to Dr. Stahl for providing me with a copy of this document and others from this file.

own … of running the risk of seeing the contract rescinded owing to the non-fulfillment and being replaced with some firm in the United States of America.

Messrs. Vickers Limited have also recently experienced difficulties in exporting war material from this country to Spain, although identical material which was placed with the Bethlehem Steel Corporation on a sub-contract, was going forward from the United States to Spain without difficulty.[79]

Additionally, Barker wrote to the British Ambassador in Madrid, Sir Esme Howard, outlining the problem. "You will of course realize the very serious loss of prestige which my firm, in conjunction with other British Armament firms, is consequently suffering, and, unless immediate steps are taken to remove the present difficulties, such trade with Spain formerly exclusively in British hands will automatically be transferred to French and American firms."[80] The next day Sir Esme sent Barker's letter to Earl Curzon at the Foreign Office, adding "I venture to think that this is a case in which an exception should be made in favour of allowing the Spanish Government to obtain the guns in question required for the battleship 'Jamie 1.'"[81]

Subsequently Rudkin wrote to Ralph Glynn (who passed the letter to the Foreign Office) about a Spanish visit he and Barker had made:

> The chief point which came to light at our interview with Sir Esme was that, until such time as all the Allied Governments have ratified the Arms Traffic Convention, the Supreme Council of the Allies cannot invite Spain to be become a signatory to it. This point, therefore, makes the case of the armament for the Spanish battleship "Jaime 1" one of particular hardship.[82]

Vickers also shared intelligence:

> I have the authority of Officers of the General Staff in Madrid that the firm of Hotchkiss in France has delivered Machine Guns to Spain during the past twelve months, also that Schneiders are supplying 29 Howitzer Batteries, 15 c.m. calibre. I also believe I am right in saying that Spain has bought in Italy war material to the value of about 300,000,000 Pesetas.[83]

The solution to the problem was not the exception Armstrongs and Vickers sought, but a letter to Earl Curzon from the Spanish Ambassador to Britain, Alfonso Merry del Val, which explained the issues and noted "that the Government of his Catholic Majesty has decided to adhere to the convention of

---

[79] Edgcumbe, Board of Trade, Memorandum to Foreign Office, received May 17, 1920. TNA, FO 371/4419.
[80] Barker to Howard, June 4, 1920. TNA, FO 371/4423.
[81] Howard to Curzon, June 5, 1920. TNA, FO 371/4423.
[82] Rudkin to Glynn, June 10, 1920. Copied to Foreign Office. TNA, FO 371/4422.
[83] Rudkin to Glynn, June 10, 1920. TNA, FO 371/4422.

Saint-Germain regulating the traffic of arms and munitions."[84] Curzon replied that in light of this, the shipments "may be expedited as much as possible."[85] Vickers and Armstrongs could now complete their contracts. This incident shows the limits of the firms' power with the British Government. Armstrongs and Vickers were unable to get their way despite their lobbying. It took another sovereign state to move the British Government.

The Washington Conference on Naval Armaments was now convened to "contribute to the maintenance of the general peace, and to reduce the burdens of competition in armament."[86] During these negotiations, which were also a high point of British naval rivalry with the United States, Sir Trevor Dawson continued Vickers' intelligence sharing, providing the First Lord of the Admiralty with "secretly obtained" data on American orders for 97,914 gross tons of armor plate. Dawson wanted to empower the First Lord in negotiating with the Cabinet for increased naval spending, thereby favoring Vickers.[87] This failed. The government was more interested in arms control.

The outcome of the hard-fought negotiations was the Washington Naval Treaty of 1922, between the British Empire, France, Italy, Japan and the United States.[88] This instituted a ten-year "battleship holiday" of no new warship production.[89] After the holiday only twenty-year-old ships could be replaced.[90] The Treaty established a "total tonnage available to each of the five contracting powers in the 'capital ship' and 'aircraft carrier' categories based on a fixed ratio."[91] Detailed regulations on capital ship and aircraft carrier displacement and gun calibers were included to ensure a common interpretation of the rules.[92] Articles XV and XVI "prohibited the construction of vessels exceeding the treaty limitations for another (non-contracting) power, and required full details of any warship built for a foreign power to be communicated to the four contracting powers."[93] While aimed at preventing state "breakout," this also restricted naval exports.

---

[84] Merry del Val to Curzon, July 23, 1920. TNA, FO 371/4423.
[85] Curzon to Spanish Ambassador, July 31, 1920. TNA, FO 371/4423.
[86] Cited in: Jordan, *Warships*, p. xii.
[87] Davenport-Hines, "British Marketing," pp. 158–59. Citing: Dawson to Walter Long, November 1, 1920, Long Papers 716/1. Dawson was made a baronet in 1920 for "Public services in connection with Home Office, War Office, and Admiralty." Supplement to the London Gazette, January 1, 1920, p. 2. At: www.thegazette.co.uk/London/issue/31712/supplement/2.
[88] There was a parallel Four-Power Treaty between the U.S.A., the British Empire, Japan and France. Jordan, *Warships*, pp. xii–xiv.
[89] "Treaty between the British Empire, France, Italy, Japan and the United States of America for the Limitation of Naval Armament – Washington, February 6, 1922." Text in: Jordan, *Warships*, Appendix 1.
[90] Jordan, *Warships*, p. 59.
[91] Jordan, *Warships*, p. xi
[92] Jordan, *Warships*, pp. 49–54.
[93] Jordan, *Warships*, p. 56.

Armament firms assumed that the impact of the agreement would mirror previous order famines, but the Washington Treaty was an existential threat. Christopher Miller recounts, "The impending resolution to wipe out orders for many years did not reach the boardrooms of the major shipbuilding companies almost until the ink was dry on the Washington agreement, and the decision was not fully accepted for some years after that."[94] The Admiralty – itself in denial about the implications of the negotiations – was completely outmaneuvered by the Treasury and only latterly protested about the Treaty's implications for private yards.[95]

In response, the Admiralty proposed closing two of the five British armor plate and naval ordnance firms. The firms objected and a counter proposal from William Beardmore was accepted by the Admiralty: Available orders would be divided between the five firms – and only them – and a maintenance sum for the "lean years," equal to the cost of maintaining only three firms, would be divided between the five.[96] So deep was the procurement trough, it took until 1934 for every firm to receive orders.[97]

Unfortunately, "while the French and Italians had soured on naval arms limitation by the late 1920s, the British continued to observe the rules of the regime for the better part of the interwar period."[98] Even so, all contracting states strategized to continue naval developments, pushing the Treaty's boundaries.[99] Germany was evading the Versailles Treaty restrictions by building "pocket battleships" and a new round of arms racing was covertly beginning.

Though Britain constructed nineteen medium and light cruisers between 1922 and 1931, ten were built in Royal Dockyards. Of the remaining nine, Vickers got only one, though the firm was somewhat cushioned by orders for submarines, constructing twelve over the period.[100] This small government program was not enough to sustain the armament industry.

Crisis: The Threat of Going Under

After six years of unsuccessful diversifications and meager military sales, even the biggest British armament firms were in crisis. In 1915 the BoE had granted Armstrongs unlimited financial provisions.[101] This proved costly. "By 1925 …

[94] Miller, *Planning*, pp. 36, 37.

[95] Miller, *Planning*, p. 39.

[96] Hume and Moss, *Beardmores*, pp. 180, 194. According to Slaven, the warship group had been using a rota since 1923. Slaven, "War," p. 104. Additionally, as David Edgerton has noted, the Admiralty subsidized steel producers Beardmore, English Steel and Firth-Brown "to keep at least 18,000 tons of capacity; well ahead of current requirements in the 1920s and early 1930s." Edgerton, "Public Ownership," pp. 169–70.

[97] Slaven, "War," p. 95.

[98] DiCicco, "Decline," pp. 90–91.

[99] Jordan, *Warships*, pp. 108–52.

[100] Miller, *Planning*, p. 40.

[101] Cerretano, "Treasury," p. 81. Citing: Bank of England Archives, G14/21, Memorandum on Armstrong by the Branch Bank Office, May 14, 1921.

Armstrong Whitworth, which owed the BoE £2.6 million, was on the verge of bankruptcy."[102] Vickers was also in a financial crisis and Beardmores was in the worst condition. What happened next is a study in contrasts.

The Vickers Board invited an "advisory committee" of outsiders to investigate the situation. It was headed by former Board member Dudley Docker and included Reginald McKenna of the Midland Bank (a former Chancellor and First Lord of the Admiralty) and Sir William Plender of Deloitte Plender and Co., the BoE's accountants.[103] Zaharoff communicated with them about keeping Vickers afloat.[104] The real investigative work was conducted by Sir Mark Webster Jenkinson.[105] His report and recommendation to write down capital was approved by the Board, and ultimately led to a High Court petition to reduce the value of ordinary shares from £1 to 6s. 8d. (6 shillings, 8 pence) which was subsequently approved by the shareholders.[106] This mainly hit banking interests and individual shareholders.[107]

The Board also agreed to divest Vickers of the financially hazardous connection with Beardmores, selling 845,000 shares to Lady Invernairn for a mere £75,000. In 1926/7 – ironically when Canadian Vickers was beginning to profit from diversifying into turbine engines – Vickers received a low-ball offer and readily sold, losing two thirds of the value of Canadian Vickers in the process. Their Wolseley Tool and Motor Car Company went into receivership, and it was acquired by Morris for £730,000. Metropolitan-Vickers was sold to General Electric, and Vickers exited the electrical engineering field. In addition, Douglas Vickers was moved aside after thirty-eight years on the Board, becoming President, and Sir Herbert Lawrence became Chairman.[108] Together with a renewed focus on armament production, these moves saved the company.

When Armstrongs was in desperate straits in 1926, John Siddeley offered £1.5 million to buy Armstrong Siddeley, and this was gladly accepted.[109] Armstrongs' perilous position had been hidden by fanciful accounting. A 1926 financial journal complained:

> The deficiency of £891,500 in the past year [1925] as compared with a net profit of £505,250 for 1924 is but an incident in a story of misfortune and miscalculation …. Year after year … the Armstrong accounts have been published, profits announced, and dividends declared with never a suggestion or hint of impending breakdown …. The statement of the new

[102] Chandler, *Scale*, p. 343.
[103] Hume and Moss, *Beardmores*, p. 196.
[104] Zaharoff to Docker and McKenna, November 24, 1925; Zaharoff to Docker, February 3, 1926; Zaharoff to Docker, February 11, 1926. In the first draft of Vickers' responses to the Royal Commission, March 10, 1936. VA, Doc. 788.
[105] Scott, *Vickers*, pp. 156–57.
[106] Scott, *Vickers*, pp. 158–59.
[107] Williams, *Who's Who*, pp. 10–14.
[108] Chandler, *Scale*, pp. 343–44.
[109] Warren, *Armstrongs*, p. 158.

chairman, Lord Southborough, that these losses "arise on a large number of contracts and affect nearly every department of the business …" is only another way of saying that the profits claimed were much overestimated.[110]

These revelations compounded Armstrongs' problems. As the First Lord of the Admiralty drily noted in 1927: "Messrs. Armstrong, by unfortunate speculations and disastrous fresh undertakings since the Armistice, find themselves in a position where they are faced with liquidation unless some substantial government assistance can be provided."[111]

Drastic changes were made.[112] That was not enough though. It was the private BoE which acted, because the firm's debt to them was nearly £6,500,000 by 1926 (£441,597,694 in August 2022) and it could not let the firm fail.[113] BoE Governor Montagu Norman forced a reorganization in 1925 by bringing in consultant Frater Taylor, known as a "company doctor" for his success in reviving firms.[114] After Chairman Sir Glynn West resigned, d'Eyncourt and two other Board members followed suit.[115] Frater Taylor became "in effect the controller of the company."[116] The depth of Armstrongs' problems was revealed in a second report to the BoE, which estimated that the firm had around £10 million invested in "undertakings foreign to their original business, on which no return is being made or is likely to be made for some time to come."[117] The Admiralty was alarmed at the idea of losing Armstrongs' capacity, particularly because Beardmores was in terrible trouble. The idea of amalgamating Armstrongs, Vickers and Beardmores was broached with Frater Taylor, but he rejected it, though Norman and Lawrence were interested in the scheme.[118]

A joint committee of Vickers and Armstrongs was now established, under the independent chairmanship of Sir William Plender (though Steven Tolliday makes it clear that Plender was doing Norman's bidding).[119] Vickers' interests – reflecting its stronger position – dominated the committee's conclusions. During the amalgamation talks, Craven wrote to a business associate:

[110] Notes from a piece by Glukstein, "Armstrong Whitworth and Co." VA, Doc. 549.
[111] "A.F.C. (27) 3 Vickers-Armstrong Fusion Scheme. Note by the First Lord of the Admiralty covering Departmental Memorandum, 21.7.27," Report, Proceedings and Memoranda of Cabinet Committee on Armament Firms Merger 1927, p. 3. TNA, CAB 27/353.
[112] Scott, *Vickers*, pp. 161–6.
[113] Clay, *Lord Norman*, pp. 318–20.
[114] Sayers, *Bank*, p. 316.
[115] d'Eyncourt joined the Parsons Marine Steam Turbine Company. He served on the board for the next twenty years, even after joining Vickers-Armstrongs. Lillicrap, "d'Eyncourt," p. 353.
[116] Scott, *Vickers*, p. 162.
[117] Scott, *Vickers*, p. 163.
[118] Hume and Moss, *Beardmores*, pp. 202–03.
[119] Tolliday, *Business*, p. 194.

You will notice in the enclosed report of the meeting that Armstrong's had to make a terrible fuss about the Merchant Shipyard etc., which they are retaining .... This, it will be obvious to you, is for the benefit of their debenture and shareholders. For your private information, the only works they are retaining are the ones we refuse to have anything to do with.[120]

In June 1927 Plender submitted a confidential memorandum to the government about the proposed merger, stating:

> Both firms have done their utmost to compensate for lack of armament orders by undertaking commercial work, and they propose to continue to do this in an effort to help the general situation. But it cannot be too strongly emphasized that Messrs. Vickers and Armstrongs are primarily manufacturers of armament and must continue to be so unless the vast skill and experience attained is to be lost to the country.[121]

Plender requested that the government pay an annual rental on factories (with skeleton staffs) of £300,000 for five years so they would be available to meet any national emergencies. "Should the Government be unable to accept the rental proposal set out above, it is suggested that the Government should undertake either to purchase or guarantee, up to an agreed amount, profit notes of the New Company if the profits in any one of the first five years should fall below a certain agreed sum."[122] The memorandum declared that it was desirable that the profits of the new company be a minimum of £1,250,000 per annum, allowing an average share dividend of 6.75 percent, "which having regard to the special nature of the business cannot be considered an unreasonable return."[123] Vickers also wanted the government to guarantee "that firms not already engaged in the production of guns, mountings, armour plate, submarines etc. should not be asked to tender for such orders."[124] They wanted to keep the armaments oligopoly tight.

The Ministry of War's response to the proposed merger noted that "Besides being manufacturers ... [Armstrongs] with their staff, records and traditions, are also of extreme importance as designers, and from this point of view there can be no doubt their disappearance, even in peace time, would be a very serious loss."[125] There was nevertheless disquiet about Armstrongs' passivity:

---

[120] Craven to Spear, November 30, 1927. Nye Committee Hearings, Part 1. September 4–6, 1934, Exhibit 19, pp. 330–31.

[121] "Lord Plender's Report on Merger 1927," Evidence submitted, Findings of Commission and Documents complied at London Office, VA, Doc. 58, Folder 99, p. 1.

[122] A.F.C. (27) 2. Armament Firms Committee Vickers-Armstrong Fusion Scheme, Plender memorandum, p. 3. TNA, CAB 27/353.

[123] "Lord Plender's Report on Merger 1927." VA, Doc. 58, Folder 99, p. 2.

[124] A.F.C. (27) 2. Armament Firms Committee Vickers-Armstrong Fusion Scheme, Note by the Secretary of State for War, Report of a departmental examination of the question (War Office, July 18, 1927). Ministry of War memorandum on the proposed merger, point 15, p. 4. TNA, CAB 27/353.

[125] A.F.C. (27) 2. Armament Firms Committee Vickers-Armstrong Fusion Scheme, p. 1.

[W]e feel that it would be highly desirable to insist, if possible, on Armstrongs taking immediate steps to effect such a reconstruction as a condition precedent to the grant of government assistance even being
considered. This has been done by Vickers on their own initiative without
the question of a subsidy being raised, and there seems no reason why the
same course should not be followed by Armstrongs.[126]

While noting that the Treasury was dealing with financial aspects of the proposed merger deal, the Ministry (passively aggressively) stated:

Otherwise we should have thought it necessary to raise such points as the
following:-
(a) the justification for so high a capital as that proposed, vis:
£18,500,000.
(b) the ground for the assumption that the combined Company
is reasonably entitled, in view of both past results and in particular of
Armstrong's present financial position, to be enabled, by means of a
Government subsidy, to pay a dividend averaging 6¾% on its whole
capital.
(c) the prospect of earning a minimum new profit amounting to
£1,250,000 (plus 6% on any new share-capital that may be issued).
(d) the justification (i) for giving priority to the payment of a 6%
dividend on such new capital before the subsidy becomes subject to
reduction, and (ii) for limiting the share of profits in excess of the specified
minimum to be applied to such repayment of subsidy to one-half.[127]

Concerning Vickers' attempt to exclude other firms from competition, the
Ministry concluded: "The suggestion at (ii) seems to us quite unacceptable.
It would prevent us from utilising the services of any possible new comers
to the armament trade ... and it would also prevent us from making use of
the general engineering industry for the manufacture of articles, such as e.g.
tanks, which they are fully qualified to produce."[128] The War Office continued to favor government arsenals over private firms, even though during the
war the Royal Arsenals had shown that they did not have the necessary surge
capacity.[129]

There was scant support for the proposed merger conditions from the other
service departments. The Admiralty now concluded that much of Armstrongs'
capacity, save for Elswick and Openshaw, could be dispensed with because
other firms could produce hulls and engines should they be needed. Moreover,

---

[126] A.F.C. (27) 2. Armament Firms Committee Vickers-Armstrong Fusion Scheme, point 12, p. 5.
[127] A.F.C. (27) 2. Armament Firms Committee Vickers-Armstrong Fusion Scheme, point 9, p. 3.
[128] A.F.C. (27) 2. Armament Firms Committee Vickers-Armstrong Fusion Scheme, p. 5.
[129] For Hornby, however: "One important effect of the war was to emphasise the limitations
of the armament industry and the necessity of retaining some state manufacture for the
more specialised munitions." Hornby, *Factories*, p. 26.

the First Lord of the Admiralty did not consider that government involvement in the merger was warranted.[130] The Secretary of State for Air emphasized that "from the point of view of the Air Ministry the proposal made in Sir W. Plender's memorandum *might constitute a most embarrassing precedent*" because there were many aircraft firms in search of subsidies. If there was to be support for Vickers-Armstrongs, the Air Ministry favored a program of orders instead of subsidies.[131]

Given government opposition to either paying rents or providing subsidies, the firms turned to the BoE for financial support, which Governor Norman was not prepared to openly provide. This was overcome by issuing a Sun Insurance Company policy to act as a screen for the BoE's support. The policy would pay out if the new company's profits fell below £900,000 in any of the next five years. The BoE's secret role was only revealed in 1935.[132]

In sum, Vickers undertook their own reorganization to return to profitability. Armstrongs drifted, but their debts and industrial importance were such that the BoE intervened to reorganize and amalgamate the firm. Beardmores also drifted until it had to be rescued by the BoE, and the Treasury had to write off debts of £100,000.[133]

Vickers-Armstrongs Is Born

On October 31, 1927, the two firms were merged into Vickers-Armstrongs Ltd., with Vickers in control, despite Norman's desire for a more equal relationship.[134] The working assumption was that "all the assets of the company should be abandoned unless they are economical and remunerative under peace conditions."[135] The aircraft businesses of the two firms – the Vickers Works at Weybridge and the Armstrong Siddeley Works in Coventry – were not combined.[136] Additionally, Vickers Ltd. and Armstrong-Whitworth Ltd. continued to exist as separate entities with their own chairmen. At Armstrong-Whitworth the BoE appointed Guy Dawnay as Chairman and George Ionides as Vice-Chairman, and both also sat on the Board of Vickers-Armstrongs.[137] As the *Times* declared in November 1927, "It would be hard to name an amalgamation

[130] A.F.C. (27) 3. Vickers-Armstrong Fusion Scheme. Note by the First Lord of the Admiralty covering Departmental Memorandum, July 21, 1927.
[131] A.F.C. (27) 4. Vickers-Armstrong Fusion Scheme. Note by the Secretary of State for Air. July 27, 1927, p. 1. Emphasis in original.
[132] Tolliday, *Business*, p. 195.
[133] "William Beardmore and Company Limited." Evidence submitted, Findings of Commission and Documents complied at London Office, VA, Doc. 58, Folder 86.
[134] Tolliday, *Business*, p. 195.
[135] Clay, *Lord Norman*, pp. 320–23.
[136] Grant, *Depression*, p. 72.
[137] Tolliday, *Business*, p. 196.

in industry of equal importance."[138] Soon after Vickers-Armstrongs was able to pay a small annual dividend.[139]

A new management team was now assembled. General the Hon. Sir Herbert Lawrence, GCB became Vickers-Armstrongs Chairman, also chairing Vickers Ltd.[140] Lawrence brought to the role military, banking and business experience. He had been on the Vickers Board since 1921 and its Chairman from 1926. Lawrence retained former submariner Charles Craven, who had been recruited by Trevor Dawson in what Scott considers "the last of his great services to the company" (Dawson died suddenly in 1931).[141] Lawrence recognized Craven's many talents, including his popularity with the workers and his tenacity in securing contracts. In the early 1930s Craven described his job: "[T]here is no real salesmanship required, but very delicate negotiations are continually taking place."[142] Another Vickers man who stayed was Frederick Yapp, who subsequently joined the Board in 1935.[143] Sir Eustace Tennyson d'Eyncourt joined Vickers-Armstrongs as a constructor and salesman. Another Armstrongs man, Sir George Hadcock, became a director. When Vickers subsequently acquired all the capital of Vickers-Armstrongs, Hadcock remained on the Board as a technical consultant, a role he held until his death in 1936.[144]

Sir Mark Webster Jenkinson had joined the Vickers Board during the amalgamation negotiations, succeeding Sir Vincent Caillard as Financial Controller.[145] Despite his obvious financial acumen and management nous, "some of his more Belgravian colleagues at Vickers found his accent and attitudes rather too redolent of Sheffield."[146] Luckily, Vickers-Armstrongs' culture followed Vickers in valuing talent over background. Robert Micklem had served in the Royal Navy and was recruited in 1928 as a general manager for Elswick, having previously been associated with Vickers' Cooke Troughton and Sims, Ltd. "During the period of depression on Tyneside a number of new industries were introduced at Elswick through Sir Robert's foresight."[147] Sir Huw Ross Kilner joined the firm in 1930. He had served in the Royal Artillery during the Great War, followed by

---

[138] Scott, *Vickers*, p. 168. Citing: *The Times* (London), November 4, 1927.

[139] "Vickers-Armstrongs Dividends Paid between Date of Incorporation of Company and 31st December 1935," Evidence submitted, Findings of Commission and Documents complied at London Office, VA, Doc. 58, Folder 80.

[140] Scott, *Vickers*, p. 392.

[141] Scott, *Vickers*, p. 160.

[142] Davenport-Hines, "British Marketing," p. 146. Citing: Craven, memorandum of March 28, 1931. VA, Microfilm R 212.

[143] Scott, *Vickers*, p. 260. His father and his son also worked for Vickers.

[144] d'Eyncourt, "Obituary," p. 143.

[145] At the end of his Vickers career Caillard sought Churchill's help in securing a place on the Suez Canal Board. Caillard to Churchill, August 17, 1927. CHAR 2/153/32.

[146] Davenport-Hines, "Jenkinson."

[147] "Commander Micklem."

four years in the War Office and five years as a gunnery instructor. At Vickers-Armstrongs he began as Special Director and General Manager of the Southern Engineering Works, in 1936 becoming a director there.[148]

Another important appointment was General Sir James Fredrick Noel Birch, who joined the Board in 1927. Birch brought an illustrious Army record, including as an artillery adviser to Field Marshal Haig in France from 1916 (therefore overlapping with Sir Herbert). Immediately prior to joining Vickers-Armstrongs he was Master-General of Ordnance and had overseen Woolwich's creation of the experimental Birch Gun, "the world's first practical self-propelled artillery piece."[149] This combined a standard 18-pound field gun with a Vickers Mark II medium tank chassis. When the Birch Gun met opposition from the Royal Regiment, he joined Vickers-Armstrongs.[150] Birch managed their land equipment sales. In Davenport-Hines' view, Birch's arrival led to improved relations with the government, where he "hectored War Office brass-hats with the freedom of an old friend."[151]

Vickers-Armstrongs now concentrated on armaments, putting the era of diversification behind it.[152] They mothballed the Walker Yard.[153] Two interesting and farsighted acquisitions followed. First, Vickers-Armstrongs moved into tanks. They sought to work with Carden-Loyd on their light tanks. In early discussion over the firm's models, "They stated, as Sir Noel already knew, that Vickers are not the only people trying to get hold of them. Carden-Loyd could have got just as good terms elsewhere – in fact better terms."[154] Nevertheless, in 1928 Vickers-Armstrongs absorbed the firm. Sir John Carden, an "aristocratic self-taught engineer," was also interested in light aviation.[155] He took over designing lighter tanks (later developing the "Flying Flea" plane) and C. O. Woodward worked on heavier tanks.[156] As well as being an exceptional engineer, Carden was an Old Harrovian and an Irish baronet, boosting Vickers-Armstrongs' elite connections. The immediate consequence of this acquisition was a March 1928 War Office order for a small quantity of Carden-Loyd Mark VI tanks, which spurred more innovations and overseas sales, viewed by Vickers-Armstrongs as a gateway to machine gun sales.[157]

---

[148] "Obituary: Major Sir Hew Ross Kilner."
[149] Zabecki, "Great Guns," p. 82.
[150] Smithers, *Rude Mechanicals*, p. 8.
[151] Davenport-Hines, "British Marketing," p. 160.
[152] Scott, *Vickers*, pp. 166–68.
[153] It was reopened in 1931 for the construction of the civilian vessel, *Monarch of Bermuda*. "Vickers Armstrongs & Co Ltd; Plans of ships built at the Walker Yard; 1946–1969," TWA DS/VA.
[154] "Carden-Loyd," Army Sales Committee 1.1.28–1.6.28. VA, Microfilm R 286.
[155] Edgerton, *Britain's*, p. 242.
[156] Edgerton, *Warfare*, p. 134; Scott, *Vickers*, p. 188.
[157] Birch to Craven, September 24, 1930. VA, Microfilm R 286.

Vickers alone made the second acquisition, buying Supermarine Ltd. of Southampton. Supermarine's successes in the biennial Schneider Trophy competitions in 1922 and 1927 were excellent adverts for their seaplanes and encouraged Vickers' interest.[158] They acquired the firm in November 1928 and in June 1931 renamed it Supermarine Aviation Works (Vickers) Ltd.[159] Supermarine continued to race, winning the 1929 and 1931 Schneider Trophies and setting a new world speed record – 407 miles per hour – in 1931.[160] With the acquisition came Squadron Commander James Bird, but, more crucially, the talented engineer R. J. Mitchell, who turned to designing fighter aircraft.

Despite getting some support from the Air Ministry, Vickers' aircraft production was underperforming. In 1930, former Chief of Air Staff Lord Trenchard assessed their aviation business. His report was critical of Captain Acland, who headed aviation (and who left soon after) and the Chairman's son Oliver Vickers (who remained!), noting that they had ignored the government aircraft acquisition cycle and failed to have a new Vickers model ready for procurement in 1930.[161] Vickers Aviation and Supermarine were now put under the leadership of Sir Robert McLean, who reported directly to the Vickers Board. He was described as "a man of granite integrity and austere independence of mind" and was at times an abrasive character.[162]

Consolidations followed in other sectors. Vickers-Armstrongs kept control of their railway carriage works by amalgamating their rolling stock with Cammell Laird's, creating the Metropolitan Cammell Carriage Company, which thereafter became moderately profitable.[163] There was fundamental consolidation in shipping at Vickers-Armstrongs and across the sector.[164] After 1921 merchant shipping orders declined below prewar levels. For 1920–1939 the combined output of merchant tonnage from Armstrongs and Vickers-Armstrongs was 6.1 percent of British production.[165] As Britain's share of global production was also declining, this was disquieting.[166] Competition was fearsome: "[E]ach of the larger firms in turn, when short of work ... [would take on] an important contract with practically no charges."[167]

In 1928 the secretive Shipbuilding Conference was formed with twenty-seven members, including Vickers-Armstrongs; this rose to fifty-one firms by 1930.[168]

[158] Beaver, *Spitfire*, pp. 54–56; "Supermarine."
[159] Scott, *Vickers*, p. 181.
[160] Souvenir Programme for the 1931 Schneider Trophy Contest. VA, Doc. 1909; "Crocks," p. 3.
[161] Davenport-Hines, "British Marketing," p. 165.
[162] Scott, *Vickers*, p. 200.
[163] Miller, *Planning*, p. 42.
[164] Johnman, "Large Manufacturing," p. 24.
[165] Jamieson, *Ebb Tide*, p. 58.
[166] Hornby, *Factories*, p. 20.
[167] Slaven, "Shipyard," p. 197.
[168] Turner, "Politics," p. 8.

Members signed a 1929 memorandum of understanding which began: "[I]t is the desire of the industry to put an end to the present suicidal competition with the object of each firm obtaining a fair share of such Admiralty work as is available at a reasonable price."[169] Members drew lots to establish the order in which they would get shipbuilding contracts. Vickers-Armstrongs was the penultimate firm on the cruiser engine list.[170] The aim was to harmonize supply and demand while preventing debilitating competition.[171] The industry's intent was clearly at odds with the Admiralty's wish to maintain competition and retain capacity that could be used in an emergency.[172] By 1936 the firms wanted to make the ring permanent, "on the same lines as the Trade Associations which other specialised industries have repeatedly been urged by the government to form in protection of their interests."[173]

In parallel, consolidation in shipbuilding was achieved through an unusual degree of industrywide cooperation, without the government (though the BoE was the hidden hand).[174] In February 1930 the Shipbuilding Conference created a rationalization company, National Shipbuilders Security Ltd. (NSS), to buy up excess shipyards and sell the sites for other uses. Craven was on the NSS Board.[175] As Vickers-Armstrongs subsequently reported to the Royal Commission: "The specialist warship building firms are all members ... and through that organisation are taking all practicable measures on their own initiative to reduce redundant capacity in the various districts."[176] The NSS was under the chairmanship of Sir James Lithgow. The Conference sought the support of the BoE, but Governor Norman merely agreed to help the NSS obtain financing.[177]

A total of thirty-eight shipyards were closed over nine years, a third of national capacity.[178] Tyneside lost nine shipyards between 1921 and 1937.[179] In 1935 the Walker Yard was mothballed again, and three former Armstrongs

---

[169] "Opening Statement at Hearing by Sir Charles Craven," Evidence submitted, Findings of Commission and Documents complied at London Office, VA, Doc. 58, Folder 123.

[170] Private Memorandum, December 5, 1934, and Memorandum of Agreement February 23, 1934. "Particulars of War Shipbuilders and Warship Machinery Agreements," Evidence submitted, Findings of Commission and Documents complied at London Office, VA, Doc. 58, p. 1.

[171] Slaven, "War," p. 95.

[172] Miller, *Planning*, pp. 75–76.

[173] "Particulars of War Shipbuilders and Warship Machinery Agreements," Evidence submitted, Findings of Commission and Documents complied at London Office, VA, Doc. 58, p. 3.

[174] Miller, *Planning*, pp. 71–73.

[175] Miller, *Planning*, p. 73.

[176] "Particulars of War Shipbuilders and Warship Machinery Agreements," p. 3.

[177] Slaven, "War," pp. 95–98.

[178] For details see: Slaven, "War," Table 4.9, pp. 98–100.

[179] Dunkley, "Ships," p. 20.

yards were closed.[180] Vickers-Armstrongs then bought Palmers' Hebburn facility from NSS for £85,000 (£6,719,036 in August 2022).[181] As Miller concluded, Vickers-Armstrongs did well: It sold a redundant yard, got one it wanted "and made a profit of £40,000 in the bargain, while the NSS lost £15,000."[182] Vickers-Armstrongs was able "to increase workload for surviving firms by about half, and … there was also a saving in cost of up to five per cent."[183] The firm invested in new plant and equipment at Barrow, meaning the shipyard weathered the depression better than most.[184]

The national decline in warship production capacity – consistently a private sector prerogative – was particularly stark: "In 1914, there were twelve armament firms capable of producing major warships: by 1933, only Vickers remained capable of fulfilling large orders for major war vessels."[185] The number of firms engaged in armaments production plummeted: "Of the thirty or more great arms factories that had supplied the [state] with its guns, ammunition, tanks and trucks during the First World War, only Vickers Armstrong and the royal arsenals remained in existence by 1930."[186] As Vickers-Armstrongs was now the only firm manufacturing gun mountings, it had "a monopoly by default."[187] This made them more important to the state, though their difficult relations with the government belied that.

Vickers-Armstrongs now pursued a new strategy of divestment. A major rationalization came in steel, which by 1926 was seen as a liability given the global outlook for heavy industry.[188] Vickers-Armstrongs' steel interests were combined with the Sheffield businesses of Cammell Laird, creating the English Steel Corporation (ESC), chaired by Craven, in 1928. As Tolliday noted, this was a "de-merger of the armament combines."[189] In 1929 Lawrence and Webster Jenkinson sought to capitalize on a scandal that had left United Steel vulnerable to acquisition. However, BoE Governor Norman opposed this because he did not want Vickers in the driving seat of rationalization, and the scheme fell through.[190] Subsequently Taylors of Trafford Park and Industrial Steels Ltd. joined the ESC. Later, Lawrence successfully opposed Norman's ambitious plans to merge the ESC with Firths and John Browns.[191]

---

[180] Miller, *Planning*, pp. 113–14. A total of 300,000 tons of naval capacity was "sterilized" by the NSS before rearmament began. Miller, *Planning*, p. 117.
[181] Slaven, "War," p. 102. Citing: National Maritime Museum, "National Shipbuilders Security Ltd.," Minutes March 27, 1935.
[182] Miller, *Planning*, p. 119.
[183] Slaven, "War," p. 102.
[184] Parkinson, "Shipbuilding," p. 96.
[185] Maiolo, "Anglo-Soviet," p. 353.
[186] Bond and Murray, "British," p. 103.
[187] Miller, *Planning*, p. 48.
[188] Hornby, *Factories*, p. 17.
[189] Tolliday, *Business*, p. 36.
[190] Tolliday, *Business*, pp. 191–92.
[191] Tolliday, *Business*, p. 195.

The ESC set about rationalizing production, updating equipment and ending duplication to meet the challenges from international producers.[192] Armstrongs' Whitworth Street works was an early casualty of rationalization. Reflecting Vickers' organizational culture, the ESC also undertook a major investment program during the 1930s, reinvigorating research and development. Ironically, the BoE found that Vickers-Armstrongs and the ESC ignored its advice and "in the end was merely an unwilling accomplice of those concerns' own development plans, which were not very much to the Bank's taste."[193] While initially in debt, by 1934 the ESC was making a profit and was to become "one of the most successful merger schemes in this period."[194] As previously noted, Vickers sold their electrical engineering interests (Metropolitan Vickers) to Associated Electrical Industries and Wolseley to Morris.[195] Dudley Docker was instrumental in the Metropolitan Vickers transfer and for his role earned £50,000 (£3,530,492 in August 2022), "at the time more than most Chairmen of large corporations would expect to earn in a year."[196]

Parts of the government were now providing some assistance to firms. Between 1926 and 1928 Vickers-Armstrongs was one of five armor firms provided with an annual Admiralty maintenance allowance of £155,000 (which included some orders). A 1928 meeting of representatives of Vickers, Beardmores, Browns and Cammell Lairds heard that in 1925–26 this meant armor cost £62 per ton, and in 1926–27 £77 per ton. However, by 1928 the Admiralty's armor needs were very low, making the cost of armor "up to about £360 per ton, or a total lump sum of £103,000 more than if last year's prices per ton were adhered to."[197] Informal discussions with DNC Sir William Berry had centered on the need for the armor firms to not quote prices based on the existing formula as "there would be a great danger of the arrangement falling through, and he looked to the firms to help them in some way." The firms made the expected sacrifices. There were several rounds of negotiations, during which "with regard to the rebates payable to the Admiralty, of £21 per ton on excess tonnage of British armour, and £15 per ton on all foreign armour, it was thought that these should be suspended until the amount sacrificed by the firms had been recovered."[198] In aircraft, despite industrial support from the Air Ministry and the ability to switch between civil and military production, in 1930 total industry output was only 1,453 aircraft and the sector was in "desperate straits."[199]

---

[192] Tweedale, *Steel City*, pp. 247–49.
[193] Tolliday, *Business*, p. 197.
[194] Tweedale, *Steel City*, p. 253.
[195] Johnman, "Large Manufacturing," p. 24.
[196] Hannah, "Takeover," p. 47, ff. 8.
[197] Minutes of a Meeting held at Vickers House, February 10, 1928, p. 1. VA, Microfilm R 286.
[198] Minutes of a Meeting held at Vickers House, February 10, 1928, pp. 2–3. VA, Microfilm R 286.
[199] Figure from Hornby, *Factories*, p. 18; Bond and Murray, "British," p. 104.

The War Office again prioritized the Royal Arsenals and minimized relationships with armament firms. Vickers-Armstrongs pursued a familiar – always polite – argument with the War Office about reserve capacities. The War Office wrote to Chairman Lawrence that the Ordnance Council "recognize that with the present amount of Government work, the new firm may not feel justified in incurring heavy capital expenditure for the modernization of plant with a view to cheapening production costs; but they trust that the reserve productive capacity of both the constituent firms will as far as possible be retained intact in readiness for an emergency." The War Office also reserved the right to spread what work there was on spare parts for tanks between the Royal Ordnance Factories and private firms, but "nevertheless recognize the force of the contention that the originators of the designs have some claims to preference, and they propose as far as practicable to allot a reasonable share of future orders for such parts to the new firm, provided that the price and delivery offered are satisfactory."[200] Once again the War Office was shifting risk onto the firm. Sir Noel Birch's response was expressed in a handwritten note on the letter: "This fellow is a pedantic ass."[201]

Vickers-Armstrongs' Army Sales Committee proposed that Birch talk to Lawrence about their response to the War Office,

> with a view to pointing out to the … War Office that Vickers-Armstrongs have an agreement with the Admiralty with regard to the reservation of plant for the production of Admiralty requirements of Guns and Mountings, and have informed the Admiralty semi-officially that, at present at any rate, the new Company has no intention of making any reduction in its productive capacity which would interfere in any way with its arrangements with the Admiralty. It is suggested that the War Office should be informed that, although the Firm will naturally make every endeavour to meet the War Office wishes in a similar respect, the Directors, *as paid servants of the shareholders*, cannot countenance keeping idle plant for any lengthy period without some guarantee of work or some other form of compensation.[202]

The Committee noted they had received War Office orders for tank parts "to about 25% of the tenders submitted. The Committee are not satisfied that this proportion is a 'reasonable share.'" They also agreed that Birch should "see the Permanent Under-Secretary of State to the War Office, pointing out that the firm is dissatisfied with this proportion and asking if there is any reason why it should not be increased," and that a "reasonable share" of work was not commensurate with the War Office's hope that "we shall be able to keep the whole of our machinery intact for Army use."[203]

[200] Creedy, War Office to Lawrence, February 7, 1928. VA, Microfilm R 286.
[201] Creedy to Lawrence, February 7, 1928. VA, Microfilm R 286.
[202] Army Sales Committee February 9, 1928. VA, Microfilm R 286. Emphasis added.
[203] Army Sales Committee February 9, 1928. VA, Microfilm R 286.

Vickers had seen major downturns before, and the firm's approach had always been to innovate in anticipation of increased production. However, such was the shortage of business and finance that Vickers-Armstrongs now did this in a more limited way. Birch reported on tanks in 1928: "I have only just fully taken over all this track business, and the first thing that strikes me most forcibly is the total absence of research."[204] He declared that, overall, "Vickers-Armstrongs have a great deal to contend with. The Government do not allow them any direct facilities. The War Office has set up a second-hand business on its own I am informed they are selling guns. The English Bankers set up Skoda and Skoda is now supplying China with War Machines etc. etc. etc. What a life!"[205]

From the start Birch was concerned that Vickers-Armstrongs' marketing was inadequate. In 1928 the firm created a book of photographs that, at Birch's instigation, was to be provided to all British military attachés.[206] They also built models of key products.[207] Birch wanted pamphlets of "a convenient size and 'snappy' form" for advertising in South America, not an "encyclopedia."[208] Customers could visit factories and see Vickers-Armstrongs products in action.[209] Subtle advertising was employed there. Birch sent Erith two big maps to have "framed and put up in some conspicuous position," explaining that "So many foreigners arrive in my office and seem to think that our efforts in the war were purely naval. These maps may help to disillusion them."[210]

The new firm had to decide which agents to retain. They still faced some class prejudices. Davenport-Hines quotes a naval attaché's judgment from 1926: "[A]ll the Vickers people seem to be rather slippery, rather what shall I say, not perhaps quite the right class. The opinion may be wrong, but it is certainly held at the legations."[211] Vickers brought a military-minded approach.[212] As Birch emphasized: "On the Military and Air Armament side the dealings are now practically entirely with the General Staff, therefore providing that they are otherwise suitable, military officers of good general education are almost essential as sellers."[213] Birch began rationalizing Vickers-Armstrongs' overseas agents. Some familiar figures were retained. In 1927 Vickers presented Zaharoff with a silver and gilded cup recognizing fifty years of service "in connection with the

[204] Birch to Swinton, September 11, 1928. VA, Microfilm R 286.
[205] Birch to Swinton, September 11, 1928. VA, Microfilm R 286.
[206] Minutes of the Army Sales Committee, February 9, 1928. VA, Microfilm R 286.
[207] Minutes of Special Meeting of Army Sales Committee, February 9, 1928. VA, Microfilm R 286.
[208] Birch to Sim, February 15, 1929. VA, Microfilm R 286.
[209] "Visit of Colombian Minister to Crayford Works," October 17, 1932; Birch to Lopez, October 27, 1932. VA, Microfilm K 613.
[210] Birch to Wilson, November 22, 1929. VA, Microfilm R 286.
[211] Davenport-Hines, "British Marketing ," p. 161. Citing: Captain Salmond to Commander Lang, January 24, 1926. FO 371/111222.
[212] Scott, Vickers, p. 260.
[213] Birch to Sim, May 19, 1930. VA, Microfilm R 286.

Company."[214] Soon after, Zaharoff wrote to Webster Jenkinson: "Now that the newspapers find that I no longer interest their readers, they either make out that I am retiring, or am dying, and I should tell you that as far as Vickers – my Alma Mater – is concerned, I hope to die in harness."[215] He eventually did.

Birch was unimpressed by many at Vickers Aviation, reporting: "In Roumania the agent recently appointed is a gaol-bird. In Latvia, a Communist. In Turkey, a gentleman called Buck, who is not allowed inside the British Ministry as he faked some figures for training pilots. Major Jullerot also appointed General Livingston, but wisely pushed him on to Vickers-Armstrong."[216] Unsurprisingly, Livingston was one of the first to be dismissed by Birch. Subsequently Livingston complained that Vickers had lost many deals in Latin America by not matching Italy's commission levels.[217] Birch also raged against Michel Clemenceau (son of the French wartime premier) being the head of sales, judging that he had not done enough to position Vickers Aviation over the previous nine to ten years, and declaring, "I consider it nothing short of madness to keep a Frenchman in charge of an English sales department."[218]

For Greek business, the choice was clear to their accountants in Athens, as Mr. Triandafyllides – formerly the agent for Armstrongs – was younger and more energetic than Vickers' agents Agelanto and Soteropouls.[219] Birch was clear too, because Triandafyllides had sold more, and he considered Agelanto's renumeration "excessive." They also represented the rival French aviation firm Breguet, considered a bad optic by Birch. However, there was dissent from Craven, who alluded to a £1,500,000 naval order planned by Greece, from Yapp (though he was circumspect about the large order as "It is considered unlikely that this large programme could be financed") and later from Dawson. Birch was supported by Hadcock.[220] The compromise was to appoint Triandafyllides for Army and air orders but to keep Agelanto and Soteropouls for "Marine only," until June 30, 1930, to win the large order. On July 1, 1930, with no naval order in sight, Triandafyllides became their sole agent. Vickers-Armstrongs Royal Commission evidence confirms Birch's concerns about excessive

---

[214] Lawrence to Royal Commission, March 11, 1936. "Vickers Ltd.: evidence; note by Secretary," TNA, T 181/56; "Zaharoff Presented with a Silver Gilded Cup," press cutting, October 12, 1927. VA, Microfilm 19A, Folio 553.

[215] Zaharoff to Webster-Jenkinson, November 2, 1927. VA Microfilm 19A, Folio 553.

[216] Birch to Sim, January 17, 1930. VA, Microfilm R 286.

[217] His memoir discussed working for Vickers. "Hot Air in Cold Blood by Brig-Gen. Guy Livingston C.M.G." p. 239. Evidence Prepared for the Bankes Committee. VA, Doc. 57, Folder 46, p. 1.

[218] Birch to Sim, January 14, 1930. VA, Microfilm R 286.

[219] Russell & Co (Athens) to Hadcock, February 8, 1928. VA, Microfilm R 286.

[220] Extract from Army Sales Committee Minutes, February 3, 1928; Minutes of the Army Sales Committee, February 17, 1928; Birch to Hadcock, March 3, 1928. VA, Microfilm R 286.

commissions. After Triandafyllides assumed the role, the commissions paid to him in 1931 were £447.3.4. compared to £5,655.6.3 to Agelanto in 1930.[221]

Vickers-Armstrongs then sent "Responsible Officials" to various parts of the world. Webster Jenkinson was irritated with the Armstrongs team:

> We are not going to get orders for Vickers-Armstrongs by sitting still in the London Office, but must have the proper sales campaign organized …. If the visits are paid as suggested we shall be able to find out whether the agents are the right people with the necessary influence to obtain orders, and, at the same time, wave the flag and convince the responsible authorities that we are able to undertake any work entrusted to us at prices which appear favourable with our foreign competitors.[222]

One of the earliest deputations saw d'Eyncourt head for South America.

In addition to gingering up their marketing, Vickers-Armstrongs resumed a traditional strategy, colluding with other armament firms to fix prices. Miller has provided the definitive account of the Warship Building Committee (WSBC) ring.[223] As Vickers-Armstrongs subsequently explained to the Royal Commission: "The Warship builders have also, from time to time, made temporary arrangements amongst themselves in respect to various types of new Admiralty construction, which have had the effect of ameliorating to some extent the foregoing National difficulties as well as of improving their own position."[224] This considerably underplays their behavior. The WSBC continuously operated between 1926 and 1942 and systematically provided a rotation of work and profit sharing sufficient to keep all the members in existence.[225] The WSBC initially focused on destroyers and helping the warship manufacturers win export orders, but by 1930 it covered orders over "£600,000 for hull and machinery only, for the Admiralty and Dominion navies."[226] It also considered export orders. For example, in 1936 it was agreed that "Vickers-Armstrong, Cammell Laird and John Brown will each forfeit their next turn in the Rota, following their Argentine orders."[227] Whereas in the 1920s the WSBC had prevented competition from undercutting prices but brought little profit, by the 1930s members were realizing some profits, and when rearmament began, the firms earned considerable profits. The WSBC ensured that 10 percent profit

[221] "Vickers Limited and Vickers-Armstrongs Agents," Evidence Prepared for the Bankes Committee. March 1935. VA 58, p. 6.
[222] Notes on Webster-Jenkinson to Zaharoff, from Microfilm No. 19a 553, VA, Doc. 788.
[223] Miller, *Planning*, especially Chapter 4.
[224] "Particulars of War Shipbuilders and Warship Machinery Agreements," Evidence Prepared for the Bankes Committee. VA, Doc. 58, Folder 101, p. 3.
[225] Miller, *Planning*, especially pp. 47–76.
[226] Miller, *Planning*, p. 51 and p. 56. Citing: Glasgow University Archives (GUAS), GD319/12/7/6, Meeting of Warship Group, December 1930.
[227] Miller, *Planning*, p. 63. Citing: GUAS, GD319/12/7/6, "Destroyer Rota Arrangements – SECRET," 9 October 1936.

was included in all bids, including that of the firm they organized to win.[228] According to Miller, there is no decisive evidence that the Admiralty knew about the WSBC in its early days or knew that it had endured beyond the initial three-year rota, which concluded in 1929.[229] While Craven regularly attended WSBC meetings for Vickers-Armstrongs and reported to the WSBC any useful intelligence he gathered from his interactions with the Admiralty, there is no record of the WSBC in the Vickers Archive, which is extremely suspicious.[230]

In 1928 the firm struck a three-year agreement with M. Klement Ruzicka, on behalf of a Czechoslovakian firm associated with Škoda, "regarding the elimination of competition between us for the sale of Machine rifles." Vickers-Armstrongs was buying guns to sell itself. The deal was conditional upon Vickers-Armstrongs placing an order for 36,000 rifles and carbines with Usinea d'Armes Techodelovaues Societe Anonyme & Brno. The firms agreed to not compete for the same orders and to "pay to the other Company commission, the amount of which is to be agreed but shall not be less than S 10 [Austrian schillings] or more than S 20 per weapon, for each weapon for which an order is secured."[231] As well as collusion, this shows that Vickers-Armstrongs lacked a good machine gun of its own manufacture to sell.

Crisis: The Great Depression

The amalgamation did not end Vickers-Armstrongs' problems. In 1928 Churchill made the Ten-Year-Rule self-perpetuating. Procurement austerity was further exacerbated by the Great Depression, which began in 1929, striking the industrial cities particularly hard, throwing millions out of work and bankrupting many companies. British defense expenditure "reached its lowest absolute figure in 1932–3."[232]

One tactical argument Vickers-Armstrongs now used in correspondence with the British Government was to make an explicit link between maintaining the firms' health through exports and Britain's ability to mobilize for future war. In communications with the Chief of the Imperial General Staff, Field Marshal Milne, Birch declared that Britain "must pay just as much attention to the industrial mobilisation for war as we do to our armed forces and act accordingly."[233] He made this point repeatedly in his correspondence with government officials.

---

[228] Miller, *Planning*, pp. 65–66. Citing: GUAS, GD319/12/7/6, Craven to Brown, 20 April 1931.
[229] Miller, *Planning*, pp. 53–54.
[230] Miller, *Planning*, p. 64.
[231] Birch to Usinea d'Armes Techodelovaues Societe Anonyme & Brno, February 15, 1928. VA, Microfilm R 286.
[232] Dunbabin, "British Rearmament," p. 588, ff. 5.
[233] Birch to Sir George Milne, CIGS [Chief of the Imperial General Staff], April 1929. VA, Microfilm R 286. Also cited in Davenport-Hines, "British," p. 161.

In 1929 Vickers-Armstrongs contacted the Board of Trade requesting that the Export Credit Guarantees Scheme be extended to armaments, which would assist the firm in securing export orders.[234] Birch had been told that the Conservatives were wary of doing so because of expected resistance from the Labour opposition. Birch told Deputy Chairman George Gall Sim that he proposed to write to Colonel Walter Guinness, "the only man Baldwin will listen to." Birch said: "[I]f you agree, I think that we should try Baldwin. Do you think it is any use trying anybody on the Labour side as well?" [235] A draft letter was enclosed asking Guinness whether "Mr. Baldwin could be persuaded to approach the Prime Minister with a view to getting an agreed clause inserted." The draft went on to explain Vickers-Armstrongs' problems: "Italy has collared all the work done … simply by the extension of the Export Credits Scheme to Armaments." Consequently, "Italy has a reserve in the event of war which England is deprived of. Further, English workmen are penalized by the action of the Government." Birch added: "The one thing that this Government is anxious about is the future of men employed in armaments, and this fact is being continually impressed upon them by the Labour Members in the munition areas."[236] Sim replied:

> I see no harm in your letter to Guinness, although I doubt if it will do much good. We have definite assurance from various members of the Cabinet that they are interested in pushing our proposals for the extension of the Export Credits for Armaments, but this involves an alteration of the *Act*, whereas the scheme which the Government have at present is merely, as I understand, for an extension of the financial provision for a further period.[237]

As Sim predicted, this attempt by Vickers-Armstrongs to use leverage on the government elite failed, showing the limits of the firm's relational power.

Vickers-Armstrongs saw Spain as a potential export market. Birch wanted to pitch Vickers tanks to Madrid, but Zaharoff urged caution, saying that the time was not right. Later Birch begged Zaharoff to bring in a Spanish tank order and in response Zaharoff offered Birch some introductions.[238] When Sir Robert McLean was planning to market aircraft to Madrid, Zaharoff suggested that he not be involved because "the Spanish Authorities might think that I am endeavouring to monopolize everything Spanish, and this might interfere with our existing business." He explained:

[234] "Armaments – Request for extension of Export Credits Guarantees Scheme to assist in securing foreign orders," Board of Trade, Office of the Chief Industrial Adviser, 1929. TNA, BT 56/18.
[235] Birch to Sim, April 7, 1930. Enclosing draft letter to Sir Walter Guinness. VA Microfilm R 286.
[236] Draft letter to Sir Walter Guinness, April 7, 1930. VA Microfilm R 286.
[237] G. Sim to Birch, April 7, 1930. VA Microfilm R 286. Emphasis in original.
[238] Birch to Zaharoff, September 3, 1931; Zaharoff to Birch, September 7, 1931. VA Microfilm 19a 55 and Doc. 786.

The Spaniards are difficult people to deal with, and if we press them, they immediately shut up like oysters, and think that we are endeavouring to force them, and my policy has always been to induce them to believe that they are having it entirely their own way, and this line of conduct has hitherto been most successful and satisfactory.[239]

Moreover, "Printed technical matter and persuasion will not go far, but the moment you know you have something which is superior to what they possess, strike quick and hard, and, once you have obtained their confidence, you can rely on them for years to come."[240] Zaharoff also urged Sir Robert McLean to "spend a little money on officials" to secure Spanish work.[241] Clearly bribery was still a tactic the firm would consider using.

In May 1931 Vickers-Armstrongs opened their redesigned London showroom.[242] The new cinema room showed films about their weapons, which were also shown abroad.[243] Despite all these marketing efforts, Lawrence explained to shareholders in 1932:

The general world-trade depression and the reduction in armaments under the pressure of public opinion, both in this and other countries, have affected adversely your Company's trading results. The net profit is £574,493, a reduction of £201,433 compared with 1930 – and allows the payment of a dividend of 5% on the Ordinary Share capital, although no transfer to Reserve Fund is possible on this occasion.[244]

Vickers-Armstrongs wanted the 1932 iteration of the Export Credit Scheme extended to include armaments.[245] Deputy Chairman J. B. Neilson wrote twice to the Controller General of the Department of Overseas Trade requesting that armament firms be granted "ordinary commercial treatment" and access to the scheme to help them to sell abroad.[246] The Government was unmoved. Lawrence then sent copies of both letters to the Secretary of the Committee of Imperial Defence, Sir Maurice Hankey, along with a hard-hitting cover letter seeking the Committee of Imperial Defence's support as "The question of trade has been treated merely from a commercial point of view."[247] Lawrence included a subtle threat:

[239] "Aviation: Spanish Correspondence 1929–1936." VA, Doc. 571.
[240] "Aviation: Spanish Correspondence 1929–1936." VA, Doc. 571.
[241] "Aviation: Spanish Correspondence 1929–1936." VA, Doc. 571.
[242] *The Times*, May 29, 1931. Cited in: Union of Democratic Control, *Secret International*, pp. 13–14.
[243] "Films for selling," VA, Microfilm K 616, Folio 249.
[244] Chairman's speech, April 4, 1932. "Papers and Notes of Sir Herbert Lawrence at Hearing," Evidence Prepared for the Bankes Committee. VA, Doc. 58, Folder 126.
[245] "Armament Sales Abroad, 1930–1938." VA, Doc. 776.
[246] J. B. Neilsen, Vickers Armstrongs to Department of Overseas Trade, September 20, 1932. VA Microfilm R 286.
[247] Lawrence to Secretary of Committee of Imperial Defence, October 4, 1932. VA Microfilm R 286.

Practically every requisite of the three fighting services is manufactured by Vickers, and large research and experimental establishments are maintained. It is not too much to say that unless this organisation is continued, (and from its nature it is inevitably one of the most expensive organisations to maintain) the forces of the Crown must suffer severely in the event of war.

He reprised Armstrongs and Vickers' wartime contributions in production, the management of National Factories and the provision of personnel to the state. Lawrence equated the interests of Vickers-Armstrongs and the state:

> The British Government often asks Vickers "what can you produce and in what time in the event of war?" The answer to this question must be a constantly diminishing quantity unless a steady flow of work can be maintained in the factories. Large technical staffs cannot be kept in idleness, and the upkeep of empty, or practically empty, factories is heavy. Orders which Vickers have passed owning to restrictions have undoubtedly been placed abroad, and Britain is poorer in consequence, her national defence has suffered, and her ability to secure commercial and armament trade abroad weakened.[248]

He closed by asking "for further assistance, and, if possible, that they [Vickers-Armstrongs] may be placed on equal terms with their competitors of other countries."[249] This message likely chimed with Hankey, who was concerned about Britain's military-industrial capacity.[250] Nevertheless, the third Scheme excluded munitions of war by statute.[251] Vickers-Armstrongs lacked influence over the political process.

Despite being party to international naval arms control agreements and ongoing negotiations, Britain began planning for war. "In 1931, an unofficial committee of businessmen was created to secretly advise the government on the industrial effects of rearmament."[252] Notably, Vickers-Armstrongs was not involved. In 1932 the Ten-Year-Rule governing British procurement was revoked.[253] Nevertheless, initially not much changed as the Treasury "remained convinced that the financial dangers out-weighed the military."[254] The powerful Committee of Imperial Defence was constantly monitoring German military-industrial progress and considering British military-industrial

---

[248] Lawrence to Secretary of Committee on Imperial Defence, October 4, 1932. VA Microfilm R 286.

[249] Lawrence to Secretary of Committee on Imperial Defence, October 4, 1932. VA Microfilm R 286.

[250] Roskill, *Hankey, Vol III*.

[251] Dietrich, "British," p. 244.

[252] Coghlan, "Armaments," p. 205.

[253] Postan, *British*, p. 9. Committee of Imperial Defence Secretary Hankey had been advocating cancelling the Ten-Year-Rule in 1931 and more strongly in 1932. Roskill, *Hankey*, pp. 27, 38–39.

[254] Dunbabin, "British Rearmament," p. 589.

capacity.[255] In 1933 a Defence Requirements Committee was established and Prime Minister Ramsay MacDonald asked the Committee of Imperial Defence for a report on the state of the private armaments industry.[256] That report rang alarm bells within the government.

In 1935 there was a difficult interaction with the War Office over the government's desire to produce a foreign gun, the Bren, at Enfield rather than purchasing the Vickers Berthier gun or the Vickers machine gun. Birch advocated for the Vickers machine gun, but the Master-General of the Ordnance was unimpressed: "[W]e do not care about your air-cooled machine gun. I am informed that the cooling is not as good as we require."[257] The War Office's Major General H. A. Lewis was kinder, but still negative: "I think our main trouble is that Vickers naturally like their Maxim and V.B. designs, whereas we prefer the Bren." He offered to help the firm get a representative on the Small Arms Committee: "It will help your people to keep 'au fait' with our trend of thought."[258] At the request of the Army Council, Vickers-Armstrongs produced a statement about the potential impact of Enfield manufacturing a foreign gun. They responded:

> The prestige of Vickers-Armstrongs Limited as the leading machine gun manufacturers would receive a serious blow. This would undoubtedly have an effect on the prospects of selling the Vickers Berthier gun to foreign governments and might have a marked effect on sales of other classes of machine guns. The loss to Vickers-Armstrongs Limited would be particularly heavy as it is clear that the future land machine business lies principally in the light machine gun.[259]

Vickers-Armstrongs also suggested that acquiring their gun would: enhance the prospect of exports, thereby having a positive impact on employment and the retention of skilled men, "whose services would be invaluable in training the large number of work-people necessary in a national emergency"; ensure that their Crayford facilities would be available in times of national emergency; and keep Enfield busy with up to 50 percent of the contract.[260] The British Army was unpersuaded and took the Bren. Subsequently Vickers-Armstrongs was

---

[255] See, for example, the Committee of Imperial Defence meeting of May 31, 1934. Committee of Imperial Defence, Minutes of the 264th Meeting, May 31, 1934. Committee of Imperial Defence, Minutes of Meetings November 9, 1933 to October 28, 1937. TNA, CAB 2/6.

[256] Miller, *Planning*, p. 88. Citing: "The Position of Private Armaments in British Defence," 10 March 1933. TNA, CAB60/13, PSO359.

[257] Hugh Elles to Birch, July 10, 1935, "Guns – Interviews etc. Manufacture 1934–45." VA, Doc. 662, Folio 240.

[258] H. A. Lewis, Director of Artillery to Birch, August 12, 1935, VA, Doc. 662, Folios 242–43.

[259] "Vickers Berthier Gun," undated, statement for the Army Council from Vickers-Armstrongs. VA, Doc. 662, Folios 66–67.

[260] "Vickers Berthier Gun," Folio 66.

permitted to market the Vickers Berthier gun in the Dominions, and it was adopted by the British Indian Army.[261]

Sir Robert McLean was skirmishing with the Air Ministry, which had issued a specification (Number G/4/31) for a General-Purpose Aircraft. Vickers submitted two proposals, one for a biplane with a normal wing construction and a geodetic fuselage, and another for a geodetic monoplane.[262] The Air Ministry – against Vickers' preference – ordered the biplane – and production began. The Vickers Board nevertheless decided to make the monoplane as a private venture for a cost of £30,271 (£2,407,991 in August 2022). The biplane flew in 1934 and the Air Ministry ordered 150. In 1935 the monoplane flew, exceeding the performance of the biplane. McLean lobbied to have the monoplane adopted instead of the biplane, writing to Air Vice Marshall Sir Hugh Dowding: "Meanwhile and until you decide whether we shall be allowed to switch over from the biplane to the monoplane, I do not wish to proceed with the work on the biplane because in my view it is not a modern machine."[263] On September 10, 1935, Supermarine was told by the Ministry to stop work on the biplane and commence with the monoplane, which became the Wellesley. Vickers Supermarine subsequently produced 176 Wellesley planes.

Crisis: More Arms Control

When the Washington Treaty seemed to be falling short in 1927, new negotiations were convened in Geneva. Britain proposed including large submarines in a new agreement, threatening Vickers-Armstrongs' business. As Lord Beatty explained to the Committee of Imperial Defence, "at Washington they had advocated the abolition of the submarine. If this could be accepted, destroyer requirements could be considerably reduced."[264] In 1929 Craven voiced Vickers-Armstrongs' fears about submarine orders being lost in an exchange of letters with Laurence Spear of Electric Boat:

> Your note regarding the limitation of armaments is very interesting, and I can assure you I am extremely anxious about some of our present contracts. Although the papers say that certain submarines have been cancelled, nothing has yet taken place although there is always a possibility of it happening. However, we shall know our fate within the next week or two.[265]

[261] Lewis to Birch, February 20, 1936. VA, Doc. 662, Folio 277.
[262] Vickers innovator Barnes Wallis had developed geodetic design for aircraft.
[263] H. Scrope, *Golden Wings*. Cited in: Webb, *Never*, VA, Doc. 1900, Section II p. 105.
[264] "Reduction and Limitation of Naval Armaments Forthcoming Conference of Naval Powers," Committee of Imperial Defence, Minutes of the 227th Meeting, May 20, 1927, p. 4. TNA CAB 2/7.
[265] Craven to Spear, July 13, 1929, Nye Committee Hearings, September 5, 1934, p. 201 and exhibit 129, p. 408.

Craven's passivity here contrasts with subsequent allegations that armament firms actively sought to influence the outcomes of these negotiations.[266]

Ultimately the Geneva negotiations failed, but new negotiations were hosted by Britain, which still favored restricting large submarines. After making concessions on the maximum number of British cruisers, negotiations were successful, resulting in the 1930 London Naval Treaty, which included tonnage limits on submarines.[267] As Basil Collier has noted, the various national armament firms were powerless to prevent the Treaty's passage.[268] Henry Carse of Electric Boat explained to the U.S. Congress' Nye Committee the effects of disarmament negotiations on business: "They have held it up, especially the effort of Great Britain to do away with submarines, and it has certainly affected our line of business very substantially."[269]

The Disarmament Conference in Geneva opened in 1932 and included negotiations over military airpower. The British Government supported the conference's aim of limiting the maximum size of military aircraft and postponed developing new bombers until the proposed restrictions were withdrawn in 1934. Even before that, Vickers had submitted designs for what became the Wellington which ignored the Geneva Disarmament weight limits.[270]

Vickers-Armstrongs' Admiralty orders were now given subject to the outcomes of disarmament negotiations. For example, in 1933, when the Admiralty was drip-feeding armament firms with work, Vickers-Armstrongs were told their design for a large submarine had been accepted – subject to the outcome of the arms control negotiations. Craven wrote to Electric Boat:

> [T]hey will have the right to withdraw their promised order for the second ship if Geneva or any other troublesome organization upsets the large submarine. In view of this, I am not saying anything publicly about the *Clyde*, and I would suggest that it would be wise that Spear should not let the information get into the hands of your Navy Department until after I can tell you that we really have a proper contract.[271]

The Admiralty followed through however, and HMS *Clyde* was launched at Barrow in March 1934. *Clyde* had a standard displacement of 1,850 tons, and a full load displacement of 2,206 tons, putting her just outside the 2,000 tons

---

[266] Oral evidence of William Arnold-Forster Day II, citing Sir Charles Craven's letter disclosed at the Nye Committee (Exhibit 22 at the Royal Commission), Evidence Prepared for the Bankes Committee. VA, Doc. 58, p. 26.

[267] "International Treaty for the Limitation and Reduction of Naval Armament – London, April 22, 1930." In: Jordan, *Warships*, Appendix 2.

[268] Collier, *Arms*, p.14.

[269] Nye Committee Hearings, Part 1, 4 September 1934, p. 31.

[270] Fearon, "Aircraft," pp. 233, 239.

[271] Craven to Carse, January 6, 1933, Nye Committee Hearings, September 4, 1934, p. 32 and exhibit 23, p. 333.

limit.[272] By 1934 more domestic and international work was coming in, with Elswick's gun mounting department half full and Barrow's over two thirds full.[273]

The mid-1930s British arms embargoes added to Vickers-Armstrongs' difficulties. Whereas past British embargoes had been designed to either retain arms for state use or prevent weapons reaching enemies, now they were used for political purposes.[274] For Vickers-Armstrongs the result was the same though: lost sales. Birch used his government contacts in 1933 when the British were considering imposing an embargo on Japan on the (incorrect) assumption that other League of Nations members would do the same. This issue was a hot potato for the government, and it was passed several times between the Disarmament Subcommittee of the Cabinet and the full Cabinet.[275] Peace groups and newspapers such as the *New Statesman* and the *Manchester Guardian* put the government under immense pressure to act as Japan defied the League with continued aggression against China. Counterlobbying came from Vickers-Armstrongs. Cabinet Secretary Sir Maurice Hankey recorded in his diary: "General Sir Noel Birch, formerly Master-General of the Ordnance and a great help to our Principal Supply Officers Committee, now on the Board of Vickers, wrote me that they had already lost £500,000 worth of prospective orders, which might (for the whole country) reach £2 millions before the end of the week. I passed this information on." The Prime Minister responded, suggesting that the embargo would be ended. Hankey added: "He told me to give Birch a hint not to let go the orders in prospect before Monday – which I did by personal interview yesterday afternoon."[276] However, Vickers-Armstrongs lobbying failed. An embargo was imposed on February 27 only to be rescinded on March 13 after other League members had not followed suit. Four embargoes were imposed: the China and Japan embargo of 1933; the Chaco embargo of 1934–35; the Italo-Ethiopian embargo of 1935; and the Spanish embargo of 1936.[277] The politics over the Sino-Japanese embargo shows that while Vickers-Armstrongs now had excellent contacts within the top ranks of the civil service, this did not enable the firm to prevail on issues where public opinion was a bigger factor for the government. This reflected another predicament Vickers-Armstrongs faced.

[272] Akermann, *British Submarines*, p. 305.
[273] Scott, *Vickers*, p. 220.
[274] Atwater, "British," pp. 304–05.
[275] Thorne, "Quest," pp. 129–49.
[276] Sir Maurice Hankey diary entry, March 4, 1933. Cited in: Roskill, *Hankey* vol. III, pp. 74–75.
[277] "Exports of Arms and Export Licences," Evidence Prepared for the Bankes Commission, VA, Doc 57, Folder 29.

Crisis: The Anti-Armament Firm Movement

In the immediate post-war years Vickers' Dawson had been glancingly affected by involvement with the British Cellulose and Chemical Manufacturing Company, which made cellulose acetate, or "dope," which was used on aircraft and airships. The firm had granted six penny shares to several investors who purchased risky debentures. Among that group were Dawson, Vickers Ltd. and Albert Vickers (with a token one 6d share). Subsequently these shares became worth £10 each, a massive profit that was investigated by a government committee in 1919. While Vickers did not look good, others involved had looked much worse. The scandal eventually subsided.[278]

By the late 1920s, however, public concern about armament firms' wartime profits was growing. Collier identified the Great Depression as a catalyst for renewed anger against armament firms.[279] For Anthony Sampson, the Allies were glad to have somewhere else to lay the blame for the war.[280] David Anderson identified press attention to the Chaco War and Germany's withdrawal from the League's Disarmament Conference as other causes.[281] Pressure was also coming from radical Members of Parliament seeking reduced spending on armaments.[282] Even in the 1930s, though, the government seemed to think that there was a powerful check on armament firms' profits from any rearmament contracts: In the words of Permanent Secretary to the Treasury Sir Warren Fisher, "the supreme interest of the stockholders is the integrity of the State ... from destruction by external force."[283] This complacency was also found in the Admiralty, which, while it had the right to inspect the financial record of all firms that supplied the Navy, failed to do so between 1929 and 1940.[284] The public was much more skeptical than the government.

Vickers-Armstrongs were alert to the dangers. In July 1929 Birch wrote to Craven about an armament exhibition planned in Buenos Aires for eighteen months' time: "I do not know if you have read Thomas' speech [James Henry Thomas MP] in the 'Times' this morning, but ... the big question will arise over this exhibition whether the Labour Party, if in power, which I hope to God they won't be, will let us export for it." He concluded by telling Craven to "get Bromley to ask Thomas up to Barrow and stuff him full of wine and cigars

---

[278] Coleman, "War Demand," pp. 205–27.
[279] Collier, *Arms*, pp. 5–6.
[280] Sampson, *Arms Bazaar*, p. 70.
[281] Anderson, "British," p. 8.
[282] See for example, "Disarmament," House of Commons Debate, March 8, 1932, *Hansard*, Vol. 262, cc. 1717–69. At: http://hansard.millbanksystems.com/commons/1932/mar/08/disarmament.
[283] Peden, *Arms*, p. 132. Citing: Fisher to Chamberlain, December 2, 1935, TNA, T 171/324.
[284] Miller, *Planning*, p. 61.

for a week!"[285] A subsequent letter to Birch stated: "With regard to the question of the M.P.'s at Newcastle, I am working through the chief Trades Union man up there as his power with the M.P.'s is very much more than mine."[286] While the trade unions could usefully lobby the government to save jobs, there was growing militancy among Elswick workers. They began to produce their own magazine questioning the international trade in weapons and their firms' role within it. *The Gun* was published monthly and by May 1935 there had been twenty issues.[287]

In 1932 Webster Jenkinson sent Zaharoff the Union of Democratic Control's exposé *The Secret International*.[288] Zaharoff responded: "[A]gree with you that 25% of the facts and 75% of the conclusions are incorrect, yet many of the allusions are correct."[289] In 1933 Archibald Fenner Brockway's influential Labour Party pamphlet *The Bloody Traffic* was published, followed in 1934 by Engelbrecht and Hanighen's *Merchants of Death*. Vickers-Armstrongs combed through each of these sources, rebutting the allegations wherever possible but admitting when an allegation was correct.[290] The case against armament firms was gaining momentum.

The investigations of the League of Nations into armament firms produced more smoke than fire. Nevertheless, the allegations stuck. During the League's 1927 Geneva negotiations, three U.S. warship manufacturing firms had employed a lobbyist, William Shearer. When this came to light (when Shearer sued over nonpayment of wages), it revealed the role that his employers had played in opposing disarmament. American public opinion was outraged, leading to the United States Congress initiating the 1934 Nye Committee investigations.[291]

The prewar practice of establishing stable prices and maintaining profits through cartels and armament rings attracted ire. The public mood in Britain was further ratcheted up by revelations from the Nye Committee about the behavior of Vickers, Imperial Chemical Industries and smaller British armament firms. As U.S. Secretary of State Cordell Hull noted, the Committee's "publicity director kept a stream of so-called 'news' flowing out to the press

---

[285] Birch to Craven, July 6, 1929. VA Microfilm R 286.
[286] Vickers Armstrongs (Bromley?) to Birch, July 20, 1929. VA Microfilm R 286.
[287] "No. 20," *The Gun* – published by the militant group of workers at Elswick, May 3, 1935. TWA, D.VA/67/5; "No. 8" *The Gun* – published by the militant group of workers at Elswick, November 9, 1934. TWA, D.VA/67/1.
[288] *Secret International*.
[289] Zaharoff to Webster Jenkinson, July 28, 1932. VA, Doc. 786.
[290] "Arms and the Men," Folder 32; "The Bloody Traffic by Fenner Brockway," Folder 33; "Merchants of Death," Folder 34; "The Secret International – Armament Firms at Work," Folder 35. Each has annotations giving Vickers' response to their allegations. Evidence Prepared for the Bankes Commission. VA, Doc. 57, Folders 32–35; Engelbrecht and Hanighen, *Merchants of Death*, p. 3; Brockway, *Bloody Traffic*.
[291] "Shearer, Skoda, and Swedish Air Force cases (war scares)," 1935. TNA, T 181/40.

of this and other countries."[292] Vickers' behavior looked particularly bad. Evidence was gathered from Vickers' American submarine partner Electric Boat, and it became clear that Craven had been far too frank (and too boastful?) in his correspondence with them.[293] The Nye Committee was regaled with stories about Vickers' collusion with Electric Boat, the behavior of Zaharoff and allegations that the King of England helped Vickers to win a contract in Poland, and revisited the firm's known bribing of a Japanese Admiral in 1912–13.

Some of the slipperiness of Vickers' management was exposed when a letter from Craven to Spear of Electric Boat was produced and its recipient cross-examined. Written in October 1927, Craven's letter tells Spear of an Admiralty inquiry for between one and three submarines, explaining that he will make Armstrong-Whitworth put in a slightly higher bid and ensure that the work came to Barrow.[294] Craven's letter also declared,

> I also think that perhaps it would be worth while putting forward a tender for six boats, the total number to be built. I have had a word with the director of contracts at the Admiralty, who is a friend of mine, and who would like this. He, I know, tried to get us the order for all five submarines last year.[295]

A subsequent letter from Craven shared information on the bid process "from an absolutely reliable but very secret source." This source had provided detailed information on the bids, how many boats each had tendered for and on their bid prices. Craven also reported, "For your private information, I was in a position to look after Armstrong's and keep them out of the picture on this occasion."[296] Senator Nye asked Spear: "Although Vickers is a British concern, in this particular case they were not opposed at all to 'ganging up' when it is to their advantage to drive a better bargain with their own government?" Spear responded: "I presume not, I do not know."[297] Despite growing interdependence with the state, Vickers-Armstrongs clearly still acted in its own interests. This letter was subsequently quoted verbatim in the House of Commons by Clement Attlee. He commented,

> Here is an ordinary business letter written by Sir Charles Craven. I do not suppose that he is bluffing, but he says that the Director of Contracts is a friend of his. It may not be corrupt at all, but there is a serious question, when you have firms like this, of the relationship of people in Government offices to the firm.[298]

[292] Hull, *Memoirs Vol. 1*, p. 399.
[293] Nye Committee Hearings, Part 1, September 4, 1934, pp. 26–27.
[294] Nye Committee Hearings, Part 1, September 4, 1934. pp. 26–28, and exhibit 18, p. 330.
[295] Nye Committee Hearings, Part 1, exhibit 18, p. 330.
[296] Craven to Spear, November 30, 1927. Nye Committee Hearings, Part 1, exhibit 19, pp. 330–31.
[297] Nye Committee Hearings, Part 1, September 4, 1934, p. 27.
[298] Clement Attlee MP, House of Commons Debate, Volume 293, November 8, 1934, cc. 1295. At: http://hansard.millbanksystems.com/commons/1934/nov/08/private-manufacture-of-and-trade-in-arms.

A 1932 telegram revealed at the Nye Committee created a sensation across the Atlantic. The telegram, to the Driggs Ordnance and Engineering Company head office, from Ziemba, Driggs' agent in Poland, read in part: "King of Great Britain summoned our Ambassador in London and intervened in 3-inch or 75mm 50-cal gun on New Mobile Mount letter Dec. 15th, 1928, contract."[299] The King stood accused of assisting Vickers-Armstrongs' efforts to win a contract described by Louis Driggs as pending to his company (though no contract had been awarded).[300] When asked at the hearing what the King was doing in "playing salesman", Driggs merely answered, "I think he was just helping them out of the depression."[301] The allegation was met with strong denials from the British Government and the Polish Embassy in London. Foreign Secretary Sir John Simon declared the King to be "perfectly incapable of having any connection with this incident," describing it as a "silly story."[302] Nevertheless, Cordell Hull received "one of the strongest protests I had yet received. Sir Robert Vansittart, the Acting Foreign Secretary, expressed his Government's deepest indignation and resentment."[303]

Less reported upon was Driggs' other remark: "That is just part of the same gesture that the British royalty has been indulging in lately in using the Prince of Wales down in Argentina; he is their best salesman they say, and creates good will and it is a gesture of the royal family interesting itself in British business."[304] The British state's interests had increasingly aligned with those of exporters, resulting in an important marketing development. The British royal family had become involved in trade promotion, undertaking international tours aboard Royal Navy ships.[305]

The Prince of Wales and Prince George had undertaken an official 18,000-mile "trade tour" of South America in 1931, including a visit to Argentina designed to counteract the country's growing relationship with Germany.[306] The Prince of Wales had opened the British Empire Trade Fair, inspected the Military Academy and watched flying displays.[307] On his return, British newsreels had declared him "Britain's Best Salesman."[308] There were also suggestions that the

---

[299] Unsigned telegram to Driggs Ordnance, from Warsaw, January 20, 1932. Nye Committee Hearings, Part 2, Exhibit 223, p. 544. Ziemba's identity was revealed in Driggs' testimony, p. 495.

[300] Nye Committee Hearings, Part 2, pp. 501–02.

[301] Nye Committee Hearings, Part 2, p. 496.

[302] Bringe, *Findings*, p. 30. Citing: *News Week*, Vol. 17, No. 4 (September 17, 1934).

[303] Hull, *Memoirs*, p. 380.

[304] Nye Committee Hearings, Part 2, p. 496.

[305] d'Eyncourt, *Shipbuilder's*, pp. 130–31; *British Pathé News*, "Prince of Wales," 1924; Wise, *Royal Navy*, p. 190.

[306] *British Pathé News*, "The Princes."

[307] Camera footage, "1931 British Empire State Visit to Argentina by Prince of Wales and Prince George." At: www.youtube.com/watch?v=ZYFs1QveqUM.

[308] *British Pathé News*, "The Princes."

prince had facilitated aircraft sales to Chile during his 1931 visit. The President of
the American Curtiss-Wright airplane company suggested that he had to act in
Chile to counteract the effects of the prince's visit.[309] Nevertheless, even staunch
British critics of the arms trade concluded that while the prince had helped to
secure Brazilian railway contracts for British firms, "there is no evidence that his
services have been similarly utilized in the arms trade." That said, they did note
that members of the royal retinue were shareholders in Vickers Ltd.[310] British
armament firms remained completely silent on all these accusations.

The Nye Committee revealed that from 1912 Zaharoff had an agreement
with Electric Boat and Vickers that he would get 5 percent commission on any
Spanish submarine sales. As Carse of Electric Boat explained: "The Spanish
business was his business. He secured that business and he held it against very
keen competition."[311] Carse also acknowledged that this "was … not an out-
of-the-way commission on securing any important business."[312] Zaharoff's
commission on Spanish business for Electric Boat between 1919 and 1934 was
$766,099.74[313] As this was during a slump in armament sales, this figure fed pub-
lic outrage. Spear had to explain how it was that Zaharoff's 1925 commission was
bigger than Electric Boat's, responding, "It is the only case I know of."[314]

On bribery, Spear informed the Nye Committee: "[T]here is a general impression that what we would call bribery and which they do not is pretty general practice in most South American countries … it was my opinion that you could not
do business with South America without paying a good many commissions."[315]
A March 1927 letter from Spear to Craven was revealed, passing some Chilean
work to Vickers. He offered "a little unsolicited and perhaps superfluous advice
which is that I would not be too modest about the price and would cover into it a
substantial amount in excess of the 10 percent above referred to, my own experience being that at the last minute something extra is always needed to grease the
ways."[316] The hearings also provided insights into Vickers' activities in Brazil in
the 1920s, via an official U.S. source obtained by Electric Boat. The source noted
that Rear Admiral Souza de Silva "is in the pay of British naval constructors, had
received a stipend amounting to $110 a month from them for work that he had
previously done in obtaining contracts for naval construction, particularly for
two large vessels which the British built some years ago for Brazil."[317]

[309] *A Monthly Digest.*
[310] Williams, *Who's Who*, pp. 13–14.
[311] Nye Committee Hearings, Part 1, 4 September 1934, p. 24.
[312] Nye Committee Hearings, Part 1, 4 September 1934, p. 36 and exhibit 23-A, p. 333.
[313] Nye Committee Hearings, Part 1, p. 21, and exhibit 17, p. 329.
[314] Nye Committee Hearings, Part 1, 4 September 1934, p. 48.
[315] Nye Committee Hearings, Part 1, 5 September 1934, p. 117.
[316] Nye Committee Hearings, Part 1, 5 September 1934, p. 119. Citing: Spear to Craven, March
       3, 1927, exhibit 68, pp. 117–19.
[317] C. S. McNeir in Washington to Carse, May 7, 1923, exhibit 102, pp. 389–90. $110 in 1923
       equates to £7,393.26 per month in August 2022.

As the World Disarmament Conference was flailing in Geneva in 1933, the results of the first British "peace ballot," which polled select regions on public attitudes to unilateral disarmament, were announced at the Labour Party conference. The results – which even the instigators thought should be treated with some caution – favored disarmament by a margin of 14 percent.[318] Subsequently a ballot by the Illford branch of the League of Nations Union and the *Illford Recorder* canvassed local views about the Locarno Treaties, disarmament and the arms trade. The response was overwhelmingly for the League. Startlingly, more people had voted in the poll than in local elections.[319] The final question on the Illford ballot was: "Should the manufacture of armaments by private enterprise be prohibited?" Of the 26,000 respondents, 80.9 percent voted yes.[320] Lord Rothermere's pro-rearmament press empire ran similar ballots through its local papers, hoping to invalidate the Illford results. Percentages of between 72 and 90 in the five cities covered answered yes to the identical question on prohibiting private armaments manufacture: not the result Rothermere wanted.[321] These experiences galvanized the League of Nations Union, churches and women's peace groups to campaign for a national "peace ballot."[322] Clumsy politicking by the government ensured that otherwise fragmented groups coalesced in support of the ballot. The 1934 "National Declaration on the League of Nations and Disarmament," or peace ballot, asked the public five questions, including: "Should the manufacture and sale of armaments for private profit be prohibited by international agreement?" Of the 11,640,066 people who participated (38.2 percent of the adult population), there was an overwhelming margin of 10,489,145 (90.1 percent) in favor of nationalization, compared with 780,350 (6.7 percent) against.[323]

Two days before the first results of the peace ballot were to be announced, Prime Minister MacDonald felt compelled to establish a Royal Commission on the Private Manufacture of and Trade in Arms and Munitions of War, chaired by Sir John Bankes.[324] The Cabinet thought the Bankes Commission would quell public demands for action, even though it had limited the scope of inquiry and the powers of the body.[325] This attempted deflection was clearly understood by opponents: "It is difficult to escape the conclusion that the National Government, in setting up a commission with restricted powers, is acting as the protector of the powerful interests behind the armament firms."[326] The Bankes Commission

---

[318] These two paragraphs draw heavily from Ceadel, "First," pp. 810–39.
[319] "The 'Peace Ballot' of 1934–35."
[320] Ceadel, "First," p. 813.
[321] Ceadel, "First," p. 816.
[322] "Perils," p. 5.
[323] Ceadel, "First," pp. 832.
[324] King George V's Royal Warrant to the Royal Commission on the Private Manufacture of and Trading in Arms, February 20, 1935. CHAR 2/247/2; Ceadel, "First," p. 820; Anderson, "British," pp. 5–37.
[325] Anderson, "British," pp. 12 and 14.
[326] Williams, *Who's Who*, p. 46.

lasted eighteen months, assessed submissions from more than fifty major organizations and held twenty-two public sessions.

Vickers-Armstrongs took their defense at the Bankes Commission extremely seriously, not just because of the reputational danger, but because the Commission was considering whether the solution to the problem was to simply nationalize production and thereby take profits, seen as the evil element, out of the equation. There was also extensive debate in the Commons over whether to nationalize the armament firms.[327] While a broad variety of allegations were made about the activities of these firms, and particularly against Vickers, the debate coalesced into one about whether to abolish the private manufacture of armaments. On this issue Vickers-Armstrongs, Beardmores and the government were on the same side: They were opposed to nationalization.

In response to requests for documentation, Vickers-Armstrongs assembled extensive data and submitted to the Commission "a volume of typed and printed papers running to 337 pages."[328] Vickers-Armstrongs made a précis of the allegations laid against them in evidence to the Bankes Commission, fifty-five issues in all (cross-referenced by witness and submission paper), and then provided information to their witnesses so that they could refute – or blunt the impact of – each in turn.[329] In the presentation of information for their defense, Vickers-Armstrongs was careful in what it provided. While the firm provided ample statistics for the wartime production of warships, artillery and ammunition at both Vickers and Armstrongs, they provided no figures for turnover or profits during the bumper war years (though they paid extra taxes on those profits).[330] Nevertheless, their figures on capital expenditure went back to 1910, long before rearmament.[331] In a confidential annex to the Royal Commission, Vickers provided an analysis of their profit and loss accounts for 1930–1934 inclusive, showing that they incurred significant costs in merging Vickers and Armstrong-Whitworth.[332] The accounts showed that in these years they consistently made more than 43 percent of their profits on financing rather than weapons production. In 1930 54.23 percent and in 1934 56.78 percent of the

---

[327] House of Commons Debate, Volume 293, November 8, 1934, cc. 1299–1323. At: http://hansard.millbanksystems.com/commons/1934/nov/08/private-manufacture-of-and-trade-in-arms.

[328] Note by the Secretary, "Messrs. Vickers Ltd. Evidence," Bankes Commission. TNA T 181/56. Also at VA, Docs. 57, 58, 59 and 60.

[329] Evidence Prepared for the Bankes Committee, Volume III. VA, Doc. 59, Folder 131.

[330] "Output of Vickers Limited and Sir W. G. Armstrong Whitworth and Co. Ltd., During War Years," Evidence Prepared for the Bankes Committee. VA, Doc. 58, Folder 91.

[331] "Statement of Capital Expenditure," Evidence Prepared for the Bankes Committee. VA, Doc. 58, Folder 96.

[332] Confidential Annex, Appendix 4A, "Statement Showing Declared and Adjusted Profits or Losses for 1930, 1931, 1932, 1933, 1934 and An Estimate of the Proportion Attributable to the Production of Arms and Munitions of War," pp. 29–33. TNA, T 181/56.

profit came from financing.[333] Further, the figures given for expenditures on plant, labor and research, experimental work and development, and ventures that failed were provided for the periods 1929 (or 1930) to the end of 1934.[334] That is, Vickers-Armstrongs gave the figures for the period when profits were at a historically low ebb, dividends to shareholders were depressed, and the consequences of their disastrous diversification strategies and the costs of their subsequent merger were most evident in the form of heavy losses. To hammer home their importance to the state, Vickers-Armstrongs presented evidence as to how much more the British Government would have had to pay for weapons if the firm had not also exported abroad, provided a document on the "subsidy" provided by the state to the Royal Ordnance Factories, and submitted cost comparisons of warship building between the Royal Dockyards and the private sector – which obviously favored the firms.[335]

Vickers-Armstrongs revealed full details of payments to Zaharoff.[336] While these commissions were extremely large, there was no strong evidence that they were hidden or illicit. There is only one hint in the Vickers Archive that Zaharoff may have also been getting underhand payments, and this was not provided to the Commission. Zaharoff claimed that he had lost money in an early deal in Russia concerning submarines and that Issac Rice of Electric Boat had authorized that he be repaid. In correspondence with Dawson, Zaharoff complained:

> I have refrained from sending this in hopes that by demurring I might get paid ... will the C- send me a cheque for the equivalent as I do not care to put it into my account for fear of a *certain* Clarke of Rice, & [Co.] will you write *privately* to Rice about it so that he can understand the entry in your account to him, and this entry should be veiled.[337]

Zaharoff stood accused of being a "merchant of death."[338] Consequently, members of the Vickers-Armstrongs Board advised ending Zaharoff's remuneration

---

[333] "Vickers Ltd. Evidence: Notes by the Secretary," July 1935 onwards. Confidential Annex on Profits, p. 28. TNA, T 181/56.

[334] "Vickers Group Research, Experimental and Development Expenditure for Five Years Ended 31st December, 1934," Folder 65; "Unprofitable Ventures in Peace Products Since 1918," Folder 79; "Vickers-Armstrongs Dividends Paid between Date of Incorporation of Company and 31st December, 1935," Folder 80; "Expenditure on Armament Patents 1930–1935," Folder 95. Evidence Prepared for the Bankes Committee, VA, Doc. 58; Treasury file "Vickers Ltd. Evidence: Notes By the Secretary," July 1935 onwards. TNA, T 181/56.

[335] "Foreign Work and Charges," Folder 93; "Subsidy to Royal Ordnance Factories," Folder 110; "Comparison of Costs of Warship Construction 1925–1934 between Dockyard and Private Manufacture," Evidence Prepared for the Bankes Committee, VA, Doc. 59, Folder 137.

[336] "Commissions Payable to Sir B. Zaharoff" seems to cover the period 1920–52 (post-1936 paid to his estate). VA, Doc. 787.

[337] Zaharoff to Dawson, undated. VA, Doc. 786. Emphasis in original.

[338] Allfrey, *Man*; McCormick, *Peddler*; Thayer, *War Business*, pp. 26–31; Stanley and Pearton, *International Trade*, pp. 3–4.

and association with the firm. Colonel Maxwell passed this suggestion to Chairman Lawrence, who, Scott reports, "at once very firmly said that 'the day I leave the chair they can do what they like. Until then we will keep that arrangement that we have made.' ... General Lawrence, although he himself much disliked the publicity and mystery-man side of Zaharoff, had a high sense of what the Company owed to his abilities."[339] Lawrence's Royal Commission correspondence reflected this:

> There is no desire on the part of the present management of Vickers Lim-
> ited to minimize in any way the importance of Sir Basil to the Vickers
> Company in pre-war days .... Bearing in mind the conditions of business
> in those remote times, it is submitted that the attempts made to portray Sir
> Basil as a type of salesman or representative now employed by the company
> in the vastly altered conditions of to-day are meretricious and unfair.[340]

However, given that Zaharoff was technically still working for the firm – they had made a new agreement to pay his expenses in February 1927 – was still receiving commissions and was still being consulted by them in 1929, this is a sleight of hand.[341] Even after his death in November 1936, Vickers paid substantial commissions to Zaharoff's estate until at least 1952.[342]

In this opening statement Sir Charles Craven announced: "In view of the acquisition by Vickers Limited of the whole of the capital of Vickers-Armstrongs Limited and the elimination thereby of outside shareholders in that Company, Vickers-Armstrongs Limited was on the 19th December, 1935, changed from a Public Company to a Private Company, and on the 1st January, 1936 the Board of the Company was reconstituted."[343] This timing is suspicious, coming as it did between the announcement of the Royal Commission and its convening. Becoming a private company was a defensive move that got rid of public shareholders who might have questioned the firm's behavior.

Representatives of British firms appeared voluntarily before the Commission and sought to appear as innocuous as possible.[344] They enjoyed limited success, particularly Craven, whose vague testimony, flippant responses and demeanor were poorly received.[345] This, and the stiff questioning of the Commissioners, led to Vickers' submitting multiple letters of clarification, providing extra materials

---

[339] "Zaharoff and Lawrence" undated paper in J. D. Scott's hand, in VA, Doc. 788.
[340] H. A. Lawrence, Chairman of Vickers Ltd., to the Royal Commission on the Private Manufacture of and Trading in Arms, March 11, 1936, p. 3. "Vickers Ltd.: evidence; note by Secretary," TNA, T 181/56.
[341] Lawrence, to the Royal Commission, March 11, 1936. Enclosure, p, 9; "For entertaining a certain person in Monte Carlo ... £9.14.6.," Birch to Sim, March 27, 1929. VA, Microfilm R 286.
[342] "Commissions Payable to Sir B. Zaharoff," VA, Doc. 787; "Arms King Dead."
[343] "Opening Statement by the Chairman of Vickers Ltd.," Evidence Prepared for the Bankes Committee, VA, Doc. 58, Folder 122, pp. 1–2.
[344] Anderson, "British," p. 19.
[345] "Craven Belittles."

and, eventually, to uncomfortable private interviews with the Commissioners. According to Miller, while "the 'prosecution' was poor ... the input from industry – particularly Vickers – nearly shot the defence in the foot."[346]

Vickers-Armstrongs representatives were confronted with correspondence showing price-fixing in South America. For example, a letter of September 23, 1923, from Spear of Electric Boat to his colleague Carse stated:

> I have advised him (i.e. Commander Aubry, agent of Electric Boat Co. in Peru) in a general way that it may be our policy to support the bid of our English friends in the Argentine and that we may also decide to have a friendly controlled bid put in from Italy .... The general idea, of course, is to fix the Italian price a little higher than Vickers' price, and if by chance they should get the order, the profit will be ample to take care of them as well as Vickers and ourselves.[347]

Interestingly, Vickers-Armstrongs offered no rebuttal to this.

The Commission focused on several arms export deals concluded by Armstrongs and Vickers, including for ammunition to Peru. In that case, the firm showed that the export was licensed, and moreover, that the Foreign Office had helped them to get the ammunition to Peru.[348] Vickers-Armstrongs' defense of this and many other deals is encapsulated in a quote from their Chairman: "As regards the whole question of the export of arms ... we cannot export anything without full permission from the Foreign Office. We have to report everything we do. Everything has to be approved by the Government of the day before we are able to do it, and that constitutes a very big restraint upon our approaching foreign powers."[349] Having once fought against export controls, they were now Vickers-Armstrongs' ultimate defense.

During these transatlantic investigations, bribes and commissions were criticized as unacceptable, even as both investigations discovered that they were routine. The Royal Commission examined a new case from Asia and re-examined several historic scandals, including Vickers' 1910 contract for the Japanese warship *Kongō*.[350] While the firm and the government had tamped down that scandal before the war, now, under renewed investigation, the *Kongō* scandal expanded

---

[346] Miller, *Planning*, p. 190.

[347] Annotated Memorandum from Yapp, Vickers concerning accusations against them. Submitted by Rachel Cowdrey to Mr. Twentyman, January 21, 1936, p. 5, referencing Arnold-Forster evidence, Day 2, Part 1, p. 399. TNA, T 181/56.

[348] "Information regarding order from Electric Boat Company for 3-inch Ammunition for Peruvian Ships." Evidence Prepared for the Bankes Committee, VA, Doc. 58, Folder 74.

[349] "Chairman's Speeches," Evidence Prepared for the Bankes Committee, VA, Doc. 58, Folder 76, p. 2.

[350] Lawrence to Secretary, with enclosures Appendix A: "Extracts from the Times," Appendix B: Parts I and II, Extracts from "The Japan Chronicle," Appendix C: "Extracts from Parliamentary Debates," February 19, 1936. "Vickers Ltd.: evidence; note by Secretary," TNA, T 181/56.

to encompass Yarrow, Weirs and Arrol too.[351] It also went higher, with revelations that Vickers' Sir James McKechnie had obtained the contract by bribing Admiral Fujii. At the hearings, Vickers-Armstrongs blamed Caillard, Dawson, Barker and McKechnie, all of whom were (conveniently) dead.[352] During questioning, Craven declared: "There is nothing in our books to show it."

A subsequent Vickers letter to the Commission provided a clarification that changed the meaning of Craven's statement: "[H]e was referring to his personal view that it having been proved that the Director in charge of the Barrow Works of the Company had bribed a foreign government official, he would have assumed that some action would have been taken in regard thereto by the Board of the Company."[353] Vickers then searched their Minute Books and the *Times* archive to find out what was reported, and interviewed two surviving Board members, neither of whom yielded anything. Vickers' Minute Books showed evidence that there were payments, run through the *Kongō* account, which matched the newspaper reports of bribes given. While Admiral Fujii was not named as the recipient of any bribes, Vickers reported that "it seems a safe assumption that the money was in fact intended for that individual."[354] Other Vickers files point to Zaharoff having also been a conduit for payments to the Admiral.[355]

The Vickers Archive contains a coded telegram, previously unrevealed, from McKechnie to B. H. Winder at the Imperial Hotel, Tokyo, dated February 1911: "Both cablegrams received please inform __ that our friend 5000 pounds is being forwarded by __ to him as second installment in payment of furniture supplied."[356] This "furniture" is very likely one of the bribery payments. This is equal to £654,612 in August 2022, and was only one of the payments, so the bribe was clearly substantial.

Subsequently, Vickers-Armstrongs was asked to report what disciplinary actions the Vickers Board had taken in response to the revelations at the 1914 Fujii bribery trial. They responded: "By this time the Great War had, of course, commenced and it is reasonable to assume that whatever the feelings and intentions of the Board were in regard to the matter the pressing needs of output of material of war would have left no time for consideration or action being taken on the matter."[357] This defense was used several times by the British Government as well as by Vickers-Armstrongs during the Commission's investigations.

---

[351] Parliamentary question, Mr. King to Mr. Churchill, "Royal Navy: Admiralty Contracts, 30 July 1914," p. 2. In Lawrence to Secretary, Appendix C: "Extracts from Parliamentary Debates." TNA, T 181/56.

[352] "Admiral Fuzii [Fujii] Case," VA, Doc. 59, Folder 133.

[353] Vickers to Secretary of the Royal Commission, 19 February 1936, TNA, T 181/56.

[354] Vickers to Secretary of the Royal Commission, 19 February 1936. TNA, T 181/56.

[355] "Admiral Fuzii [Fujii] Case," VA, Doc. 59, Folder 133.

[356] McKechnie to Winder, Coded Telegram, February 21, 1911. Letter Book No. 33, VA, Doc. 1006A, Folio 383.

[357] Vickers to Secretary of the Royal Commission, February 19, 1936. TNA, T 181/56.

The contemporaneous "Connolly case" proved difficult for Vickers-Armstrongs. A 1936 deal in China brokered by the company Jardine Matheson involved T. B. M Conolly, who had been sent out to the country by Vickers-Armstrongs in 1932 to demonstrate Carden-Loyd vehicles and stayed on as a demonstrator.[358] In the 1936 deal Conolly had added a fee of £54,000 to a tender to the Chinese Government for gunboats. A 5 percent commission had also recently been paid to a key official, General Tao, to secure the deal, but such commissions were common.[359] Conolly had been increasingly critical of Jardine's inaction in China and declared that Vickers-Armstrongs should employ him instead. In May 1936 Connolly sent an encrypted telegram to Birch: "Your competitors with my assistance have obtained contract £1,000,000.0.0. Their success assisted by passive Jardine policy."[360] Birch took the bait and Conolly was given a six-month trial. That same month, though, Conolly claimed to have been undone by Jardine's machinations against him, sending a long letter to Birch complaining of his treatment.[361] This was followed by an offer from Conolly to represent Vickers-Armstrongs to sell ground apparatus and search lights – which the firm refused – declaring that Jardine were their principals in China.[362]

Vickers-Armstrongs initially claimed at the Commission hearings that Conolly and the extra fee were all the responsibility of Jardine Matheson and that when they found out the sum quoted, they had informed the Chinese Government that the figure was too high. After Vickers-Armstrongs had provided what they hoped was conclusive evidence of their innocence, the Commission requested access to a vast array of documents. This was bargained down to two members of the Commission visiting to review two sets of papers. This visit spurred new questions, which Vickers-Armstrongs duly answered, but the Commission then requested a private meeting with representatives of the firm, where Craven, Keswick and Yapp were subject to a grilling that uncovered several inconsistencies in Vickers-Armstrongs' account, including the fact that Conolly was on their payroll.[363] Vickers-Armstrongs' behavior was roundly criticized by the Commission.

With the Bankes Commission hearings casting armament firms in a bad light, Sir Maurice Hankey swept in to assist them. His second testimony – approved of by the government and reflecting interdepartmental preparation – demolished many of the claims against the firms and the calls

---

[358] Yapp to Jardine Matheson, January 29, 1932. TNA T 181/83.
[359] Transcript of evidence taken at the private meeting, May 7, 1936, "Connolly Case," VA, Doc. 59, Folder 132, and TNA T 181/84.
[360] Conolly to Birch Telegram, May 4, 1936. VA, Microfilm K 613.
[361] Conolly to Birch, May 9, 1936. VA, Microfilm K 613.
[362] Vickers-Armstrongs to Conolly, June 10, 1936. VA, Microfilm K 613.
[363] Transcript of evidence taken at the private meeting, May 7, 1936. "Connolly Case," VA, Doc. 59, Folder 132.

for nationalization.[364] Hankey's testimony received a lot of bad press, but it reflected government concern about the deteriorating international situation, and certainly influenced the findings of the Commission.[365]

While critical of much of the behavior of armament firms and the minimal regulation of them, the Royal Commission's central conclusion was unequivocal: "The abolition of the private industry in the United Kingdom and the substitution for it of a system of State monopoly may be practicable; but it is undesirable."[366] Both Vickers-Armstrongs and the government were immensely relieved. The Interdepartmental Committee on the Report of the Royal Commission reported to the Committee of Imperial Defence that it was only prepared to accept three of the Commission's ten conclusions, and even then, had some quibbles.[367] The Committee discussed the Commission's Conclusion 7 about profits, which read: "We recommend that measures be taken to restrict the profits of armament firms in peace-time to a reasonable scale of remuneration designed not only to prevent excessive profits but to satisfy the public that they do so." Sir Maurice Hankey responded: "A great deal was already being done, and the Inter-departmental Committee suggested that it should be sufficient for His Majesty's Government to point to the assurances of the White Paper and the arrangements already made for controlling prices and securing co-ordination through the Treasury Inter-Service Committee and the Contracts Co-ordinating Committee."[368] Essentially the Committee of Imperial Defence punted the issue. The formal response to the Bankes Commission report revealed the government's priorities: "[W]ithout prejudice to the need for proper and adequate supervision of the trade, the export licensing machinery must be so administered as to eliminate unnecessary interference and delay: otherwise British firms will merely lose legitimate trade to foreign competitors."[369]

The Bankes Commission had advocated for planning for "the conscription of industry for a future war." The government's prescient response was:

> His Majesty's Government recognize that, if ever this country should again become involved in a major war, a much wider measure of control over industry would be needed than in time of peace. Indeed, this conclusion

[364] "Sir Maurice Hankey: Evidence," 1935. TNA, T 181/50; "Minutes of Meetings of Inter-Departmental Committees on the procedure in regard to Official Evidence and Consideration of the Report of the Royal Commission," 1936. CAB 16/124.
[365] Roskill, *Hankey*, pp. 246–49.
[366] Royal Commission conclusion, Chapter XII, para. 3. In Evidence Prepared for the Bankes Committee, Volume IV. VA, Doc. 60, p. 5.
[367] "Private Manufacture and Trading in Arms," Committee of Imperial Defence, Minutes of the 287th Meeting, p. 4. January 28, 1937. TNA CAB 2/7.
[368] "Private Manufacture and Trading in Arms," Committee of Imperial Defence, Minutes of the 287th Meeting, p. 9. January 28, 1937. TNA CAB 2/7.
[369] Government Response to the Findings of the Commission, VA, Doc. 60, pp. 16–17.

is plainly indicated from the experience of the Great War, and provisional plans for this purpose, ready in case of need to be presented for parliamentary approval, have necessarily to be prepared beforehand.[370]

Summary

Vickers-Armstrongs emerged from this period bruised from the combined impacts of economic depression, arms control agreements and public ire. The firm had survived relative deprivation – partly thanks to the Admiralty and Air Ministry's "drip-feeding" of contracts – but had not been able to fully pursue their classic strategy of investment during downswings. Nevertheless, with rearmament becoming the British Government's priority, Vickers-Armstrongs' investments in tanks and aircraft would soon prove vital.

The power and influence of Armstrongs, Vickers and Vickers-Armstrongs were not much in evidence. The firms were powerless to stop government inquiries into their behavior, though the British Government's increasing concern about preserving private armament manufacturing capacity helped the firms survive the scrutiny of the Royal Commission. Armstrongs and Vickers were unable to mobilize government support for their goal of gaining access to the Export Credit scheme. On this the firms were rebuffed three times, showing the limitations of their power and influence.

---

[370] Government Response to the Findings of the Commission, VA, Doc. 60, p. 16.

5

Selling Armaments in Britain 1936–1955

Vickers-Armstrongs and the Challenges
of Wartime and Peacetime

With the Royal Commission now behind them and the depression reced-
ing, Vickers-Armstrongs was once again able to fully focus on business and
the needs of their customers. They began to rebuild their exports, but then
reluctantly had to put aside the international market and turn to British rearmament in the years prior to World War Two. When war came, Vickers-
Armstrongs faced a tsunami of orders across all areas of their business and
initially struggled to meet British war needs, but ultimately rose to the occasion. In the aftermath of the war a familiar threat to the future of the firm
reemerged: nationalization.

Retooling during the Lull

Even while striving for disarmament, the government had also been considering questions of industrial preparedness for war. The Cabinet had appointed
the secret Defence Requirements Committee in 1934, with instructions to
"prepare a programme for meeting our worst deficiencies."[1] The government
was extremely concerned that Britain lacked the industrial capacity to fight the
militarized German state; even with a full mobilization of existing armament
firms, capacity would be insufficient for wartime needs. Planning therefore
began for augmenting military production in Britain. The Advisory Panel of
Industrialists, which did not include anyone from Vickers-Armstrongs, was
composed of Lord Weir, Sir James Lithgow and Sir Arthur Balfour. It sent a
memorandum to the Supply Board in February 1934 pointing out that there
were only two facilities able to produce munitions: Vickers-Armstrongs and the
Woolwich Arsenal. By contrast, in 1914 there had been six.[2] The Advisory Panel
made recommendations for improving industrial planning, including creating
shadow industrial capacities able to manufacture armaments that could free
up existing firms to work on the broader range of products necessary for any
war effort, and for placing "educational orders" so that non-armament firms

---

[1] Coghlan, "Armaments," p. 205. Citing Hancock and Gowing, *British War Economy*, p. 63.
[2] Miller, *Planning*, pp. 108–09. Citing: TNA, CAB60/14, RSC 415, "Memorandum by Lord
Weir, Sir James Lithgow and Sir Arthur Balfour," February 20, 1934.

could develop the skills to make armaments and components, which would be bottlenecked if only the major firms were able to produce them. These recommendations were subsequently accepted by the Supply Board in late April 1934, but remained confidential.[3] Reflecting government estimates of German and Japanese naval strength, the Defence Requirements Committee had concluded that a minimum of seven battleships, fifteen cruisers, four aircraft carriers and many support ships should be built.[4] However, as Miller notes, "Very few, if any, of these facts were known to WSBC [Warship Building Committee] members, in the same way the WSBC's existence was almost certainly not known to the Admiralty."[5]

Nevertheless, Vickers-Armstrongs speculated. Pursuing the standard Vickers strategy of reinvesting during lulls, the firm had already begun re-equipping their various sites for new orders. In 1934 they spent £100,000 bringing the Palmers' shipyard at Jarrow (acquired from the NSS) up to a standard to be able to handle repairs.[6] At Barrow, Vickers-Armstrongs was spending £100,000 annually on updating equipment and had maintained many unused berths, while they and Newcastle got by on merchant ship work. An important early signal of revival was the fall 1934 reopening of the mothballed Walker naval yard in preparation for building the cruiser HMS *Newcastle*, which had been approved in the 1933 Naval Estimates.

In gun mountings (the heaviest of which took three years to make), Vickers-Armstrongs was the sole British designer and maker. The cost of maintaining this capacity was significant, and primarily borne by the firm, supplemented by a trickle of Admiralty contracts. Vickers-Armstrongs' Crayford factory was similarly vital in the design and production of fire control systems, but the firm's work on this had been episodic – responding to domestic and international orders – so improvements needed to be made there too.[7]

During the mid-1930s the ESC struggled to maintain average armor production at 20 percent of output. In parallel, the ESC modernization – mostly financed by Vickers-Armstrongs – was costing close to two million pounds annually in 1935. As Scott wittily noted: "Craven had always believed in spending money in keeping the works and yards up to date, and his boldness in pursuing this policy had caused awe, admiration and alarm among colleagues, subordinates and rivals, although it was not always the colleagues who were awed or the rivals who were alarmed."[8] The signals the firm was getting from the government were decidedly mixed and made this kind of investment a real

[3] Miller, *Planning*, pp. 112; 136.
[4] Miller, *Planning*, pp. 154–55.
[5] Miller, *Planning*, p. 162.
[6] Scott, *Vickers*, pp. 217–18.
[7] Scott, *Vickers*, pp. 219–20.
[8] Scott, *Vickers*, p. 218.

risk. For example, a White Paper on Defence was published March 4, 1935, alongside the defense estimates, raising public awareness of "the vital necessity of putting our defences in order."[9] But this was followed by Britain hosting a Second Naval Disarmament Conference in December 1935 in an attempt to sustain the faltering 1930 London Naval Treaty. Though lacking Japan and Italy, a Second London Naval Treaty was signed in March 1936. It reiterated the controls on submarines and ships contained in the First London Treaty but made no headway on tonnage limits and ratios. This effectively ended the era of quantitative treaty restrictions and cleared the way for new naval construction.

Rearmament Begins

When that first public hint at rearmament came in 1935, Vickers-Armstrongs thought it was ready. As Craven recalled in a letter to First Sea Lord Admiral Sir Roger Backhouse:

> [W]e thoroughly re-equipped our group of works, as they then existed, before the Prime Minister's statement relating to defence, which was made in March 1935, so that when we heard of the naval and military programme resulting from that statement, we felt that we were fully equipped regarding plant and buildings so as to deal with that part of them which affected my company in an orderly manner.[10]

This exhibits overconfidence. After the White Paper, Vickers-Armstrongs realized that existing gun mounting capacity would be inadequate to meet new Admiralty needs. "It was agreed that ... a new gun mounting shop should be built at Barrow and that the company should put up a quarter of a million pounds for this out of its own resources, with another quarter of a million pounds for machine tools."[11]

Vickers-Armstrongs had been working on tanks as a private venture without government assistance. However,

> In October 1935 Sir John Carden ... attended a meeting at the War Office with Colonel M.A. Studd, Assistant Director of Mechanisation. Sir John left with a draft proposal under the codename "Matilda" for a small, two-man tank, armed with a single machine gun. Studd made two significant provisos. The design was to be ready within six months, and above all the new tank was to be cheap.[12]

---

[9] Defence White Paper 1935, Cmd. 4827 (March 1935); "Britain to Increase Spending on Arms"; Miller, *Planning*, pp. 113, 126 and 143–49.

[10] Scott, *Vickers*, p. 219. Quoting Craven to Backhouse; no citation given.

[11] Scott, *Vickers*, p. 222.

[12] Fletcher, *British Battle Tanks*, p. 6.

The General Staff specification number was A11, and the Vickers A11E1 was ready for testing by September 1936. In April 1938 a batch of only sixty A11E1s was ordered from Vickers-Armstrongs, and though the order doubled ten days later this was still much less than the firm had hoped for.

> This was not due to penny-pinching but a change in policy, and the final order to Vickers for the Infantry Tank Mark I, placed in January 1939, only amounted to 19 machines. The reason was that, with war now inevitable, it had been decided to produce a cannon-armed Infantry tank after all, and create up to six army tank battalions to operate them.[13]

By mid-decade Sir Herbert Lawrence was stepping back from his dual chairmanships. In January 1936 Sir Charles Craven took over as Chairman of Vickers-Armstrongs, and in July 1937 Sir Archibald Jamieson KBE, MC took over Vickers Limited. That these roles were split is an indication of the work now involved in running the two concerns.[14] Denis Webb of Supermarine recorded that subsequently:

> Sir Robert McLean our Chairman, who had been allowed by the main Vickers Board to run the aviation business on a pretty loose rein and had in fact run it as if it was his own private company, did not see eye to eye with his new boss, Charles Craven who was an ex-Naval man and liked to run a "tight ship" to use a Naval expression, and so Sir Robert departed.[15]

In 1940 Hew Kilner was made General Manager of the aircraft section and in 1944 became Managing Director (Aviation).[16]

British rearmament began sequentially, but later became synchronous and even competitive between the service – creating headaches for Vickers-Armstrongs, who needed to serve all military branches. In 1934 building aircraft was the top priority, followed by naval production, with land rearmament a much lesser priority. This ordering is often explained as the pursuit of air-power parity with Germany. Martin Ceadel also links the government's decision to prioritize the air power recommendations of the Defence Requirements Committee to the public's responses to various "peace ballots," which showed a preference for air rearmament over land rearmament.[17] This connects to the public's – and the government's – fear of German bombing (though these concerns were based on an overestimation of the destructive power of bombing).[18] On the Defence Requirements Committee, Chancellor Chamberlain argued for an aerial deterrent and successfully maneuvered to ensure that only modest

---

[13] Fletcher, *British Battle Tanks*, p. 10.
[14] Scott, *Vickers*, p. 392.
[15] Webb, *Never A Dull Moment!* VA Doc. 1900, p. 104.
[16] He was knighted in 1947. "Obituary: Major Sir Hew Ross Kilner."
[17] Ceadel, "First British Referendum," p. 821.
[18] Bialer, *Shadow of the Bomber*; Holman, "Air Panic of 1935."

sums would be allocated to naval rearmament.[19] Equipment for the Army was initially considered the lowest priority, on the assumption that it would not be engaged in a land war in Europe.[20] This assumption changed in 1938 as the likely character of any conflict became clearer.[21]

The reconstruction of the Royal Air Force was now begun. However, air rearmament was a moving target for the private firms as concerns about Germany's air force increased, leading to ever-higher production targets. Overall, the aircraft designs used relied heavily on research and development from government laboratories, rather than from private industry, therefore cleaving more to the Army procurement model, and "military R&D [research and development] contracts (in contrast to procurement funding) remained modest."[22]

Nevertheless, private firms, including Vickers Supermarine, were trying to interest the Air Ministry in their designs. Supermarine's first fighter aircraft design, designated Type 224, was supplied to the Air Ministry even though the firm was not completely happy with it. "Without waiting for the Air Ministry to complete its appraisal of the Type 224 the design team started looking into ways of improving the performance."[23] Many changes were made, including to the wing shape and width, and more powerful Rolls-Royce PV XII engines were added. The Air Ministry were interested in this version, placing a contract (specification F37/34) which was along the lines of the evolving Supermarine aircraft. Development now followed an iterative process. As Jack Davis, a senior draftsman at Supermarine, explained:

> In April 1935 the final specification F10/35 was issued. By then the Firm had clear ideas of the Air Ministry requirements, and they, in turn had some idea of what was possible. The specification called for six guns with a reference for eight and deleted the bombs. Detailed design was in progress, but as the requirements had been anticipated they were easily absorbed. Other changes, such as liquid cooling were made as detail design continued. In fact, changes went on all through the detail design and manufacturing states; thus when the machine flew it was as up-to-date as possible. However, changes, even simple, slow down manufacture and the Air Ministry showed concern at the apparent slow progress. They could not be expected to fully understand the process. In particular the knock-on effect of apparently small modifications, because modifications breed more modifications.[24]

[19] Miller, *Planning*, pp. 130–33.
[20] "Rearmament Plans," TNA at: www.nationalarchives.gov.uk/cabinetpapers/themes/rearmament-plans.htm.
[21] Minutes of the 330th Meeting of the Committee of Imperial Defence, July 21, 1938, p. 3. TNA, CAB 2/7.
[22] Mowery, "Military R&D," p. 1227.
[23] Davis, "The Basic Design of the Prototype Spitfire," Lecture at the Royal Aeronautic Society, April 4, 1984. Transcript. VA Doc. 1908, p. 2.
[24] Davis, "Basic Design," VA Doc. 1908, p. 6.

R. J. Mitchell of Supermarine and Sir Henry Royce of Rolls-Royce worked closely together on the aircraft: "The Spitfire was the end result of a team job by a well-knit body of men."[25]

Supermarine delivered a prototype to RAF Martlesham Heath on May 26, 1936, but specifications continued to change up until the Spitfire Mark 1 entered squadron service in 1938. As the Chairman of Vickers noted in 1994: "I quote this historical document that the period from the concept ... within three weeks of May 1st up to the Mk 1. no less than 400,000 man hours were spent on the design of the aircraft and 800,000 man hours were spent on the jigs and the tools."[26]

While Supermarine were putting in all these hours on developing the Spitfire, debate was raging over rearmament in general and aircraft in particular. Aircraft were "the cheapest weapon, but also the one most dreaded by the country at large."[27] The combination of "financial stringency and gestures towards disarmament" meant that in 1933 the RAF's home strength had been only "13 squadrons of fighters and 12 of bombers," despite the plan having been for a fifty-two-squadron Home Defence Force.[28] In March 1934 a modest program of new expenditure was announced, and this was revised upwards only four months later. As Lord President of the Council and spokesman for the National Government Stanley Baldwin explained to Parliament in July 1934:

> We have come to the conclusion that we cannot delay any longer measures which will in the course of the next few years bring our air forces to a level more closely approaching that of our nearest neighbours .... [W]e have decided on a programme covering the present and the four ensuing years, under which the Royal Air Force will be increased by 41 new squadrons, including those already announced in the 1934 programme. Of these 41 squadrons, 33 will be allotted to Home Defence, raising the existing 42 squadrons at home to a total of 75 squadrons. The remaining squadrons are for service with the Fleet Air Arm or abroad. The rate at which this programme can be carried out within the five years must depend upon various considerations, including finance, which I cannot specify now. We hope, however, so to space out the work, as not to make an unmanageable addition to the Estimates in any one year.[29]

Even then MPs such as Winston Churchill urged air rearmament on an even larger scale. In November 1934, making what turned out to be wildly inaccurate assumptions of the effects of German bombing on cities such as London, Churchill speculated that "One could hardly expect that less than 30,000 or

---

[25] Davis, "Basic Design," VA Doc. 1908, p. 12.
[26] Chairman's introduction, Davis, "Basic Design," VA Doc. 1908, p. 1.
[27] Dunbabin, "British Rearmament," p. 590.
[28] Holman, "Air Panic of 1935," p. 295.
[29] "Mr. Baldwin's Statement," House of Commons Debate, July 19, 1934. *Hansard*, Vol. 292, cc. 1273–78. At: https://api.parliament.uk/historic-hansard/commons/1934/jul/19/mr-baldwins-statement#column_1274.

40,000 people would be killed or maimed," though he had promised that "I shall be specially careful not to exaggerate." He complained that nothing had happened since the March announcement or the July increase.[30] Baldwin responded: "I think it is correct to say that the Germans are engaged in creating an air force" – in defiance of the Versailles Treaty: "[T]he figures we have range from a figure, given on excellent authority and from a source of indisputable authority of 600 military aircraft altogether to the highest figure we have been given, also from good sources, of something not over 1,000."[31]

The government accelerated the gradual July schedule for the RAF program again in November 1934. But in March 1935 a new panic resulted from Hitler's claim to Foreign Secretary Sir John Simon that Germany had achieved air parity.[32] In May 1935 Baldwin announced (not via the normal procedure of the annual estimates) that the number of RAF squadrons for the Home Defence Force would be tripled, with a target date of completion in 1938.[33] Bond and Murray concluded:

> Lord Swinton, Air Minister from 1935 to 1938, achieved remarkable improvements, most notably by ordering aircraft directly from the drawing board and by the establishment of the so-called shadow factory scheme. In its financial support for a reserve capacity for aircraft production, the Chamberlain government made its most sensible strategic decision of the late 1930s. One suspects, however, that this support was more a result of the scheme's relatively low cost than of strategic foresight.[34]

Vickers Supermarine were profoundly affected by the scale of government needs and had "to change from a factory largely engaged in experimental designs and seldom if ever, receiving contracts for more than six aircraft at a time to be produced at the rate of one per month, to a factory receiving orders for hundreds to be produced at a rate of 30 or more per week."[35] The Mark 1 Spitfire first entered service in 1938 and by 1939 – at the dawn of the war – Supermarine had delivered 308 Spitfires. This had increased by 1940 to 1,200 Spitfires delivered prior to the Battle of Britain.[36]

Nevertheless, in 1938, while Vickers Supermarine was seeking to win the long distance and speed records for the Spitfire in races over Germany, Lord

[30] "Debate on the Address," Mr. Churchill, *Hansard*, Vol. 295, cc. 858–71. At: https://api .parliament.uk/historic-hansard/commons/1934/nov/28/debate-on-the-address.
[31] "Debate on the Address," Mr. Baldwin, *Hansard*, Vol. 295, cc. 875–76. At: https://api .parliament.uk/historic-hansard/commons/1934/nov/28/debate-on-the-address.
[32] "German Air Parity."
[33] Holman, "Air Panic of 1935," p. 301; Shay, *British Rearmament*, p. 51. Citing Londonderry to Baldwin, Simon and MacDonald proposing new RAF expansion, October 4, 1935. Bald. #1.
[34] Bond and Murray, "British Armed Forces," p. 104.
[35] Webb, *Never A Dull Moment!* VA Doc. 1900, p. 1.
[36] Webb, *Never A Dull Moment!* VA Doc. 1900.

Swinton was pointing out "that the manufacture of the Spitfire aircraft by Messrs. Supermarine was most unsatisfactory."[37] However, this was common across the aircraft industry. For example, with the Skua made by Blackburn Aircraft for the Fleet Air Arm (and to carry the Vickers K machine gun), First Sea Lord Duff Cooper reported to the Committee of Imperial Defence that since "there seems little prospect of the firm completing the order within a reasonable time, the question of cancelling it was under consideration. The compensation which would have to be given to the firm was under discussion, but the sum involved was likely to be considerable."[38]

Turning to naval rearmament, a second White Paper of March 1936 laid out the security challenges facing Britain and announced a naval program for meeting them; out of fear of inciting domestic opposition, this was a minimal one. Even so, Britain did not begin naval rearmament until late in 1936, when the 1930 London Treaty finally expired. In December 1936, when naval rearmament finally started, strong disputes within the Admiralty over what guns to procure slowed down the process. Crucially, armament firms did not know even months in advance that a larger rearmament was beginning. "It is far from obvious that private armament manufacturers believed massive rearmament was a possibility before March 1936 …. In this regard the relationship between the Admiralty and industry is conspicuous by its absence."[39]

Nevertheless, Vickers-Armstrongs speculated, and "at the beginning of 1936, the company was proposing a capital expenditure of nearly two million on new capacity for naval requirements [including £129,000 for tanks]. On its side the Admiralty undertook to place orders for capital-ship mountings for seven ships over the next four years."[40] As ever, the government would not provide subsidies, only rewarding firms' investments with contracts. However, the WSBC was still in existence and firms continued to collude on prices to ensure profits: "[I]n 1937, the profit margins on Admiralty work were more than thirty percent, or roughly twice the level of cost increases. Indeed, these levels were about three times higher than the typical margins on naval contracts before 1936, which themselves were still far better than the razor-thin profits … in the years before the WSBC."[41]

The 1936 Admiralty program brought in intimidatingly large armor orders to a "pool" of Beardmores, ESC and Firth-Browns; this demanded the production of 168,000 tons of finished armor a year within four years, despite current total national output being 40,000 tons. The ESC was to meet 50 percent of

[37] Craven to McLean, December 3, 1938. VA 626 Folio 87; Committee of Imperial Defence, Minutes of the 308th Meeting, January 27, 1938, p. 8. TNA CAB 2/7.
[38] Committee of Imperial Defence, Minutes of the 330th Meeting, July 21, 1938, p. 7. TNA CAB 2/7.
[39] Miller, *Planning*, p. 171.
[40] Scott, *Vickers*, p. 222.
[41] Miller, *Planning*, p. 194. Citing Peebles, *Warshipbuilding*, pp. 140–42.

that tonnage. Despite Vickers-Armstrongs' heavy investments, they lacked the capacity now required. Consequently, the Admiralty financed extensions to plants in Sheffield to the tune of £1 million and the Ministry of Supply equipped a shop for the machining of tank armor. Some of the factories scheduled for scrapping in the 1931 reorganization of ESC were also brought back into full production. The firms now scrambled for the necessary resources to fill these orders as foreign firms did the same. The government expected steel firms to simply surge production, but the firms struggled to do so. For example, in January 1938 Third Sea Lord Sir Reginald Henderson reported to the Committee of Imperial Defence that "the English Steel Corporation had at the moment a large number of plates awaiting machining" but lacked the additional machine tools to do the work.[42] Vickers-Armstrongs and ESC were acutely aware of the consequences of these shortages of machine tools. Henderson reported that "the armament firms themselves had taken up the matter, but further machine tools for armour could nowhere be obtained under about sixteen months."[43]

Once naval rearmament was begun, according to the government, it proceeded apace. A former minister, Viscount Chilston, described this with pride:

> [I]n the three principal classes (battleships, aircraft carriers and cruisers) Britain laid down in 1937–1938 between two and three times the amount of tonnage of the other European naval powers put together …. But the effort might not have been so successful had it not [been] matched by an unparalleled industrial capacity, for no other country possessed such resources for warship production and naval armament as Great Britain.[44]

This statement significantly underplays the difficulties that private firms experienced in moving from two decades of austerity to a period of exponentially growing demand.

In particular, the issue of gun mounting capacity now became acute, but guns and fire control instruments were also delayed, and machine tool shortages were a constant problem.[45] The government requested Vickers-Armstrongs to work at full capacity on gun mountings, but Sir Thomas Inskip, Minister for the Co-ordination of Defence, reported to the Committee of Imperial Defence that "he had received specific figures which showed that to work to full capacity Messrs. Vickers required approximately 7,000 additional men, of which half were skilled, but they saw little prospect of that under present conditions." It was also noted that highly skilled workers were required to make fire control

---

[42] Committee of Imperial Defence, Minutes of the 306th Meeting, January 13, 1938, p. 3. TNA CAB 2/7.

[43] Committee of Imperial Defence, Minutes of the 306th Meeting, January 13, 1938, p. 3. TNA CAB 2/7.

[44] Haigh, Morris and Turner, *Armed Peace or War?* p. 35. Citing Toynbee *Survey.*

[45] Lloyd Jones and Lewis, "A Call to Arms"; "Machine Tool Orders," p. 22.

instruments.[46] In 1939 Vickers-Armstrongs' old Whitworth Street site was sold to the Admiralty, which "erected new buildings and installed plant for gun and gun-mounting production."[47] During the war, Vickers-Armstrongs managed this shadow factory for the government.

Despite this, Vickers-Armstrongs made the transition more easily than most, particularly in terms of shipbuilding. As a former employee recalled, Vickers' fortunes were already improving at Barrow: "[I]t was just about the time that rearmament orders came in that the shops were in any case being filled with civilian work. There was still a good deal of civilian and marine engineering in 1936."[48] By 1937 Craven was commenting to Sir Robert McLean, who then still headed the aviation division, that "I am being inundated with applications from retired Officers with similar qualifications."[49] During this period Craven also received recommendations on behalf of war veterans from both Sir Roger Keys (whom he had served under) and Lord Mountbatten.[50] Vickers-Armstrongs needed skilled workers more than retired officers, however.

The battleship *King George V*, to be the new flagship of the Commander in Chief of the Fleet, was laid down at the Walker Yard on January 1, 1937 (and was built to the 35,000-ton limit of the Washington Naval Treaty). On December 20, 1937, Vickers-Armstrongs got an order for the HMS *Nigeria* (to their Fuji-class design) also to be built at the Walker Yard.[51] However, in January 1938, according to Sir Reginald Henderson, machine tool shortages were slowing production and the Admiralty roughly estimated "that the two battleships [including *King George* V] and aircraft carriers at present on the slips might be 6 to 12 months late."[52] The *King George* V was launched on February 21, 1939 by the King and Queen.[53] First Sea Lord Admiral Sir Roger Backhouse also attended the reception following the launch.[54] HMS *King George* V was commissioned on December 11, 1940.[55] This was four months before Cammell Laird's *Prince of Wales*, which was also laid down on January 1, 1937.

HMS *Nigeria* was laid down on February 8, 1938, launched on July 18, 1939, by Lady Hankey and commissioned on September 23, 1940, so some delays

[46] Committee of Imperial Defence, Minutes of the 308th Meeting, January 27, 1938, p. 3. TNA CAB 2/7.
[47] Tweedale, *Steel City*, p. 251.
[48] Barrow recollections of Mr. V. H. Crozier, VA, Doc. 596, Folio 123.
[49] Craven to McLean, May 5, 1937. "Craven, Sir Charles – Letters 1937–41," VA, Doc. 626, Folio 15.
[50] Keys to Craven and Mountbatten to Craven, 1938. VA, Doc. 626, Folios 91 and 98.
[51] Konstam, *British Light Cruisers*, pp. 28–31.
[52] Committee of Imperial Defence, Minutes of the 306th Meeting, January 13, 1938, p. 2. TNA CAB 2/7.
[53] *British Pathé News*, "Royal Visit."
[54] *Shipbuilder and Marine Engine-Builder*, Vol. 46 (1939), p. 163.
[55] Chesneau, *Conway's*, p. 15.

were compensated for at the yard.[56] Subsequently, the Fuji-class ships HMS *Jamaica* and *Uganda* were ordered from Vickers-Armstrongs. HMS *Jamaica* was ordered on March 1, 1939, laid down at Barrow on April 28 that year, launched on November 16, 1940, and commissioned on June 29, 1942. HMS *Uganda*, also ordered on March 1, 1939, was laid down at Walkers on July 20 of that year, launched on August 7, 1941, and commissioned on January 3, 1943.[57] In December 1939 Barrow got an order for HMS *Spartan*, a Dido-class cruiser.[58] Other battleships of the King George V class were built by John Browns, Swan Hunter and Fairfields. All were in service by June 1942. This meant that Britain was largely reliant on old battleships when the war opened in 1939, as most of the ships ordered in 1937 had not yet been commissioned.[59]

The work of the Advisory Panel of Industrialists might have been expected to presage wider armament firm involvement in planning for and implementing rearmament, but this was not the case. Indeed, it was only in 1937 that Craven and others were appointed to a Shipbuilding Consultative Committee.[60] After the decline of the interwar years, it was obviously difficult for firms to quickly reach "surge" capacity again.[61] However, to Miller, "the fact that bottlenecks existed and mistakes were still being made in the finished product in 1937 was a failure of policy, not of industry."[62]

Even after the creation of the Shipbuilding Consultative Committee, their reports initially languished, due to government adherence to economic and business orthodoxy, which prioritized "normal" business over rearmament. It was only in 1938, after the March *Anschluss*, when the Cabinet agreed to cancel the core assumption that rearmament should not impede the course of "normal trade," that industry was instructed to give priority to rearmament. All three services were now able to place contracts with industry.[63]

Thereafter there was extensive government planning for extending military capacity through: providing additional plant and factories to existing armament firms; making additions to the Royal Ordnance Factories, and creating new ones; and converting civilian industries to military production, known as the "Shadow Factories" scheme.[64] This latter scheme was a crucial means of addressing the shortages of factories, plant and skilled labor revealed in the planning for war. The scheme was initially developed for military aircraft

---

[56] Colledge and Warlow, *Ships*, p. 514.
[57] Colledge and Warlow, *Ships*, pp. 250; 399–400.
[58] Konstam, *British Light Cruisers*, pp. 28–31.
[59] Miller, *Planning*, p. 208.
[60] Miller, *Planning*, p. 199. Citing TNA, SUPP3/18, "Interim Report of the Shipbuilding Consultative Committee," Appendix I.
[61] Jamieson, *Ebb Tide*, p. 187, ff. 31.
[62] Miller, *Planning*, p. 197.
[63] Postan, *British War Production*, p. 87; Miller, *Planning*, p. 206.
[64] Rogers, *Shadow Factories*.

production and the major civilian industry utilized was the burgeoning motor industry.[65] Now that the Air Ministry was free to tap the full capacity of the aircraft industry, Vickers-Armstrongs worked with the Ministry to establish a "widespread subcontracting system for the manufacture of aircraft. This system, it is said, will feed the component parts of certain specified types of aircraft already ordered into a new central factory to be built and controlled by Vickers-Armstrongs."[66] This was the Chester factory. In October 1939 Supermarine was the recipient of production programs for bombers and fighters planned by the Air Council.[67] Vickers-Armstrongs assisted in other ways too, for example, by addressing supply shortages; in November 1938 Craven was reaching out to ICI Metals and James Booth & Co. Ltd (Vickers was a shareholder) about getting sufficient Duralumin for the shadow aircraft factories. Both firms responded positively to Craven's overtures.[68]

Nevertheless, bringing in outside producers to armaments was not as easy as the government hoped. As the Chairman of Vickers noted in retrospect, discussing the vast amount of work to perfect the Spitfire:

> So therefore, all this effort was put in at that stage of the Mk 1. from 1934, you could see that those of us who were around before the war took it as a big joke when a certain William Morris, later to become Lord Nuffield said "huh, I can produce Spitfires like shelling peas." But it took him a long time after the beginning of the war before he ever produced his first aircraft.[69]

Later the Shadow Factories scheme was extended to the other services and to other industries. Interestingly, the lessons of the mobilization for the Great War – when armament firms had (over)extended themselves and many "National Factories" had been purpose-built for them – were learned. The government planned primarily to repurpose existing industrial capacity, which could seamlessly switch back to civilian production once war was over, avoiding the overcapacity of the 1920s.

Within the Army, the years of austerity had led to a retreat to a culture of avoiding innovation because of its likely costs. "The service had also been starved of development funds and required the manufacturers of armaments to consider the cost implications of weapons under development to an extent which resulted, to give but one example, in the complete erosion of the lead that Britain had once enjoyed in the field of armoured fighting

---

[65] "The Cabinet Papers 1915–1982, Defence Policy 1933–1939, End of Disarmament and Defence Requirements."

[66] "New Arms Campaign," p. 32.

[67] Craven to Under Secretary of State, Air Ministry, October 26, 1939. VA, Doc. 626, Folio 124.

[68] Craven to Clarke, Messrs. James Booth & Co. Ltd, November 9, 1938; Craven to Lord McGowan, ICI Metals, November 9, 1938. Sir Charles Craven Letters 1937–41. VA, Doc. 626, Folios 67–76.

[69] Chairman's introduction, Davis, "Basic Design," VA Doc. 1908, p. 1.

vehicles."[70] Consequently, by the early 1930s the British military was hardly mechanized, with only four tank battalions (compared to 136 infantry battalions) and twenty cavalry regiments, only two of which were armored car regiments.[71] Inevitably, the Army therefore also lacked a well-developed production capacity for armored fighting vehicles and tanks for use if war loomed. This was a crisis when in 1937 rearmament of the Army was beginning.

In 1923 the Tank Design Department in the War Office had been closed and "but for the solitary and pioneering efforts of the designers at Vickers-Armstrongs the country would have possessed no facilities for the design and development of armoured vehicles."[72] In 1931 Vickers-Armstrongs had debuted a Carden-Loyd amphibious light tank from their Chertsey tank development facility.[73] These Vickers-Armstrongs interwar tank investments paid off to an extent. As Benjamin Coombs noted, "Tank development was intrinsically linked to experimentation at Vickers-Armstrongs and technical advances in the motor and metallurgical industries."[74] Vickers had kept a design shop in Sheffield and had doubled-down investing in a new shop (no. 136) for tank production, so it was ready when government orders began to arrive for the Valentine tank.[75] This was the Matilda Senior. Although it was not designed or manufactured by Vickers-Armstrongs, but by the Vulcan Foundry, it used a co-axial, water-cooled Vickers .303 machine gun (or the .5 Vickers), and a Vickers-Armstrongs-designed suspension system (developed for the Medium C tanks for Japan in 1928) which had been lent to Vulcan during the design stage. Matildas were manufactured by Vulcan and by five other firms pressed into tank production, but there were many production delays.[76]

Vitally, a new employee at the War Office, Admiral Harold Brown, decided to try to avoid the Committee of Imperial Defence system altogether to try and make progress on tanks.

> Late one night in 1937, with the Controller of the Navy, Reginald Henderson, Brown devised a plan between them and Sir Charles Craven to take over an entire site belonging to Vickers exclusively for War Office tank work while allowing the Admiralty free rein over the rest. To assist, Craven put a substantial portion of the design department at Vickers at Brown and Henderson's disposal, and together they developed what Brown later described as a "most valuable asset."[77]

---

[70] Haigh, Morris and Turner, *Armed Peace*, p. 21.

[71] Liddell-Hart, *Memoirs*, Vol. I, pp. 223–28. Cited in Haigh, Morris and Turner, *Armed Peace*, p. 13.

[72] Postan, *British War Production*, p. 7.

[73] *British Pathé News*, "Demonstration."

[74] Coombs, *British Tank Production*, p. 4.

[75] "Tanks, Guns and Bombs ... War Output of Elswick and Scotswood," nd [c. 1960?] TWA, D/VA/49/4/1.

[76] Fletcher, *British Battle Tanks*, p. 13.

[77] Miller, *Planning*, p. 201.

Miller records that "Brown … remarked that he owed an 'eternal debt of gratitude to Craven,' who 'gave every possible assistance, both as regards design and production' to him and his department in times of need."[78] Along with Henderson of the Admiralty and Air Chief Marshal Sir Wilfred Freeman, Brown initiated regular unofficial working lunches with Craven and Lithgow, where interservice supply issues were worked out. As Miller reports, "From this Craven, Lithgow, Rebbeck [Harland and Wolff] and Henderson began to informally allocate shipbuilding capacity as a 'shadow committee,' and it would be to them Brown would go if he wanted use of some shipbuilding capacity that had been allocated to the Admiralty."[79] The group was informally known as 'the boilermen' and their gentlemen's agreements were infinitely more efficient than the formal government process.

When the Treasury finally stopped trying to restrain military spending in the spring of 1939, a bottleneck emerged as armored vehicle capacity was inadequate and "the army had no choice but to convert railway engine workshops and other civil engineering works to military production – a process that was both lengthy and expensive."[80] Consequently, at the outbreak of the war the Army was at a very difficult point: "Not only was the available force so small, but the first British panzer divisions were only slowly being formed, with all the teething troubles of organisation and equipment."[81] In 1939 the Vickers-Armstrongs amphibious L1E3 tank was completed for testing.

> It was ordered by the War Office but Sir Noel Birch, once Master General of the Ordnance … was very anxious to generate more interest in amphibious tanks and may well have used some of his old Army contacts to secure the order. There is no evidence to suggest that the British Army needed such a tank, or indeed were very interested in it (except the statement in the Mechanization Experimental Establishment's … report that the General Staff had asked for 100, having abandoned the idea of acquiring ordinary light tanks with attachable floats).[82]

Vickers-Armstrongs' Export Dilemma

While it might seem that rearmament in Britain would be a pure opportunity for Vickers-Armstrongs, from the firm's perspective it was also a crisis in terms of their export markets.

The firm's concerns were threefold. First, they felt they should be reaping the benefits of the work they had put in to rebuilding diplomatic relationships

---

78 Miller, *Planning*, p. 203. Citing Brown, "Reminiscences," II, p. 143.
79 Miller, *Planning*, p. 203.
80 Bond and Murray, "The British Armed Forces," p. 103.
81 Barnett, *Britain*, p. 420.
82 Fletcher, *British Battle Tanks*, p. 5.

around the world. As Commander Craven complained to Lord Chatfield in 1939, "Although no value is attached to the item in Vickers-Armstrongs' balance sheet, our foreign business and connections constitute a valuable portion of our good-will, and this asset has been formed in the same way as our other assets, namely by the expenditure of much energy and money."[83] Second, the firm had pursued its standard strategy of developing and expanding research and development dur-ing the interwar depression, in 1936 telling the Royal Commission that it was spending £200,000 a year on research.[84] Birch declared in his half-yearly report for 1936, "We now have up-to-date models and the advantage of having carried out costly and intensive research and I feel certain that but for the pressure of Government orders, and in spite of Germany having entered the foreign market, our business this year would have increased and probably have gone on increas-ing."[85] These expensive developments certainly did feature on the firms' interwar balance sheet and now Vickers-Armstrongs was not reaping the benefits of this strategy. Third, Vickers-Armstrongs was very concerned that not being able to meet the needs of foreign customers would harm those relationships, making it hard for the firm to resume business after rearmament was complete.[86]

While Vickers-Armstrongs had fought to make export sales in the difficult interwar period, as Jonathan Grant remarks, by 1936 it "found itself in the strange position of purposefully not seeking trade abroad."[87] With the deterio-rating strategic environment, Vickers-Armstrongs was getting inquiries from Turkey for tanks and costal guns (which the Admiralty forbade it to supply), and for artillery from Denmark, Finland, Greece, Holland, Iraq, Paraguay, Romania and Siam.[88] Sir Noel Birch complained in the second half of 1936 of having to turn down land armament orders worth £1 million, and in summer 1937 reported that once again the firm "had to turn down 'good foreign busi-ness prospects' to the amount of approximately £1 million." By the end of 1937 he estimated the value of prospective business lost at "practically £3 million."[89]

Vickers-Armstrongs ran into problems in February 1938, when the Air Ministry was threatening to block the firm from selling the "K"-class gun abroad. Sir Noel Birch argued against the proposed restriction based on British prepared-ness for war. He explained, "We must sell abroad where we can …. [U]nless we have some gun to sell abroad, you will find nobody at the bench for industrial mobilisation."[90] A few months later he expostulated that "We have got to get this

83   Craven to Lord Chatfield, August 1, 1939. VA, Doc. 863.
84   Royal Commission evidence, p. 353. Cited in Edgerton, *Warfare State*, p. 121.
85   VA, Microfilm K 611. Cited in Stone, "Lesser European Powers," p. 240.
86   Craven to Lord Chatfield, August 1, 1939. VA, Doc. 863.
87   Grant, *Between*, p. 194.
88   Grant, *Between*, p. 194, citing "Half-yearly Report on Military and Air Armaments," July–December 1936. VA, Doc. 183.
89   Stone, "Lesser European Powers," p. 240. Citing: VA, Microfilm K 611.
90   Birch to Sir W. R. Freeman, February 18, 1938. VA, Doc. 603, Folio 42.

[machine gun] market back with thin times ahead, and this is most important for the British Empire if we are going to find men at the bench when the next war starts."[91] In March 1938 the specific issue was an order from Portugal for artillery. By this time the government had instituted a Sub-Committee on Armament Orders from Foreign Countries. In March the Committee of Imperial Defence discussed the issue of Portuguese orders. The country had not yet committed to the Allied cause, and Sir Robert Vansittart noted that "Unless something was done, not only was the order for the Portuguese artillery equipments at stake, but our whole position in relation to the supply of arms to Portugal would be prejudiced."[92] There was agreement that filling the order was desirable, as long as it did not interfere with British orders, and Chairman of the Supply Board Sir Arthur Robinson reported "it was contemplated that Messrs. Vickers could begin gun deliveries to Portugal in 1940."[93] The Committee of Imperial Defence agreed that this would happen only after Portugal had pledged herself to the Allied cause and gave "a formal assurance to the effect that all contracts for armaments and ammunition of calibres larger than rifles and light machine guns would be placed in Great Britain, it being made clear that this definition should include aircraft and their equipment, and also naval material."[94]

Vickers-Armstrongs had been asked to sound out the Portuguese authorities about how payments would be handled on a long-term order such as this. There was also a more general discussion of armament exports, with Sir Maurice Hankey asking "whether we are making any provision at all to deal with all the foreign orders to which we were committed. If not, it would take years and years." Leslie Hore-Belisha, the Secretary of State for War, responded that the government had "made no provision for capacity to meet this type of order, which not only came from Portugal, but also from Egypt, Iraq and Belgium, to say nothing of the Dominions." But "he considered it would be wise to allocate a pool of capacity to meet foreign orders."[95] Sir Reginald Henderson informed the Committee of Imperial Defence that "the Admiralty was being pressed to undertake orders from Turkey, which country was presumably as important as Portugal. They also had demands from Chile." And there was general agreement that a priority list for exports needed to be established.[96]

In the summer of 1938, the question of extending the export credit scheme to cover armament exports was raised at the Committee of Imperial Defence.

> *Sir Robert Vansittart* expressed the anxiety of the Secretary of State for Foreign Affairs as to whether we are speeding up our rearmament programme

[91] Birch to G. Calder, Air Ministry, May 9, 1938. VA, Doc. 662, Folio 382.
[92] Minutes of the 314th meeting of the CID, p. 7. March 24, 1938. TNA, CAB 2/7.
[93] Minutes of the 314th meeting of the CID, p. 8. March 24, 1938. TNA, CAB 2/7.
[94] Conclusions, Minutes of the 314th meeting of the CID, 8. March 24, 1938. TNA, CAB 2/7.
[95] Minutes of the 314th meeting of the CID, p. 8. March 24, 1938. TNA, CAB 2/7.
[96] Minutes of the 314th meeting of the CID, p. 8. March 24, 1938. TNA, CAB 2/7.

sufficiently to ensure the safety of the country. He referred to Lord Halifax's letter of the 27th April, which suggested that the time had come for
extending to arms export the export credits plan. Lord Halifax thought
that this question should be re-examined. *Mr. Stanley* reminded the Committee that only a year ago it had been decided to exclude armaments from
the export credits scheme.

The Committee agreed to "invite the Board of Trade to re-examine and
report on the question of the extension to arms export of the Export Credits
plan."[97]

Vickers-Armstrongs' anxieties were not only about exports. By 1939 there was
the question of the fate of the agents they had working in Europe and beyond,
especially two brothers, the Sakowskis, who had worked for the firm in Riga and
Tallinn. As a British Foreign Office official noted on the file: "The two Sakowskis
are very different characters. C.J., who has gone to Germany, is a bit of a rascal, but
A. is honest to the satisfaction of the firm and also to the best of my knowledge."[98]
Vickers had requested that both agents be given visas by the Home Office, but
the latter replied that the firm had given insufficient reasons for the visa to be
granted. Subsequently, the British Embassy in Riga reported that C. J. Sakowski
had left for Germany.[99] Vickers-Armstrongs informed the British Government
that "we have now received a communication from the Latvian War Office, confirming that Mr. [C. J.] Sakowski has left for Germany. We have therefore severed
our connection with him."[100] Not covered in the Foreign Office file was the question of what C. J. Sakowski knew of Vickers-Armstrongs' weapons systems and
sales activities that might be useful to the German Government. Better news from
the firm was that Mr. Alexander Sakowski, who had worked for the firm for seventeen years in Estonia intended to continue to do so.[101]

As Glyn Stone concluded of armament exports: "Between 1936 and 1939,
despite the massive increase in weapons production, British arms firms sold
precious few of their products abroad. Although they had Foreign Office support, these firms failed to persuade the service departments to release equipment, essentially the latest models, for export. This was a source of great
disappointment, not least for Vickers-Armstrong."[102] Nevertheless, they had
no time to mourn since British needs were mounting.

[97] Minutes of the 330th Meeting of the Committee of Imperial Defence. July 21, 1938, pp.
3–4. TNA, CAB 2/7. Italics in original.

[98] Comment of L. C. [possibly Collier?] on file "Baltic States 1939." TNA, FO 371/23610.

[99] C. W. Orde, British Legation Riga to Viscount Halifax, November 14, 1939. TNA, FO
371/23610.

[100] To Under Secretary of State for Foreign Affairs from Vickers-Armstrongs Chief Foreign
Representative, November 28, 1939. TNA, FO 371/23610.

[101] To Under Secretary of State for Foreign Affairs from Vickers-Armstrongs Chief Foreign
Representative, November 28, 1939. TNA, FO 371/23610.

[102] Stone, "The British Government," p. 239.

World War Two

From early 1939 the government and industry went hell-for-leather for rearmament. As Miller notes, "Throwing ever-increasing sums at the problem was not a particularly good solution in 1939, however, for there was precious little spare capacity in established industries to cope with demand. As such, the period between February and the declaration of war was as much about building whatever could be built with the capacity available as it was about meeting strategic priorities."[103] In the immediate run up to war a contract had been placed with Vickers Supermarine for Spitfire aircraft. A Supermarine employee, Denis Webb, recalled that "between Munich and the outbreak of war we just about completed our first Production Contract for 310 'Spitfires'. Neville Chamberlain's much despised 'scrap of paper' had given a good return."[104]

As *Vickers News* recounted:

> The wise and far-seeing policy laid down by the late Sir Charles Craven, with the able assistance on the spot of Sir Robert Micklem and later Mr. P. Muirhead, had seen to it that when the curtain rose on the 3rd September 1939, it found Elswick Works fully equipped with modern machinery and with shops which had been reconstructed and were in every way ready to undertake full production.[105]

As in the past, Vickers-Armstrongs had anticipated the coming demand and was ready to benefit from the new largesse from the government.

With war's outbreak Britain returned to the tradition of requisitioning. Six Jurua-class destroyers being built for Brazil were commandeered and redesignated as Havant-class: the *Harvester* and *Hurricane* from Vickers-Armstrongs, the *Havant* and *Havelock* from Whites, and the *Hesperus* and *Highlander* from Thorneycroft.[106] Vickers-Armstrongs also saw two I-class ships commandeered – the *Inconstant* and *Ithuriel*, originally ordered for the Turkish navy.[107] In 1940 Supermarine was instructed to not supply eleven finished Spitfires to Turkey as contracted, but to make the small changes necessary for them to be RAF standard, and to send them to Castle Bromwich to enable the shadow factory to be up and running and producing the promised "ten in June."[108] The appearance of success clearly mattered to the government.

---

[103] Miller, *Planning*, p. 207.
[104] Webb, *Never A Dull Moment!* Part II, p. 119. VA, Doc. 1900.
[105] Cited in "Tanks, Guns and Bombs ... War Output of Elswick and Scotswood," nd [c. 1960] TWA D/VA/49/4/1.
[106] *Hurricane, Harvester* and *Havant* were sunk in June 1940, and March and December 1943, respectively, whereas *Havelock, Hesperus* and *Highlander* survived the war and were broken up in 1946–47. Chesnau, *Conway's*, p. 40.
[107] Wragg, "Royal Navy," p. 99.
[108] Webb, *Never A Dull Moment!* p. 137.

From the early months of World War Two the British Government became much more interventionist in the running of armament and steel firms, as these companies were now a vital part of the war effort. However, it seems that during the war government intervention "stopped at the factory gates." As a review of Michael Postan's official history of British war production noted, Postan seemed to regret that there was little attempt by the Ministry of Aircraft Production "to inquire into production arrangements at the factories and by research and analysis to find the most efficient methods of manufacture, and then induce or perhaps even direct the firms to adopt them."[109] However, Denis Webb's experience at Supermarine was that the Ministry interfered too much.[110]

The government took control of steel production, but this time with a strategy of maximizing production at existing plants and filling shortages from imports rather than spending several years building new factories (draining manpower and resources).[111] The government paid for further extensions at ESC, which was the main producer of alloy steels for tank armor, turrets, gun forgings and the aircraft industry. ESC Director Bill Pugh noted that "Every Spitfire had a River Don crankshaft forging and each one was quite a job."[112]

British shipbuilding struggled to keep pace with the demand for warships and later for merchant vessels (many of which were being lost due to the success of the German U-boat campaigns). Such was the need for vessels that the Royal Navy repurposed fifty-six merchant vessels as armed merchant cruisers.[113] Early in the war the Admiralty gained control of the industry, but this brought problems too, specifically that of "confused Admiralty control."[114] The naval shipbuilding industry could not match demand, which far exceeded official expectations. To aid the industry, the Navy built shadow factories to make naval ordnance, for example, the Admiralty Fuse Factory built outside Borehamwood, Hertfordshire.[115]

"Confused control" was evident not only in the Admiralty. Vickers-Armstrongs (and their subsidiary Cooke Troughton and Sims, Ltd.) complained to the Air Ministry in 1941 about the "unnecessarily various forms of agreement which are submitted to them" in the context of the various government assistance schemes. In response, the Air Ministry sought to establish a standard agreement to use with the Vickers Group.[116] There were also ongoing discussions within the Ministry about the percentage of profits that

---

[109] Devons, *Economica*, p. 282.
[110] Webb, *Never a Dull Moment!* VA, Do. 1900.
[111] Tweedale, *Steel City*, p. 300.
[112] Tweedale, Steel City, p. 304. Citing: Interview with Bill Pugh, June 29, 1992.
[113] Wragg, "Royal Navy," p. 99.
[114] Jamieson, *Ebb Tide*, p. 58.
[115] Hornby, *Factories and Plant*, Chapter II "Shipbuilding and Admiralty Production."
[116] Note on file, D of C (G) [Director of Contracts (Guns)], "Vickers-Armstrongs (Standard Form of Agreement)," TNA, AVIA 22/2925.

Vickers-Armstrongs should be allowed to take, creating uncertainties at the firm.

Soon after the war began government procurement requests began to sharply escalate. At Elswick, Vickers-Armstrongs was "continually pressed to extend our commitments and this forced us to expand our boundaries"; it took over a nearby trading estate, erecting new buildings where cartridge cases were manufactured and enlarging one of these buildings to accommodate propeller production. Between October 1942 and the end of the war, three and a half million cartridge cases were produced by Elswick.[117] The Scotswood factory in Newcastle went from a monthly output of three 25-pounder field guns in February 1940 to a peak maintained over a considerable period of over 100 25-pounders per month. By the close of the war the Elswick and Scotswood plants employed nearly 32,000 people.

Vickers-Armstrongs also set up and ran a shadow factory at Crook, County Durham, retooled to produce variable speed gear units.

> We had a very difficult task indeed to introduce the engineering trade to this particular district. There was no background of any description of an engineering nature and the bulk of the population travelled some distance to shadow factories, leaving a remnant not too suitable for us to convert into skilled craftspeople. However, patience and skill surmounted all the teething troubles and once it settled down this particular factory put up an excellent production record.[118]

While the making of shell casings could be done by general engineering firms, the filling of the shells was a specialist activity. To increase their capacity to fill ammunition, Vickers-Armstrongs extended their Thames Ammunition Works at Dartford and purchased a new site at Crayford in Kent.[119] Harold Evans notes:

> Vickers' ability to move quickly into mass production had been vitally important: from the outbreak of war in September 1939 to the end of 1940 the Crayford Works alone produced nearly 20,000 machine and gas-operated guns, about half the national production, and in the field of artillery Vickers as a whole supplied some two thirds of the national output during the same period.[120]

During the early years of World War Two the British aircraft industry struggled to keep pace with the demand for combat aircraft.[121] Vickers Supermarine

---

[117] "Tanks, Guns and Bombs ... War Output of Elswick and Scotswood," n.d. [c. 1960?], TWA, D/VA/49/4/1.

[118] "Tanks, Guns and Bombs ... War Output of Elswick and Scotswood," TWA, D/VA/49/4/2.

[119] "Additional Ammunition Filling Capacity: extension to Thames Ammunition Works of Vickers-Armstrongs Ltd.," Ministry of Aviation, 1939–48. TNA, AVIA 22/2530.

[120] Evans, *Vickers*, p. 21.

[121] Postan, *British War Production*, pp. 163–74.

was immediately under significant pressure to rapidly increase production and managed to deliver 1,200 Spitfires prior to the Battle of Britain in July 1940, as well as producing 225 Walrus flying boats. Nevertheless, the firm was criticized for its slow rate of production. Loyal employee Denis Webb's exasperation with this criticism is clear: "I would only like to add to the 'case for the defence' by laying a very large portion of the blame on the British public, who for years had been demanding disarmament and then, when madmen appeared in Europe, expected industry to save their necks at the last moment."[122]

Vickers-Armstrongs experienced "outside" firms and shadow factories taking on increasing amounts of wartime production as the war progressed.[123] That said, traffic was not all in that direction. In May 1940 Vickers-Armstrongs took over managing the large Spitfire factory at Castle Bromwich after control was taken away from the car manufacturer Nuffield (William Morris' firm). This diluted the management left at Vickers Supermarine even further.[124] Even as shadow factory production increased there was consolidation of the number of factories in use. For example, at Supermarine in 1942 subcontract work was spread over 250 firms all over England, but by 1944 this had been reduced to 136.[125]

German bombing raids also had an impact on production. Along with other aircraft production facilities, a Vickers factory in the Home Counties was bombed on September 4, 1940 and Supermarine was subject to a heavy raid on September 26, 1940.[126] Vickers then faced the added complication of the dispersal of Vickers production and its supply firms. This dispersal had been designed by the Ministry of Aircraft Production to protect capacity from aerial bombardment (particularly in the south of England), but it multiplied the management challenges for Vickers-Armstrongs. As Denis Webb recounted, for Supermarine this involved dispersing production of Spitfires to around forty workshops spread up to fifty miles apart – while maintaining full output.[127] While the ESC sites were not bombed, "expenditures and outlays were heavy, despite government support," as were those of other northern steel producers:

> Eliminating glare from the furnaces (a Bessemer blow could be seen for miles in the skies on a clear night) and the slag heaps was a major problem and expense. Pressure for output from operatives under worsened conditions meant improved welfare amenities. Thus works "maintenance" costs soared …. There was to be no massive lift to dividends, as had occurred at some firms during the First World War.[128]

[122] Webb, *Never A Dull Moment!* Part II, p. 121.
[123] Postan, *British War Production*, pp. 400–01.
[124] Webb, *Never A Dull Moment!* pp. 134–28.
[125] Webb, *Never A Dull Moment!* Part II p. 185.
[126] Postan, *British War Production*, p. 164.
[127] Webb, *Never A Dull Moment!* pp. 1–2.
[128] Tweedale, *Steel City*, p. 305.

In the early stages of the war tanks were not given the same priority as aircraft and it was not until July 1941 that tanks were afforded equal priority. Thereafter there was government coordination on the need for machine tools, toolmaking and, to an extent, skilled labor for aircraft and tanks.[129] Although the production of tanks was improving, their quality was not equal that of German tanks in terms of speed and firepower, and would not be so for two to three more years.[130] "The earlier neglect of tank design and development made itself felt in the difficult years of 1940 and 1941; and despite subsequent efforts of the Ministry of Supply it continued to affect tank development throughout the war."[131] However, just as the government had given Vickers-Armstrongs a de facto interwar monopoly on tank work, it took this away again early in the war, bringing in shipbuilders, rolling stock makers and truck makers to produce models. As additional firms, such as Nuffield Mechanizations, became involved in design and development and as the shadow factories came online, Vickers-Armstrongs became less central to tank production. Ironically, the problems the "outside" firms had in producing tanks led to tanks being taken on by a Royal Ordnance Factory in 1944.[132] British forces also used many U.S. Grant and Sherman tanks.[133] The eventual result of these combined efforts would be that the British Army became the only fully mechanized army in the world. However, achieving that required a massive industrial effort.

For Vickers-Armstrongs the six-year war effort involved: warship and submarine production; extensive gun mounting work; the installation of new plant into existing factories (some of which had to come out of mothballs) for artillery manufacturing; designing and producing tanks; working with shadow firms on tanks, armored cars and aircraft production; shell filling; the production of small arms; cartridge production; and working with and managing various government shadow factories.

At the same time as all this activity, many of the firm's senior management went to work *pro bono* for the government, leaving the Vickers-Armstrongs' management stretched very thin.[134] For example, Charles Craven and Alexander Dunbar became sequential Controllers-General at the Ministry of Aircraft Production.[135] Craven was initially seconded to the Air Ministry as Civil Member of the Air Council for Development and Production. In May 1940, when the Ministry of Aircraft Production was formed, he transferred there as Industrial Advisor to the Minister and Chairman of the Supply

---

[129] Postan, *British War Production*, p. 184.
[130] Postan, *British War Production*, p. 185 and pp. 187–88.
[131] Postan, *British War Production*, p. 189.
[132] Postan, *British War Production*, p. 427.
[133] Edgerton, *Warfare State*, p. 81.
[134] Scott, *Vickers*, p. 309.
[135] Edgerton, *Britain's War Machine*, p. 229.

Board. Subsequently Craven returned to Vickers, having clashed with Lord Beaverbrook, a controversial figure who subsequently left the Ministry of Aircraft Production to become Minister of Supply.[136] Six months later, on June 15, 1941, Prime Minister Churchill personally telephoned the chair of Vickers and asked that Craven be released to return to the government, where he became Controller General of the Ministry for Aircraft Production (now under Col. John Moore-Brabazon) and then the chair of the Munitions Management and Labour Efficiency Committee.[137] Craven again returned to Vickers-Armstrongs in 1942, having been given a baronetcy; he was succeeded in government by (Sir) Alexander Dunbar, who served for a year.[138] Craven died in 1944, having aged prematurely due to the stress of government work.[139] He was succeeded as Chairman of Vickers-Armstrongs by Sir Frederick Yapp. Sir Robert Micklem returned as Deputy Chairman in 1944 after two spells in government service, including heading the Department of Tank Production in the Ministry of Supply and chairing the Tank Board.[140] Therefore, during the war Vickers-Armstrongs' extremely complex management operation was being run without the help of key figures from the firm's naval, tank and air-craft sectors. While many civilian firms lent personnel to the government, to do so while producing vital armaments was an impressive achievement.

The Early Postwar Period

Sir Fredrick Yapp saw Vickers-Armstrongs through the end of the war, holding the chairmanship from November 1944 until August 1946. He was succeeded by Sir Robert Micklem, who understood the business well. Jamieson continued to helm Vickers Limited, and in 1945 Lieutenant-General Sir Ronald Weeks, KCB, CBE, DSO, MC, TD joined the Board. He had been Deputy Chief of the Imperial General Staff from 1942, with responsibility for Army organization and equipment, and brought a stellar reputation for organizational efficiency and energy.[141] He arrived at a pivotal point. With the end of the war Vickers and Vickers-Armstrongs faced an – entirely predictable – drastic reduction in orders as "armament demands fell from the insatiable to the negligible."[142] The British Government planned to disarm by stages (in contrast to the period

---

[136] Trevor Westbrook, the general manager of Vickers Aviation, also joined the Ministry of Aircraft Production and then moved to the Ministry of Supply. Thereafter he joined De Havilland. Edgerton, *Warfare State*, p. 154, ff. 30.

[137] Webb, *Never A Dull Moment!* Part II pp. 135–36; Postan, *British War Production*, pp. 138 and 260, ff. 2.

[138] Edgerton, *Warfare State*, p. 154.

[139] Scott, *Vickers*, p. 307.

[140] Smithers, *Rude Mechanicals*, p. 119.

[141] Evans, *Vickers*, p. 18.

[142] Evans, *Vickers*, p. 21.

after World War One) and involved Vickers-Armstrongs in several civilian projects, while asking the firm to retain some capacity in armaments such as torpedoes. Vickers-Armstrongs had formed a committee to consider the problems the firm would face in the postwar world. The committee recommended that the firm follow the domestic strategy that had brought them success in the past – developing by investing in new equipment. The firm now spent over £7,000,000 across all their different sites.[143]

One of their first acts was to exercise the "Break Clauses" they had in contracts with subcontractors, many of which were civilian firms. As Vickers Supermarine employee Webb commented: "I had to operate the 'Break Clause' on many firms .... Sudden cancellations could cause severe hardships both to the firm and the employees and so I always tried to gear the run down to the contractors' resumption of his peace time work."[144] Another important move was the reconsolidation of Supermarine after the dispersal that had been necessary during the war. Hew Ross Kilner traveled to Supermarine to discuss the situation, saying "in effect ... that the sole purpose of the firm was to make money for the shareholders and we could not do this if spread all over the place in uneconomic dispersed sites so we would have to get under one roof as soon as possible."[145] Vickers-Armstrongs was reorientating to prioritizing shareholders and a broader array of customers once again.

The aircraft division made a successful transition from war to peacetime production, thanks to the demand for civilian air travel, which the company met with the Viking twin-engine derivative of the Wellington bomber. In its three years of production 165 Vikings were produced, including four for the Royal Flight. In 1948 their Viking flew from London to Paris in a record-breaking thirty-four minutes.[146] This was followed by the George Edwards-designed turbo-prop Viscount, which was aided by £1.5 million in state development monies and was a tremendous success, ultimately earning the government £3 million in royalty payments.[147] Vickers Supermarine toppled the London–Paris record in 1952 and challenged the speed record again in 1953.[148]

On top of this successful civilian airliner the firm developed three new military fighters: the Valetta, the Varsity and the Valiant. There was also an unexpected case of Vickers-Armstrongs refusing funding from the Ministry of Supply. The Ministry offered £1,000,000 toward the development of a civilian aircraft to replace the Viscount. The money was offered upfront in return for a royalty (as had been done with the Viscount). Scott recounted that

[143] Scott, *Vickers*, p. 309.
[144] Webb, *Never A Dull Moment!* Part II, p. 195.
[145] Webb, *Never A Dull Moment!* Part II, p. 213.
[146] *British Pathé News*, "London to Paris."
[147] Evans, *Vickers*, p. 23.
[148] "Attempt," *Londonderry Sentinel*, p. 3.

"the company had felt the royalty on the Viscount to be onerous, and they did not accept this offer. The *Vanguard* remained a purely private venture."[149] Vickers-Armstrongs had such a strong sense of the value of its work, it would not accept the government's terms.

Rearmament had helped to conceal the long-term decline of the British shipbuilding industry, particularly in civilian production.[150] Reflecting the organizational culture of Vickers-Armstrongs, the naval yards at Barrow and Elswick were modernized, allowing them to diversify into meeting civilian demand, especially for tankers, but also for prestigious liners. In the late 1940s and early 1950s the yards built the *Himalaya* and *Chusan* for the Peninsular and Oriental Steam Navigation Company, the *Orcades*, *Oronsay* and *Orsova* for the Orient Steam Navigation Company and the French liner *Île de France*.[151] For Ellerman Lines, Vickers-Armstrongs built the combination liners and merchant ships *City of Port Elizabeth*, *City of Exeter*, *City of York* and *City of Durban*, which were launched in 1953.[152] As this book closes in 1955, Elswick was building the *Empress of England*, which was delivered in 1957 and the *Empress of Canada*, delivered to Canadian Pacific in 1961.[153]

In terms of naval production, the firm continued to receive British Government orders, primarily for submarines. The firm benefited from German experimentation on using hydrogen peroxide for propulsion, resulting in the (ultimately unsuccessful) experimental submarines *Explorer* and *Excalibur*.[154] This failure turned Barrow toward submarine propulsion by nuclear energy, an important strand of the yard's work to this day.

At government behest the firm took over the aircraft shadow factories in Blackpool and Chester, repurposing them to build the prefabricated housing needed to compensate for stock lost due to bombing. More ambitiously, the government wanted Vickers-Armstrongs' engineering division to convert from tank production to tractor production. As with past civilian diversifications, this was ultimately disastrous, though this time the firm was less to blame. Vickers-Armstrongs converted American Sherman tanks into tractors named Shervicks to work on the government's African groundnut production scheme. They were promised initial orders of 500 annually, rising to 1,000. Further, the government orchestrated Vickers-Armstrongs' design and production of a commercial heavy tracked vehicle, the Vickers Vigor for the groundnut scheme and later, a lighter Vickers Vikon. Unfortunately, the government scheme collapsed at a point when there was no turning back for

---

149 Scott, *Vickers*, p. 342.
150 Parkinson, "Shipbuilding," p. 84.
151 "SS Chusan."
152 Miller, *British Ocean Liners*, p. 80.
153 Miller, *British Ocean Liners*, pp. 76 and 92.
154 Evans, *Vickers*, p. 23.

Vickers-Armstrongs, so they persisted and "for well over a decade the tractor project hung around Vickers' neck like the proverbial albatross before the
corpse was expensively interred."[155] After the groundnut scheme foundered,
production persisted for some time before "Vickers finally withdrew from the
commercial tractor business in the late fifties, having lost over £9 million on the
venture but not before going full circle in the swords-into-ploughshares business by trying to sell an armoured, air-portable version [of the Vikon] to the
Ministry of Defence."[156]

Vickers-Armstrongs themselves initiated a civilian diffusion by buying a
substantial holding in the firm Powers Accounting Machines Ltd., which they
had been a subcontractor for since the end of the war, reasoning that "accounting machinery might just be what was required to fill gunnery-control capacity."[157] This gave the firm a business that was to later become – through various
mergers – very important in the British production of computers. The ESC was
also facing an empty order book having "relied almost entirely on armaments
both before and during the War and … neglected overseas markets. It did not
return to its normal rhythm until 1948."[158]

In April 1949 Sir Archibald Jamison stepped down from the chairmanship of
Vickers Ltd.; his successor was Board member Lord Weeks. In the early 1950s
the firms suffered two personnel blows. First, in 1952 Sir Robert Micklem had
to resign as Chairman of Vickers-Armstrongs due to ill health and died soon
after.[159] He was succeeded by Sir James Reid Young. Then in 1953, Sir Hew
Kilner, who had overseen aviation interests for Vickers, died soon after retiring.[160] There was a changing of the guard at the firms just as the domestic and
international environments were changing too. While the downturn in orders
and Vickers-Armstrongs' response to it were predictable, the firm now faced a
stiff challenge from the newly elected Labour Government.

Crisis: The Threat of Nationalization

Four state interventions in armament firms between 1919 and 1945 had been
harbingers of things to come. First, the Shorts Airship Works at Cardington
had been nationalized in 1919, becoming the Royal Airship Works. Second, after
years of failing to increase efficiency at warship builders Short Brothers and
Harland Ltd. of Belfast, the firm was nationalized in 1943. As Leonard Tivey
noted, with Shorts "Even the powerful wartime controls were found inadequate

---

[155] Evans, *Vickers*, p. 22.
[156] Foss and McKenzie, *Vickers Tanks*, pp. 148–49, quotation on p. 149.
[157] Scott, *Vickers*, p. 311.
[158] Tweedale, *Steel City*, p. 308.
[159] "Sir Robert Micklem," p. 27; Scott, *Vickers*, p. 392.
[160] "Obituary: Hew Ross Kilner."

and had to be surpassed."[161] The nationalization was made on the grounds that Shorts' inefficiency endangered the war effort.[162] Third, S. G. Brown Ltd., makers of precision instruments, was nationalized during the war.[163] Finally, Frank Whittle's Power Jets engine manufacturing firm – which was only "nominally private" due to the massive government investments in the firm – was also nationalized in 1944, creating Power Jets (Research and Development) Ltd.[164] As Hermione Giffard noted, the Minister of Aircraft Production, Stafford Cripps, wanted the nationalized firm to be as far as possible self-supporting through "arranging profitable outlets for its intellectual or physical products."[165] The Treasury's acquiescence to the move was secured by defining the nationalization as a temporary wartime expedient to be reviewed when the war ended.[166] In 1945, after review, the nationalized company was recreated as a Government Research Establishment concentrating on basic research and no longer manufacturing jet engines.[167] Also, as discussed in Chapter 4, in the 1930s at the Bankes Commission and in Parliament there had been calls to nationalize armament firms, but the British Government had seen these off.

While the 1930s focus on nationalizing armament firms had gone, the issue of public ownership of the means of production remained, with the Labour Party championing the move to nationalize key industries. Potentially, one of those industries was steel, affecting the ESC and therefore Vickers-Armstrongs. World War Two had left the state accustomed to being "highly interventionist and directive."[168] This attitude would empower a new government to implement major changes. There had been a lot of doubt about Labour's plans because iron and steel had been a late addition to the Party's 1945 election manifesto's list of industries for nationalization, with other industries prioritized.[169]

[161] Tivey, *Nationalisation*, p. 39.
[162] Howlett, "'Thin End of the Wedge?'" p. 438.
[163] Tivey, *Nationalisation*, p. 39.
[164] W. Jenkins (Ministry of Aircraft Production) to Arthur Fforde (Treasury), March 13, 1945. TNA, T 161/1240, Folder: Jet Propulsion Power-Jets Ltd.; Giffard, *Making Jet Engines*, quotation on p. 173, and pp. 155–56, 173–75; Nahum, *Frank Whittle*, pp. 95–106.
[165] "A Suitable Mandate for Power Jets (R&D) Ltd.," TNA, AVIA 10/142. Cited in Giffard, *Making Jet Engines*, p. 173, ff. 128.
[166] F. G. Lee (Treasury) to Tucker, February 10, 1944; Sir Bernard W. Gilbert to the Permanent Secretary of Ministry of Aircraft Production, February 17, 1944. TNA, T 161/1240, Folder: Jet Propulsion Power-Jets Ltd. The Treasury reluctantly accepted giving the new Director, Dr. Roxbee Cox, a five-year term. B. Trend (Treasury) to Sam Brown (Ministry of Aircraft Production), March 30, 1944. TNA T 161/1240, Folder: Jet Propulsion Power-Jets Ltd.
[167] Wilmot to Morrison, December 17, 1945 with attached note; M. T. Fleet to M. Bailey (Ministry of Supply), December 21, 1945. TNA, T 161/1240, Folder: Jet Propulsion Power-Jets Ltd.
[168] Edgerton, *Warfare State*, p. 145.
[169] Burk, *First Privatisation*, pp. 17–18.

Nevertheless, after winning the 1945 election the Labour Government decided to push ahead with steel nationalization.

This obviously had major implications for Vickers-Armstrongs and Cammell Laird's holdings in the ESC. The steel nationalization was very controversial. According to Scott, however, "In the political battle that had now been joined, Vickers played no part. The industry was represented by the British Iron and Steel Federation."[170] Under the chairmanship of Sir Andrew Duncan, who had no background in steel, it was the Federation which argued the case against nationalization.

The Boards of both Vickers-Armstrongs and the ESC considered it to be an engineering firm rather than as just a steel producer and hoped that the firm would either avoid nationalization altogether or that only parts of it would be nationalized. They set about planning contingencies to hive off some parts of the firm to "save" them and applied to the Ministry of Supply for the exclusion of some parts of the firm from nationalization.[171] The Chairman of the ESC reinforced this view to their shareholders, stating that the firm was "essentially an engineering works." As Geoffrey Tweedale Recounts:

> Nationalization – which the directors were unable to prevent – was an amputation, seriously disrupting its close technical collaboration with other parts of the Vickers group. The Weybridge aircraft division, for example, relied on its intimate daily association with the River Don to solve various technical problems far more quickly than if the ESC had been an outside firm. The Vickers' board estimated that the Government was going to nationalize the ESC to get – at most – one fifth of it.[172]

Consequently, any nationalization would be extremely disruptive to the many functions of the firm. In 1948, Vickers-Armstrongs withdrew from the £3.7 million capital investment they had been planning for the ESC in anticipation of the nationalization. At the same time, the Labour Government was managing the parliamentary process to bring about nationalization despite the opposition to it. As Scott commented: "Perhaps if Vickers had had their minds more on politics and less on what had been their own business they would have deduced from this that the government would never consider any compromise proposals from individual firms."[173]

After much politicking, the Iron and Steel Act passed in November 1949. During a debate on the issue, Leader of the Opposition Winston Churchill promised to reverse it when the Conservative Party regained power: "It will be one of our first steps to remove it from the Statute Book, and to allow the steel industry to continue its splendid career … without being dragged into party

---

[170] Scott, *Vickers*, p. 330.
[171] "English Steel Corporation and Nationalisation," VA, Doc. 457.
[172] Tweedale, *Steel City*, p. 309; Scott, *Vickers*, p. 333.
[173] Scott, *Vickers*, p. 332.

politics by the fanatics of obsolete and discredited Socialistic doctrines."[174] Steel firms took heart from this. Even after the Act had passed, many assumed it would not be implemented because either the Labour Party would lose the 1950 election, or a new Labour Government would be too weak to act.

However, Labour narrowly won the 1950 election and it "came as an unpleasant shock to the industry to be told by [George] Strauss [Minister of Supply] in July 1950 that the Government intended to put the act into operation," despite having a parliamentary majority of only five.[175] In response, firms tried to slow the process in the hope of a further election and a Conservative victory, hardly interacting with the newly nationalized entity, the Iron and Steel Corporation of Great Britain. In fact, the Federation "and its members dragged their feet to such good effect" that relations with the Iron and Steel Corporation nearly broke down.[176]

In the end, to Vickers-Armstrongs' consternation, the government nationalized the whole of the ESC. The government took over all the shares but left the steel firms intact. Like other firms, Vickers-Armstrongs was compensated for the nationalization, but it came in the form of £22,000,000 stock in the Iron and Steel Corporation of Great Britain. However, "company structures and managements were left untouched by nationalization and plans to rationalize the industry made little headway. As one ESC director put it: 'In the early 1950s we didn't know we were nationalized. We just carried on as normal.'"[177]

While this was going on the Vickers-Armstrongs Board was considering its strategy. In terms of finance, the Board was debating what to do with the compensation they were slated to get and was pondering the likely fate of the stocks in the newly nationalized industry. Their stock in the Iron and Steel Corporation of Great Britain immediately plummeted by £1,880,000 and Vickers-Armstrongs swiftly sold it before there were greater losses. In terms of their products, the firm were discussing ways to ensure that they did not produce the same things as the newly nationalized industry and were concerned about whether the ESC would attempt to use their trademarks. There were also questions about the ESC's relationship with Vickers (Eastern), covering India and Pakistan, and what new sales agreements would need to be put in place.[178] By December 1950 Vickers-Armstrongs was playing hardball and demanding that the nationalized ESC "quit and deliver up possession of such parts of the premises known as Vickers House."[179]

[174] House of Commons Debate, *Hansard*, Col. 2045. November 16, 1949. https://api.parliament.uk/historic-hansard/commons/1949/nov/16/iron-and-steel-bill#S5CV0469P0_19491116_HOC_297.

[175] Burk, *First Privatisation*, p. 2.

[176] Burk, *First Privatisation*, p. 27.

[177] Tweedale, Steel City, p. 310. Citing: Interview with Bill Pugh, June 29, 1992.

[178] "English Steel Corporation and Nationalisation," VA, Doc. 457.

[179] Vickers-Armstrongs to ESC, December 18, 1950. "English Steel Corporation and Nationalisation," VA, Doc. 457.

During the first quarter of 1951 Vickers-Armstrongs was also fighting with the Iron and Steel Corporation, trying to avoid being completely severed from the ESC and trying to retain certain key units, using arguments about the national interest and the need for rearmament as justifications for retaining these.[180] The firm were also demanding from the government a "special dividend" under the Act as compensation for their losses. They were also trying to prevent their accounts from being made public and they did not want the ESC figures to appear on the consolidated balance sheet of Vickers. Essentially, Vickers-Armstrongs was staging a rearguard action to undermine the 1949 Act. Interestingly, their partners Cammell Lairds were less willing to fight, showing how much more the ESC mattered to Vickers-Armstrongs.[181]

The attempt to hive off certain parts of the ESC for Vickers-Armstrongs and Cammell Lairds continued into April. This persistent campaign was beginning to bear fruit by June 26, 1951, when the Iron and Steel Corporation agreed to some parts of the ESC remaining with Vickers-Armstrongs.[182] In October the firm was still disentangling the relationship between the ESC and their international holdings, encountering problems in Pakistan when the ESC's new agents, Greaves Cotton, could not get enough money to pay for the stock they had agreed to buy from Vickers Pakistan. This was all happening as the fall of the Labour Government looked increasingly likely, raising the possibility that Vickers-Armstrongs might soon want to reverse some of these complicated transactions.

Opportunity: Denationalization

With another election in prospect, there were behind-the-scenes machinations over the future of steel ownership, with the British Iron and Steel Federation being lobbied by its members for the return of the industry to private hands.[183] After the fall of Labour in October 1951, the Conservative Party declared its intention to reverse the nationalization of steel and began working to achieve it. There were real questions, though, about how the nationalization could be "unscrambled." The Conservatives faced the tricky political issue of "returning ownership of the companies to the private sector," yet retaining "enough public control to satisfy the Opposition and thereby, it was hoped, prevent the renationalisation of the industry" – something that Labour had already pledged to do.[184]

Even as they were still wrangling over a "special dividend" in 1953, Vickers-Armstrongs saw an opportunity to buy back the ESC. In June 1953 Cammell

---

[180] Weeks to Strauss, January 12, 1951. "English Steel Corporation and Nationalisation, January–March 1951," VA, Doc. 458.

[181] "English Steel Corporation and Nationalisation, January–March 1951," p. 16. VA, Doc. 458.

[182] "English Steel Corporation and Nationalisation, April–June 1951," pp. 31–35 and 78. VA, Doc. 459.

[183] Burke, *First Privatization*, p. 4.

[184] Burke, *First Privatization*, p. 5.

Laird agreed that it was interested in reacquisition.[185] The Vickers-Armstrongs Board decided that if the price was right, they would reacquire the firm with Cammell Lairds as their junior partners. Vickers-Armstrongs set up a committee under Chairman Weeks to consider reacquisition. It set about trying to discover the current profitability of the ESC, and the state of the plant (especially the rolling stock) since they had handed it over to the government. The firm now made some strategic arguments about the age of the plant and the drop in profitability likely in the future, all designed to help reduce the price that they and Cammell Lairds would have to pay. Moreover, a memorandum declared that Vickers-Armstrongs' three-year pursuit of a "special dividend" had arisen out of a "drafting oversight in the Act." Further, "it was never intended that such a payment should be permitted. It may be that, if there was no denationalization, the Directors would have a duty to their shareholders to maintain the claim, but this does not seem to be so necessary on a re-acquisition."[186] Scott notes that the committee was more concerned with the financial aspects of any deal and did not pay much attention to politics (despite some on the Board having opposed reacquisition because of the danger of subsequent renationalization).[187]

The negotiation with the Iron and Steel Realisation Agency over reacquiring the ESC was "prolonged and difficult" because the government did not want to be seen to be making a loss on the deal, but the financial situation had changed, and the value of the ESC had lessened.[188] Sir John Morison was negotiating with firms over reacquisition and reported in September 1953 that Guest Keen Nettlefold and Vickers Cammell Laird, "indicated that they were willing purchasers. But that there was a wide disagreement over price."[189] By October a deal with Vickers Cammell Laird was imminent.[190] It took until June 1954 for the deal to be completed, with Vickers-Armstrongs paying £10,000,000 and the government recovering the rest of the money from new debentures and preference shares (underwritten by Morgan Grenfell) issued to the public.[191] Nevertheless, the iron and steel industries remained more regulated than they had been prior to nationalization. Once again, the tide of government regulation did not retreat to its previous position.

Luckily for Vickers-Armstrongs, they regained the firm at the start of a boom in the British steel industry, and in the late 1950s the ESC "customarily returned

---

[185] "English Steel Corporation Ltd. Nationalisation and De-nationalisation, June–September 1953." VA, Doc. 460.
[186] "English Steel Corporation Ltd.," p. 47. "English Steel Corporation Ltd. Nationalisation and De-nationalisation, June–September 1953." VA, Doc. 460.
[187] Scott, *Vickers*, p. 334.
[188] "English Steel Corporation Ltd. Nationalisation and De-nationalisation, September 1953–April 1954." VA, Doc. 461.
[189] Burke, *First Privatization*, p. 109.
[190] Burke, *First Privatization*, p. 131.
[191] Scott, *Vickers*, pp. 334 and 335; Burke, *First Privatization*, p. 142.

profits of £4–5 million."[192] The expectation was of an ever-expanding demand for steel, and reflecting the Vickers-Armstrongs' organizational culture of investment, the ESC planned an expansion into a modern custom-built facility in Tinsley Park.[193] Such was national demand in the 1950s, tool steel firms such as ESC did not have to work to market their wares. A director of a Sheffield steel firm explained: "With the Iron and Steel Board setting prices ... selling was a gentleman's existence, with Sheffield operating as a big cartel. Orders were reported first to the respective trade association and committee and at the end of the day they would tell you what prices to quote. The price-fixing was incredible."[194] Thus, by the close of the era, the state was empowering private firms to behave in a way that previous governments had spent several generations fighting against!

In terms of domestic politics, as Tivey showed, the British Iron and Steel Federation, Vickers-Armstrongs and the ESC were trying to navigate very difficult political waters:

> The story of the nationalisation and denationalisation of the iron and steel industry reflects a clash of principles more clearly than does any other major episode in postwar politics. The Labour Party was sharply divided from Conservatives and Liberals on the issue; nationalisation was forced through against bitter and determined resistance; compromises were rejected; and it was reversed as soon as its opponents had power to do so.[195]

However, the issue of ownership of the ESC did not end there – although this book does – because the Labour Party remained committed to a nationalization program, including the renationalization of steel. Vickers-Armstrongs was involved (through the Federation of British Industries and later the Confederation of British Industries) in collective efforts to resist this agenda. In addition, Vickers-Armstrongs independently lobbied for the steel industry to remain in private hands. These efforts were unsuccessful, however, and steel was again nationalized by the Wilson Government in 1967 (though it was not making a profit then) with the creation of the British Steel Corporation. That firm was to be denationalized by the Thatcher Government in September 1988, becoming British Steel plc.

Crisis/Opportunity: Rearmament

A further production feast came in the early 1950s. Ostensibly this was for the Korean War, though Edgerton makes the case that the real military buildup

---

[192] Tweedale, *Steel City*, p. 323.
[193] Tweedale, *Steel City*, p. 333. Unfortunately, expectations of endless demand – found across the steel industry in Britain – proved disastrously wrong in the 1960s.
[194] Interview with Gordon Polson of Brown Bayley, November 21, 1991. Cited in Tweedale, *Steel City*, p. 330.
[195] Tivey, *Nationalisation*, p. 55.

was actually in Europe.[196] At Vickers-Armstrongs, international contracts had once again to be set aside for emergency national procurement; at the end of 1951 armament work was at three times the level of the late 1940s and fully half the staff were employed on military work.[197] For Vickers Supermarine:

> [T]he Korean War caused panic in high places as we [Britain] really had no jet combat aircraft to match any potential enemy and because the Hawker first production aircraft was still about a year from flying with no guarantee it would be successful, we were, in 1950[,] given a contract for production "Swifts" which were almost identical to VV119 but with a reheated "Avon" and two 30mm Aden guns mounted in the belly of the fuselage. This was the armament specified by the Ministry. This contract was in effect an insurance measure in case the "Hunter" failed to come up to scratch.[198]

However, there were problems with the Swifts and therefore disputes with the Air Ministry.[199]

Vickers-Armstrongs again rose to the production challenge and had more government help than in the past to do so. As the century covered by this book closes, the relationship between Vickers-Armstrongs and the state was changing yet again, with the Cold War inducing a closer relationship between them than had previously been the peacetime norm. The two actors had shifted from being independent to becoming interdependent. Edgerton has shown that in the postwar period the government was conducting more research and development, mostly in industry but increasingly in its own laboratories and centers, such as the new Government Research Establishment, using a greatly expanded workforce. Military research and development now took up a greater proportion of funding than it had before the war.[200]

In 1955, where this book ends, Vickers-Armstrongs underwent a major reorganization, splitting into four distinct companies, covering shipbuilding, engineering, aircraft making and tractor production (this last company a much smaller one). Ironically, Sir Mark Webster Jenkinson's 1922 report for Vickers had advocated exactly this change. This division reflected the reality that these units – or "Kingdoms" as Harold Evans called them – already enjoyed a lot of internal power and independence.[201] The firm's 1955 profit was the best on record and the dividend to shareholders, though fixed at 10 percent, was in fact an increase over the 15 percent declared in 1952 and 1953.[202] The firm was described by the *Times* as "a thriving and well-knit organisation, worthy of its distinguished past."[203]

---

[196] Edgerton, *Warfare State*, p. 103.
[197] Scott, *Vickers*, pp. 357–58.
[198] Webb, *Never A Dull Moment!* Part III, p. 301.
[199] Webb, *Never A Dull Moment!* Part III, pp. 302–05.
[200] Edgerton, *Warfare State*, p. 104.
[201] Evans, *Vickers*, p. 19.
[202] Evans, *Vickers*, p. 26.
[203] Cited in Evans, *Vickers*, p. 26.

At the close of this study in 1955 Major-General Sir Charles Dunphie, CB, CBE, DSO took the reins of Vickers-Armstrongs.[204] A new Chairman took the helm of Vickers Ltd. in 1956, but his surname is familiar: Edward George William Tyrwhitt Knollys, Second Viscount, GCMG, MBE, DFC. His father, the first Viscount, had served as Private Secretary to the Prince of Wales (subsequently Edward VII), in which capacity he organized the Prince's visit to Sir William Armstrong at Cragside in 1884 (see Chapter 2), and had served as Private Secretary to King George V between 1910–1913.[205] While the appointment of the Second Viscount could be viewed as a mere return to the firm's elite strategy, Knollys had a strong background in banking and insurance. He had been on the Vickers Board for several years before assuming the chairmanship.[206]

---

[204] Scott, *Vickers*, p. 392.

[205] "Knollys," Oxford Dictionary of National Biography. At: www.oxforddnb.com/view/10.1093/ref:odnb/9780198614128.001.0001/odnb-9780198614128-e-34350.

[206] Scott, *Vickers*, p. 365.

PART II

Selling Abroad

6

Foreign Policies for Selling
Armaments to Latin America

British armament firms operating in Latin America and elsewhere got very little help from their home government; they were on their own. Consequently,
Armstrongs – and later Vickers – needed to generate commercial, political and
legal intelligence and build relationships in the region. Although most of the
Latin American states had been independent since the mid-1820s, the firms were
operating in choppy political waters. In terms of internal power shifts, Robert
Scheina counted seventeen uprisings with naval participation between 1890 and
1955 (and there were many others without naval help).[1] Successful naval revolts
might result in new sales, but unsuccessful naval revolts or naval participation
in general uprisings could have a chilling effect on future sales as politicians
punished rebels and avoided empowering future opponents. Even without
rebellions, in most Latin American countries constitutionally Presidents served
only one term, making a degree of political change inevitable.[2] Armstrongs and
Vickers had to be attuned to these political evolutions and revolutions.

They also had to be attentive to changes in interregional relationships; if
these turned sour, this could lead to new sales for the firms, and they benefited
handsomely in those times. Alternatively, if such relationships improved – and
the British Government often encouraged this – sales opportunities would dis-
appear. The Latin American market was therefore an exhilarating mix of risk
and reward.

Additionally, the economic situation of the region veered between boom
and bust. The ability of Latin American states to finance armaments purchases
largely depended on where they were in the debt cycle. The states oscillated
between being lent money by European houses and then defaulting on those
loans, which inevitably turned off the loan pipelines for a time. Rory Miller
identified three cycles of lending to Latin America: The first peaked in 1872 and
was halted by a number of government defaults on loans; the second began in
the late 1870s, when Argentina, Brazil, Chile, Mexico and Uruguay were able
to raise new loans, terminating with a financial crisis in Argentina and the collapse of Barings Bank in London in 1890; the third began with the new century

[1] Scheina, *Latin America*, Appendix 2, pp. 294–96.
[2] Miller, *Britain*, p. 138.

and reached its apex in 1913.[3] During the fat times, armament firms made major deals, but at the point of default, they were in significant financial jeopardy and got no support from the British Government.

Another factor in doing any business in the region was the routine use of bribery in business, as Sir Edmund Monson had noted in 1886: "All speculations and enterprises … depend for their preliminary success upon the readiness of the promoters to bribe the wire-pullers of the Government."[4] In 1890 John Baring, of the eponymous banking firm, reported from Argentina that the "bribery and corruption is really quite awful."[5]

Armstrongs' first contact with Latin America came in 1862 when Brazil sought to purchase the Armstrong Gun, a sale the British Government blocked.[6] Nevertheless, many warships built in Britain for Latin America began to carry Armstrong Guns, and Armstrongs' direct relationship with Chile began in 1864 with gun purchases.[7]

After the American Civil War (1861–65), the British Government had been forced through arbitration to compensate for the damage to Union shipping the Birkenhead-built *Alabama* had caused after Britain had (passively) allowed the ship to sail. Thereafter the government was extremely wary of British neutrality being compromised by the commercial activities of armament firms.[8] There are several relevant features of the *Alabama* experience. First, the onus was on the state potentially affected by the armament export to provide evidence to the British Government that British armaments firms were making problematic armaments exports. Second, the government did not then see itself as obligated to systematically track the export behavior of private armament firms. Third, the case led to the passing of the 1870 Foreign Enlistment Act (which included §8 on not breaking neutrality), the Customs and Tariff Act of 1876 (§138) and the amended 1879 Customs and Inland Revenue Act (§8).[9] The British Government therefore had new tools to control the behavior of armament firms. Finally, several of the government players involved in the case were more senior officials when the next major tests came in Latin America. For example, Foreign Office Minister Lord Tenterden had been the British Agent in the *Alabama* arbitration, and this left him wary of Britain being caught again in breach of its obligations as a neutral state.

In 1874, when Chile faced the threat of war with Argentina and Bolivia, the *Almirante Cochrane*, which was being built by Earle of Hull, was hurriedly sent

---

[3] Miller, *Britain*, pp. 120–25.
[4] Monson's 1886 reply to a Foreign Office circular. Cited in Platt, *Finance*, pp. 332–33.
[5] Miller, *Britain*, p. 154. Citing John Baring, writing to his father, Lord Revelstoke, February 1890.
[6] Morgan, *Legacy*, p. 166.
[7] Bastable, *Arms*, p. 112.
[8] *The Case of Great Britain*; Cross, *Lincoln's Man*; Carroll, "Diplomats"; Milton, *Lincoln's Spymaster*; Atwater, "British," pp. 292–317.
[9] Evidence prepared for the Bankes Commission, VA, Vickers Doc. 57, Folder 29.

to Chile, even though it was incomplete, to avoid being caught by a British neutrality declaration. After the threat subsided in 1877, the warship returned to Hull for completion, and was armed with Armstrongs', electrically fired, rifled, muzzle-loading guns, as her sister ship *Blanco Encalada* had been. Indeed, most of Chile's and some of Peru's ships were armed with Armstrong guns when war erupted between the two.[10]

When war looked likely between Peru, Chile and Bolivia in 1879, the British Foreign Office informed the belligerents that it was anxious to avoid war and offered its "friendly offices" for arbitration.[11] The parties refused.[12] Nevertheless, Sir Julian Pauncefote declared: "It is almost worth making another attempt at pacification in the interests of British commerce which must suffer very much by a continuance of hostilities between such fiery and unscrupulous belligerents."[13] To the Foreign Office, "the vast British interests involved" mattered more than armament sales.[14] In late May the Chilean Government appealed to Britain to help prevent the Peruvian Government from purchasing one or more ironclad warships from Turkey, which would "place their navy in a position of superiority over Chili," and in "consideration of the damage that the warlike operations of Peru were doing to British interests." The Foreign Office said it was "impossible" for Britain to be involved "without departing from that attitude of neutrality to which we desire to adhere between the two belligerents."[15] But British neutrality was about to be severely strained by the activities of British armament firms.

In 1879 Armstrongs had six warships for export under construction. This case provides an interesting snapshot of relations between Armstrongs and the British Government. The issue was first raised in July 1880 by Colonel Almonte of the Legation of Peru in London, who informed the Foreign Office that "we have reason for supposing that some vessels of war were being constructed at Newcastle on Tyne for Chile" and that the vessels "are to be armed with two 10-inch guns constructed on Armstrong's new method. One of the vessels being in a fit condition to be launched."[16] A "private source" of Pauncefote's

---

[10]   Sater, *Andean Tragedy*, pp. 96–103.

[11]   Pauncefote to Pakenham (Santiago), No. 13, April 17,1879. TNA, FO 16/201. Folios 31–32; Telegram to the Chilean and Peruvian Governments, No. 13, April 17, 1879. TNA, FO 16/201. Folios 48–49.

[12]   The Peruvian Government expressed "gratitude for the offer, but stated that as hostilities have commenced, they cannot at present accept it." Pauncefote to Pakenham, May 15, 1879. TNA, FO 16/201, Folio 42.

[13]   Pauncefote to Salisbury, May 20, 1879, TNA, FO 16/201.

[14]   Foreign Office "Peru and Chile," on visit of Mr. Pividal, April 15, 1879. TNA, FO 16/201. Folios 46–47.

[15]   Foreign Office to Pakenham, No. 19, May 27, 1879. FO 16/201. Folios 55–56. "Chili" was a common spelling of the time.

[16]   Almonte to Pauncefote, July 12, 1880. TNA, T 1/13046.

suggested that one was for Chile, three were for Peru and two were for China.[17] The Foreign Office asked the Treasury Secretary Sir Ralph Lingen to direct local customs officials to "enquire and report respecting the vessels in question, and to exercise all vigilance in order to prevent any breach of the Foreign Enlistment Act in connection with them."[18]

Meanwhile Sir Charles Russell, who held Peruvian bonds, sought to persuade the Foreign Office to prevent munitions going to Peru (because Peru would need loans to pay for them).[19] In January 1881 Almonte reported to the Foreign Office: "I am given to understand that at least [one] of these vessels is shortly to sail for Chile without having her guns on board."[20] This prompted Lord Tenterden to write to Lingen at the Treasury on January 13 about "the opinion of the Law Officers ... that immediate orders must be taken to detain the ship ... which is supposed to be intended for Chile. If the reports are true it is another Alabama and the consequences of any delay may be most serious."[21]

Under Treasury orders, Inspector Hicks of the Tyne Water Guard boarded a ship at Armstrongs' Elswick yard, and the Collector of Customs Saunders reported that the steamer already had five guns on board.[22] On January 14 the Collector was reporting that the "Steamer with guns" had left Elswick and was now "moored to [the] wharf at Wallsend Slipway. She is incomplete."[23] This raised the specter that she might be able to evade the 1870 Act and steam away.

The government needed definitive information on the destination of the nearly completed ship. As Lord Tenterden cautioned, "there may be claims for damages if it turns out that after all the ship we have laid hands on is not the right one or is not built for war purposes."[24] The Treasury also feared an over-hasty seizure, but according to Lingen:

> [M]y Lords think it not unimportant to ask you to bring to the notice of the Secretary of State a communication which My Lords received from the late Earl Russell in 1873 after the Alabama arbitration in which he emphasises his regret that he did not apply to the Admiralty to support the action of the customs.
> ... [I]t seems to them [the Lords] to be important that the escape of a vessel contrary to the provision of the Foreign Enlistment Act 1870 should be rendered so nearly impossible in the presence of superior force as to remove the temptation of undertaking it.[25]

[17] Pauncefote to the Permanent Secretary to the Treasury, July 19, 1880. TNA, T 1/13046.
[18] Pauncefote to Lingen, July 17, 1880. TNA, T 1/13046.
[19] Kiernan, "Foreign Interests," pp. 15–16.
[20] Almonte to Pauncefote, January 9, 1881. TNA, T 1/13046.
[21] Tenterden to Lingen, January 13, 1881. TNA, T 1/13046.
[22] Saunders to the Foreign Office, January 12, 1881. TNA, T 1/13046.
[23] Telegram, Collector of Customs at Newcastle to Lord Fred K. Cavendish, Treasury. Received January 14, 1881. TNA, T 1/13046.
[24] Note from Tenterden to Lingen, January 14, 1881. TNA, T 1/13046.
[25] Lingen to Tenterden, January 15, 1881. TNA, T 1/13046.

Subsequently the Treasury received a copy of a letter from new Foreign Secretary Lord Granville to the Admiralty "requesting that measures may be taken to prevent the escape of the vessel from custody."[26] This was an escalation, as previously only local Customs Officials and the Water Guard had been involved.

The local Customs Collector was given instructions: "If vessel is in a state to put to sea, the Treasury wishes her to be detained by any means necessary to ensure her detention until further orders."[27] The Foreign Office also contacted the Collector of Customs at Newcastle "to call his attention by telegram to the powers which he is authorized to exercise under Clause 22 of the Foreign Enlistment Act to call in aid if necessary to render the detention an effective one."[28] On January 15, 1881, it was reported that a vessel "has accordingly been detained since yesterday by the local authority under §2.4 of the Foreign Enlistment Act at Wallsend."[29] Commander Pipon visited the ship and noted that there were several guns and 30 tons of coal on board. He concluded, "The ship being in my opinion quite fit to go to sea, I considered it advisable to post two C. [Coast] guard men on board."[30]

Lingen reported that the Treasury Law Officers had determined that

> the Secretary of State's Warrant had better not be issued until further information is obtained, but that they see no objection to addressing to whomsoever has the control of the vessel a communication to the effect that *the vessel is being detained on the ground that the government has reason to believe that she is intended to be employed in the service of Chili, and asking whether the persons to whom the communication is addressed have any observations to make.*

The Law Officers added that "no direct question should be put, as it might be said that the answer tended to criminate the persons addressed. They also suggest that your officer in charge of the vessel should be directed to do nothing to interfere with her completion."[31] Lacking definitive information on the ships' destination, the Treasury was unsure of the legality of holding the ship, even though it had ordered it be held. Similar conclusions were being reached at the Foreign Office, where their Law Officers concluded: "It appears to us that the information before your lordship leads to an almost certain conclusion that the vessel in question is intended to be used for the purposes of warfare, but the

---

26 Pauncefote to the Permanent Secretary to the Treasury, January 15, 1881. TNA, T 1/13046.
27 Telegram from the Treasury to the Collector of Customs at Newcastle, January 14, 1881. TNA, T 1/13046.
28 Note from Du Cane Foreign Office to Lingen, January 14, 1881. TNA, T 1/13046.
29 Pauncefote to the Admiralty, January 15, 1881. TNA, T 1/13046.
30 Commander Pipon to the Admiralty, January 17, 1881. TNA, T 1/13046.
31 Lingen to the Commissioners of Customs, January 17, 1881. TNA, T 1/13046. Emphasis in original.

evidence to establish the fact that the vessel is to enter the service of Chili is at present very slight."[32]

The Foreign Office therefore went back to Colonel Almonte at the Peruvian Legation.[33] He reported that the ship was to be called the *Esmeralda* and Captain Lynch and Admiral Simpson of the Chilean Navy were in England to oversee the vessel's finishing.[34] The Foreign Office reported this to the Treasury, including Almonte's claim that some at Armstrongs thought the export "would not be contrary to the Foreign Enlistment Act as it would not have her armament on board."[35]

Throughout, Armstrongs was wholly cooperative, providing information to the Collector of Customs, and directly to the Foreign Secretary.[36] The Collector reported he had "seen Sir William Armstrong, who in presence of his partner Capt. Noble, informed me that they had contracted for six ships, three of one class and three of another, five for China and one for Chili, but by terms of contract, copy produced to me, no delivery to take place to Chilean authorities whilst that state at war."[37] Sir William directly informed Granville that: "not only by the clause in our contracts, but by repeated communications with the Chilian authorities we have informed them that the vessel cannot be delivered while their country is at war – and the Chilian authorities have no intention of taking delivery of the ship while such a state of affairs continues."[38] Armstrongs was entirely obeying the law. Nevertheless, there was still anxiety in the Treasury that the ship (the fastest cruiser in existence[39]) might slip away.

These concerns were further heightened when Mitchells and Company requested that the ship be moved from their slipway so as to not hold up local businesses.[40] Armstrongs also requested that the Foreign Office "will also state what guarantee will be required from us, that the vessel shall not be delivered to the Chilian or other foreign authorities without your lordships['] sanction."[41] The Foreign Office had recently received assurances from the Chilean Minister at Court that the vessel would not be delivered while Chile was at war.[42] Moreover, the Foreign Office reported as follows:

32 Hershell, Law Officer of the Crown, to Earl Granville, January 13, 1881. TNA, T 1/13046.
33 Granville to the Secretary to the Treasury, January 14, 1881. TNA, T 1/13046.
34 Amonte to Earl Granville, January 14, 1881. TNA, T 1/13046.
35 Granville to the Secretary to the Treasury, January 14, 1881. TNA, T 1/13046. This letter reported that Almonte had been reprimanded for not furnishing comprehensive information!
36 Saunders, Collector at Newcastle, to the Customs House, London, January 18, 1881. TNA, T 1/13046.
37 Saunders to Secretary, Custom House London, Telegram, January 17, 1881. TNA, T 1/13046.
38 William Armstrong and Co. to Earl Granville, January 17, 1881. TNA, T 1/13046.
39 "A Great Victorian," p. 27. TWA, D/VA/74/3/2.
40 Mitchell and Co. to Earl Granville, Telegram, January 17, 1881; Mitchell and Co. to Saunders, January 17, 1881. TNA, T 1/13046.
41 William Armstrong and Co. to the Earl Granville, January 17, 1881. TNA, T 1/13046.
42 Foreign Office to the Treasury, January 18, 1881. TNA, T 1/13046.

Messrs. Armstrong have undertaken to sign a declaration and give security that the vessel in question shall not leave the Tyne before the termination of the war, without the presumption of Her Majesty's Government.
Lord Granville is advised by the law officers that, in these circumstances,
the vessel should be allowed to go off the slipway without prejudice to the
right of detention. His Lordship is further advised that Messrs. Armstrong
should be allowed to make a declaration under §8 of the Foreign Enlistment Act. The law officers are of opinion that every consideration should
be shown to Messrs. Armstrong, as there is no actual proof that the particular vessel in question is destined for Chili, and it is probable that they
intended to act properly in the matter.[43]

The ship was therefore allowed to move off the slipway, but local officials
deemed "it prudent to retain the assistance of the two Coast Guard men ...
[who] will remain on board pending further orders."[44] Armstrongs subsequently requested permission to take the ship for sea trials, with Coast Guard
officials onboard, which the Foreign Office and Treasury agreed to.[45]

Arrangements were being made for Armstrongs to execute a monetary
bond stating – on pain of forfeit – that no warships would be provided to
Chile while she was at war. The precedent was the 1874 Samuda case restricting
exports of ships to Turkey while she was at war with Russia (see Chapter 8).[46]
Armstrongs readily agreed when the government finally asked them for a
bond. There was much intragovernmental correspondence about the language
for the bond and the tone of the letter. The Treasury's Law Officer was particularly concerned about "the spirit in which the Government should deal with
Messrs. Armstrong. I have thought it advisable to forward the draft of a letter which I propose should be sent to Messrs. Armstrong with the proposed
bond ... and might be sent from their Lordships by their Secretary rather than
by their Solicitor."[47] When the letter and bond were sent to Armstrongs, they
swiftly complied, and the *Esmeralda* was placed in dry dock until the conflict
ended. Despite the upstanding behavior of the firm, Treasury and Customs
officials remained deeply skeptical of Armstrongs and maintained a Water
Guard watch on the *Esmeralda*. Due to Chile's financial woes the warship never
reached Latin America but was later sold to Japan.[48]

During these events the British Government accepted no obligation to track
armament firms' exports. Nevertheless, it was noted that this lack of tracking

---

[43] Tenterden, to Treasury, January 17, 1881. TNA, T 1/13046.
[44] Saunders to Treasury, January 19, 1881. TNA, T 1/13046.
[45] Lingen to the Commissioner of Customs, January 26, 1881. TNA, T 1/13046.
[46] Stephenam to Treasury, February 2, 1881, enclosing a copy of the Samuda Bond, dated July
       19, 1877. "Suspected Ships of War for Chile and China," 1880–81. TNA, T 1/13046.
[47] Stephenam to the Secretary of the Treasury, February 2, 1881. TNA. T 1/13046.
[48] The *Idzumi* and *Idzumo* earned fame as part of the Japanese fleet that defeated the Russian
       navy in 1905. "Ships Built for the Japanese Navy," TWA, D/VA/21 Folios 1 and 3; McKen-
       zie, *W. G. Armstrong*, pp. 96 and 101.

had implications for the collection of customs duties.[49] The government subsequently decided that they needed to systematically monitor all types of armaments being exported by British firms.

Late in the War of the Pacific the United States sought to pressure Chile by deploying warships to Valparaíso. However, British Representative Spenser St. John reported that the demonstration went "almost unnoticed."[50] This was because, as the Admiralty had observed in 1881, "The Chilian Government ... having three ironclads, and the United States Government being deficient in that particular, it would be out of the power of the latter effectively to coerce the former Power."[51]

Armstrongs had courteously interacted with Chilean officials throughout, and the *Esmeralda* incident did not harm their relationship with Chile. This was impressive, because, as Victor Gordon Kiernan recounts, "Chile did not emerge from the war in any mood of gratitude or docility towards England, nor England in any mood of admiration or respect for Chile."[52] It was vital for Armstrongs to be seen to be independent of the British Government so as to avoid getting caught up in the cooling of official relations with Chile.

The firm's success was demonstrated in 1883, when Armstrongs provided a detailed marketing memorandum on "Armoured and Protected Ships" at the request of the Chilean navy's Captain Lynch – an interlocutor with Armstrongs over the *Esmeralda* – "for use in pressing for the construction of an armoured ship."[53] This new requirement reflected the pace of technological change; the *Esmeralda* would have been eclipsed before it was delivered. The Armstrongs' memorandum provided a detailed review of recent developments in ship design and protection, and advised that one firm should do all of the work, on the grounds that "the necessary provisions for most economically working into one design the several features of armament, armour, and speed can at once be made, and subsequent alterations avoided."[54] This was an attempt to forestall Chile copying the Admiralty policy of splitting ship, armor and gun orders. In 1885 Armstrongs was advertising its talents in a letter to the Peruvian Consul, noting it was able to build both warships and armaments and could "ensure both economy and rapidity in the completion of vessels."[55]

In the 1880s Armstrongs' relationship with Brazil blossomed. An early sale was a torpedo boat destroyer which Armstrongs had bought when the makers, the Defence Vessel Construction Co., went out of business, and sold as

49 Tenterden (Foreign Office) to Lingen, January 17, 1881. TNA, T 1/13046.
50 Kiernan, "Foreign," p. 31. Citing St. John to Granville, March 1, 1882. TNA, FO 61/339.
51 Kiernan, "Foreign," p. 31. Citing Admiralty to Foreign Office, Confidential November 10, 1881, TNA, FO 61/337.
52 Kiernan, "Foreign," p. 35.
53 Manning, *William White*, p. 109. Citing White to F. H. Swan, April 25, 1883.
54 Manning, *William White*, p. 111.
55 Bastable, *Arms*, p. 115. Citing Letter to Peruvian Consul, January 31, 1885. TWA, 31/2689.

the *Gustavo Sampaio* in October 1883.[56] Brazil also bought *Tiradentes* and *República*, designed by their naval architect Phillip Watts, in 1891.[57] The two Armstrong ships found themselves on opposite sides in the Brazilian Naval Revolt of 1893–94.[58] During the revolt Armstrongs was negotiating with the government to build three additional cruisers, clinching the deal in November 1894.[59] However, after defeating the rebels, the government decreased support for the Brazilian navy, fearing more mutinies.

During the 1890s Armstrongs benefited from border tensions in the region, particularly between Argentina and Chile, creating more and more powerfully protected cruisers for both, even as the British Government was trying to ease tensions.[60] Robert Lawrie Thompson represented Armstrongs in Chile, where he had "special advantages for obtaining orders," and in Argentina from 1890.[61] Armstrongs' speculative building of a protected cruiser paid off in May 1890 when Argentina purchased it as the *Veinticinco de Mayo*. A year later Armstrongs sold her an improved cruiser, the *Nuevo de Julio*.[62] Argentina also bought several ships from Ansaldo of Italy.

Chile was concerned that Argentina and the United States might ally against her. The 1891 revolution, which involved the Chilean navy, toppled President Balmaceda's government.[63] The revolution did not harm the relationship with Armstrongs, though, and in 1892 the firm sold Chile the Watts-designed protected cruiser *Blanco Escalada*. The ship had been laid down as a stock cruiser and work got underway while Chile considered the tender. Sir Edward Reed was advising the Chilean Commission and asked for many costly modifications.[64] The *Blanco Escalada* sale was likely attributable to Thompson's work. In an August 1892 contract renegotiation with Armstrongs, he agreed generous commission levels: "Both in South America and in further Asia '2 per cent commission on the cost of hulls and engines of orders for war vessels for Chile; 5 per cent on orders for other war materials ... [and] £1,000 towards expenses.'"[65] Thompson was clearly an important element of Armstrongs' regional marketing.

The arms race continued in November 1893 when Argentina bought a protected cruiser, the *Buenos Aires*, which Armstrongs had speculatively laid down.[66]

[56] Initially the *Aurora*. Brook, *Warships*, p. 166.
[57] "Republica and Tiradentes," p. 190; "Final Trials of 'Tiradentes,'" p. 330.
[58] Wilson, *Ironclads*, pp. 35–36, 39.
[59] Morgan, *Legacy*, pp. 155–60.
[60] Pauncefote to Pakenham (Santiago), "Convention between Chile and Argentine Republic," Draft. January 31, 1879. FO 16/201 Folios 13–14.
[61] Ferris, *War Traders*, p. 17.
[62] Scheina, *Latin America*, p. 46.
[63] Wilson, *Ironclads*, pp. 16–18.
[64] Brook, *Warships*, p. 81.
[65] Ferris, *War Traders*, p. 17. Citing *The Times*.
[66] Brook, *Warships*, p. 82.

This came shortly after many Argentinian sailors had revolted against the government, which might have been expected to halt the deal. Some of the cost of the vessel was paid for by Argentine public subscription, so clearly the navy remained popular.

Chile responded in August 1895 by buying a protected cruiser that had been under construction at Elswick for Brazil (who had missed their first payment); this became the *Ministro Zenteno*.[67] After selling the original *Esmeralda* to Japan to raise funds, in 1895 Chile ordered an armored cruiser (also called *Esmeralda*) and four torpedo boats from Armstrongs. There was considerable back and forth between Armstrongs and Santiago on the design of the new *Esmeralda*, with Chile wanting a belted cruiser 1,200 tons heavier than Armstrongs' tender, to be delivered two months sooner. The customer won and the heavier cruiser was delivered in September 1896.[68] As the first ship to cruise without sails, the *Esmeralda* was a sensation and was toured by the Prince of Wales.[69]

In parallel with the *Esmeralda* discussions, Armstrongs was negotiating with Chile over a September 1895 tender for a fast cruiser. The Chilean Naval Commission was acting from Paris and Philip Watts presented three designs to them there. After significant negotiation between Watts and the Commission over the design and armament, the *O'Higgins* was laid down in March 1896 and launched in May 1897.[70] In early February 1898 the Chilean Ambassador requested that four Chilean officers training on British ships at the Mediterranean station be allowed to come to Britain to join the *O'Higgins*; the Admiralty agreed.[71] The ship was delivered in July 1898 and cost £700,000 (£101,126,262 in August 2022).[72] This was incredibly fast construction and reflected Chile's concern that war was imminent. The Chilean Government also asked Armstrongs to tender for a 2,400 ton "school ship," leading to the Watts-designed *General Baquedano*.[73] In July 1898 the Board of Customs notified the Foreign Office that Armstrongs had launched the *General Baquedano*, armed with "four 4.7inch quick-firing guns, two 12-pounder quick-firing guns, two 6-pounder quick-firing guns, and an 18 inch torpedo tube," asking if the Secretary of State wished steps to be taken to prevent the ship from sailing.[74] The answer was no, and the ship was delivered to Chile in August 1899.[75]

---

[67] Brook, *Warships*, p. 83; Scheina, *Latin America*, p. 47.
[68] Brook, *Warships*, p. 102.
[69] Wright, *Chinese*, p. 53; Brook, *Warships*, p. 53.
[70] Brook, *Warships*, pp. 103–07. An earlier corvette, also called *O'Higgins*, had been built by Ravenhill in 1866. It carried Armstrong guns.
[71] Foreign Office to Admiralty, February 5, 1898; Macgregor, Admiralty to Foreign Office, February 15, 1898. TNA, FO 16/322.
[72] "New Chilean Cruiser."
[73] Brook, *Warships*, p. 218.
[74] Prowse, Board of Customs to Under Secretary, Foreign Office, July 7, 1898. TNA, FO 16/322.
[75] Foreign Office to Customs (with copy to Minister Gana), August 24, 1898. TNA, FO 16/322.

As tensions increased, the British Government became involved in diplomacy to end the standoff – potentially thwarting Armstrongs' interests – and Argentina and Chile agreed to submit their southern border dispute to British arbitration. While a dispute over Punta de Atacama was solved, the southern border arbitration proved more difficult, and the protagonists began to purchase warships once again. Argentina turned to Ansaldo of Italy, and, according to intelligence passed to Lord Curzon from Anthony Gibbs and Sons in Valparaíso, were "said to be treating with Armstrong for the ironclad *Juan de Austria* originally intended for Spain."[76] As Gibbs had previously been Armstrongs' ambassador-agents in Chile, this information was credible. While British businesses in Chile, including Rothschild and Gibbs, appealed for further British arbitration of the dispute, the Chilean Government declared her readiness to negotiate via the *Times* newspaper.[77] The British Government was also directly approached by Chile for assistance in establishing a new arbitration with Argentina.[78] In September 1898 Chile formally proposed to Argentina that they begin arbitration, and at the same time Rothschild reported to Britain that if the process failed, Chile intended to call up 25,000 national guardsmen on October 1.[79] Gibbs and Sons contacted the Foreign Office to express their concern about the "extreme gravity of the situation."[80] By October the Admiralty was reporting that the Chilean Naval Squadron was "actively drilling, and frequently carrying out target practice, the torpedo boats and destroyers getting under weigh daily," although "Chili was in great straits for want of money, with excessive armaments and standing Navy having strained her resources."[81]

Chile again turned to Armstrongs. The firm had been speculatively building a sister ship, a "stock Yoshino," to the protected cruiser *Takasago*. Potential buyers included Italy, Japan and Turkey, but Chile purchased it in early 1902, named it the *Chacabuco* and sailed it in King Edward VII's Coronation Review.[82] Also in 1902 Chile purchased another Armstrongs speculative build, the destroyer *Capitan Thompson*.[83]

Tensions between Argentina and Chile continued to bubble, and both were planning new warship purchases. In 1901, when Sir Edward Reed was in Chile for health reasons, he met with Chilean naval officials to discuss the design and purchase of two battleships.[84] Reed worked with Armstrongs and Vickers

[76] Extract from Gibbs and Sons, Valparaíso to Antony Gibbs and Sons, June 4, 1898. TNA, FO 16/322.
[77] "Chile and Argentina," clipping in TNA, FO 16/322.
[78] Villiers to Salisbury, July 12, 1898; Villiers memo July 16, 1889. TNA, FO 16/322.
[79] Telegram to Rothschilds from Valparaíso, September 13, 1889. TNA, FO 16/322.
[80] Anthony Gibbs and Sons to Bertie and Villiers, September 16, 1889. TNA, FO 16/322.
[81] Macgregor Admiralty to Under Secretary of State, Foreign Office, October 25, 1898. TNA, FO 16/322.
[82] Brook, *Warships*, pp. 91–92.
[83] Brook, *Warships*, pp. 172–73.
[84] Brook, *Warships*, p. 130.

to finalize the designs for identical "lightweight" battleships, the *Constitución* and the *Libertad*. They were to be delivered in eighteen months by Elswick and Barrow, the speed of construction a reflection of Chile's security concerns. These orders further sped up the arms race with Argentina and marked Vickers' entry to the Latin American market.

British economic interests in Argentina and Chile were significant and were threatened by the disarray that tensions were causing.[85] These interests were judged far more important than British armament sales (which were themselves substantial) and the British Government again offered to mediate the dispute.[86] This time negotiations were successful.

The 1902 "Pacts of May" agreed between Argentina and Chile contained three different pacts, the third of which covered naval armaments. The two states agreed to: stop buying new warships for a period of five years; provide eighteen months' notice if they intended to purchase a ship in that timeframe; reduce their fleets within a year; and delay by two months the delivery dates they had agreed for warships under contract (i.e., the near-compete Chilean battleships built by Armstrongs and Vickers). This latter clause, Article IV, was in place "[i]n order to facilitate the transfer of pending contracts," that is, to enable the British government to buy the warships. Armstrongs and Vickers had produced innovative, well-protected ships with impressive armaments that at nineteen knots were faster than anything else then afloat.[87] J. D. Scott commented: "No wonder that the Admiralty did not wish to see these notable products of British yards go to a foreign navy, even to a power so uninvolved in the European naval arms race at Chile was."[88] Initially the British Government declined to buy them for £1,100,000 each, declaring them unsuitable for Admiralty needs. However, after Russia offered to buy them from Chile, Britain changed her mind (fearing Russia would then threaten Japan). After initially resisting a proposal from the House of Commons to buy the ships itself, that is exactly what the Admiralty reluctantly did, renaming them HMS *Swiftsure* and HMS *Triumph*. Armstrongs and Vickers allowed the Admiralty to buy the ships incomplete, selling both for £1,875,000 (£256,152,508 in August 2022). The government subsequently refused Japan's request to buy them.[89]

In 1906 Vickers launched the cruiser-scout *Almirante Grau*, built for Peru. The British Government had been unaware of this program.[90] In January

---

[85] A 1898 memorandum reported that it was not possible to "ascertain with any accuracy the amount of British capital – which is believed, however, to be very large – invested in the two Republics," September 14, 1898. TNA, FO 16/322.

[86] Scheina, *Latin America*, p. 51.

[87] "Launches," p. 72.

[88] Scott, *Vickers*, p. 54.

[89] Brook, *Warships*, p. 130.

[90] "Paper 2785: Messrs. Vickers Sons and Maxim Limited building two Cruiser-scouts for Peruvian Government," 1906. TNA, FO /372/26/35.

1906 the Consul General, Alfred St. John, reported that Peru had received a loan from Germany for another vessel and that the contract had gone to Vickers.[91] Peru's Admiral Carajal oversaw the building of the fast cruiser *Coronel Bolognesi* at Barrow. Its trials were very successful.[92] A naval journal reported: "This vessel has many features which will commend her to such naval powers as Peru ... as the vessel combines with the exceptionally high speed of 24 knots, a considerable armament, including two weapons, each firing a 100-pound shell at a velocity effective against unarmored craft at three miles range."[93] Vickers provided everything, "even to the provision of shot and shell and powder."[94]

The failure of a naval rebellion in 1894 precipitated the Brazilian service going into decline for a decade.[95] That year Brazil had signed a contract with Armstrongs for three protected cruisers, but after Brazil missed the initial payment Armstrongs sold one to Chile. The second, the *Almirante Barroso*, completed her trials in April 1897 and sailed for Brazil. The third, the *Amazonas*, was laid down in December 1897 and left Elswick in March 1898. Two weeks later Brazil sold her to the United States, and the ship became the USS *New Orleans*.[96] Another Armstrongs' second-class cruiser for Brazil, the *Almirante Abreu*, was also sold to the United States in March 1898, becoming the USS *Albany*.

In 1904 Brazilian elites agreed to reinvigorate the navy to showcase the nation's power. Armstrongs was already in informal discussions with Rio, and had prepared proposals on "Armoured clads, Armoured Cruisers and Coast Defence Ships for Brazil."[97] Krupp was also competing for orders, strongly supported by the Kaiser.[98] Within the Brazilian Government there were debates over whether to go with a big ship navy or to have many smaller, faster ships – following the *Jeune École* model; the latter approach initially triumphed.[99] The ambitious plan was to procure up to twenty-eight ships of various types, with most of the ships to be acquired in Britain. A sum of $31,250,000 (£903,465,158 in August 2022) was allocated in 1904 for the construction of three battleships, three armored cruisers and some smaller war vessels.[100] According to Armstrongs' designer d'Eyncourt, "My firm had excellent agents out there,

[91] "Fast Cruiser for Peruvian Government," January 4, 1906. TNA, FO 368/39/2 Folios 3–4.
[92] "Peru: New Cruisers," p. 1293.
[93] "Peru: British-Built Cruiser," pp. 683–84.
[94] "Peru: New Cruisers," p. 1294.
[95] Scheina, *Latin America*, pp. 66–76.
[96] Brook, *Warships*, p. 86.
[97] Topliss, "Brazilian Dreadnoughts," p. 241.
[98] Yorulmaz, *Arming*, pp. 164–65.
[99] For more on this model see: Røksund, *The Jeune École*.
[100] Livermore, "Battleship Diplomacy," p. 32. Citing "Information on file concerning the Brazilian battleships," March 16, 1907, U.S. Navy Department archives, general correspondence, Office of Naval Intelligence, case 8079.

Messrs. Walter Bros., who had been in business in Rio for a number of years and knew pretty well all there was to know about Brazil."

D'Eyncourt traveled to Rio several times and "experienced most agreeable relations with the authorities on all matters."[101] N. M. Rothschilds and Sons in Brazil played a vital role, wielding "immense power in Brazilian financial circles at this time and ... in fact [they] underwrote the loan for the new naval program."[102] Rothschilds ran the tender process from their London office, sending out the invitation to tender for battleships, armored cruisers, torpedo boat destroyers and submarines, and receiving the various bids in spring 1905. Armstrongs and Vickers bid jointly for battleship and armored cruiser orders, with Vickers to build the latter. However, the Brazilian Government then decided not to procure armored cruisers.

The first three Brazilian battleships were ordered from Armstrongs in 1905 and the firm shared the order with Vickers. Morgan attributes this to concerns about rivals such as Krupp.[103] According to a confidential Armstrong Whitworth document from around 1906, the firms had "arrangements ... as regards foreign orders. They have been as far as possible with a view of dividing the work equally between the two firms – but this obviously, cannot be done in all cases. The object underlying them is, of course, to prevent unnecessary cutting of prices and where possible, to bring the work to England."[104] Among the agreements listed were the following:

Chili	A. and V.
	On Battleships.
	Builder pays 3% on Hull.
	Builder pays 12½% on Armament.
	Builder pays £6-10-0 per ton on Hull Armour.
	Builder pays £15-0-0 per ton on Shield Armour.
	Maker pays 7½% to non-maker on Coast Defence Guns and Mountings.
Argentina	Agreement to work together. Present ships being built in U.S.A. and no details are at present fixed.
Brazil	On previous ships profit was divided; for present ship A. will pay V 3% on Hull.
	12½% on Armament.
	£10 per ton on Hull Armour.
	£15 per ton on Shield Armour.
	V. pays A. 3½% on Propelling Machinery.[105]

---

[101] d'Eyncourt, *Shipbuilder's*, p. 55.

[102] Topliss, "Brazilian," p. 243.

[103] Morgan, *Legacy*, p. 160.

[104] "Armstrongs and Vickers (about 1906 to 1913)," Confidential memorandum signed by A.M.W. of Armstrongs, undated. "War Work," VA, Doc. 551.

[105] "Armstrongs and Vickers." Emphasis in original.

By November 1906 Armstrongs' Chief Naval Architect Josiah Perrett was reporting good progress at both yards.[106] However, the appearance of HMS *Dreadnought* dramatically changed Brazil's plans, enabling the "big ship" faction to triumph in Brazil and initiating a new Latin American arms race. The existing contract with Armstrongs was canceled, the completed building work was dismantled, and in 1906 Brazil awarded new contracts to Armstrongs, initially for two powerful dreadnoughts, the *Minas Gerais* and the *São Paulo*.[107] A third dreadnought, the *Rio de Janeiro*, was to be ordered later. Chile and Argentina reacted, canceling their 1902 nonaggression pact, an action which gave them the freedom (though not the money) to rearm in response.

The firms again divided the Brazilian dreadnought contract. Armstrongs was to build the first dreadnought and provide all armor, guns and ordnance; Vickers was to build the second dreadnought and the engines for both ships. Though the share of the work had been agreed, the division of the profits had not been. In May 1907 Armstrongs laid the keel for the *Minas Gerais*. Work was slowed down by strikes at the Elswick Yard, leading to a six-month delay in her launch. On September 10, 1908, she was named by Senora Regis de Oliveira, the wife of the Brazilian Minister to Britain. John Meade Faulkner reported that the launch went off with "great precision and éclat." Explaining: "She is the largest ship of war ever launched in English waters. There is now a very large permanent Brazilian colony in Newcastle – and a great many more Brazilians came for the occasion, from all parts. At a dinner which Admiral Bacellar [head of the Brazilian Naval Commission in Britain] gave, we sat down one-hundred thirty people."[108] Even after the *Minas Gerais* was launched, completion "work was slowed by constant difficulties in gaining the approval of the design by the Brazilian representative," Admiral Bacellar.[109] The Commission spent many months monitoring building work in Newcastle and observing armor trials run by Armstrongs.[110] On April 19, 1909, the *São Paulo* was launched by Vickers at Barrow. Again, Senora Regis de Oliveira named the ship and there were many South American diplomats and naval officers present.[111]

In parallel Armstrongs were building Brazil two scout cruisers, the *Bahia* and the *Rio Grande Do Sul*. These Perrett-designed ships were laid down in August 1907 and completed their final trials three years later.[112] Brazil was also negotiating with Armstrongs for battleships to rival the American ships that

[106] Perrett, "Report to Meeting of Directors to be Held in London on Thursday, November 15, 1906." In "Elswick Shipyard Reports Books Nos. 1 and 2, 1883–1913," VA, Doc. 1158.
[107] Wise, *Royal Navy*, p. 35.
[108] Falkner to S. Rendel, No. 31/3727, "Elswick Papers 18, Letters January – December 1908." TWA, 31/3700–3733.
[109] Topliss, "Brazilian," p. 254.
[110] Morgan, *Legacy*, pp. 153 and 180–88; "The New," pp. 214–16.
[111] *New York Times*, April 20, 1909.
[112] Brook, *Warships*, p. 194.

Argentina was buying. The price was around £20 million and d'Eyncourt was central to the negotiations.[113] Albert Vickers asked Noble "if you will be good enough to place the engines with us as for the other two ships."[114]

The year 1910 saw Vickers working with their accountants to finalize the distribution of profits on the Brazilian orders of 1908. By January Armstrongs had not shared the total profit figure for the *Minas Gerais* and the likely profits on the *São Paulo* were also unknown. It is unclear from the correspondence if Vickers thought Armstrongs were merely being inefficient or if there were other motives.[115] In August 1910 Vickers London headquarters were questioning Barrow as to what had been agreed about costs and profits on this Brazilian work. They were preparing for a meeting with Armstrongs to negotiate "an equitable arrangement" for dividing the profits. London asked: "Have we ever made a firm quotation to them for the construction of the Machinery of the 'Minas Geraes', or was it simply arranged verbally with Mr. Perrett, Mr. McKechnie and Mr. Dunn, and a profit price of £270,000 given Mr. Perrett as the approximate figure?"[116] The meeting did not solve the issue and this "murky profit-sharing agreement" was wrangled over for many subsequent years.[117]

In 1908 Armstrongs launched two 1,000-ton armored river gunboats for Argentina, the Perrett-designed *Rosario* and *Parana*.[118] Argentina now responded to Brazil's move into dreadnoughts by setting up a competition for two innovative battleships, with an option for a third. Armstrongs were invited to tender for the *Rivadavia* and *Moreno* contracts.[119] Initially the hub for the competition was London, with a Naval Commission under Admirals Garcia and Lagos traveling to Europe in January 1909, but it later shifted to Buenos Aires.

In 1908 d'Eyncourt traveled to Argentina for Armstrongs. The firm faced fierce competition for the dreadnought order, with more than thirty firms from seven countries submitting bids.[120] He recalled that "there was strong competition for the order between my own firm and a United States firm that was well backed by the U.S. Government."[121] The competition for the battleship contract was protracted, eventually involving sixty-seven individual tenders for the warships.[122] The President of Newport News Shipbuilding complained that "The political influence of foreign powers is being exerted in a very forceful

---

113 Bastable, *Arms*, p. 114.
114 Albert Vickers to Noble, November 19, 1909. VA Doc. 1005, Folio 30.
115 Caillard to Peat, January 25, 1910. Letter Book 31, VA Doc. 1005, Folios 251–53.
116 Vickers to Directors at Barrow, Strictly Confidential, August 11, 1910. Letter Book No. 32. VA, Doc. 1006, Folio 143.
117 Morgan, *Legacy*, p. 175.
118 Brook, *Warships*, p. 41.
119 Lillicrap, "Eustace," p. 342.
120 Livermore, "Battleship," p. 35; "Argentine," pp. 234–35.
121 d'Eyncourt, *Shipbuilder's*, p. 52.
122 Wise, *Royal Navy*, p. 36.

manner … the King of Italy, the German Emperor, and the force of British diplomacy are being made use of."[123] As intended, this provoked the U.S. Government to support American firms, offering Argentina access to high-technology torpedo tubes, a fire-control system and various other sweeteners designed to secure the deal.[124] There was pro-American sentiment in the prominent newspaper *La Prensa*, which gleefully reported that the British-leaning Naval Commission had requested bribes from one of the British firms bidding on a torpedo contract.[125] Although the bribes were not paid, this damaged all the British firms bidding on Argentinian naval contracts and weakened the standing of the Naval Commission.

Another source of concern for Armstrongs and the British Government was the Argentinian approach to tendering. They ran several rounds to select and combine the best features offered by firms, which then became the basis for the next round and were shared with other bidders. Britain was concerned that this meant a loss of both Admiralty and private firm technologies and knowledge to foreign rivals.[126]

There were so many changes to the tenders that d'Eyncourt had to return to Newcastle to consult with the Board. In 1909, only a few days after he returned to Buenos Aires and submitted the new designs, it was announced that Massachusetts' Fore River Shipbuilding Company had won the contract. For d'Eyncourt, "After all the trouble and expense of the prolonged efforts my firm and I had made, this was a depressing … disappointment to me."[127] Fore River Shipbuilding agreed a total price of £2,200,000 (£291,061,152 in August 2022), saving Argentina £224,000 (£31,752,126 in August 2022) on each ship.[128] In the *Times* a British shipbuilder explained the reason for the American firm's low tender – £78.3 per ton compared to Armstrong's £87.4 per ton: The firm was "hungry for work," lacking domestic orders. By contrast, "on the other side were two British firms already in possession of large orders from the British Admiralty and Brazil, and secure in their expectation of further large and profitable orders … in view of the coming enlargement of British shipbuilding programmes."[129] This sanguine view of Armstrongs' prospects is belied by the efforts the firm devoted to the competition.

Argentina then requested that Vickers assist in the creation and financing of a dry dock and repair facility at La Plata. Albert's response reveals the firm's pique:

[123] Livermore, "Battleship," p. 35. Citing Orcutt to McHarg, July 21, 1909, State Department File Argentina.
[124] Scheina, *Latin America*, p. 83.
[125] Livermore, "Battleship," p. 36.
[126] Scheina, *Latin America*, pp. 82–84.
[127] d'Eyncourt, *Shipbuilder's*, p. 54.
[128] Scheina, *Latin America*, p. 83.
[129] Platt, *Latin America*, p. 205. Citing *The Times*, Engineering Supplement, February 16, 1910, p. 13 b, c.

> You are no doubt aware of the great disappointment occasioned in this country through the order for the two Argentine battleships having just been placed in the United States, and partly this feeling and partly the fact that an undertaking such as proposed does not appeal to the general public here but more especially to special firms connected with the work in question render it advisable not to reckon on any British financial cooperation.[130]

In 1908 Brazil sought to cancel the third dreadnought order with Armstrongs as her economic position had weakened and as Argentina had made overtures (via Rothschilds) to her to avoid a dreadnought race between them. Rothschilds now acted as "honest broker" between state and firm, Alfred Rothschild eventually convening a meeting between Saxton Noble and John Meade Falkner of Armstrongs, and Leopold and Neuman of the Brazilian Government. A compromise was agreed, postponing the dreadnought building for three years. However, this was rejected by the Armstrongs Board, spearheaded by an angry Lord Stuart Rendel.[131] Ten months later Brazil again asked to postpone the third battleship, because of fresh economic problems.

Brazil took delivery of the two dreadnoughts in 1910 and the arms race in South America intensified. Chile put out a tender for two dreadnoughts. Jon Wise recounts: "The tendering process for the ship was again intense and accompanied by accusations of the use of unfair practices by the British."[132] American Lieutenant Commander Neely complained that "there was being carried out in Chilean newspapers systematic propaganda against American naval materials …. In frequent editions of these newspapers, an attack on our powder, guns, or other material was given prominent place."[133] Armstrongs won the order. Lord Rothschild, financial agent for Chile, wrote to First Lord Winston Churchill:

> [I]t must be self-evident to all that should unfortunately war break out while ships of this calibre are being built or are near completion in English shipyards, the English Government would in such untoward circumstances be able to purchase these ships and thus replenish their Navy; that is, I believe, one of the chief reasons why both the American and German Governments are anxious to secure these contracts.[134]

The Chilean dreadnoughts *Almirante Lattore* and *Almirante Cochrane*, laid down in 1911 and 1913, respectively, were still under construction in 1914 when war began. As predicted by Lord Rothschild, the British Government commandeered

---

[130] Albert Vickers to Marcus Agrelo, May 12, 1910. Letter Book No. 32, May 12. VA, Doc. 1006, Folio 1.

[131] Topliss, "Brazilian," p. 248.

[132] Wise, *Royal Navy*, p. 37.

[133] Scheina, *Latin America*, p. 84. Citing General Correspondence of the Secretary of the Navy, letter from U.S. Secretary of State to U.S. Secretary of the Navy, November 28, 1911, enclosure 1 of 5, November 1911, p. 4.

[134] G. Miller, *Straits*, p. 220. Citing Lord Rothschild to Churchill, May 8, 1912. *Winston Spencer Churchill Comp.* II, pt. iii, pp. 1549–50.

them; they became HMS *Canada* and HMS *Eagle*. The Admiralty also took over two Chilean destroyers, "the *Lynch* and *Condell*. They are the largest of their class in the world, displacing 1,850 tons, and on trial have done over 32 knots. They are armed with six 4in. guns and three 18in. torpedo tubes."[135] The British compensated Chile with five Holland torpedo boats in 1917 and by returning a modernized *Almirante Lattore* in 1920 (her crew immediately participated in a mutiny).[136]

In early August 1910 d'Eyncourt returned to Brazil to try to complete the promised third dreadnought order, but now German firms were competing for the contract. For d'Eyncourt, "The negotiations … were slow and uncertain, and the original design I submitted had to be modified on the spot many times."[137] Part of the problem d'Eyncourt faced was a disagreement between the Minister of Marine in Rio and Admiral Bacellar in Newcastle.[138] The negotiations and design changes took several months, with d'Eyncourt changing the size, number and arrangement of the ship's guns to see off the German challenge. Clive Trebilcock records: "The contract … was landed by d'Eyencourt's ability to redesign her on the spot as the largest warship of the pre-1914 world, outbidding entirely the Kaiser's personal protest that not even the Imperial Navy, let alone the *Brazilian* navy, needed leviathans of these proportions."[139] As d'Eyncourt recorded, "this carried the day and we were given the order, which it gave me enormous satisfaction to cable home to Armstrongs."[140] The contract, worth £2,864,000 (£374,961,734 in August 2022), was signed in October 1910.[141] While Armstrongs secured the order, Brazil never received the ship.

Work was begun on the *Rio de Janeiro* in 1910 but was repeatedly held up by political, financial and technological issues. In politics, the "Revolt of the Lash" mutiny broke out over the Brazilian navy's use of corporal punishment and general mistreatment of personnel.[142] Sailors aboard the two new dreadnoughts rebelled and killed the captain of the *Minas Gerais*, among others.[143] The rebels were joined by the crews of the *Bahia* and *São Paulo*.[144] The *Minas Gerais* (with eighteen British engineers continuing to man the engines) threatened to fire on Rio, a potent threat given the powerful guns on the new ship, and eventually did so. Ironically, d'Eyncourt was in the city at the time and reported later that the guns had done "a great deal of damage."[145] This dulled the government's

---

[135] "Ex-Foreign Warships," p. 6.
[136] Scheina, *Latin America*, pp. 85, 355, ff. 19; Brook, *Warships*, pp. 147–48.
[137] d'Eyncourt, *Shipbuilder's*, p. 58.
[138] Topliss, "Brazilian," p. 256.
[139] Trebilcock, *Vickers Brothers*, p. 127. Emphasis in original.
[140] d'Eyncourt, *A Shipbuilder's*, p. 58.
[141] Topliss, "Brazilian," p. 257.
[142] Morgan, *Legacy*, p. 209.
[143] Scheina, *Latin America*, p. 81.
[144] Brook, *Warships*, p. 195.
[145] d'Eyncourt, *Shipbuilder's*, p. 160.

enthusiasm for dreadnoughts. In economics, the collapse of coffee and rubber prices, and the general economic downturn meant that Brazil missed some installments and Armstrongs suspended work on the *Rio de Janeiro*. Also, the Foreign Office denied Brazil's request for a loan.[146] Technologically, the specifications from Brazil changed several times, and each new demand led to time-consuming design revisions and a new laying-down. The size of warships and guns was growing so fast that Brazil eventually realized the third ship would be obsolete before it was delivered. According to d'Eyncourt, the *Rio de Janeiro* "began her wavering career when she was not more than half completed, at which point for some obscure reason the Brazilians sold her."[147] Rothschilds oversaw the sale. After a scuffle between European powers eager to buy her, the ship was sold to Turkey in December 1913 and became the *Sultan Osman*. It was never delivered, being commandeered in 1914 and becoming HMS *Agincourt*.[148]

Brazil subsequently ordered an even larger dreadnought, the *Riachuelo*, from Armstrongs, along with two corvettes.[149] The *Riachuelo* was to be 30,000 tons and to mount 15-inch guns.[150] However, the ship had to be canceled before it was laid down as Brazil could not afford it. This enabled Argentina to set aside her plans for a third dreadnought, quelling the arms race.[151] This was bad news for Armstrongs and Vickers. Nevertheless, "the Argentine, Brazilian, and Chilean dreadnoughts took their place among the most powerful ships in the world and often excited the envy of other navies, including those of the builders."[152]

Vickers sought other sales, with mixed success. In 1910–11 she offered Ecuador a 3,650-ton cruiser with two submerged torpedo tubes and twenty-two guns of various dimensions. However, Ecuador bought nothing.[153] Around the same time Vickers prepared a run of four protected cruiser designs for Peru, eventually building the *Almirante Grau* class. Peru was then considering more ships, and Vickers prepared a new protected cruiser design (designated 371). However, Peru settled on second-hand warships instead.[154] The Argentinian market was also difficult for Vickers. They contacted their agents in Buenos Aires in May 1912 about a potential sale, explaining:

> At the last moment French financiers and industrialists have withdrawn from concession arrangements. We have immediately taken up the matter with financiers in London and there is a possibility of success. In the

146 Platt, *Finance*, p. 20
147 Morgan, *Legacy*, p. 175.
148 Brook, *Warships*, p. 140.
149 "Brazilian Battleship," p. 14.
150 Scheina, *Latin America*, p. 82.
151 Scheina, *Latin America*, p. 354, ff. 10.
152 Scheina, *Latin America*, p. 85.
153 Friedman, *British Cruisers*, p. 272.
154 Idem.

meantime, if absolutely necessary we authorize you to sign a contract with the Government provided our liability in the event of failure is limited to our guarantee deposit.[155]

With the finance in question no sales were forthcoming.

Vickers did secure a contract with Brazil to build three George Thurston-designed monitors, the *Javary*, *Solimoes* and *Madeira*. In 1914, when the monitors were ready for delivery, they were commandeered by the British Government, becoming HMS *Severn*, *Mersey*, and *Humber*.[156] After Brazil declared war on Germany, she received British and U.S. naval missions and significant U.S. help in making her fleet battle-ready. Both the *São Paulo* and *Minas Gerais* were overhauled at U.S. expense, enabling the Americans to evaluate British equipment.[157]

The onset of war in Europe had ended British financing to Latin America. British Government controls on all exports and attempts to marginalize the German businesses in Latin America "aroused considerable resentment in the region."[158] This, and Britain's weakness at war's end, left the region ripe for increased American influence. Nevertheless, London "resented US attempts to hinder the De Brunsen Mission, which was despatched in 1918 to rebuild Britain's commercial relations with South America."[159] The "temporary" withdrawal of the Royal Navy's South American Squadron in spring 1921, "dictated by financial stringency," signaled Britain's weakness.[160] The deposing of Britain as a major financial and trading power in the region made the task of selling armaments even more challenging for Armstrongs and Vickers. The Brazilians dispensed with their British naval mission in 1922, while ties with the United States strengthened. Nevertheless, neither power would supply Brazil with the warships she wanted – acquisitions that would allow her to match Argentina's from Italy – citing Article 18 of the 1922 Washington Naval Treaty.[161]

While a few aircraft sales were made, including nineteen Vickers' Vixen Vs to Chile, naval business was hit because Latin American states were reluctant to accept the ships authorized for sale under the Treaty, as they were not top-of-the-line warships.[162] The Foreign Office was so committed to the Naval Treaty that they would not even supply Chile with ships set to be scrapped (Chile offered Easter Island in exchange), despite the pleas of Chargé d'Affaires John Cecil Sterndale Bennett in the Santiago Embassy that the "Present moment

[155] Vickers to Percy Grant and Co., Coded Telegram May 21, 1912. Letter Book 14, VA, Doc. 1011, Folios 87–88.
[156] "Obituary: Sir George Thurston," p. 153.
[157] Scheina, *Latin America*, p. 134.
[158] Miller, *Britain*, p. 182.
[159] Miller, *Britain*, p. 184.
[160] Memorandum for the Board, "South America – British Naval Policy," TNA ADM 167/76.
[161] Wise, *Royal Navy*, p. 110.
[162] Andrews and Morgan, *Vickers Aircraft*, pp. 8–9.

is exceptionally favourable for consolidating British influence here."[163] The Foreign Office held firm.[164]

According to Seward Livermore, in the period 1905–25, "The competition for the business was fierce and unscrupulous. The European firms of established reputation had the support of their respective governments, which never hesitated to exert diplomatic pressure to influence the award of contracts to their own nationals."[165] However, the British Government was heavily criticized by British firms for failing to do just that. British armaments sales to the region became rare because of the indebtedness of many Latin American countries and the strong international competition for orders. For example, a Brazilian submarine order which Vickers-Armstrongs sought went to Italy as the firm could not match Ansaldo's price.[166] In Peru, U.S. diplomats "protested successfully against an armaments contract with Vickers."[167] British Diplomatic Service reluctance to support British companies once again came under fire after a trade mission headed by Viscount d'Abernon visited the region in 1929.[168] In the interwar years armament firms were seeking to diversify production, so there were also attempts to supply non-military goods to the region.[169]

In 1926 Argentina passed the Naval Procurement Act, which authorized the spending of £15 million. The lion's share went to Spanish and Italian firms, with few orders for Vickers-Armstrongs. Did diplomatic disputes hinder the firm in the Argentine competition? Wise concluded that "There is no hard evidence to suggest that diplomatic tensions between Britain and Argentina worked directly against the fortunes of British shipbuilding firms at this time." Indeed, he noted that the British Government refrained from protesting Argentina's establishment of a wireless station on the disputed Laurie Island until the Director of Naval Intelligence confirmed that British firms were unlikely to secure a major part of the Argentinian naval program.[170]

Despite the difficult market conditions, in 1926 d'Eyncourt went back to South America for Armstrongs, visiting Peru, Chile, Brazil and Paraguay. Sailing to New York, d'Eyncourt met his old friend, Major Ivo Crawford, an ambassador-agent for Vickers, and they traveled to Peru together. There they met the British Minister Lord Hervey, who "was very popular locally, and most

---

[163] Bennett telegram to Vansittart, June 24, 1926. "Purchase of War Vessels by Chilean Government," June 24, 1926. TNA, FO 371/11122; Bennett to Vansittart, June 24, 1926. TNA, FO 371/11122.

[164] Vansittart to Bennett, July 26, 1926. TNA, FO 371/11122.

[165] Livermore, "Battleship," p. 31.

[166] Wise, *Royal Navy*, p. 110.

[167] Miller, *Britain*, p. 192.

[168] Department of Overseas Trade, *Report*, p. 7.

[169] See the *Armstrong Whitworth Record*, Spring 1930. TWA, D/VA/65/1.

[170] Wise, *Royal Navy*, pp. 95–96.

helpful in putting us in touch with the necessary authorities."[171] While enjoy-
able, the trip did not yield much business for Armstrongs, but d'Eyncourt and
the firm valued maintaining relations with statesmen in the region.

Vickers had more luck. While in Peru, Major Crawford got wind of potential
sales in Bolivia, and set off for La Paz, where he cooperated with Mr. O'Malley
Davis, "a Financial Agent already in touch with the Bolivian Government."
According to Vickers' submissions to the Bankes Commission, "During the
discussions in La Paz Major Crawford had meetings with the President, Chief
of General Staff, Minister of Finance, Minister of War and Members of the
Cabinet. Certain of these meetings were attended by the British Minister in
La Paz."[172] The relationship between the firm and the British Government had
clearly evolved; now the Diplomatic Service was assisting British armament
firms in their search for sales.

In May 1927 O'Malley Davis became the Bolivian ambassador-agent for
Vickers, at a 2.5 percent commission rate on the first deal and for any further
orders for the next eight years. He hosted many Vickers officials over the subsequent months and years. O'Malley Davis and Major Crawford eventually
secured Bolivian gun orders for Vickers-Armstrongs: "The original contract
called for the supply of Gas Shells, but we intimated our inability to supply on
the grounds that the use of asphyxiating gases was prohibited by international
law."[173] Unusually, the contract stipulated that the goods should be shipped out
under the British flag, in order to protect them under international law if they
were seized. This was because Britain might embargo Bolivia.

In early 1926 the Foreign Office and Department of Overseas Trade found
themselves involved in efforts to induce Armstrongs, Vickers and Beardmores
to work together in Chile, at the request of the Ambassador there. Vickers confirmed that they were asking their agents to work with Armstrongs' agents.[174]
From the start, Beardmores was the least cooperative – which is ironic given its
involvement with Vickers – with their agent in Santiago declaring that cooperation was "impossible."[175] Later, the British Government sought to induce them
to also work with Yarrows.[176] Vickers replied positively to the suggestion.[177]
Among the possible sales were submarines, though Vickers was interested in
marketing aviation too.[178] However, by August the Chilean Minister of Marine

[171] d'Eyncourt, *Shipbuilder's*, p. 158.
[172] "Embargo: List of orders we could have accepted from the Bolivian Authorities if the
     embargo had not been enforced," Evidence Prepared for the Bankes Commission, VA,
     Doc. 58, Folder 102, Folios 2 and 3.
[173] "Embargo," Folio 8.
[174] Dawson to Department of Overseas Trade, December 31, 1925. TNA, FO 371/11122.
[175] Foreign Office memorandum, January 19, 1926. TNA, FO 371/11122.
[176] Crowe to L. I. G. Leveson of Vickers, March 27, 1926. TNA, FO 371/11122.
[177] Leveson to Crowe, March 30, 1926. TNA, FO 371/11122.
[178] For example, Captain Broom of the Aviation department travelled out in the summer of 1926.
     "South America: Proposed Visit of Captain Broom," August 13, 1926. VA, Microfilm R 286.

was reporting that the plans were "in abeyance" due to economic problems.[179] When the situation improved, Chile accepted tenders for the boats, and the Cammell Laird tender was far lower than any other offer. Nevertheless, Vickers got the sale.

This anomaly was focused on by the 1934 U.S. Nye Committee as an example of inflated prices, thanks to correspondence between Craven and Spear of Electric Boat. Vickers' response to the allegation at the Bankes Commission painted a different story, however. Craven explained:

> The reference to Chilean Submarines is in connection with a telegram received from our Agents informing us that Cammell Lairds had quoted very much below us. I accompanied Sir Trevor Dawson when he went to see Mr. Hitchens, the chairman of Cammell Lairds, who informed us that his Agent had given him our prices. When Sir Trevor divulged the figure we had quoted it was clear that the Agent had given him a figure very considerably below the price we had quoted and very considerably below the cost of production. Cammell Laird had assumed that if the price given by their Agent was good enough for us, it was good enough for them and they quoted a figure slightly below that price. On Sir Trevor Dawson showing Mr. Hitchens the actual figures, he at once saw that the Agent had misinformed him and withdrew his tender.[180]

Chile ordered six Vickers submarines (Electric Boat had passed the order to Vickers, as they were already building submarines for Peru). By 1928 Vickers had delivered three and a submarine depot ship, but had not yet been paid.[181] This, for Scott, is the explanation for Craven's words to Spear: "I am trying to ginger up the Chileans to take three more boats."[182]

Vickers was involved in a long-running competition to sell submarines to Brazil. This brought her into conflict with Electric Boat, her erstwhile ally. Such was Electric Boat's desire to secure the sale, she offered Vickers an "interest in the Brazilian business if they would withdraw" their own bid.[183] Vickers refused and later competed for the contract against Cammell Lairds, though neither British firm secured the order.

In the 1920s all potential armaments sales had to be approved by the British Government. The Foreign Office valued naval treaties more than exports, thwarting the firms. For example, when Chile inquired about purchasing warships from British yards in the 1930s, the government was the major point of contact. Vickers-Armstrongs expected to be a strong contender and bid on two 8,000-ton cruisers with twelve 6-inch guns. Within the government, the Board

---

[179] Bennett to Sir Austen Chamberlain, August 24, 1926. TNA, FO 371/11122.

[180] Re: Exhibit 125, p. 405. "Replies to American Enquiry Exhibits – Sir Charles Craven," VA, Doc. 58, Folder 118, p. 5.

[181] "A New Submarine"; "Almirante Simpson"; "With the Church's."

[182] Scott, *Vickers*, p. 244. Citing Nye Commission, Craven to Spear, 1928.

[183] United States Senate, "Report," p. 233.

of Trade, the Admiralty and Ambassador Cavendish-Bentinck in Buenos Aires were loath to lose these sales, but the Foreign Office's interest in naval arms control prevailed and the sales were blocked.[184] This was extremely disappointing to Vickers-Armstrongs, who were concerned about their future relationship with Chile. The Foreign Office worked to ensure that the other Treaty signatories would not build Chile cruisers. The Admiralty suggested to Chile that a Treaty-compliant Fuji-class cruiser with a 6-inch gun would meet their needs, but Santiago was unconvinced.[185] In the end, the onset of World War Two forced Chile to shelve her acquisition plans.

Vickers-Armstrongs' (British & Foreign) Army Sales Committee had been informed in early 1928 that "Both Schneider and Skoda have obtained trial orders for a Battery of artillery in Argentina, and we have not."[186] These were dark times for Vickers-Armstrongs, which was newly amalgamated and experiencing terrible troubles in armament development, production and marketing. Birch informed the Army Sales Committee that he was deeply troubled by the lack of Latin American artillery orders on the firm's books and "considered that we must make a desperate push to get orders from South America." Birch twice interviewed their ambassador-agent Brig.-General Guy Livingstone and "was entirely dissatisfied with the situation in South America as far as Army sales were concerned," concluding that Livingstone needed to be replaced.[187] The Executive Committee therefore approved the dispatch of Colonel Kinsman on a "special mission to Argentina to follow up diplomatic and financial pressure, and to Uruguay where he [Birch] considered that orders were possible. Light equipment would be offered for sale in each case. He feared, however, that we were too late in Argentina."[188] The Foreign Office confirmed in April that the French had obtained an artillery order from Argentina, but it was decided that Col. Kinsman "should proceed to South America to prepare the ground for future orders, especially with regard to Tanks and Armoured Cars, etc."[189]

The British Government was increasingly aware of how valuable exports were to maintaining a defense industrial base. Thus, in February 1928, when Argentina and Uruguay declared their intention to update their artillery, the Foreign Office proactively reached out to General Sir Noel Birch

> to enquire whether you would desire this department to telegraph, at your expense, to His Majesty's Representatives at Buenos Aires and Montevideo requesting them to inform the Argentine and Uruguayan Governments of

[184] "Cruisers for Chile: enquiries and proposals," 1936–38. TNA, ADM 116/3920.
[185] Wise, *Royal Navy*, p. 102.
[186] Minutes of the (British and Foreign) Army Sales Committee, January 19, 1928. VA, Microfilm R 286.
[187] Minutes of (British and Foreign) Army Sales Committee, January 27, 1928, p. 1. VA, Microfilm R 286.
[188] Minutes of Army Sales Committee, February 24, 1928. VA, Microfilm R 286.
[189] Minutes of Army Sales Committee, April 2 and 3, 1928, p. 3. VA, Microfilm R 286.

Messrs. Vickers competence to undertake the manufacture of guns of any caliber and to take any action possible in order that Vickers-Armstrong may be invited to tender for the works in question.[190]

The Foreign Office's belief in export controls was obviously limited to naval orders.

Vickers-Armstrongs' production problems affected business with Bolivia. Birch subsequently referred to "the disaster of the Bolivian equipment," where the order was very late and the guns were not adequately tested before export.[191] When Bolivia eventually got the guns, they did not work well. Nor did the Škoda guns supplied in substitution. Under the Hayes Agreement Vickers-Armstrongs had to pay all the modification costs and sent out Major Briggs to oversee the work. Even after this, there was "another unfortunate occurrence from Bolivia in connection with Breech mechanisms," where the tripping piece was fracturing. Retrospectively the same problem was discovered at Erith.[192]

Vickers-Armstrongs also struggled with a Bolivian contract for vehicles mounted with 75 mm field and mountain batteries. Bolivia resisted Vickers-Armstrongs' attempts to reduce the number of vehicles, saying that any change to the contract would have to be dealt with through the Bolivian courts. Vickers-Armstrongs decided to stick with the initial contract.[193] In January 1929 Birch wrote to Craven: "Please give the Bolivian order your earliest and immediate attention, as you and only you know where and how the ginger can be applied. From what I can make out the Drawing Office is terribly behind …. The Bolivians are urging delivery and all the works can do is to promise six or seven months."[194]

In 1928 Vickers was also experiencing difficulties securing a cruiser sale to Peru. As Birch recorded: "It is well to note that an American Naval Mission lives in Peru, and so they are in an advantageous position as far as getting orders is concerned."[195] The British Embassy suggested that Vickers-Armstrongs may have offered bribes.[196] However, when the case was discussed at the Nye Committee, it became apparent that the bribes had been requested by an American officer. Notwithstanding, it was intimated that Vickers-Armstrongs was prepared to go to great lengths to win Peruvian sales.

In September 1929 General Dias, the Inspector-General of the Chilean army, was due to visit the Vickers-Armstrongs factories at Erith. Birch declared:

---

[190] Foreign Office to Birch, February 28, 1928. VA, Microfilm R 286.
[191] Birch to Wilson, November 21, 1929. VA, Microfilm R 286.
[192] Wilson to Birch, June 3, 1930, p. 2. VA, Microfilm R 286.
[193] Minutes of (British and Foreign) Army Sales Committee, January 27, 1928, p. 2. VA, Microfilm R 286.
[194] Birch to Craven, January 10, 1929, and Birch to Craven, February 26, 1929. VA, Microfilm K 613.
[195] Birch to Taylor and Sim, January 26, 1928. VA, Microfilm R 286.
[196] "Vickers Armstrong, Ltd. Contract for Construction of Destroyers," 1928. TNA, FO 177/481.

I want you to make his visit as impressive as possible. I thought perhaps you could meet us at the drawing office, or send somebody to meet us there, spend about half an hour there, and then go to see the machine guns being manufactured. The more work there is going on in the shop the better. We have a telegram from Colonel Kinsman this morning saying that our prospects of getting the Vickers Machine Gun accepted for Chile are good, so we want to impress this fellow as much as we can.[197]

The result was a contract for an air-cooled machine gun, which was produced quickly leading to praise for Erith: "[M]y appreciation of the excellent results achieved, which have got the firm out of a serious difficulty and which will undoubtedly redound to our credit throughout South America, one of our most important markets."[198] The gun had another important impact; walking through the Erith works with the Chilean delegation, a British Army official saw the gun and was interested in it for use on armored fighting vehicles. Subsequently a deputation from the Directory of Mechanization came to see the machine gun in action.[199]

In February 1930 the first Argentine military mission in six years visited Barrow.[200] During the visit the mission was able to examine some equipment headed to the War Office.[201] In 1930 there was to be a big exhibition in Buenos Aires, and Birch was keen that Vickers-Armstrongs put on a really strong showing: "I think the importance of this exhibition is enormous, and we should spend every penny necessary to make it a great success." Birch pondered the implications of a change in government in Britain: "[T]he big question [that] will arise over this exhibition [is] whether the Labour Party, if in power, which I hope to God they won't be, will let us export for it."[202] Securing armaments sales to the region remained very challenging. In 1932, the British Ambassador in Chile wrote:

Things are rotten out here and for the moment there is nothing we can do for you. We haven't got the Chileans to pay for what has already been bought, and they certainly can't afford to order anything else. It has been a hard year and I am worn out with protests and requests. It's like banging one's head against a brick wall.[203]

During the 1930s Vickers-Armstrongs sought to strengthen their relationship with Colombia. Minister Senor Don Alfonso Lopez visited the Weybridge

[197] Birch to Wilson, September 17, 1929. VA, Microfilm R 286.
[198] Neilson to Wilson, October 29, 1930. VA, Microfilm R 286.
[199] Demonstration of Vickers 7 mm Air-cooled Land Service Gun (Chilean type), July 15, 1931. VA, Microfilm R 286.
[200] Craven to Birch, January 18, 1930. VA, Microfilm K 613.
[201] Birch to Craven, February 19, 1930. VA, Microfilm K 613.
[202] Birch to Craven, July 6, 1929. VA, Microfilm K 613.
[203] Davenport-Hines, "The British Marketing," p. 168. Citing Sir Henry Chilton to Bridge, February 1932, VA, Microfilm R 310. Microfilm is missing from the Archive.

works in October 1932.[204] Lopez was interested in building up Colombian aviation after the initiation of war by Peru, and "General Caddell is, therefore, preparing a scheme for the organisation of a small Air Force with Repair and Maintenance Depots." Lopez was also interested in anti-aircraft guns and wanted Vickers to quote.[205] The Minister was given a tour of the Crayford works later that month, and the firm submitted to him quotes on Victoria and Virginia aircraft.[206] No sales resulted. Two years later two engineers and two Colombian army officers visited the Chertsey works to examine tractors and tanks.[207]

In pursuit of naval orders, Vickers-Armstrongs' ambassador-agent Mr. Leveson traveled to Bogotá in May 1934. He was assisted by Vickers-Armstrongs' local ambassador-agent, Captain Fanning. While it was easy for Leveson and Fanning to meet the President and the President-elect, the Minister of War was more elusive. T. J. Anderson, the Commercial Secretary at the British Embassy, eventually arranged it. Leveson concluded that the firm would not get orders for aircraft sales (the Americans had cornered the market) or riverboats (as Vickers' models were too big, though Yarrow might get a sale), but there were possibilities in seagoing vessels and army material.[208] The Americans and Škoda were offering partial financing of their orders. Leveson recorded: "I said unfortunately we were manufacturers and had no financial support from our Government but would look into the question."[209] He returned from Colombia hopeful about ship orders, but noted: "After carefully considering the many factors in the case I have come to the conclusion that Captain Fanning is not a good Agent for us and not likely to get many orders."[210] In 1937 a delegation of cadets from Colombia visited the Crayford works, focusing their visit on fire control and machine guns.[211] However, by this point Colombia was turning to Germany for armaments.

Major Briggs was in Bolivia in June 1934 when Britain imposed an embargo on both Bolivia and Paraguay. According to Vickers-Armstrongs, the embargo "at first … concerned more particularly the issue of new licences, and we actually made shipments up to and including July 1934 on existing licences which up to that time had not been withdrawn."[212] Vickers was defending itself against charges that they had broken British policy in supplying arms to Bolivia.

[204] Representatives report by G. Sinclair, October 17, 1932. VA, Microfilm K 613.
[205] Sinclair to Yapp, October 17, 1932. VA, Microfilm K 613.
[206] "Visit of Colombian Minister to Crayford Works," October 17, 1932. VA, Microfilm K 613.
[207] Representatives report of Kinsman, March 27, 1934. VA, Microfilm K 613.
[208] Leveson to Vickers-Armstrongs, April 28, 1934. VA, Microfilm K 613.
[209] Leveson, "Colombia: Second Report," May 4, 1934. VA, Microfilm K 613.
[210] Leveson, "Colombia: Notes Re Agency to Accompany Third Report." VA, Microfilm K 613.
[211] Representatives report of G. M. Clunes, January 13, 1937. VA, Microfilm K 613.
[212] "Embargo," Folios 6 and 8.

The issue hinged on whether the embargo covered just new licenses or existing ones; Vickers-Armstrongs clearly interpreted this question as covering the former, their opponents the latter.

At the Nye Committee hearings, Senator Bone remarked negatively on European firms' use of women and their lack of ethics, to which Alfred Miranda of the American Armament Corporation replied: "They go out after the business and if there is a certain way in which these people expect to do business, they just cater to it."[213] Vickers-Armstrongs' activities in Latin America were exposed in a most unflattering light. For example, a letter from Craven said: "During the last few days by skillful manoeuvering we have managed to get some of our competitors' prices in the Chilean competition put up, and so may have prevented a real price-cutting war which would have resulted in our taking the boats at a loss."[214] Vickers-Armstrongs tried to hold its corner though, informing the Royal Commission that it had lost many potential Bolivian sales due to the British arms embargo of June 1934.[215] Nevertheless, the image of the firm was now tarnished in Britain and America.

In 1932 Vickers-Armstrongs supplied Brazil with the training ship *Almirante Saldanah* for £316,000.[216] Brazil also sought to purchase cruisers from either Britain or America, but both refused on the grounds that they were signatories to the Washington Naval Treaty. In 1936, recognizing the Treaty's constraints, Brazil ordered six slightly modified H-class destroyers, two to be built by Vickers-Armstrongs.[217] Unfortunately for Brazil, the ships were commandeered by Britain at the onset of war. The *Jurua* and *Japura* became HMS *Harvester* and HMS *Hurricane*.

In 1935 Vickers-Armstrongs won an Argentinian tender for a light cruiser for training, *La Argentina*. Although it was launched in 1936, completion was delayed by two years due to Vickers-Armstrong being pressured to prioritize Admiralty rearmament programs.[218] A consortium of John Browns, Cammell Lairds and Vickers-Armstrongs won Argentinian contracts for seven modified G-class destroyers. All were launched and commissioned in 1937–38 despite the pressures of British rearmament.

From the mid-1930s Chile was seeking a cruiser. There were extensive discussions between the Chilean navy, the British Embassy in Santiago, the Foreign Office and the Admiralty over this. John Browns and Vickers-Armstrongs were pursuing the contracts, but by 1937 only Vickers-Armstrongs had put

[213] Nye Committee Hearings, Part 3. September 10, 1934, p. 649.
[214] Nye Commission, Exhibit No. 125. Also cited in the House of Lords, *Hansard*, March 27, 1935, Vol. 96, Col. 375.
[215] Evidence Prepared for the Bankes Commission, VA, Doc. 58, Folder 102.
[216] Buxton and Johnston, *Battleship Builders*, p. 40.
[217] Wise, *Royal Navy*, p. 111.
[218] Wise, *Royal Navy*, p. 98.

in a provisional tender.[219] The firm was largely a bystander to the negotiations within and between governments, but several times provided the British authorities with information on the status of the deal in Santiago.[220] The Admiralty supported Vickers-Armstrongs, suggesting the firm be permitted to bid on the contract in anticipation that the "cruiser holiday" of the major naval powers would end. Should it remain in place, the Admiralty suggested that Vickers-Armstrongs could simply withdraw its bid. However, this was vetoed by the Foreign Office, which wanted to signal that the "cruiser holiday" should endure, did not wish to be seen to be breaking the spirit of that agreement and thought that a subsequent withdrawal of tender would be embarrassing.[221]

In March 1938 the Admiralty informed Vickers-Armstrongs that Chile was about to invite tenders for two 8,500-ton cruisers with 8-inch guns, but "My Lords desire that you should not submit a tender for these ships."[222] Britain was observing the restrictions of the unratified 1936 London Naval Treaty. Before ratification, Chile tried to persuade Britain to slip the order through, but the government would not. Britain tried to persuade Chile to buy 6,000-ton cruisers with 6-inch guns instead, but the Chilean navy wanted the larger vessels and guns, in part for prestige (to match Argentina) but also because their small navy needed the bigger guns for effective operations. Even after they had been refused the right to buy from Britain, the pro-British Chilean navy kept alive the idea of buying the cruisers from Britain.[223] Stephen Holmes in Ottawa secretly informed the Dominions Office in May 1938 that Canadian Vickers had been approached by Chile to construct two cruisers.[224] Dominion Office official Dixon inquired about the legality of Canada supplying the ships.[225] Subsequent inquiries by the Canadian High Commission revealed that Canadian Vickers had not quoted on any cruisers.[226]

The Foreign Office put pressure on Germany and Sweden to refuse Chilean requests for cruisers.[227] Nor did Britain want the vessels built by the Dutch or Finns, as it was clear that there was significant German involvement in their shipbuilding industries. Ideally the Foreign Office did not want Italy to

[219] Mitcheson, Commercial Secretary Santiago, to Secretary of State for Foreign Affairs, September 24,1937. "Cruisers for Chile: enquiries and proposals," TNA, ADM 116/3920.

[220] Yapp to Henderson, Controller of the Navy, April 7, 1938, enclosing Morrison to Yapp, March 31, 1938; Yapp to Henderson, June 10, 1938, enclosing Morrison, Santiago to Yapp, May 20, 1938. TNA, ADM 116/3920.

[221] Foreign Office to Admiralty, March 8, 1938. TNA, ADM 116/3920.

[222] Phillips, Admiralty to Messrs. Vickers-Armstrongs Ltd., March 29, 1938. TNA, ADM 116/3920.

[223] Bentinck, Santiago to Viscount Halifax, March 11, 1938. TNA, ADM 116/3920.

[224] "Extract from a secret letter from Mr. Holmes, Ottawa, to Mr. C. W. Dixon, Dominions Office, dated 4th May 1938." TNA, ADM 116/3920.

[225] Phillips, Admiralty to Dixon, June 3, 1938. TNA, ADM 116/3920.

[226] Mason to Dixon, Dominions Office, August 30, 1938. TNA, ADM 116/3920.

[227] Minute sheet No. 1, July 26, 1938. TNA, ADM 116/3920.

build either and sought to inculcate in them the spirit of the London Naval Treaty. When it looked likely that Finland or the Netherlands would get the contract, their shipyards began to contact British firms about supplying sub-components, for example, boilers from Yarrow. This was a dilemma for the government, as "we should … have no legal powers to prohibit the export of machinery etc. which would not come under the Arms Export Prohibition Order."[228] Vickers-Armstrongs replied to Chilean overtures: "[W]e regret to inform you that the provisions of the London Naval treaty of 1936, and other bilateral treaties, preclude us from making an offer for the supply of this arma-ment for cruisers to the displacement you refer to."[229] They provided this correspondence to the Controller of the British Navy.[230] Chile then enquired about having the Dutch build the cruisers, but buying the 8-inch armaments, ammunition and fire-control system from Vickers.[231] The issue rumbled on for three years. In January 1939 Chile requested British Export Credits to buy the cruisers. They were rebuffed. The Export Credits Guarantee Department in the Foreign Office had not allocated Chile any credits and armaments were explic-itly excluded from eligibility for support.[232]

British records show that Vickers-Armstrongs was refused several export licenses during this period. Vickers Aviation Ltd. was denied a license to sell six armed bombers to Brazil in November 1930 because "Brazil in a state of revolu-tion," and Vickers-Armstrongs' request to sell Bolivia spare parts for various machine guns and 75 mm guns, plus 100 new machine guns was refused in June 1934 due to "Participation … in the arms embargo against Bolivia and Paraguay."[233] Vickers-Armstrongs was, though, able to sell anti-aircraft guns and ammunition to Argentina and Peru in the 1930s.[234]

During World War Two there were no Vickers-Armstrongs sales to Latin America and relationships with the region languished. Postwar, Vickers-Armstrongs wanted to resume exporting armaments, but the market was now challenging, due to U.S. competition. Now the British Government and Vickers-Armstrongs were closely aligned, facing the common threat of U.S. attempts to exclude them from the market. The United States, now the more powerful nation, had ambitions for the standardization (i.e. Americanization)

---

[228] Minute sheet 1, October 17, 1938. TNA, ADM 116/3920.

[229] Yapp, Vickers-Armstrongs to Renard, Chargé d'Affaires, Chilean Embassy, July 22, 1938. TNA, ADM 116/3920.

[230] Yapp to Henderson, July 22, 1938. TNA, ADM 116/3920.

[231] Jones, Admiralty to Holman, Foreign Office, August 4, 1938. TNA, ADM 116/3920.

[232] Export Credits Guarantee Department to Foreign Office, January 24, 1939. TNA, ADM 116/3920.

[233] Board of Trade to Bankes Commission, November 18, 1935. "II Statement of Cases in Which Applications for Licenses to Export Have Been Refused with Reasons for Refusal during the Period 1st January 1929, to 30th September, 1935." "Armaments Export Con-trol, Board of Trade Memoranda, 1935." TNA T 181/34.

[234] Buxton and Johnston, *Battleship Builders*, p. 40.

of all training and equipment across Latin America in the name of hemispheric defense, through the Inter-American Military Cooperation Act.[235] Foreign Secretary Ernest Bevin reminded Secretary of State James Byrnes: "[A]bout a month ago, your Department approached our Embassy in Washington in connexion with the visit to Brazil of Mr. Levison [sic] of Vickers, and suggested we ought to renounce our old-established trade in armaments with the Latin American countries, because it might lead to an arms race, and would interfere with the orderly development of inter-American defence plans."[236] Clearly the marketing activities of the Vickers-Armstrongs ambassador-agent had triggered an American response. A subsequent British backgrounder explained: "The Americans asked us last December [1945], without suggesting any compensation, in effect to yield to them a monopoly on the Latin American arms market. We politely declined this suggestion."[237]

The British Government was interested in Venezuela, despite it being a military junta, recognizing its plentiful oil revenues. "The Navy had sent HMS *Corsair* to attend the anniversary celebrations of a long-forgotten Venezuelan general in February 1945, a ceremony not attended by US warships. This gesture was later acknowledged by the president."[238] While the Admiralty considered Venezuela's request for the loan of a destroyer, the Embassy in Washington reported that the United States was sending a naval mission to Venezuela, concentrating minds in the British Government.[239] U.S. objections were not what scuppered the destroyer deal, however. Shortages within the British Navy led them to prioritize their own needs. The Admiralty informed the Naval Attaché in Venezuela that "Technical difficulties now make it necessary to cancel the suggestion regarding loan of a destroyer tentatively made .... You should inform Venezuelan authorities accordingly and say that [the] Admiralty would be pleased to offer advice should they wish to consider placing an order for new construction with a building firm in the U.K."[240] The Venezuelans then sought the loan or sale of a frigate from the British Navy. A month later the attaché in Caracas was cabling that he was receiving "urgent enquiries from this end."[241] Negotiations proceeded haltingly over the loan of HMS *Odzani*.

---

[235] Hadow, British Embassy, Washington to Perowne, South American Department, Foreign Office. October 16, 1946. Ships for Venezuelan Government, 1946–49. TNA ADM 1/21140.

[236] Bevin to Byrnes, January 14, 1946. "American: South American 1946, General File No. 29." TNA, FO 371/52086.

[237] "Latin America: Supply of Armaments," October 12, 1946. Paper b, p. 1. "American: South American 1946, General File No. 29." TNA, FO 371/52086.

[238] Wise, *Royal Navy*, p. 121; "Contracts (25), Ships for Venezuela Government, 1946–49." TNA, ADM 1/21140; "Sale by Vickers Armstrong Ltd. Of two destroyers to Venezuela, 1950." TNA, FO 371/81813.

[239] Hadow to Perowne, October 16, 1946.

[240] Director of Naval Intelligence to Naval Attaché, Caracas, July 15, 1947. TNA ADM 1/21140.

[241] Note to Abercrombie, September 19, 1947; Caracas to DNI [Director of Naval Intelligence], October 15, 1947. TNA ADM 1/21140.

Then, in February 1948, Venezuelan attention shifted to a cruiser, HMS *Scylla*, but this too was stymied, leading to the Admiralty suggesting "that a similar ship might be built for Venezuela by, say, Vickers" as an idea "worth further consideration."[242]

The experiences of Vickers-Armstrongs in securing the Venezuelan naval deal were not unlike those with the British Government, involving many hold-ups and changes of fortune. From late 1946 Vickers-Armstrongs were pressing the British Government for decisions on whether they could supply armaments to Paraguay and Venezuela, informing the Ministry of Supply "that they may lose the business if a decision is not given in a reasonable time."[243] Nevertheless, it took them several years to secure a deal.

Vickers-Armstrongs strongly lobbied to sell two destroyers to Venezuela, supplying the Admiralty with drawings and asking in April 1948 for a decision on whether they would be licensed to construct the vessel.[244] In the summer of 1948 Vickers-Armstrongs' ambassador-agent Gordon Clunes secured an undertaking from the Venezuelan Minister of Defense that the firm would be invited to tender to construct a Dido-class cruiser; the invitation came in October 1948.[245] Vickers-Armstrongs again approached the Admiralty, asking if they would be licensed to build the ship and for permission to use Admiralty drawings for the Dido class in their tender (as they had done before). The Admiralty took several months to decide. Meanwhile Venezuela was anxious for a cost estimate, prompting the Foreign Office to ask for the issue to be expedited.[246] Vickers was granted permission to use the Admiralty drawings in January 1949.[247] By 1950 Vickers and the British Government were working together to secure the deal, showing the extent to which the relationship between the firm and the government had evolved.

The Embassy in Caracas gave Vickers-Armstrongs considerable help. Ambassador Sir John Magowan reported in January 1950 that "Commander Cunningham [of Vickers-Armstrongs] and members of my staff have had

[242] Note February 24, 1948, on file "H.M.S. Scylla: proposed sale to Venezuela." TNA ADM 1/21140.

[243] Imports and Exports, Ministry of Supply to Mr. Bruce, South American Department, Foreign Office. December 23, 1946. "American: South American 1946, General File No. 29." TNA, FO 371/52086.

[244] Vickers-Armstrongs Ltd., "Design for Cruiser" December 29, 1948; Leveson to Sir Charles Simeon, April 27, 1948. TNA, ADM 1/21140.

[245] Cecil, Foreign Office to Gillingham, Admiralty, August 20, 1948; Ogilvie-Forbes, British Embassy Caracas to Leveson, Vickers-Armstrongs, August 10, 1948; Robinson, Caracas to Foreign Office, "Dido Class Cruisers," September 28, 1948; Robinson, Caracas to Foreign Office, October 7, 1948, and translated letter for Venezuelan Ministry of Defence. TNA ADM 1/21140.

[246] Leveson to Admiralty, October 20, 1948; Leveson to Gillingham, December 30, 1948; Cecil, Foreign Office to Gillingham, January 11, 1948. TNA ADM 1/21140.

[247] Abercrombie to Vickers, January 19, 1949. TNA ADM 1/21140.

several interviews with the Chief of Staff." A sticking point was Venezuela's concerns about the level of its revenue from oil. "I am seeking an interview with the President of the Junta as soon as possible and will endeavor to remove any misunderstanding or ill founded concern which may exist about the United Kingdom's oil policy and general trade exchange with Venezuela."[248] However, the deal stalled only a day later: "Commander Cunningham reported that the contract for the destroyers had been postponed for at least two months, and possibly indefinitely. The reasons were economic: The United Kingdom substitution policy [sterling oil for dollar oil], and a report that the United States was about to impose a tax on imports of Venezuelan oil."[249] Cunningham returned to Britain thinking there was nothing to be done. Luckily Ambassador Magowan discovered that the hiatus would likely last only a couple of months.[250]

In the meantime, Vickers-Armstrongs' Commander Sir Robert Micklem and Cunningham met with Treasury officials to explain the Venezuelan position on oil and to advocate for a change in British policy. This meeting was a clear attempt by the firm to influence the British Government's agenda. A Treasury official reported:

> The cause of the Venezuelan concern had been the recently announced reduction of output by oil companies in Venezuela, attributed directly or indirectly to British oil policy, particularly to that announced on 20th December, 1949, of shutting out a certain amount of dollar oil from the sterling area and replacing it with imports from sterling sources. Vickers Armstrong explained that the Venezuelan action towards them in suspending negotiations about the purchase of the two destroyers could, of course, not be expected by them to reverse H.M.G.'s policy. Sir R. Micklem explained that they had now called to put the position before H.M.G.[251]

Micklem and Cunningham produced four cuttings from Venezuelan newspapers which showed American bias by suggesting a causal connection between British oil refinery projects and cutbacks in oil production in Venezuela. The Treasury took this publicity issue quite seriously, particularly the "American biased descriptions of our oil policy" and forwarded to the Foreign Office Vickers-Armstrongs' translations of the articles.[252] At the meeting Cunningham had also pointed out that the cost of the destroyers was "not very large compared to the very considerable deficit in the Anglo-Venezuelan

[248] Magowan to Foreign Office, telegram No. 6, January 26, 1950. Americas/Venezuela (hereafter AV) 1213/1. TNA, FO 371/81813.
[249] "Announcement of Commander Cunningham," January 27, 1950. Minute AV 1213/2. TNA, FO 371/81813.
[250] Magowan to FO, telegram No. 7, February 2, 1950. AV 1213/3. TNA, FO 371/81813.
[251] Rudd (Treasury) to Benchley (FO), "Likelihood of purchase by Venezuela of Vickers Armstrong destroyers," February 6, 1950. TNA, FO 371/81813. AV 1213/4. Folio 2.
[252] Lambert (Treasury) to Brenchley, and enclosures, March 14, 1950. TNA, FO 371/81813. AV 1213/6.

balance of payments in Venezuela's favour." Cunningham had made that point before to the Foreign Office, which repeated it to their ambassador in Caracas.[253] Vickers-Armstrongs' attempt at agenda resetting via the Treasury was not a success, however.

It was agreed there was nothing that the government could effectively do about this in the meantime, despite the desirability of a Venezuelan order earning the equivalent in dollars and providing employment at Vickers-Armstrongs. "Sir Wilfred Eady promised that we would let Vickers-Armstrong know as soon as any definite results came out of the oil negotiations in Washington, or as soon as any general improvement in the situation ... might be reported by our Ambassador in Venezuela."[254]

While this was not the change in British policy that Vickers-Armstrongs needed to secure the deal, they were in no doubt as to the government's sympathy for their position. Indeed, in March 1950 Micklem wrote to the Foreign Office to "convey to you our appreciation of the very considerable help we have received from H.E. the British Ambassador to Venezuela and his staff and in particular Mr. Malcolm Gale, the Commercial Attaché."[255]

By March the Embassy Chancery had identified both an opportunity and a potential problem for the destroyer deal. The opportunity was the Congressional mid-term elections, which would make it hard to pass U.S. legislation with members wanting to recess early to campaign. "It is therefore conceivable that an opportunity to revive the Vickers contract might be squeezed in before June 30th, when the current Venezuelan budget will expire."[256] The problem identified was a possible counter-bid from Yarrows, whose representative, Mr. Gibson, was no fan of Commander Cunningham. The Chancery met with Gibson and "begged him, mentioning warships but not destroyers, not to encourage the Venezuelans to play Yarrows and Vickers off together." They reported that "Gibson was attentive but non-committal." Yarrows did give Venezuela specifications for two destroyers but did not submit a formal tender.[257]

The Chancery had offered to advise Cunningham on whether it made sense for him to travel out to Caracas, in order "to save him another fruitless errand."[258] Later the Chancery provided some potentially valuable intelligence,

---

[253] Draft of FO to H.M. Ambassador Caracas, February 8, 1950. TNA, FO 371/81813. AV 1213/6.

[254] Rudd to Brenchley, February 6, 1950. TNA, FO 371/81813. AV 1213/4. Folio 3.

[255] Micklem to Sir William Strang, March 6, 1950, and response, March 8, 1950. TNA, FO 371/81813. AV 1213/5.

[256] Chancery Caracas to American Department, March 17, 1950. TNA, FO 371/81813. AV 1213/7.

[257] Chancery to American Department, March 17, 1950. Yarrows later received a contract for two river boats. Gale thought this was due to an intervention by one of the Naval Mission sent to Barrow. British Embassy Caracas, September 6, 1950. TNA, FO 371/81813. AV 1213/20.

[258] Chancery to American Department, March 17, 1950.

suggesting that the Foreign Office might like to warn Vickers-Armstrongs that their local agent, REPEX, headed by Señor Perez Pisante, who "has forged a brilliant financial career by introducing a foot into every camp," had engaged a former employee of the American Embassy, Alan S. Kipping. They reported, "We cannot yet estimate Mr. Kipping's precise status or importance in Señor Perez Pisante's group of firms, but it looks as though he is paid well enough to frequent the best hotels."[259] The Americas Department telephoned this intelligence to Ross at Vickers-Armstrongs to pass to Cunningham, who was "about to leave on a tour of S. America."[260]

Additionally, the Italian firm Ansaldo was pushing for the Venezuelan contract and offering to accept half the cost in oil. Ambassador Magowan also noted, "Another 'consideration' was, of course, the presence of a U.S. Naval Mission, and the obligations, moral and otherwise, incumbent on Venezuela as a result of the Rio Treaty of Mutual Defence. At one stage the Americans made an effort to preserve hemispheric autarky by pressing for award of the contract to Canadian Vickers."[261]

In response to an inquiry from Foreign Office official Robin Cecil as to why the deal had stalled yet again, Ambassador Magowan sent a long letter explaining what the problem was and how he had helped to solve it.[262] The issue was political. Vickers-Armstrongs' local agents, REPEX, were headed by Perez Pisante, who was regarded by the junta as a "double-crosser" for his past association – and possible current support for – opposition groups. Pisante had recently applied to Magowan for help in securing a meeting for Vickers-Armstrongs with the Minister of Defense. This was an unusual request as an ambassador-agent was supposed to possess the connections necessary to secure meetings. The ambassador had told Pisante that he had been unable to get the meeting, then explained in person to the newly arrived Cunningham that Pisante was now the obstacle to negotiations and that nothing would move until "an assurance was received that Perez Pisanty [Pisante] had been eliminated as agent and barred from any prospect of commission when the contract was signed."[263] As Magowan recounted, "Cunningham, whose authority from his principals included (somewhat to my surprise) life and death power over agents, thereupon said he would act at once to eliminate Perez Pisanty."[264] The ambassador even sent a telegram to Vickers-Armstrongs – via the Foreign Office – telling them to no longer deal with REPEX. The Foreign Office also telephoned Yapp at

[259] Chancery to American Department, April 28, 1950. TNA, FO 371/81813. AV 1213/8.
[260] Note from May 9, 1950, on "Suspended Vickers Armstrong negotiations." TNA, FO 371/81813. AV 1213/8.
[261] Magowan to Cecil, June 27, 1950. TNA, FO 371/81813. AV 1213/16.
[262] Magowan to Cecil, June 3, 1950, Folios 1–4. TNA, FO 371/81813. AV 1213/11.
[263] Magowan to Cecil, June 3, 1950, Folio 3.
[264] Magowan to Cecil, June 3, 1950, Folio 3.

Vickers-Armstrongs with the instruction.[265] Ambassador Magowan concluded his letter, "I have promised that my Commercial Department would continue to take an interest in the transaction and be at the disposal of both Vickers and the Ministry of Defence as a channel for exchanges about the arrangement for the resumption."[266]

Subsequently, the firm received helpful intelligence from the Embassy on Venezuela's negotiator, Napoleon Dupouy, his standing with the junta, and on the state of the Venezuelan budget (urging them to sign quickly in the current fiscal year). Ambassador Magowan advanced the deal by explaining to Venezuelan ministers the value of purchasing weapons in non-dollar countries, and that the end of petrol rationing in Britain meant more potential oil sales there.[267]

The Foreign Office itself was now working on behalf of Vickers-Armstrongs. This began when Cunningham and Yapp called there to consult on the Venezuelan request that the contract for destroyers should not be signed by the Venezuelan Ambassador in London, and that "Furthermore, the Venezuelan Ambassador is *not* even to be kept informed."[268] The irregularity of this request had the firm concerned and they asked for the British Embassy in Caracas to clear that point up. The Foreign Office added their own questions, wondering if the Venezuelan Ministry of Defense was acting without the knowledge of the Ministry of Foreign Affairs.[269] Ambassador Magowan cleared up the issue, which concerned the internal politics of the Venezuelan Government and was not a matter for concern.[270] Magowan played a further facilitating role for Vickers-Armstrongs: passing the final terms for payment installments from the Venezuelan Ministry of Defence to Vickers-Armstrongs; subsequently confirming that the contract would be signed by Cunningham in Caracas; communicating formally to REPEX that their contract was terminated; and later passing to Cunnningham a request from Frederico Ponce of REPEX for some payment for his labors.[271] Despite his involvement, the ambassador deftly

[265] Note from 5 June on "Request that Vickers be informed that Commander Cunningham wishes them to cease correspondence with Repex," June 2, 1950. TNA, FO 371/81813. AV 1213/9.

[266] Magowan to Cecil, June 3, 1950, Folio 4.

[267] Magowan to Foreign Office, June 8, 1950. Telegram No. 52. TNA, FO 371/81813. AV 1213/10.

[268] "Sale of Vickers Destroyers to Venezuela, Rifles to Caracas," Tel. No. 49. June 9, 1950. TNA, FO 371/81813. AV 1213/10. Emphasis in original.

[269] Foreign Office to Caracas, Confidential telegram No. 93, June 13, 1950. TNA, FO 371/81813. AV 1213/10.

[270] Magowan to Foreign Office, Confidential telegram No. 54, June 17, 1950. TNA, FO 371/81813. AV 1213/12.

[271] Magowan to Foreign Office, Confidential telegram No. 55, June 19, 1950; Foreign Office to Caracas, Confidential telegram 103, June 20, 1950. AV 1213/13; Foreign Office to Vickers Armstrongs, June 22, 1950. TNA, AV 1213/14; Vickers Armstrongs to Under-Secretary of State for Foreign Affairs, June 26, 1950. AV 1213/15; Sale of Destroyers to Venezuela, July 19, 1950, AV 1213/19. TNA, FO 371/81813.

avoided attending the contract-signing ceremony, sending Second Secretary Gale to both translate for Cunningham and make a speech about this deal being "an important contribution to progress in the task of broadening and strengthening ... economic relations" between the two countries.[272] The final agreement was secured by bribery: Vickers-Armstrongs immediately made a very large secret payment into an American bank account held by members of the junta.[273]

At the conclusion of the deal Ambassador Magowan reported to the Foreign Office that Dupoy had been able "to give a very optimistic account of his impressions of Britain to the President of the Military Junta and to the Minister of Defence."[274] This prompted the Foreign Office to note that "Certainly Vickers did Dupouy proud; they even took him to Ascot!"[275]

The importance of the contract to the British Government was not that Vickers-Armstrongs earned money, but rather that the sale would help the balance of payments and potentially save some hard currency from being used on oil.[276] In the context of a different ship deal, Foreign Office official Robert Cecil revealingly reported to the Treasury: "A maximum effort to secure this order for British shipyards would be in line with the drive to increase exports to dollar markets in Latin America .... Venezuela is, fortunately, a market where we can continue to sell without being embarrassed by insistent requests to purchase in proportion."[277] Clearly, the Government's help to armament firms was instrumental. Regardless, the net effect was that the Foreign Office gave Vickers-Armstrongs significant help to secure the Venezuelan deal.

It took Vickers-Armstrongs four years to secure the contract for three destroyers. During that time Venezuela endured various changes of government, including one involving a successful coup.[278] The completion of the vessels was not smooth sailing either, and the Venezuelan Ambassador complained repeatedly that the destroyers' completion was being held up. Venezuela did grant Vickers-Armstrongs a six-month extension on delivery, ostensibly to allow for the prioritizing of Royal Navy ships for the Korean War. The British Government identified the problems at Vickers-Armstrongs as a shortage of special quality steel for the hulls and a lack of highly skilled labor. However, the issue extended to the sub-contractors whose supplies (such as voltage regulators) were necessary for the destroyers. The government sought to expedite the

---

[272] Magowan to Secretary of State, No. 52, June 29, 1950. TNA, FO 371/81813. AV 1213/18.

[273] Cecil to Magowan, June 27,1950. Folios 1–2. TNA, FO 371/81813. AV 1213/16.

[274] Cecil to Magowan, June 27, 1950. Folio 2.

[275] "Report on the bids made ...," June 27, 1950, TNA, FO 371/81813. AV 1213/16.

[276] Magowan to Secretary of State for Foreign Affairs, June 24, 1950. AV 1213/17. TNA, FO 371/81813.

[277] Cecil to Stevenson, July 23, 1952. "British offer to supply naval escort vessels to Venezuela; Competition from Italy." TNA, FO 371/97674.

[278] Wise, "Securing," p. 121.

sub-components, telling contractors to prioritize Venezuelan supplies as if they had been ordered by the Admiralty.[279] The Foreign Office was concerned that the continuing delays might impact the chances of a Thornycroft consortium getting a contract for escort vessels.[280] The ambassador in Caracas "was afraid that the delays at Barrow-in-Furness would not encourage the Venezuelan authorities to place orders in this country."[281] The Venezuelan Minister of Defense also complained to the Embassy about the delays, while also dangling the prospect of orders for two troop transporters and after that for three submarines.[282] These would, of course, be of great interest to Vickers-Armstrongs.

In response to the threats and entreaties from the Venezuelan Government, the Admiralty had given "some degree of priority ... to the construction of destroyers for Venezuela over and above the priority given to orders for the Royal Navy."[283] Other Admiralty actions included an offer to supply armaments at the expense of the British frigate conversion program, and the "release of armoured plates from [the] current H.M. Dockyards programme which should assist Vickers to meet [the] promised January 53 launching date of [the] first destroyer." It was noted that the Admiralty offer should be kept secret as it was "a divergence from normal principles and may attract criticism or request for similar treatment from other quarters if generally advertised."[284] In October 1952 the Board of Trade was reporting to the Caracas Embassy that "Following recent talks with Vickers and as a direct result of Admiralty assistance, launching date for first destroyer now fixed for 19th November 1952. Ambassador's wife in London has already been invited to perform the ceremony."[285]

This was an unprecedented effort by the British Government to fulfill the Vickers-Armstrongs contract and to secure the escort ship order for the Thornycroft consortium, reflecting the very high value placed on dollar currency (rather than the health of the firms). Vickers-Armstrongs worked hard to complete the destroyers and to mend diplomatic fences with the Venezuelans. Ambassador Urquhart recounted that Venezuelan official Napoleon Dupouy "had found the Minister literally purring over a scale model of the destroyer which had been sent out to him. That sort of gesture means a great deal in a set-up such as we have here, where the Minister of Defence, one man, has so much power to decide where contracts go."[286]

[279] Hanna, Admiralty to Jackson, Foreign Office, February 6, 1952. TNA, FO 371/97674.
[280] Cecil to Watson, Admiralty, July 25, 1952. "British offer to supply naval escort vessels to Venezuela; Competition from Italy." TNA, FO 371/97674.
[281] Barclay to Ambassador Urquhart, August 16, 1952. TNA, FO 371/97674.
[282] Ambassador Urquhart to Barclay, September 5, 1952. TNA, FO 371/97674.
[283] Minute by Cecil, September 25, 1952. TNA, FO 371/97674.
[284] Board of Trade telegram to Ambassador, Caracas, September 29, 1952. TNA, FO 371/97674.
[285] Board of Trade telegram to Ambassador, Caracas, October 10, 1952. TNA, FO 371/97674.
[286] Ambassador Urquhart to Cecil, October 16, 1952. TNA, FO 371/97674.

Despite this very significant British Government assistance to business, and the Thornycroft consortium spending £15,000 to try to win the order, the Foreign Office recorded in November that the firms were losing hope of securing the deal to build the escort vessels (renamed "light destroyers" at Venezuelan Ministry insistence). One official noted that "there are no new arguments to put forward [to Venezuela] and I expect the Italians have simply offered a bigger bribe."[287] Ultimately, the contract for six escort vessels went to Ansaldo in late 1952. By December, though, the Board of Trade were reporting to the Foreign Office that Napoleon Dupouy was to arrive in January to meet with Vickers-Armstrongs and noting the Admiralty had given Vickers permission to offer to Venezuela a modern-class submarine. Vickers-Armstrongs were reported to be working on plans for such a submarine, and also for a cruiser.[288] In 1956 a new destroyer was formally handed over to Venezuela and other orders were in the works.[289]

In the late 1940s Britain and America clashed over the issue of armaments for Argentina. They had a secret "Gentleman's Agreement" not to supply armaments to Argentina (and to the Dominican Republic), in part because of concerns about Nazis being sheltered by Argentina and the nature of the Peron government, but these issues were also manipulated by Washington to support the U.S. standardization agenda. The United States – from the British government perspective – tried a number of tacks to keep the British out, including failing to provide any details on the standardization plan or a timetable for it, and failing to detail what Argentina needed to do for them to be eligible for arms sales again.[290] There was also rhetorical interest from both governments for attempts to agree a worldwide arms traffic control convention, but, as the President of the Board of Trade Sir Stafford Cripps concluded, "U.S. policy does not contemplate so much an embargo on the export of arms to Latin America, as a monopoly by the U.S. of the Latin American arms market. Such a monopoly we are not prepared to concede."[291]

The British Government wanted to sell warships to Argentina, as this would bring valuable hard currency, business and employment, and re-establish an important relationship interrupted by the war. This situation created clear common interests between them and Vickers-Armstrongs.[292] The first shift was

---

[287] "Escort Vessels for Venezuela," November 20, 1952. TNA, FO 371/97674.

[288] Armstrong to Young, December 12, 1952. TNA, FO 371/97674.

[289] "Vickers-Armstrongs."

[290] Sir Rex Lepper [Buenos Aires] to Foreign Office, September 3, 1946. "American: South American 1946, General File No. 29." TNA FO 371/52086.

[291] Draft, Cripps to Sir George Nelson of English Electric, "Sale of Arms to Latin America," October 1946; "American: South American 1946, General File No. 29." TNA FO 371/52086.

[292] Wise, *Royal Navy*, p. 233, ff. 12. Citing "Sale of Arms to South American Countries," Economic Policy Meeting, April 1948. "Trade in Armaments with Latin America," TNA, PREM 8/766.

the government giving permission for the English Electric subsidiary Marconi to fit Type-291 radars onto Argentinian navy ships. The reason given was that the radar was not "warlike materiel" and therefore could be supplied; this earned £100,000 in hard currency. In the same letter to the Board of Trade in which English Electric asked permission to make the sale, Managing Director Sir George Nelson mentioned that a Latin American country had been inquiring about buying 100 de Havilland Vampire aircraft, potentially generating more than £2,000,000 in hard currency.[293] By November it was clear that the country in question was Argentina, and taking this forward would raise tensions with the United States.

In the midst of this struggle for armaments markets and influence, the Foreign Office and Admiralty were surprised to learn in 1946 that Vickers-Armstrongs had apparently made a deal with Brazil to sell her three cruisers.[294] In the minutes accompanying that correspondence, Mr. Butler noted:

> As we know, complete standardisation on U.S. equipment, starting with naval equipment, is the U.S. plan, and it becomes more and more clear, that some L-A countries are reluctant to accept this proposition, to which an order for three British cruisers would be a considerable blow …. It seems highly unlikely that such a proposition exists, but we shall hear via the Admiralty from Vickers.

Mr. Murray commented: "Even if (as is most likely) the Brazilians want three cruisers from us, we should have to think very carefully before supplying them, and make sure the matter was coordinated within the framework of U.S. defence plans, and not left cutting across them."[295] Upon further inquiry, it turned out that Leveson had offered Brazil three cruisers but they had not been accepted as Rio anticipated getting three U.S. surplus cruisers "practically for free."[296]

In November 1946 Leveson took Murray of the Foreign Office South America Department out to lunch and briefed him on his recent travels in the region.[297] Murray subsequently recorded Leveson's views on the likelihood of Argentine naval purchases (good, though any aircraft carrier contract would likely go to a U.S. firm), Brazil's acquisitions from the United States (it was hard to turn down the bargains on offer) and Chile's financial situation (they had wasted money on second-hand acquisitions and hoped to be in a position

---

[293] Nelson to Cripps, "American: South American 1946, General File No. 29." TNA FO 371/52086.

[294] Hadow [Washington] to Perowne, September 23, 1946. "American: South American 1946, General File No. 29." TNA FO 371/52086.

[295] "U.S. Plans for Hemisphere Defence," Minutes, in Butler and Murray's handwriting. "American: South American 1946, General File No. 29." TNA FO 371/52086.

[296] Leeper telegram to Foreign Office, November 4, 1946. "American: South American 1946, General File No. 29." TNA FO 371/52086.

[297] Misspelled as Levison in these documents.

to talk seriously to Vickers-Armstrongs in about a year).[298] Murray asked Leveson about regional acceptance of the standardization agenda and whether "they would in future purchase all the equipment for their armed forces in the United States. He said that so far as naval circles were concerned there was no acceptance of this view."[299] The lunch alerted the government to Vickers-Armstrongs' interests and provided the Foreign Office with intelligence that (once verified by the Admiralty) was shared with their embassies in the region, and Ambassador Balfour in Washington.[300]

In 1947 Argentina had requested tenders for a large naval order worth £20 million and maybe more, an attractive prospect for many firms. There was an argument within the British Government as to whether the private yards should be able to respond. The government was inching toward support for arms sales to the region and the ending of the "Gentleman's Agreement" with the United States[301] J. V. Perone of the Foreign Office noted in a letter to Ambassador Balfour that "the Chancellor of the Exchequer and the President of the Board of Trade have both been pressing the Secretary of State very hard personally for the termination of the 'Gentleman's Agreement', in particular connection with the Argentine naval construction programme for importing combat aircraft."[302]

Armament firms were also lobbying hard on the issue. In January 1947 Leveson had a conversation with Treasury officials about competition for the forthcoming Argentinian naval order, and Vickers-Armstrongs' hesitation to bid without government assurances of support for the bid.[303] Thornycrofts were also asking the Admiralty about the government position on them bidding on Argentinian contracts.[304]

In January the "Gentleman's Agreement" was finally set aside and Vickers-Armstrongs had permission to bid on the naval orders. The Foreign Office reported, "The Argentine Government recently expelled a number of Germans and decreed the deportation of some fifty more." As Argentina was now meeting her obligations, she could be treated like other South American countries.[305]

[298] "Supply of Arms to Latin America – Argentine, Chile, and Brazil," November 25, 1946. "American: South American 1946, General File No. 29." TNA FO 371/52086.
[299] "Supply of Arms to Latin America – Argentine, Chile, and Brazil," November 25, 1946. "American: South American 1946, General File No. 29." TNA FO 371/52086.
[300] Handwritten memo from Perowne, Foreign Office. November 26, 1946. TNA FO 371/52086.
[301] Bevin to Atlee, "Naval Armaments for Argentina" and "Argentine Naval Construction Programme," memorandum, January 15, 1947. TNA PREM 8/766.
[302] Perone to Balfour, January 20, 1947. "South American 1947 Argentina, File No. 76." TNA, FO 371/61138.
[303] Treasury to Perone, January 6, 1947. "South American 1947 Argentina, File No. 76." TNA, FO 371/61138.
[304] Thornycroft to the Secretary of the Admiralty, December 4, 1946; Thornycroft to Murray, December 4, 1946. "American: South American 1946, General File No. 29." TNA FO 371/52086.
[305] "Argentine Naval Construction Programme," January 15, 1947. TNA PREM 8/766, pp. 1–2.

Secretary Bevin noted: "There may be a row with America over this. I am quite ready to face it, for we must earn hard currency where we can, and the American attitude on this question is quite unreasonable."[306] Later the Prime Minister was reminded that armaments were "a 'high conversion' export giving a very big return on the imported raw materials used."[307] However, Ambassador Lord Inverchapel reported from Washington that "[Dean] Acheson has suggested to me that our termination of the gentleman's agreement was understood by him only to refer to replacements for Argentine Navy. He fears that the rumour which had reached State Department of an offer by Messrs. Vickers to build cruisers for the Argentine Government will 'give his people fits.'"[308] The British regarded this "misinterpretation" by Acheson as "not unlikely … calculated, in the hope of drawing us as regards our intentions."[309] Inverchapel also reported on the U.S. navy's desire to dispose of 2,000 surplus naval vessels to Latin America. However, this was not acknowledged as a threat to potential British naval sales.

In a further diplomatic tussle, the Americans declared they were shocked and angered by British plans, announced in May 1947, to sell Meteor jet aircraft to Argentina, which Secretary Marshall described as "so dramatic a weapon."[310] Foreign Secretary Bevin reminded Marshall that he had explained in January that "we no longer regarded it as appropriate to maintain this agreement [the "Gentleman's Agreement"] and that we proposed to treat Argentina hencefor-ward in all respects on the same footing as other Latin American countries."[311] A ministerial meeting discussed Secretary Marshall's response but noted, "It was difficult to resist the conclusion that the attitude of the United States Government in this matter was determined by a desire to establish a monopoly in the supply of armaments to the South American countries."[312]

However, there was another threat to Western armament sales to Argentina: the Soviet Union. In June, Bevin reported to Lord Inverchapel that the American Ambassador had shared intelligence on a Soviet barter deal with Argentina, swapping captured German armaments for foodstuffs.[313] The Cabinet's Economic Policy Committee met the same day and focused exclu-sively on aircraft orders.[314] An appendix to the minutes reveals why, noting of

---

[306] Bevin to Atlee, Telegram No, 881 from Moscow, April 20, 1947. TNA PREM 8/766.
[307] Brooks to Atlee, "Arms for Latin America," April 8, 1948. TNA PREM 8/766.
[308] Inverchapel to Foreign Office, Telegram No. 2131. April 9, 1947. TNA PREM 8/766.
[309] Sargent to UK Delegation to Council of Ministers, Moscow (Bevin was traveling), April 11, 1947. TNA PREM 8/766.
[310] Personal message Marshall to Bevin, Telegram No. 4964, May 18, 1947. TNA PREM 8/766.
[311] Personal message Bevin to Marshall, Telegram No. 4981. May 18, 1947. "1948 Exports," TNA PREM 8/766.
[312] "Sale of Armaments to Argentine Government," Notes of a Meeting of Ministers, May 19, 1947. "1948 Exports." TNA PREM 8/766, p. 3.
[313] Bevin to Inverchapel, June 4, 1947. TNA PREM 8/766.
[314] One hundred Meteors were sold to Argentina.

the naval sales, "These orders did not materialize," with Argentina now seeking surplus vessels from the government, not new warships.[315] The Argentine market was now lost to Vickers-Armstrongs.

In 1951 Vickers-Armstrongs began to negotiate seriously to build two Almirante-Class destroyers for Chile, competing with Thornycrofts for the £9 million contract. The Foreign Office was wary because Chile was short of sterling; however, Vickers-Armstrongs secured the deal, and the *Almirante Riveros* and *Almirante Williams* were delivered in 1960.

In 1953 Vickers asked for permission and help to sign a barter deal with Brazil, selling Viscount passenger planes in return for iron ore.[316] The Ministry of Supply was opposed and the Board of Trade in favor.[317] America was offering Export Import Credits to Brazil to secure the business, but that did not move British opponents. The dispute ended when the Foreign Office and Treasury sided with the Ministry of Supply.[318] Vickers was informed that the deal would not be sanctioned – despite Brazil having been allowed to privately barter raw cotton for seventy Meteor jets from the Gloster Aircraft Company.[319]

Conclusion

This chapter has shown Armstrongs and Vickers' foreign policy strategies in action. They built resilient relationships in Latin America, used ambassador-agents, competed against – but also aligned with – other firms to secure deals, provided access to finance and bribed as necessary to secure sales. The rewards were generally prosperous relationships in the region spanning ninety years.

Early on the firms were completely independent actors, and the British Government was a bystander. The firms freely made deals without even informing the government and concluded some sales that the government opposed. As Miller concluded: "Between 1870 and 1914 ... the key actors in the relationship between Latin America and Britain were businessmen, not the government."[320] Lacking institutional support increased the risks for armament firms, especially given the expense of their products and the chronic indebtedness of many Latin American states. However, for Armstrongs and Vickers the rewards made calculated risks worth it.

---

[315] "Sale of Arms to South American Countries," Minute of the 13th Meeting of the Economic Policy Committee, April 9, 1948. Confidential appendix, "Present Outstanding Orders and Enquiries." TNA PREM 8/766.

[316] "Anglo/Brazilian Trade," March 28, 1953. Americas Office, Brazil Desk, 1151/70. TNA, FO 371/103232.

[317] Peter Young (Board of Trade) to C. J. A. Whitehouse (Ministry of Supply), April 16, 1953. Americas Office, Brazil Desk 1151/70. TNA, FO 371/103232.

[318] Symons to Young, April 17, 1953. 1151/70. TNA, FO 371/103232.

[319] *Economist*, Vol. 166 (1953), p. 435.

[320] Miller, *Britain*, p. 68.

After the Great War the major problem Armstrongs and Vickers faced in Latin America was that the British Government's commitment to arms control extended to restricting sales to the region. The arc of the relationship between the firms and the British Government had shifted, and Armstrongs and Vickers were now limited by government export policies and preferences.

The arc bent further in World War Two, and in its aftermath the British Government and Vickers-Armstrongs worked together to regain market share in the Latin America. The British Government ended the "Gentleman's Agreement" with the United States, allowing armament sales to Latin America because of the hard currency Britain was losing when buying agricultural goods from the region. British Government help to Vickers-Armstrongs had nothing to do with the firm *per se.*

What does the firms' engagement in Latin America tell us about the power that Armstrongs and Vickers wielded vis-à-vis the British Government? First, the firms did hold and exercise some relational power and got some (albeit unsystematic) help from the state. However, once the government had decided on an important but unfavorable policy – such as international arms control in the 1920s – the firms lacked the power to overturn that decision, even in a peripheral market such as Latin America. Thus, there were clear limits to even the amount of the "first face" of power (see Introduction) that Armstrongs and Vickers held.

In terms of armament firms' agenda-setting power, there is little evidence they had any in their Latin American dealings. Even in 1950, when the two were closely aligned, Vickers-Armstrongs' attempt to change British Government policy on payment for Venezuelan oil failed. Even the prospect of destroyer sales was not sufficient to change the British Government's economic calculations. In this case, in effect, the firm was used by Venezuela to lobby for a change they wanted from the British Government; this hardly demonstrates the power of Vickers-Armstrongs.

If there was little evidence of agenda-setting in terms of the "second face" of power, then there is even less evidence of the firm having had any ideological power in its relationship with the British Government as played out in Latin America.

7

Foreign Policies for Selling Armaments to Asia

This chapter examines the records of Armstrongs and Vickers in selling armaments in Asia. As part of their foreign policy strategies, and independent of the British Government, the firms built diplomatic relationships with states in the region using their own ambassador-agents and reaped impressive rewards for their labors. At the start of the era Armstrongs pioneered many gun and warship deals with China and Japan. Armstrongs created lasting relationships with key Chinese and Japanese government officials, and many of the firm's managers received state decorations for their services. After Vickers moved into warship production just before the turn of the century, they also began to secure lucrative contracts in the region, sometimes in competition and sometimes in alliance with Armstrongs.

In the early part of the era, Armstrongs enjoyed some advantages in trying to secure sales to China due to the personality and energy of Robert Hart, who, though a British citizen, worked assiduously for the Chinese Government as the Inspector General for Customs between 1863 and 1910.[1] The heyday of the relationship between Hart and Armstrongs was the 1870s and 1880s. Marshall Bastable has described Sir Robert as "one of Elswick's most productive foreign ambassadors."[2] Not only did Hart facilitate Armstrongs' sales but his support also enabled the Tyneside firm to avoid the bribery usually necessary to secure armaments deals in China.[3] His approach was not universally popular, as Hart reported to his Inspector General representative in London, James Duncan Campbell:

> Sir W. Armstrong's agents at Honkong (Sharpe & CO.) have written me a lengthy letter, almost protesting against my having passed them by, and saying that Sir W.A. & Co. would rather receive my orders through them via H'kong, than direct from my own representative (yourself) in England.

---

[1] Hart later received a British knighthood. Drew, "Sir Robert," pp. 6–7.
[2] Bastable, *Arms*, p. 151.
[3] Hart reorganized the collection of customs revenues across China, so that local officials lost their "time-honored 'rake-off,'" making him unpopular with local officials. Drew, "Sir Robert," pp. 11–12.

In reply I simply acknowledge receipt. I suppose the manufacturer has said to the agent: "pretty fellow you are not to catch it when there *is* an order given!"[4]

Campbell acted as building supervisor of the Staunch gunboats and cruisers made for China.[5] It seems that Armstrongs offered commissions and shares to both Hart and Campbell for their facilitation of warship sales. Hart commented to Campbell: "I see no objection to *your* holding shares. I should like some myself, but as it would not be quite the thing for *me* to have them, I shall not ask for any."[6] A later letter from Hart declared: "I have not yet found time to write my promised letter about the percentage allowed by Sir W.A & Co., but I ought to say here that my instinct is *against* every one of the ways you suggest for its expenditure."[7] Campbell must have become a shareholder as he subsequently sold his shares when Armstrongs was contracted to build the Chinese fleet in the mid-1870s. Unfortunately for him, when the news of the Chinese contracts became public, the value of Armstrongs' shares increased significantly, magnifying the sense of financial loss that Campbell experienced.[8]

Later, both Armstrongs and Vickers benefited from the help of Nicholas O'Conor, the British Ambassador to China between 1892 and 1895 (the year in which he was knighted). He took Foreign Secretary Lord Salisbury and his successor Earl Rosebery's instructions to assist British firms very seriously. O'Conor explained his work in China:

> I have, while in charge, always gone on the principle that to be efficient and to render the best service within their power to British commerce they [diplomats] ought not only to report commercial matters to the foreign office and to Her Majesty's legation, but also to be on the lookout to show British merchants and traders when and how to take advantage of commercial openings, and, if necessary, to introduce British commercial agents willingly, yet with just discrimination, to the local authorities.[9]

This enlightened attitude to trade was not typical of the Diplomatic Service.

In 1863 Imperial China had purchased directly from the British Admiralty "a compact squadron of seven steamers capable of serving as a war fleet," plus

---

[4] Hart to Campbell, Letter 131, 9 July 1875. In Fairbank, Bruner and Matheson, *I.G.*, p. 199; Campbell "efficiently and loyally" directed the special agency of the Chinese customs in London; "a more competent man could not have been found." Drew, "Sir Robert," p. 16.

[5] Brook, *Warships*, p. 51.

[6] Hart to Campbell, Letter 390, 10 December 1882. Fairbank, Bruner and Matheson, *I.G.*, p. 435.

[7] Hart to Campbell, Letter 149, 21 April 1876. Later he wrote, "As for commissions, I think it would be better not to take them." Letter 185, 2 November 1877. Fairbank, Bruner and Matheson, *I.G.*, pp. 219 and 253.

[8] Fairbank, Bruner and Matheson, *I.G.*, p. 435.

[9] O'Conor to Earl of Rosebery, March 6, 1886. "Correspondence," Communication No. 45, p. 61.

equipment, to be headed by a European – Chinese Naval Commander-in-Chief, Sherard Osborn. However, things had gone awry with the deal and due to fears that the ships might end up in the hands of pirates, the Japanese or the American Confederacy, Captain Osborn returned the ships to England, a course widely approved of there.[10] This unfortunately left the Imperial Chinese somewhat poorer and no better defended. The debacle also led to the dismissal of the reckless Horatio Nelson Lay, then Chinese Inspector General of Customs, who had assembled the fleet in Britain, and the appointment of his deputy, Robert Hart, to the role in November 1863.[11]

The first reference to Armstrongs' products in Hart's letters to Campbell comes in 1874:

> Will you find out what would be the cost of *two* 20-pounder Armstrong guns (*muzzle loaders*), and also of *two* of less caliber – say 10- or 12-pounders or thereabouts, also muzzle loaders. I want these light guns to take the place of the *40-pounders* Forbes put in the Papita and Condita (Feihoo and Ling Feng). *Telegraph the cost in round numbers*: I shall telegraph and order, most possibly, in reply.[12]

As Hart subsequently explained to Campbell: "This Formosa affair has given everything a little fillip, and the Mandarins are ready to try iron-clads, monitors, catapults, cross-bows, Krupps, *old clo's* – and anything else that anybody will tell them to acquire."[13] The incident was a Japanese raid on Taiwan in retaliation for the murder of Japanese sailors there three years earlier. This punitive raid was the first overseas deployment of the Imperial Japanese Navy and it suggested that China's hold on Taiwan was fragile.

The next development shows that early in this era the British Government sometimes provided some help to connect potential buyers with British armament firms, though it did not show any sense of duty to – and even signaled skepticism about – the firms. A 1875 letter from Sir Thomas Wade of the Peking Legation to Foreign Secretary the Earl of Derby noted that the Chinese, having been discouraged in their attempts to buy a vessel of war from the Admiralty, were now enquiring if there would be any objections to China having men of war constructed in private yards.[14] Mr. Wade reported the conversation: "I said none, but that the Chinese Government would do well to have a competent agent both to choose the builders and to watch the progress of the vessel. An officer of our Navy might be the best agent, and, it was even possible

---

[10] Wright, *Chinese*, pp. 15–18; Morse, *International Relations*, pp. 34–48.
[11] van de Ven, *Breaking*, pp. 41–43.
[12] Hart to Campbell, Letter 88, 11 April 1874. Fairbank, Bruner and Matheson, *I.G.*, p. 153. Emphasis in original.
[13] Hart to Campbell, Letter 102, 26 June 1974. Fairbank, Bruner and Matheson, *I.G.*, p. 170. Emphasis in original.
[14] A Legation was a second-ranked mission headed by a minister.

that the Admiralty might consent to name some one as fit for the necessary surveillance."[15]

The Chinese Government was interested in Armstrongs' innovative Staunch gunboats. The Viceroy of Chihli, Li Hung-chang (Li Hongzhang) – who became an important figure shaping the Qing Empire's foreign policy and military modernization – authorized Inspector General Hart to buy four from Armstrongs in 1875.[16] Peter Brook recounts, "As neither Hart nor Campbell had any shipbuilding expertise it was left to the honour of Armstrongs to provide value for money."[17] Armstrongs was charged with preparing their own ship-building contracts, which they then treated and signed as though prepared by Campbell. "One of the contract stipulations was that Armstrongs were to 'pro-vide guns of the very best make which had duly passed the British Government test.'"[18] The Admiralty consented to help China find suitable officers and crew to take the gunboats to China after the ships had passed the necessary trials and inspections. As a contemporary account reported, "As these gunboats were a novelty from the point of view of the size of the guns carried in relation to the tonnage of the ships the Admiralty were eager for their own information to wit-ness the results of the tests."[19]

The four gunboats, known in Britain as *Alpha, Beta, Gamma* and *Delta* (they were nicknamed the "alphabet gunboats"), were a great success in China. Inspector General Hart reported to Campbell on Li Hongzhang's response to the first two: "*Li* has memorialized reporting arrival of steamers, and says they are excellent. The Yamen [Foreign Office] told me to thank you for all your trouble and pains. I hope the '*Gamma*' and '*Delta*' will come along quickly."[20] The second two arrived six months later, and while they included some impor-tant design improvements – including carrying a "monster" 12.5-inch, 38-ton muzzle-loading rifle – Hart nevertheless grumbled:

> I saw the vessels in Hongkong. To my eye, they had not arrived in point of neatness and cleanliness, in as respectable a condition as the Alpha and Beta were on reaching Tientsin, and, although their officers made a more favourable impression than those of the A and B, their crews were far behind the A's and B's in appearance. Their engineers were the roughest looking lot of low-class mechanics I have met out here.[21]

[15] Thomas Francis Wade in Peking to the Earl of Derby, 23 February 1875. TNA, FO17/697, Folios 218–219.
[16] Chu and Liu, *Li Hung-chang*, pp. 70 and 97.
[17] Brook, *Warships*, p. 28.
[18] "Gunboats for China, 1876–1881," VA, Doc. 626, p. 3.
[19] "Gunboats for China, 1876–1881," p. 5.
[20] Hart to Campbell, Letter 160, 14 December 1876. Fairbank, Bruner and Matheson, *I.G.*, p. 230.
[21] Hart to Campbell, Letter 179, 1 July 1977. Fairbank, Bruner and Matheson, *I.G.*, p. 245; Wright, *Chinese*, p. 44.

The Chief Naval Architect of the British Admiralty described the alphabet gunboats as "the best of their kind, the newest and most powerful afloat," and noted the improvements made between the first and the second pair. According to an Armstrongs account, "Their safe arrival in China was regarded by the Admiralty as a great achievement; in fact, as Rendel remarked, they were quite startled by it."[22] Four more gunboats were ordered by China, to include all the advances available, which meant that they would be made of steel, not iron, and double-ended, enabling them to steam backwards as well as forwards. Each gunboat cost £32,500.[23] Soon after two were ordered by the Governor of Shantung and one by the Viceroy of Canton. The *Iota*, *Kappa* and *Lambada* cost £33,000 each. The *Times* noted in July 1879 that on paper the armaments of the last seven alphabets were more powerful than the heaviest guns the Royal Navy had on HMS *Dreadnought*.[24]

While China now had Staunch gunboats for defense, she lacked sufficient warships capable of taking offensive action. The Newcastle yard of Charles Mitchell and Co., a close neighbor to Armstrongs (and which would subsequently amalgamate with the firm), were commissioned to build two lowcost ram cruisers (heavily armed, with armor fore and aft but without vertical armor) of a new design by George Rendel. The *Chao Yung* and the *Yang Wei* used Rendel's basic design, applied to the *Arturo Prat* being built for Chile, but with two extra boilers, greater speed and 10-inch Armstrong canons protected from the weather by gun shields (which, however, limited their range and angle of fire). Delivery of these ships was delayed because they became entangled in a dispute between Armstrongs and the British Government over ships possibly being built for Chile while the country was on the brink of war (see Chapter 6). The issue took time to sort out, but the rams left Newcastle on August 9, 1881, and reached China in mid-October. Armstrongs also assisted China in making fortification guns after their indigenously produced guns burst, though the resulting guns did not match the standard of European gunnery, which was innovating fast.

In parallel Armstrongs was building a relationship with China's potential enemy, Japan. This had started in 1872, when the Iwakura Mission was in Britain to examine modernization; one of the industrialists they had met was Sir William.[25] During that Mission, the Japanese visitors were shown around the Elswick works by Noble.[26] Five years later, Tokyo was regarding the buildup of the Peiyang (Beiyang) fleet, sponsored by Li Hongzhang, with some concern and was seeking more naval protection. In 1880 Armstrongs launched the

[22] "Gunboats for China, 1876–1881," p. 6.
[23] "Gunboats for China, 1876–1881," pp. 6–7.
[24] Brook, *Warships*, p. 29. Citing *The Times*, July 25, 1879.
[25] Pearse and McCooey, *Companion*, p. 161.
[26] Diary, 10th May 1886, ff. 184. Ruxton, *Diaries*.

Tsukushi for Japan; this ship had originally been built as the *Arturo Prat*. The low-cost cruiser arrived in Japan in 1883.

After initially relying on Sir Robert Hart, in 1880 Armstrongs sent out Major Bridgford, formerly of the Royal Marine Artillery, as their ambassador-agent. Robert Hart pronounced:

> B. has breakfasted and dined with me, and is one of the pleasantest men I have met for years: he is well informed, has been about a good deal, – has seen much and met many, – and can reproduce all in better English than one usually hears. I have enjoyed his gossip immensely but I have nothing for him to do in particular. I shall ask Detring to introduce him to *Li*, and also get his advice about storing the projectiles, etc., etc., etc.

He subsequently noted: "*Li* is pleased with *Bridgford*, and says A. *& Co.* do well, in addition to supplying good guns etc., to send out a competent man to see that Customs use them and keep them as they ought to be used and kept."[27] Hart's appraisal of Bridgford likely changed soon after when he was told that future sales would be negotiated between Li and Armstrongs via Bridgford and Jardine, Matheson & Co., diminishing his own role in the process.[28]

The firm's marketing efforts continued, and George Rendel's memoranda about the naval defense of China were influential in winning Armstrongs an 1880 order for torpedo boats.[29] When a Chinese Admiral visited Britain in 1881, he was "given the grand tour: presented at Court, visitations to the royal dock-yards, and Woolwich with the usual banquets and complimentary speeches."[30] He also toured Elswick's factories and dockyards. This was an effort by Armstrongs to win an order which Krupp's agents – and the many Chinese officials they had bribed – wanted for the German firm. Major Bridgford in Peking was anxious that the firm impress the Admiral with the greatness of British naval strength and expertise, which he saw as key to Armstrongs getting the sale.[31] In 1881 some of Sir William's speeches were translated into Chinese and published the following year in Peking.[32]

Armstrongs continued to seek orders in Japan, for example, by entertaining the Japanese Legation at Cragside in January 1884.[33] Chief Constructor William White wrote a specification memorandum for the Japanese Naval Commission under Admiral Ito, resulting in the 1883 contracts for the *Naniwa* and

[27] Hart to Campbell, October 27, 1880 (Letter 303), and Hart to Campbell (Letter 305), November 18, 1880. Fairbank, Bruner and Matheson, *I.G.*, pp. 345–46 and 347.
[28] Bastable, *Arms*, p. 153. Citing TWA, 31/3120.
[29] Hart to Campbell, October 27, 1880 (Letter 303). Fairbank, Bruner and Matheson, *I.G.*, p. 346.
[30] Bastable, *Arms*, p. 115.
[31] Bridgford Report, December 23, 1880. TWA, 31/2689.
[32] Arthur Gart to Armstrong, July 21, 1882. TWA, DF/A/3/8.
[33] Japanese Legation to Armstrong, January 19, 1884. TWA, DF/A/3/12.

Takachiho cruisers.[34] The design used, though based on the Elswick design, was customized by Sasō Sachū, showing that Japan's capacity for design and production was expanding. While the cruisers were being built on the Tyne in 1885 (and after White had returned to the Admiralty as DNC), there was a European war scare, leaving the Japanese concerned that their ships might be commandeered by the British Government. White reported to First Sea Lord Sir Astley Cooper Key, "I discovered, as we anticipated, that the Japanese are very anxious to have these ships themselves as soon as possible; and I think, from a casual remark made, that, if the transfer were insisted upon, the Japanese would look for ample monetary compensation."[35] As it was, the scare passed and the ships were delivered to Japan.

After the 1884 French bombardment of the Foo-Chow (Fuzhou) naval dockyard – ironically, the facility had been built with French help – Hart and Campbell worked to prevent a wider conflict with China and bring about peace. They were aided in Britain by Stuart Rendel, who lobbied the British Government on behalf of Hart's peace plans, contacting Lord Granville directly. Gladstone, however, was not prepared to become involved, to Hart's frustration. According to Rendel, the British began to fear that the Qing Government might fragment, removing the buffer between India and Russia.[36] Faced with this impasse, Hart acted himself, dispatching Campbell to France, ostensibly to deal with a small issue – the French capture of a Chinese lighthouse tender *Feihe*, which benefited all shipping by supplying lighthouses – but in reality to open the door to peace.[37] Campbell briefed Rendel (and, through him, Lord Granville) before he left for the continent. By this means Hart and Campbell negotiated peace between China and France, and along the way legitimated the role of the Inspector General in China's international relations.[38] The action also deepened the relationship between Rendel and Hart, and therefore between the Inspector General and Armstrongs.

The French bombardment, opening the Sino-French War (1884–85), was the culmination of increasing French activism in Indo-China. The French navy easily destroyed twenty-two Chinese ships spurring China to make, as opposed to talk about, further warship purchases. "The Southern mandarins [senior bureaucrats] discussed these events with some British merchants, whose influence with them was perhaps greater because it was unofficial; and inquiries came to Armstrong's through several of these firms."[39] One of the agents made it clear that bribes would have to be paid, as well as commissions, adding 10 percent to any estimate.[40]

---

34 Manning, *William White*, pp. 118–21.
35 Manning, *William White*, p. 176. Citing White to Cooper Key, April 10, 1885.
36 Rendel, *Personal Papers*, pp. 243–66.
37 Michie, *Englishman*, pp. 333–34.
38 van de Ven, *Breaking*, p. 115.
39 Manning, *William White*, p. 155.
40 Manning, *William White*, p. 156. Citing Agent in Shanghai, January 21, 1885.

Krupps was also seeking this order. William White wrote a detailed memorandum on the naval defense of China, which Campbell passed to Robert Hart.[41] The latter was again influential on Armstrongs' behalf because he believed it was in the best interests of China; he rejected commissions, preferring to ensure that China could buy weapons at a lower price.[42] Although those Chinese bureaucrats seeking bribes plotted against Hart, on this occasion they failed and he was able to persuade the Chinese to buy Armstrongs cruisers instead of Krupp ironclads.[43] White designed two protected cruisers for China, the *Chih-Yuen* and *Ching-Yuen*, which were launched at Elswick in 1886.[44] In the same year Hart attempted to send more business to Armstrongs, telegraphing detailed specifications via Campbell for the costs and schedules for three steamers. However, this was not successful.[45]

Between the 1850s and the 1880s British Government engagement with Asia was designed to open up the countries to the world and promote free trade (not specifically trade with Britain) on the assumption these changes would bring benefits to all. Nevertheless, responding to accounts of German Government activities in Japan, on August 2, 1885, Prime Minister Lord Salisbury cabled the British Legation in Tokyo, "In cases where foreign Representatives interfere to the detriment of British commercial interest, you are at liberty to give the latter your support."[46] He sent the same message to O'Conor in China in January 1886.[47] Months later, "Lord Rosebery in fact told the Marquis Tseng [Zeng Jize], on ratifying a convention in 1886, that he was against governments putting pressure on other governments to obtain commercial advantages in a narrow sense, but that all we desired was a 'fair field and no favour.'"[48] However, this British Government policy could not withstand the pressure exerted by other European legations in Asia, which strongly represented the interests of their own national firms.

When the Chinese announced a plan to purchase a significant amount of armaments in 1886, Sir Robert Jardine, of Jardine, Matheson & Co., lobbied Foreign Secretary Lord Rosebery that British manufacturers of armaments and railways needed more support from the government to secure contracts in China.[49] This came while Parliamentary Under-Secretary James Bryce was investigating what more the government could do to support British trade and commerce (see Chapter 2).[50] In February 1886 the London Chamber of

---

[41] Manning, *William White*, pp. 140–44.
[42] "Gunboats for China, 1876–1881," VA, Doc. 626, pp. 3–4.
[43] Bastable, *Arms*, p. 120.
[44] Noble to Stuart Rendel, October 11, 1886. TWA, 31/2810.
[45] Campbell to Rendel, December 21, 1886. TWA ,31/2819.
[46] Platt, *Finance*, p. 272.
[47] Salisbury to O'Conor, January 26, 1886. In "Correspondence."
[48] Rosebery to O'Conor, May 6, 1886. Communication No. 47. In "Correspondence."
[49] Platt, *Finance*, p. 59.
[50] Bryce Minute, February 9, 1886. "Foreign Office: Political and Other Departments: General Correspondence before 1906," TNA, FO 17/1035.

Commerce wrote to the Marquis of Salisbury about support for British firms
in China, declaring:

> At a time when the Chinese Government is engaged in providing arma-
> ments on a large scale, and is now to contemplate large expenditure for
> railway and other industrial undertakings, it is of the utmost importance,
> in the interests of British trade, as well as of the merchants who have at
> much expense established themselves in China, that they should have the
> firm support and assistance of Her Majesty's representatives at Peking.[51]

The Chamber further stated that if this support was withheld, the trade would
certainly go to Germany or the United States. This request came at a time of
increased Foreign Office interest in supporting trade, and reinforced the mandate for the Diplomatic Service to support British firms. Nevertheless, the
laissez-faire ideology and culture of the Diplomatic Service still inhibited the
activities of British Embassies and Legations in the region.

Responding to pressure from Sir Robert Jardine, the Foreign Office facilitated the temporary transfer of a member of the China Consular Service to
work with the firm. As David McLean reported, "The firm, anxious to gain
the exclusive agency in China of Armstrong, Mitchell, and Company, had
approached consul Spence, at Taiwan, with an offer of six years' employment
in January 1886." [52] The Treasury put up a fight about how long Spence could
be away from government, and the agreement with the Foreign Office was for
four years' absence. Spence soon proved his worth to Jardine, Matheson &
Co., within three months securing a deal for Armstrongs to provide thirty-one
steel, breech-loading, heavy guns for the defense of Formosa.[53] "The price was
fixed at Tls. [Taels] 600,000, [£18,227,734 in August 2022] to be paid in three
instalments, and included the cost of carriages, projectiles, packing cases and
freight." The guns were all delivered, tested and approved by spring 1889.[54]
Another Armstrongs deal with China saw them supply 7-inch breech-loading
guns for coastal defense; China actually mounted these on a locally produced
cruiser.[55]

Following the launch of the *Naniwa* and *Takachiho* in 1885, the Japanese warship business was lost: "French diplomats, the Paris banks, and the arms syndicate took it right out of English hands."[56] Crucial to this switch was the 1886

51 Kenric Murray to Salisbury, February 5, 1886. In "Correspondence," Communication
No. 1, p. 1; London Chamber of Commerce to Foreign Office, February 3, 1886. "Foreign
Office: Political and Other Departments: General Correspondence before 1906," TNA, FO
17/1035.
52 McLean, "Commerce," p. 472.
53 McLean, "Commerce," p. 473. Citing Jardine, Matheson & Co. to Armstrong, Mitchell &
Co. Ltd., April 19 and 28, 1886. Jardine Matheson Papers, B.6, Vol. 52.
54 "Armstrong Guns," p. 522.
55 Wright, *Chinese*, p. 69.
56 Hymans, "Why Recognize?" pp. 66–67. Citing Ropp, *Modern Navy*, p. 71.

appointment of Louis-Emile Bertin, a French naval engineer, as chief advisor at the Yokosuka yard, one of five Naval Districts of the Imperial Japanese Navy. Under his influence, the Japanese adopted the *Jeune École* naval theory and began procuring their warships from France. Armstrongs complained loudly to the Foreign Office that it was losing Japanese contracts to the French. As Jacques Hymans records: "Their cries caught the ear of Lord Salisbury, who wrote to the British legation in Tokyo in July 1887 to apply his 1885 rule of leveling the playing field for British business in pursuit of naval contracts."[57] However, Ambassador Sir Francis Plunkett replied that the decision to hire Bertin had reflected a Japanese strategic decision to adopt the French *Jeune École* model. "Under such circumstances, little or no diplomatic pressure is required to turn naval contracts towards France sooner than elsewhere. I fear, therefore, that I have no locus standi to make any useful representation on this point."[58] Plunkett thought that British firms were losing naval orders because of the deteriorating relationship between the Japanese leadership and British diplomats in Tokyo, and this was why they had turned to France. He sought to improve relations by offering to provide British naval officers to teach at the Naval College in Japan and in a new Naval Cadet School. As a result, in 1887 Captain John Ingles arrived in the country to teach British naval theory. Ingles and Bertin quickly became serious rivals.

While relations between the Japanese Government and the British Legation were strained, this was not true of relations between the Japanese Government and Armstrongs, which remained very positive. The firm was contributing to Japanese modernization and "some forty or fifty young Japs of high social position have been articled as pupils to Sir William Armstrong, Mitchell and Company at Elswick."[59] There had also been high-level Japanese visitors to Cragside and Elswick, including Chief Engineer Yashida T. in April 1886, the Minister of Marine General Count Saigo in September 1886 and future Prime Minister Saito Makoto in the same month.[60]

In 1891 Armstrongs was invited by Japan to tender for a 4,200-ton cruiser, and in November the design – by Philip Watts – was accepted with some modifications.[61] The British Legation (and Hymans) attributed this to Britain's improved relationship with the Japanese Government, but Armstrongs' independent diplomacy certainly played a role.[62] When she was launched in 1892, the *Yoshino* was the fastest cruiser in the world, making 23 knots in trials.[63]

In 1893 O'Conor in Peking informed Foreign Secretary Earl Rosebery that China was intending to add two cruisers to the Southern Fleet and that the

[57] Hymans, "Why Recognize?" p. 67.
[58] Cited in Hymans, "Why Recognize?" p. 67.
[59] Dolman, "Notable," p. 581.
[60] M. Conte-Helm, *Japan*, pp. 60–62.
[61] Brook, *Warships*, p. 79.
[62] Hymans, "Why Recognize?" p. 68.
[63] Wilson, *Ironclads*, p. 59; Wright, *Chinese*, p. 87; Brook, *Warships*, p. 79.

new Chinese Minister to London, Kung Chao Yuan (Gong Zhaoyuan), "had no doubt he would be authorized by the Viceroy of Nanking to have these ships built in England."[64] While Armstrongs would seem to be the natural home for further Chinese orders, Sir Edward Grey had informed Benjamin C. Browne, Chairman of Hawthorne Leslie (Newcastle upon Tyne) of the potential for an order. Browne wrote afterwards to Sir Edward, "I am very much obliged to you for the information as to the Chinese Cruisers and I have at once written to see what we can do in the matter, our difficulty is that all our Chinese work has been done through Elswick, but I hope this may be got over."[65]

However, neither British firm secured the order. In March 1894 O'Conor reported to the new Foreign Secretary Earl Kimberly that an order for four torpedo boats had actually been placed with the German firms Vulcan Works and M. Schichau.[66] Noting his previous optimistic dispatch, he stated that "it is much to be hoped that those British firms, who are directly interested in such matters will see their way to approaching Kung Jajên upon his arrival in Paris and before he has committed himself to giving any part of the order in France, so as to secure these contracts."[67] O'Conor reflected on his role in this issue, commenting:

> It will be as well perhaps that my name should not be connected with any information on this subject which may be conveyed to Messrs. Armstrong or other British shipbuilding firms – at all events it should not come around to the Chinese Minister. Hitherto I have carefully refrained from the sort of "touting" for Government orders which distinguished so much the late German Minister, Monsieur von Brandt, and I think it is in the interests of England that I should continue in this course …. [I]t gives me a good position from which to interfere if at any time I notice that an undue proportion of orders for naval armaments are going to Germany – or France.[68]

Marginalia shows that Earl Kimberley authorized that this information be provided to Captain Noble at Armstrongs, but specifying "not stating source of information."[69]

Armstrongs responded to O'Conor's prompting and China's urgent need for boats and, as they did not have a stock torpedo gunboat under construction, scrambled to buy a model from Whites of Cowes.[70] In six months the gunboat

[64] O'Conor to Rosebery, December 31, 1893. TNA, FO17/1158, Folios 411–412. Text has "Kung Jajên." I am grateful to Dr. Edward McCord for noticing this error.
[65] Browne to Grey, November 18, 1893. TNA, FO 800/36. Folio 76.
[66] Also recorded at "Purchase of 4 Torpedo Boats in Germany for Southern Squadron," Chinese Secretary's Office, Misc. No. 23 of 1894. "Chinese Secretary's Office: Sino-Japanese War: Denunciation of Li Hung-chang," 1894. TNA, FO 233/119.
[67] O'Conor to Kimberley, March 24, 1894. TNA, FO17/1193, Folio 40.
[68] O'Conor to Kimberley, March 24, 1894, Folios 40–41.
[69] O'Conor to Kimberley, March 24, 1894, Folio 39.
[70] Wright, *Chinese*, pp. 107–08.

Sea Serpent was substantially rebuilt, strengthened and armed with the latest Armstrong 3.75-inch, 25 pounder, quick-fire guns.[71] This was an extremely speedy completion.

In 1894 Armstrongs was involved in fresh export issues relating to sales to Japan and China. Two years previously Armstrongs had signed a "treaty" with Japan for a "torpedo catcher," and on July 31, 1894, the *Tatsuta* had hastily sailed for Japan, manned by a crew provided by the firm, indicating an urgent departure. On 1 August Japan formally declared war on China. On 6 August Armstrongs sold the *Sea Serpent*, renamed the *Fei Ting*, to John Palmer, Jr., an agent for China.[72] As the *Fei Ting* had been bought after war was declared, on 13 September the Board of Customs detained the *Fei Ting*. In November 1894 the *Tatsuta* was detained by the British authorities in Aden, "but shortly afterwards the British government indicated that they were prepared to release her and hand her over to Japan."[73] Having completed her steam trials while in custody, she was taken over by a Japanese crew and released. The *Fei Ting* was not released until June 1895, two months after the end of the Sino-Japanese War. Ten months later, when she was undergoing trials, she still had Armstrongs engineers on board.[74] China's intention to quickly obtain the ship was therefore thwarted – not by any action by Armstrongs – but by British Government policy. What is interesting is that Armstrongs was consistently regarded by both protagonists as a helpful actor whom they still wanted to work with – quite the diplomatic feat!

On August 26 Sir Robert Hart had prophesied that China would be defeated by Japan in battle and lose many men: "[W]e have no reserves, no spare … guns, rifles or ammunition, and such being the case, I shall probably 'cut in' and arrange things the moment an opportunity presents itself for – the sooner we are out the better!"[75] Hart's forebodings were proved justified and by mid-September the Chinese position was dire; the Battle of the Yalu River had seen most of China's warships sunk and Japan in command of the Yellow Sea, and the situation on land was worsening. In early October 1894 Lord Stuart Rendel sought to use his good offices as an emissary between the Foreign Office and Hart to try to end the conflict. Hart also directly telegraphed Foreign Secretary Lord Kimberly to urge an intervention to prevent Japan advancing on Peking.[76]

The Armstrongs records show that Francis Bertie (Assistant Under-Secretary of State) asked Stuart Rendel to call on him in early October.[77] Two days later Rendel received two important telegrams from Hart (via Campbell) that he

---

[71] Wright, *Chinese*, p. 107.
[72] Brook, *Warships*, p. 170.
[73] Brook, *Warships*, p. 168.
[74] Wright, *Chinese*, p. 108.
[75] Quoted in Campbell to Rendel, October 8, 1894, TWA, 31/3913.
[76] Otte, *China*, p. 39.
[77] Bertie telegram to Rendel, October 3, 1894. TWA, 31/3903.

wished to share with the government.[78] At the same time, O'Conor was urging the Foreign Office to act (likely in collaboration with Hart).[79] In response, Prime Minister Lord Rosebery acted swiftly, reporting to Rendel, "I have already sent a cipher telegram to Kimberly to suggest instant action on certain lines. A copy is going to Murray which you can see."[80] Rendel followed up with a letter to Rosebery the same day that advocated following Hart's advice and acting quickly, "because at any moment the U.S.A. in Pekin might nip in and take our place."[81] The next day Rosebery responded, "With regard to your telegram I am in communication with my colleague but I cannot see how we should be justified in separate action except on one particular point."[82] The problem was how to bring China to capitulate and end the war – something they were seeking to do – but without any loss of status.[83] There was a flurry of correspondence on October 11, begun when Rendel wrote to Rosebery that "China will agree to pay the bill. It is merely a function of how to put it. Hart is the man to find the face-saving [formula]."[84] While Rosebery was ready to act, the Foreign Secretary was not. The British Government let the conflict continue. Rendel's intervention to aid Hart had little impact on British Government policy, although nothing did influence this for months to come.

Armstrongs had supplied ships to both sides in the conflict. DNC William White (who had designed two ships for each side while at Armstrongs) and experts around the world followed the conflict closely as, despite the number of warships in existence, there had not been a naval war for many years and the technologies were untested in combat.[85] Foreign warships – including HMS *Severn* and HMS *Edgar* – observed the twenty-three-day siege of Weihaiwei from nearby.[86] The Japanese navy triumphed.[87] As a Chinese Government account noted drily: "On the announcement of hostilities, military experts and all who had a knowledge of foreign questions were unanimous in thinking that Japan would be crushed like an ant under the wheel of a cart .... The result has strangely falsified all these predictions."[88] While on paper the Chinese navy

---

[78] Campbell telegram to Rendel, 11.35 a.m., October 5, 1894. TWA, 31/3904; Campbell telegram to Rendel, 12.30 p.m., October 5, 1894, TWA, 31/3905.

[79] Otte, *China*, p. 41.

[80] Rosebery telegram to Rendel, October 6, 1894. TWA, 31/3907.

[81] Rendel to Rosebery, October 6, 1894. TWA, 31/3909.

[82] Rosebery telegram to Rendel, October 7, 1894. TWA, 31/3908; Rendel to Rosebery, October 8, 1894. TWA, 31/3914.

[83] Skřivan and Skřivan, "Great Powers," p. 29.

[84] Rendel to Rosebery, October 11, 1894. TWA, 31/3917.

[85] Manning, *William White*, pp. 339–40.

[86] Wright, *Chinese*, pp. 100, ff. 2 and 105, ff. 8.

[87] Wright, *Chinese*, pp. 88–96.

[88] "Memorial denouncing Li Hung-chang (Original through H.M.'s Consul at Tientsin)," C.S.O., Misc. No. 68, December 3, 1894, p. 4. "Chinese Secretary's Office: Sino-Japanese War, Denunciation of Li Hung-chang," TNA, FO 233/119, Folio 211a.

looked respectable, "the Empress Dowager had used the naval maintainance [sic] fund to embellish the Summer Palace, so that the well-equipped Japanese navy made short work of destroying it."[89] The Japanese army inflicted serious damage too, and carried out massacres at Port Arthur, something that Hart had expressed "fears and forebodings" about to Rendel.[90] One consequence of the resounding Chinese defeat was the fall of the friend of Armstrongs, Li Hongzhang. A denunciation against him declared: "The mortification of grief must be attributed to the blind incapacity and haughty distain of Li Hung-chang to whom the soldiers owe their death and the country its ruin."[91]

Accounts sent to Britain described the damage inflicted by the Japanese quick-fire guns on the Armstrong-built protected cruisers *Chi Yuan* and *Ching Yuan*, "scattering sheaves of splinters over the ship, setting her frequently on fire, and riddling everything not protected by armour or below water."[92] In the battle of Yalu River, China lost eight out of its twelve warships, the poorly maintained Armstrong ships being significantly slower than when delivered; their the wooden fixtures and layers of varnish made them very vulnerable to fires started by shells. Only China's two German-made battleships proved resilient to Japanese ordnance.

Japan's decisive victory led Admiral Ito to write to DNC White to extol the "illustrious constructor, to whose talents are due the late successes of our *Naniwa* and *Takachiha*."[93] White's reply, likely reflecting the position of the British Government, which he once again served, declared: "The news of your gallant fight at Weihaiwei has just come to hand. It stirs one's blood to read of what your torpedo flotilla has done in such weather and under such conditions."[94] Sir William and Andrew Noble were awarded the Order of the Sacred Treasure of the Rising Sun in 1895, for assistance rendered during the Sino-Japanese War.[95]

Interestingly both sides were keen to continue purchasing from Armstrongs, an indication of the neutral way in which each perceived the firm. Japan continued an existing warship contract for two advanced cruisers. The *Yashima*

---

[89] Tenney, "Reminiscences of Li Hung-Chang," p. 12. Charles Daniel Tenney Papers.

[90] Campbell to Rendel, November 25, 1894. TWA, 31/3974.

[91] "Memorial denouncing Li Hung-chang," Précis, Folio 212a; "Decree Censoring Li for Dilatoriness in the War with Japan, C.S.O. Misc. No 43," September 17, 1894. Translation from *Peking Gazette*. "Chinese Secretary's Office: Sino-Japanese War, Views of foreign officers in Chinese fleet on punishment of …," TNA, FO 233/119; "Denunciation of Li Hung-chang," C.S.O. Misc. No. 13 of 1895. January 1895. Chinese Secretary's Office: Sino-Japanese War: Denunciation of Li Hung-chang, 1894. TNA, FO, 233/119/68.

[92] "Von Hammelkeu's Report of Naval Action off Yaloo [Yalu] – given to Admiral by his clerk," C.S.O. Misc. No. 55, undated, p. 11. "Chinese Secretary's Office: Sino-Japanese War, Denunciation of Li Hung-chang," TNA, FO 233/119, Folio 176.

[93] Manning, *William White*, p. 340. Citing Ito to White, December 23, 1894.

[94] Manning, *William White*, p. 341. Citing White to Ito, February 11, 1895.

[95] Diary May 10, 1886, ff. 184. Ruxton, *Diaries*. Citing Conte-Helm, "Armstrong, Vickers and Japan."

protected cruiser, closely modeled on an Admiralty design and very similar to the contemporaneous *Fuji* designed by the Thames Iron Works (but claimed as Watt's work), was launched in 1896 and delivered in 1897.[96] The ship had an innovative armored shield to protect the guns. Initially laid down as a stock cruiser but with modified armament compared to her sister, the *Takasago* was launched in 1897.[97] As Roger Parkinson drily comments: "Once again leading-edge British technology was immediately available to a foreign power that could pay for it."[98]

Li Hongzhang was soon restored to prominence in China and charged with negotiating peace with Japan.[99] Although chronically short of money due to the war indemnity it had to pay Japan, China was keen to rebuild her navy and to benefit once again from Armstrongs' expertise; it clearly regarded the firm as an apolitical – and helpful – actor. However, Hart was opposed to new naval purchases because of China's shortage of money. The Chinese leadership ignored Hart's advice and sought loans to pay for the equipment. There were negotiations with the Hong Kong and Shanghai Banking Corporation and Deutsche-Asiatische Bank to lend the Imperial Government £16,000,000. At the same time China was negotiating with Russia over a loan.[100] British bankers were also competing for the loan and there was discussion about China's readiness to give up Formosa to get the money. The Chinese Secretary's office obtained a private letter from Mr. Bristow (likely of the Pekin Syndicate Limited) to Claude Maxwell MacDonald (to become British Minister in China in 1896) about a loan. This was followed by a letter from Bristow to O'Conor which mentioned that the Chinese planned to buy warships with the loan.[101] In the end, however, a loan was taken from Russia; the British Government accepted this but the German Government was very unhappy about it, wanting to maintain influence over China. Subsequently, China negotiated – within weeks – an additional loan from German merchants.[102] Armstrongs was obviously concerned that any purchases made with German loans would be of ships made in German shipyards.

---

[96] Brook, *Warships*, pp. 119 and 123.
[97] Brook, *Warships*, p. 89.
[98] Parkinson, *Late Victorian*, p. 184.
[99] "Full Powers Granted to Li Hung-chang for Negotiating Treaty of Peace with Japan," C.S.O. Misc. No. 35 of 1895. "Chinese Secretary's Office: Sino-Japanese War, Views of foreign officers in Chinese fleet on punishment of …," TNA, FO 233/119.
[100] "Chinese Secretary's Office: Finance: Memo on proposal of Hong Kong and Shanghai Banking Corp. and …," 1895. TNA, FO 233/120/101; FO 233/120/104; FO 233/120/105; "Chinese Secretary's Office: Finance: Russo-Chinese loan agreement," TNA, FO 233/120/96.
[101] "Abstract: Enclosed in private letter from Mr. Bristow dated March 22, 1895, the document was addressed to Mr. Macdonald by someone in Peking." C.S.O. Misc. No. 39 of 1895. FO 233/120; "Précis of letter to Mr. Macdonald – described in his covering letter to Mr. Bristow as No. 4. Enclosed in Mr. Bristow's letter to Mr. O'Conor of March 25/95." C.S.O. Misc. No. 45A. TNA, FO 233/120.
[102] "Copy of Telegram to His Excellency Hsü, June 30, 1895." C.S.O. Misc. No. 66. TNA, FO 233/120.

In 1896 the rehabilitated Li Hongzhang traveled to Russia for the coronation of Tsar Nicholas II (and to conclude a secret treaty for the extension of the Trans-Siberian Railway through Manchuria), and then to Germany, France, Belgium, Britain and the United States. All the major armament firms were involved in the British tour by Li Hongzhang, who had become Grand Secretary in August 1895.[103] The red carpet was rolled out across Britain. This tour opened the possibility of new naval sales, though Li Hongzhang was said to want loans to build railways too.[104] Sigmund Loewe of Maxim-Nordenfeld was seeking money for China from financiers Ernest Cassel and Rothschilds, so that China could buy guns from his firm. Loewe had leased the Pinner estate of Mrs. Beaton (of cookbook fame) and entertained Li Hongzhang and his entourage there. During their stay, "Squads of Chinese dragging machine guns about and firing them with more relish than discrimination were to be found at all daylight hours."[105] Photographs show that a Maxim gun demonstration completely destroyed a tree.[106] Hongzhang's Maxim-Nordenfeld visit also included entertainment at the Empire Theatre.[107]

Li Hongzhang's visit to Armstrongs included trips to three different sites: the Ordnance Works, where he watched a torpedo discharge on the jetty; the Elswick Shipyard; and the Steel Works.[108] In Glasgow he and his entourage, along with the Lord Provost, visited Messrs. Neilson & Co.'s works.[109] In Chester he met Mr. Gladstone.[110] Li Hongzhang also spent three days at Vickers' new Barrow shipyard and was feted with a program of activities, included being serenaded by the firm's brass band. He inspected the shipyard and the "H.M. First-Class Cruiser *Niobe* and four 30-knot Torpedo Boat Destroyers, now under construction."[111] Later he met the Duke of Devonshire at the Furness Abbey Hotel.[112] Having toured Lake Windermere on a steamer

---

[103] "Li Hung-chang to Peking as Grand Secretary, August 28, 1895." C.S.O. Misc. No. 84. TNA, FO 233/120.

[104] "Real Mission of Li Hung Chang," p. 6.

[105] Notes of an interview with Sigmund Loewe's daughter Mrs. Orbach, January 19, 1959. VA, Doc. 788.

[106] Photograph, "Maxim Gun Demonstration, to Chinese Ambassador Li Hung Chang at Pinner in 1896, with Albert Vickers and Sigmund Loewe," www.alamy.com/stock-photo-maxim-gun-demonstration-to-chinese-ambassador-li-hung-chang-at-pinner-26818695.html.

[107] Program of entertainment from the Empire Theatre, including a demonstration of M. Trewey's Lumière Cinématographe. VA, 1933, Loewe Papers C/10.

[108] Program for the visit of His Excellency Li Hung Chang to the Elswick Works, August 20, 1896. VA, Doc. 1911.

[109] "Photograph of His Excellency Li Hung Chang and suite arriving at Messrs Neilson and Co.," August 26, 1896. TNA, COPY 1/426/442.

[110] "Photograph of Mr. Gladstone and Li Hung Chang," August 18, 1896. TNA, COPY 1/426/261.

[111] "Visit of His Excellency Li Hung Chang, August 15–17, 1896: printed program; Barrow; VIP visit," 1896. Cumbria Archive Center, Kendal, WDSo, 108/A 2513/Kerr PR 1/002, p. 3.

[112] "Photograph of His Grace the Duke of Devonshire and Li Hung Chang," August 20, 1896. TNA, COPY 1/426/276.

provided by the Furness Railway (no doubt hoping for contracts), he met two Members of Parliament, Victor Cavendish and R. F. Cavendish, at the Belsfield Hotel Bowness.[113] Li Hongzhang also observed the Royal Naval Review at Spithead, dined with royalty, attended Parliament and was awarded the Grand Knight Cross of the Victorian Order by the Queen. At the Foreign Office Li Hongzhang, dressed in a yellow jacket and peacock feather, was carried by chair up the great staircase to the Secretary of State's room. "In the middle of the second flight the little procession stopped, and much to our wonderment, the chair was put down. Then one of the suite solemnly stepped forward and wiped Li Hung Chang's nose, and the procession continued on its way."[114] In his diary, however, the only part of the trip Li Hongzhang recorded was his meeting with Gladstone, whom he deeply admired.[115]

Armstrongs' diplomacy was somewhat effective as China accepted their tender to supply two Watts-designed protected cruisers, though the bulk of orders went to the German firms Vulcan and Schichau. The 4,300-ton Armstrongs cruisers were named *Hai Chi* and *Hai Tien*, and cost £336,659 each [£48,635,809 in August 2022].[116] They reached China in August 1899. Vickers, however, received no orders.

Although the relationship between the British and Japanese governments languished between 1895 and 1900, the same was not true of relations between Japan and Armstrongs. In May 1896 Noble traveled to Japan. It seems that many were curious about the purpose of his trip, with Hammond of the Legation sending a secretary to ask Noble why he had come to Japan.[117] During a dinner party at Secretary of Legation Gerard Lowther's, Ambassador Sir Ernest Satow easily extracted the truth and telegraphed it back to London:

> Sir Andrew Noble told me that Japanese anxious with regard to Russia, and the real object of his visit is to agree with them about increase of their navy beyond what is sanctioned by Parliament. Armstrongs to build ships ostensibly not for Japan, and to keep them in stock, as it were. Particularly desirous to have a ship that can beat *Rurik*. Has told them he can build one 2000 tons less, with less coal capacity, which they do not need to be so large as that of *Rurik*, 3 knots more speed and 18 broadside guns instead of 15. So that they would have the weatherage of her. The Japs want to be strong enough to cope alone with Russia.[118]

During his trip, the Noble party was also entertained at Armstrongs' ambassador-agent Balthasar Münster's house, and at the homes of prominent

[113] "Photograph of group of guests of R.F. Coy at Belsfield Hotel Bowness, Including Li Hung-Chang," August 20, 1896. TNA, COPY 1/426/277.
[114] Tilley and Gaselee, *Foreign Office*, pp. 141–42.
[115] Mannix, *Memoirs*, pp. 177–81.
[116] Wright, *Chinese*, pp. 111 and 113–14.
[117] "Journal of Sir Ernest Satow," May 18, p. 9A. TNA, PRO 30/33/16/1.
[118] "Journal of Sir Ernest Satow," May 23, p. 12. TNA, PRO 30/33/16/1.

Japanese officials Okura, Oyama and Saigo, among other places.[119] Meanwhile Noble telegraphed back to Armstrongs to lay down two stock cruisers, and work began on updating the design from the Chilean *O'Higgins* blueprints. Several iterations were sent to Tokyo before the Imperial Navy agreed to a design for a heavier cruiser, with more armaments and speed than the *O'Higgins*. The first cruiser was laid down nine months before the order was finally received.[120]

Noble actively conducted diplomacy with both China and Japan. A June 1897 letter to Sir William from Noble recounts that he was kept in the city for an extra day and "had an interview" with the Chinese Ambassador in London, who seems to have been angling for an invitation to Cragside, and who wanted to see Noble again the following week. In the same letter Noble noted that he had been "chiefly occupied in London arranging [ship?] contents with the Japanese Govt."[121]

Of lesser importance to Armstrongs or Vickers was the relationship with Siam (Thailand), but the connection brought a trickle of sales over the period. In 1894, when Siam feared war with the French, it turned to Armstrongs and bought guns "off the shelf."[122] In 1897 King Rama V visited Armstrongs' shipyard. This turned out to be Sir William's final visit to Elswick.[123] King Rama also stayed at Cragside. This visit by the King seems to have led to further sales of Armstrong guns to the Siamese navy as it sought to "Westernize," through the addition of the guns to wooden steamships.[124]

In 1898, when British Government policy shifted further in support of British industry in China due to the "war of concessions," the firms championed by the British Embassy were active in railways, mining and the financing of loans.[125] The comparatively less lucrative armaments exports did not occupy much Embassy time. What came to dominate the thinking of every foreigner was the Boxer Rebellion of 1900, which had been brewing for some months, fueled by floods and famine. As Marshall Bastable has noted, Armstrongs voluntarily gave the Foreign Office a list of Krupp and Armstrong guns that had been supplied to China.[126] The subsequent taking of the Taku forts and dockyard by an alliance of foreign forces meant that China lost most of her ships, which were split between the allies.[127] In 1904–05, when China was once again rebuilding her fleet, the orders for small gunboats went not to European firms but to Japan.

[119] "Journal of Sir Ernest Satow," May 11, p. 6, May 13, p. 6A, May 15, p. 7, and May 27, p. 12A. TNA, PRO 30/33/16/1.
[120] Brook, *Warships*, pp. 107–09; Milanovich, "Armored Cruisers," p. 73.
[121] Noble to Armstrong, June 13, 1897, TWA, DF/A/1/24/1.
[122] Dolman, "Notable," p. 582.
[123] Frederick Varney, Siamese Legation to Armstrong, August 10, 1897. TWA, DF/A/3/17; Fairbairn, *Elswick*, VA, Doc. 593, p. 97.
[124] Black, *Naval*, p. 41.
[125] Platt, *Finance*, p. 294.
[126] Bastable, *Arms*, p. 216, ff. 48. Citing Noble to Bertie, November 3, 1900. TNA, FO 17/1449.
[127] Wright, *Chinese*, pp. 117–18.

Japan was increasingly concerned about being able to withstand any Russian naval attacks. Through combat experience Japanese naval experts had realized that the French *Jeune École* strategy, which relied on the use of torpedo boats against heavily armed warships, had serious weaknesses. This spurred a new naval building program. In 1897 Vickers hosted a Commission from the Japanese Legation, who were shown around the Barrow Yard and then entertained to lunch. A local magazine subsequently reported, "It is probable this visit of the Japanese Commission ... will mean new business to Barrow."[128] This came to pass. In 1898 Japan placed an order with Vickers for a powerful battleship, the *Mikasa*, for delivery in 1902. The Japanese ship was prioritized over the Admiralty's *Euryalus*, much to the annoyance of DNC William White.[129] Thanks to this chicanery, the *Mikasa* was completed in two and a half years, being launched in 1900 and commissioned, as promised, in 1902.

Armstrongs, with their well-established relationship with Japan, received orders for the battleship *Hatsuse*, the Asama-class cruisers *Asama* and *Tokiwa*, and the armored cruisers *Idzumo* and *Iwate*.[130] Japan also ordered the warships *Asahi* from John Brown and *Shikishima* from the Thames Ironworks. These two warships, the *Mikasa* and the *Hatsuse*, had Elswick-designed heavy mountings.[131] All the ships were paid for with China's £30,000,000 indemnity for losing the Sino-Japanese War. The *Idzumo* was launched on September 19, 1899, and finished a year later.[132] The *Hatsuse*, with a displacement of 15,000 tons, was launched at Elswick on June 27, 1899.[133] The *Iwate* was launched at Elswick in 1900.

The importance of these purchases from Armstrongs and Vickers was shown in the Japanese naval victory over Russia in 1904. As reported in 1906:

> The task that confronted the little Japanese Navy at the outbreak of the recent war was simply stupendous. By the book, and on paper, it was simply impossible of accomplishment. Theoretically, by the laws of all naval strategy, that Navy should have been at least three times as large as it was to accomplish with certainty, the work that confronted it.[134]

That Japan triumphed – and captured many Russian ships – was a great advertisement for the products of Armstrongs and Vickers. Even Russia sought to buy from them during the conflict, and in 1905 Zaharoff cemented a deal for Vickers to create the major Nicolaieff naval dockyard in Russia, and for

---

[128] "Barrow," p. 105.
[129] Manning, *William White*, pp. 411–12.
[130] "Launch of Japanese Battleship Hatsuse," photographs, date unknown. TWA, D.VA/24/4.
[131] Brook, "Armstrong Battleships," p. 278.
[132] "Armoured Cruiser Idzumo launched in 1899," 1899. TWA, D.VA/21/3.
[133] *Shields Daily Gazette*, June 27, 1899, p. 3.
[134] "The Japanese Navy," p. 325.

Barrow to build the Russian-designed *Rurik*.[135] Moreover, the performance of the *Mikasa*, Admiral Tōgō's flagship throughout the Russo-Japanese War, cemented Vickers arrival as a competitor to Armstrongs and other warship manufacturers. Albert Vickers was sent a photograph of Admiral Tōgō as a memento of the *Mikasa*.[136] Vickers' designer George Thurston earned the Order of the Rising Sun for his work for Japan.[137]

In 1904, before the conflict with Russia, Japan had ordered two battleships, one each from Vickers and Armstrongs. Armstrongs' *Kashima* was designed by their architect Josiah Perrett (from G. G. Mackrow's basic design) and was launched in 1905.[138] The Vickers' ship, *Katori*, was slightly smaller but more heavily armed.[139] Both underwent trials in 1906 overseen by the Japanese Special Commission in Britain under Captain Tanaka and Captain Fujii, the *Kashima* using the Admiralty run off the Tyne, and the *Katori* in the Irish Sea.[140] Together the battleships were considered to be "a splendid advance on even the ships of our [Britain's] *King Edward VII* class."[141] This was particularly true of the armaments. In building the *Kashima* in two years and two months, Armstrongs had given "a performance worthy of the high traditions of the company, and four months within the contract time."[142]

That said, the Vickers' ship was more highly praised. The *Katori* was feted for her record-breaking fighting power and speed.

> Built and completed in every respect for war by Messrs. Vickers Sons and Maxim, Limited, she represents what may be regarded as the highest conception, prior to the late war, of what a battleship should be; and the anticipations of the design have been more than fulfilled during the searching tests as to guns and speed made by the Japanese naval authorities in this country, terminating with most successful ordnance trials.[143]

The guns and gun mountings benefited from "many improvements in detail, as a result of experience and experiment."[144] This reflected the Vickers' organizational culture of innovation and was a serious challenge to Armstrongs, which had previously been the only firm able to build complete armed warships.

---

[135] "Trials of the 'Rurik,'" p. 346. As Norman Friedman records, the Vickers designs 160A and 160B were marked as "large armoured cruisers for Z.Z." This was Zaharoff's nickname, so he was likely involved in securing the sale. Friedman, *British Cruisers*, p. 268. On the Nicolaieff dockyard see Trebilcock, "British Armaments," pp. 263–67.

[136] Albert Vickers to Commander Kato, November 26, 1909. Letter Book 31, VA 1005, Folio 46.

[137] "Obituary: Sir George Thurston," p. 153.

[138] "First Class Battleship Kashima," 1905. TWA, D.VA/21/4.

[139] Brook, "Armstrong Battleships," pp. 268 and 279–81.

[140] "First Class Battleship Kashima," 1905. TWA, D.VA/21/4.

[141] "Japan: Kashima," p. 673. Citing *Engineering*.

[142] "Japan: Kashima," p. 676. Citing *Engineering*.

[143] "Katori," p. 682.

[144] "Japan Katori," p. 677.

In September 1907 there was an accident onboard Armstrongs' *Kashima* during target practice. The starboard 10-in turret gun exploded, resulting in what Captain Murakami (an "informer" cited in a U.S. naval intelligence report) described as a "great loss of life and injury," mostly due to the jet of flames exiting the turret.[145] The explosion seemed to mirror one that the United States had experienced on the USS *Georgia*. Office of Navy Intelligence personnel visited Newcastle to discuss the *Kashima* incident with Noble and Captain Lloyd, Armstrongs' Director of Ordnance.[146]

Around 1906 Armstrongs and Vickers agreed a work and profit share arrangement on orders for Japan:

Japan   A. and V. partners with Tanko Company in Seiko Sho.
        All work to be divided in equal shares.
        In the case of the Cruiser now being built by V. They pay A.:-
            3% on Hull.
            3½% on Engines.
            12½% on Armament.
            £10 per ton on Hull Armour
            £15 per ton on Shield Armour.[147]

In 1908 news broke that the Chinese navy was to be reorganized and rebuilt, and firms from around the world responded with a flood of tenders. In 1909 the Chinese Naval Commission toured countries with shipbuilding industries. While in Britain Admiral Sah, one of the heads of the Commission, was awarded the KCMG. Vickers' Head Office arranged for the Commission to stay at the Furness Abbey Hotel, where the firm arranged a firework display. Head office cautioned Barrow over the arrangements: "[W]e wish you to carefully consider the matter most secret" and "to refrain in any way from letting our intention become known, as we do not wish either the press, or the public (and, of course, any of our competitors), to be aware of this."[148] The Commission visited both Elswick and Barrow.[149]

The following year both Armstrongs and Vickers won contracts from China to build training cruisers (a third contract with a promise of more orders went

---

[145] Brook, "Armstrong Battleships," pp. 279–81. Citing U.S. Navy Office of Naval Intelligence Report concerning the Kashima's 1907 10-inch gun powder explosion. U.S. National Archives, RG38, entry 98 series 1 (1886–1939) Box 1260, file #07-672.

[146] Brook, "Armstrong Battleships," p. 281. Citing Office of Naval Intelligence Report.

[147] "Armstrongs and Vickers (about 1906 to 1913)," confidential memorandum signed by A. M. W. of Armstrongs, undated. "War Work," p. 3. VA, Doc. 551.

[148] Vickers to the Directors, Barrow, November 26, 1909. Letter Book 31, VA 1005, Folios 44–45.

[149] Wright, *Chinese*, pp. 123–24. In Italy, the Commission was also entertained by Royalty. It awarded a contract for the *Qing Po* to the Gio. Ansaldo and Armstrongs Company (an alliance formed in the 1890s). Fang and Ceccarelli, "On the Warship by Ansaldo," pp. 223–33.

to the New York Shipping Company, part of the Bethlehem Steel Corporation). The Armstrongs protected cruiser *Chao Ho* was designed by Josiah Perrett. He based the hull on a model developed at the Admiralty experimental tank where he used to work; there seems to have been no sense that the knowledge he had obtained there was proprietary. The Vickers' *Ying Swei* was a protected cruiser also built to Perrett's design. Once the *Chao Ho* was completed by Armstrongs in 1911, there was a lengthy dispute with China over the cost of delivering her to Asia. The Chinese Revolution of October 1911 led to the new Republican Government entering negotiations to sell two of the three training ships, though eventually Chinese loans were renegotiated and in 1913 the *Chao Ho* and *Ying Swei* were accepted by China, arriving in March and April, respectively.[150] Although intended as training cruisers, the two ships were the most modern in the Chinese Republican Navy.

Also in 1913 the new government went on a naval purchasing spree, ordering four cruisers and eighteen destroyers. None of the orders went to Armstrongs, Vickers or the New York Shipping Company. China placed the orders with Vulcan of Stettin, Stablimento Technico of Trieste and CNT Montfalcone. Richard Wright speculated that the Chinese Republican Government did not want to be tied by the previous government's commitment to buy more from the Bethlehem Steel Corporation, and it is also likely that they wanted to draw a line under the relationships and naval networks of the disgraced government.[151] The ships were never delivered to China, however, as the Great War began, and the warships were commandeered. After this, China had no money for major ship purchases for a decade and was consumed by civil war.

Vickers' relationship with Japan continued apace and in 1909 Vickers informed Electric Boat that they were manufacturing three sets of machinery for them, "for which prices are so good that you may count the order equal to three boats."[152] There was a sniff of new sales in the air in May 1910. In response Vickers sent a breathless telegram to James Vickers, via the Traveller's Club in Paris: "We wish you go to Japan on company's business starting next Monday week can you go of course taking your wife with you if you wish please wire whether you can do as your ticket must be taken at once and when you will be back in London."[153] Vickers and Armstrongs both tendered for the contract and – reflecting their agreement – kept their prices in line.[154]

In 1911 Japanese hero Admiral Tōgō and General Nogi were in Britain for the crowning of King George V, and took part in the Spithead Coronation

[150] Brook, *Warships*, pp. 219–20; Wright, *Chinese*, p. 131.
[151] Wright, *Chinese*, pp. 132–33.
[152] Albert Vickers to Isaac Rice, November 16, 1909. Letter Book No. 31. VA Doc. 1005, Folios 7–9.
[153] Albert Vickers to James Vickers, May 26, 1910. Letter Book No. 32. VA, Doc. 1006, Folio 32.
[154] Vickers to Owens, August 1, 1910. Letter Book No. 32. VA, Doc. 1006, Folio 130.

Review. While in London Admiral Tōgō revisited the ship on which he had trained decades before.[155] He also attended a banquet in his honor given by the Royal Navy Club. Among the guests were Sir Charles Ottley (soon to join the Armstrongs Board) and William Charles Dundas of Armstrongs.[156] Additionally, "Admiral Heihachiro Tōgō made a point of visiting the Armstrong works."[157] The Newcastle visit included the Admiral being entertained by Noble, Lady Armstrong and Dundas.[158] During his British stay, Tōgō also visited Glasgow, the yards of Yarrow, Browns in Edinburgh and Vickers' Barrow Works.[159]

Japan is the only state considered in this book that developed an independent warship-building industry. The last ship she purchased was Vickers' George Thurston-designed *Kongō*, ordered in response to Britain's commissioning of Armstrongs' HMS *Invincible* in 1908. The new British capital ships had rendered all Imperial Japanese Navy ships obsolete.[160] The *Kongō* was laid down at Barrow in 1911 and commissioned in 1913. This was followed by three more that were built in Japan from the Thurston design.[161] Thereafter both Armstrongs and Vickers only offered designs to Japan for home production.[162] The acquisition of the *Kongō* contract by Vickers was controversial and subsequently marred by bribery allegations (see Chapter 4).

The Republican Government in China was heavily indebted and fell behind on its payments to all firms. In 1914 George Morrison, Political Adviser to the President of the Republic, wrote to the Imperial Chancellor that it was hard to understand why China could have a surplus of revenue from the Salt administration (a state institution)

> when the Government are repudiating or expressing their inability to pay Treasury Bills as they mature in London. Cases cited to me are those of the two great English firms of Armstrongs and Vickers. The effect is injurious to the credit of China. The total amount is not great. The effect of paying them from current revenue would be of great value to China.[163]

It is not clear if the Chinese Government heeded this advice, but in May 1914 the Chinese Government was negotiating a loan from the Bethlehem Steel Trust

[155] "Admiral Togo," p. 1. After training with the Royal Navy, Tōgō had joined Samuda Brothers in 1877 for work experience.
[156] "Banquet," p. 11.
[157] *Encyclopedia*, p. 41.
[158] "Admiral Togo," *Geordie Japan* blog.
[159] "Admiral Togo Received," p. 3; "Admiral Togo in Glasgow," p. 6; "Admiral Togo Pays Visit to Rosyth," p. 1.
[160] Hackett, Kingsepp and Ahlberg, "IJN Battleship KONGO."
[161] Lengerer, "Kongô Class."
[162] Friedman, *British Battleship*, p. 149.
[163] G. E. Morrison to Yüan Shih-kai, July 17, 1914. In Hui-Min, *Correspondence*, pp. 340–41.

for £6,000,000, with one third in cash and two thirds to pay for the construction of a naval docks.[164]

In 1919 Vickers loaned £1,803,200 to the Chinese government of Duan Qirui at 8 percent interest to enable them to buy twenty-four Vimy and twenty Avro aircraft, as well as spare parts.[165] This loan was a new development, reflecting the difficult economic times being experienced by both suppliers and recipients. Importantly, the sale was approved by the British Government only five months after an Arms Embargo Agreement against China had been agreed with the United States.[166] The government justified the Vickers deal as involving planes for "commercial use only."[167] The decade-long embargo on arms sales to China was begun out of fears that arms left over from the Great War would spark more civil conflict in China. The embargo was leaky as not all countries were involved, but it was reluctantly adhered to by British armament firms, locking them out of the Chinese underground market. In 1922 Vickers eventually rebuffed an approach from the Chinese to buy ten fast scouting planes.[168] According to Anthony Chan,

> Vickers even attempted to circumvent the British government by utilizing its overseas subsidiaries. But the British position was firm. The Canadian government, for example, told R. S. Griffith of Vickers Ltd., Canadian Agency, Montreal, that the export of airplanes was not permitted without departmental approval. Since Canada was part of the British Empire, it supported the Arms Embargo Agreement of 1919.[169]

Vickers was alarmed when the Chinese Government defaulted on a payment for the 1919 aircraft deal. According to the British Government representative in the Chinese Aeronautical Department, the Vickers head office was not behaving well in its efforts to ensure payment was made.[170] The firm agreed a revised loan agreement with China, but by 1923 the Chinese had defaulted on at least three payments to Vickers and the agreement was in tatters.

At the cessation of the embargo in April 1929, a Chinese–British naval agreement was signed to bring a British Naval Mission to aid Nationalist China with training and assistance in developing her navy, and there were hopes that some sales might result.[171] In October 1929 Admiral Tu Hsi-Kwei (Du Xigui) visited

[164] Mr. King to Sir E. Grey, House of Commons Debate, May 21, 1914. *Hansard*, Vol. 62, cc. 2107–08.
[165] Chan, *Arming*, p. 79.
[166] Chan, *Arming*, p. 54.
[167] Chan, *Arming*, p. 150. Citing Vickers to Foreign Office, March 3, 1921. TNA, FO 371/6583.
[168] H. B. Donaldson report November 15, 1922, enclosed in Vickers to Foreign Office, December 29, 1922. TNA, FO 371/9196.
[169] Chan, *Arming*, p. 154, ff. 43. Citing R. R. Farrow, commissioner of customs and excise to the acting deputy minister, Department of Militia and Defence, Ottawa, February 1, 1923. TNA, FO 371/3107.
[170] "Dossier 8163 (Vickers Loan), Vol. V," April 1, 1922–March 31, 1924. TNA, FO 228/3559.
[171] Wright, *Chinese*, p. 151.

Table 7.1 *Armstrongs and Vickers' guns sold to China**

Type	Bore	Shell (lbs)	Gun (tons)	Maker	Date
Rifled breech-loader	4.7	40	1.75	Armstrongs	1860s
Rifled breech-loader	3.75	20	1.7	Armstrongs	1860s
Muzzle-loading rifle	12.5	810	38	Armstrongs	1870s
Muzzle-loading rifle	11	535	26/35	Armstrongs	1870s
Muzzle-loading rifle	7	115	6.5	Armstrongs	1870s
Muzzle-loading rifle	4.7	40	1.75	Armstrongs	1870s
Breech-loading	10	400	25	Armstrongs	1880s
Breech-loading	7	120	7	Armstrongs	1880s
Breech-loading	6	100	4.5	Armstrongs	1880s
Breech-loading	5	50	2	Armstrongs	1880s
Breech-loading	4.7	40	1.32	Armstrongs	1880s
Quick-firer	3.75	25	-	Armstrongs	1895
Quick-firer	8	250/210	-	Armstrongs	1900
Quick-firer	4.7	45	-	Armstrongs	1900s
Quick-firer	1.46	1	-	Maxim	1900s
Quick-firer	3	14	-	Armstrongs	1910s
Anti-aircraft	1.57	2	-	Vickers	1920s
Anti-aircraft	1.46	1	-	Vickers	1920s

*Extract from: "Appendix A Chinese Naval Guns," Wright, *Chinese*, pp. 195–96.

Vickers as part of his Naval Mission to see what was available for purchase from the major naval powers. At Barrow, Admiral Du Xigui inquired about China purchasing a 6,000-ton cruiser capable of 30 knots and equipped with 8-inch guns. The Chinese wanted the ship in twenty-four months for a price of £1.5 million. The British Foreign Office had concerns about the Nationalist Government's ability to pay for the ship, but the Cabinet made no objection to the Vickers negotiation, while warning the firm about China's indebtedness.[172] Talks between Vickers and the Nationalist Government were abandoned in September 1930, however, whereupon the Chinese turned to Harima of Japan for the ship.[173] Ironically a British Naval Mission arrived the next month. It remained in China until 1936, without yielding any sales to British firms.

The relationship between Armstrongs and China spanned more than six decades and survived several changes of regime. Table 7.1 illustrates the armaments sales of Armstrongs, and later Vickers, to China.

---

[172] "Dossier 93 Chinese Navy," 1929. TNA, FO 228/4079; "Dossier 93F-G Chinese Navy," 1929. TNA, FO 228/4080.
[173] Wright, *Chinese*, pp. 152–53 and 155.

The interwar multilateral naval arms control agreements affected British exports as well as domestic procurement. During the early 1920s both Vickers and Armstrongs put much energy into diversifying away from armaments (see Chapter 4). These diversification strategies were reinforced by the fact that the firms knew there would be few orders from Asia; Japan could now build her own warships and armaments, and China was short of money. In addition to diversifying, Vickers again lent money, £40,000 to China, and their ally Marconi made an even bigger loan. Both were to enable China to buy Marconi electrical equipment. Once China began to default on payments, the British Government's machinery to help recover monies owed to British firms swung into action.[174] This was a stark contrast to earlier decades, when a firm would have had no such help.

As the newly amalgamated Vickers-Armstrongs struggled to make sales in 1928 it was proposed to send Anthony Vickers to Japan in search of naval orders. However, the firm's Executive Committee was wary of this, and requested "an estimate of the cost and a clear statement of the purpose of the journey, as the object stated in the Minutes of the Admiralty Sales Committee does not appear sufficient to justify the expenditure."[175] This is an indication of the depths to which the company had sunk; in the past, such a sales trip would have not needed approval or a clear purpose. When the purpose was elucidated – that Vickers should spend a year in Japan and then be based in the London Office dealing with Japanese delegations – the Army Sales Committee enthusiastically concurred, especially as for £1,000 in expenses the firm might win many times that in sales.[176] Vickers-Armstrongs in their pursuit of sales also entertained a group of Japanese at the Savoy Hotel.[177] A year later Vickers-Armstrongs agreed to host a Japanese Inspectorate official, Captain Osachi, at Erith for three weeks while he studied machine gun manufacture, because "there is a chance of the Japanese Army acquiring a licence from us for the manufacture of the Vickers gun."[178] The following August a delegation visited Erith to examine drawings and descriptions.[179]

In 1914 Siam had ordered a gunboat, the *Ratanakosindra*, from Armstrongs.[180] The ship was laid down at Elswick but then dismantled to free up the slip for British war production. A decade later, Armstrongs built the gunboat to a revised design for Siam, and it went through final trials in August 1925. The *Ratanakosindra* departed for Siam in October 1925.[181] Vickers built a sister ship,

---

[174] "Dossier 46S Vickers and Marconi Loans," January 1926–February 1927. TNA, FO 228/3083.
[175] Note to Birch, March 2, 1928. VA, Microfilm R 286.
[176] Minutes of Army Sales Committee, March 2, 1928, No. 45, pp. 3–4. VA, Microfilm R 286.
[177] Birch to Sim, January 10, 1929. VA, Microfilm R 286.
[178] Birch to Wilson, November 22, 1929. VA, Microfilm R 286.
[179] Birch to Watson, August 8, 1930. VA, Microfilm R 286.
[180] Gardiner, *Eclipse*, p. 46.
[181] Brook, *Warships*, p. 42.

the *Sukothai*, for the country, completed in 1929.[182] After the amalgamation, Vickers-Armstrongs built a large gunboat for Siam, the *Sukhodaya*, which was launched in November 1928 by Madame Nunkae Bahiddha, wife of the Siamese Chargé d'Affaires in London.[183] In March 1930 the gunboat was inspected by Siamese naval officers at Barrow, and it sailed for Siam a day later.[184] During the interwar period Vickers-Armstrongs managed to sell Siam armaments for two sloops being built for them at Japanese yards, plus anti-aircraft guns and ammunition.[185] Despite making few sales, relations remained cordial; for example, in December 1937 Commander Craven attended an event at the Siamese Legation.[186] Vickers-Armstrongs was able to provide a file of intelligence on Siam to the British Government early in World War II.[187]

A 1930 memo from the First Lord of the Admiralty to the Cabinet suggested that their decision of October 1929 to disallow the disposal of surplus weapons to private firms for sale abroad had likely cost a sale to China. Vickers-Armstrongs were chasing an order for a large cruiser, but their inability to supply shipborne anti-aircraft guns had inhibited the negotiations.[188] Certainly the British Government refused firms' requests for licenses to export rifles and machine guns to China in 1929. Later such requests were refused on the basis that "the export of war materials ex-Government surplus stores to Foreign Governments was regarded as undesirable at this time."[189] With this disincentive, and given other developments in the region, armament sales by British firms never achieved their previous levels after the interwar depression.

By the mid-1930s the Chinese business was moving along again, however. In 1935 a Vickers-Armstrongs' employee in China was at Canton assembling predictor trailers and preparing to receive "the first two tractors (mediums)" there.[190] The same year, a Chinese Army General and government official, Fang Seu-Ping, accompanied by Colonel-in-Chief Chang of the 19th Army, visited the works at Crayford, Weybridge, Barrow and Elswick. The Chinese had a

---

[182] Brook, *Warships*, pp. 23, 42.
[183] *British Pathé News*, "British Built"; "'Sukhidayo.'" Cumbria Archive, Barrow, BDB 16/NA/5/7.
[184] Craven to Directors, March 15, 1930. VA, Microfilm K 613.
[185] Buxton and Johnston, *Battleship*, p. 40.
[186] Craven to Supermarine. VA, Doc. 626, Folio 32.
[187] Intelligence on Siam. VA, Microfilm K 616, Folio 30.
[188] Wise, *Royal Navy*, pp. 50, 218, ff. 32. Citing "Memorandum by First Lord of Admiralty," September 22, 1930. TNA, BT 56/18.
[189] Among the firms' denied licenses were Le Personne and Co., R. J. Adgey of Belfast and Soley Armament Co. Ltd. Confidential, Board of Trade to Bankes Commission, "II Statement of Cases in Which Applications for Licenses to Export Have Been Refused with Reasons for Refusal during the Period 1st January 1929, to 30th September, 1935." "Armaments Export Control, Board of Trade Memoranda, 1935." TNA, T 181/34.
[190] Cox to Armstrongs-Vickers Chertsey, September 22, 1935. VA, Microfilm K 613.

"General interest in armaments, chiefly anti-aircraft and tanks." A report of the visit recorded that General Fang "mentioned the possibility of considerable orders coming from China, who are apparently going to make extensive armament purchases in the near future."[191] The Chinese visit was followed up on in March 1936 by their representative, Brigadier-General K. E. Haynes. In preparation for the visit Vickers-Armstrongs noted in passing to the Foreign Office that "the German Military Mission had been photographing our tanks and tractors out there and asked him [a Jardine, Matheson & Co. agent] if the Japanese did not object to this. He thought they might but nothing had been brought to the notice of Jardine Mathesons about it. He said there were about 60 Germans there."[192] Clearly, this was in the tradition of intelligence sharing between the firm and the British Government, and indicates the extent to which European strategic considerations resonated as far afield as Asia.

General Haynes' visit was facilitated by Jardines, who "spared no effort in helping in the negotiations"; their officials accompanied him everywhere. General Haynes' subsequently reported:

> On 19th May I had an interview with the Generalissimo Chiang Kai Shek at his private house outside Nanking. He told me that he had read my reports and recommendations and that he and his advisers agreed with them, and that he wishes me, before anything definite was settled, to discuss details with Generals Yui and Hsu. This is what I had been endeavouring to do at every opportunity.

He recounted that in his previous meetings with General Yui, he "seemed more inclined at times to talk about Chinese philosophy or English poetry than armaments." Haynes' good work seems to have been undone, however, when the "question of dates of delivery put an end to everything … it is unfortunate that the overload in the armament industry in England throws the work into Germany."[193] Vickers-Armstrongs was busy with rearmament work for the British Government, and Birch bitterly complained of the business they had lost – including in China – as a consequence.[194]

Even though the sales had fallen through, members of the Chinese delegation to the Coronation visited the Crayford works in May 1937, to examine "Machine guns, especially Light Machine Guns," and Elswick and Barrow: "Visit arranged at the request of the War Office. Particular interest shown in Tanks. Probability of orders for 6-ton Tanks."[195] In November 1938 China was

[191] Representatives Report by Gordon Clunes, November 29, 1935; "Report on General Fang's Visit." VA, Microfilm K 613.
[192] Vickers-Armstrongs to Sir Victor Wellesley, December 12, 1935. VA, Microfilm K 613.
[193] "Report on Visit to China," September 15, 1936. VA, Microfilm K 613.
[194] Second Six-Month Report, 1936. VA, Microfilm K 611.
[195] Representatives report of Kinsman, May 25, 1937; Representatives report of Captain Craven, May 31, 1937. VA, Microfilm K 613.

granted £3 million in export credits.[196] However, while China now had the means to purchase Vickers-Armstrongs' armaments, the British Service Staffs were unwilling to allow weapons to go abroad, thwarting the Foreign Office's attempts to support important allies.

Even after Japan became self-sufficient in warship production the connection with Vickers-Armstrongs did not end, as they had become a partner to the Japan Steel Works (admittedly the source of the bribery scandal over the *Kongō*) and maintained a stake in the company. They also employed former military officers there as agents.[197] These became awkward connections during World War Two, when the Vickers-Armstrongs' claim became defined as "property in enemy territory"; the Hongkong and Shanghai Banking Corporation acted on their behalf.[198] After the war, several staff who had worked in Tokyo pre-war on behalf of Vickers-Armstrongs sought financial support from the firm, detailing the hardships they had endured because of their connections to the firm. While Vickers-Armstrongs gave an initial settlement to the three former employees, in 1951–52 the staff were seeking more because they could not find employment.[199] The relationship with the Japan Steel Works sputtered to life again in 1952, with the active assistance of the British Embassy in Tokyo. The Admiralty granted permission for representatives of the firm to visit Vickers-Armstrongs, although in the end the representatives did not travel to Britain.[200]

Conclusion

Armstrongs and Vickers built lasting independent relationships with Asian governments that survived various strategic developments, including changes in British Government policies. The firms were viewed in the region as independent too, as illustrated by Armstrongs emerging with relationships unscathed from the Sino-Japanese War despite having supplied armaments to both sides. Interestingly, key figures from the firm became involved in high-level diplomacy with the British Government to try to end the conflict. Here the firm acted as an equal, not as a supplicant. Moreover, the firms' relationships did not necessarily follow the variations of British Government policies. For example, the firms' relationships with Japan did not drift between 1895 and 1900 when government-to-government relationships did.

---

[196] Stone, "British Government," p. 235. Citing Committee of Imperial Defence 338th meeting, November 17, 1938. TNA, CAB 2/8.

[197] In the mid-1930s their representative in Japan, Admiral Yutani, was criticizing the performance of the anti-aircraft gun for the navy in comparison to the Hotchkiss gun. Yutani to Vickers-Armstrongs, no date, "Guns – Interviews etc. Manufacture 1934–45," VA, Doc. 662.

[198] March 7, 1952, "Property in Enemy Territory," VA Doc. 890. Also, "Property in Enemy Territory," on Japan and Rumania. VA, Doc. 891.

[199] "Property in Enemy Territory – Japanese Supplement 1951–53," VA, Doc. 892.

[200] "Property in Enemy Territory," VA Doc. 890.

Nevertheless, over a century of relations between Armstrongs and Vickers with China, Japan and Siam we see the gradual intervention of the British state via both positive assistance to the firms to make exports, and negatively through the imposition of export controls and strategic arms embargoes. Whereas at the start of the era the firms really were independent actors with minimal state involvement, as the remit of the British state grew and it took on more domestic and foreign responsibilities, so the relationships with each firm thickened. While the firms lost their autonomy, they still had some power in the relationship with the British state through their increasing interdependence, which gave them some power, albeit not on the scale they had at the dawn of their independent existences.

Foreign Policies for Selling Arms to the Ottoman Empire/Turkey

Armstrongs and Vickers confronted many challenges in the Ottoman armaments market and experienced more changes of fortune there than in the foreign markets previously discussed. Over the century considered in this book there were two overriding problems for the firms in doing business with the Ottoman Empire. The first was the Empire's constant indebtedness. The Ottomans always needed loans to buy weaponry and had a habit of falling behind on payments. The second problem was that British Government followed its own diktats and was not afraid to cross the Ottoman rulers, doing so frequently in the late nineteenth century. This meant that Armstrongs – and later Vickers – despite pursuing independent policies, were many times disadvantaged by being seen as British firms. This chapter is therefore in some ways a case study showing the limitations of the firms' independent diplomacy and marketing. However, Armstrongs – accidentally – discovered a route around the problem of guilt by association, and for a time profited handsomely from that strategy.

The two firms experienced roller-coaster relationships with the Empire, with many peaks and troughs – some even coming in the same year. Bribery and intrigue surrounded every sale and deals were done and undone at will.[1] The firms coped with the demand for "*backsheesh*" by paying it, as every successful firm did. The intrigue was more challenging as it created a truly capricious environment. For much of the century the firms got no intelligence or assistance from the British state, disadvantaging them against their foreign competitors. To prosper in this market the firms had to be constantly attuned to Ottoman politics, pay *backsheesh* and be ready to change their local interlocutors when people fell in or out of favor. A hallmark of the firms' approaches was that they never stopped trying to make sales to the Ottoman Empire.

---

[1] In 1890 Colonel Chermside of the Embassy in Constantinople reported to Fane at the Therapia Embassy that Krupp's agent, Menshauser, was "reported to thoroughly understand dealing with the Turkish Departments and that gratuities or commissions are arranged, even with some of the minor Ordnance Department officials so that orders to his firm are not obstructed in the way that many others are." Chermside to Fane, 5 July 1890. FO 78/4276, Folio 256.

Even when internal politics were against them, they kept demonstrating their wares and seeking sales, indicating that the market was always sufficiently lucrative to justify their attention.

Armstrongs pioneered a way into the Ottoman Empire's armament market in the 1860s via British warship manufacturers. Later Armstrongs sought to make warship deals itself, but it was challenging to secure sales. There had been a British commercial maritime relationship with the Empire since the late 1830s, when British engineering firms began supplying engines and boilers for Ottoman navy ships being built in Ottoman docks.[2] Early warship orders went to British firms, notably the Thames Iron Works and Samuda Brothers "as Turkey had largely put itself into the hands of the British Government for the building of an ironclad fleet."[3] The Empire "had decided to have the guns made upon the Government pattern at the Elswick works." As Stuart Rendel recalled, "It was left to me to negotiate the contracts as the London representative of the firm direct with Musurus Pasha, the Turkish Ambassador."[4] This contract provided Armstrongs with an entrée into the Ottoman market and the firm secured its first gun order from the Empire in 1864.[5] By 1867 the Ottoman order had increased to £150,000 (a good sum).[6] The Empire had contracted with Napiers of Glasgow to build three ironclads and Armstrongs agreed to supply the guns "so far as she can pay."[7] This codicil reflected the fact that the Empire's finances were overstretched and they wanted more international loans, though investors and bankers were increasingly wary of working with the insolvent regime.[8] When the ships were ready, Armstrongs was still owed significant money for the guns, and a further £900 for the ammunition. Sir William Armstrong did not want to deliver the guns until he knew that the money for them had arrived in Britain, sending Stuart Rendel to meet the Turkish Ambassador to "explain these matters to him in the most delicate way."[9] Rendel received sufficient assurance from the Ambassador for the guns to be transferred, and the Ottoman Empire's four new ironclads, delivered in 1865 by Napiers and the Thames Iron Works, carried Armstrong Guns.[10]

A new gun contract negotiated by Stuart Rendel in 1866 provided the firm with some protection against late payments. The contract involved three equal payments from Turkey: a down payment; a payment while production was

[2] Langensiepen and Güleryüz, *Ottoman*, p. 1.
[3] Fairbairn, *Elswick*, p. 70.
[4] Rendel, *Personal Papers*, p. 279.
[5] Fairbairn, *Elswick*.
[6] Bastable, *Arms*, p. 112. Citing TWA, Armstrong to Rendel, 31/56 and 31/59.
[7] Stuart Rendel, TWA, 31/1934. Also cited in Bastable, *Arms*, p. 113.
[8] Ottoman debt was not a new phenomenon. "Correspondence Respecting the Ottoman Loans of 1858 and 1862," *Parliamentary Papers*, 1874, LXXVI; "Correspondence Respecting the Various Ottoman Loans," *Parliamentary Papers*, 1876, LXXXIV.
[9] Bastable, *Arms*, p. 129. Citing TWA, 31/106.
[10] Langensiepen and Güleryüz, *Ottoman*, p. 133; Gardiner, *Conway's*, p. 389.

underway; and a final payment before the completed guns were delivered.[11] Despite these precautions, it was even more difficult than before to extract the final installment of £55,000 from the Turks. Sir William contemplated selling the guns elsewhere, and Italy's urgent need for guns for its war with Austria meant that this is what happened.[12] Interestingly, it seems at this point that the firm had no qualms about selling guns to a country at war.

The 1869 twin-screw ironclads *Avnillah*, built by the Thames Iron Works, and *Muin-i Zaffer*, built by Samuda Brothers, each carried "four 12-ton rifle Armstrongs guns in a central battery."[13] Armstrong guns also provided the firepower for three ironclads built for Egypt but seized by Constantinople in 1870, named *Asar-i Tevfik*, *Lüft-ü Celil* and *Necm-i Şevket*.[14] The *Asar-i Tevfik* and *Necm-i Şevket* were built by SA des Ferges et Chantiers de la Méditerranée, La Seyne and armed with eight nine-inch, muzzle-loading, Armstrong guns. The *Lüft-ü Celil* was built by Chantiers et Atelier de la Gironde and carried a succession of Armstrong guns. Clearly, the international renown of the firm's guns was now bringing in orders. In 1875, however, European bankers' hesitance about dealing with the indebted regime proved justified when the Ottoman Empire went bankrupt, leading directly to several American gun manufacturers going bankrupt themselves.[15] Armstrongs was not unduly affected and continued to seek Ottoman contracts.

In 1869 Royal Navy Lieutenant Henry Felix Woods had entered the Sultan's service. Woods Pasha worked with several other British citizens, including Augustus Charles Hobart (Hobart Pasha) in the Ottoman Admiralty, and Vinicombe Pasha and Frost Pasha, who worked with him on torpedoes.[16] Under Sultan Abdülaziz there were about 200 British engineers working in the Ottoman navy. Having British citizens in the naval service might have been expected to lead to more sales to British firms; however, these men set their nationality aside when serving the Ottoman Empire. By contrast, the German military advisers, most particularly Colmar Freiherr von der Goltz Pasha, were important advocates for German armaments purchases. Goltz Pasha's position in the Ottoman Army gave him access to confidential information on products offered by foreign firms to the Empire. "He then secretly shared this specific technical information with some German armament firms, an act that amounted to industrial espionage."[17] Moreover, as Goltz Pasha was directly attached to the Imperial Military Household, he had special opportunities to interact with key officials

[11] Bastable, *Arms*, p. 129. Citing TWA 31/133.
[12] Bastable, *Arms*, pp. 130–31.
[13] Martin, *Statesman's*, p. 467.
[14] The ironclads also carried some smaller Krupp guns. Langensiepen and Güleryüz, *Ottoman*, p. 137.
[15] Achtermeier, "Turkish."
[16] Zhukov and Vitol, "Origins," p. 225. Citing Woods, *Spunyarn*, pp. 36–37 and 49. "Pasha" indicates that they were of high rank in the Ottoman Empire.
[17] Yorulmaz, *Arming*, p. 8. See especially pp. 68–96.

in the Yildiz Palace and influence their thinking. The new Sultan, Abdülhamid II (1876–1909), brought many more British officers into the service in 1876–77, hoping that this would bring Britain into a brewing conflict with Russia on the side of the Empire. To his disappointment, this did not happen.[18] Subsequently the Ottoman navy had to undertake steep cost-cutting measures; the first to go were foreign personnel, most of whom were gone within three years.[19]

As tensions mounted between the Ottoman Empire and Russia in 1877, the detachment of British officers was clear. Woods Pasha recounted:

> One might have thought Turkey was an "El Dorado," by the way "inventors" and concession-hunters flocked to Constantinople ... We had a great deal of trouble during the Russo-Turkish war and afterwards, and as chief of such torpedo services as we had, I was very much worried at times in getting rid of them, especially when there were supported by their country's representative.[20]

This, naturally, meant that British armament firms were not his chief problem.

With the outbreak of hostilities between Russia and Turkey in April 1877, the British Government's 1870 Foreign Enlistment Act, which banned weapons supplies to countries at war, was again tested. Foreign Secretary Lord Derby requested that the Treasury instruct its customs officers to regularly report on whether ships of war were being built for the belligerents so that he could consider whether or not the Act should be applied.[21] Armstrongs was busy completing a gunboat and two ironclads for Constantinople, all of which had been ordered in 1876.[22] As Marshall Bastable recounts, on April 28, the British Government issued a Proclamation of Neutrality, triggering the Foreign Enlistment Act's embargo on supplying armaments. While the gunboat had already departed from Armstrongs, the two ironclads were still at the Elswick yard. The Empire urgently wanted the ironclads. Sir William's solicitors appealed to the government to be allowed to deliver the warships,

> on the grounds that the contract had been signed before the war began. The two ships cost £76 350 and Armstrong claimed he would lose 5 per cent of that if delivery was a month late and 2½ per cent for each succeeding month. Armstrong's solicitors explained to Derby that the company "have been assured and believe that neither of the Corvettes in question is in fact intended or likely to be employed in the Military or Naval Service of either belligerent."[23]

[18] Grant, "The Sword," p. 22.
[19] Komatsu, "Financial Problems," pp. 215–16.
[20] Woods, *Spunyarn*, pp. 192–93.
[21] Bastable, *Arms*, p. 215. Citing Derby to Treasury, April 26, 1877. TNA, FO 78/2664.
[22] Gardiner, *Conway's*, p. 389.
[23] Bastable, *Arms*, p. 215. Citing Radcliffe, Cator and Martineau to Derby, May 3, 1877. "General Correspondence before 1906, Ottoman Empire. Domestic Various," TNA, FO 78/2664.

Armstrongs' ship sales lists show no ironclads going to Turkey at this time, so the firm's appeal to the British Government obviously fell on deaf ears.

Other shipbuilders fared better; the Blackwall-based firm of Samuda Brothers had agreed to sell two armor-clad corvettes to Turkey. The initial solution was for Samuda Brothers to issue a £10,000 bond to the British state agreeing not to supply the warships until hostilities ended.[24] However, in 1878 the Royal Navy bought those warships from Samuda, together with one from the Thames Iron Works (these became HMS *Superb, Belleisle* and *Orion*), because the British feared they would become embroiled in their own war with Russia.[25] Despite not getting the British ships, the Ottoman Empire had the better naval force for the conflict with Russia. The Empire's equipment was not matched by the quality of leadership and training in the Ottoman navy, however, and Russia was victorious.

One potential opening for the firms came because Abdülhamid's diplomats were often left unpaid for months on end due to the Empire's finances.[26] This opened the way for bribery by British armament firms, though they still faced the obstacle of increasing German influence over the military through advisors such as Lt. Col. Kohler Pasha, predecessor to Goltz Pasha.[27] The Germans were also adept at providing *baksheesh*.[28]

Unfortunately for the firms, Sultan Abdülhamid was unhappy at the British Government's indifference to his country's defense. The subsequent British occupations of Cyprus in 1878 and Egypt in 1882 further soured relations with the Empire, as did the British Government's advocacy of a return to the parliamentary system that Abdülhamid had suspended in 1878.[29] The British stance in favor of the unification of Bulgaria in 1885 was yet another mark against her in the eyes of the Sultan. This friction with the Ottoman Empire created a difficult environment for British armament firms. For example, in July 1886 the Ottoman Empire had an Armstrongs stock ship under offer, but later withdrew.[30]

Nevertheless, one British firm did make sales: Des Vignes of Chertsey. The relationship began with the January 1886 contract with Des Vignes for two torpedo boats, which the Empire would pay for in installments.[31] The *Mahabbet* and

---

[24] Stephenam to the Secretary of the Treasury, February 2, 1881, enclosing a copy of the Samuda Bond, dated July 19, 1877. "Suspected Ships of War for Chile and China," 1880–81. TNA, T 1/13046.

[25] Gardiner, *Conway's*, p. 18; Langensiepen and Güleryüz, *Ottoman*, p. 136.

[26] Gürpinar, *Ottoman*, p. 93.

[27] Ayvazoğlu, "Military Modernization."

[28] Yorulmaz, *Arming*, pp. 205–06 and 220.

[29] Otte, *Foreign Office*, pp. 124 and 158.

[30] Brook, *Warships*, p. 61.

[31] Bankruptcy case of Maudsley, Field & Co., engine makers for the Turkish torpedo boats. The parties settled. "Queen's Bench," p. 635.

Satvet, armed with Whitehead torpedoes, were delivered at the end of 1886.[32] According to the British Naval Attaché, Captain Henry Kane, "The contract price of these boats is £11,000/. Each. They took the contract much too cheap, and as a consequence cannot get their money and are, I hear, nearly ruined."[33] Des Vignes followed that contract in 1887 with the sale to Turkey of a former pleasure steamer, *Scirocco*, as a torpedo boat, renamed *Timsah*. Des Vignes also sold the Empire two Nordenfelt submarines. Nordenfelt had ordered several sets of machinery from Barrow in 1885 and 1886; one set was used on a Turkish submarine, the other on a Greek submarine.[34] The *Abdülhamid* submarine was shipped out in pieces to be assembled in Constantinople.[35] The submarines "were ordered by the Sultan himself, and out of his privy purse, not out of naval funds …. His Majesty has already paid, not only for the value of the material obtained from England, but the cost of putting them together here, the latter operation having taken three times as long and cost three times as much as the estimate."[36] The *Abdülhamid* became famous as the first to successfully fire a live torpedo under water. This was followed by *Abdülmecid*, which was lost at sea.[37] Unfortunately, the submarines were not very effective – or stable – and disappointed the Sultan, rusting away in an Ottoman port before eventually being sold for scrap.[38] Of course, the submarines' inadequacy did not help other British firms make the case for new sales.

As British influence continued to decline, Germany was increasing her influence in the Ottoman Empire, particularly with the army. According to Zhukov and Vitol, "as early as 1883 the Turkish government changed its allegiance from Armstrong to Krupp and Mauser."[39] Krupp monopolized orders for artillery and Mauser orders for infantry rifles. One factor favoring Mauser and Germany was their willingness to provide credit, for example, in 1893 providing the Empire with the credit to buy 201,000 new rifles.[40]

British firms in all economic sectors found it difficult to make sales to the Ottoman Empire. This was partly because, as the Consul in Constantinople

---

[32] "Turkey: Torpedo Boats," in Laird Clowes, *Naval*, pp. 577–78; Grant – following some official British government sources – identified Des Vignes as French. Grant, *Swords*, p. 28. However, the British Naval Attaché in Turkey identified the boats as "lately built in England by Desvignes." Captain Henry C. Kane, "Turkish Fleet and Dockyards, 1886," December 6, 1886, p. 9. Naval Intelligence Department No. 127. TNA, ADM 231/10. The Maudsley bankruptcy case confirms this.

[33] Kane, "Turkish Fleet and Dockyards, 1886," p. 10.

[34] "Plans of Nordenfelt submarines & Plenty Steam Engines," VA, Doc. 737.

[35] Jones, "Garrett-Nordenfelt," p. 29; Scott, *Vickers*, p. 62.

[36] Kane, "Turkish Fleet and Dockyards, 1886," p. 12.

[37] Zhukov and Vitol, "Ottoman," pp. 228–31.

[38] Goldstone, *Going Deep*, p. 86.

[39] Zhukov and Vitol, "Ottoman," p. 223.

[40] Grant, "The Arms Trade," p. 28.

reported in 1882, the Ottomans expected *backsheesh* for every concession.[41] As Naval Attaché Kane noted in his 1886 report on tenders for orders by German shipbuilders, this would involve "paying all the backsheesh demanded by everyone concerned, and they are many, from the Minister of Marine downwards."[42] Nevertheless, in 1886 Sir Edward Thornton, the Ambassador in Constantinople, batted away complaints from British merchants:

> Englishmen complain that in Turkey Germans are getting the advantage of them in point of trade, and attribute it to the want of assistance from Her Majesty's diplomatic and consular officers …. I have been painfully impressed by the conviction that English merchants are indeed being driven out of the field by Germans, but that the latter attain this superiority, not by protection from their authorities but by their own unaided and independent energy, by the greater economy of their establishments, and by downright hard work on the part of both chief and subalterns.[43]

This attitude made it difficult for British firms to secure any help in Constantinople. Two years later in 1888 Armstrongs' agent in Turkey complained about the disadvantage the firm was at compared to Krupp.[44] A similar complaint was made in the same year by ammunition maker Kynoch of Birmingham, who criticized the inactivity of Ambassador Sir William White, compared to his German counterpart.[45]

Even worse for Armstrongs and Vickers, British Government foreign policy interests and principles again came to positively hamper their ability to operate successfully to counteract the near dominance of Germany in the Ottoman arms market.[46] After the 1895 massacre of Armenians in the Ottoman Empire, the British Government spoke out forcefully, leading to her diplomats being cold-shouldered. This was in stark contrast to the Kaiser, who visited Abdülhamid and remained friendly with the Sultan.[47] The Foreign Office also decried the situation in Macedonia and the treatment of minorities, and spoke out on other issues, further irritating the Sultan.[48]

In addition, by the 1890s Constantinople was a difficult environment to work in due to the "indifference, incompetence and corruption in court, in the

---

[41] Consul Wrench in Constantinople to Rosebery, April 26, 1882, Consular Report No. 64. In *Correspondence*, p. 64.

[42] Kane, "Turkish Fleet and Dockyards, 1886," p. 10.

[43] Thornton to Rosebery, May 1, 1886. Consular Report No. 46, May 1, 1886. *Correspondence*, p. 41.

[44] A. H. Leak to Elswick, October 10, 1888. TWA, 31/4187.

[45] Yorulmaz, *Arming*, p. 35. Citing Sanderson to Fergusson, May 12, 1888. TNA, FO 78/4022.

[46] Grant, "The Sword," p. 25.

[47] Platt, *Finance*, pp. 187–88; Yorulmaz, *Arming*, p. 137.

[48] See, for example, O'Conor to Lansdowne, April 4, 1903, and O'Conor to Lansdowne, August 28, 1903, in Gooch and Temperley, *British Documents*, pp. 56 and 61–63.

government and at navy headquarters."[49] Nevertheless, Armstrongs continued
to seek sales there, and Vickers now began to compete with them in that search.
In this situation, the armament firms did their best to be viewed as independent
of the British state, a task made easier by the lack of support they received from
the Embassy and Legations.

During the Greco-Ottoman War of 1897, British and German naval officials
inspected the Ottoman navy and reported on the state of the fleet, which was
terrible. This soon became widely known, exposing the Empire's weakness.
This revelation jolted Sultan Abdülhamid into setting up a Naval Commission,
which recommended the modernization of old warships and the building
abroad of six new ones. "After the report has [had] been presented to the
Sultan, there followed a round of diplomatic intrigues and industrial double-
dealing, with Abdülhamid playing off one potential warship supplier against
another."[50]

Armstrongs played a major role in this ruthless diplomacy. While the Krupp
firm was negotiating with the Ottoman Government over a contract to mod-
ernize eight armored warships and build two battleships and two cruisers, "The
German tender … [was] leaked by Istanbul to Krupp's competitor, Armstrong
of Elswick (Armstrong had been discretely promised the contract as compensation for the [recent] Krupp artillery orders). With the Ottoman navy minister
on its side, Armstrong was able to tender 2m gold lira, some thirty percent
under Krupp's offer."[51] The Armstrongs' tender was unrealistic if everything
planned was to be built, but the firm calculated that the Ottomans were
being overambitious and only two cruisers would actually be ordered. While
Armstrongs appeared to have secured the contract, official German complaints
of corruption led to the dismissal of the Ottoman navy minister and new officials taking over the procurement commission.

The new procurement plans were even more ambitious, and Krupp withdrew from the competition because they "had found the vessels in such poor
condition that reconstruction is neither practicable, financially possible or
profitable."[52] In January 1898 Armstrongs was told to expect an order for a
cruiser and two large torpedo boats, with the modernization of the armored
warships to be done in Istanbul. Once again Armstrongs seemed to be sitting
pretty, but another round of intrigue began.

As the Empire did not have the money for new purchases, the government's attention turned to refitting existing ships. This time it was Italy that
intervened, via an October 1898 meeting between the Italian Ambassador and
Abdülhamid about the compensation owed to Italy for the losses of Italians

---

[49] Langensiepen and Güleryüz, *Ottoman*, p. 8.
[50] Langensiepen and Güleryüz, *Ottoman*, pp. 9–10.
[51] Langensiepen and Güleryüz, *Ottoman*, p. 10.
[52] Langensiepen and Güleryüz, *Ottoman*, p. 10.

caught up in the Armenian massacres. The Sultan hoped to meet those claims through placing armament orders in Italy and in other claimant states.[53] Italy was therefore asked for proposals to refit two ironclads, *Mesûdiye* and *Asar-i-Tevfik*. The Ansaldo yard submitted a tender that included new guns provided by Armstrongs. However, the *Asar-i-Tevfik* contract actually went to Germania (a Krupp yard) after a further intervention from Kaiser Wilhelm II, in "a blatant attack intended to disrupt a finished contract between Ansaldo and the Ottoman Naval Ministry."[54]

While it looked as though Armstrongs was now locked out of the Ottoman warship market, this was not in fact the case, thanks to a strategic move they had made elsewhere. To maintain access to the Italian market, the firm had entered a temporary alliance with Ansaldo of Genoa. This alliance strongly favored Armstrongs. When Ansaldo secured the Ottoman *Mesûdiye* modernization contract, Armstrongs got the lion's share of the reconstruction work.[55] Stemming again from the Sultan's approach to indemnity repayment, a 1900 contract to repair eight ironclads, for which Armstrongs had independently tendered, went instead to Ansaldo. Thanks to the cover provided by the alliance with Ansaldo, Armstrongs continued to secure important Ottoman orders.

In response to a parliamentary question about this contract from Sir Ellis Ashmead Bartlett, MP for Sheffield (Vickers' home town), the Under Secretary of State for Foreign Affairs replied: "Her Majesty's Ambassador at Constantinople has already brought the claim of a British firm to the notice of the Sultan, and His Excellency has since been authorised to express the hope that British firms may receive a fair share in the orders for war material given by the Turkish Government."[56] The Sheffield MP and investor had experienced his own problems with the Empire, but was likely unaware that Armstrongs was Ansaldo's partner in refitting those ironclads.[57]

In a change of fortune, Armstrongs received significant assistance from Sir Nicholas O'Conor (now British Ambassador to Turkey and accustomed to facilitating sales thanks to the experience he gained during his tour in China, as discussed in Chapter 7), as they sought to conclude a stalled warship deal in 1901. As John Meade Falkner of Armstrongs reported from Constantinople of Sir Nicholas, "He is obligingness itself – and says that he thinks we ought to wait a few days, before he plays the trump card of a strong remonstrance to the Sultan."[58]

[53] Noppen, *Ottoman*, p. 5.
[54] Yorulmaz, *Arming*, pp. 174–75; Langensiepen and Güleryüz record the 1903 refit as fitting all Vickers guns in the *Mesudiye*. *Ottoman*, pp. 11 and 135.
[55] The 1875 Thames Iron Works' ironclad was also fitted with new Vickers guns. Attilio, "Reconstruction," p. 208.
[56] House of Commons, Parliamentary Questions, June 21, 1900, *Parliamentary Debates*, Vol. 84, pp. 626–27.
[57] Yorulmaz, *Arming*, pp. 158–59.
[58] Falkner to Noble, April 23, 1901. TWA, DF/NOB/3/1/1.

Armstrongs subsequently received a contract for the cruiser *Hamidieh* (initially known as the *Abdülhamid*) and two non-military contracts for a yacht and a state barge. It seems, though, that the contract was actually secured not because of Sir Nicholas' efforts but because the Americans were pressing Turkey to make good the losses that U.S. citizens had suffered during the Armenian massacres; these losses had been indemnified by the U.S. Government. The "Sublime Porte, in order to 'save face' agreed to order a cruiser from America [the *Mecidiye*], the price of which was to include the amount of the indemnity; the same agreement was made with England."[59] Nevertheless, Sir Nicholas' coupling of state and firm interests helped Armstrongs succeed. The *Hamidieh* was an excellent advertisement for Armstrongs' work, whereas the Cramps-built *Mecidiye* had stability problems that meant it rarely put to sea.[60] Also unfortunate for American firms was that their government's show of force – sending a cruiser to İzmir to pressure the Empire to pay its debts – backfired as the Sultan subsequently refused to buy from U.S. firms.[61]

In 1902 Armstrongs and Ansaldo struck a new deal with the Ottoman navy to refit the *Muin-i-Zafar* and *Feth-i-Bülend*, both of which had been contracted to Krupp two years previously. Constantinople also leased part of the Tersane-I Amire shipyard on the Golden Horn to the two firms and allowed their foreign staff to work there. They also got an order for torpedo boats. In 1904 d'Eyncourt and Faulkner traveled to Turkey to hand over to the government the cruiser *Hamidieh*, the Sultan's new yacht, the *Erthogrul*, and a state barge, the *Seughudlu*.[62] D'Eyncourt described this as "a more or less diplomatic mission …. It was also part of my mission to try to get further orders for warships and perhaps some guns."[63] Armstrongs were offering to build a sister ship to the *Hamidieh*. The Minister of Marine asked d'Eyncourt to extend his stay and inspect and report on the condition of the greater part of the Turkish fleet. D'Eyncourt recalled:

> It was hardly possible to refuse such a request, so we agreed to stay, and the job took several months, which was made as pleasant as possible by the hospitable Turks. Many of the ships I examined were in bad condition and much too old to give good service under what were always "modern conditions", and I had to exercise a considerable amount of tact in wording my report.[64]

On the completion of this work, he was awarded a Third Class Medjidieh.[65]

---

[59] Taylor, "Turkish Naval," p. 41.
[60] Langensiepen and Güleryüz, *Ottoman*, p. 11.
[61] Yorulmaz, *Arming*, p. 191.
[62] "State Barge Seughudlu, built in 1903 for the Turkish Sultan," Photograph, 1903. TWA, D.VA/24/6; "The Erthogroul," Photograph, undated. TWA, D.VA/24/5.
[63] d'Eyncourt, *Shipbuilder's*, p. 48.
[64] d'Eyncourt, *Shipbuilder's*, p. 50.
[65] Lillicrap, "Eustace," p. 342.

Armstrongs and Ansaldo agreed to formally establish a joint venture in September 1904, creating Gio Ansaldo Armstrong & Co.[66] By 1905 the firm had transformed the *Mesûdiye*, "from a military point of view, [an] almost valueless ironclad, into very formidable ship."[67] They had also completed four Turkish 25-knot torpedo boats and had a further seven nearing completion.[68]

The joint venture with Ansaldo was intended by Armstrongs to be a means to retain access to the Italian domestic market, where nationalism was leading to calls to buy only goods manufactured in the country.[69] Ansaldo was motivated by the desire for access to steel from Armstrongs' Puzzuoli Works.[70] The very positive unintended outcome for Armstrongs from the venture was exports. In 1908 *The Naval Annual* was reporting that "the aggregate displacement of naval ships built by Ansaldo-Armstrong for foreigner's amounts to 38,258 tons, while for the Italian Navy it only amounts to 12,520 tons."[71] The joint venture also had the effect of neutralizing a firm that had been a fierce competitor to Armstrongs in foreign markets, and of giving Armstrongs the distinct advantage of having another identity to use in foreign markets, such as Turkey, that were difficult for firms identified as British.

It seems that Sir Nicholas O'Conor's enthusiasm for supporting Armstrongs waned. As Bastable recounts, by 1904 Falkner was reporting that "As a rule he shows himself difficult and contemptuous of all things commercial."[72] When the interests of the firm and the state overlapped, O'Conor was more helpful, for example, aiding Armstrongs in getting £98,791 in overdue payments from the Ottomans, but extracting from that £63,000 for the indemnity still owed to British businesses that had lost property in the Armenian massacres.[73]

While the Sultan was interested in obtaining a sister ship to the *Hamidieh* from Armstrongs, the Empire could not pay for it. To cover for this Abdülhamid declared his concern that "British influence in the navy has become too obvious and consideration should be given to offers from other countries."[74] In 1907 Ansaldo got the contract to build the ship, named *Drama*. Armstrongs once again benefited from the deal. In addition, French yards received orders for destroyers and gunboats in 1906, and Germany delivered two torpedo cruisers and a refitted *Asar-i Tevfik* – for a "ridiculously low price" – the cost of winning

---

[66] TWA, 31/3654.

[67] Attilio, "Reconstruction," p. 208.

[68] Likely they were the *Akhisar* and *Alpagot*, completed in 1904, the *Anatalya*, *Urfa*, *Ankara* and *Tokad*, completed in 1906, and the *Draç*, *Kütaliya*, *Musul*, *Sivrishiar* and *Sultanishar*, completed in 1907.

[69] Warren, *Armstrongs*, pp. 122–25.

[70] Segreto, "More Trouble," pp. 318 and 333, ff. 12.

[71] "Ansaldo-Armstrong," in Brassey, *Naval*, pp. 164–65.

[72] Bastable, *Arms*, p. 217. Citing Falkner to Rendel, July 10, 1904, TWA, 31/7051.

[73] Bastable, *Arms*, p. 218.

[74] Langensiepen and Güleryüz, *Ottoman*, p. 12.

a big artillery contract.[75] Thus the Sultan balanced the claims of other countries, but did nothing for British firms.

Around 1906 Armstrongs, Vickers and John Brown & Co. made an "arrange-ment as regards foreign orders" that covered Turkey, where the agreement was recorded to have been successful. The ad hoc consortium was informally known as the British Group.[76] The profit sharing was agreed as follows:

Turkey   The group consists of A., V. & J. B. & Co, and deals with the present
          programme. One ship has been ordered so far.
          V. build Hull and Machinery at agreed price.
          A. & V. divide Armament.
          A., V. and B. divide Armour.
          A. and V. divide Shafting etc.
          V. standout for Hull and Engines of next ship.
          It is not thought that Hull and Engines will shew any material profit.[77]

The three firms' hopes to directly secure Turkish business were again initially hobbled by the British Government's foreign policy choices. As O'Conor noted in the "Annual Report for Turkey" of 1907, even his enthusiasm and support for British commercial interests could not overcome the Sultan's position that the "policy of His Majesty's Government with regard to Macedonia, Armenia, and other oppressed nationalities is objectionable and even hateful."[78] By contrast, Germany appeased the Sultan and consequently secured many commercial and industrial concessions, among them a monopoly over munition supplies for the Turkish army.[79] Germany also trained many Turkish army officers.[80]

The British Government provided a Naval Mission from 1907 to 1910 but this did little to improve the situation. There was frustration in the Constantinople Embassy. Gerald Fitzmaurice, the Chief Dragoman, wrote privately to William Tyrrell (Sir Edward Grey's private secretary and confident) in 1908 that, for the last few years,

> our policy, if I may so call it, in Turkey has been, and for some time to come will be, to attempt the impossible tasks of furthering our commercial interests while pursuing a course (in Macedonia, Armenia, Turco-Persian Boundary &c.) which the Sultan interprets as being pre-eminently hostile in aim and tendency. These two lines are diametrically opposed and conse-quently incompatible with one another .... Every big trade &c. concession is regarded as an Imperial favour to be bestowed on the seemingly friendly, a category in which, needless to say, we are not included.[81]

[75] Langensiepen and Güleryüz, Ottoman, pp. 12–13.
[76] Trebilcock, Vickers Brothers, p. 125.
[77] "Armstrongs and Vickers," confidential memorandum signed by A. M. W. of Armstrongs, notated "about 1906 to 1913." "War Work," VA, Doc. 551, pp. 2–3.
[78] O'Conor, "Hamidian Diplomacy," p. 43.
[79] O'Conor, "Hamidian Diplomacy," p. 43.
[80] Surtees, "Turkish Army," p. 35.
[81] G. H. Fitzmaurice to Tyrrell, April 12, 1908. In Gooch and Temperley, British, p. 247.

Bound by British strategic and humanitarian interests, the most the Embassy in Turkey could do for armament firms was try to ensure they received equal treatment. There were some minor British successes; with government help, Kynoch of Birmingham secured a contract for cartridges, and the Bolton Iron and Steel Co. secured a rifle contract.[82] However, the major armaments contracts all went to firms from other countries.

In 1907 the British Naval representative in Turkey noted:

> The ordering of some modern submarines is in contemplation for the defence of the Dardanelles and the Bosphorus; there is a rumour that the agents of Messrs. Krupp are trying to get the order …. There is a further rumour, as yet unconfirmed, that a number of young Turkish officers will be admitted to the German navy for training. In view of these rumours and facts, it would seem advisable to endeavor to place orders for submarines in England or America, and to offer to train the officers in the British or American navy if anywhere.[83]

Arthur Vere, Vickers' representative in Constantinople, was aware that one of the factors limiting armaments sales to Turkey was the country's indebtedness. He was also aware of the creeping influence of the Germans, a development undesirable for his firm and for the interests of the British state. In 1906 Vere therefore began to maneuver to establish an Anglo-French financial and commercial syndicate, with each country forming a syndicate which would combine to bid on concessions in the Ottoman Empire.[84] Sir Edward Grey gave the scheme his approval in January 1907. "If successful the relative decline in British investment in Turkey might thus be halted, and the growth of German influence over the Porte checked."[85] Of course, Vere was also likely hoping for armaments contracts for Vickers.

In the same year Ambassador O'Conor, with an eye on the disastrous state of Turkish finances, noted: "By dint of vigorous pressure, the Italian Embassy has secured for the firm of Ansaldos, in Genoa, an order for a cruiser." This was the *Drama*. He acknowledged that this "act of folly" broke a promise made by the Sultan

> some years ago to Armstrong's, that the next ships should be built by them. I have been careful not to let His Majesty lose sight of this fact, but I have not seen my way to press for an order for the British firm …. *I should be loth to make the commission of an act of folly by the Sultan an excuse for urging him to commit another.* I have, however, made it known that His Majesty's Government expects compensation in one form or another for the violation of a promise given by the Sultan himself.[86]

---

[82] Platt, *Finance*, p. 190.
[83] Taylor, "Turkish," p. 42.
[84] Hamilton, *Bertie*, p. 167.
[85] Hamilton, "Britain and France," p. 126.
[86] O'Conor, "Hamidian Diplomacy," p. 47. Emphasis added.

Thus, Armstrongs benefited from its alliance with Ansaldo but also stood to gain directly if O'Conor could create business for the British Group.

Vere's Anglo-French "Ottoman Society" syndicate, or "Industrial Entente," as the scheme was known in the Foreign Office, was overtaken by events, however. The Young Turk Revolution of 1908 offered Britain a potential clean slate in diplomacy. Grey expressed no regrets: "I cannot feel any sympathy for Abdul Hamid. His reign has been absolute, during it large numbers of his subjects have been massacred, and all his subjects have been rendered more or less miserable by corrupt misgovernment." Ambassador Lowther in Constantinople was in agreement: "Abdul Hamid's system of Government during the thirty odd years preceding July last was responsible for so much blood-shed and misery that his removal was more than justified."[87]

Britain hoped that the Anglo-French syndicate would now flourish. However, it floundered thanks to the apathy of the Imperial Ottoman Bank (an Anglo-French institution with significant German involvement in Constantinople), French dithering and problems with the staff of the London branch of the Ottoman Society.[88] British financiers such as Sir Ernest Cassel – in whom Vere had put a lot of faith but who had become disillusioned with the scheme – began to work directly with the new regime on a new National Bank of Turkey.[89] This was not received well in Paris and Vere's scheme fell apart.[90] A 1908 request to the British Government to assist in persuading British bankers to lend the new Turkish Government a million Turkish pounds failed because the government could not persuade any British bankers to try to raise the money.[91]

While the new regime held out the promise of new armaments contracts, it was still difficult for Armstrongs and Vickers to secure them. Expectations that German influence would be lessened after the revolution were wrong. In fact, younger German-trained officers came into positions of authority.[92] Also, as Grey explained to Falkner, the new Ottoman mode of deciding contracts using sealed tenders made the issue of price a real component in decision making, as shown in a large order for field and mountain artillery ammunition that Armstrongs was underbid on by the four other competitors.[93] By 1909 there was recognition that Britain needed to be more proactive against German commercial interests in the Ottoman Empire. However, "Ambassadors before the First

[87] Grey to Lowther, April 30, 1909. FO 800/79/146, Folio 307; Lowther to Grey, Private, May 12, 1909. TNA FO 800/79/146, Folio 314.
[88] Hamilton, *Bertie*, pp. 166–72; Kent, "Agent of Empire?," pp. 367–71.
[89] Kent, "Agent," pp. 370–71. Citing Sir Adam Block Memorandum, November 3, 1908, enclosed in Lowther to Grey, November 10, 1908. TNA, FO 371/549; Campbell to Vere, November 28, 1908. TNA, FO 371/547.
[90] Hamilton, "Britain and France," pp. 126–27.
[91] Platt, *Finance*, p. 193.
[92] Yorulmaz, *Arming*, p. 209.
[93] Yorulmaz, *Arming*, pp. 238–39.

World War were recognised by their Foreign Office chiefs as being required
to promote British interests in a difficult diplomatic setting of two regimes,
[which] with only a brief lapse in 1908–9, were pro-German and anti-British."[94]

The most that the ambassadors would do was request equal treatment for
British firms.[95] Even then, the concessions targeted were railways, banks and
petroleum, not armaments. During that "brief lapse," Grey wrote twice to
First Secretary Charles Murray Marling in Constantinople requesting that he
provide aid to Falkner of Armstrongs and Barker of Vickers as they and John
Browns pursued orders from the Turkish navy.[96] A year later, Grey was contacting Ambassador Gerard Lowther on behalf of the two firms.[97] Early in 1909 a
new Naval Attaché arrived in Constantinople and Lowther reported: "Admiral
Gamble seems to be a splendid fellow but is quite horrified at the indescribable
mess he finds here and the empty coffers are not encouraging for his work."[98]

In 1910 British Government diplomacy again disappointed the Ottomans, as
well as Armstrongs and Vickers. The Empire, afraid of the new armored cruiser
that the Greeks were soon to launch, were desperate to obtain a ship to protect
Crete and her other islands. A new naval program was endorsed by the Cabinet
in early 1910. However, the British Admiralty refused the Ottoman request to
sell them a modern ship, relying on the advice of the head of the Naval Mission,
Rear-Admiral Gamble, that the Ottomans were incapable of managing modern
vessels and that they should receive simpler models.[99] Gamble then resigned –
because his advice was being ignored in Turkey – and Ambassador Lowther
reported to the Foreign Office that "the Turks will be rather sick at our not
being able to sell them ships and then losing our Admiral."[100] This rebuff by the
British Government had predictable effects, as reported by Lowther: "[T]hey
have got 4 destroyers in Germany and American and German builders are
swarming like locusts around the [Ottoman] Admiralty now."[101]

Armstrongs and Vickers were also part of that swarm. Grey wrote to Lowther
in February 1910 recommending to him Falkner, whom he had recently met. He
recounted to Lowther that he had told Falkner that the Embassy could not favor
any particular British group, "But as in this case Falkner is acting for a group
which includes Armstrong's and Vickers, who are I suppose the two greatest

---

[94] Kent, *Great Powers*, p. 174.
[95] Platt, *Finance*, pp. 217–18.
[96] Grey to Marling, November 2, 1909, on aid to Barker and citing a letter written on behalf
      of Falkner "the other day." TNA, FO 800/79/146, Folio 397.
[97] Telegram Grey to Lowther concerning: The Admiralty: orders for the Turkish naval ships
      to Armstrong Vickers Group. 28 February 1910. TNA, FO 800/79/147 Folios 406–08.
[98] Lowther to Grey, February 8, 1909, TNA, FO 800/79/146, Folio 287.
[99] Miller, *Straits*, p. 78. Citing Lowther to Hardinge, January 18, 1910. TNA, FO 800/192.
[100] Miller, *Straits*, p. 78. Citing Lowther to Hardinge, February 1, 1910. TNA, FO 800/192.
[101] Miller, *Straits*, p. 78. Citing Lowther to Hardinge, February 1, 1910. TNA, FO 800/192.

firms of the kind in this country, his group is obviously one to which all proper support can be given without hesitation." Grey also made clear to Falkner that "we are not of opinion that the Turks can wisely afford to spend large sums on building a navy, and therefore we cannot press them to do so; but that you [Lowther] would do your best to secure whatever orders the Turks themselves decided to give should be placed here." During their meeting Falkner had explained to Grey that the competition was very keen in Constantinople and that the Americans "were especially keen competitors, and seemed to be willing to make sacrifices in order to keep their yards at work."[102] Vickers and Armstrongs were aided by developments in the international armor pool. Vickers reported by telegram to Barker in Turkey: "Paris meeting reduced price at which makers may estimate when tendering for foreign ships to 85 per ton they also reduced percentage payable to pool from 20 to 12.5 tell Falkner." This meant Vickers and Armstrongs could lower their bids on warships to Turkey.[103]

In a negotiation with Armstrongs the new navy minister, Halil Pasha, offered to pay the shipbuilders 5 m gold lira for two battleships and an armored cruiser; far more than the Ottoman Treasury could afford. "When the government learned of these unauthorised dealings the navy minister was dismissed on 3 May 1910."[104] This was a blow to Armstrongs. The next move was equally inauspicious for the British Group – the Turkish Government accepted some ancient warships from Germany. Ambassador Lowther wrote to Grey,

> I hope the Turks will not get too uppish with their two new (old) German ships. [Rear-Admiral H.P.] Williams thinks they will be useful and he could not, for technical reasons, advise his conferees to agree to take ships of the "Royal Sovereign" [pre-dreadnought] class. It seems a real pity for many reasons that we could not dispose of something that would suit the Turks.[105]

Thus, even while the British Group was seeking to sell dreadnoughts, the Naval Mission in Turkey was skeptical of the Turkish navy's ability to handle an even older make of destroyer.

In trying to secure this contract Barker and Vere were permitted to offer discounts on the original price, because the international pool (cartel) had reduced payment levels. An important proviso was added:

[102] Grey to Lowther, Private, February 18, 1910. TNA, FO 800/79/146, Folio 405.
[103] Coded Telegram Vickers to Barker (Constantinople), April 28, 1910. Letter Book No. 31, VA, Doc. 1005, Folio 452.
[104] Langensiepen and Güleryüz, *Ottoman*, p. 14.
[105] Lowther to Grey, Private, August 10, 1910. TNA, FO 800/79/146, Folio 428. In September Ambassador Lowther noted, "the danger now is that having their two best ships and guns German they may continue on those lines …. However, as the Admiralty could not see their way to helping there is nothing to be said." Lowther to Grey, September 21, 1910. TNA, FO 800/79/146, Folio 436.

If necessary absolutely however you may reduce price of each battleship by further 30,000 pounds sterling and cruiser by 30,000 pounds sterling but sincerely trust you will not find it necessary to go as low as this especially as if original prices were considered satisfactory by British Admiralty *it would be dangerous to our British Admiralty English business if it became known we accept orders at such reduced prices.*[106]

In June 1910 Basil Zaharoff was reporting from St. Petersburg to Vickers: "Referring to my letter of last Wednesday regarding Turkish ships, we and Armstrongs yesterday signed preliminary contract in Constantinople for ships of British Superb class."[107] Zaharoff had obviously been brought in to help close the deal. The Superb class were dreadnoughts, so the firms were selling the Ottomans ships that the British Naval Mission had specifically opposed as being far too advanced for them. These international negotiations also necessitated knowing British Government attitudes to geostrategic issues. For example, as Bastable recounts, in 1910 Falkner "quipped to Stuart Rendel, 'I am dining with Sir Edward Grey tonight to talk Turkey.'"[108]

The Ottoman market had now become attractive to other British shipbuilders. In June Barker was reporting to Vere (who was also his father-in-law) about other British firms seeking entry to the Ottoman naval market. He reported to Constantinople:

> Have seen Foreign Office who are sending to-day to British Ambassador telegram embodying their views which are that Armstrongs were first in the business and that the British Government will support no other firms except Armstrongs and allied firms because this might lead to throwing open the business to tender and thus it being lost to England and going to some foreign country. Foreign Office also writing in the above sense to Fairfield who have applied to them for support.[109]

In this case British Group members Vickers and John Browns were considered "allied firms" and thus eligible for support. The Coventry Ordnance Works was another potential seller, though Vickers thought they were not serious contenders, with Caillard declaring their plants and financial resources to be "ridiculously small and inadequate," particularly as the Turks wanted repayments on the deal to run over a decade.[110] A month later the Vickers London office wrote to Armstrongs' Elswick works: "We already know the Foreign Office and the Admiralty are dead in our favour, and will not give any support to the other people."[111]

---

[106] Coded Telegram Vickers to Barker, April 30, 1910. Letter Book No. 31, VA, Doc. 1005, Folios 458–59. Emphasis added.
[107] Telegram Zaharoff to Vickers, June 10, 1910. Letter Book No. 32, VA, Doc. 1006, Folio 49.
[108] Bastable, *Arms*, p. 218. Citing Falkner to Rendel, 4 August 1910, TWA, 31/7089.
[109] Barker to Vere, June 17, 1910. Letter Book No. 31, VA Doc. 1005, Folios 498–99.
[110] Caillard to Vere, July 8, 1910. VA, Microfilm 307.
[111] Vickers to Elswick, July 16, 1910. Letter Book No. 32, VA, Doc. 1006, Folio 83.

While the Foreign Office was providing some support to the firms against British rivals, the Naval Mission in Turkey continually advocated for more modest ships, such as torpedo boats. In direct contradiction of this, Vickers, Armstrongs and Ellis (of the Atlas Steel Works Sheffield) in July funded a £300 press campaign in the Ottoman Empire advocating for the dreadnought purchases.[112] Later that month Zaharoff was congratulating Barker on his successes in that difficult market.[113] While the British Government would not actively support the dreadnought sales, the firms nevertheless sought Admiralty help in another direction. In August Vickers wrote a memorandum to V. W. Bradley about sales and sought to have the Admiralty block the Empire from purchasing from Germany.[114]

In the autumn of 1910 Armstrongs and Vickers were still in hot pursuit of the Ottoman order. Vickers' Barker in London wrote to Vere to reintroduce him to Captain Mumtaz Bey, who had been in England on a "special mission" and was a friend of Muhmoud Chevkey Pache (Pasha). He reported: "I have every reason to believe he can be of great use to you in this question of the naval order for Turkey" and "I have no doubt that some business will result from the recommendations that Captain Mumtaz Bey has to make to his Government after what he has seen during his trip."[115] In October Albert Vickers was reporting to William Beardmore: "[W]e have now received a request for our delegates to go to Constantinople to complete the transaction. I am telling you this in all secrecy, as a Director of the Vickers Company."[116] In London in March 1911 Albert Vickers reported that their representative were "all dining tonight with Saxton Noble [of Armstrongs], who is giving a dinner to the Turkish Commission, and all are to dine with me tomorrow night at my house."[117]

However, there were still problems in finalizing the contracts, with lots of intrigue going on within the Ottoman regime. In December Barker was discussing with Falkner and Ellis the need for Vere (whom he also called "Vera") in Constantinople to provide a retainer to someone with the code name "Safety." As Barker explained to Charles Ellis:

> Vera writes to me that it is very important that we should for six months pay the little Turk, who used to bring us all the information about our business there, especially as he is now a persona grata with the new Minister of

---

[112] Vickers to Falkner (Armstrongs), July 8, 1910. Letter Book No. 32, VA, Doc. 1006, Folio 73.

[113] "Frank Barker has certainly managed that business well … and kindly congratulate him for me." Zaharoff to Albert Vickers, July 28, 1910. VA, Microfilm 307.

[114] Caillard to V. W. Bradley, August 1, 1910. Letter Book No. 32, VA, Doc. 1006, Folios 126–27.

[115] Barker to Vere, September 22, 1910. Letter Book No. 32, VA, Doc. 1006, Folio 182.

[116] Vickers to Beardmore, October 6, 1910. Letter Book No. 32, VA, Doc. 1006, Folio 202.

[117] Albert Vickers to Zaharoff, March 6, 1911. Letter Book No. 33, VA 1006A, Folio 418–19.

Marine. Vera suggests that we should pay him £25 per month. The man he is referring to is Safety. Falkner is entirely in accord with me, and I hope *you* also will agree.[118]

The "little Turk" was later identified as Zorab, a member of the Turkish opposition.[119]

In January 1911 Barker and Falkner traveled to Turkey, apparently taking with them Foreign Office instructions.[120] When Barker returned to London, Falkner stayed on, attempting to finalize the deal. In February Vere was authorized by Barker to "allocate £125 between the two persons for services rendered."[121] Barker also telegraphed to Vere in Constantinople: "With reference to Mr. Saxton Noble's telegram you might enlist support of Turkish Minister of Finance in view of heavy reduction I have obtained. You might also endeavour to get 4.5 per cent instead of 4."[122]

During Falkner's stay in Constantinople he was rather put out when Lowther told him: "[H]e [Lowther] is only concerned that the ships go to *some* English firm, and that he has no brief for our group or for any other individual."[123] Nevertheless, Lowther did help Armstrongs and Vickers by obtaining confirmation that the Turkish Government were planning to buy hulls, engines and armor from the firms, but reported that the gun contract would not be decided until a commission had reported on the best choices. Moreover, Falkner reported: "Considering the circumstances[,] British Ambassador thinks we should sign as suggested [in] my telegram yesterday if we get chance on Monday. This is in accordance with my views."[124] The circumstance was a concern that the Turkish Government could backslide on the deal.

Barker demurred, though, concerned that Turkey was demanding too much, and telegraphed in code to Falkner in February:

> I may repeat my strong personal view(s) when suggestion was made before departure that promises suggested ... will result in our selling our birth-right. If there is any idea(s) of prompting Turkish Minister of Marine to make such suggestion[,] we will show great weakness and it will interfere with action [of the] Foreign Office and as the Turkish Minister of Marine cannot accept unless other ministries consent decision must be delayed

---

[118] Quotation from Barker to Ellis, December 19, 1910, Folio 148. Emphasis in original. See also Barker to Falkner, December 19, 1910, Folio 139; Barker to Vere, December 19, 1910. Letter Book No. 33, VA, Doc. 1006A, Folio 147.

[119] January 1911, Letter Book No. 33, VA, Doc. 1006A, Folio 166.

[120] Vickers to Falkner, January 20, 1911. Letter Book No. 33, VA, Doc. 1006A, Folio 210.

[121] Barker to Vere, Telegram February 10, 1911. Letter Book No. 33, VA, Doc. 1006A, Folio 275.

[122] Coded Telegram, Barker to Vere, February 20, 1911. Letter Book No. 33, VA, Doc. 1006A, Folio 379.

[123] Falkner to Saxton Noble, January 16, 1911. Emphasis in original. TWA, DF/NOB/3/5.

[124] Coded Telegram from Meade Falkner to Vickers, February 11, 1911. Letter Book No. 33, VA, Doc. 1006A, Folio 294.

and you will receive emasculated offer. My view is to accept suggestion subject to confirmation [by] London when final official written offer from Turkish Minister of Marine with cabinet decision or through British Ambassador is made[.] [W]e thus gain time for Foreign Office action with regard to guns[.] [A]m doing everything possible to try to meet your recommendation.[125]

Vickers telegraphed to Falkner later that day, reemphasizing this: "Have seen all partners concerned who are strongly of the opinion that we must again consult Foreign Office to-morrow before replying."[126] Meanwhile, Gamble's replacement in Constantinople, Rear-Admiral Williams, was irritated that the Turks were ignoring the Mission's consistent advice to acquire modest vessels and were still seeking dreadnoughts.

Later in February Barker telegraphed to Vere: "Our heartiest congratulations [to] you and Falkner on having defeated Oscar Wilde."[127] Presumably this was a reference to an opponent in the Turkish deal. In May and July 1911 the Ottomans placed contracts for two 23,000-ton dreadnoughts, the *Reshad-i-Hamiss* from Armstrongs and the *Medmed Resad V* from Vickers. Langensiepen and Güleryüz record that "thanks to the intervention of Cemal Pasa [Pasha] an order was place with Vickers for a battleship ... at a cost of 1.5m gold lira."[128] The contract for the Vickers dreadnought, renamed the *Reshadieh*, was won by providing a loan equal to the full cost of the ship to the Ottoman regime through the Glyn Mills bank. Vickers also provided Turkey with six months of interest-free credit to get the venture underway.[129] It had taken the British Group a year and a half to secure the contracts.

Even after that all was not plain sailing. According to Miller: "The Armstrong's ship was laid down in December 1911, but work was suspended the following year when the company demanded a better guarantee of payment and the contract was then cancelled."[130] Construction of the *Reshadieh* was "stopped pending developments" in November 1912, a few weeks after the outbreak of the Balkan War (October 1912–October 1913), but good progress was made once work was resumed. There was a second suspension of work at Vickers due to a Turkish default on loan payments, leading to speculation that the British Admiralty might buy the ship.[131] Subsequently, though, the ship was

---

[125] Barker to Falkner in Constantinople, February 12, 1911. Letter Book No. 33, VA, Doc. 1006A, Folios 288–92.

[126] Coded Telegram, Vickers to Falkner, 9.30 p.m., February 12, 1911. Letter Book No. 33, VA, Doc. 1006A, Folio 296.

[127] Coded Telegram Barker to Vere, February 23, 1911. Letter Book No. 33, VA, Doc. 1006A, Folio 391.

[128] Langensiepen and Güleryüz, *Ottoman*, p. 17.

[129] Trebilcock, *Vickers Brothers*, p. 130.

[130] Miller, *Straits*, pp. 82 and 88.

[131] "Built for Turkey," p. 10.

paid for by patriotic Turks of the Naval Society. The *Reshadieh* was so big that no existing dock in Turkey was able accommodate her.

In spring 1912 Vickers was working on the subcontracts for the Turkish deal and slyly offered different firms' different levels of commission on the same armaments order.[132] Vickers and Armstrongs had a workshare agreement for the *Reshadieh*, with Vickers building the ship at Barrow. This led to considerable disquiet on the Armstrongs Board, with Stuart Rendel being particularly critical of the deal with Vickers.[133] Another reversal for Armstrongs was the September 1911 Italian attack on Turkey, which initiated a year-long war. This obviously meant that Gio Ansaldo Armstrong & Co. was no longer an effective vehicle for Turkish warship contracts, and in 1912 the alliance was formally dissolved.

In 1913, while the *Reshadieh* was under construction at Barrow, the Ottomans began seeking an already completed dreadnought. Like Russia, Italy and Greece, the Ottomans were interested in the *Rio de Janeiro*, which was being built by Armstrongs for Brazil but was now unaffordable to the country because of the collapse in rubber prices. The Turkish Ambassador in London, Tewfik Pasha, really wanted the battleship. Greece wanted it too. As Istanbul had already promised Armstrongs more work, she had some advantage in the negotiation. However, Armstrongs had to contend with the European strategic implications of any sale of the *Rio de Janeiro* and the views of the British Government, which sought to impose their will on the firm.

Concerns about the potential sale were first seriously raised when Britain learned that Italy had requested from Armstrongs a ten-day option to buy the ship, but the concerns came from the French, who were extremely anxious about a member of the Triple Alliance getting the dreadnought.[134] The French therefore decided to fund Greece to buy the dreadnought. As Miller recounts:

> The French also wanted Armstrong's, the builders, to be warned to delay the completion of the sale, which Grey thought might take place early on Monday morning, 24 November [1913], in which case he proposed to ask Sir George Murray of Armstrong's "at once to await further communication from the Admiralty." Suddenly the matter had become so urgent that, on Sunday 23rd, Churchill sent a telephone message to Battenberg declaring that the Foreign Office should be told the Admiralty regarded it as "most important" that Greece should purchase the ship and Armstrong's "should be warned at once not to conclude alternative bargain."[135]

[132] Letter Book No. 12, 1912. VA, Doc. 1010, Folios 740 and 741.
[133] Brook, *Warships*, p. 143.
[134] Miller, *Straits*, p. 181.
[135] Miller, *Straits*, p. 182. Citing Telegram Battenberg to Churchill, November 22, 1913; and Telephone Message from Churchill to Battenberg, November 23, 1913. TNA ADM 1 8365/8.

However, that is eventually what Brazil did.

Two weeks later the Armstrongs' agent in Brazil was informing the Foreign Office that a mysterious new power had bid on the dreadnought. Three days later the Brazilian Government informed the British Legation that a deal had been completed, but "the Brazilian Government also do not know to what power."[136] On December 15 the new owner was formally unveiled by Ambassador Mallet in Constantinople: it was Turkey. Ironically, Perrier, a French bank, had loaned the Ottomans the million-pound deposit. The Ottoman naval hero Captain Raouf Orbay sailed to Britain to make the final arrangements with Armstrongs, completing them on December 23, 1913. Again, public subscriptions in Turkey helped to pay for the ship, which was renamed the *Sultan Osman I*. Here we have a case of money having more sway than the British Government's exhortations to Armstrongs to sell to Greece. As Miller reports:

> [T]he French were cynical enough to believe that the sale was not uncon-
> nected with the recent concession awarded by the Turks to Armstrong's
> and Vickers for the reorganization of the Ottoman dockyards. This suspi-
> cion would not have been weakened when, at the beginning of May 1914,
> Armstrongs clinched a new Turkish order for a third dreadnought for the
> Ottoman Navy.[137]

Late in 1913 Armstrongs and Vickers negotiated a secret agreement to coop-
erate on securing orders in

> Roumania, Turkey, Greece, Bulgaria, Servia, Albania and Montenegro
> ... for warships submarine boats and naval and military armaments and
> materials of all kinds with the exception of aircraft and their accessories,
> Maxim automatic Guns and rifle caliber guns and shall divide equally the
> execution of all orders and also the cost of obtaining and executing the
> same and the profit or loss resulting therefrom.[138]

It confirmed the agents they would jointly use in Turkey: "ALL matters the subject of this agreement relating to Roumania and Turkey shall be dealt with through Messrs. A. & H. Vere [Harry, Arthur's son] in Constantinople whose remuneration shall be mutually agreed upon by the said Companies and shall ... be borne by the said Companies in equal shares."[139] The secret agreement was signed on December 31, 1913, by Sir Percy Girouard for Armstrongs and Sir Vincent Caillard for Vickers, and was to run for three years.

In an effort to prevent the Ottoman Empire from siding with Germany, Rear-
Admiral Limpus, now the British Naval Attaché, persuaded Armstrongs and

---

[136] Miller, *Straits*, p. 182. Citing Robertson to Foreign Office, No. 23, December 8, 1913. TNA ADM 1/8365/8; Robertson to Foreign Office, No. 25, December 11, 1913.

[137] Miller, *Straits*, p. 184.

[138] "Agreement."

[139] "Agreement," Provision 2, pp. 1–2.

Vickers to bid to build all the naval installations for the new battleship. "Both firms sent their leading negotiators to Turkey, Vickers sending Sir Vincent Caillard, and Armstrongs sending a former Director of Naval Intelligence and Secretary to the Imperial Defence Committee, Sir Charles Ottley."[140] Caillard, who had previously worked for the Ottoman Public Debt Administrative Council and spoke Turkish, was successful, negotiating "the important contract for the reconstruction of the Turkish Fleet, dockyards and arsenals."[141] The concession was to last thirty years. According to Grant, "Vickers' supremacy showed in the firm's success in capturing the huge docks concessions within Russia and Turkey."[142] Given the secret agreement between the firms, Armstrongs did not lose out, however. The Imperial Ottoman Docks, Arsenals and Naval Construction Company had a Board composed of five English and four Turkish directors.[143] The chairman was Sir Adam Block, who had been the British delegate and President of the Council of Administration of the Ottoman Public Debt and was "long known as an advocate of Anglo-Turkish friendship," according to the Turkish Naval Minister.[144] The other British directors included Sir Charles Ottley of Armstrongs. The new firm had to see off a strong challenge from Germany for Turkish battleships to be built in Germany, which they did by threatening to withdraw from the whole contract until Turkey capitulated.[145] The Turkish government had the controlling share of the capital, with the minority holding divided between Armstrongs and Vickers. There was also an issue of £600,000 bonds in July 1914; the two firms took up £100,000 and the general public took the rest.[146]

At this point Anglo-Turkish relations were looking very healthy. The Ottoman Empire took a naval construction loan from Armstrongs, Vickers and the National Bank of Turkey (a British institution) and, in parallel, Admiral Limpus "was busy reorganising the Turkish navy."[147] In May 1914 the British Group successfully negotiated contracts with the Empire for the third dreadnought, and for six destroyers and two submarines. The dreadnought order was particularly controversial as the British Government were opposed to it on the basis that the Turks could not afford it and that it would stoke further the tensions with Greece. The Turks – and Armstrongs and Vickers – blithely ignored these concerns. In July 1914 Vickers and Armstrongs took over the Government Naval Construction works in Constantinople. This was regarded as a very public recognition that the two states had become increasingly close. However, this did not last.

---

[140] Gilbert, *Winston*, p. 269.
[141] Scott, *Vickers*, p. 78; "Obituary Sir Vincent."
[142] Grant, "Arms Trade," p. 38.
[143] "Vickers Turkish Undertaking," p. 12.
[144] Djemal Pasha, *Memories*, p. 100.
[145] Grant, "The Sword," p. 31.
[146] Scott, *Vickers*, p. 85.
[147] Kent, "Great Britain," pp. 179 and 184.

According to the new Naval Minister Djemal Pasha, "My main purpose was to get the *Sultan Osman*, the construction of which in England was almost finished, into the Sea of Marmora and to fix a definite time for the delivery of the battleship *Reshadieh*, which had been ordered even before the war with Italy and the building of which had suffered one delay after another."[148] According to the Turks, the *Sultan Osman* was expected to be delivered at the end of July and the *Reshadieh* at the beginning of 1915.[149] However, in response to rumors in Paris and "other Continental centres" that the ships were to be delivered early, the British Press Association reported from official sources that "the facts are that the delivery of the ships is contracted for towards the end of October and in November, and the contracts cannot possibly be completed before the contractual dates."[150] This was an attempt to dampen Turkish expectations.

Some of those delays to the *Sultan Osman* were caused by the various Ottoman government departments' handling of the detailed design of the dreadnoughts, combined with the leisurely approach of the officials overseeing construction at Armstrongs. As Richard Hough recounts: "They arrived at their office, itself separated by some miles from the dirt and clamour of their battleship, at ten in the morning, drove into Newcastle for a leisurely lunch at one of the hotels, and had left for the day by three in the afternoon." This approach likely amused both workers and management at Armstrongs, as did the fact that "apparently satisfied with the fighting prowess of their vessel, they were preoccupied with its creature comforts rather than its guns."[151] By March 1914 other Turkish supervisors had arrived. According to an Armstrongs' joiner, they were very respectable, "calling everyone 'Effendi' and hustling us along politely but getting in the way all the time."[152] The Turkish Government was now intent on expediting the arrival of their two ships. Unfortunately for Armstrongs, the British Government wanted exactly the opposite. Raouf Bey, recalled to Constantinople for consultations, reported to Djemal Pasha that "the English were in a very peculiar frame of mind. They seemed to be always searching for some excuse for delaying the completion and delivery of our warship."[153]

Armstrongs tried to balance the opposing forces of her customer and her government. At Elswick,

> As the summer advanced, the sense of urgency became more marked. Still more men were transferred to the *Sultan Osman* .... By late June, with only a few days left before she was due to leave for her trials, there were more

[148] Djemal Pasha, *Memories*, p. 91.
[149] Djemal Pasha, *Memories*, pp. 94–95.
[150] "The Turkish Dreadnoughts," p. 21.
[151] Hough, *Big Battleship*, p. 89.
[152] Hough, *Big Battleship*, p. 90.
[153] Djemal Pasha, *Memories*, p. 104.

than a thousand men at work from before seven to five-thirty in the evening, when the night shift took over. There was no pause at weekends.[154]

The return of Raouf Bey to Newcastle ratcheted things up further, and now his focus was on the fighting power of the dreadnought. Twelve of the fourteen big guns had been fitted, "But two of them were still being proved, it was said, and there was a succession of hold-ups with the new hydraulic controller, which promised well but because of its radical design was causing further delay. Armstrongs reassured their clients that all would be well, and increased still further the labour force."[155] Some inquisitive workers at Armstrongs were asking questions: "At the ordnance shop, for instance, the last two guns were ready, now satisfactorily proved, ready for installation. And all the gunsights had been completed. Why, one or two men were asking, weren't they being fitted?"[156] Djemal Pasha sought to overcome the (apparent) problem that the two guns would not be ready in time for the dreadnought's sea trials. "I declared my readiness to allow the trials to proceed without the two guns, which could then be fitted in Constantinople."[157]

What further slowed things down, however, was the surprising decision that the required dry-docking of the ship was to be done at the Admiralty's Devonport dockyard.[158] Plymouth was the furthest possible place for the work to be done, and the *Sultan Osman* was "the first Turkish warship that has been in Devonport for a number of years."[159] Worse for Turkey, when the ship was at Devonport, the firemen contracted by Vickers went on strike over not being given the 24-hour wages they had been promised.[160] This was possibly the only time that the British Government approved of a strike. Then, when the dry-dock work was completed, for reasons baffling to the Turks, the ship did her timed trials eighty miles north of Newcastle, at St. Abb's Head. "The captain could only assure them that he was merely following orders, received from Armstrongs."[161] After three days kept in a Scottish port by heavy fog, on July 22 the *Sultan Osman* returned to the Walker Yard. "Captain Raouf Bey was there to greet her, anxious and resentful at the delay, and commanding from Armstrong's officials the immediate fitting of her last guns, of her ammunition and her gunsights to make her ready for combat."[162]

[154] Hough, *Big Battleship*, p. 92.
[155] Hough, *Big Battleship*, p. 94.
[156] Hough, *Big Battleship*, p. 95.
[157] Djemal Pasha, *Memories*, p. 104.
[158] "Turkish Battleship."
[159] "Sultan Osman I: Turkey's," p. 8; "The Turkish Navy," p. 4.; "Sultan Osman I: Turkish," p. 7. BNA; Hough, *Big Battleship*, p. 95.
[160] "Sultan Osman I: Contractor's," p. 8.
[161] Hough, *Big Battleship*, p. 115.
[162] Hough, *Big Battleship*, p. 116.

Retrospectively Djemal Pasha darkly declared: "The Greeks themselves realised the situation only too well, and did everything they possibly could to prevent the arrival of the *Sultan Osman* in Stambul."[163] Indeed, British newspapers reported diplomatic speculation in Constantinople that when the dreadnought was ready to leave for Turkey, Greece would declare war on her, obliging the British to withhold the ship.[164]

However, in the end, the obstacles faced by the Turkish Government in getting the dreadnoughts came from Britain. As early as September 1913 the Admiralty had been eyeing the *Sultan Osman I* and *Reshadieh* for commandeering should there be a war with Germany. The *Reshadieh*'s firepower exceeded anything the Royal Navy possessed, making her an attractive target for acquisition. As the *Army and Navy Gazette* noted that month, "From an offensive standpoint, the *Reshadieh* is, if anything, ahead of her time. She must have been designed early in 1911, and while her displacement compares with that of the *King George V*, of 1910–11, her armament is superior to that of the *Iron Duke*, of 1911–12, than which she is 3,000 tons smaller."[165] Moreover, there were already "rumours of a probable transfer" due to questions over whether the Turks could actually pay for the *Reshadieh*.[166] As the *Sheffield Daily Telegraph* reported in September 1913, the Turkish Government would take the ship "if the funds permit. If not, the vessel becomes a marketable commodity, and, being built in Great Britain, our own Government has some sort of preemption upon her of which they would certainly take advantage if there was a probability of the ship passing into the hands of a potentially hostile power."[167] The way the British obtained the ship was not predicted, however.

Under the shadow of war, in late July 1914 Turkish sailors arrived at Elswick, waiting in the steamer *Neshid Pasha* to take over their new ship. Intelligence was passed to the British Admiralty by the Foreign Office on July 29, 1914, that the *Sultan Osman* was "being equipped with coal today and is under orders to proceed to Constantinople as soon as possible, though still unfinished."[168] Clearly the situation was reaching a critical point.

A meeting between Sir Arthur Wilson, who was advising the Admiralty, and the Foreign Office senior legal adviser reached the uncomfortable conclusion that the ship was "unquestionably the property of the Turkish Government even if not yet in commission and flying the national flag. Further, there was no peacetime precedent for seizing a foreign man of war."[169] To deal with the problem, Wilson reported, the first line of maneuver was the firms: "[I]f action

---

[163] Djemal Pasha, *Memories*, p. 96.
[164] "A Warship," p. 12.
[165] "Turkey's New," p. 2.
[166] "Built for Turkey," p. 10.
[167] "The Reshadieh," p. 3.
[168] Gilbert, *Winston*, pp. 270–71. Citing Eyre Crowe to Admiralty, July 29, 1914.
[169] Miller, *Straits*, p. 220.

is desired it should take the form of getting the builders to prevent by some means or other the ship being commissioned." If more was needed, then the Government should negotiate with the Ottoman Empire, and if that failed, the dreadnoughts should be taken by force while also compensating the Empire and "risking the result of such action."[170]

At Winston Churchill's instigation, on July 30 the Foreign Office "pressed" Armstrongs to "put all difficulties in the way of hoisting the flag."[171] Armstrongs did so, but the Ottomans were similarly pressing them for a swift completion of the deal. Third Sea Lord Admiral Moore reported to the Admiralty that the Ottomans wanted Armstrongs to hoist their flag on the warship on Saturday August 1, and that the firm's agent in Constantinople had wired that the final £800,000 installment owed on the ship was to be deposited in a British bank on 30 or 31 of July.[172] That payment would make it impossible for Armstrongs to stall the handover any longer.

The firm was further embroiled in the interstate drama by Grey's decision that "representations to the Turkish Ambassador should not come first [before commandeering]. The firm should, when they had no other means of delaying action, inform the Turkish representatives of the decision of H.M. Govt."[173] Consequently, Churchill called Sir Percy Girouard and Saxton Noble of Armstrongs to a meeting, at which he informed them that the *Sultan Osman* could not be commissioned nor allowed to leave the Tyne. He warned them that "This fact should be kept secret until the last moment, and there was no reason why the money due should not be accepted."[174] This latter instruction would become a bone of contention in the future. Churchill also wrote directly to Elswick: "As a result of consultation with the Law Officers of the Crown, Messrs. Armstrong should be informed that they must understand that in view of the present circumstances, the Government cannot permit the ship to be handed over to a Foreign Power or commissioned as a public ship of a Foreign Government or to leave their jurisdiction."[175]

As Miller recounts, Captain Power, the Superintendent of Contract Built Ships on the Tyne, was instructed to take any steps necessary to prevent the ship's departure and was permitted to use local troops to enforce the order. One hundred Sherwood Foresters had been sent to the yard on the pretext of guarding the British superdreadnought HMS *Malaya*. On the morning of

---

[170] Miller, *Straits*, p. 220. Citing Wilson to Churchill, July 29, 1914. TNA, ADM 137/800 Section II.

[171] Miller, *Straits*, p. 220. Citing Moore to Churchill, July 30, 1914. TNA, ADM 137/800 Section II.

[172] Miller, *Straits*, p. 221. Citing Moore to Churchill, July 30, 1914. TNA, ADM 137/800.

[173] Miller, *Straits*, p. 221. Citing Memorandum to Sir Arthur Wilson, July 30, 1914. TNA, ADM 137/800 Section II.

[174] Memorandum to Sir Arthur Wilson.

[175] Hough, *Big Battleship*, p. 121; Scott, *Vickers*, p. 111.

August 1, one of the missing guns was being placed aboard the *Sultan Osman*. Captain Power received an urgent call from Armstrongs at noon, stating that the final installment was shortly to be paid and the Turks then planned to raise their flag on their ship. In preparation for this meeting, Power had written two letters for Armstrongs, both instructing the firm not to hand over the ships, but the second also stating that, if necessary, a threat of force could be made against the Turks. He gave both to the firm's representatives. These letters put the onus on the firm to ensure that the Turks did not take over the *Sultan Osman*, with the second stating, "I beg that you yourselves communicate this decision to the Turkish officials with a view to minimising any awkward incidents, and avoid unnecessary publicity."[176]

Some two hours later confirmation was received of the final Turkish payment and the firm was called into action. As Miller relates,

> One of the Armstrong's directors immediately went aboard the ship, located Captain Raouf and invited him to the director's private residence. "It was considered a wiser, as well as more graceful act, to make this communication in private rather than on board ship," recorded Power. Raouf Bey was informed of the situation by the directors and shown the first letter; lest there be any doubt, Captain Power confirmed the Admiralty's decision. "Rauf Bey took the matter in the way we hoped" reported Power, "though evidently he was deeply moved, and he at once telephoned the Turkish Ambassador in London."[177]

British sailors now boarded and commandeered the dreadnought. The Turkish Ambassador immediately protested to Sir Arthur Nicholson of the Foreign Office, who told Tewfik Pasha, "The Admiralty had, I believed, taken possession temporarily of her – as it would have been discourteous to have taken any steps once the Turkish flag had been hoisted and a Turkish crew placed on board."[178] The same commandeering occurred at Barrow, where the *Reshadieh* was ready for commissioning. The Turkish crew was waiting "among uncertainty and rumours, and after a few days their ship was whisked from under their noses. It was an episode the Turks would not forget. They were bitterly angry."[179] The embargo was doubly galling for Ambassador Tewfik Pasha, first because his daughter, Naile Hanoum, had launched the ship at Barrow the previous September; at the celebration lunch he had declared that "he could not help thinking that with such a mighty weapon his country would be able to protect itself more efficaciously and benefit in consequences of the blessings of peace

---

[176] Miller, *Straits*, p. 223. Citing Power to Admiralty, August 1, 1914. TNA ADM 137/800, Section II.

[177] Miller, *Straits*, p. 223. Citing Power to Admiralty, August 1, 1914. TNA ADM 137/800, Section II.

[178] Gilbert, *Winston*, p. 271. Citing Nicholson Memorandum.

[179] Scott, *Vickers*, p. 110.

which the whole civilized world was anxious and desirous to see maintained."[180] Second, the contract had been bound for Krupp before Vickers won it at the eleventh hour, a decision he now rued.[181] The two ships became HMS *Agincourt* and HMS *Erin*.[182] In an interesting act of foreshadowing, when Armstrongs was completing the last-minute task of changing the Portuguese "tallies" (instruction plates) to Turkish on the *Sultan Osman* the firm had the perspicacity to put an English translation on the reverse side of every brass plate.[183]

The Ottoman Empire had ordered two submarines from the British Group in April 1914, which they had subcontracted out to Beardmores. The E-class submarines never made it to the building stage, however, due to the outbreak of war, with the production materials being redirected for the submarines HMS *E25* and HMS *E26*.[184] Turkey had ordered a pair of scout cruisers from the British Group in May 1914, and they suffered a similar fate, being cannibalized for the British war effort.[185] These appropriations irked the Turks because the Ottoman regime was formally still a neutral power, and particularly because the firms had each received part-payments on the contracts and the money was not immediately returned.

The commandeering of the dreadnoughts – recommended by Churchill – had been accepted by the Cabinet on July 31. The action had the effect of engendering Turkish anti-British feeling, and added to Germany's influence in Constantinople – the opposite effect of what the ship sales had been initially designed to do. The *Tasfiri-Efkiah* newspaper carried a story about the British seizure entitled "A Thousand Curses," stating that though Turkey was neutral, "it is, however, painful to note that without our having yet taken any steps towards mobilization, England has already dealt us a first blow in laying an embargo on our Dreadnought ('Sultan Osman')."[186] The Ottoman Empire complained publicly that the action was contrary to international law, even though by the time the complaint appeared in British newspapers the country was at war. The *Sheffield Independent* reported, "The British Government has answered that it is obliged in the public interest to retain ships in course of construction for foreign nations in England, and that full compensation will be given."[187] Reuters in Constantinople highlighted the fact that the *Sultan Osman*

---

[180] "Turkey's Big Ship," p. 7.
[181] Gilbert, *Winston*, p. 271. Citing Nicholson Memorandum.
[182] "Naval Additions," p. 5.
[183] Hough, *Big Battleship*, p. 95.
[184] Gardiner, *Conway's*, p. 393.
[185] Brook, *Warships*, pp. 200–01.
[186] "Seizure by H.M.G. of Sultan Osman (Newspaper article)," October 15, 1914. A translation of a newspaper article from the *Tasfiri-Efkiah* was provided by Irvin & Sellers of Bootle, bobbin makers. They provided the initial intelligence on the Turkish reaction to the seizure on October 6 and sent a translation of the article to the government on October 10. TNA, ADM 137/881/2 Folios 173–76.
[187] "The Sultan Osman," p. 1. The paper's headline story was "World's Greatest Battle Opens."

was "purchased by national subscription" and its seizing "caused a feeling of irritation among the Turkish population, although in official circles the difficulties of Great Britain in such matters were recognised."[188] That being said, there were suggestions in the *Times* reports that some of the Turkish irritation was because "Unless it gave explanations, the Turkish Government would come in for sharp criticism for having spent money uselessly."[189] This would certainly explain the subsequent Turkish complaints about the monies they alleged they had lost as a result of the commandeering.

What was particularly infuriating to Djemal Pasha was that he felt he had been misled by Armstrongs. As he explained to Beaumont of the Admiralty on August 6, "when the contract for the ship was being drawn up the Ottoman Government wished to insert a clause providing for a fine of £1 million, payable by Armstrong's should the ship be embargoed, but were persuaded otherwise by the written opinions of Ottley, Caillard 'and another' that no such right of embargo existed."[190] On the same day Djemal Pasha had been even clearer – and more petulant – with Harry Vere of Armstrongs, threatening to never place another order in Britain and to cancel the docks contract.[191] Grey wrote to Ottley of Armstrongs to find out if there was any truth to Djemal's complaint. Two days later Caillard, Ottley and Barker called at the Foreign Office to discuss the matter. According to Ottley, the request to insert a clause for compensation if the ships were embargoed had been discussed once with Djemal, but in March 1914, in the context of the new Turkish building program, that is, months after the *Sultan Osman* had been bought. Even then, the firm "absolutely declined to consent to the imposition of any penalty." The firm had also taken the time to obtain a legal opinion on the question from a King's Counsel, who had concluded that the British Government had no right to seize a ship being built in Britain for a foreign power during peacetime.[192] Despite that (and the Foreign Office lawyers initially made the same judgment), the ship had indeed been embargoed from export.

At the meeting Caillard, Ottley and Barker – all experts on Turkey – offered the Foreign Office advice on how to mollify Turkey enough that she would remain neutral in the war, even if she did not ally with Britain. They advocated promising to eventually pay the full price of the two dreadnoughts, to return the reconditioned ships or substitutes at the end of the war and to acknowledge

---

[188] Reuters, "Turkey's," p. 3.
[189] Times Telegram, "Turkish," p. 3.
[190] Miller, *Straits*, p. 237. Citing Beaumont to Grey, No. 493, August 7, 1914. TNA, ADM 137/HS19.
[191] Miller, *Straits*, p. 237. Citing Beaumont to Grey, No. 489, August 6, 1914. TNA, ADM 137/HS19.
[192] Miller, *Straits*, p. 266. Citing Ottley to Crowe, August 11, 1914, with an enclosed letter from Armstrongs to Mr. Duke, KC MP, and Duke's opinion, dated April 22, 1914. TNA, FO 371/2137/38132.

Turkey's current territorial possessions.[193] The British Government was indeed considering how to mollify the Ottomans. Churchill and Asquith agreed a formula to be put to Enver Pasha, which included the return of the reconditioned ships or full payment for them at the end of the war if they were sunk, paying the expenses of the Turks sent to Newcastle to collect the dreadnought and paying the government £1,000 a day "compensation" for as long as Britain kept the ships.[194]

Nevertheless, later in August the Ottoman Empire was protesting to the British Government that Armstrongs had not returned a payment they made on the *Sultan Osman* just before it was commandeered. This enraged Armstrongs' Sir Charles Ottley, who complained directly to Churchill about this "fantastically untrue" statement. Ottley even went to the Turkish Embassy in London, confronting the Naval Attaché there and forcing him to admit that Ambassador Tewfik had informed Constantinople by wire of the repayment by Armstrongs, describing the whole incident as "a regrettable mistake, due to the inefficiency of the telegraph communications."[195] While Miller says that "the last remittance of $700,000 had been returned," this would have been £100,000 less than Admiral Moore said the Turks had paid in the final installment, despite Nicolson having promised Ambassador Tewfik Pasha that "he would not lose his money."[196] The Turks actually lost even more on the deal. To make up the shortfall in public donations for the ships they had taken out loans at punishing interest levels, meaning that Vickers estimated that together the *Sultan Osman* and *Reshadieh* in the end cost the country $6,893,000, of which Turkey had already paid Armstrongs and Vickers $3.6 million.[197] Eventually, after negotiations to keep Turkey neutral seemed to be failing, the Admiralty declared that if Turkey went to war the two ships would be forfeited completely.[198] This is what happened. After being defeated in the war, Turkey was barred under the Treaty of Lausanne from seeking compensation for the two lost dreadnoughts.[199]

In July 1914 Grey was questioned in Parliament about the British Ambassador's role in creating the Imperial Ottoman Docks, Arsenals and Naval Construction Company, to which he replied, "This agreement was the

---

[193] Miller, *Straits*, p. 266. Citing Minutes by Clarke and Crowe, August 11, 1914. TNA, FO 371/2137/38132.

[194] Miller, *Straits*, p. 290 and ff. 2, p. 302. Citing Grey to Mallet, No. 398, August 19, 1914. TNA, ADM 137/800.

[195] Miller, *Straits*, p. 291 and ff. 4, p. 303. Citing Ottley to Churchill, August 21, 1914, *Winston Spencer Churchill Comp. Vol. III, pt. I*, pp. 47–48; and Grey to Mallet, no. 411, August 21, 1914, TNA, ADM 137/800.

[196] Miller, *Straits*, p. 238 and p. 223. Citing Nicholson to Grey, August 1, 1914. TNA, FO 371/2137/36825.

[197] Miller, *Straits*, p. 297. Citing Vickers to Foreign Office, August 20, 1914. TNA FO 371/2137.

[198] Miller, *Straits*, p. 297. Citing Admiralty to Treasury, September 23, 1914. TNA FO 371/2137/52468.

[199] Barlas and Güvenç, "To Build," p. 152.

result of private negotiations between the Turkish Government and the firms interested in which His Majesty's Government had no participation."[200] In addition to ignoring the catalytic role of the British Naval Mission in forming the new company, this was a clear signal to Armstrongs and Vickers that they were being left holding this particular baby. The Ottoman Dock Company was seized by the Turkish Government in November 1914.[201] In the House of Commons the same month a question was asked by Joseph King about the Company and whether this British company had continued to operate until the outbreak of hostilities with Turkey. Grey replied:

> The company in question is Ottoman, not British. I presume that up to the outbreak of War the company carried out operations in accordance with its contract, but I have no reason to suppose that these operations, of which the provision of munitions of war was to form a subsequent and subsidiary part, were in any way detrimental to the interests of His Majesty's Government.[202]

When Turkey took over the firm, Armstrongs and Vickers gallantly accepted liability – "as the fortune of war" – and compensated the British shareholders, buying back their £500,000 in bonds for what they cost, plus interest, despite having no formal obligation to do so.[203]

With Turkey's defeat in the war, Vickers were able to recover their rights to the Ottoman Dock Company and, having obtained a National Bank of Turkey overdraft, began work in April 1920.[204] However, the bitter legacy of the commandeering still haunted their relationship with the Turkish Government. By 1921 the Ottoman Docks, Arsenals and Naval Construction Company was losing money. In June 1923 "representatives of Messrs. Armstrongs and Vickers had returned from Angora [Ankara], having, it was stated, failed to reach an understanding in regard to recognition of the principle of the concession granted in 1913 for re-organization of the Turkish arsenal and dockyards at the Golden Horn." A week later came a sharp message from Constantinople: "[T]he Angora Government has decided to claim from the shipbuilders concerned the first payment made by the old Government at Constantinople for the construction of the Dreadnought, Sultan Osman."[205] According to Scott, the lack of profits and a mounting overdraft led to Vickers and Armstrongs leaving their operations there in October 1923. A few months later the firms paid off the £29,215 overdraft (equal to £1,963,449 in August 2022).[206]

[200] House of Commons Debate, July 30, 1914, *Hansard*, Vol. 65, cc. 1534–35.
[201] Scott, *Vickers*, p. 149.
[202] House of Commons Debate, November 17, 1914, *Hansard*, Vol. 68, cc. 310–11.
[203] Scott, *Vickers*, p. 86.
[204] Scott, *Vickers*, p. 149.
[205] "Seized Warship," p. 6.
[206] Scott, *Vickers*, pp. 84–86 and 149.

In the same year Vickers was involved in negotiations with Turkey for the reconditioning of the cruiser *Goeben*, renamed the *Yavuz*, and new naval construction, including submarines. A concern for the Turkish Government – clearly in light of their experience in the Great War – was possible confiscation or sequestration of Turkish vessels under construction in Britain if conflict broke out. In response to a September 1923 inquiry from Vickers, the Admiralty declared:

(i)   In the case of this country going to war before the contract was completed, we would be debarred under Article XVII of the Washington Treaty from seizing any vessel under construction for Turkey. The completion of the vessels, however, might be delayed by British war requirements.

(ii)   In the case of Turkey going to war before completion of the contract, it would certainly be necessary that any vessels under construction for Turkey should be interned.[207]

By 1924 several British, American, French and Italian firms had made offers to the Turkish navy. The Vickers' offer of five submarines was "conditional on the scrapping of the *Yavuz* [battlecruiser] in five years."[208] Despite British Government assurances that ships destined for Turkey would not be confiscated, Barrow was unsuccessful in securing the contract for reconditioning the *Yavuz*, which went to French yards.[209] For the firm, however, worse was to come. "The British-Turkish rift over the status of Mosul in September 1924 had an immediate impact on the submarine deal …. [W]hen the Turkish government invited bids for one submarine, Vickers-Armstrong's bid was eliminated par principe."[210] The successful bidder was a Dutch shipyard that had been set up by three German shipbuilders to evade the restrictions of the Treaty of Versailles.[211]

The quarrels between the Turkish Government and Armstrongs and Vickers continued. The Turkish Government sued Armstrongs' agent in Constantinople, Harry Vere, claiming that he had not complied with the March 1913 contract to supply ammunition and torpedoes (even though the dreadnoughts they were to be used on had been commandeered). In 1927 the Atatürk Government was pursuing a claim against Armstrongs and Vickers over the ship the Admiralty commandeered, the *Reshadieh*.[212] The British Government

[207] Foreign Office to Board of Trade, February 29, 1929. TNA, FO 371/13817. Citing Foreign Office to Vickers, September 18, 1923.
[208] Güvenç and Barlas, "Atatürk's," p. 11. Citing Service Historique de la Marine, Vincennes, Carton 1BB7/150, Bulletin de Informations Militaires (Turquie), No. 292, August 12, 1924.
[209] Epstein, *Statesman's*, p. 1328.
[210] Güvenç and Barlas, "Atatürk's," p. 11.
[211] Barlas and Güvenç, "To Build," p. 148.
[212] Lavison and Caillard to the Under Secretary of State for Foreign Affairs, January 11, 1927. TNA, ADM 116/2589.

became involved and the Treasury Solicitor's Department defended the two firms before the Mixed Arbitral Tribunal.[213] Dr. Brown, the Treasury Solicitor, was successful in getting the cases dismissed in December 1928.[214] Even with this case settled, there remained the question of the monies due to Turkey from deposits paid to Vickers and Armstrongs on the March 1914 naval orders.

After Sir Trevor Dawson had tested the waters with the Treasury, the newly amalgamated firm of Vickers-Armstrongs requested that the British Government pay the £10,754 costs (£759,338 in August 2022) that the firm had incurred by 1929 in defending itself against the Turkish claims.[215] The Admiralty agreed that some compensation should be supplied, but the Treasury balked at the amount the firm was claiming.[216] In the end, Vickers-Armstrongs was paid £5,500 (£399,578 in August 2022) "compensation," which was to be paid from the Navy Vote as the Treasury refused point blank to provide the money.[217]

Despite these disputes with Turkey, in a 1929 competition for a new gun, the Turkish military commission visited both Vickers-Armstrongs and Schneider to consider their wares. Vickers-Armstrongs eventually got the sale.[218]

In terms of new Turkish construction, a 1929 proposed order was for four destroyers, six submarines and six submarine chasers, valued at "about two and a half million pounds sterling" – an enticing prospect at a time of depressed orders – and Turkey wanted only tenders for all the work.[219] British firms Yarrow and Hawthorne Leslie were interested in the contract and an official from the Turkish Ministry of National Defence had suggested that they form a syndicate to bid on the deal. As Ambassador Clerk speculated from Constantinople, "I believe Vickers to be the only British firm capable of building all three types of craft, and they may therefore prefer to play a lone hand."[220] By April Vickers had agreed to work with Thornycroft (which had expertise in destroyers) to try to secure the Turkish contract.[221]

While Vickers had advantages against other British rivals, it was disadvantaged compared to bidders such as Ansaldo. First, during this period the British Government viewed arms exports through the lens of international

[213] Flint to Armstrong Whitworth and Vickers Ltd., February 9, 1927. TNA, ADM 116/2589.
[214] "Anglo-Turkish," p. 13.
[215] Baddeley to Brown, July 2, 1929; Dawson to Secretary of the Admiralty, June 28, 1929. TNA, ADM 116/2589.
[216] Brown to Baddeley, July 17, 1929. TNA, ADM 116/2589.
[217] Nind Hopkins, Treasury, to Secretary of the Admiralty, March 29, 1930. TNA, ADM 116/2589.
[218] Nye Committee Hearings, Part 2, testimony of Mr. Driggs, pp. 507–08.
[219] Note on file, January 29, 1929. "Desire of Turkish Government to Purchase Destroyers, Submarines and Submarine Chasers," FO 371/13817, Folio 68; Clerk to Chamberlain, February 21, 1929. FO 371/13817, Folio 80.
[220] Clerk to Chamberlain, January 24, 1929. FO 371/13817, Folio 70.
[221] Memorandum from the Department of Overseas Trade, April 13, 1929. FO 371/13817, Folios 99–100.

disarmament negotiations, leading them to exercise self-restraint over potential exports. That said, in the case of Turkey in 1929 the Foreign Office saw "the great desirability of securing for this country orders of the kind contemplated."[222] Second, the Turks still remembered the embargo placed on their dreadnoughts in 1914, and – despite assurances – remained wary of Armstrongs and Vickers. On this, the Board of Trade suggested that Vickers look at getting insurance from Lloyds of London as it was impossible for the British Government to provide a definite guarantee of war reimbursement for any case except that of Britain and Turkey going to war.[223] Finally, the greatest hurdle Vickers faced in the deal was that the British Government would not provide any direct finance to the Turkish regime to facilitate the purchases. At the urging of Sir George Clerk in Constantinople, in early March the Foreign Office was in principle ready to encourage British banks contemplating loaning Turkey the money to "take the plunge."[224] While Vickers' banking contacts were robust compared to those of other British firms, as Dawson explained to the Department of Overseas Trade, the Turkish Government wanted a generous payment schedule: "2% of value of contract on signature of contract. 2% in 1929–1930, 5% in 1930–1931 and about 13% of Treasury bonds each year for the next seven years." From their perspective it carried considerable risk. The firm's counterproposal was: "20% of the value of the contract during construction period of 3 years. Balance in Turkish Treasury bonds payable over 6 years from date of contract." Dawson explained that "Sir Herbert Lawrence considers the Turkish proposals impossible, yet it is feared that the Italian competitors may with the indirect support of their government, accede to them."[225]

In this meeting Dawson asked what indirect help the British Government could give to Vickers and was told that if he requested it, they could confidentially provide him with the views of the Embassy in Constantinople as to the financial situation in Turkey. This he immediately did, and received a response from the Department of Overseas Trade "on the distinct understanding that no responsibility for the result attaches to this Department or His Majesty's Embassy." The letter cited verbatim from a February 21 letter to the Foreign Office from Ambassador Clerk. He began with a pertinent observation:

> The various vessels are to be completed and delivered within two years and it would seem more or less certain that the Turkish Treasury bills maturing during that period would be met. It would be less safe, however, to

---

[222] Foreign Office Memorandum for the Department of Overseas Trade, February 5, 1929. FO 371/13817, Folio 75.

[223] Memorandum from the Board of Trade to the Department of Overseas Trade, March 20, 1929. FO 371/13817, Folio 88.

[224] Note on file by W. Knight, March 1, 1929. "Proposed Supply of Destroyers and Submarines to Turkish Government," FO 371/13817, Folio 79.

[225] Memorandum from the Department of Overseas Trade to the Foreign Office, April 13, 1929. FO 371/13817, Folios 98–102.

count on equal punctuality once the ships are delivered to the Turkish
Government. No *deliberate* intention on the part of the Turkish Government to fail to meet its obligations is to be anticipated. The possibility is
rather a lack of funds for the purpose.

While this was rather bleak, Clerk declared that "three considerations lead His
Majesty's Ambassador to the conclusion that the Turkish Government, both
could, and would, pay." These considerations were: increasing Turkish revenue; the moderate cost of the vessels when spread over ten years; and the desire
of Turkey to avoid the blow to its credit that any default would cause.[226] The
British Government also sought to encourage Vickers to seek banking help to
deal with the difficult Turkish terms. After the London branch of the Ottoman
Bank refused to help, Vickers did not pursue Ambassador Clerk's suggestion of
the Turkish Government bank, Ish Bankasi, which he thought could not refuse
to discount its own Government's bonds.[227] The Foreign Office thought it
"most unfortunate ... that Armstrong Vickers preferred to lose the order rather
than have recourse to the Turkish Government bank."[228] Vickers-Armstrongs
clearly thought the risks too great.

While Vickers had thought the Italians would undercut them on cost,
Ambassador Clerk reported that "Messrs. Armstrong Vickers' price was
£100,000 lower than that of their Italian competitor."[229] Nevertheless, the
Italians secured the contract thanks to the financial terms they offered, though
the actual order was reduced considerably from the initial Turkish plan. The
Italian loan was more of an indication of the improved relationship between
Fascist Italy and Turkey than a statement of faith in Turkish finances.

Despite being frozen out of the Turkish naval market, Vickers-Armstrongs
were benefiting from Krupps being formally excluded from the international
armaments market. Sir Noel Birch had been informed by General Emin Pasha
of the military's intent to move to standard weapons systems.[230] If Vickers-
Armstrongs could secure some of these gun contracts, it would ensure their
place in the Turkish market for decades. The firm demonstrated various types
of guns to a Turkish Mission at the Eskmeals testing ground in Cumbria in
March 1928. J. Rose of Vickers-Armstrongs reported that the Turks were
impressed by all they saw. In particular, a "very convincing demonstration
was given of the Predictor [for anti-aircraft guns] and the Turks also expressed
themselves as very satisfied with the instrument. They informed our Turkish
representative that it was their intention to recommend the purchase of 40 – 3"

226 Farrer, Department of Overseas Trade to Messrs. Vickers-Armstrongs Ltd., April 13,
1929. FO 371/13817, Folios 103–04. Citing Clerk to Chamberlain, February 21, 1929. FO
371/13817, Folio 80. Emphasis in original.
227 Clerk to Chamberlain, June 10, 1929. FO 371/13817, Folio 106.
228 Note on file by W. Knight, June 14, 1929. FO 371/13817, Folio 105.
229 Clerk to Chamberlain, June 10, 1929.
230 Grant, *Depression*, p. 76. Citing Vahid Bey to Birch, March 23, 1928. VA, Microfilm K 617.

High Angle Equipments and 20 Predictors." Later, the Turkish Mission was entertained at Abbey House, Barrow. "Owing to the special arrangements made by Commander Craven, both at his house and at the works, for the reception of this mission, the visit was a very great success … the Turkish Mission … expressed how very delighted they were with what they have seen and the kindness which has been shown to them."[231] Rose then followed the mission back to Ankara to pursue orders.[232]

However, Vickers-Armstrongs lost the mountain gun orders to Bofors, whose final agreement was £570,000 cheaper than the British tender (£39,800,408 in August 2022).[233] Nevertheless, the firm was still in competition for the anti-aircraft gun order, and in May 1929 Sir Noel Birch and Sir Trevor Dawson headed to Ankara in pursuit of the deal. As Grant recounts, "Although Turkey's financial position was not the most robust, Vickers recognized that the Turks had never defaulted in respect of payments for munitions of war."[234] This rather glosses over the near-constant experiences of Armstrongs and Vickers in struggling to keep Turkey to payment schedules, and likely reflects the desperation to secure the gun deals for the firm. Ironically, some major impediments to securing the deal were the monies the firms still owed to Turkey for the installments the state had paid on the aborted 1914 naval shipbuilding program and – in the other direction – the ongoing dispute over what Vickers-Armstrongs was owed by Turkey for the losses they incurred on the Ottoman Dock Company. In terms of the naval program,

> The Turks wanted either the execution of the contract or repayment of the amount received with interest. Vickers-Armstrong knew it had an indefensible position. The British judge on the Mixed Tribunal offered the firm his legal advice that if Vickers-Armstrong contended the case, it would lose the action. Therefore, he urged the firm to settle the matter without delay so as to avoid suffering a great blow to its prestige.[235]

The Vickers-Armstrongs Board took the decision to settle the claims, assuming that new contracts with Turkey would compensate for the losses.[236] This cleared the way for Vickers-Armstrongs if sales orders could be won.

The British Chancery understood what needed to be done to successfully conclude business in Constantinople. As Grant recounts, in 1927 the Chancery was explaining to the Embassy what was required if British firms were to win

---

[231] Rose to Leveson, March 19, 1928. VA, Microfilm R 286.
[232] Minutes of Army Sales Committee, April 2 and 3, 1928, p. 5. VA, Microfilm R 286.
[233] Grant, *Depression*, p. 77.
[234] Grant, *Depression*, p. 79. Citing "Turkish Business, Minute No. 232 (G.G. Sim)," Minute Book of Board Meetings, Minutes, May 1, 1929. VA, Doc. 1223.
[235] Grant, *Depression*, p. 78.
[236] Grant, *Depression*, p. 79. Citing "Turkish Business, Minute No. 232 (G.G. Sim)," Minute Book of Board Meetings, Minutes, May 1, 1929. VA, Doc. 1223.

aircraft business there – "agents on the spot in Ankara, ready with specifications, price-lists, short-time credits, and who could, 'go in for hospitality and personal contact with the Turkish deputies and cabinet on an extensive scale.' The Chancery also advised that all these materials should be printed in Turkish." Noting Turkish concerns about British reliability, the Chancery advised that "much can be done to overcome this fear by the judicious use of 'palm oil' [bribes] which need neither concern His Majesty's Government nor reduce the profits of manufacturing companies to vanishing point."[237] From 1926 Armstrongs had been represented there by Captain A. V. Lander OBE, who later represented Vickers too. At the instigation of the head office, in January 1928 Lander took on a former Turkish officer, A. Vahit Bey, who was accustomed to the ways of business in Constantinople. In June 1928, however, the Turkish National Assembly passed a rule forbidding Turkish ex-officers from engaging in business connected to national defense. From then on, Vahit Bey acted as an informal aide to Lander.[238]

Thanks to efforts on many fronts from representatives at Vickers-Armstrongs' head office and in Constantinople, the firm broke into the Turkish gun market with the July 1929 order for sixty-four of their Predictor anti-aircraft guns, valued at £385,000. This contract was highly sought after; Herbert Allen of the American Driggs Ordnance Company wrote to his firm's headquarters explaining that he had lost the contract to Vickers-Armstrongs because "The Vickers crowd are the dirtiest opponents here. They have almost an entire Embassy in number working for them and use women of doubtful character freely."[239] The Driggs firm had been confident of securing the contract, writing as such to the U.S. Government, even before the Turkish Mission had tested the gun.[240]

With the door now opened by the anti-aircraft gun sales, Birch went in search of bigger orders. This was facilitated in December 1929 by Vickers-Armstrongs handing over £150,000 in final settlement of all debts between the firm and the Turkish Government. The immediate result was a contract for seventy 75 mm guns, and prospects for more orders.

Despite these successes, the firm still complained about the lack of British Government support, which, in their view, was costing them orders. From

---

[237] Grant, *Depression*, pp. 136–37. Citing Chancery at Constantinople to British Embassy Constantinople, November 14, 1927. TNA FO 371/12323.

[238] "A.V. Lander – Turkey," March 1, 1935. Folder 1, VA, Doc. 57.

[239] Allen to Drigg, January 22, 1929. Exhibit 219 p. 538. Nye Committee Hearings, Part 2, September 7, 1934; Driggs wrote to Allen discussing Captain Osann coming to Turkey to help Allen so "You will not feel you are playing a lone hand against the Vickers crowd." Driggs to Allen, February 22, 1929. Nye Committee Hearings, Part 2. September 7, 1934. Exhibit 205, p. 528.

[240] Driggs to U.S. Chief of Bureau of Ordnance, February 13, 1929. Nye Committee Hearings, Exhibit 227, p. 498.

Vickers-Armstrongs' perspective, financing was key. James Wilson of the Erith branch of Vickers-Armstrongs complained to the Treasury in 1929 that

> over £3,000,000 worth of armament work for Turkey and Greece had been lost by his firm to Italy owing to the inadequacy of credit arrangements. He reported that whilst in Italy the Government guaranteed such contracts up to 80%, in this country there was no guarantee of any kind and if the resources of a firm plus the credit which banks were prepared to allow were insufficient to meet the credit required the contract would be lost.[241]

In 1930 Vickers-Armstrongs put forward to Turkey two proposals for a major refit and modernization of the *Hamidieh*, which was then twenty-eight years old. Their offers were not taken up by the regime.[242] In the same year Turkey placed an order for two new destroyers directly with Italy, not bothering with a competition, even though they had been dissatisfied with the first two that Italy had delivered.[243] This illustrates the importance of both geopolitics and the major loan from Italy that underpinned the deal, neither of which Vickers-Armstrongs could compete with.

From July 1929 the firm was handling the anti-aircraft guns order.[244] Reflecting the relative decline within Vickers-Armstrongs, these orders were not easily fulfilled, despite the need for them. Noel Birch admonished Commander Craven: "Please do not forget that the date of delivery of the first Turkish equipments is November 1930. We have to deliver four equipments by that date."[245] Subsequently Vickers was asked to provide a gun for trials, but the firm had trouble producing the breech block and mechanism in time.[246] There were also financial issues. In June 1930 Birch was writing in exasperation about a repeat order: "Those blooming Turks! They have now wired for fresh financial terms, which I am going to recommend the Chairman not give them, involving 25% only being paid on delivery, the next 25% being paid six months later, finishing payments in 1935."[247] In November 1931 Noel Birch was complaining about the Vickers-Armstrongs 75 mm gun being unfairly criticized by the Turkish inspection team.[248]

In Constantinople things were not all smooth sailing. In August 1933 Vickers-Armstrongs' agent Lander was expelled from the country under a cloud – he

---

[241] Dartford-Turfleet Tunnel and Unemployment Conference, Report on a Deputation to the Treasury, November 6, 1929. VA, Microfilm R 286.

[242] Brook, *Warships*, p. 97.

[243] Barlas and Güvenç, "To Build," p. 157.

[244] Craven to Birch, July 3, 1929. VA, Microfilm K 613; Buxton and Johnston, *Battleship*, p. 40.

[245] Birch to Craven, October 13, 1929. VA, Microfilm K 613.

[246] Birch to Wilson, May 14, 1930. VA, Microfilm R 286.

[247] Birch to Craven, June 28, 1930. VA, Microfilm K 613.

[248] Birch to V. Vahid Bey, November 26, 1931, "Guns – Interviews etc. Manufacture 1934–1945," VA, Doc. 662, Folios 24–28.

was alleged to have engaged in bribery, which he vehemently denied.[249] Interestingly, the problems with Lander did not extend to the Vickers-Armstrongs company, whose Mr. Leveson returned from Constantinople with the news that "I received from the Ministry of Defence personally the confirmation that Mr. Lander's expulsion from Turkey was a personal question and that they had no complaints against the firm."[250] While in Turkey, Leveson also met with Vehit Bey and agreed that he would be appointed Vickers-Armstrongs agent from January 1, 1934. This did not endure, however, as in March "it came to our notice, from an indirect source, that Vehit Bey was no longer a person grata with the Government." Consequently, the firm twice sent representatives to Turkey to search for a new agent, and Fethi Halil Bey was appointed.[251]

Vickers made its first overseas aircraft sales – important to create a market for their air armaments – to Turkey.[252] In 1934 Vickers Supermarine delivered six R. J. Mitchell-designed Southampton Mk. II flying boats to Turkey. The country had first seen these flying boats in 1927 when trials were completed in the Mediterranean.[253] As the delivery date approached, there were many telegrams to decode and encode between the Hampshire office and the Turkish Government.[254] Vickers Supermarine subsequently supplied Turkey with six Seagull Vs (a model better known as the Walrus) – single-engine amphibious biplanes.[255]

By 1934 Turkey had come to perceive Italy as a threat, particularly after Mussolini's speech about wanting to move into Africa and Asia. Turkey therefore lost their major source of subsidized shipbuilding and, along with Greece, sought financial help from Britain to strengthen her navy.[256]

> The countries' joint plea for British credits, however, was not received enthusiastically in London on two counts. The lack of funds was a first restraining factor. London was still reluctant to spend even on its own naval programs. Additionally, the British Government was still bound by the restriction in the 1921 Trade Facilities Act which prohibited the use of credits for armaments exports. Second, the British were the champions of world-wide disarmament.[257]

While the Admiralty wanted to have orders for British shipyards, the Foreign Office was not keen.

---

[249] "British Arms Man Ousted," p. 16.
[250] "A.V. Lander – Turkey," March 1, 1935. Folio 4.
[251] "A.V. Lander – Turkey," March 1, 1935. Folio 4.
[252] Grant, *Depression*, p. 145.
[253] Smith, *Supermarine*, p. 48.
[254] Webb, *Never*, pp. 70–75.
[255] Stemp, *Kites*, p. 39.
[256] Grant, *Depression*, p. 168.
[257] Güvenç and Barlas, "Atatürk's," p. 22.

In addition to using ambassador-agents, Vickers-Armstrongs' records show thirty-four visits to the country by head office representatives between February 1924 and September 1934, indicating how valuable the Turkish market was in the difficult interwar years.[258] During the investigations of the Nye Committee and the Royal Commission, critics made much of the behavior of the firms in providing bribes to influential officials to ensure that they either directly approved arms sales or acted as interlocutors on the firms' behalf with higher-level officials who could approve sales. In Turkey this was not just common practice but was the only way to secure sales (and important concessions such as railway contracts). Consequently, Armstrongs, Vickers and other British firms paid the necessary "*backsheesh*," as did international firms. Viewed from the vantage point of the mid-1930s the behavior looked distasteful, but it was the common practice in all business sectors and was not illegal in Turkey.

By 1936 the British Government's attitude to Turkey had shifted because of the strategic situation. Now Turkey was seen as an ally against Italy in the Eastern Mediterranean and was to be protected from German domination. Nevertheless, the new British priority of domestic rearmament meant that Vickers-Armstrongs still did not secure Turkish export orders. A proposed July 1936 contract for eight tanks for Turkey had to be turned down at the demand of the British War Office, and the Admiralty also instructed Vickers-Armstrongs to decline a request for 15-inch costal defense guns.[259] Now, however, the firm saw a profound shift in its relationship with the British Government, with the firm now getting significant help from Whitehall.

Vickers-Armstrongs was trying to recover money now owed to the firm by the Turks and sought the help of the British Government in early October 1936.[260] The issue was the final payment on a 1929 armaments agreement (likely the contracts for Predictors, anti-aircraft guns and 75 mm guns). Even Vickers-Armstrongs admitted that "Certain difficulties arose in regard to the supply of the material but these were eventually met" and the contract had finally been fulfilled in 1933.[261] Before completion, and due to the Turkish Government's financial difficulties, in 1932 an appendix contract with a modified payment schedule had been agreed by A. V. Lander for Vickers-Armstrongs and Kekai Bey for the Ottoman Government.[262] However, the Turkish Government had again fallen behind in payments, and another

---

[258] "Vickers Limited and Vickers-Armstrong Limited: Principal visits abroad of a general character made by Directors, Sales Representatives and Senior Officials 1919 to 1934," Folder 3, VA, Doc. 57.

[259] Grant, *Depression*, p. 194. Citing Howard to FO, July 23, 1936, TNA, FO 371/20371 and Phillips to Air Ministry and Board of Trade, December 2, 1937, TNA, ADM 116/4195.

[260] "British Embassy, Angora file: Vickers Armstrongs, Ltd." TNA, FO 195/2516.

[261] Reid Young to Welch, Board of Trade, October 7, 1936. "Angora File." TNA, FO 195/2516.

[262] Appendix Contract, May 31, 1932. "Angora File." TNA, FO 195/2516.

schedule had been agreed in 1934, using maturing bonds to make the payments, with a final large payment in sterling due on October 1, 1936.[263]

This 1934 payment schedule had been adhered to by the Turkish Government up until the final payment. Vickers-Armstrongs learned about the Turkish failure to pay from their bank, Glyn Mills, on October 3. Glyn Mills had received a communication from the Ottoman Bank in London that "Ministry of Finance will make settlement remittance ... sterling 103900 as cover[ed] by clearing."[264] This was a reference to the Anglo-Turkish Trade and Clearing Agreement of June 4, 1935, for the liquidation of commercial debts.[265] The Turks wanted their final payment to be paid out of the Clearing Agreement. The failure to pay the firm came just days after the Clearing Agreement had come into force.

Vickers-Armstrongs immediately appealed to the British Government for help, thereby setting off an internal discussion about whether the Clearing Agreement could and should be used in this way. Interestingly, and in contrast to years past, there was no suggestion that Vickers-Armstrongs should be told to solve its own problems with Turkey. A serious issue with the Clearing Agreement route was that by May 1936 the Turkish account was already in debt by £600,000; by April 1937 it was fifteen months in arrears.[266] The Board of Trade and the Treasury were of the opinion that "the payments due on the bonds given by the Turkish Government to Messrs. Vickers Armstrong Limited constitute financial payments and as such are not proper to be transferred through the Anglo-Turkish Clearing, the purpose of which is the liquidation of commercial debts."[267] In response the Foreign Office, seeking out the strongest arguments that could be used by the Embassy in Ankara to bring the Vickers-Armstrongs claims, went into detail about how the Clearing Agreement could be variously understood and the ambivalence that could allow the Turkish Government to make an argument for using that route.[268]

The British Government coalesced around the position that the Turks could not use the Clearing Agreement, though they were hesitant about saying why. The instruction to the Embassy from the Secretary of State merely said, "I shall be glad if you will now approach the Turkish Government with a view to securing the payment of this bond otherwise than through the machinery set up by the Anglo-Turkish Trade and Clearing Agreement."[269] The Foreign Office

---

[263] Ministry of Finance of the Turkish Republic copy of Bond to Vickers Armstrongs, July 12, 1934, Ankara. "Angora File." TNA, FO 195/2516.

[264] Ottoman Bank to Messrs. Glyn Mills & Co., October 3, 1936. "Angora File." TNA, FO 195/2516.

[265] Also known as the Trade and Payments Agreement of 1935.

[266] Millman, *Ill-Made*, pp. 111 and 115.

[267] St. Quintin Hill, Board of Trade to Under Secretary of State, Foreign Office, October 20, 1936. "Angora File." TNA, FO 195/2516.

[268] Baggallay to Welch, Board of Trade, October 29, 1936; Baggallay to Morgan, Angora, October 29, 1936. "Angora File." TNA, FO 195/2516.

[269] Stendale Bennett to Morgan, November 13, 1936. "Angora File." TNA, FO 195/2516.

decided that the arguments against the use of the Agreement should be held in reserve until needed, but were in little doubt that they would be needed.[270]

In parallel, Commander Craven was planning to visit Ankara, and Vickers-Armstrongs sought the help of the Board of Trade, relaying news from Glyn Mills that the Ankara Branch of the Ottoman Bank interpreted the Anglo-Turkish Clearing Agreement as "being against the point of view upheld by us."[271] The firm's communication concluded: "[A]s the matter is causing us grave concern we are anxious that every possible pressure should be brought to bear on the Turkish Government to meet its obligations to us."[272] Craven also met a Foreign Office official to discuss the proposed trip. He was advised to "call upon the Director General of the 'Mouvements des Fondes' at the Ministry of Finance." He was also told of the British Government's agreed position that the final payment should not be made from the Clearing Agreement.[273] However, while in Ankara Craven did not visit the Director of the 'Mouvements des Fondes' but was reportedly "waiting for the Embassy to take action."[274] One of the notes on this Foreign Office minute responded: "Then, subject to the CS's [Chief Secretary's] views, I suppose we shall have to make representations to TG [Turkish Government]." A further minute noted that Craven "went on to say that he had been offered several new orders but that he had been unwilling to accept any of them."[275] This was in line with the British Government's prioritization of domestic rearmament.

The British Embassy in Ankara subsequently petitioned the Turkish Ministry of Foreign Affairs on behalf of Vickers-Armstrongs, using many of the arguments of the Board of Trade and the Treasury. It made clear that "His Majesty's Government consider therefore that the final payment like its predecessors should be made from other sources, that is to say either out of the sterling which, under article 9 of the Anglo-Turkish Trade and Clearing Agreement, is left at the free disposal of the central bank in a sub-account 'E', or from other sources."[276]

From 1936 onwards Turkey sought to retain her independence and play Germany and Britain off against each other while attracting extra-European bidders (i.e., the United States) for a large naval program of ten submarines, four destroyers, twelve aircraft and nine heavy guns.[277] By 1937 the Turkish preference was for British arms, but they needed credit to purchase them, a sticking

---

[270] Baggalley to Morgan, November 14, 1936; Minute Sheet, 453/3/36. December 3, 1936. "Angora File." TNA, FO 195/2516.

[271] Ottoman Bank, Ankara to Glyn Mills & Co., November 26, 1936. "Angora File." TNA, FO 195/2516.

[272] Reid Young to Welch, November 26, 1936. "Angora File." TNA, FO 195/2516.

[273] Minute Sheet, December 6, 1936. "Angora File." TNA, FO 195/2516.

[274] Minute Sheet 453/5/36, December 9, 1936. "Angora File." TNA, FO 195/2516.

[275] Minute Sheet 453/6/36, December 12, 1936. "Angora File." TNA, FO 195/2516.

[276] British Embassy Turkey to Ministry of Foreign affairs, December 14, 1936. "Angora File." TNA, FO 195/2516.

[277] Grant, *Depression*, pp. 196–97.

point with the British Government.[278] Late in the year Turkey approached Vickers directly in search of 15-inch guns. The Admiralty demanded that Vickers turn down the order. As the Foreign Office commented, "It is too much to expect that the Admiralty would allow their own rearmament plan to be sacrificed to Turkish desires."[279] However, geopolitics ended Turkey's balancing strategy – and Britain's detached attitude. In March 1938, after Germany had annexed Austria, Turkey again sought help from Britain, finding that the British Government had now changed her attitude to providing credits for armaments.

In December the Turkish Chief of Naval Staff, Captain Rifat Özdes, came to London with the county's naval shopping list, hoping to pay through the Clearing Agreement. By March 1938 Sir Reginald Henderson informed the CID that "the Admiralty was being pressed to undertake orders from Turkey."[280] In April 1938 Vickers-Armstrongs' informed the Foreign Office that Turkey had directly approached the firm about naval purchases. "Vickers was willing to accept 10 per cent down, 10 per cent on completion, and the rest to follow, but they would *not* accept payment through the clearing."[281] Sir Frederick Yapp had informed the Admiralty in the same month that Vickers needed a guarantee of payment from the British Government if the Turks defaulted.[282] By this time – in anticipation of the British Government providing credits – serious negotiations were proceeding between Vickers and Turkey over the construction of four destroyers, four submarines and four escort vessels, and the reconditioning of ten 13.5-inch guns provided by the Admiralty (the 15-inch guns the Turks wanted being unavailable). These developments caused considerable angst within the British Government, as the Clearing Agreement was hopelessly behind demand and factions within the government remained opposed to extending credit to Turkey. In the end, though, the strategic importance of Turkey, in the event of war with Germany, proved decisive.[283] In May 1939 the British Government allowed Turkey a £6 million credit for war materials, overriding the conditions of the 1921 Trade Facilities Act – something that British armament firms had been lobbying for since 1921![284]

By this stage there was a clamor for British armaments: from lesser European powers such as Turkey and Greece, from China and Siam, and from countries in Latin America. Consequently, between November 1938 and July 1939, there

---

[278] Millman, *Ill-Made*, p. 120. Citing Eden to Loraine, January 30, 1936. TNA FO 424/280.

[279] Millman, *Ill-Made*, p. 426, ff. 80. Citing Colville Minute, December 3, 1937. TNA, FO 371/20865.

[280] Minutes of the 314th meeting of the CID, p. 8. March 24, 1938. TNA, CAB 2/7.

[281] Millman, *Ill-Made*, p. 122. Citing Mounsey Minute, April 1, 1938. TNA, FO 371/21930. Emphasis in original.

[282] Grant, *Depression*, p. 198.

[283] Baggallay Minute, December 31, 1937. TNA, FO 371/20865; Millman, *Ill-Made*, pp. 122–24.

[284] "Armament Sales Abroad, 1930–1938," VA Doc. 776.

were extensive discussions within the British Government over which countries should receive priority in arms exports and what export credits should be
advanced to those allies. Turkey's position in the pecking order shifted several
times, but in July 1939 it was settled at fourth in importance for British arms
exports.[285] In July 1939 the Government formally amended the Export Credit
Guarantee Act of 1939 to allow credits to be spent on armaments. As Lord
Templemore explained to the House of Lords:

> Owing to the developments of the international situation which have taken
> place since that Act was passed last February, the Government decided
> that further steps were required to preserve the commercial and economic
> relations between the United Kingdom and other friendly nations .... It
> is inevitable in present circumstances that a considerable proportion of
> these goods should be material and equipment for defence purposes.[286]

Of the total of £60 million guaranteed by the Act, up to £10 million could be
spent on armaments. Nevertheless, the Army and Air Force chiefs remained
reluctant to divert supplies from British rearmament to allies.

The Admiralty was more flexible. By 1938 they were willing to offer Turkey
two guns, which would be diverted from an Admiralty order for Spain being
completed by Vickers.[287] Additionally, having initially signaled its willingness
to contemplate Turkish warship orders only if they were not urgently needed, by
April 1938 the Admiralty were prepared to delay the British naval rearmament
program in order to meet Turkey's urgent requirements.[288] The Foreign Office
was now also in favor of British firms building for Turkey, despite the difficulties involved, because they considered that she would be an important potential ally if the international situation deteriorated.[289] Just over half the credits
Turkey had been granted, £3.6 million, was earmarked for her naval program,
to include four destroyers, four submarines and two minelayers. Vickers-
Armstrongs signed the destroyer contract in March 1939; they would build two
and Denneys the other two.[290] They signed the contract for four submarines a
few days later.[291] Turkey had wanted to increase the submarine order to eight
boats, but the Admiralty would not even consider that.[292] Vickers-Armstrongs

[285] Stone, "British Government," pp. 233–38.
[286] House of Lords Debate, July 21, 1939. *Hansard*, Vol. 114, cc. 341–66.
[287] Admiralty to Captain Aydinalp, August 26, 1938. TNA, ADM 116/4494; Vickers to Admi-
       ralty, January 12, 1940. "Ships and Armaments: Arrangements for Supply to Turkey, Vol.
       5," TNA, ADM 116/4197.
[288] Güvenç and Barlas, "Atatürk's," pp. 26 and 27. Citing TNA, ADM 116/14198 M02082138,
       March 12,1938, and TNA FO 371/121918 E2274167144, April 14, 1938.
[289] Baggallay to Admiralty, January 4, 1938. "Ships and Armaments: Arrangements for Sup-
       ply to Turkey," 1936–1940. TNA, ADM 116/4195.
[290] Millman, *Ill-Made*, p. 489, ff. 30. Citing Aras to FO, March 27, 1939. TNA, FO 371/23297.
[291] Millman, *Ill-Made*, p. 489, ff. 31. Citing Aras to FO, March 30, 1939. TNA, 371/23297.
[292] Millman, *Ill-Made*, p. 489, ff. 31. Citing ADM to FO, February 7, 1938. TNA, FO 371/21930.

also signed a contract with Turkey for 13.5-inch and 15-inch guns.[293] In the short term Turkey was to be supplied with tokenistic amounts of anti-aircraft defense equipment.[294] The contract for the refortification of the Bosphorous Strait that had been expected to go to Krupps went to Vickers-Armstrongs after Atatürk himself ensured that the Krupp sketches were shared with British firms so they too could tender.[295] While the British firms accepted these naval orders, the onset of the World War Two meant that they were not completely fulfilled. In March 1941 the sub-contractor Denneys delivered the *Sultanhisar* and the *Demirhisar* destroyers, but the two I-Class destroyers from Vickers-Armstrongs, the *Mauvenet* and the *Gayeret*, were commandeered, becoming HMS *Inconstant* and HMS *Ithuriel*.[296] Turkey only got two of the four submarines she had been promised, the first two, *Burek Reis* and *Ulic Ali Reis*, being diverted for Admiralty use in October 1941.[297] Turkey received their *Oruc Reis* and *Murat Reis* in April 1942, thirteen months behind schedule.[298] She did not receive any of the four escorts she had been pledged. Turkey later made claims against Vickers-Armstrongs for the loan of personnel for trials on the destroyers and submarines commandeered by the Admiralty.[299]

During 1938 to 1940 Vickers was in negotiations with Turkey (and the British Government) over the sale of Spitfires.[300] The deal was complicated for many reasons. First, as it was wartime, the Air Ministry controlled the production line and would have to agree to release the aircraft. Second, Spitfire production was now dispersed far beyond Vickers Supermarine to various shadow factories. Third, to fill the order the firm would need to obtain spare parts from various British Government departments. Fourth, royalties had to be paid on the aircraft's Colt Browning 303 guns; a formula was eventually reached with the Air Ministry for paying and recovering the monies from Vickers. Finally, the deal was to be financed through the Export Credit Fund.[301] If that was not enough, the Merlin engines for the aircraft were made by Rolls-Royce – who were concerned about the financial risks of supplying Turkey – and suggesting

---

[293] Millman, *Ill-Made*, p. 490, ff. 46. Citing Aras to FO, March 30, 1939. TNA, FO 371/23297.
[294] Stone, "British Government," pp. 244 and 246.
[295] Millman, *Ill-Made*, p. 136.
[296] Wragg, "Royal Navy," p. 99; Millman, *Ill-Made*, Appendix C, p. 389. Citing NAA to FO, October 20, 1941. "Turkey: Supply of Ships, Armaments and Stores, 1941–1943," TNA, ADM 116/4876.
[297] Millman, *Ill-Made*, Appendix C, p. 389. Citing NAA to FO, October 20, 1941.
[298] Millman, *Ill-Made*, Appendix C, p. 389. Citing ADM 116/4876.
[299] "Settlement of Turkish Armament Credits: withdrawal of claim against Vickers-Armstrong Ltd. for loan of personnel," 1954–57, TNA, ADM 1/25431.
[300] "Turkey Spitfire Aircraft Correspondence Part 1," VA, Doc. 352.
[301] Air Ministry to Vickers-Armstrongs, 31 January 1940; Marsh-Hunn Supermarine to Wonfor Vickers-Armstrongs, April 23, 1940; Reid, British Air Ministry, to Marsh-Hunn, April 16, 1940; Marsh-Hunn to Reid, April 23, 1940. "Turkey Spitfire Aircraft Correspondence Pt. 1." VA, Doc. 352.

that Vickers assume all that risk. Vickers pushed back against this, arguing that "Rolls-Royce should accept payment under the same terms as ourselves and take their share of whatever risk there is."[302] The complexities of the deal were evident in the meeting between Vickers, the Air Ministry and the Turkish Air Attaché held in January 1940.[303] With everything mediated through the British Government, the deal was very complex. Turkey had pushed Vickers to begin production before there was a formal contract and was immediately pressing for deliveries, but production soon fell behind the ambitious schedule.[304] Moreover, British needs remained predominant. The Spitfires for Turkey were eventually delivered, but behind schedule. As the war ended, Vickers-Armstrongs was also fulfilling a Turkish order for costal defense systems.[305]

   In 1945 Britain was victorious but financially exhausted. Rather than providing military and economic aid to her allies, Britain became a major recipient of Marshall Plan aid from the United States. Britain's hold on her Empire was increasingly shaky and her ability to project power was in doubt. Additionally, the alliance that had defeated Nazism had collapsed into acrimony and the Soviet Union was now regarded with increasing concern. Prime Minister Attlee privately wrote to Ernest Bevin late in 1946:

> I do not think that the countries bordering on Soviet Russia's zone viz. Greece, Turkey, Iraq and Persia can be made strong enough to form an effective barrier. We do not command the resources to make them so …. I think, therefore, that we have got to be very careful in taking on military obligations in Greece and Turkey when the U.S.A. only gives economic assistance.[306]

   In 1946–7 British defense expenditure had to be cut, and one of the casualties was military support for Greece and Turkey. The end of British aid drew in the United States because of the concerns about Soviet intentions towards the Middle East.[307] The consequence was the 1947 Truman Doctrine, which provided military aid, including weapons, to Turkey and Greece. By 1950 the United States was now the main supplier of arms to Turkey.[308] Nevertheless in that year Vickers was hoping to buy the Spitfires back from Turkey and sell them Attackers instead.[309] Without financial support from the British

[302] Ormonde Darby, Rolls Royce to Vickers, 19 April 1940; Wonfor to Marsh-Hunn, 25 April 1940. VA, Doc. 352.
[303] "Turkish Armaments Credit (1939) Agreement," notes of a meeting at the Air Ministry, January 19, 1940. VA, Doc. 352.
[304] Wonfor to Under Secretary of State, February 15, 1940; Göker, Turkish Air Attaché to Marsh-Hunn, April 25, 1940. VA, Doc. 352.
[305] "Southern 1946 Turkey," TNA, FO 371/59298.
[306] Attlee to Bevin, Private and Personal, December 1, 1946. TNA, FO 800/475, ME/46/22, p. 59–60.
[307] Uslu, *Turkish-American*, p. 68.
[308] Deveraux and Schrecker, *Formulation*, p. 49.
[309] "1950 Turkey," TNA, FO 371/87987.

Government, however, the deal was dead. This was the functional end of Vickers-Armstrongs' relationship with the Turkish state, which received subsidized United States arms as a member of NATO from 1952 onwards.

Conclusions

The relationship between Armstrongs, Vickers and the Ottoman Empire/ Turkey was very long lived but a roller-coaster compared to the relationships built in the Asian and Latin American markets. Two major reasons account for this. First, there was the knotty issue of finance, which haunted the relationship between British armament firms and the Turkish state for the century discussed here. The second reason was the impact of the British state's strategic interests and priorities on the firms. Compared to Asia and Latin America, the Ottoman Empire was of more immediate interest and came to be of strategic significance to Britain much sooner than those further-flung markets.

Conclusions

Assessing Armstrongs and Vickers' Independence
and Power in Relation to the British State:
A Military–Industrial Complex?

This book has examined the domestic and international behaviors of Armstrongs and Vickers over the course of one hundred years to assess their independence and power in relation to the British state and foreign governments. The firms experienced three primary challenges in dealing with the British state: strong resistance to assisting them based on *laissez-faire* ideology and free trade orthodoxy; class prejudice; and the deep resistance – sometimes even hostility – of key government departments toward them. Consequently, the British state provided no assistance or subsidies to armament firms, which were necessarily independent and sank or swam by their own actions. Internationally, for Armstrongs and Vickers the challenge was gaining access to foreign elites and competing to make sales against firms which did receive help from their home governments. Over time, Armstrongs and Vickers developed a suite of strategies and tactics to meet these domestic and international challenges.

First, Armstrongs and Vickers' prime strategy was to cultivate relationships with the British state. Armstrongs developed a very successful elite approach. Pioneered by William Armstrong, this became the firm's most consistent strategy. The elite strategy evolved from developing military inventions of interest to the elite and royalty; this was deepened by charitable giving and Liberal politics. Elite relationships were supplemented by the tactic of interchanging high-level personnel with the government, mostly with the Admiralty. Vickers wanted to use an elite strategy but encountered much greater resistance from the elite. Here the contrast with Armstrongs is instructive. The Vickers family were primarily interested in being businessmen and their politics swiftly became Conservative; Sheffield was a provincial city, whereas Newcastle was – thanks to men like Sir William – an increasingly grand regional capital.[1] Vickers was more successful at building relations with civil servants and military officers, who appreciated

---

[1] Wilson, *Middle Class Housing*, p. 226.

the firm's technical expertise. To compensate for being unable to use an elite strategy, Vickers developed the successful tactic of being useful to the state through intelligence sharing. Over time government class prejudices softened and Vickers' superior products drew the firm and the state closer together.

Second, as firms developed armaments they wanted sell abroad, building relationships with elites in foreign countries was necessary for securing sales. Rarely did an armament sell itself, though the Armstrong Gun did so at the dawn of the era.[2] Internationally Vickers was able to build elite relationships more easily than at home as British class prejudice held less sway in foreign capitals. To aid their strategies of international elite relationship building, Armstrongs and Vickers used two additional tactics: employing agents; and giving commissions and bribes. Both tactics were used consistently, but Vickers was the more obviously successful at winning contracts aided by "palm oil" or "grease."

The third major strategy of the armament firms was to exclude competitors from markets, keeping oligopolies tight and prices high. Initially Armstrongs, as the premier British armament firm, was able to ignore challengers to its position. However, Vickers was such a strong competitor by the turn of the century (facilitated, in the eyes of shareholder Stuart Rendel, by missteps at Armstrongs) that the two firms reached a truce and began cooperating to exclude challengers such as the nascent Coventry Ordnance Works, created in 1905. To do this Armstrongs and Vickers tried to insert exclusionary language into contracts with the British Government. However, the government consistently blocked these attempts, as Chapters 3–4 showed. Ironically, in the interwar years Vickers-Armstrongs became an oligopolist by government approval when firms in key sectors of the armament industry, such as manufacturers of gun mountings and warships, consolidated or exited the market.

A fourth strategy was to collaborate and even collude with other armament firms. In addition to Armstrongs and Vickers collaborating to try to keep others out of the domestic market, there were domestic and international "rings" and "trusts" that colluded to set prices. Some of these arrangements were known about – for example, agreements with the Admiralty to maintain five armor plate and naval ordnance firms during the interwar period (see Chapter 4). However, many such arrangements were secret. Revelations about international collusive strategies badly rebounded on Vickers-Armstrongs in the 1930s, but the secret Warship Building Committee continued to operate in Britain until 1942. For decades these collusive behaviors served Armstrongs and Vickers well.

[2] Bastable, *Arms*, p. 110.

A vital issue for armament firms was how to respond to famines in the armament market. The fifth strategy, diversification, was developed in response to
this problem. Armstrongs and Vickers at various points diversified into different markets (through exports), international partnerships and licensing deals,
and made technological and sectoral diversifications, even moving into civilian
products. This strategy brought mixed results. While exporting armaments was
never a bad strategy for them, international partnerships and subsidiaries were
much less successful, as is shown in Table 9.1.

Table 9.1 *Armstrongs and Vickers' armaments subsidiaries**

Armstrongs' international subsidiaries	Vickers' international subsidiaries
Italy	Spain
Pozzuoli Works, 1886, to build warships and guns. Managed by George Rendel and Captain (later Rear-Admiral) Count Albini, staffed by Elswick workers.	*Placencia de las Armas*, registered as English in 1887. Inherited from Maxim-Nordenfelt with the merger of 1897. Not profitable until 1911, when it got contracts from a new Vickers concern in Spain. Association ended in 1935.
Gio Ansaldo-Armstrongs & Co., shipbuilding company of Genoa, 1904 (dissolved in 1911).	*La Sociedad Española de Construccion Naval*, founded in 1909. A subsidiary of the British Group (Vickers, Armstrongs, John Browns). Terminated in 1943.
Società Anonima Italiana Whitehead, 1914–23, a joint venture with Vickers, 50 percent each.	
Japan	Japan
Nihon Seiko Sho (aka *Japan Steel Works*) ordnance works in Muroran. A Japanese Government initiative, 1907, jointly with Vickers and Japanese firms. Received government orders but was hardly profitable by 1914. Terminated in 1941.	*Nihon Seiko Sho* (aka *Japan Steel Works*) ordnance works in Muroran. A Japanese Government initiative, 1907, jointly with Armstrongs and Japanese firms. Received government orders but was hardly profitable by 1914. Terminated in 1941.
Austro-Hungary	Austro-Hungary
Whitehead Torpedo Fiume, 1906–14. A joint venture with Vickers; Armstrongs had a 75 percent stake.	*Whitehead Torpedo Fiume*, 1906–14. A joint venture with Armstrongs; Vickers had a 25 percent stake.

Table 9.1 (*cont.*)

Armstrongs' international subsidiaries	Vickers' international subsidiaries
<u>Turkey</u>	<u>Italy</u>
Ottoman Dock Company, jointly with Vickers. Constituted in 1913 but confiscated in 1914; returned 1918, but closed due to unprofitability in 1923.	*Vickers-Terni Società Italiana d'Artiglieria ed Armamente* company. Founded with Italian firms in 1905, with Vickers providing all artillery designs and technical aid. The Spezia factory was finished in 1910. Not profitable by 1914. The technical aid agreement ended December 31, 1930. Terminated in 1935.
	Società Anonima Italiana Whitehead 1914–23, a joint venture with Armstrongs, 50 percent each.
<u>France</u>	<u>Russia</u>
Société Française de Torpilles Whitehead, 1913. A joint venture with Vickers, Armstrongs had a 75 percent stake.	*Chantiers Nicolaiev,* 1912–17. Vickers was to provide technical assistance and had a 10 percent stake alongside French and Russian financiers.
	Tsaritsyn Gun Foundry Vickers was invited to design and build three battleships by the Russian Government. Constituted in September 1913. After the Russian Revolution in 1917, Vickers sold the firm to the new government, while also providing new equipment for the factory and signing a fifteen-year agreement to provide technical aid to the new Tzaritzin Ordnance Works in return for a fixed commission.
	Whitehead Company, 1914–17. A joint venture with Armstrongs; Vickers held a 25 percent stake.
<u>Russia</u>	<u>France</u>
Whitehead Company, 1914–17, joint venture with Vickers, Armstrongs held a 25 percent stake.	*Société Française de Torpilles Whitehead,* 1913. A joint venture with Armstrongs, Vickers held a 25 percent stake.
	<u>Romania</u>
	Uzinele Metalurgice din Copșa-Mica și Cugir S.A., 1924–25.
	S.A. Aciéries et Domaines de Reșița Copsa Mica. The result of a 1921 approach from the government to Vickers. Teamed up with local firm Resita. A disastrous investment (technical aid and machinery only).

Table 9.1 *(cont.)*

Armstrongs' international subsidiaries	Vickers' international subsidiaries
	Estonia
	Reval Naval Works Anglo-Baltic Shipbuilding Co., 1921–23. Vickers made some direct investments into Reval.
	Poland
	Starachowice Mining Company. To manufacture guns and ammunition, a 1920 agreement with Schneiders of France.
	Serbia
	Société Serbe Minière et Industrielle (Sartid) with the Yugoslav Government. Vickers was directly associated 1922–34, having an equity shareholding but no management control. Expected government orders but there were none in the 1920s. By 1932 Sartid were doing only civilian work – but still paid no dividends – so Vickers sold out in 1934.
	Turkey
	Ottoman Dock Company, jointly with Armstrongs. Constituted in 1913 but confiscated in 1914; returned 1918, but closed due to unprofitability in 1923.
	Canada
	Canadian Vickers. Founded in 1911 to build warships and aircraft. Vickers owned until 1927. In 1956 Vickers again bought control of the company, betting on good orders.

*Civilian subsidiaries from the interwar years have not been included. Sources: J. Reid Young, Vickers Ltd. to Secretary, Royal Commission, November 11, 1936, p. 1; "Vickers Ltd.: evidence; note by Secretary," TNA, T 181/56; Trebilcock, *Vickers Brothers*, pp. 133–35; Scott, *Vickers*, pp. 84–85.

Most subsidiaries and partnerships were developed in the Edwardian era, and Vickers was the entrepreneurial force behind many of them.[3] Why was sharing technology, plant and machinery considered good strategy and not a liability? First, in some cases it was the only way to maintain market access

[3] Trebilcock, "British Armaments," pp. 256 and 258.

and reap profits. This was true in Italy and Tsarist Russia. Second, when these arrangements were negotiated with a government, the buyer paid generously for access to patents and technologies. For Vickers, "The Tsaritsyn project carried with it a 3 million rouble design fee and 10 per cent of the gunmaking profits over a guaranteed decade's worth of work, while a very similar profit-taking scheme was agreed at Terni."[4] The Nikolayev deal would bring Vickers £45,000 for its drawings and £75,000 for each dreadnought battleship produced, and the Tsarist state was promising regular orders.[5] Third, many deals with foreign governments to establish local firms came with guaranteed orders for multiple years. This reduced the risk involved in the deal, with the state often accepting a clause that if the agreed orders were not placed, the foreign firm would be compensated. However, such deals still carried risks, as Vickers found out when their assets were seized after the Russian Revolution. Russia did not pay Vickers back until 1986.[6] Fourth, forming a partnership with a foreign firm could eliminate a potential rival. This certainly was the effect – though not the intent – of Armstrongs' 1904 Ansaldo combination. Up until then Ansaldo had been a fierce competitor for sales in the Turkish market. Finally, the spirit of the Edwardian Age may have bred an attitude where the firms were so sure of innovations to come that they felt secure in handing over their latest technologies. For example, Vickers had no problem in promising Russia an arsenal that was "the most recent, the most modern and most effective which would be produced in any country of the world … excepting England."[7] Many of the Vickers agreements were of ten-year duration, showing their time horizons for profits. This belief in innovation went together with the risk-taking entrepreneurial ethos at Vickers.[8]

Diversifications into new sectors of the armament market (near diversifications) were often successful – for example, Armstrongs' sectoral diversification from guns into naval ships, and Vickers' move from machine guns into tanks. Diversifications into new sectors of civilian markets (far diversifications) were spectacularly unsuccessful, as the interwar experiences of both Armstrongs and Vickers showed (see Chapter 4).

The sixth strategy was financing. Armstrongs initially chose not to get involved in helping customers secure loans, whereas Vickers consistently did so and showed real strength in facilitating funding. Only when the two firms

---

[4] Trebilcock, *Vickers Brothers*, p. 135.

[5] Gatrell, *Government*, p. 238.

[6] After the 1986 treaty signed between Britain and Russia for partial reparations on interests lost in the Russian Revolution, Vickers' claims were resubmitted, resulting in an ultimate payout of £178,905.45, calculated to be 54% of the total debt owed, and described by C. W. Foreman (Commercial Director of Vickers PLC in 1989) as "Not a bad Christmas present and worth the effort!" Foreman to Scrope, December 18, 1989. VA, Doc. 1219A.

[7] Evidence Prepared for Bankes Commission. VA, Doc. 51.

[8] Davenport-Hines, "Vickers," p. 68.

began to work together in international markets did Armstrongs really become involved with financing, and then as Vickers' junior partner. As many potential customers lacked money, securing funding often became key to securing international sales, as the case of Turkey showed (see Chapter 8). Of course, the strategy could backfire when a customer defaulted on loans, but Vickers carefully insulated themselves against this eventuality.

The final strategy used by Armstrongs and Vickers was innovation, the lifeblood of any business. Initially Armstrongs was the leader here, developing innovative products that the British Government could not ignore. From the start Vickers was good at innovating in production techniques, and later developed an eye for acquiring firms with innovative products and for licensing important international innovations. By the turn of the century Armstrongs was losing their innovatory edge, while Vickers was sharpening theirs. Vickers developed a particular strategy of innovating during lulls in the market; this was a risky approach, but one that served them well. This became part of Vickers' DNA and it carried over into Vickers-Armstrongs – for example, in their interwar preparations for rearmament (see Chapter 5).

Over the period 1855 to 1955 Armstrongs, Vickers and the British state each went through profound evolutions, and these eventually brought the actors closer together. For armament firms, the process was one of expansion and professionalization, replacing family firms with limited liability companies and institutional shareholders, achieving greater scale, licensing inventions, acquiring other firms, developing more rigorous management structures and responding to more regulation from the government. For the British Government, the evolution was toward significantly greater involvement in all areas of domestic life. Particularly relevant here is the government's evolving approach to managing economic issues, and therefore businesses, shifting away from *laissez-faire* thinking toward becoming much more interventionist. In parallel, government regulation was a tide coming in. In times of war, government management of firms expanded; export controls and domestic regulations were tightened. This never retreated to prewar levels and was ratcheted up further when the next crisis came along. These evolutions should be borne in mind as this chapter now returns to the conceptual framework laid out in the Introduction, dealing first with the idea of firms as independent actors.

Independence?

Were Armstrongs and Vickers independent actors? This study makes clear that at least up until the late interwar period, and arguably up to nationalization, Armstrongs, Vickers and other armament firms were independent actors.

British Government behaviors show that they regarded the firms as independent (and lesser) actors. At the outset, the British Government felt free to manipulate the armament firms in terms of orders, expecting them to bear the costs of expanding factories and creating machine tools to meet urgent needs, and to cope without compensation with the sudden loss of government orders. The British Government effectively shifted the risks of innovation onto the private firms. This stance was justified by adherence to *laissez-faire* ideology and reinforced by the inherent class bias of the British Government. This meant that Armstrongs and Vickers lurched from order famines to order feasts, each in its way a crisis for them. To smooth out their order books, Armstrongs and Vickers sold freely on the international market and tried to price their domestic products to compensate for their research, development and manufacturing expenses. The British Government consistently sought to protect the Royal Armories and Dockyards at the expense of the firms' interests, and the War Office always favored giving orders to the Royal Arsenals, except in absolute emergencies.

On the other side of the coin, Armstrongs, Vickers and other armament firms – precisely because they were regarded as independent actors – faced very few inhibitors. There were minimal regulations impinging on their activities: few rules on company behavior in terms of their shareholders and workers, no stringent rules on official secrets, no prohibitions on providing bribes abroad and minimal rules limiting armaments exports. Even when export restraints were first instituted, they were moderate. Moreover, the firms made very good profits when domestic and international orders came in. While the British Government was the firms' best customer, it was not their only customer, giving bold entrepreneurs much freedom of maneuver.

What were the domestic implications of the independence of British armament firms? For Armstrongs and Vickers, it meant that they were wary in their domestic engagements with the government; they knew that the state was only looking out for its own interests and would happily sacrifice the firms to protect those interests. Armstrongs, as the pioneer, was the first to experience being cast aside – denied British Government gun orders for sixteen years – and Vickers' had a similar experience in the 1890s when they expanded plant in the firm expectation of orders and then did not receive any. As was shown in Chapters 2–5, this was a common cycle that the firms experienced. Consequently, Armstrongs and Vickers tried to write contracts with the British Government that priced their goods to compensate for past and future shortages of orders, leading to tussles with the government over contract terms and profit levels (sometimes even when they had been specified in the contract). Armstrongs and Vickers also strategized to keep competitors out of the domestic market, whereas the government wanted more options. The firms had secret agreements over prices (e.g., over armor plate) and structured bids so that certain firms won government competitions (and shared the consequent profits). All these strategies went against the interests of the British Government and show that the firms were thinking as independent actors.

For the British Government the implications of the armament firms' independence were generally positive; they could be used when necessary and ignored when not. The government did not need to provide subsidies but could reward armaments innovators with contracts. The firms were certainly nimbler and more innovative than the Royal Arsenals and produced more cheaply than the Royal Dockyards and Arsenals, but the existence of both public and private providers gave the government levers to use over each. When the government needed the firms, it could use its economic persuasion (i.e., the promise of profits) to get what it wanted, but it had no obligations when the firms were not needed. When the firms' prices were too high, the government could use the Arsenals as benchmarks, or invite other firms to bid on contracts, thereby using competition to keep prices in check.

Internationally, their independence enabled the firms to send their own ambassador-agents out to places of their choosing around the world to build relationships that the British Government played no part in. Indeed, until well after the turn of the century the firms did not seem to be particularly defined by the British Government's foreign policies.[9] As was shown in Chapters 6–8, Armstrongs and then Vickers became active in key international markets and achieved significant successes. In Latin America, Asia and the Ottoman Empire the firms operated as independent actors unfettered by government controls or foreign policy diktats. Armstrongs and Vickers pursued their own interests and sometimes made deals that the British Government did not approve of; for example, the firms several times sold unnecessarily advanced warships to Latin American countries, fueling arms races (see Chapter 6). Armstrongs and Vickers developed their own foreign policies that did not change – even when the British Government's interests did – and built surprisingly enduring relationships that withstood political upheavals such as coups, successions and dramatic changes in leadership.

Nevertheless, there were challenges for the firms. Chapter 8 showed that in Turkey the British Government's stance on minority rights, advocacy of a return to the Parliamentary system and denunciation of Ottoman behavior in Macedonia and Armenia, as well as Britain's occupation of Cyprus and Egypt, all created a very difficult environment for the firms (and indeed the British Embassy in Ankara). To secure sales, the firms had to be seen as independent by Ankara. In this they were not successful, with the bulk of sales going to German and Italian firms, whose home governments could better tolerate the behavior of the Ottoman regime. For a time Armstrongs stumbled on a solution to this dilemma: Having aligned with Ansaldo to retain access to the Italian market, they reaped unexpected bonuses in the Ottoman Empire, where Ansaldo was

---

[9] Further, in the 1880s and 1890s, as the United States began to seek to build a modern navy to meet the threats from Britain and France, British and French firms happily supplied them with armor and gunnery technologies! Cooling, *Gray Steel*, p. 67.

receiving substantial orders. For around a decade Armstrongs received helpful cover from this alliance. The connection came to a sudden end in September 1911, when Italy attacked Turkey, leading to a year-long war and the dissolution of the Armstrongs–Ansaldo alliance.

An independent foreign policy was exhibited when an armament firm undertook an action reflecting its own preferences, not those of the British Government. During the dreadnought era, the policies of Armstrongs and Vickers defied the interests of the British Government. The firms wanted to sell dreadnoughts and the Ottoman Empire wanted to buy them. The British Government was concerned about Turkish indebtedness and the Ottoman navy's ability to handle dreadnoughts, favoring sales of more modest ships. These points were made to the firms, but they and their buyer ignored them. As the sales did not go against British law, the firms were free to sell what they pleased. In the Ottoman Empire, as in South America, Armstrongs and Vickers acted on their independent foreign policies.

In the twentieth century the British state and Armstrongs and Vickers still sometimes acted as independent actors. The government abandoned the armament firms after the Great War, favoring their diversification into other industries, on the assumption that arms control agreements lessened the need for military preparedness. That said, the regulation of armament firms never returned to prewar levels, much to the disappointment of Armstrongs and Vickers. In the interwar period the armament firms again formed "rings" to divide orders and sustain profits, in defiance of state interests. However, as rearmament began, the two actors drew together again for the war effort. After the war the tide of regulation remained strong, and after the nationalization of the English Steel Corporation, Vickers-Armstrongs was firmly tied to the British state. Having traced the arc of the state–firm relationship from independence to interdependence, we now return to the question of power.

Power?

The Introduction to this volume laid out a "three faces of power" framework for assessing the degree of power and influence possessed by Armstrongs and Vickers, and a set of propositions derived from that framework. These are now discussed in turn.

The first two propositions concern the "first face of power." This is a situation where one actor uses its power over another to make something happen; this is also described as relational power. There is ample evidence in this book of discussions over armament orders taking place between the British Government and Armstrongs and Vickers, meaning that the firms had access to the government and therefore potentially some relational power. A compelling military product, such as a new gun or better armor plate, gave firms something that the government wanted and was prepared to negotiate over. Armstrongs and

Vickers' relational power was boosted by the fact that there were only a small number of firms able to successfully develop new military products and make sufficient investments in the expensive infrastructure needed for manufacturing them. They sought to bolster that relational power by building connections with elites, keeping challengers out of the armament market and resisting government attempts to share their armament innovations with other firms.

Notably though, in their early years, Armstrongs and Vickers' relational power with the British Government derived solely from their armament products, not their roles in the economy. Until *laissez-faire* thinking within the British Government began to weaken after the turn of the century, the state was formally indifferent to the firms' economic heft.

The first proposition is:

- If Armstrongs and Vickers had relational power in relation to the British Government, there will be evidence of successful interactions in the records of the firms and the state, for example, showing the firms successfully negotiating over relevant issues.

The records of Armstrongs, Vickers and the British Government provide significant evidence of them negotiating over armament deals. However, as was shown in Chapters 2–5, the firms rarely got all they wanted from these negotiations with the state. For example, through contract language the War Office and Admiralty rebuffed the firms' efforts to exclude their competitors from bidding on future contracts and rejected the firms' ideas about the expansive scope of their patents. These and other examples suggest that Armstrongs and Vickers' relational power was somewhat limited. This is explored more in the second proposition:

- Armstrongs and Vickers will have been shown to have strong relational power if they have influenced the British Government to act in their favor. The firms should win victories or concessions on issues such as subsidies, costs, profits, competition, penalty clauses in procurement contracts, export controls, patent rules, taxation levels, etc.

A repeated request from armament firms was that the British Government provide them subsidies and sales help equal to that provided to French, German and later American armament firms by their respective governments. However, except for a little seed funding to Joseph Whitworth and William Armstrong to develop guns for the Crimea campaign, subsidies and research and development monies were not given to either Armstrongs or Vickers until late in the era. Rather, after the firms had invested in the research and development to create a product, the government might grant them a contract (though this was not assured). The government's *laissez-faire* ideology ruled out subsidies to armament firms. Even after *laissez-faire* faded, the allergy to subsidies remained, as was shown in the government reactions to initial proposals for the merger of Vickers and Armstrongs (discussed in Chapter 4). The government left the merger issue to the private Bank of England to sort out.

Throughout the period covered in this book, the British Government and the armament firms tussled over the size of contracts, the spread of contracts among firms, the profits allowed on contracts and royalties on the firms' inventions. That Armstrongs and Vickers were able to dispute these at all is an indication that they held some power in their relationships with the British Government. However, as Chapters 2–5 showed, the British Government was a strong opponent and thwarted the interests of the two firms in various ways. These included enforcing Treasury-induced parsimony in military spending, bringing new armor manufacturers into the process to keep prices low (though Vickers was an early beneficiary of that policy), dividing contracts for ships and guns to ensure accountability, dividing orders between firms, sharing firms' patents with their competitors and disputing prices. As the domestic market was a monopsony, the British Government was in a good position to demand terms from the armament firms. Also, the British Government could – and did – ally with public opinion in times of crisis to limit the profits of Armstrongs and Vickers.

Nevertheless, the armament firms had some arrows in their quiver too, because there were a limited number of firms who could undertake the advanced processes necessary for the production of armaments. Bringing new industrial players into the field took time and a lot of money, so it was not a policy to be undertaken lightly by the government. Firms had responses to the government's attempts to limit the costs of procuring armaments, particularly secret price-fixing agreements and armament "rings" to divide contracts in difficult times. The government did not always know about the price-fixing agreements, but it was aware of the costs of doing business with the firms – hence the addition of new suppliers to keep competition keen and prices down.

Armstrongs and Vickers enjoyed mixed success in their attempts to maximize domestic procurement contracts and the profits on them. Sometimes they were clearly successful – for example, when Armstrongs held a monopoly over naval gun production and Vickers was one of only two producers of advanced armor. At other times they completely failed, as in 1905 when Armstrongs and Vickers tried to keep the Coventry Ordnance Works outside of the circle of approved contractors, and in the run-up to the Great War when Beardmores began to contract for guns and airships. In the latter cases, Vickers' part-ownership of Beardmores softened the blow, but Sheffield had nevertheless wanted to keep contracts exclusively for Vickers.

In summary, in negotiating on all these issues, Armstrongs and Vickers demonstrated that they held some relational power in relation to the British Government. However, that power had limits and sometimes the firms did not get their way at all, though more often the outcome was a compromise of some form, either agreed overtly or achieved by covert counter-manipulations by the firms and the government.

The "second face of power," also described as agenda-setting power, can be formulated as a proposition:

- In Armstrongs and Vickers' relationships with the British Government, the second face of power will be in evidence if the two firms were able to put favorable issues, such as more military spending or generous profit levels, on the agenda and to keep negative issues, such as investigations into their behavior or limits on their profits, completely off the agenda.

How effective were the firms in setting the agenda in their favor so that they got contracts, public subsidies and help with selling abroad? Surprisingly, given the legends of the armament firms, there is no evidence of Armstrongs and Vickers having successfully exercised agenda-setting power in their relationship with the British Government. If Armstrongs and Vickers had agenda-setting power, they would never have experienced order famines and undoubtedly would have consistently received subsidies from the state, which they did not. The Selbourne Program of 1902 is sometimes presented as showing the power of armament firms to influence the agenda. However, the firms themselves were not decisive here; it was the combination of public opinion whipped up by magazines such as the *Pall Mall Gazette* and organizations such as the Navy League that led to Parliamentary pressure for more naval spending. That is, public opinion was most important. Even this agenda-setting was only a temporary "win" because the proposed warship spending was significantly winnowed down over the subsequent six years.

Vickers-Armstrongs did not have the power to keep issues off the agenda. There are several important examples of their failure to keep potentially damaging issues from being acted upon. The first example, from the early post-World War One period, was the firms' complete failure to keep plans for deep cuts in international armaments off the table. If Armstrongs and Vickers had agenda-setting power, they would not have allowed international arms control to become a British Government priority, nor for it to remain so until 1936. The firms were passive observers of those negotiations and did not seem to have inside knowledge of what was occurring (possibly because the Admiralty was insufficiently focused on the dangers of further naval arms control agreements). Arms control was particularly harmful to the armament firms' interests, but they could not prevent it dominating British policy. While there was a lot of concern about armament firms' attempts to prevent international arms control agreements, and allegations that they undermined the First World Disarmament Conference, the firms had no success in the former; the problems at the Disarmament Conference ultimately lay with the states, not with firms.

Secondly, Vickers-Armstrongs was unable to keep the issue of their wartime profits and past domestic and international behaviors off the agenda in the 1930s, when public opinion was shown to be a formidable force. The Royal

Commission (Bankes) hearings provided spectacularly unflattering revelations about the past behavior of Vickers and Vickers-Armstrongs. The firm and the government were caught on the back foot by the public popularity of proposals to nationalize armaments production. Vickers-Armstrongs and the British Government fought to avoid the Bankes Commission concluding that the nationalization of the private armament firms was the only way forward. Notably though, there is no evidence of the government and Vickers-Armstrongs working together to blunt the impact of the Royal Commission and its findings. However, common interests certainly saw them working in parallel to resist critics' calls for fundamental changes. A decisive intervention came not from the firms but through Sir Maurice Hankey's second testimony to the Commission (supported by government preparation), as discussed in Chapter 4. What saved firms was interdependence; neither the firms nor the government wanted fundamental changes in the production and procurement of armaments given the likelihood of war.

Finally, in the post-World War Two period, firms such as Vickers-Armstrongs were powerless to keep the issue of nationalization off the Labour Government's agenda. While Vickers-Armstrongs did not play the politics of the day particularly well, it is not clear that they could ever have prevented the nationalization of the English Steel Corporation. The firm could only respond to the agenda, not set it.

Considering the "third face of power," or ideological power, this is formulated as a proposition:

- In the relationship between Armstrongs, Vickers and the British Government, the firms will show ideological power if there is evidence of the British Government unquestioningly adopting the interests of the firms in terms of issues such as military spending, armaments sales at home and abroad, profit levels and subsidies.

In the official records of Armstrongs, Vickers, Vickers-Armstrongs and the British Government, there is no evidence that the armament firms exercised the "third face of power." Rather, there is consistent evidence that the firms and the state had different and competing interests, leading to extensive negotiations between them. Further, at times the British Government adopted policies that were inimical to the interests of armament firms, such as the "Ten-Year Rule," which dominated procurement decisions between 1919 and 1932, and interwar international naval arms control negotiations. This is a far cry from the firms holding the ideological power. Rather, in times of acute national tension, as in the Boer War, the Great War and World War Two, the armament firms unquestioningly took the side of the British Government, showing that ideological power lay with the state, not the firms.

Summarizing the power of armament firms, the strongest evidence is that Armstrongs and Vickers had some relational power, cresting at the "first face" of power in their relationship with the British Government. Agenda-setting was beyond them, and ideological power was far out of their reach – despite the claims of their critics.

A British Military–Industrial Complex?

What are the implications of these findings for claims about a British military–industrial complex stretching back to the late nineteenth century? That the British Government had relations with armament firms is not itself sufficient evidence to conclude that such a complex existed. Rather, the nature of the relationships between individual armament firms and the state needs to be investigated. In this in-depth examination of relations between Armstrongs, Vickers and the British state from 1855 to 1955, the types of common interests that indicate the existence of a military–industrial complex were not found. Even in dealings with these most important armament firms, the British Government consistently prioritized their own interests over those of the firms and resisted all claims for assistance.

During the century covered in this book Armstrongs and Vickers experienced periods of order famines and order feasts precisely because there was no true confluence of interests between the firms and the state. The British Government regarded them as firms to be used when necessary and otherwise left to their own devices. Even during wars, when interactions between the British state and the firms were at their most intense, there were disputes over orders, prices and taxes. Indeed, during the Great War Vickers and Armstrongs deceptively disguised their profits to depress their tax bills.

Looking at the period up until the Great War British Government adherence to *laissez-faire* meant that a military–industrial complex could not take root – the ideology inoculated key departments of state against it. Rather, relationships with armament firms were premised solely on distance and utility. Interactions between the British Government and armament firms were (politely) conflictual: The government and the firms dueled over contract awards, using new firms, prices, royalties and patents. While over time there was a "thickening" of the relationships between Armstrongs, Vickers and the British state, their interests remained distinct and often in conflict. Indeed, some of that "thickening" was due to the increasing regulation of armament firms, necessitated precisely because the two actors had distinct interests and the state wanted to rein in the firms.

Moreover, Armstrongs and, to a greater extent, Vickers and then Vickers-Armstrongs were subject to departmental snobbery well into the 1930s, another factor that inhibited the growth of a military–industrial complex. Curiously, some of this disparaging behavior lingered even after the nationalization that birthed the British Steel Corporation and drew the state and Vickers-Armstrongs into constant dialogue.

Armstrongs' strategy of elite relationship building could be seen as an attempt to *build* a military–industrial complex, but even Armstrongs' apparent successes at this – shown by exchanges of key personnel with the government – did not notably bring the firm benefits beyond those earned by their products. The personnel who transferred to the government were rigorous in adhering to state norms and behaviors, and so consistently adopted the distance from their old firm that the state valued. Similarly, Vickers' use of intelligence sharing was an attempt to curry favor with the state, but while the government utilized the intelligence that the firm provided, Vickers nevertheless faced reversals in not receiving the orders that they expected. The British Government always preserved a distance from both Armstrongs and Vickers and consistently worked solely in its own interests. Essentially the argument for a British military–industrial complex fails for the firms and periods covered in this book.

BIBLIOGRAPHY

"1930 Industrial Britain: Vickers-Armstrongs Limited," *Grace's Guide*. At: www
.gracesguide.co.uk/1930_Industrial_Britain:_Vickers-Armstrongs

"1931 British Empire State Visit to Argentina by Prince of Wales and Prince
George." At: www.youtube.com/watch?v=ZYFslQveqUM

Achtermeier, W. O. "The Turkish Connection: The Saga of the Peabody-Martini
Rifle," *Men at Arms Magazine*, Vol. 1, March/April 1979.

Adams, G. *The Politics of Defense Contracting* (Washington, DC: Council on
Economic Priorities, 1981).

Adams, R. J. Q. "Delivering the Goods," *Albion: A Quarterly Journal Concerned
with British Studies*, Vol. 7, No. 3 (1975), pp. 232–44.

"Admiral Togo," *Dundee Evening Telegraph*, July 12, 1911. BNA.

"Admiral Togo in Glasgow," *The Scotsman*, July 14, 1911. BNA.

"Admiral Togo Pays Thanks to Newcastle Shipyards," *Geordie Japan* blog. At:
https://geordiejapan.wordpress.com/2012/04/06/285/

"Admiral Togo Pays Visit to Rosyth," *Dundee Evening Telegraph*, July 14, 1911.
BNA.

"Admiral Togo Visits His Old Training Ship," *Dundee Evening Telegraph*, June 29,
1911. BNA.

"A Great Victorian: Sir Andrew Noble," *Armstrong Whitworth Record*, Spring 1932.
TWA.

"Agreement (with covering letter) Vickers and Sir WG Armstrong Whitworth
& Co., for development of Naval and Military business in the Balkan States,"
December 31, 1913. BDB 16/L/1219, Cumbria Archive and Local Studies Centre,
Barrow-in-Furness.

Akermann, P. *Encyclopedia of British Submarines 1901–1955* (Penzance: Periscope
Publishing, 2002).

"Albert Vickers," *1918 Institution of Mechanical Engineers Obituaries*. At: www
.gracesguide.co.uk/Albert_Vickers#cite_note-6

Aldcroft, D. H. "Early History and Development of Export Credit Insurance in
Great Britain," *The Manchester School*, Vol. 30, No. 1 (1962), pp. 69–85.

Allfrey, A. *Man of Arms: The Life and Legend of Sir Basil Zaharoff* (London:
Weidenfeld & Nicolson, 1989).

The Arbitrator; A Monthly Digest of News of Social Significance, Vol. 16, No. 10
(October 1934).

Anderson, D. G. "British Rearmament and the 'Merchants of Death': The 1935–36 Royal Commission," *Journal of Contemporary History*, Vol. 29, No. 1 (1994), pp. 5–37.

Anderson, D. G. "The International Arms Trade: Regulating Conventional Arms Transfers in the Aftermath of the Gulf War," *American University Journal of International Law and Policy*, Vol. 7, No. 4 (1992), pp. 749–805.

"Andrew Noble and Elswick," *Page's Magazine*, September 1902, p. 266. In *Grace's Guide: British Industrial History*. At: www.gracesguide.co.uk/ Andrew_Noble&oldid=829079

Andrews, C. F. and E. B. Morgan. *Vickers Aircraft since 1908* (London: Putnam, Reprinted 1989).

"Anglo-Turkish Arbitral Tribunal: Four Claims Dismissed," *The Times*, December 20, 1928.

"Argentine Republic," *Hazell's Annual, 1910* (1910).

"Armor Plate Cheaper in This Country," *Journal of the American Society of Naval Engineers*, Vol. 18, No. 4 (November 1906), p. 1225.

Arms and Explosives, April 1909.

Arms and Explosives, Monthly Trade Report, 1903–5.

"Arms King Dead," *Derby Daily Telegraph*, November 27, 1936. BNA.

"Arms and the Men," *Fortune Magazine*, March 1934.

"Armstrong Guns for Formosa and the Pescadores," *The Chinese Times*, Vol. 3, August 17, 1889.

Armstrong Whitworth Record, Vol. 1, No. 1 (Spring 1930).

Arnold, A. J. "'In the Service of the State?' Profitability of the British Armaments Industry, 1914–24," *Journal of European Economic History*, Vol. 28, No. 2 (Fall 1998), pp. 285–314.

"Attempt on Air Speed Record," *Londonderry Sentinel*, September 24, 1953. BNA.

Attilio, D. "The Reconstruction of the Turkish Fleet," *Marine Engineering*, Vol. 10, No. 69300 (May 1905).

Atwater, E. "British Control Over the Export of War Materials," *The American Journal of International Law*, Vol. 33, No. 2 (April 1939), pp. 292–317.

"A Warship That May Cause a War," *The Sphere*, June 13, 1914. BNA.

Ayvazoğlu, E. "Military Modernization Efforts by Sultan Abdülhamid II," *Academic Perspective Journal*, April 23, 2014.

Baack, B. and E. Ray. "The Political Economy of the Origins of the Military Industrial Complex in the United States," *Journal of Economic History*, Vol. 45, No. 2 (1985), pp. 369–75.

Bacharach, P. and M. S. Baratz, "Two Faces of Power," *American Political Science Review*, Vol. 56, No. 4 (December 1962), pp. 947–52.

"Banquet to Admiral Togo," *Army Navy Gazette*, July 8, 1911.

Barlas, D. and S. Güvenç, "To Build a Navy with the Help of Adversary: Italian-Turkish Naval Arms Trade, 1929–32," *Middle Eastern Studies*, Vol. 38 (2002), pp. 143–69.

Barnett, C. *Britain and Her Army* (London: Allen Lane & Penguin, 1970).

Barnett, C. *The Audit of War* (Basingstoke: Macmillan, 1986).

Barnett, C. "The Audit of the Great War: On British Technology," in J.-P. Dormois and M. Dintenfass (eds.), *The British Industrial Decline* (London: Routledge, 1999), pp. 103–13.

Barnett, M. and Duval, R. "Power in International Relations," *International Organization*, Vol. 59, No. 1 (2005), pp. 39–75.

Barnes, C. H. *Shorts Aircraft Since 1900* (London: Putnam, 1967).

"Barrow," *Marine Engineer and Naval Architect*, Vol. 19, June 1, 1897.

Bastable, M. J. *Arms and the State: Sir William Armstrong and the Remaking of British Naval Power, 1854–1914* (Aldershot: Ashgate, 2004).

Bastable, M. J. "From Breechloaders to Monster Guns," *Technology and Culture*, Vol. 33, No. 2 (April 1992), pp. 213–47.

"Beardmore Locomotives," *Beardmore News*, Vol. 2, No. 5 (May 1920); Vol. 2, No. 6 (June 1920).

Beaver, P. *Spitfire People* (Sherbourne: Evro Publishing, 2015).

Beeler, J. F. *British Naval Policy in the Gladstone-Disraeli Era, 1866–1880* (Stanford, CA: Stanford University Press, 1997).

Bialer, U. *Shadow of the Bomber* (London: Royal Historical Society, 1980).

Black, J. *Naval Warfare* (London: Rowman & Littlefield, 2017).

"Bolsover Hill, 1851–1899," Sheffield City Council, *Picture Sheffield*. At: https://picturesheffield.com/frontend.php?keywords=Ref_No_increment;EQUALS;s29522&pos=41&action=zoom&id=92525

Bond, B. and Murray, W. , "The British Armed Forces, 1918–39," in A. R. Millett and W. Murray (eds.), *Military Effectiveness: Vol. II, Interwar Period* (Cambridge: Cambridge University Press, 2010), pp. 98–130 .

Boyce, R. "Economics and the Crisis of British Foreign Policy Management, 1914–45," in D. Richards and G. A. Stone (eds.), *Decisions and Diplomacy* (London: Routledge, 1995), pp. 9–42.

Brailsford, H. N. *The War of Steel and Gold* (London: G. Bell and Sons Limited, 1915).

Branfill-Cook, R. *X.1: The Royal Navy's Mystery Submarine* (Barnsley: Seaforth Publishing, 2012).

Brassey T. (ed.) *The Naval Annual 1908* (Portsmouth: Griffin & Co., 1908).

"Brazilian Battleship to be Built on the Tyne," *Birmingham Daily Post*, July 10, 1914. BNA.

Bringe, J. W. *The Findings of the Nye Committee on the Munitions Industry in the United States* (Madison: University of Wisconsin, 1938).

"Britain to Increase Spending on Arms," *Manchester Guardian*, March 4, 1935. At: www.theguardian.com/century/1930-1939/Story/0,,126998,00.html

"British Arms Man Ousted by Turkey: Vickers-Armstrongs Agent is Deported 3 Days After Return from England," *New York Times*, August 4, 1933. p. 16. At: https://timesmachine.nytimes.com/timesmachine/1933/08/04/105797255.html?pageNumber=16

"British Cellulose Inquiry," *Aeronautics*, Vol. 17, August 21, 1919, p. 194.

British Pathé News, "King George V Naval Review," June 24, 1911.

British Pathé News, "A New Submarine Called The Captain O'Brien Is Launched from Vickers Shipyard, Cumbria," October 14, 1928.

British Pathé News, "King George V Naval Review," June 24, 1911.

British Pathé News, "HMS Hermes Designed for Seaplane Carrier, Launched 1919," September 15, 1919.

British Pathé News, "The Prince of Wales in South America," 1924.

British Pathé News, "Almirante Simpson and Capitan Thompson, 1929," January 17, 1929.

British Pathé News, "With the Church's Blessing, 1929," October 24, 1929.

British Pathe News, "British Built Gunboat for Siam," November 21, 1929.

British Pathé News, "The Princes Home Again," April 30, 1931.

British Pathé News, "Demonstration of New Amphibious Tank Design from Vickers-Armstrong," November 2, 1931.

British Pathé News, "Royal Visit to Tyneside," February 23, 1939.

British Pathé News, "London to Paris Flight Sets New Record for Channel Crossing, 1948," July 29, 1948.

British Pathé News, "Vickers-Armstrongs Hand over New Destroyer to Venezuela," February 20, 1956.

Brockway, A. F. *The Bloody Traffic* (London: Gollancz, 1933).

Brook, P. "Armstrong Battleships for Japan," *Warship International*, Vol. 22, No. 3 (1985), pp. 268–82.

Brook, P. *Warships for Export* (Gravesend: World Ship Society, 1999).

Brown, P. F. *Reminiscences of the War of 1861–1865 Reissue* (Charleston, SC: Nabu Press, 2012).

"Built for Turkey. Will Britain Buy Her?" *Manchester Courier and Lancashire General Advertiser*, September 4, 1913. BNA.

Burk, K. *The First Privatisation* (London: Historian's Press, 1988).

Buxton I. and I. Johnston, *The Battleship Builders* (Barnsley: Seaforth Publishing, 2013).

Ceadel, M. "The First British Referendum," *English Historical Review*, Vol. 95, No. 377 (October 1980), pp. 810–39.

Cain P. J. and A. G. Hopkins, *British Imperialism: 1688–2000* 2nd ed. (New York: Longman, 2001).

"Canada Steamship Lines Limited," *The Scotsman*, March 29, 1917. BNA.

Carr, J. C. and W. Taplin, *History of the British Steel Industry* (Oxford: Basil Blackwell, 1962).

Carroll, F. M. "Diplomats and the Civil War at Sea," *Canadian Review of American Studies*, Vol. 40, No. 1 (2010), pp. 117–30.

"Cars of Today," *The Times*, January 1924, p. 78.

Castell Hopkins, J. *The Life of King Edward VII* (London: W. E. Schull, 1910).

Cerretano, V. "The Treasury and the Industrial Intervention of the Bank of England, 1921–9," *Economic History Review*, Vol. 62, No. 1 (2009), pp. 80–100.

"Chair of Flying," *The People*, July 14, 1918. BNA.

Chivers, C. J. *The Gun* (New York: Simon and Schuster, 2010).

Chan, A. B. *Arming the Chinese* (Vancouver: University of British Columbia Press, 1982).

Chandler, A. D. *Scale and Scope* (Cambridge, MA: Belknap/Harvard University Press, 1990).

Chesnau, R. (ed.), *Conway's All the World's Fighting Ships 1922–1946* (Greenwich: Conway Maritime Press, 1980).

"Chile and Argentina," *The Times*, July 7, 1898.

Chinn, G. M. *The Machine Gun, Vol. 1* U.S. Bureau of Ordnance, Department of the Navy (Washington, DC: Government Printing Office, 1951).

Chu, Samuel and Kwang-Ching Liu (eds.), *Li Hung-chang and China's Early Modernization* (New York: M. E. Sharpe, 1994).

Clay, Sir H. *Lord Norman* (London: Macmillan, 1957).

Cochrane, A. "Obituary: Lord Armstrong," *Northern Counties Magazine*, Vol. 1 October 1900– March 01, pp. 324–29.

Cochrane, R. *The Romance of Industry and Invention* (Edinburgh: W. R. Chambers Ltd., 1897). Project Gutenberg. At: www.gutenberg.org/files/38329/38329-8.txt

Coghlan, F. "Armaments, Economic Policy and Appeasement," *History*, Vol. 57, No. 190 (June 1972), pp. 205–16.

Coleman, D. C. "War Demand and Industrial Supply," in Winter, J. M. (ed.) *War and Economic Development* (Cambridge: Cambridge University Press, 1975), pp. 205–27.

Colledge, J. J. and Warlow, B. *Ships of the Royal Navy: The Complete Record* (Havertown, PA: Casemate, 2010).

Collier, B. *Arms and the Men* (London: Hamish Hamilton, 1980).

"Colonel Dyer," *Grace's Guide.* At: www.gracesguide.co.uk/Colonel_Dyer

"Colonel Thomas Edward Vickers," 1915 *Institution of Mechanical Engineers Obituaries.* At: www.gracesguide.co.uk/Thomas_Edward_Vickers#cite_note-10.

"Commander Sir Edward Robert Micklem C.B.E., R.N., ret.," *Proceedings of the Institution of Mechanical Engineers*, Vol. 167 (1953). At: www.gracesguide .co.uk/Edward_Robert_Micklem

"Companionship in Arms": Speeches Delivered in London on April 12, 1917 (New York: George H. Doran Co, 1917).

"Company Meetings: Vickers, Limited," *The Scotsman*, December 23, 1921, p. 3. BNA.

Conte-Helm, M. *Japan and the North East of England* (London: Bloomsbury, 1989).

Conte-Helm, M. "Armstrong, Vickers and Japan," in Nish, I. (ed.), *Britain and Japan: Biographical Portraits*, Vol. 1 (Folkestone: Japan Society, 1994), pp. 92–105.

Contributed. "The Work of the Export Credits Guarantee Department," *Managerial Finance*, Vol. 2, No. 1 (1976), pp. 50–51.

Cooling, B. F. *Grey Steel and Blue Water Navy* (Hamden, CT: Archon Books, 1979).

Coombs, B. *British Tank Production and the War Economy, 1934–1945* (London: Bloomsbury, 2013).

Cooper, N. Evidence to Committees on Arms Exports, July 12, 2012. At: www .publications.parliament.uk/pa/cm201213/cmselect/cmfaff/419/419we02 .htm#footnote_1

"Coronation Festivities. Great Naval Review at Spithead," *The Argus*, June 26, 1911. BNA.

"Correspondence Respecting the Question of Diplomatic and Consular Assistance to British Trade Abroad, Parts I and II," *AKA Bryce Memorandum*. June 1886. *Parliamentary Papers*, Cmnd. 4779–1 (London: Harrison and Sons, 1886).

"Craven Belittles Arms Sales Peril," *New York Times*, January 10, 1936, p. 13. At: https://timesmachine.nytimes.com/timesmachine/1936/01/10/88624326 .html?pageNumber=13

"Crocks and Crazes: Mr. Mitchell's Triumph," *Staffordshire Sentinel*, September 5, 1931. BNA.

Cross II, C. F. *Lincoln's Man in Liverpool* (DeKalb, IL: Northern Illinois University Press, 2007).

Crow, D. *A Man of Push and Go: George Macauley Booth* (London: Rupert Hart-Davis, 1965).

Cutler, "Corrigall v. Armstrong, Whitworth and Co. Ltd.," *Reports of Patent, Design, Trade Mark and Other Cases*, Vol. XXII, No. 10, May 10, 1905, p. 268.

Dahl, R. A. *Who Governs?: Democracy and Power in an American City* (New Haven: Yale University Press, 2005).

Dalrymple, W. *The Anarchy* (London: Bloomsbury, 2020).

Davenport-Hines, R. P. T. "Vickers as a Multinational Before 1945," in G. Jones (ed.), *British Multinationals: Origins, Management, and Performance* (London: Gower, 1986), pp. 43–74.

Davenport-Hines, R. T. P. "The British Marketing of Armaments, 1885–1935," in R. T. P. Davenport-Hines (ed.), *Markets and Bagmen: Studies in the History of Marketing and British Industrial Performance, 1830–1939* (London: Gower, 1987), pp. 146–91.

Davenport-Hines, R. T. P. "Vickers and Schneider," in A. Teichova, M. Lévy-Leboyer and H. Nussbaum (eds.), *Historical Studies in International Corporate Business* (Cambridge: Cambridge University Press, 1989), pp. 123–34.

Davenport-Hines, R. T. P. *Business in the Age of Depression and War* (London: Frank Cass, 1990).

Davenport-Hines, R. P. T. "Jenkinson, Sir Mark Webster (1880–1935)," in L. Goldman (ed.), *Oxford Dictionary of National Biography* (Oxford: Oxford University Press, 2010). Online at: www.oxforddnb.com/view/10.1093/ref: odnb/9780198614128.001.0001/odnb-9780198614128-e-48717?rskey= mnjlsB&result=1

"Definitions of Sir William George Armstrong's Duties as 'Engineer for Rifled Ordnance' and Forms of his Appointment," signed by Sir William Armstrong, February 23, 1859. Wiltshire and Swindon History Center, 2057/F8/V/A/32.

Department of Overseas Trade, *Report of the British Economic Mission to Argentina, Brazil, and Uruguay* (London: HMSO, 1930).

Deveraux, D. R. and C. Schrecker, *The Formulation of British Defense Policy towards the Middle East, 1948–56* (New York: St. Martin's Press, 1990).

Devons, E. "Review of: Postan, British War Production," *Economica*, Vol. 20, No. 79 (August 1953), pp. 279–82.

Dewar, G. A. B. *The Great Munition Feat* (London: Constable and Company Ltd., 1921).

Dietrich, E. B. "British Export Credit Insurance," *The American Economic Review*, Vol. 25, No. 2 (June 1935), pp. 236–49.

DiCicco, J. M. "Decline, Disengagement and Shaping the Periphery," in E. Rhodes, J. M. DiCicco, S. S. Milburn and T. C. Walker, *Presence, Prevention, and Persuasion* (Lanham, MD: Lexington Books, 2004), pp. 65–122.

Directory of Iron and Steel Works of the United States and Canada Vol. 18 (New York: American Iron and Steel Institute, 1916).

Djemal Pasha, *Memories of a Turkish Statesman – 1913–1919* (New York: George H. Doran Company, 1922).

Dolman, F. "Notable Men and their Work: Lord Armstrong, C.B., and Newcastle-upon-Tyne," *The Ludgate*, Vol. 5, No. 6 (1894), pp. 571–82.

Drew, E. B. "Sir Robert Hart and His Life Work in China," *Journal of Race Development*, Vol. 4, No. 1 (July 1913), pp. 1–33.

Driver, H. *The Birth of Military Aviation: Britain, 1903–1914* (Woodbridge: Boydell Press, 1997).

Dunbabin, J. P. D. "British Rearmament in the 1930s," *The Historical Journal*, Vol. 18, No. 3 (September 1975), pp. 587–609.

Dunkley, M. "Ships and Boats: 1840–1950," *Historic England* (July 2016).

d'Eyncourt, E. H. W. "Obituary: Sir George Hadcock," *Royal Society*, December 1, 1936. At: https://royalsocietypublishing.org/doi/pdf/10.1098/rsbm.1936.0010

d'Eyncourt, Sir Tennyson E. H. W. *A Shipbuilder's Yarn* (London: Hutchinson & Co., 1948).

Edgerton, D. *England and the Aeroplane* (Basingstoke: Macmillan, 1991).

Edgerton, D. "Public Ownership," in R. Millward and J. Singleton (eds.), *The Political Economy of Nationalisation, 1920–1950* (Cambridge: Cambridge University Press, 1995), pp. 164–88.

Edgerton, D. *Warfare State* (Cambridge: Cambridge University Press, 2006).

Edgerton, D. *Britain's War Machine* (Oxford: Oxford University Press, 2011).

"Edward Vickers," *Grace's Guide*. At: www.gracesguide.co.uk/Edward_Vickers#cite_ref-13

Eisenhower, President D. D. "Farewell Address." Transcript, 1961. At: www.ourdocuments.gov/doc.php?flash=false&doc=90&page=transcript

Elgin Commission, Minutes of Evidence Taken Before the Royal Commission on the War in South Africa (1903), *Parliamentary Papers*, Cd. 1790.

"Elswick Naval Mountings," *The Engineer*, January 26, 1900.

"Elswick Works, Newcastle, Part 1 (1847–1882)," BAE Systems, Heritage. At: www.baesystems.com/en/heritage/elswick-works----newcastle

"Elswick Works, Newcastle, Part 2 (1882–1928)" BAE Systems, Heritage. At: www.baesystems.com/en/heritage/elswick-works----newcastle-part-2

Encyclopedia of the Industrial Revolution in World History, Vol. 3 (Lanham, MD: Rowman & Littlefield, 2014).

Engelbrecht, H. C. and F. C. Hanighen, *Merchants of Death* (New York: Dodd, Meade & Co., 1934).

Epkenhans, M. "Military-Industrial Relations in Imperial Germany," *War in History*, Vol. 10, No. 1 (2003), pp. 1–26.

Epstein, M. (ed.) *The Statesman's Yearbook 1930* (London: Macmillan, 1930).

Epstein, K. C. *Torpedo: Inventing the Military-Industrial Complex in the United States and Great Britain* (Cambridge, MA: Harvard University Press, 2014).

Evans, H. *Vickers: Against the Odds 1956–1977* (London: Hodder and Stoughton, 1978).

"Evidence Submitted, Findings of Commission and Documents Complied at London Office for the Use of the Witnesses of the Vickers group of Companies Together with Supporting Correspondence and Data," Volume I, VA, Doc. 57.

"Evidence submitted, Findings of Commission and Documents Complied at London Office for the Use of the Witnesses of the Vickers Group of Companies Together with Supporting Correspondence and Data," Volume III, VA, Doc. 59.

"Ex-Foreign Warships," *Army and Navy Gazette*, August 8, 1914.

Fang Y. and M. Ceccarelli, "On the Warship by Ansaldo for Chinese Imperial Navy," in C. López-Cajún and M. Ceccarelli (eds.), *Explorations in the History of Machines and Mechanisms* (Cham: Springer, 2016), pp. 223–34.

Fairbairn, A. R., *Elswick (Sir W.G. Armstrong, Whitworth & Company Limited)*, VA Doc. 593.

Fairbank, J. K., K. F. Bruner and E. M. Matheson (eds.), *The I.G. in Peking*, Vol. I (Cambridge, MA: Belknap Press, 1975).

Fairbrother, T. J. *John Singer Sargent* (New Haven: Yale University Press, 2000).

Fearon, P. "Aircraft Manufacturing," in N. K. and D. H. Aldcroft (eds.), *British Industry* (London: Scholar Press, 1979).

Ferris, G. H. *War Traders* (Manchester: National Peace Council and The Labour Press Ltd., 1913).

"Final Trials of the Brazilian Cruiser 'Tiradentes,'" *The Marine Engineer*, Vol. 14, October 1, 1892.

Flynn, J. T. *Men of Wealth* 1941 (Germany: Ludwig von Mises Institute, 2007), Section VIII. At: http://mises.org/daily/2687/The-Merchant-of-Death-Basil-Zaharoff

"Foch Professorship at Oxford," *The Times*, March 21, 1918.

Foss, C. F. and P. McKenzie, *Vickers Tanks* (Wellingborough: Patrick Stephens, 1988).

"France and the Olympic Games," *Belfast News-Letter*, April 25, 1914. BNA.

French, D. *British Economic and Strategic Planning, 1905–1915* (London: George Allen and Unwin, 1982).

Freeth, F. A. "James Swinburne, 1858–1958," *Journal of the Royal Society*, 1960.

Freeth, F. A. "Swinburne As an Expert Witness," *Journal of the Royal Society*, 1960.

Fletcher, D. *British Battle Tanks* (London: Osprey Publishing, 2017).

Friedman, N. *British Cruisers of the Victorian Era* (Barnsley: Seaforth Publishing, 2012).

Friedman, N. *The British Battleship 1906–1946* (Annapolis, MD: Naval Institute Press, 2015).

Gardiner R. (ed.) *Conway's All the World's Fighting Ships 1860–1905* (Greenwich: Conway Maritime Press, 1979).

Gardiner, R. *The Eclipse of the Big Gun: The Warship 1906–1945* (Greenwich: Conway Maritime, 2004).

Gardiner R. and A. Lambert (eds.) *Steam, Steel and Shellfire: The Steam Warship, 1815–1905* (Annapolis, MD: Naval Institute Press, 1992).

Gatrell, P. *Government, Industry and Rearmament in Russia, 1900–1914* (Cambridge: Cambridge University Press 1994).

"German Air Parity Is Called Remote," *New York Times*, April 28, 1935, p. 5. At: https://timesmachine.nytimes.com/timesmachine/1935/04/28/95069238.html?pageNumber=5

Glukstein, S. M. "Armstrong Whitworth and Co.," *The Financial Review of Reviews*, Vol. XIX, No. 154 (July–September 1926).

Grant, Sir A. J. *Steel and Ships: The History of John Brown's* (London: Michael Joseph, 1950).

Grant, J. "'Merchants of Death'," *Origins: Current Events in Historical Perspective*, Vol. 6, No. 3 (December 2012). At: https://origins.osu.edu/article/merchants-death-international-traffic-arms?language_content_entity=en

Grant, J. A. *Between Depression and Disarmament* (Cambridge: Cambridge University Press, 2018).

Grant, J. A. "The Sword of the Sultan," *Journal of Military History*, Vol. 66, No. 1 (January 2002), pp. 9–36.

Grant, J. A. "The Arms Trade in Eastern Europe, 1870–1914," in Stoker and Grant, *Girding*, pp. 25–42.

Grant, J. A. *Rulers, Guns and Money* (Cambridge, MA: Harvard University Press, 2007).

"General Sykes Visits Flying Boat Factory," *Beardmore News*, Vol. 2, No. 6, June 1920.

Gilbert, M. *Winston S. Churchill, Vol. III: The Challenge of War, 1914–1916* (Boston: Houghton-Mifflin, 1971).

Goldblat, J. *Arms Control* (London: Sage, 2002).

Goldstein, E. R. "Vickers Limited and the Tsarist Regime," *The Slavonic and East European Review*, Vol. 54, No. 4 (October 1980), pp. 561–71.

Goldstone, L. *Going Deep: John Philip Holland and the Invention of the Attack Submarine* (New York: Pegasus Books, 2017).

Gooch, G. P., and H. Temperley (eds.), *British Documents on the Origins of the War 1898–1914*, Vol. V (London: HMSO, 1928).

Gooch G. P. and H. Temperley (eds.), *British Documents on the Origins of the War 1898–1914*, Vol. IV (London: HMSO, 1929).

Güvenç, S. and D. Barlas, "Atatürk's Navy," *Journal of Strategic Studies*, Vol. 26, No. 1 (2010), pp. 1–35.

Hackemer, K. *The U.S. Navy and the Origins of the Military-Industrial Complex, 1847–1883* (Annapolis, MD: Naval Institute Press, 2001).

Hackett, B. S. Kingsepp and L. Ahlberg, "IJN Battleship KONGO." At: www.combinedfleet.com/kongo.htm

Haigh, R. H., D. S. Morris, and P. W. Turner, *Armed Peace or War?* (Sheffield: Hallam University Press, 2003).

Halsted, Rear-Admiral E. P. *The Armstrong Gun: A Rejoinder to the Letter of Sir William Armstrong*, 27 November, 1861 private pamphlet (1862).

Halstead, Rear-Admiral E. P. *England's Navy Unarmed* (Westminster: J. B. Nichols & Sons, 1864).

Hamilton, J. *The Misses Vickers* (Sheffield: Sheffield Art Department, 1984).

Hamilton, K. A. "Britain and France, 1905–1911," in Hinsley, *British Foreign Policy*, pp. 113–32.

Hamilton, K. *Bertie of Thame: Edwardian Ambassador* (Woodbridge: Royal Historical Society and Boydell Press, 1990).

Hamilton, Sir R. V., *Naval Administration* (London: George Bell and Sons, 1896).

Hancock W. K. and M. M. Gowing, *British War Economy* (London: HMSO, 1949).

Hannah, L. "Takeover Bids in Britain Before 1950," in Davenport-Hines, R. T. P. *Business in the Age of Depression and War* (London: Frank Cass, 1990), pp. 40–52.

Harkavy, R. E. *Arms Trade and International Systems* (Cambridge, MA: Ballinger, 1975).

Hayward, K. *British Aircraft Industry* (Manchester: Manchester University Press, 1989).

Heywood, A. "The Armstrong Affair," *Revolutionary Russia*, Vol. 5, No. 1 (1992), pp. 53–91.

Heywood, A. *Modernizing Lenin's Russia* (Cambridge: Cambridge University Press, 2004).

Heald, H. *William Armstrong* (Newcastle upon Tyne: Northumbria Press, 2010).

"Help Rolling In," *Nottingham Evening Post*, January 15, 1925. BNA.

Hinsley, F. H. (ed.) *British Foreign Policy Under Sir Edward Grey* (Cambridge: Cambridge University Press, 1977).

Hislam, P. A. "Russia's New Addition to Her Navy," *Scientific American*, Supplement, Vol. 66, No. 1714, November 7, 1908, p. 290.

History of the Ministry of Munitions, Vol. I: Industrial Mobilizations, 1914–15 (London: His Majesty's Stationery Office, 1922).

History of the Ministry of Munitions, Vol. III: Finance and Contracts (London: His Majesty's Stationery Office, 1922).

History of the Ministry of Munitions, Vol. XII: The Supply of Munitions (London: His Majesty's Stationery Office, 1922).

Hobhouse, H. (ed.), *Crystal Palace and the Great Exhibition* (London: Continuum, 2004).

Hobsbawm, E. *Age of Empire 1875–1914* (New York: Vintage Books, 1989).

Holman, B. "The Air Panic of 1935," *Journal of Contemporary History*, Vol. 46, No. 2 (April 2011), pp. 288–307.

"Honouring Sir James McKechnie," *The Engineer*, January 25, 1918.

Hopkins, Castell J. *The Life of King Edward VII* (London: W. E. Schull, 1910).

Horn, M. *Britain, France and the Financing of the First World War* (Montreal: Kingston, 2003).

Hornby, W. *Factories and Plant* (London: Her Majesty's Stationery Office & Longmans, 1958).

Howlett, P. "'The Thin End of the Wedge?'," in R. Millward and J. Singleton (eds.), *The Political Economy of Nationalisation, 1920–1950* (Cambridge: Cambridge University Press, 1995), pp. 237–56.

Hough, R. *Admirals in Collision* (Penzance: Periscope Publishing, 2003, first published 1959).

Hough, R. *Big Battleship* (Penzance: Periscope Publishing, 2003, first published 1966).

House of Commons, Parliamentary Questions, June 21, 1900, *The Parliamentary Debates*, Vol. 84.

House of Commons, Various Parliamentary Debates and Parliamentary Questions, *Hansard*.

Howe, A. *Free Trade and Liberal England 1846–1946* (Oxford: Clarendon Press, 1997).

Hui-Min, L. *Correspondence of G.E. Morrison 1912–1920*, Vol. 2 (Cambridge: Cambridge University Press, 1978).

Hull, C. *Memoirs of Cordell Hull*, Vol. 1 (New York: Macmillan, 1948).

Hume, J. R. and M. S. Moss, *Beardmore: A History of the Scottish Industrial Giant* (London: Heinemann, 1979).

Hymans, J. E. C. "Why Recognize?," *Korean Journal of International Studies*, Vol. 12, Special Issue (May 2014), pp. 49–78.

"Imperial Ottoman Docks, Arsenals, and Naval Construction Company," House of Commons Debate, November 17, 1914, *Hansard*, Vol. 68, cc. 310–11.

"Imperial Ottoman Docks Company," House of Commons Debate, July 30, 1914, *Hansard*, Vol. 65, cc. 1534–35.

International Inventions Exhibition, Official Guide, 3rd ed. (London: William Clowes & Sons, Ltd., 1885).

International Exhibition 1862: *Official Catalogue of the Industrial Department*, 3rd ed. (London: Truscott, Son & Simmons, 1862).

"In the Garden at Edgwarebury House," *The Tatler*, July 16, 1930.

"In the Honours List," *Beardmore News*, Vol. 2, No. May 5, 1920.

"Investigate British War Company Now Starting Work in United States," *Drug and Chemical Markets*, August 14, 1918.

Irving, R. J. "New Industries for Old?," *Business History*, Vol. 17, No. 2 (1975), pp. 150–75.

Jamieson, A. G. *Ebb Tide in the British Maritime Industries* (Liverpool: Liverpool University Press, 2003).

"Japan: Kashima," *Journal of the American Society of Naval Engineers*, Vol. XVIII No. 2 (May 1906), in section pp. 640–86.

"Japan Katori," *Journal of the American Society of Naval Engineers*, Vol. XVIII No. 2 (May 1906), in section pp. 640–86.

Johnman, L. "The Large Manufacturing Companies of 1935," in Davenport-Hines, R. T. P. *Business in the Age of Depression and War* (London: Frank Cass, 1990), pp. 20–39.

Johnson, M. "The Liberal Party and the Navy League," *Twentieth Century British History*, Vol. 22, No. 2 (2011), pp. 137–63.

Jones, R. W. "The Garrett-Nordenfelt Submarines," *Warship International*, Vol. V, No. 1 (Winter 1968), pp. 26–38.

Jordan, J. *Warships After Washington* (Barnsley: Seaforth Publishing, 2011).

Jordan, J. and S. Dent (eds.), *Warship 2013* (London: Conway, 2013).

"Katori (Japanese)," *Journal of the American Society of Naval Engineers*, Vol. XVIII No. 2 (May 1906), in section pp. 640–86.

Kent, M. "Agent of Empire?," *The Historical Journal*, Vol. 18, No. 2 (June 1975), pp. 376–89.

Kent M. (ed.) *The Great Powers and the End of the Ottoman Empire* (London: George Allen and Unwin, 1984).

Kiernan, V. G. "Foreign Interests in the War of the Pacific," *The Hispanic American Historical Review*, Vol. 35, No. 1 (February 1955), pp. 14–36.

King-Hall, S. *My Naval Life, 1906–1929* (London: Faber and Faber, 1952).

"Knollys," *Oxford Dictionary of National Biography*. At: www.oxforddnb.com/view/10.1093/ref:odnb/9780198614128.001.0001/odnb-9780198614128-e-34350

Komatsu, K. "Financial Problems of the Navy during the Reign of Abdülhamid II," *Oriente Moderno*, Vol. 81, No. 1 (2001), pp. 209–19.

Konstam, A. *British Light Cruisers* (Oxford: Osprey Publishing, 2012).

"Labour's Splendid Achievement," *Sheffield Independent*, December 21, 1915. BNA.

Laird Clowes, G. S. (ed.) *Naval Pocket Book Vol. VIII* (London: W. Thacker & Co., 1908).

Lambert, A. *Admirals* (London: Faber and Faber, 2008).

Langensiepen B. and A. Güleryüz, *Ottoman Steam Navy 1828–1923* (London: Conway Maritime Press, 1995).

"Launches of Three Warships," *The Engineer*, January 16, 1903.

League of Nations, *Report Presented to the Third Assembly by the Third Committee*, League of Nations document A.124.1922.IX (Third Assembly, Plenary meeting, Annex 24).

LeClair, D. *Supervising a Revolution: British Ordnance Committees, Private Inventors, and Military Technology in the Victorian Era*, unpublished Ph.D. thesis, University of Houston, 2015. At: https://uh-ir.tdl.org/handle/10657/1254

Lengerer, H. "Battlecruisers of the Kongô Class," in Jordan, J. (ed.), *Warship 2012*, (London: Conway, 2012), pp. 142–61.

Liddell-Hart, B. H. *Memoirs*, Vol. I (London: Cassell, 1965).

Lillicrap, C. S. "Eustace Tennyson d'Eyncourt, 1868–1951," *Obituary Notices of Fellows of the Royal Society*, Vol. 7, No. 20 (November 1951), pp. 341–54. At: https://royalsocietypublishing.org/doi/10.1098/rsbm.1951.0005

Livermore, S. W. "Battleship Diplomacy in South America," *Journal of Modern History*, Vol. 16, No. 1 (March 1944), pp. 31–48.

Livingston, G. *Hot Air in Cold Blood* (London: Selwyn and Blount, 1933).

Lloyd-Jones R. and M. J. Lewis, "A Call to Arms," in R. Lloyd-Jones and M. J. Lewis, *Albert Herbert Ltd and the British Machine Tool Industry, 1887–1983* (London: Routledge, 2006), pp. 125–48.

Lloyd-Jones R. and M. J. Lewis, *Arming the Western Front* (London: Routledge, 2016).

London Gazette, July 25, 1902.

"Lord Kitchener at Sheffield". *The Times*. No. 36887. London. October 1, 1902, p. 9.

Lounger, "Club Talk," *Sporting Times*, October 15, 1921.

Lukes, S. *Power* (London: Macmillan, 1974).

Lyon, H. "The Relationship between the Admiralty and Private Industry in the Development of Warships," in Ranft, B. (ed.) *Technical Change and British Naval Policy, 1860–1939* (London: Hodder and Stoughton, 1977), pp. 37–64.

McCormick, D. *Peddler of Death* (New York: Holt, Rinehart and Winston, 1965).

McDermott, J. "'A Needless Sacrifice,'" *Albion*, Vol. 21, No. 2 (Summer 1989), pp. 263–82.

McKendrick, N. "General Introduction: In Search of a Secular Ideal," in Trebilcock, C. *Vickers Brothers: Armaments and Enterprise 1854–1914* (London: Europa Publications, 1977), pp. ix–xxxiv.

McKenzie, P. *W. G. Armstrong* (Morpeth: Longhirst Press, 1983).

McLean, D. "Commerce, Finance, and British Diplomatic Support in China, 1885–86," *Economic History Review*, Vol. 26, No. 3 (1973), pp. 464–76.

McNeill, W. H. *The Pursuit of Power* (Chicago: University of Chicago Press, 1982).

MacDonagh, O. "Nineteenth-Century Revolution in Government: A Reappraisal," in Stansky P. (ed.) *Victorian Revolution: Government and Society in Victoria's Britain* (New York: New Viewpoint, 1973), pp. 5–25.

"Machine Tool Orders At Highest Since 1937," *New York Times*, April 15, 1939. At: https://timesmachine.nytimes.com/timesmachine/1939/04/15/91565742.html?pageNumber=22

Maiolo, J. A. "Anglo-Soviet Naval Armaments Diplomacy Before the Second World War," *English Historical Review*, Vol. CXXIII, No. 501 (2008), pp. 351–78.

Maiolo, J. and T. Insall, "Sir Basil Zaharoff and Sir Vincent Caillard," *The International History Review*, Vol. 34, No. 4 (December 2012), pp. 819–39.

Manchester, W. *The Arms of Krupp* (Boston: Little, Brown & Co., 1964).

Manning, F. *The Life of Sir William White* (New York: E. P. Dutton & Co., 1923).

Mannix, W. F. (ed.) *Memoirs of Li Hung Chang* (New York: Houghton Mifflin, 1913).

Marder, A. J. "English Armament Industry and Navalism in the Nineties," *Pacific Historical Review*, Vol. 7, No. 3 (September 1938), pp. 241–53.

Marder, A. J. *Fear God and Dread Nought, Vol. I: The Making of an Admiral, 1854–1904* (London: Jonathan Cape, 1952).

Marder, A. J. *Fear God and Dread Nought, Vol. II: Years of Power, 1904–1914* (London: Jonathan Cape, 1956).

Marshall, S. "Tools of War: Vickers F.B.5 'Gunbus,'" *Military Historian* blog, May 15, 2018. At: https://military-historian.squarespace.com/blog/2018/5/15/tools-of-war-vickers-fb5-gunbus#_ftn10

Martin, F. (ed.), *Statesman's Year-Book 1881* (London: Macmillan, 1881).

"Messrs. Armstrong, Mitchell & Co.," *Industries and Iron*, Vol. VII. July to December, 1889. October 4, 1889, p. 327.

Michie, A. *An Englishman in China During the Victorian Era, Sir Rutherford Alcock*, Vol. II, (London: William Blackwood & Sons, 1900).

Milanovich, K. "Armored Cruisers of the Imperial Japanese Navy," in J. Jordan (ed.),*Warship 2014* (London: Conway, 2014), pp. 83–84.

Miller C. *Planning and Profits* (Liverpool: Liverpool University Press, 2018).

Miller, G. *Straits* (Hull: University of Hull Press, 1997).

Miller, H. W. Jr. *Picture History of British Ocean Liners* (New York: Dover Publications, 2001).

Miller, R. *Britain and Latin America in the Nineteenth and Twentieth Centuries* (New York: Longman, 1993).

Millett A. R. and W. Murray (eds.), *Military Effectiveness: Vol. II, Interwar Period* (Cambridge: Cambridge University Press, 2010).

Millman, B. *Ill-Made Alliance* (Montreal: McGill-Queen's University Press, 1998).

Milton, D. H. *Lincoln's Spymaster* (Mechanicsburg, PA: Stackpole Books, 2003).

Morgan, Z. R. *Legacy of the Lash* (Bloomington: Indiana University Press, 2014).

Morley Committee, *Parliamentary Report of the Committee Appointed to Inquire into the Organization and Administration of the Manufacturing Departments of the Army 1887*. Cmd. 5116.

Morris, A. J. A. *Edwardian Radicalism* (London: Routledge, 1974).

Morse, H. B., *The International Relations of the Chinese Empire, Vol. II: The Period of Submission, 1861–1893* (London: Longmans, 1918).

Mowery, D. C. "Military R&D and Innovation," in B. H. Hall and N. Rosenberg (eds.), *Handbook of the Economics of Innovation*, Vol. 2 (Amsterdam: Elsevier, 2010), pp. 1219–56.

"Mysterious Zaharoff in London," *Sunday Post*, October 25, 1925. BNA.

"Mystery Man of Europe: Sir Basil Zaharoff Pilloried in the Commons," *Daily Express*, August 17, 1921.

"Mystery Millionaire," *Derby Daily Telegraph*, September 24, 1924. BNA.

Nahum, A. *Frank Whittle* (Cambridge: Icon Books, 2004).

National Maritime Museum, "National Shipbuilders Security Ltd.," *Minutes* March 27, 1935.

"Naylor, Hutchinson, Vickers and Co.," *Grace's Guide to British Industrial History*. At: www.gracesguide.co.uk/Naylor,_Hutchinson,_Vickers_and_Co

"Naval Additions: Two Dreadnoughts," *Western Morning News*, August 5, 1914. BNA.

"Naval Matters Past and Prospective: Tributes to Sir William White," *The Marine Engineer*, Vol. 23, London, December 1, 1901, p. 355.

"Naval Summary," *Illustrated Naval and Military Magazine* Vol. VI, No. 23 (November 1890), pp. 465–70.

Navy Appropriation Account: 1916–17 (London: HMSO, 1918).

"New Arms Campaign Revealed in Britain: Vickers-Armstrongs," *New York Times*, October 23, 1938, p. 32. At: https://timesmachine.nytimes.com/timesmachine/1938/10/23/98866494.html?pageNumber=32

"New Chilean Cruiser: The Almirante O'Higgins," *New York Times*, July 26, 1898, p. 5.

"New Warships: Speeding up the Work of Construction: Activity at Vickers," *Sheffield Independent*, August 6, 1914. BNA.

Noble, M. D. *A Long Life* (Newcastle: Andrew Reid & Co., 1925).

Noppen, R. K. *Ottoman Navy Warships* (Oxford: Osprey Publishing, 2015).

Nye Committee, *Munitions Industry, Hearings before the Special Committee Investigating the Munitions Industry, United States Senate, 73rd Congress, Pursuant to S.Res. 206 A Resolution to Make Certain Investigations Concerning the Manufacture and Sale of Arms and Other War Munitions, Part 1*, September 4–6, Part 2, September 7, 1934 (Washington, DC: Government Printing Office, 1934). At: https://archive.org/details/munitionsindustr1ll4unit

"Obituary: Commander Sir Arthur Trevor Dawson," *1931 Institution of Mechanical Engineers: Obituaries*. At: www.gracesguide.co.uk/Arthur_Trevor_Dawson

"Obituary: Josiah Vavasseur," *1908 Institution of Mechanical Engineers: Obituaries*. At: www.gracesguide.co.uk/Josiah_Vavasseur#cite_note-2

"Obituary: Josiah Vavasseur," *The Engineer*, November 20, 1908. At: www.gracesguide.co.uk/Josiah_Vavasseur#cite_note-2

"Obituary: Major Sir Hew Ross Kilner," *The Engineer*, August 7, 1953. At: www.gracesguide.co.uk/Hew_Ross_Kilner

"Obituary: Sir Andrew Noble," *Institution of Civil Engineers*, 1916. At: www.gracesguide.co.uk/Andrew_Noble

"Obituary: Sir Edward Robert Micklem," *The Engineer*, May 16, 1952. At: www.gracesguide.co.uk/Edward_Robert_Micklem

"Obituary: Sir Frederick Bramwell," *Institution of Mechanical Engineers*, 1903. At: www.gracesguide.co.uk/Frederick_Joseph_Bramwell

"Obituary: Sir George Thurston," *The Engineer* (January–June 1950), p. 153. At: www.gracesguide.co.uk/George_Thurston

"Obituary: Sir William Siemens," *1884 Institution of Civil Engineers: Obituaries*. At: www.gracesguide.co.uk/William_Siemens#cite_note-10

"Obituary, Sir William Henry White," *Minutes of the Proceedings of the Institution of Civil Engineers*, Vol. 192 (1913). At: www.icevirtuallibrary.com/doi/abs/10.1680/imotp.1913.17629

"Obituary: Sir Vincent Caillard, *Engineering*, March 28, 1930. At: www.gracesguide.co.uk/Vincent_Henry_Pensalver_Caillard

"Official Documents: Convention for the Control of the Trade in Arms and Ammunition, and Protocol," *The American Journal of International Law*, Vol. 15, No. 4 (October 1921), pp. 297–313.

O'Conor, Sir N. "The Hamidian Diplomacy," *Annual Report for Turkey for 1907*, in Gooch, G. P., and H. Temperley (eds.), *British Documents on the Origins of the War 1898–1914*, Vol. V (London: HMSO, 1928), pp. 20–25.

O'Hara, V. (ed.) *On Seas Contested* (Annapolis, MD: Naval Institute Press, 2014).

Otte, T. G. *The China Question* (Oxford: Oxford University Press, 2007).

Otte, T. G. *The Foreign Office Mind* (Cambridge: Cambridge University Press, 2011).

"Our Supplementary Arsenal: The Shipbuilding Department," *Pall Mall Gazette "Extra"*, No. 15, March 17, 1885, pp. 2–6.

Oxford Dictionary of National Biography (Oxford: Oxford University Press, 2010).

Packard, E. F. *Whitehall, Industrial Mobilisation and the Private Manufacture of Armaments*, Unpublished Ph.D. thesis, London School of Economics, July 2009. At: http://etheses.lse.ac.uk/46/1/Packard_Whitehall_industrial_mobilisation_and_the_private_manufacture_of_armaments.pdf

Padfield, P. *Guns at Sea* (New York: St. Martin's Press, 1974).

Pamphlets on the European War, Vol. 64 (University of California, 1917).

"Parliamentary answer of Sir Edward Grey to Mr. King," July 23, 1914. *Hansard*, Vol. 65, cc. 626–627.

Parkinson, J. R. "Shipbuilding," in N. K. Buxton and D. H. Aldcroft (eds.), *British Industry between the Wars: Instability and Industrial Development, 1919–1939* (London: Scholar Press, 1979), pp. 79–102.

Parkinson, R. *The Late Victorian Navy* (Woodbridge: Boydell Press, 2008).

Payne, R. *Private Spies* (London: Arthur Baker Ltd., 1967).

Pearse B. and C. McCooey, *Companion to Japanese Britain and Ireland* (London: Japan Society, 1991).

Pearton, M. *Diplomacy, War and Technology Since 1830* (Lawrence, KA: University of Kansas, 1984).

Peden, G. C. *Arms, Economics and British Strategy* (Cambridge: Cambridge University Press, 2007).

Peebles, H. *Warshipbuilding on the Clyde, 1889–1939* (Edinburgh: John Donald, 1987).

"Perils of Private Manufacture of Armaments," *Nottingham Journal*, February 2, 1935, p. 5. BNA.

"Peru: New British-Built Peruvian Cruiser," *Journal of the American Society of Naval Engineers*, Vol. XVIII, No. 2 (May 1906), pp. 683–86.

"Peru: New Peruvian Cruisers," *Journal of the American Society of Naval Engineers*, Vol. XVIII, No. 4 (November 1906), pp. 1291–94.

Picard, L. "The Great Exhibition," The British Library, October 14, 2009. At: www.bl.uk/victorian-britain/articles/the-great-exhibition#

Platt, D. C. M. "The Role of the British Consular Service in Overseas Trade," *Economic History Review*, Vol. 15, No. 3 (1963), pp. 494–512.

Platt, D. C. M. *Finance, Trade and Politics in British Foreign Policy, 1815–1914* (Oxford: Clarendon Press, 1968).

Platt, D. C. M. *Latin America and British Trade 1806–1914* (London: A & C Black Ltd., 1972).

Pollard, S. "*Laissez-Faire* and Shipbuilding," *Economic History Review*, New Series, Vol. 5, No. 1 (1952), pp. 98–115.

"Pom Poms in the Boer War." At: www.bwm.org.au/pom_poms.php

Postan, M. M. *British War Production* (London: HMSO and Longmans, Green and Co., 1952).

"*Queen's Bench Division – May 15th. Maudslay and Others V. Ashby and Others*" (London: Waterlow & Sons Ltd, 1888).

"Real Mission of Li Hung Chang," *Chicago Tribune*, September 1, 1896, p. 6. At: http://archives.chicagotribune.com/1896/09/01/page/6/article/real-mission-of-li-hung-chang

Reese, P. *Men Who Gave Us Wings* (Barnsley: Pen & Sword Aviation, 2014).

Rendel, S. *Personal Papers of Lord Rendel*, ed. by F. E. Hamer (London: Ernest Benn Limited, 1931).

"Report of the Parks Committee Relative to Jesmond Dene," *Proceedings of the Council of the City and County of Newcastle-Upon-Tyne* (Newcastle upon Tyne: J. Dowling & Sons, 1899), pp. 434–35.

Report of the Enquiry into the Royal Ordnance Factories, Woolwich, Reports to the Minister of Munitions. Second Interim Report, November 22, 1918. House of Commons, Cmd. 229, March 1919.

"Republica and Tiradentes," *The Marine Engineer*, Vol. 14, July 1, 1892, p. 190.

Reuters, "Turkey's Dreadnought: Irritation at Great Britain's Action," *Western Daily Press*, August 13, 1914. BNA.

Richardson, Sir A. *Vickers Sons and Maxim, Limited* (Strand, London, privately printed, 1902).

Ritchie, S. *Industry and Airpower* (Abingdon: Routledge, 1997).

Rogers, D. *Shadow Factories* (Solihull: Helion & Co. Ltd., 2016).

Rogers, S. "Interest Rates in the UK Since 1694," *The Guardian*, January 10, 2013. At: www.theguardian.com/news/datablog/2011/jan/13/interest-rates-uk-since-1694#data

Røksund, A. *The Jeune École: The Strategy of the Weak* (Leiden: Brill, 2007).

Ropp, T. *Development of a Modern Navy* (Annapolis, MD: Naval Institute Press, 1987).

Roskill, S. *Hankey: Man of Secrets, Vol. III: 1931–1963* (London: Collins, 1974).

Royal Commission on the Civil Service, "Minutes of Evidence, April 29, 1914 – July 16, 1914." *Parliamentary Papers*, Cmnd. 7749.

"*Royal Naval Exhibition 1891: The Illustrated Handbook, and Souvenir*" Pall Mall Gazette "*Extra*", No. 56 (1891).

Royal Naval Exhibition 1891, *Official Catalogue and Guide* (London: W. P. Griffith and Sons, 1891).

"Rush to Make Munitions," *Leeds Mercury*, June 29, 1915. BNA.

Russell Young, J. *Around the World with General Grant*, Vol. 1 (New York: The American News Company, 1879).

"Russia: Armored Cruiser Rurik," *Journal of the American Society of Naval Engineers*, Vol. XVIII, No. 4 (November 1906), pp. 1294–304.

Ruxton I. (ed.), *The Diaries of Sir Ernest Satow* (Morrisville, NC: Lulu Press Inc., 2013).

Sampson, A. *Arms Bazaar* (London: Hodder and Stoughton, 1975).

Sater, W. *Andean Tragedy* (Lincoln: University of Nebraska Press, 2007).

Sayers, R. S. *Bank of England 1891–1944* (Cambridge: Cambridge University Press, 1976).

Scheina, R. L. *Latin America: A Naval History, 1810–1987* (Annapolis, MD: Naval Institute Press, 1987).

Schofield, P. *Industry and Society: A Study of the Home Front in Barrow-in-Furness during the First World War*, Unpublished Ph.D. thesis, University of Central Lancashire, 2017. At: https://clok.uclan.ac.uk/22471/1/22471%20Schofield%20Peter%20Final%20e-Thesis%20%28Master%20Copy%29.pdf

Scott, C. P. *C. P. Scott, 1846–1932, Making of the Manchester Guardian* (London: Frederick Muller Ltd., 1946).

Scott, J. D. *Vickers: A History* (London: Weidenfeld and Nicolson, 1962).

Scott J. D. and R. Hughes. *Administration of War Production* (London: HMSO, 1955).

Segreto, L. "More Trouble than Profit," *Business History*, Vol. 27, No. 3 (November 1985), pp. 316–37.

"Seized Warship: Angora to Make Claim on Elswick Firm," *Hartlepool Northern Daily Mail*, June 23, 1914. BNA.

Shay, R. P. Jr. *British Rearmament in the Thirties* (Princeton, NJ: Princeton University Press, 1977).

"Sheffield, 2nd October 1889," *Industries and Iron*, Vol. VII. July to December, 1889. October 4, 1889, p. 327.

"Sheffield's Case: Still Carrying Heavy Burdens," *Sheffield Daily Telegraph*, December 31, 1925. BNA.

"Shell Shortage: Incompetence in High Places," *Dundalk Examiner and Louth Advertiser*, July 3, 1915. BNA.

"Shell Shortage," *The Globe*, September 8, 1915. BNA.

"Sir Robert Micklem," *New York Times*, May 14, 1952, p. 27.

Simmonds, A. G. V. *Britain and World War One* (London: Routledge, 2013).

Simpkin, J. "Hiram Maxim," *Spartacus Educational*. At: https://spartacus-educational.com/FWWmaxim.htm

Skřivan, Sr. A. and A. Skřivan, Jr., "Great Powers and the Sino-Japanese War 1894–1895," *Prague Papers on the History of International Relations*, Vol. 2 (2015), pp. 16–44.

Slaven, A. "A Shipyard in Depression: John Browns," *Business History*, Vol. 19, No. 2 (1977), pp. 192–217.

Slaven, A. *British Ship Building 1500–2010* (Lancaster: Crucible Books, 2013).

Slaven, A. "War and Depression: 1914–1938," in Davenport-Hines, R. T. P. (ed.) *Business in the Age of Depression and War* (London: Frank Cass, 1990), pp. 122–47.

Smith, C. *Supermarine* (Stroud: Amberley Publishing, 2016).

Smithers, A. J. *Rude Mechanicals* (London: Leo Cooper, 1987).

"Some Recent Portraits of Society Interest," *The Tatler*, May 1, 1918.

South Kensington Museum, *Catalogue of Ship Models and Marine Engineering in the Museum* (London: Eyre and Spottiswoode for HMSO, 1889).

"SS Chusan," Peninsular and Oriental. At: www.pandosnco.co.uk/chusan.html

Stahl, D. "Decolonization of the Arms Trade," *History of Global Arms Transfer*, Vol. 7 (2019), pp. 3–19.

Stanley, J. and M. Pearton, *International Trade in Arms* (London: Chatto and Windus, 1972).

Stansky, P. (ed.) *Victorian Revolution: Government and Society in Victoria's Britain* (New York: New Viewpoint, 1973).

Steiner, Z. "The FCO and Changing Times," in G. Johnson (ed.) *The Foreign Office and British Diplomacy* (Abingdon: Routledge, 2005), pp. 13–30.

Stemp, P. D. *Kites, Birds & Stuff: Supermarine Aircraft* (Morrisville, NC: Lulu Press Inc, 2011).

Stevenson, D. *Armaments and the Coming of War* (Oxford: Oxford University Press, 1996).

Stoker D. J. Jr. and J. A. Grant, *Girding for Battle* (Westport, CT: Praeger, 2003).

Stone, D. R. "Imperialism and Sovereignty," *Journal of Contemporary History*, Vol. 35, No. 2 (2000), pp. 213–30.

Stone, G. "The British Government and the Sale of Arms to the Lesser European Powers," in E. Goldstein, and B. J. C. McKercher (eds.) *Power and Stability: British Foreign Policy, 1865-1965* (Abingdon: Routledge, 2013), pp. 237–70.

"Sudden Death of Colonel Dyer," *Dover Express*, March 25, 1898. BNA.

"'Sukhidayo,' Siamese gunboat, built at Barrow," 1929. Cumbria Archive and Local Studies Centre, Barrow, BDB 16/NA/5/7.

"The Sultan Osman: Turkish Resentment of our Embargo," *Sheffield Independent*, August 13, 1914. BNA.

"Sultan Osman I: Contractor's Firemen Strike at Devonport," *Western Morning News*, July 11, 1914. BNA.

"Sultan Osman I: Turkey's New Battleship to be Docked at Devonport," *Western Morning News*, June 26, 1914. BNA.

"Sultan Osman I: Turkish Super-Dreadnought Docked at Devonport," *Western Morning News*, July 10, 1914. BNA.

Sumida, J. T. *In Defence of Naval Supremacy* (Boston: Unwin Hyman, 1989).

"Supermarine Aviation Works: Share Capital Acquired by Vickers," *Western Mail*, December 3, 1928. BNA.

Surtees, Col. H. C. "The Turkish Army as a Military Factor," November 16, 1906. In Gooch, G. P., and H. Temperley (eds.), *British Documents on the Origins of the War 1898-1914*, Vol. V (London: HMSO, 1928), pp. 34–38.

Taylor, Commander. "Turkish Naval Policy and Armaments," *Annual Report for Turkey 1907*, in Gooch, G. P., and H. Temperley (eds.), *British Documents on the Origins of the War 1898–1914*, Vol. V (London: HMSO, 1928), pp. 40–42.

Taylor, G. D. "Negotiating Technology Transfers within Multinational Enterprises," in G. Jones (ed.) *The Making of Global Enterprise* (London: Frank Cass, 1994), pp. 127–58.

Tennent, Sir J. E. *Story of Guns* (London: Longman, 1864).

Tenney, C. D. "Reminiscences of Li Hung-Chang," *The Papers of Charles Daniel Tenney*, Dartmouth College Library. At: https://collections.dartmouth.edu/teitexts/tenney/diplomatic/ms794-011-diplomatic.html

Thayer, G. *The War Business* (London: Weidenfeld and Nicolson, 1969).

"The Armstrong & Whitworth Trials," *Newcastle Journal*, May 10, 1864. BNA.

The Cabinet Papers 1915–1982, "Defence Policy 1933–1939, End of Disarmament and Defence Requirements," National Archive. At: www.nationalarchives.gov.uk/cabinetpapers/themes/end-of-disarmament-defence-requirements.htm

The Case of Great Britain: As Laid Before the Tribunal of Arbitration Convened at Geneva Concluded at Washington, May 8, 1871 (Washington, DC: Government Printing Office, 1872).

The Electrical Review, Vol. 51, No. 1, September 19, 1902.

"The Facts About Shell Shortage," *Birmingham Daily Post*, August 10, 1915. BNA.

"The Great Need: Organisaton of Nation's Skilled Workers," *Taunton Courier and Western Advertiser*, June 9, 1915. BNA.

"The Great War Exhibition at the Crystal Palace," *Beardmore News*, Vol. 2, No. 7, July 1920.

"The Late Sir Trevor Dawson, Bart," *1931 Institute of Metals: Obituaries*. At: www.gracesguide.co.uk/Arthur_Trevor_Dawson

The Near East, Vol. 13 (1917).

"The 'Peace Ballot' of 1934–35," Churchill College, Cambridge. At: www.chu.cam.ac.uk/archives/education/churchill-era/exercises/appeasement/peace-ballot-1934-35/

"The Great War Exhibition at the Crystal Palace," *Beardmore News*, Vol. 2, No. 7, July 1920.

The International, Vol. 10 (London, Moods Publishing Company, 1916).

"The Japanese Navy after the War," *Journal of the American Society of Naval Engineers*, Vol. XVIII, No. 1 (February 1906), pp. 325–31.

"The Naval Exhibition," *The Engineer*, Vol. 51, January–June 1891, May 1, 1891, pp. 530–33.

"The New Brazilian Battleships and Their Armour," *Engineering*, Vol. 86, August 14, 1908.

"The Reshadieh: Messrs. Vickers' Latest in Battleships," *Sheffield Daily Telegraph*, September 3, 1913. BNA.

"The Sheffield District," *The Engineer*, Vol. 69, February 21, 1890, p. 161.

"The Shell Shortage," *Taunton Courier and Western Advertiser*, June 23, 1915. BNA.

"The Shell Shortage: Mr. Asquith Explains Reasons," *Dundee Courier*, July 6, 1915. BNA.

The Statist, March 26, 1910. BNA.

"The Sultan Osman: Turkish Resentment of our Embargo," *Sheffield Independent*, August 13, 1914. BNA.

"The Trials of the Armoured Cruiser 'Rurik,'" *Engineering*, September 11, 1908, Vol. 86.

"The Truth About the Shell Shortage," *Sheffield Weekly Telegraph*, June 28, 1919. BNA.

"The Turkish Dreadnoughts," *Manchester Courier and Lancashire General Advertiser*, June 24, 1914. BNA.

"The Turkish Navy: Battleship Sultan Osman I Leaves Tyne To-day," *Newcastle Journal*, July 7, 1914. BNA.

"The Whitehead Torpedo in Action," *The Engineer*, Vol. 51, May 1, 1891.

"Thomas Edward Vickers," *Grace's Guide*. At: www.gracesguide.co.uk/ Thomas_Edward_Vickers#cite_ref-5

Thorne, C. "The Quest for Arms Embargoes: Failure in 1933," *Journal of Contemporary History*, Vol. 5, No. 4 (1970), pp. 129–49.

Tilley, Sir J. and S. Gaselee, *Foreign Office* (London: G. P. Putnam's Sons Ltd., 1933).

Tivey, L. J. *Nationalisation* (London: Jonathan Cape, 1966).

Times Telegram, "Turkish Protest about the Sultan Osman," *Sunderland Daily Echo and Shipping Gazette*, August 13, 1914. BNA.

Tolliday, S. *Business, Banking, and Politics* (Cambridge, MA: Harvard University Press, 1987).

Topliss, D. "The Brazilian Dreadnoughts, 1904–1914," *Warship International*, Vol. 25, No. 3 (1988), pp. 240–89.

Townsend, P. *Duel of Eagles* (New York: Simon and Schuster, 1970).

Toynbee, A. J. (ed.) *Survey of International Affairs*, Vol. III (Oxford: Oxford University Press, 1953).

Trebilcock, C. "A 'Special Relationship' – Government, Rearmament, and the Cordite Firms," *The Economic History Review*, Vol. 19, No. 2 (1966), pp. 364–79.

Trebilcock, C. "British Armaments and European Industrialization, 1890–1914," *The Economic History Review*, Vol. 26, No. 2 (1973), pp. 254–72.

Trebilcock, C. "Radicalism and the Armament Trust," in Morris, A. J. A. (ed.) *Edwardian Radicalism* (London: Routledge & Kegan Paul, 1974), pp. 180–201.

Trebilcock, C. *Vickers Brothers: Armaments and Enterprise 1854–1914* (London: Europa Publications, 1977).

Trebilcock, C. "War and the Failure of Industrial Mobilisation," in J. M. Winter (ed.) *War and Economic Development* (Cambridge: Cambridge University Press, 1975), pp. 139–64.

"Trials of the H.M.S. *Dreadnought*," *Journal of the American Society of Naval Engineers*, Vol. XVIII, No. 4 (November 1906), pp. 1206–10.

"Turkish Battleship Leaves the Tyne," *Newcastle Evening Chronicle*, July 7, 1914. BNA.

"Turkey's Big Ship: Reshadieh," *Sheffield Daily Telegraph*, September 4, 1913. BNA.

"Turkey's New Battleship," *Army and Navy Gazette*, September 6, 1913. BNA.

Turner, J. (ed.) *Businessmen and Politics* (London: Heinemann, 1984).

Tweedale, G. *Giants of Sheffield Steel* (Sheffield: Sheffield City Libraries, 1986).

Tweedale, G. *Steel City* (Oxford: Clarendon Press, 1995).

Union of Democratic Control, *The Secret International* (London: Union of Democratic Control, 1932).

United States Senate, "Report on the Activities and Sales of Munitions Companies," *Senate* Report, Vol. 1, 1936.

Uslu, N. *The Turkish-American Relationship* (London: Nova Science, 2003).

Van de Ven, H. *Breaking With the Past* (New York: Columbia University Press, 1914).

"Vickers and the Turkish Undertaking," *Sheffield Daily Telegraph*, July 10, 1914. BNA.

Vickers, D. *History of Vickers*, five drafts, 1920. VA Doc. 762.

"Vickers Company Chronological Aircraft List." At: www.militaryfactory.com/aircraft/contractor.asp?thisCompany=Vickers

Vickers, T. *Minutes of Evidence, Report of the Royal Commission on the Depression of Trade and Industry*, Second Report (London: HMSO, 1886).

"Vickers, Sons and Maxim, Limited," *The Statist*, Vol. 59, March 23, 1907.

"Vickers, Sons and Maxim, Limited," *The Economist*, Vol. 66, No. 3369, March 21, 1908, p. 628.

"War Profits and the Next Budget," *Taunton Courier and Western Advertiser*, June 23, 1915. BNA.

Warren, K. *Armstrongs of Elswick* (Basingstoke: Palgrave Macmillan, 1989).

Warren, K. *John Meade Falkner, 1858–1932* (Lewiston, NY: Edwin Mellen Press, 1995).

Walker, R. J. "Progress Made in the Application of the Parsons Turbine to Marine Propulsion," *The Steamship*, Vol. 17 (March 1906), pp. 170–202.

Webb, D. Le P. *Never a Dull Moment! A Personal History of Vickers Supermarine 1926–1960* (unpublished manuscript, 1994). VA, Doc. 1900.

Webster-Jenkinson, M. *Bookkeeping for Retail Grocers* (London: Gee & Co., 1905).

West, W. J. *The Quest for Graham Greene* (New York: St. Martin's Press, 1998).

Wheeler, M. *The Athenaeum* (New Haven: Yale University Press, 2020).

"When Lord Inchcape Won 100 Francs," *Hartlepool Northern Daily Mail*, July 20, 1931. BNA.

White, A. P. *Formation and Development of Middle-Class Urban Culture and Politics: Sheffield 1825–1880*, Unpublished Ph.D. thesis, University of Leeds, 1990. At: https://core.ac.uk/download/pdf/43783.pdf

White, C. A. *British and American Commercial Relations with Soviet Russia* (Chapel Hill: University of North Carolina Press, 1992).

Wilson, A. N. *Victorians* (London: Arrow Books, 2003).

Wilson A. W. and Lewendon, R. J. *Story of the Gun* (Woolwich: Royal Artillery Institution, 1985).

Wilson, H. W. *Ironclads in Action*, Vol. II, 5th ed. (Boston: Little Brown, 1898).

Wilson, N. M. *The Development of Middle-Class Housing in Western Sheffield during the Nineteenth Century*, unpublished Ph.D. thesis, University of Sheffield, 1998. At: https://etheses.whiterose.ac.uk/15124/1/680820.pdf

Williams, W. H. *Who's Who in Arms* (London: Labour Research Department, 1935).

Wise, J. "Securing 'The Ripest Plum,'" in Jordan, J. and Dent, S., *Warship 2013* (London: Bloomsbury, 2013), pp. 120–24.

Woods, Sir H. F., *Spunyarn from the Strands of a Sailor's Life* (London: Hutchinson & Co., 1924).

Wragg, D. "The Royal Navy," in V. O'Hara (ed.) *On Seas Contested* (Annapolis, MD: Naval Institute Press, 2014), pp. 96–102.

Wright, R. N. J. *Chinese Steam Navy* (London: Chatham, 2000).

Yorulmaz, N. *Arming the Sultan* (London: I. B. Tauris, 2014).

Zabecki, D. T. "Great Guns!" *MHQ: Quarterly Journal of Military History*, Vol. 27, No. 1 (Autumn 2014), pp. 76–84.

Zhukov, K. and A. Vitol, "The Origins of the Ottoman Submarine Fleet," *Oriente Moderno*, Vol. 81, No. 1 (2001), pp. 221–32.

INDEX

Abdul Hamid. *See* Abdulhamid, Sultan
Abdülhamid, Sultan, 292, 294, 295, 298
Admiralty
  and aircraft, 28–29, 96–97
  and armament export policy, 3
  and armament orders, 95
  and armor plate firms, 58
  and armor plate negotiations, 64, 86,
    120–23, 127–29
  and Armstrongs' aiming rifle, 76
  Armstrongs relations with, 27, 31,
    35–36, 47–48, 51, 53, 54, 58, 79,
    85, 140
  and artillery orders, 58–59, 67–68, 70
  and Elswich pattern aiming rifle, 76–78
  and fire control system purchase, 7
  and knowledge about profits, 183
  and price controls, 303–304, 337
  procurement model, 87, 94, 146–47,
    153, 162, 175, 185, 194, 220
  and rearmament plans, 183–84
  and rearmament programs, 241
  recruitments to, 50, 53, 54
  reliance on private firms, 27–29
  and royalty payments, 64–74, 88–92
  in Second World War, 191, 331–33
  and support of contractors, 9, 31, 86,
    142–43, 149, 183
  and the Washington Naval Treaty
    (1922), 138
  and the WSBC, 154, 177
  and warships, 17, 44, 224, 231
  and Whitehead Torpedo Co., 7
  support of contractors, 28
  Vickers agreement with, 84
  Vickers relations with, 27, 31, 32,
    35–36, 58–59, 64, 79, 85, 328, 331

Advisory Panel of Industrialists (DRC),
  176
Afghanistan, 54
Air Ministry, 4, 9, 149
aircraft, 114, 180, 181, 195, 199, 240
Alabama incident, implications of, 214
Almirante Abreu (Brazilian second
  class cruiser), 225
Almirante Barroso (Brazilian protected
  cruiser), 225
Almirante Cochrane (Chilean
  dreadnought), 214, 230
Almirante Grau (Peruvian cruiser
  scout), 224
Almirante Lattore (Chilean
  dreadnought), 230, 231
Almirante Saldanah (Brazilian training
  ship), 241
Amazonas (Brazilian protected
  cruiser), 225
Ansaldo, 84, 98, 100, 221, 223, 234, 248,
  252, 296, 297, 321, 341
Argentina, 241
  Ansaldo orders, 221
  arms race with Chile, 223–24
  detente with Chile, 224
armament exports
  British Government policy on, 3–4,
    215, 234, 257, 322
  interwar years, 126
armament firms
  and the State, 4, 5, 8–10, 26–27, 83, 150
  foreign policy of, 3, 24
  independence of, 5–6
  interwar years, 9
armament production, regulation of,
  4, 11

www.ingramcontent.com/pod-product-compliance
Ingram Content Group UK Ltd.
Pitfield, Milton Keynes, MK11 3LW, UK
UKHW032035171224
452612UK00004B/8